Organizational Behavior

MANAGING PEOPLE AND ORGANIZATIONS

Gregory Moorhead

ARIZONA STATE UNIVERSITY

Ricky W. Griffin

TEXAS A & M UNIVERSITY

HOUGHTON MIFFLIN COMPANY   BOSTON   TORONTO

GENEVA, ILLINOIS   PALO ALTO   PRINCETON, NEW JERSEY

Senior Associate Editor: *Susan Kahn*
Editorial Production Manager: *Nancy Doherty Schmidt*
Production/Design Coordinator: *Sarah Ambrose*
Senior Manufacturing Coordinator: *Priscilla Bailey*
Marketing Manager: *Robert D. Wolcott*

Cover design: Edda V. Sigurdardottir, Greenwood Design Studio; **cover image**: Robert Delaunay, *Simultaneous Contrasts: Sun and Moon (Soleil, lune, simultane 2).* 1913, dated on painting 1912.

Photo credits: *Chapter 1:* p. 3: Jeff Smith, p. 8: Bob Daemmrich, p. 14: Steven Pumphrey/Stock, Boston; *Chapter 2:* p. 27: Gale Zucker/Stock, Boston, p. 32: Joseph B. Treaster/New York Times Pictures, p. 39: Bob Sacha; *continued* on p. 592.

Printed in the U.S.A.
Library of Congress Catalog Card Number: 94-76531
ISBN: 0-395-70898-2

123456789-RM-97 98 96 95 94

Brief Contents

Contents

II.   INDIVIDUAL PROCESSES IN ORGANIZATIONS   50

3.   Foundations of Individual Behavior   50

6.   Learning-Based Perspectives on Motivation   128

III.   ENHANCING PERFORMANCE IN ORGANIZATIONS   154

7.   Designing Jobs for Individuals and Teams   154

8. Performance Measurement and Rewards   180

9. Managing Stress and Interpersonal Conflict   204

V. ORGANIZATIONAL PROCESSES AND CHARACTERISTICS

17.   Organization Culture   438

18.   Organization Change and Development   466

VI.   INTEGRATING INDIVIDUALS, GROUPS, AND ORGANIZATIONS

Preface

The field of organizational behavior, still in its infancy as a science, remains full of competing and conflicting models and theories. There are few laws or absolute principles that dictate proper conduct for organizational members or predict with certainty their behaviors. The role of human resources in the long-term viability of any business or not-for-profit enterprise is nevertheless recognized as enormously significant. Other resources—financial, information, and material—are also essential, but only human resources are virtually boundless in their potential impact (positive or negative) on the organization.

The primary objectives of the previous editions of *Organizational Behavior: Managing People and Organizations* were to provide some of the tools and insights necessary to understand and analyze the characteristics of human beings and organizational situations in order to contribute to the long-run survival of an enterprise. We hope that the earlier editions also initiated in readers some degree of excitement and enthusiasm for the field of organizational behavior. Responses from many instructors, students, and other readers have indicated that the previous editions did indeed accomplish these objectives.

In this fourth edition we have built on this solid foundation in several ways. First, we have updated the research on all of the topics discussed in the book. We have also utilized current examples from real organizations to illustrate how research and new developments in the field apply to the everyday situations of typical organizations. We introduce several new theories and approaches that improve and add to the understanding of people and situations in organizations. We have shortened the overall length of the book—without sacrificing its comprehensive nature—by more concisely summarizing some of the older theories and approaches, while expanding coverage of current topics. In addition, we have added an entirely new chapter on "Managing Diversity in Organizations" due to the importance of this topic in organizations today. We also have carefully edited and rewritten major portions of the book in an effort to enhance its readability and interest level. In response to feedback from students and instructors, some topics and several chapters have also been reorganized.

In every way the book is contemporary in its topics, examples, research, and readability. We hope that our enthusiasm for the field of organizational behavior is contagious and will promote motivation to learn more about the dynamic nature of the behavior of people in organizations.

Improved Organization and Coverage

Organization of the Fourth Edition

The organization and coverage in this edition represent a fine tuning and improvement over the third edition that was based on extensive consideration. We asked users and nonusers of the book to review the third edition and answer a set of specific questions about it. Based on these responses, plus other comments from current users of the book, we made several changes. First, the order and grouping of chapters have been revised from the third edition. The order changes we made in the third edition were not as popular as we expected. Therefore, we have reorganized more along the lines of the second edition with significant consideration given to new developments in the field.

The content of *Organizational Behavior*, Fourth Edition, is divided into one introductory part and five more general parts that emanate from the characteristics of the field: individual processes in organizations, enhancing performance in organizations, interpersonal processes in organizations, organizational process and characteristics, and emerging dimensions of organizational behavior. Chapter 1 in Part I discusses basic concepts of the field, the importance of the study of organizational behavior, and a brief history of the field. Chapter 2 develops a managerial perspective on the field of organizational behavior. The four chapters in Part II focus on key aspects of individual processes in organizations: individual differences and perception, and three common perspectives of motivation—need-based perspectives, process-based approaches, and learning-based perspectives. Part III, also consisting of four chapters, deals with how managers and organizations can enhance individual performance through job design, through performance measurement and reward systems, by managing stress and conflict, and through decision making, creativity, and innovation. Important interpersonal processes—group and intergroup dynamics, leadership and influence processes, and interpersonal communication—are discussed in four chapters in Part IV. Processes and characteristics of organizations are presented in four chapters in Part V—basic dimensions of organization structure, organization design, organization culture, and organization change and development. Part VI includes two chapters that address two emerging issues in organizational behavior—international aspects of organizations and managing diversity in organizations. Two appendices at the end of the text discuss research methods in organizational behavior and career dynamics.

At the same time we reorganized material, we significantly shortened the book without sacrificing its comprehensive coverage and readability. This was accomplished by summarizing some of the older, classic topics, thereby leaving room for more coverage of current topics. Beginning with a comprehensive list of topics in the field, both classic and new, we conducted an extensive survey of what coverage users wanted to see in a current text. The most apparent result of this survey is the addition of a new chapter on managing diversity in organizations. To make room for this chapter we combined our coverage of organization structure, design, environment, and technology into two chapters (Chapters 15 and 16) instead of three and combined our discussion of group and intergroup processes into one chapter (Chapter 11) instead of two. As a result of our market survey, we also changed the sequence of several chapters to improve the logical flow of the text and to group topics into more related categories. For example, goal setting is included as part of the motivation topics in Chapter 5; the chapter on performance appraisal was significantly changed to focus on performance management rather than performance appraisal techniques, and coverage of reward systems was included in Chapter 8; power and politics were included as part of influence processes related to leadership in Chapter 13; conflict was combined with stress in Chapter 9; and topics related to innovation were moved from the technology chapter and combined with decision making and creativity in Chapter 10.

Important Topics and Key Themes

To further respond to the needs of OB instructors and students, we have enhanced the coverage of specific topics and themes.

Diversity in the Workplace   In this edition we have endeavored to show the importance of diversity issues in understanding organizational behavior in three ways. First, an entirely new chapter, "Managing Diversity in Organizations" (Chapter 20), is included. Second, many chapters include a boxed feature entitled "Diversity in the Workplace" that describes how real companies are dealing with diversity related to the topic of the chapter. Finally, throughout the text we have included as many examples of diversity as possible.

International Emphasis   In this edition we have continued to show the international nature of organizational behavior. This has been accomplished in three ways. First, we include an entire chapter, "International Aspects of Organizations" (Chapter 19). Second, many chapters include a boxed insert entitled "International Perspective" that describes how a topic or concept is applied internationally. Finally, we have tried to include as many international examples as possible throughout the text.

Ethics   Ethical issues continue to be of interest and importance in the study and practice of management. For that reason, we lay a foundation for the discussion of ethics as it relates to organizational behavior issues in Chapter 2. Throughout the text we include examples of ethical issues when appropriate, including the use of "The Ethical Dilemma" boxed inserts.

Skills   In order to help prepare students for their careers, we believe it is important for students to learn and practice management skills. To this end we have included, along with many application-oriented pedagogical features, boxed inserts called "Developing Management Skills."

Features of the Book

Readability and Ease of Use

We believe that readers will find that the fourth edition continues to be engaging and accessible. Without sacrificing the level of sophistication with which the content is treated, the language of the text is aimed at the student. In addition, a variety of pedagogical features are included to guide students through the text and help them gain a full understanding of the concepts.

Contemporary Focus

The theory and research on each topic in this text represent state-of-the-art thinking. Currently popular topics are worked into discussions throughout the book.

Examples are included to illustrate the current use of these ideas and concepts. As noted above, ethical, diversity, and international issues are all covered extensively. Total Quality Management (TQM) is also discussed in several chapters and is given an in-depth discussion in the chapter on performance management and rewards. Other current topics such as empowerment, superleadership, and procedural justice are also included.

We have also thoroughly updated the examples used throughout the text. All of the real-world cases in this edition are new.

Applications

Throughout the book the companies cited in examples, cases, and boxed items represent a blend of large, well-known and smaller, less well-known firms, in order to show the applicability of the material in all types of organizations. Each chapter opens with a brief critical incident, which provides a concrete example of an issue in organizational behavior, and closes with two cases, one of which is from a real organization and the other of which is hypothetical. The boxed inserts are of four types: ethics, skills, diversity, and international, and are built around what organizations are doing in these areas. All of these examples and the pedagogical features of the text combine to give students both an understanding of how the concepts apply to the real world and also an opportunity to practice the concepts for themselves.

Pedagogical Aids

The learning process is facilitated by several features of this book, many of which have already been mentioned. Each chapter opens with a chapter outline and a list of chapter objectives and closes with a section entitled "Summary of Key Points." At the end of each chapter are several discussion questions, designed to stimulate discussion among students. An experiential exercise is included at the end of each chapter to help students make the transition from textbook learning to real-world application. In addition, the end-of-chapter cases are designed to assist in this transition. Figures, tables, and photographs offer visual support for the text content. And a running marginal glossary and a complete glossary at the end of the book provide additional support for identifying and learning key concepts.

Supplemental Materials

The fourth edition is accompanied by a complete package of teaching and learning support materials.

The **Instructor's Resource Manual** includes for each chapter a synopsis, objectives, lecture outline, text discussion questions with possible responses, case summaries with possible responses to questions, notes on the experiential exercises, a mini-lecture, and references for additional experiential exercises. Also included are a section on learning and teaching ideologies, suggested course outlines, suggestions on how to use the minilectures, a video guide, a list of the color transparencies, and a transition guide to help current users of the third edition move easily to this new edition.

The **Test Bank** has been thoroughly revised and contains multiple-choice, true/false, completion, matching, and essay questions for every chapter. Each question is accompanied by a text page reference and learning level indicator. A computerized version of the test bank is available to allow instructors to generate and change tests easily on the computer.

A set of color **transparencies** includes 100 figures and tables both from and outside the text.

Special efforts were invested in developing a set of **videos** that enhance the teaching package that accompanies the text. We have selected a video segment to be used with each part of the book. The topics discussed in the video segments focus on key topics of organizational behavior: ethics, motivation, conflict, creativity, communication, quality, and international management. The videos present both real-world examples and skill-based perspectives. A video guide with teaching suggestions for each video is included in the *Instructor's Resource Manual*.

OB in Action: Cases and Exercises, Fourth Edition, by Janet W. Wohlberg and Gail Gilmore, contains additional cases and exercises to help student bridge the gap between theory and practice. The authors bring their extensive experience in both university classroom and executive training and development settings to their work in creating this new edition. This book is divided into seven parts: Individual Processes in Organizations; Interpersonal Processes in Organizations; Enhancing Individual and Interpersonal Processes; Integrating Individual, Groups, and Organizations; Negotiation; International Aspects of Organizational Behavior; and Career Management. The new edition features several pieces on diversity and sexual harassment, strengthened part introductions, and more multipart cases. An *Instructor's Resource Manual* provides detailed notes on how to use the material in the classroom.

Acknowledgments

Although this book bears the name of two authors, numerous people have contributed to it. Through the years we have had the good fortune to work with many fine professionals who helped us sharpen our thinking about this complex field and to develop new and more effective ways of discussing it. Several reviewers were also important to the development of the fourth edition. Their contributions were essential to helping us identify areas in need of reworking or minor fine tuning. Any and all errors of omission, interpretation, and emphasis remain the responsibility of the authors. We would like to express a special thanks to the following reviewers for taking the time to provide us with their valuable assistance:

Abdul Aziz
College of Charleston

Steve Ball
Cleary College

Brendan Bannister
Northeastern University

Greg Baxter
Southeastern Oklahoma State University

Mary-Beth Beres
Mercer University Atlanta

Allen Bluedorn
University of Missouri Columbia

Murray Brunton
Central Ohio Technical College

John Bunch
Kansas State University

Mark Butler
San Diego State University

Richaurd R. Camp
Eastern Michigan University

Dan R. Dalton
Indiana University Bloomington

T. K. Das
Baruch College

Thomas W. Dougherty
University of Missouri Columbia

Cathy Dubois
Kent State University

Stanley W. Elsea
Kansas State University

Joseph Forest
Georgia State University

Eliezer Geisler
Northeastern Illinois University

Robert Giacalone
University of Richmond

Lynn Harland
University of Nebraska at Omaha

Stan Harris
Lawrence Tech University

Nell Hartley
Robert Morris College

Peter Heine
Stetson University

William Hendrix
Clemson University

John R. Hollenbeck
Michigan State University

John Jermier
University of South Florida

Avis L. Johnson
University of Akron

Bruce H. Johnson
Gustavus Adolphus College

Gwen Jones
Bowling Green State University

Robert T. Keller
University of Houston

Michael Klausner
University of Pittsburgh at Bradford

Richard Leifer
Rensselaer Polytechnic Institute

Peter Lorenzi
University of Central Arkansas

Joseph Lovell
California State University–San Bernardino

Patricia Manninen
Northshore Community College

Edward K. Marlow
Eastern Illinois University

Edward Miles
Georgia State University

C. W. Millard
University of Puget Sound

Alan N. Miller
University of Nevada Las Vegas

Herff L. Moore
University of Central Arkansas

Robert Moorman
West Virginia University

Stephan J. Motowidlo
Pennsylvania State University

Richard T. Mowday
University of Oregon

Margaret A. Neale
Northwestern University

Linda L. Neider
University of Miami

Mary Lippitt Nichols
University of Minnesota Minneapolis

Robert J. Paul
Kansas State University

William R. Stevens
Missouri Southern State College

James C. Quick
University of Texas at Arlington

Donald Tompkins
Slippery Rock University

Bill Robinson
Indiana University of Pennsylvania

David D. Van Fleet
Arizona State University West

Hannah Rothstein
CUNY – Baruch College

Bobby C. Vaught
Southwest Missouri State University

Carol S. Saunders
Florida Atlantic University

Jack W. Waldrip
American Graduate School of
International Management

Ralph L. Schmitt
Macomb Community College

John P. Wanous
The Ohio State University

Randall S. Schuler
New York University

The fourth edition could never have been completed without the support of Arizona State University and Texas A & M University. Luis Gomez-Mejia, acting chair of the Management Department; Larry Penley, dean of the College of Business at Arizona State University; Felice Cavallini of IAL; Al Ringleb, director of the Institute for International Business Studies in Italy; and Dick Woodman, head of the Management Department and A. Benton Cocanougher, dean of the College of Business Administration at Texas A & M University facilitated our work by providing the environment that encourages scholarly activities and contributions to the field.

Several secretaries and graduate assistants were also involved in the development of the fourth edition. We extend our appreciation to Chris Neck, Phyllis Washburn, David Glew, Jennifer Miller, and Sharon Coker for their help.

We would also like to acknowledge the outstanding team of professionals at Houghton Mifflin Company who helped us prepare this book. Nancy Doherty Schmitt, editorial production manager, has been incredibly helpful and supportive throughout our association with Houghton Mifflin. During the actual development of the text itself, Susan Kahn, senior associate editor, and Kate Burden, editorial assistant, each made important contributions as they sharpened our thinking, paid attention to details, and tried to keep us on schedule.

Finally, we would like to acknowledge the daily reminders that we get from our families of the importance of our work. They equip us with perspective. When we work too much, they drag us away to play. When we play too much, they remind us of work that we must do. Mixed among swim team practices, baseball games, school functions, battles over who gets to use the car next and weekend curfews, doctor appointments, soccer games, and gymnastics practices, we devoted the time to prepare this revision! Without the support and love of our families we would not survive. It is with all of our love that we dedicate this book to them.

G. M.
R. W. G.

Organizational Behavior

CHAPTER 1

An Overview of Organizational Behavior

OBJECTIVES

After studying this chapter, you should be able to:

Define organizational behavior.

Trace the historical roots of organizational behavior.

Discuss the emergence of contemporary organizational behavior, including its precursors, the Hawthorne studies, and the human relations movement.

Describe contemporary organizational behavior—its characteristics, concepts, and importance.

Identify and discuss contextual perspectives on organizational behavior.

An understanding of what both customers and employees want is essential to a business's success. Here, Sam Walton, founder of the immensely successful Wal-Mart Stores, encourages associates to "catch the spirit" that has characterized the company since its inception in 1962.

One of the biggest success stories in the history of U.S. business was Sam Walton and the firm he founded, Wal-Mart Stores, Inc. Walton got his start in 1950 by running franchised Ben Franklin variety stores. After several years of experience, Walton developed a plan for starting a chain of discount stores in smaller towns and presented the proposal to Ben Franklin's top managers. After they rejected his plan, Walton left the firm in 1962 and opened his own store, Wal-Mart Discount City, in Rogers, Arkansas.

The firm grew slowly at first. By 1970 Walton had eighteen stores with total annual sales of around $44 million. After its first public stock offering that year, the firm began to invest heavily in an automated distribution center and an advanced computerized inventory tracking and merchandise reordering system. These innovations, in combination with Walton's merchandising instincts, launched Wal-Mart on a trajectory of phenomenal growth.

By 1980, Walton was operating 276 stores and was opening dozens more each year. By mid-decade, dozens had mushroomed to hundreds and, as the 1980s drew to a close, Wal-Mart became the largest retailer in the world. Today there are over 2,000 Wal-Mart stores scattered across the country. The firm also operates hundreds of Sam's Clubs, large warehouse membership clubs, and several Hypermart U.S.A. stores and Wal-Mart Supercenters, combining general merchandise and groceries.

How did a simple retailer from rural Arkansas pull all this off? Walton himself was probably asked this question hundreds of times, right up until his death in 1992. And he always gave the same answer: "Our people and the way they're treated and the way they feel about our company. The attitude of our employees, our associates, is that things are different in our company, and they deserve the credit."

Always self-effacing and humble, Walton had the ability to know what people—employees and customers alike—wanted from his business. And he did everything in his power to give it to them. These keen insights into human behavior served him in good stead and helped create a retailing giant. They also made him one of the most respected managers in the country.[1]

■ ■ ■ ■

Sam Walton's success was based on a number of different factors, including his skills as a retailer, his own hard work and motivation, and his understanding of the importance of other people. He cared deeply about the people who work for Wal-Mart, and he knew that those people would be the major factor in the ultimate success of his business. Indeed, no manager can succeed without the assistance of others. Thus, every manager—whether responsible for an industrial giant like General Electric, IBM, or Mobil; the Boston Celtics basketball team; the

1. "America's Best CEOs," *Industry Week*, December 2, 1991, pp. 28–41; and Patricia Sellers, "Companies That Serve You Best," *Fortune*, May 31, 1993, pp. 74–88.

Mayo Clinic; or a local Pizza Hut restaurant—must strive to understand the people who work in the organization.

This book is about those people. It is also about the organization itself and the managers who operate it. The study of organizations and of the collection of people within them together comprise the field of organizational behavior. In this introductory chapter, we begin with a comprehensive definition of organizational behavior and a framework for its study. Then we trace the field's historical roots and its emergence as an independent field. Next, we discuss contemporary organizational behavior and present an overview of the rest of this book. Finally, we examine several contextual perspectives that provide a general framework from which we can develop a more comprehensive examination of human behavior at work.

The Meaning of Organizational Behavior

Organizational behavior (OB) is the study of human behavior in organizational settings, the human behavior-organization interface, and the organization itself.

Organizational behavior (OB) is the study of human behavior in organizational settings, the interface between human behavior and the organization, and the organization itself.[2] Although we can focus on any one of these three areas, we must remember that all three are ultimately necessary for a comprehensive understanding of organizational behavior. For example, we can study individual behavior (such as the behavior of Sam Walton or of one of his Wal-Mart employees) without explicitly considering the organization. But because the organization influences and is influenced by the individual, we cannot fully understand the individual's behavior without learning something about the organization. Similarly, we can study organizations (such as Wal-Mart itself) without focusing specifically on the people within them. But again, we are looking at only a portion of the puzzle. Eventually we must consider the other pieces as well as the whole.

Figure 1.1 illustrates this view of organizational behavior. It shows the linkages among human behavior in organizational settings, the individual-organization interface, the organization, and the environment surrounding the organization. Each individual brings to an organization a unique set of personal characteristics, experiences from other organizations, and personal background. In considering the people who work in organizations, therefore, organizational behavior must look at the unique perspective that each individual brings to the work setting. For example, suppose that Texas Instruments hires a consultant to investigate employee turnover. As a starting point, the consultant might analyze the types of people the firm usually hires. The goal of this analysis would be to learn as much as possible about the nature of the company's workforce as individuals—their expectations, their personal goals, and so forth.

But individuals do not work in isolation. They come in contact with other people and with the organization in a variety of ways. Points of contact include managers, coworkers, the formal policies and procedures of the organization, and various changes implemented by the organization. Over time, the individual too changes as a function both of personal experiences and maturity and of work experiences and the organization. The organization, in turn, is affected by the presence

2. For a discussion of the meaning of organizational behavior, see Larry Cummings, "Toward Organizational Behavior," *Academy of Management Review*, January 1978, pp. 90–98. For recent updates, see the annual series *Research in Organizational Behavior* (Greenwich, Conn.: JAI Press), edited by Larry Cummings and Barry Staw.

FIGURE 1.1

The Nature of
Organizational Behavior

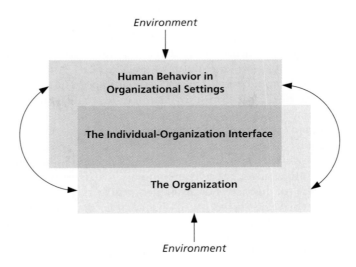

and eventual absence of the individual. Clearly, then, the study of organizational behavior must consider the ways in which the individual and the organization interact. Thus, the consultant studying turnover at Texas Instruments might next look at the orientation procedures for newcomers to the organization. The goal of this phase of the study would be to understand some of the dynamics of how incoming individuals interact with the broader organizational context.

An organization, of course, exists before a particular person joins it and continues to exist after he or she has left. Thus, the organization itself represents a crucial third perspective from which to view organizational behavior. For instance, the consultant studying turnover would also need to study the structure and culture of Texas Instruments. An understanding of factors such as the performance evaluation and reward systems, the decision-making and communication patterns, and the design of the firm itself can provide added insight into why some people choose to leave a company and others elect to stay.

Thus, the field of organizational behavior is both exciting and complex. Myriad variables and concepts accompany the interactions just described, and together these factors greatly complicate the manager's ability to understand, appreciate, and manage others in the organization. They also provide unique opportunities to enhance personal and organizational effectiveness. The key, of course, is understanding. To provide a groundwork for this understanding, we look first at the historical roots of organizational behavior.

Historical Roots of Organizational Behavior

Management is a relatively new field of study, having emerged only within the last 100 years.

Many disciplines, such as physics and chemistry, are literally thousands of years old. Management has also been around in one form or another for centuries. For example, the writings of Aristotle and Plato abound with references and examples of management concepts and practices. But because serious interest in the study of management did not emerge until the turn of the twentieth century, organizational behavior is only a few decades old.[3]

One reason for the relatively late development of management as a scientific field is that few large business organizations existed until around a hundred years ago. Although management is just as important to a small organization as it is to a large one, large firms provided both a stimulus and a laboratory for management research. Second, many of the first people who took an interest in studying organizations were economists who initially assumed that management practices are by nature efficient and effective; therefore, they concentrated on higher levels of analysis such as national economic policy and industrial structures.

Interestingly, many contemporary managers today have come to appreciate the value of history. For example, managers glean insights from Homer's *Iliad*, Machiavelli's *Prince*, and Chaucer's *Canterbury Tales*. And some organizations, such as Polaroid and Wells Fargo, have even designated corporate historians. Indeed, management history is so popular today that the publishers of *Forbes* and *American Heritage* recently joined forces to introduce a new magazine called *Audacity—The Magazine of Business Experience*, dedicated to business history. The *Global Perspective* summarizes how a recent article from that magazine sheds light on the plight of automakers today.

Scientific Management

Scientific management, popular during the early twentieth century, was one of the first approaches to management. It focused on the efficiency of individual workers.

Key contributors to scientific management included Frederick W. Taylor, Frank and Lillian Gilbreth, Henry Gantt, and Harrington Emerson.

Taylor identified a phenomenon he called soldiering—the practice of working considerably slower than one can.

One of the first approaches to the study of management, popularized during the early 1900s, was **scientific management**. Individuals who helped develop and promote scientific management included Frank and Lillian Gilbreth (whose lives were portrayed in a book and a subsequent movie, *Cheaper by the Dozen*), Henry Gantt, and Harrington Emerson. But Frederick W. Taylor is most closely identified with scientific management.[4]

Early in his life, Taylor developed an interest in efficiency and productivity. While working as a foreman at Midvale Steel Company in Philadelphia from 1878 to 1890, he became aware of a phenomenon he called *soldiering*—or employees' working at a pace much slower than their capabilities. Because managers had never systematically studied jobs in the plant—and, in fact, had little idea how to gauge worker productivity—they were completely unaware of this practice.

To counteract the effects of soldiering, Taylor developed several innovative techniques. For example, he scientifically studied all the jobs in the Midvale plant and developed a standardized method for performing each one. He also installed a piece-rate pay system in which each worker was paid for the amount of work he completed during the workday rather than for the time spent on the job. (Taylor believed that money was the only important motivational factor in the workplace.) These innovations boosted productivity markedly and are the foundation of scientific management.

After leaving Midvale, Taylor spent several years working as a management consultant for industrial firms. At Bethlehem Steel Company, he developed several

3. Daniel A. Wren, *The Evolution of Management Thought*, 4th ed. (New York: Wiley, 1994), Chapter 1. See also Stephen J. Carroll and Dennis A. Gillen, "Are the Classical Management Functions Useful in Describing Managerial Work?" *Academy of Management Review*, January 1987, pp. 38–51; and Daniel A. Wren, "Management History: Issues and Ideas for Teaching and Research," *Journal of Management*, Summer 1987, pp. 339–350.
4. Frederick W. Taylor, *Principles of Scientific Management* (New York: Harper, 1911).

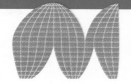

GLOBAL PERSPECTIVE

Using History to Understand Today's Business World

The rise and fall of the British sports car industry provides fascinating glimpses into the auto industry that are still relevant to big automakers today. At the end of World War II, the British government pressured firms such as MG and British Leyland to export their products to the United States in return for hard currency. Because so many U.S. soldiers had seen British sports cars like the MG Midget, Triumph, and Jaguar for the first time during the war, their popularity boomed and Britain sent thousands of the cars to the United States. Indeed, until the early 1960s, England was the largest automobile exporter in the world.

But British manufacturers refused to invest in new technology for their plants. Instead, they continued to rely on both old model designs and labor-intense methods of production. For example, British auto plants were among the last in the world to install automated assembly lines. During the 1960s, productivity and quality steadily declined in their factories while labor costs rose rapidly.

The introduction of the Ford Mustang in 1963 fueled an amazing period of growth in sports car sales. MG, British Leyland, and Jaguar should have been poised to capitalize on this growth, but in fact just the opposite happened. They remained on the sidelines, never knowing quite what to do, while Japanese firms—most notably Datsun (now Nissan)—pushed ahead aggressively. The Datsun Z series helped redefine the U.S. sports car market, and the British were left in the dust. By the dawn of the 1980s, only Jaguar was still making sports cars in Britain, and it was eventually swallowed by Ford.

SOURCE: Timothy R. Whisler, "Defeating the Triumph," *Audacity*, Fall 1993, pp. 16–25. Reprinted By Permission of AMERICAN HERITAGE Magazine, a division of Forbes, Inc., © Forbes, Inc., 1993.

efficient techniques for loading and unloading rail cars. At Simonds Rolling Machine Company, he redesigned jobs, introduced rest breaks to combat fatigue, and implemented a piece-rate pay system. In every case, Taylor claimed his ideas and methods greatly improved worker output. His book, *Principles of Scientific Management*, published in 1911, was greeted with enthusiasm by practicing managers and quickly became a standard reference.

Scientific management quickly became a mainstay of business practice. It facilitated job specialization and mass production, thus profoundly influencing the U.S. business system. Taylor had his critics, however. Labor opposed scientific management because of its explicit goal of getting more output from workers. Congress investigated Taylor's methods and ideas because some argued that his incentive system would dehumanize the workplace and reduce workers to little more than drones. Later theorists recognized that Taylor's views of employee motivation were inadequate and narrow. And recently there have been allegations that Taylor falsified some of his research findings and paid someone to do his writing for him. Nevertheless, scientific management represents an important milestone in the development of management thought.[5]

5. For critical analyses, see Charles D. Wrege and Amedeo G. Perroni, "Taylor's Pig-Tale: A Historical Analysis of Frederick W. Taylor's Pig-Iron Experiment," *Academy of Management Journal*, March 1974, pp. 6–27, and Charles D. Wrege and Ann Marie Stoka, "Cooke Creates a Classic: The Story Behind Taylor's Principles of Scientific Management," *Academy of Management Review*, October 1978, pp. 736–749. For a more favorable review, see Edwin A. Locke, "The Ideas of Frederick W. Taylor: An Evaluation," *Academy of Management Review*, January 1982, pp. 14–24.

This is a view of the busy trading room of the New York headquarters of First Boston, a leading investment bank. The bank's 6,000 employees provide financial services to corporate clients worldwide. Large companies like First Boston rely at least partially upon classical bureaucratic structures to maintain efficient operation.

Classical Organization Theory

Classical organization theory focused on how organizations can be structured most effectively.

Important contributors to classical organization theory included Henri Fayol, Lyndall Urwick, and Max Weber.

The concept of **bureaucracy**, as described by Weber, was an early universal approach to organization structure. A bureaucracy is a logical, rational, and efficient model of organizations.

During this same era, another perspective on management theory and practice was also emerging. Generally referred to as **classical organization theory**, this perspective was concerned with structuring organizations effectively. Whereas scientific management studied how individual workers could be made more efficient, classical organization theory focused on how a large number of workers and managers could be most effectively organized into an overall structure.

Major contributors to classical organization theory included Henri Fayol, Lyndall Urwick, and Max Weber. Weber, the most prominent of the three, proposed a "bureaucratic" form of structure that he believed would work for all organizations.[6] Although today the term **bureaucracy** conjures up images of paperwork, red tape, and inflexibility, Weber's model of bureaucracy embraced logic, rationality, and efficiency. Weber assumed that the bureaucratic structure would always be the most efficient approach. (Such a blanket prescription represents what is now called a *universal approach.*) Table 1.1 summarizes the elements of Weber's ideal bureaucracy.

In contrast to Weber's views, contemporary organization theorists recognize that different organization structures may be appropriate in different situations. As with scientific management, however, classical organization theory played a major role in the development of management thought, and Weber's ideas and the concepts associated with his bureaucratic structure are still interesting and relevant today. (Chapters 15 and 16 discuss contemporary organization theory.)

6. Max Weber, *Theory of Social and Economic Organization,* trans. A. M. Henderson and T. Parsons (London: Oxford University Press, 1921).

TABLE 1.1

**Elements of Weber's
Ideal Bureaucracy**

Elements	Comments
1. Rules and Procedures	A consistent set of abstract rules and procedures should exist to ensure uniform performance.
2. Distinct Division of Labor	Each position should be filled by an expert.
3. Hierarchy of Authority	The chain of command should be clearly established.
4. Technical Competence	Employment and advancement should be based on merit.
5. Segregation of Ownership	Professional managers, rather than owners, should run the organization.
6. Rights and Properties of the Position	These should be associated with the organization, not the person who holds the office.
7. Documentation	A record of actions should be kept regarding administrative decisions, rules, and procedures.

The Emergence of Organizational Behavior

The central themes of both scientific management and classical organization theory were rationality, efficiency, and standardization. The roles of individuals and groups in organizations were either ignored altogether or given only minimal attention. A few early writers and managers, however, recognized the importance of individual and social processes in organizations.[7]

Precursors of Organizational Behavior

Robert Owen, Hugo Munsterberg, and Mary Parker Follett were among the first to recognize the importance of individual behavior to organizations.

In the early nineteenth century, Robert Owen, a British industrialist, attempted to improve the condition of industrial workers. He improved working conditions, raised minimum ages for hiring children, introduced meals for employees, and shortened working hours. In the early twentieth century, the noted German psychologist Hugo Munsterberg argued that the field of psychology could provide important insights into areas such as motivation and the hiring of new employees.[8] Another writer in the early 1900s, Mary Parker Follett, believed that management should become more democratic in its dealings with employees. An expert in vocational guidance, Follett argued that organizations should strive harder to accommodate their employees' human needs.

The views of Owen, Munsterberg, and Follett, however, were not widely shared by practicing managers. Not until the 1930s did notable change occur in management's perception of the relationship between the individual and the workplace.

7. Raymond A. Katzell and James T. Austin, "From Then to Now: The Development of Industrial-Organizational Psychology in the United States," *Journal of Applied Psychology*, 1992, Vol. 77, No. 6, pp. 803–835.
8. Hugo Munsterberg, *Psychology and Industrial Efficiency* (Boston: Houghton Mifflin, 1913); and Wren, *The Evolution of Management Thought.* See also Frank J. Landy, "Hugo Munsterberg: Victim or Visionary?" *Journal of Applied Psychology*, 1992, Vol. 77, No. 6, pp. 787–802.

At that time, a series of now classic research studies led to the emergence of organizational behavior as a field of study.

The Hawthorne Studies

The **Hawthorne studies,** conducted between 1927 and 1932, led to some of the first discoveries of the importance of human behavior in organizations.

The **Hawthorne studies** were conducted between 1927 and 1932 at Western Electric's Hawthorne plant near Chicago. (General Electric initially sponsored the research but withdrew its support after the first study was finished.) Several researchers were involved, the best known being Elton Mayo and Fritz Roethlisberger, Harvard faculty members and consultants, and William Dickson, chief of Hawthorne's Employee Relations Research Department.[9]

The first major experiment at Hawthorne studied the effects of different levels of lighting on productivity. The researchers systematically manipulated the lighting of the area in which a group of women worked. The group's productivity was measured and compared with that of another group (the control group) whose lighting was left unchanged. As lighting was increased for the experimental group, productivity went up—but, surprisingly, so did the productivity of the control group. Even when lighting was subsequently reduced, the productivity of both groups continued to increase. Not until the lighting had become almost as dim as moonlight did productivity start to decline. This led the researchers to conclude that lighting had no relationship to productivity—and at this point General Electric withdrew its sponsorship of the project!

In another major experiment, a piecework incentive system was established for a nine-man group that assembled terminal banks for telephone exchanges. Proponents of scientific management expected each man to work as hard as he could to maximize his personal income. But the Hawthorne researchers found instead that the group as a whole established an acceptable level of output for its members. Individuals who failed to meet this level were dubbed "chiselers," and those who exceeded it by too much were branded "rate busters." A worker who wanted to be accepted by the group could not produce at too high or too low a level. Thus, as a worker approached the accepted level each day, he slowed down to avoid overproducing.

After a follow-up interview program with several thousand workers, the Hawthorne researchers concluded that the human element in the workplace was considerably more important than previously believed. The lighting experiment, for example, suggested that productivity might increase simply because workers were singled out for special treatment and thus perhaps felt more valued. In the incentive system experiment, being accepted as a part of the group evidently meant more to the workers than earning extra money. Several other studies supported the overall conclusion that individual and social processes are too important to ignore.

Like the work of Taylor, the Hawthorne studies recently have been called into question. Critics cite deficiencies in research methods and offer alternative explanations of the findings. Again, however, these studies were a major factor in the advancement of organizational behavior and are still among its most frequently cited works.[10]

9. Elton Mayo, *The Human Problems of Industrial Civilization* (New York: Macmillan, 1933); and Fritz J. Roethlisberger and William J. Dickson, *Management and the Worker* (Cambridge, Mass.: Harvard University Press, 1939).
10. Alex Carey, "The Hawthorne Studies: A Radical Criticism," *American Sociological Review,* June 1967, pp. 403–416; and Lyle Yorks and David A. Whitsett, "Hawthorne, Topeka, and the Issue of Science versus Advocacy in Organizational Behavior," *Academy of Management Review,* January 1985, pp. 21–30.

Human Relations Movement

The Hawthorne studies provided the foundation for the **human relations movement**. Human relationists believed that employee satisfaction is a major determinant of performance.

The Hawthorne studies created quite a stir among managers, providing the foundation for an entirely new school of management thought that came to be known as the **human relations movement**. The basic premises underlying the human relations movement were that people respond primarily to their social environment, that motivation depends more on social needs than on economic needs, and that satisfied employees work harder than unsatisfied employees. This perspective represented a fundamental shift away from the philosophy and values of scientific management and classical organization theory.

One prominent human relations writer, Douglas McGregor, developed the concepts of **Theory X** and **Theory Y**. Theory X takes a negative and pessimistic view of workers, whereas Theory Y takes a more positive and optimistic approach. McGregor advocated the Theory Y style of management.

The values of the human relationists are perhaps best exemplified by the works of Douglas McGregor and Abraham Maslow.[11] McGregor is best known for his classic book *The Human Side of Enterprise*, in which he identified two opposing perspectives that he believed typified managerial views of employees. Some managers, McGregor said, subscribed to what he labeled **Theory X**. Theory X, which takes a pessimistic view of human nature and employee behavior, is in many ways consistent with the tenets of scientific management. A much more optimistic and positive view of employees is found in **Theory Y**. Theory Y, which is generally representative of the human relations perspective, was the approach McGregor himself advocated. Assumptions of Theory X and Theory Y are summarized in Table 1.2. The questions in *Developing Management Skills* provide some insights into your own inclinations toward Theory X or Theory Y viewpoints.

Abraham Maslow, another pioneer in the human relations movement, developed the well-known hierarchy of human needs.

In 1943, Abraham Maslow published a pioneering theory of employee motivation that became well known and widely accepted among managers. Maslow's theory, which we describe in detail in Chapter 4, assumes that motivation arises from a hierarchical series of needs. As the needs at each level are satisfied, the individual progresses to the next higher level.

Organizational behavior began to emerge as a mature field of study in the late 1950s and early 1960s.

Although the Hawthorne studies and the human relations movement played major roles in developing the foundations for the field of organizational behavior, some of the early theorists' basic premises and assumptions were incorrect. For example, most human relationists believed that employee attitudes such as job satisfaction are the major causes of employee behaviors such as job performance. As we explain in Chapter 5, however, this usually is not the case at all. Also, many of the human relationists' views were unnecessarily limited and situation specific. Thus, there was still plenty of room for refinement and development in the emerging field of human behavior in organizations.

Toward Organizational Behavior

Most scholars would agree that organizational behavior began to emerge as a mature field of study in the late 1950s and early 1960s.[12] That period saw the field's evolution from the simple assumptions and behavioral models of the human relationists to the concepts and methodologies of a scientific discipline. Since that time, organizational behavior as a scientific field of inquiry has made considerable

11. Douglas McGregor, *The Human Side of Enterprise* (New York: McGraw-Hill, 1960); and Abraham Maslow, "A Theory of Human Motivation," *Psychological Review*, July 1943, pp. 370–396. See also Paul R. Lawrence, "Historical Development of Organizational Behavior," in Jay W. Lorsch (Ed.), *Handbook of Organizational Behavior* (Englewood Cliffs, N.J.: Prentice-Hall, 1987), pp. 1–9.
12. See "Conversation with Lyman W. Porter," *Organizational Dynamics*, Winter 1990, pp. 69–79.

TABLE 1.2

Theory X and Theory Y

Theory X Assumptions	Theory Y Assumptions
1. People do not like work and try to avoid it.	1. People do not naturally dislike work; work is a natural part of their lives.
2. People do not like work, so managers have to control, direct, coerce, and threaten employees to get them to work toward organizational goals.	2. People are internally motivated to reach objectives to which they are committed.
3. People prefer to be directed, to avoid responsibility, to want security; they have little ambition.	3. People are committed to goals to the degree that they receive personal rewards when they reach their objectives.
	4. People will seek and accept responsibility under favorable conditions.
	5. People have the capacity to be innovative in solving organizational problems.
	6. People are bright, but under most organizational conditions their potentials are underutilized.

SOURCE: Douglas McGregor, *The Humane Side of Enterprise* (New York: McGraw-Hill, 1960), pp. 33–34, 47–48. Used with permission of publisher.

strides, although there have been occasional steps backward as well. Many of the ideas discussed in this book have emerged over the past two decades. We turn now to contemporary organizational behavior.[13]

Contemporary Organizational Behavior

Contemporary organizational behavior has two fundamental characteristics that warrant special discussion. It also consists of a generally accepted set of concepts that define its domain.

Characteristics of the Field

Researchers and managers who use concepts and ideas from organizational behavior must recognize that it has an interdisciplinary focus and a descriptive nature; that is, it draws from a variety of fields and attempts to describe behavior (as opposed to prescribing how behavior can be changed in consistent and predictable ways).

13. See Lorsch, *Handbook of Organizational Behavior,* for an overview of the current state of the field. See also the annual *Research in Organizational Behavior* series edited by Larry Cummings and Barry Staw.

Assessing Your Theory X and Theory Y Tendencies

The following questions are intended to provide insights into your tendencies toward Theory X or Theory Y management styles. Answer each of these questions on a scale of 1 to 5. Mark a 5 beside statements that you strongly agree with. Mark a 4 beside those you agree with, a 3 beside those you neither agree nor disagree with, a 2 beside those you disagree with, and a 1 beside those you strongly disagree with.

1. Most employees today are lazy and have to be forced to work hard.
2. People are only motivated by extrinsic rewards like pay and bonuses.
3. People do not like to work.
4. People generally avoid responsibility.
5. Many employees in big companies today do not accept the company's goals but instead work only for their own welfare.
6. Most people are not innovative and are not interested in helping their employer solve problems.
7. Most people need someone else to tell them how to do their job.
8. Many people today have little ambition, preferring to stay where they are and not work hard for advancement.
9. Work is not a natural activity for most people and instead is something they feel they have to do.
10. Most employees today are not interested in utilizing their full potential and capabilities.

Add up your responses to each question. If you scored 40 or higher, you have clear tendencies toward the Theory X view of management. If you scored 20 or lower, you have clear tendencies toward the Theory Y view of management. If you scored between 20 and 40, your tendencies fall in between the extreme Theory X and Y viewpoints and you have a more balanced approach. (Note: This brief instrument has not been scientifically validated and is to be used for classroom discussion purposes only.)

Contemporary organizational behavior has an interdisciplinary focus, drawing from psychology, sociology, and other related fields.

An Interdisciplinary Focus In many ways, organizational behavior synthesizes several other fields of study. Psychology, especially organizational psychology, is perhaps the greatest contributor to the field of organizational behavior. Psychologists study human behavior, whereas organizational psychologists specifically address the behavior of people in organizational settings. Many of the concepts that interest psychologists, such as individual differences and motivation, are also central to students of organizational behavior.

Sociology also has had a major impact on the field of organizational behavior. Sociologists study social systems such as families, occupational classes, and organizations. Because a major concern of organizational behavior is the study of organization structures, the field clearly overlaps with areas of sociology that focus on the organization as a social system.

Anthropology is concerned with the interactions between people and their environments, especially their cultural environment. Culture is a major influence on the structure of organizations as well as on the behavior of people within organizations.

Political science also interests organizational behaviorists. We usually think of political science as the study of political systems such as governments. But themes

No research can predict exactly what combination of variables will result in maximal employee productivity and satisfaction. Within any organizational system is a unique group of individuals, like the team that this Austin, Texas, carpenter works with, each of whom may respond differently to a given organizational system.

of interest to political scientists include how and why people acquire power, political behavior, decision making, conflict, the behavior of interest groups, and coalition formation. These are also major areas of interest in organizational behavior.

Economists study the production, distribution, and consumption of goods and services. Students of organizational behavior share the economist's interest in areas such as labor market dynamics, productivity, human resource planning and forecasting, and cost-benefit analysis.

Engineering has also influenced the field of organizational behavior. Industrial engineering in particular has long been concerned with work measurement, productivity measurement, work flow analysis and design, job design, and labor relations. Obviously these areas are also relevant to organizational behavior.

Most recently, medicine has also influenced organizational behavior in connection with the study of human behavior at work, specifically in the area of stress. Increasingly, research is showing that controlling the causes and consequences of stress in and out of organizational settings is important for the well-being of the individual as well as that of the organization.

Organizational behavior is descriptive—that is, it attempts to describe relationships between two or more behavioral variables.

A Descriptive Nature A primary goal of organizational behavior is to describe relationships between two or more behavioral variables. The theories and concepts of the field, for example, cannot predict with certainty that changing a specific set of workplace variables will improve an individual employee's performance by a certain amount. At best, theories can suggest that certain general concepts or variables tend to be related to one another in particular settings. For instance, research might indicate that in one organization, employee satisfaction and individual perceptions of working conditions correlate positively. Nevertheless, we may not know if better working conditions lead to more satisfaction, if more satisfied people see their jobs differently from dissatisfied people, or if both satisfaction and perceptions of working conditions are actually related through other variables. Also, the observed relationship between satisfaction and perceptions of working conditions may be considerably stronger, weaker, or nonexistent in other settings.

Organizational behavior is descriptive for several reasons: the immaturity of the field, the complexities inherent in studying human behavior, and the lack of valid, reliable, and accepted definitions and measures. Whether the field will ever be able to make definitive predictions and prescriptions is still an open question. But the value of studying organizational behavior nonetheless is firmly established. Because behavioral processes pervade most managerial functions and roles, and because the work of organizations is done primarily by people, the knowledge and understanding gained from the field can help managers significantly in many ways.[14]

Basic Concepts of the Field

Basic concepts of organizational behavior can be divided into five basic categories.

The central concepts of organizational behavior can be grouped into five basic categories: (1) individual processes, (2) methods for enhancing performance, (3) interpersonal processes, (4) organizational processes and characteristics, and (5) emerging dimensions. As Figure 1.2 shows, these categories provide the basic framework for this book.

Chapter 2 develops a managerial perspective on organizational behavior and represents a fundamental link between the core concepts of organizational behavior and the management of organizational effectiveness. The four chapters of Part 2 cover individual processes in organizations. Chapter 3 explores important individual differences such as personality and attitudes. Chapters 4, 5, and 6 provide in-depth coverage of an especially important topic, employee motivation in organizations.

Part 3 is devoted to methods and techniques used by managers to enhance individual and group performance in organizations. Chapter 7 discusses job design. Chapter 8 is devoted to performance measurement and rewards. Methods for managing stress and interpersonal conflict are explored in Chapter 9. Finally, decision making, creativity, and innovation are the subjects of Chapter 10.

Interpersonal processes in organizations are the focus of Part 4. Chapter 11 examines group dynamics. Leadership models and concepts are discussed in Chapter 12. Leadership and influence processes are the subject of Chapter 13. Interpersonal communication, the topic of Chapter 14, concludes this part.

Organizational processes and characteristics are the subject of Part 5. Chapter 15 describes organization structure, and Chapter 16 presents an in-depth treatment of organization design. Organization culture is discussed in Chapter 17. Finally, organization change and development are covered in Chapter 18.

Part 6 concludes the book with a discussion of two emerging dimensions of organizational behavior. Chapter 19 is devoted to the increasingly important area of international aspects of organizational behavior, and Chapter 20 explores work-

---

14. Joseph W. McGuire, "Retreat to the Academy," *Business Horizons*, July–August 1982, pp. 31–37; and Kenneth Thomas and Walter G. Tymon, "Necessary Properties of Relevant Research: Lessons from Recent Criticisms of the Organizational Sciences," *Academy of Management Review*, July 1982, pp. 345–353. See also Jeffrey Pfeffer, "The Theory Practice Gap: Myth or Reality?" *Academy of Management Executive*, February 1987, pp. 31–32.

---

force diversity in organizations. Finally, research methods in organizational behavior and career dynamics are covered in two appendixes.

The Framework for Understanding Organizational Behavior

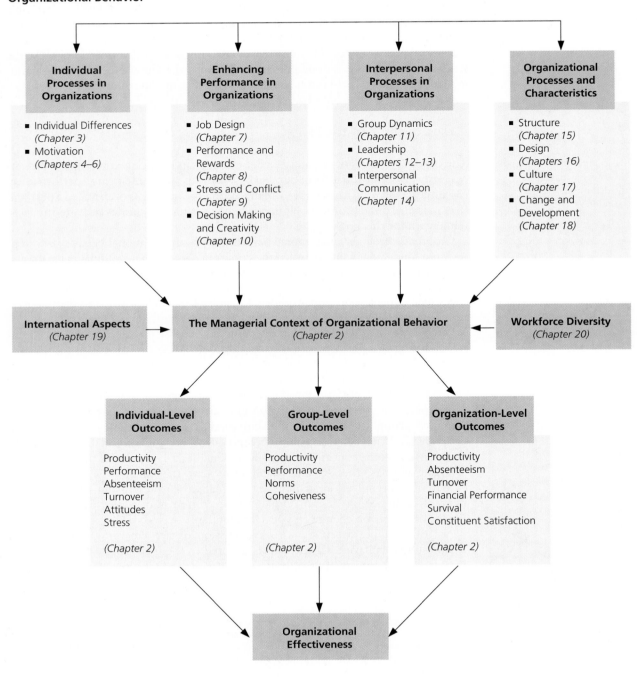

The Importance of Organizational Behavior

Although the importance of organizational behavior may be clear, we should nevertheless take a few moments to make it even more explicit. People are born and educated in organizations, acquire most of their material possessions from organizations, and die as members of organizations. Many of our activities are regulated by organizations called governments. And most adults spend the better part of their lives working in organizations. Because organizations influence our lives so powerfully, we have every reason to be concerned about how and why those organizations function.[15]

In our relationships with organizations, we may adopt any one of several roles or identities. For example, we can be consumers, employees, or investors. Because most readers of this book are either present or future managers, we adopt a managerial perspective throughout this textbook. Organizational behavior can greatly clarify the factors that affect how managers manage. It is the field's job to describe the complex human context in which managers work and to define the problems associated with that realm. The value of organizational behavior is that it isolates important aspects of the manager's job and offers specific perspectives on the human side of management: people as organizations, people as resources, and people as people.

Contextual Perspectives on Organizational Behavior

Several contextual perspectives have increasingly influenced organizational behavior: the systems approach and contingency perspectives, the interactional view, and popular-press perspectives. Many of the concepts and theories we discuss in the chapters that follow reflect these perspectives; they represent basic points of view that influence much of our contemporary thinking about behavior in organizations.

Systems and Contingency Perspectives

The systems and contingency perspectives take related viewpoints on organizations and how they function. Each is concerned with interrelationships among organizational elements and between organizational and environmental elements.

A **system** is a set of interrelated elements functioning as a whole.

The Systems Perspective The systems perspective, or the theory of systems, was first developed in the physical sciences, but it has been extended to other areas, such as management.[16] A **system** is an interrelated set of elements that function as a whole. Figure 1.3 shows a general framework for viewing organizations as systems.

15. See "Work & Family," *Business Week*, June 28, 1993, pp. 80–88, for some insights into the role of work and organizations in our everyday lives.
16. Fremont Kast and James Rosenzweig, "General Systems Theory: Applications for Organization and Management," *Academy of Management Journal*, December 1972, pp. 447–465.

FIGURE 1.3

The Systems Approach to Organizations

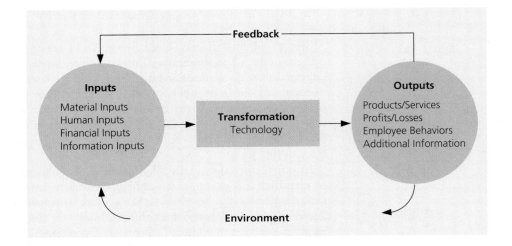

An organizational system receives four kinds of inputs from its environment: material, human, financial, and information. The organization then combines and transforms the inputs and returns them to the environment in the form of products or services, profits or losses, employee behaviors, and additional information. Finally, the system receives feedback from the environment regarding these outputs.

As an example, we can apply systems theory to Shell Oil Company. Material inputs include pipelines, crude oil, and the machinery used to refine petroleum. Financial inputs are the money received from oil and gas sales, stockholder investment, and so forth. Human inputs are oil field workers, refinery workers, office staff, and other people employed by the company. Finally, the company receives information inputs from forecasts about future oil supplies, geological surveys on potential drilling sites, sales projections, and similar analyses.

Through complex refining and other processes, these inputs are combined and transformed to create products such as gasoline and motor oil. As outputs, these products are sold to the consuming public. Profits from operations are fed back into the environment through taxes, investments, and dividends; losses, when they occur, hit the environment by reducing stockholders' incomes. In addition to having on-the-job contacts with customers and suppliers, employees live in the community and participate in a variety of activities away from the workplace. In varying degrees, at least some part of this behavior is influenced by their experiences as Shell workers. Finally, information about the company and its operations is also released into the environment. The environment, in turn, responds to these outputs and influences future inputs. For example, consumers may buy more or less gasoline depending on the quality and price of Shell's product, and banks may be more or less willing to lend Shell money based on financial information about the company.

The **contingency perspective** suggests that in most organizations, situations and outcomes are contingent on, or influenced by, other variables.

The Contingency Perspective Another useful viewpoint for understanding behavior in organizations comes from the **contingency perspective**. In the early days of management studies, managers searched for universal answers to organizational questions. They sought prescriptions that could be applied to any organization under any conditions. For example, early leadership researchers tried to discover forms of leadership behavior that would always increase employee satisfaction and effort. Eventually, however, researchers realized that the complexities of human behavior and organizational settings make universal conclusions virtually impossible. They discovered that in organizations, most situations and outcomes are contingent; that is, the relationship between any two variables is likely to be influenced by other variables.[17]

Figure 1.4 distinguishes universal and contingency perspectives. The universal approach, shown at the top of the figure, presumes a direct cause-and-effect linkage between variables. For example, it suggests that whenever a manager encounters a certain problem or situation (such as motivating employees to work harder), a universal approach exists that will lead to the desired outcome (such as raising pay or increasing autonomy). The contingency approach, on the other hand, acknowledges several other variables that alter the direct relationship. In other words, appropriate managerial action or behavior in any given situation depends on elements of that situation.

The field of organizational behavior gradually has shifted from a universal approach in the 1950s and early 1960s to a contingency perspective. The contingency perspective is especially strong in the areas of motivation (Chapters 4–6), job design (Chapter 7), leadership (Chapters 12 and 13), and organization design (Chapter 16), but it is becoming increasingly important throughout the field.

When Jim Treybig founded Tandem Computers, he had an open, laid-back management style. His office was always accessible, and he paid little attention to what others were doing. Tandem grew rapidly, but eventually problems set in. Profits started to drop, and a financial scandal occurred. Treybig soon realized that his relaxed approach would not work in a large, structured organization. Consequently, he developed a more formalized control process and adopted a clearer hierarchy. As a result, Tandem regained its lost effectiveness. Treybig learned the hard way that what works in one situation (for example, a new, small company) will not necessarily work in another (a large, established firm).

17. See Fremont Kast and James Rosenzweig (Eds.), *Contingency Views of Organization and Management* (Chicago: SRA, 1973), for a classic overview and introduction.

FIGURE 1.4

Universal Versus Contingency Approaches

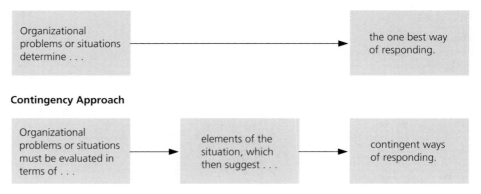

Universal Approach

Organizational problems or situations determine . . . → the one best way of responding.

Contingency Approach

Organizational problems or situations must be evaluated in terms of . . . → elements of the situation, which then suggest . . . → contingent ways of responding.

Interactionalism

Interactionalism suggests that individuals and situations interact continuously to determine individuals' behavior.

Interactionalism is a relatively new approach to understanding behavior in organizational settings. First presented in terms of interactional psychology, this view assumes that individual behavior results from a continuous and multidirectional interaction between characteristics of the person and characteristics of the situation. More specifically, **interactionalism** attempts to explain how people select, interpret, and change various situations.[18] Figure 1.5 illustrates this perspective. Note that the individual and the situation are presumed to interact continuously. This interaction is what determines the individual's behavior.

The interactional view implies that simple cause-and-effect descriptions of organizational phenomena are not enough. For example, one set of research studies may suggest that job changes will lead to improved employee attitudes. Another set of studies may propose that attitudes influence how people perceive their jobs in the first place. Both positions probably are incomplete: employee attitudes may influence job perceptions, but these perceptions may in turn influence future attitudes. Because interactionalism is a fairly recent contribution to the field, it is less prominent in the chapters that follow than the systems and contingency theories. Nonetheless, the interactional view appears to offer many promising ideas for future development in the field.

Popular-Press Perspectives

Finally, the popular press also has provided numerous new insights into the field of organizational behavior. Popular books such as *Theory Z, In Search of Excellence*, and *Corporate Cultures* all spent time on the *New York Times* best-seller list. Biographies of executives such as Lee Iacocca, Sam Walton, and Donald Trump also received widespread attention. These books highlight the management practices—many of them directly linked with concepts from organizational behavior—of successful firms like Eastman Kodak and IBM.

18. James Terborg, "Interactional Psychology and Research on Human Behavior in Organizations," *Academy of Management Review*, October 1981, pp. 569–576; Benjamin Schneider, "Interactional Psychology and Organizational Behavior," in Larry Cummings and Barry Staw (Eds.), *Research in Organizational Behavior*, Vol. 5 (Greenwich, Conn.: JAI Press, 1983), pp. 1–32; and Daniel B. Turban and Thomas L. Keon, "Organizational Attractiveness: An Interactionist Perspective," *Journal of Applied Psychology*, 1993, Vol. 78, No. 2, pp. 184–193.

FIGURE 1.5

The Interactionist Perspective on Behavior in Organizations

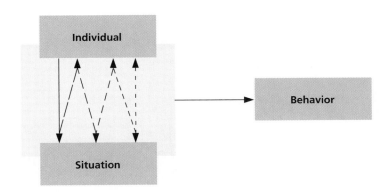

Of course, much of what these authors had to say was based on anecdotal evidence subject to different interpretations. Nevertheless, they have helped focus popular attention on many of the important issues and problems confronting business today. As a result, managers of the 1990s better appreciate both their problems and their prospects in working toward more effective organizational practices in the years to come.

Summary of Key Points

- Organizational behavior (OB) is the study of human behavior in organizational settings, the interface between human behavior and the organization, and the organization itself.
- Serious interest in the study of management first developed around the beginning of this century. Two of the earliest approaches were scientific management (best represented by the work of Taylor) and classical organization theory (exemplified by the work of Weber).
- Organizational behavior began to emerge as a scientific discipline as a result of the Hawthorne studies. McGregor and Maslow led the human relations movement that grew from those studies.
- Two characteristics of organizational behavior are its interdisciplinary focus, or its ties to psychology, sociology, anthropology, political science, economics, engineering, and medicine, and its attempts to describe, rather than prescribe, behavioral forces in organizations.
- Basic concepts of the field are divided into five categories: individual processes, methods for enhancing individual and group performance, interpersonal processes, organizational processes and characteristics, and emerging dimensions of organizational behavior. Those categories form the framework for the organization of this book. The study of organizational behavior is important because of the powerful influences organizations exert over our lives.
- Important contextual perspectives on the field of organizational behavior are the systems and contingency perspectives, the interactional view, and popular-press perspectives.

Discussion Questions

1. Some people have suggested that understanding organizational behavior is the single most important ingredient for managerial success. Do you agree or disagree with this statement? Why?
2. In what ways is organizational behavior comparable to functional areas such as finance, marketing, and production? In what ways is it different from these areas? Is it similar to statistics in any way?
3. Identify some managerial jobs that are highly affected by human behavior and others that are less so. Which would you prefer? Why?
4. Besides those cited in the text, what reasons can you think of for the importance of organizational behavior?

5. Suppose that you have to hire a new manager. One candidate has outstanding technical skills but poor interpersonal skills. The other has exactly the opposite mix of skills. Who would you hire? Why?

6. Some people believe that individuals working in an organization have a basic human right to satisfaction with their work and to the opportunity to grow and develop. How would you defend this position? How would you argue against it?

7. Many universities offer a course in industrial or organizational psychology. The content of those courses is quite similar to this one. Do you think that behavioral material is best taught in a business or psychology program, or is it best to teach it in both?

8. Do you believe that the field of organizational behavior has the potential to become prescriptive as opposed to descriptive? Why or why not?

9. Are the notions of systems, contingency, and interactionalism independent of one another? If not, describe ways in which they are related.

10. Get a recent issue of a popular business magazine such as *Business Week* or *Fortune* and scan its major articles. Do any of them reflect concepts from organizational behavior? Describe.

11. Interview a local manager or business owner. Ask if he or she relies on any "universal principles." If so, what are these principles?

EXPERIENTIAL EXERCISE

Purpose This exercise will help you develop an appreciation for the importance and pervasiveness of organizational behavior concepts and processes in both contemporary organizational settings and popular culture.

Format Your instructor will divide the class into groups of three to five members. Each group will be assigned a specific television program to watch before the next class meeting.

Procedure Arrange to watch the program as a group. Each person should have paper and a pencil handy. As you watch the show, jot down examples of individual behavior, interpersonal dynamics, organizational characteristics, and other concepts and processes relevant to organizational behavior. After the show, spend a few minutes comparing notes. Compile one list for the entire group. (It is advisable to turn off the television set during this discussion!)

During the next class meeting, have someone in the group summarize the plot of the show and list the concepts it illustrated. The following television shows are especially good for illustrating behavioral concepts in organizational settings:

Network Shows	*Syndicated Shows*
"Home Improvement"	"M*A*S*H"
"Frasier"	"Cheers"
"The Simpsons"	"The Mary Tyler Moore Show"
"Coach"	"Star Trek"
"Roseanne"	"Taxi"
"Murphy Brown"	"L.A. Law"

Follow-up Questions

1. What does this exercise illustrate about the pervasiveness of organizations in our contemporary society?.
2. What recent or classic movies might provide similar kinds of examples?
3. Do you think non-U.S. television would provide more or fewer examples of behavior in organizations?

CASE 1.1 John Malone and Tele-Communications Inc.

Although relatively few people outside of the television industry even know his name, John Malone has become one of the most powerful people in the industry. Malone runs Tele-Communications Inc. (TCI), the largest cable television company in the country. One of every five cable subscribers in the United States is a TCI customer. The firm owns cable systems in every state except Alaska.

Since the early 1980s, TCI has spent several billion dollars acquiring hundreds of cable networks around the country. TCI concentrates on mid-size and small cities, avoiding large cities with both greater competition and more regulation. Because of the vast size of Malone's cable system, networks such as MTV and ESPN go to great lengths to make their signals available to TCI. Some, like HBO, even charge TCI a lower fee than they charge most other cable companies.

Over the years, Malone has developed a reputation as a shrewd manager. He is decisive, often making major decisions in a matter of hours, and treats those close to him well. He also controls costs and makes sure that each of TCI's local firms is operated as efficiently as possible. He also has many supporters in the industry who credit him for making the cable industry more profitable for everyone. They also give him high marks for his integrity and commitment to ethical behavior.

But some of Malone's peers in the industry see him in a quite different light. Some, for example, perceive him to be a bully and others resent his taking on the role of industry spokesperson. They also think that he worries more about increasing his own personal wealth than about running his business with a long-term perspective.

Both his admirers and his detractors agree that he puts a lot of pressure on people in his firm. Malone has a clear vision of what he wants to accomplish and doesn't lightly suffer others questioning that vision. People who go to work for TCI know that they will be working long hours, be subjected to intense pressure, and be closely accountable for meeting their goals. Malone recognizes the importance of human capital to his organization, but he has been criticized for ignoring the intellectual capabilities of that capital. That is, he sometimes wants people to work hard for his goals but isn't particularly interested in listening to their ideas or understanding their own goals.

But TCI employees who succeed will also be well rewarded for their efforts. TCI pays its employees well and provides generous benefits packages. The firm's growth has also afforded ample opportunities for promotion and advancement. Job security at TCI is also better than at most firms. And the company stock-option plan has made millionaires of many of the firm's original managers.

Malone recognizes that he cannot sit still if TCI is to remain viable. The cable television industry changes continually, for example, and only firms that anticipate and fully participate in that change will be around in the future. Rapid advances in technology mean that both the transmission and the reception of cable signals will continue to change.

Soon, for instance, cable companies will be able to transmit as many as 500 channels into a home, and the customer will be able to receive multiple channels simultaneously. For example, the technology will soon exist for different family members to watch one program on a television screen, watch another pro-

---

gram on a picture-within-a-picture on the same screen, record another program on a videocassette recorder, listen to only the audio portion of yet another, and feed information from another program directly into a personal computer data bank—all at the same time.

To help prepare for the future, Malone and TCI have a number of joint ventures underway with different firms. For example, Microsoft is preparing software to help TCI customers better manage their reception technology, and Carolco Pictures is making four movies that TCI will preview on a pay-per-view basis before they open in theaters. Other joint venture partners include AT&T, McCaw, and Ted Turner. And Malone is also expanding aggressively abroad, with big operations in Britain and Germany.

Case Questions

1. What role do people play at TCI Cable?
2. How would you evaluate John Malone's approach to managing his business? To managing his employees?
3. Would you consider working for Malone? Why or why not?

SOURCES: Andrew Kupfer, "The No. 1 in Cable TV Has Big Plans," *Fortune*, June 28, 1993, pp. 92–98; "John Malone of TCI Is Formidable Player in Bid for Paramount," *Wall Street Journal*, September 27, 1993, pp. A1, A7; "Cable's King: Vital Leader or Bully?" *USA Today*, September 28, 1993, pp. 1B, 2B.

CASE 1.2   Difficult Transitions

Tony Stark just finished his first week at Reece Enterprises and decided to drive upstate to a small lakefront lodge for some fishing and relaxation. Before accepting a job with Reece, Tony had worked for the past ten years for the O'Grady Company. O'Grady had suffered through some hard times, however, and recently shut down several of its operating groups, including Tony's, to cut costs. Fortunately, Tony's experience and recommendations had made finding another position fairly easy. As he drove the interstate, he reflected on the past ten years and the apparent situation at Reece.

At O'Grady, things had been great. Tony had been part of the team from day one. The job had met his personal goals and expectations perfectly, and Tony believed that he had grown greatly as a person. His work was appreciated and recognized; he had received three promotions and many more pay increases.

Tony had also liked the company itself. The firm was decentralized, allowing its managers considerable autonomy and freedom. The corporate culture was easygoing. Communication was open. It seemed that everyone knew what was going on at all times; finding out information was easy.

The people had been another plus. Tony and three other managers went to lunch often and played golf every Saturday. They got along well both personally and professionally and truly worked together as a team. Their boss had been very supportive, giving them the help they needed but also staying out of the way and letting them work.

When word about the shutdown came down, Tony was devastated. He was sure that nothing could replace O'Grady. After the final closing was announced, he spent only a few weeks looking around before he found a comparable position at Reece Enterprises.

As Tony drove, he reflected that comparable probably was the wrong word. Indeed, Reece and O'Grady were about as different as they could be. Top managers at Reece apparently didn't worry too much about who did a good job and who didn't. Their basis for promoting and rewarding people seemed to be how long they had been there and how well they played the never-ending political games.

Maybe this stemmed from the organization itself, Tony pondered. Reece was a bigger organization than O'Grady and was structured much more bureaucratically. It seemed that no one was allowed to make any sort of decision without getting three signatures from higher up. Those signatures, though, were hard to get. All the top managers usually were too busy to see anyone, and few relied on interoffice memos for communication.

Tony also had had some problems fitting in. His peers treated him with polite indifference. He sensed that a couple of them resented that he, an outsider, had been brought in at their level after they had had to work themselves up the ladder. On Tuesday he had asked two colleagues about playing golf. They had politely declined, saying that they did not play often. But later in the week, he had overheard them making arrangements to play that very Saturday.

That was when Tony decided to go fishing. As he steered his car off the interstate to get gas, he won-dered if perhaps he had made a mistake in accepting the Reece offer without finding out more about what he was getting into.

Case Questions

1. Identify several concepts and characteristics from the field of organizational behavior that this case illustrates.
2. What advice can you give Tony? How is this advice supported or tempered by behavioral concepts and processes?
3. Is it possible to find an "ideal" place to work? Explain.

CHAPTER 2

Managing People and Organizations

OBJECTIVES

After studying this chapter, you should be able to:

Explain managerial perspectives on organizational behavior.

Describe the manager's job in terms of managerial functions, roles, and skills.

Identify major managerial challenges and relate them to organizational behavior.

Identify major organizational challenges and relate them to organizational behavior.

Identify major competitive challenges and relate them to organizational behavior.

Discuss how to manage for effectiveness from the perspective of organizational behavior.

Stephen Racioppo, a partner in New York's Anderson Consulting, uses a fiber-optic network to communicate with clients and colleagues around the world. Technology has enabled Racioppo, and many others, to conduct business in many locations at once without the assistance of on-site managers.

It's no secret that organizations today are changing. For example, the business press reminds us constantly that many companies are shrinking, becoming more quality conscious, and entering global markets. Sometimes overlooked in this hoopla, however, is the impact that these and other changes have on employees and managers in those organizations.

A number of trends are reshaping the nature of work and the jobs of managers. Traditional hierarchies are giving way to flat amoeba-like structures centered around expert specialists. New forms of technical work are creating opportunities for ambitious and motivated skilled employees. Managers are spending less and less of their time directing and supervising employees and are instead being expected to coach and coordinate work. And in many firms workers have stopped working alone and instead belong to work teams responsible for a wide array of projects, including managing their own activities.

Consider, for example, Westt, Inc. This California-based enterprise does sophisticated custom manufacturing and industrial automation with millions of dollars worth of equipment, no managers, and only ten employees. Or consider how account executives at Andersen Consulting use a fiberoptic network to keep in touch with clients and colleagues around the world. Or how the Franklin Mint recently eliminated two of five layers of management and doubled its productivity. Or how a General Electric plant in upstate New York operates three shifts a day, but has managers on duty for only one of them. The list of examples is virtually endless, but all of its entries support a simple conclusion: tomorrow's managers, more than ever before, must have a keen understanding of not only their own work but also the work of others throughout the organization.[1]

Sweeping change threatens to make yesterday's manager obsolete. But an awareness of that change and how to capitalize on it offer tomorrow's manager untold opportunity. Although the nature of managerial work varies from company to company and continues to evolve, however, one common thread permeates virtually all managerial activity: interacting with other people. Indeed, the "typical" day for most managers is almost entirely devoted to interacting with others. Thus, the management process and the behavior of people in organizations are undeniably intertwined.

This chapter relates the general field of management to the more specific field of organizational behavior. We start by developing managerial perspectives on organizational behavior. Then we characterize the manager's job in terms of its functions, roles, and requisite skills. Next, we identify and discuss a variety of managerial,

1. Walter Kiechel III, "How We Will Work in the Year 2000," *Fortune*, May 17, 1993, pp. 38–52; Shawn Tully, "The Modular Corporation," *Fortune*, February 8, 1993, pp. 106–116; and "The Technology Payoff," *Business Week*, June 14, 1993, pp. 57–68.

organizational, and competitive challenges and relate them to organizational behavior. Finally, we discuss how to manage for organizational effectiveness in the context of organizational behavior.

Managerial Perspectives on Organizational Behavior

Organizational behavior is not an organizational function or area; rather, it is a perspective that all managers can use to perform their jobs more effectively.

Managers can use organizational behavior to better understand themselves, their subordinates, their peers and colleagues, and their superiors.

Virtually all organizations have managers with titles like marketing manager, director of public relations, vice president for human resources, and plant manager. But probably no organization has a position called organizational behavior manager. The reason for this is simple: organizational behavior is not an organizational function or area. Instead, it is best described as a perspective or set of tools that all managers can use to carry out their jobs more effectively.[2]

By understanding organizational behavior concepts, managers can better understand and appreciate the behavior of those around them.[3] For example, most managers in an organization are directly responsible for the work-related behaviors of a set of other people—their immediate subordinates. Typical managerial activities in this area include motivating employees to work harder, ensuring that their jobs are properly designed, resolving conflicts, evaluating their performance, and helping them set goals to achieve rewards. The field of organizational behavior abounds with theory and research regarding each of these functions.[4]

Unless they happen to be CEOs, managers also report to others in the organization (and even the CEO reports to the board of directors). In working with these individuals, understanding basic issues associated with leadership, power and political behavior, decision making, organization structure and design, and organization culture can also be extremely beneficial. Again, the field of organizational behavior provides numerous valuable insights into these processes.

Managers can also use their knowledge from the field of organizational behavior to better understand their own behaviors and feelings. For example, understanding personal needs and motives, how to improve decision-making capabilities, how to respond to and control stress, how to better communicate with others, and how career dynamics unfold can all be of enormous benefit to individual managers. Organizational behavior once again provides useful insights into these concepts and processes.

Managers must also interact with a variety of colleagues, peers, and coworkers inside the organization. Understanding attitudinal processes, individual differences, group dynamics, intergroup dynamics, organization culture, and power and political behavior can help managers handle such interactions more effectively. Many useful ideas from the field of organizational behavior have provided a variety of practical insights into these processes.

Finally, managers also interact with various individuals from outside the organization, including suppliers, customers, competitors, government officials, repre-

---

2. Rosabeth Moss Kanter, "The New Managerial Work," *Harvard Business Review*, November–December 1989, pp. 85–92.
3. Brian Dumaine, "The New Non-Manager Managers," *Fortune*, February 22, 1993, pp. 80–84.
4. See Omar Aktouf, "Management and Theories of Organizations in the 1990s: Toward a Critical Radical Humanism?" *Academy of Management Review*, October 1992, pp. 407–431. See also Frank Rose, "A New Age for Business?" *Fortune*, October 8, 1990, pp. 156–164.

sentatives of citizens' groups, union officials, and potential joint venture partners. Virtually all of the behavioral processes already noted can be relevant. In addition, special understanding of the environment, technology, and, increasingly, international issues is also of value. Here again, the field of organizational behavior offers managers many different insights into how and why things happen.

Thus, management and organizational behavior are interrelated in many ways. Understanding and practicing management without considering the numerous areas from the field of organizational behavior is essentially impossible. And organizational behavior itself can provide a useful set of tools and perspectives for managing organizations more effectively. We now turn to the nature of the manager's job in more detail.

Management Functions, Roles, and Skills

The job of a contemporary manager can be conceptualized in many different ways.[5] The most widely accepted approaches, however, are from the perspectives of basic managerial functions, common managerial roles, and fundamental managerial skills.

Managerial Functions

The manager's job involves four basic functions: planning, organizing, leading, and controlling.

As Figure 2.1 shows, the four basic managerial functions in organizations are planning, organizing, leading, and controlling. By applying these functions to the various organizational resources—human, financial, physical, and information—the organization achieves different levels of effectiveness and efficiency.

Planning is the process of determining the organization's desired future position and the best means to get there.

Planning   The managerial function of **planning** is the process of determining the organization's desired future position and deciding how best to get there. The planning process at Sears, Roebuck, for example, includes scanning the environment, deciding on appropriate goals, outlining strategies for achieving those goals, and developing tactics to execute the strategies. Behavioral processes and characteristics pervade each of these activities. Perception, for instance, plays a major role in environmental scanning, and creativity and motivation influence how managers set goals, strategies, and tactics for their organization.

Organizing is the process of designing jobs, grouping jobs into units, and establishing patterns of authority between jobs and units.

Organizing   The managerial function of **organizing** is the process of designing jobs, grouping jobs into manageable units, and establishing patterns of authority among jobs and groups of jobs. This process designs the basic structure, or framework, of the organization. For large organizations like Sears, that structure can be extensive and complicated. As noted earlier, the processes and characteristics of the organization itself are a major theme of organizational behavior.

Leading is the process of getting the organization's members to work together toward the organization's goals.

Leading   **Leading** is the process of motivating members of the organization to work together toward the organization's goals. A Sears manager, for example, must hire and motivate people, and train them. Major components of leading

5. David H. Freedman, "Is Management Still a Science?" *Harvard Business Review*, November–December 1992, pp. 26–38.

FIGURE 2.1

Basic Managerial Functions

include motivating employees, managing group dynamics, and leadership per se, all of which are closely related to major areas of organizational behavior.

Controlling is the process of monitoring and correcting the actions of the organization and its members to keep them directed toward their goals.

Controlling   A final managerial function, **controlling**, is the process of monitoring and correcting the actions of the organization and its people to keep them headed toward their goals. A Sears manager has to control costs, inventory, and so on. Again, behavioral processes and characteristics are an important part of this function. Performance evaluation, reward systems, and motivation, for example, are all aspects of controlling.

Managerial Roles

Managers play ten basic roles in their jobs.

In an organization, as in a play or a movie, a role is the part a person plays in a given situation. Managers often play a number of different roles. Much of our knowledge about managerial roles comes from the work of Henry Mintzberg.[6]

Mintzberg identified ten basic managerial roles clustered into three general categories. Both the categories and the specific roles are listed in Table 2.1.

Three important **interpersonal roles** are the figurehead, the leader, and the liaison.

Interpersonal Roles   Mintzberg's **interpersonal roles** are primarily social in nature; that is, they are roles in which the manager's main task is to relate to other people in certain ways. The manager sometimes may serve as a *figurehead* for the organization. Taking visitors to dinner and attending ribbon-cutting ceremonies are part of the figurehead role. In the role of *leader*, the manager works to hire, train, and motivate employees. Finally, the *liaison* role consists of relating to others outside the group or organization. For example, a manager at Intel might be

6. Henry Mintzberg, "The Manager's Job: Folklore and Fact," *Harvard Business Review*, July–August 1975, pp. 49–61.

TABLE 2.1

Important Managerial Roles

Category	Role	Example
Interpersonal	Figurehead	Attend employee retirement ceremony
	Leader	Encourage workers to increase productivity
	Liaison	Coordinate activities of two committees
Informational	Monitor	Scan *Business Week* for information about competition
	Disseminator	Send out memos outlining new policies
	Spokesperson	Hold press conference to announce new plant
Decision-making	Entrepreneur	Develop idea for new product and convince others of its merits
	Disturbance handler	Resolve dispute
	Resource allocator	Allocate budget requests
	Negotiator	Settle new labor contract

responsible for handling all price negotiations with a major supplier of electronic circuit boards. Obviously, each of these interpersonal roles involves behavioral processes.

Three major **informational roles** are the monitor, the disseminator, and the spokesperson.

Informational Roles   Mintzberg's three **informational roles** involve some aspect of information processing. The *monitor* actively seeks information that might be of value to the organization in general or to specific managers. The manager who transmits this information to others is carrying out the role of *disseminator*. The *spokesperson* speaks for the organization to outsiders. For example, the manager chosen by Apple Computer to appear at a press conference announcing a merger or other major deal, such as a recent decision to undertake a joint venture with Microsoft, would be serving in this role. Again, behavioral processes are part of these roles because information is almost always exchanged between people.

Four basic **decision-making roles** are the entrepreneur, the disturbance handler, the resource allocator, and the negotiator.

Decision-making Roles   Finally, Mintzberg identified four **decision-making roles**. The *entrepreneur* voluntarily initiates change, such as innovations or new strategies, in the organization. The *disturbance handler* helps settle disputes between various parties, such as other managers and their subordinates. The *resource allocator* decides who will get what—how resources in the organization will be distributed among various individuals and groups. The *negotiator* represents the organization in reaching agreements with other organizations, such as contracts between management and labor unions. Again, behavioral processes clearly are crucial in each of these decisional roles.

The top executives of the Be-Puzzled Company, a small publisher of mystery books and puzzles, hold an informal planning meeting. Planning is an essential managerial function; companies of all sizes must develop suitable goals and strategies for achieving those goals.

Managerial Skills

Most successful managers have effective technical, interpersonal, conceptual, and diagnostic skills.

Still another important element of managerial work is the skills necessary to carry out basic functions and fill fundamental roles. In general, most successful managers have a strong combination of technical, interpersonal, conceptual, and diagnostic skills.[7]

Technical skills are those skills necessary to accomplish specific tasks within the organization.

Technical Skills   **Technical skills** are those skills necessary to accomplish specific tasks within the organization. Assembling a computer, developing a new formula for a frozen food additive, and writing a press release each require technical skills. Hence, these skills are generally associated with the operations employed by the organization in its production processes. For example, David Packard and Bill Hewlett, founders of Hewlett-Packard, started their careers as engineers. They still work hard today to keep abreast of new technology. Thus, their technical skills are an important part of their success. Other examples of managers with strong technical skills include David Glass (CEO of Wal-Mart, who started his career as a store manager) and John Reed (CEO of Citicorp, who started as a loan officer in a bank).

Interpersonal skills comprise the manager's ability to communicate with, understand, and motivate individuals and groups.

Interpersonal Skills   **Interpersonal skills** comprise the manager's ability to communicate with, understand, and motivate individuals and groups. As we have already noted, managers spend a large portion of their time interacting with others. Thus, it is clearly important that they be able to relate to, and get along with, other people. Stanley Gault, CEO of Goodyear, is one of the most admired business leaders in the United States. Part of his success is attributable to his making a

7. Robert L. Katz, "The Skills of an Effective Administrator," *Harvard Business Review*, September–October 1987, pp. 90–102.

conscious effort to get acquainted with people in the firm, treating them with dignity and respect, and always being open and direct when he talks to them.[8]

Conceptual skills are the manager's ability to think in the abstract.

Conceptual Skills   **Conceptual skills** refer to the manager's ability to think in the abstract. A manager with strong conceptual skills is able to see the "big picture." That is, she or he can see potential or opportunity where others see roadblocks or problems. Managers with strong conceptual skills can see opportunities that others miss. For example, after Steve Wozniak and Steve Jobs built a small computer of their own design in a garage, Wozniak simply saw a new toy that could be tinkered with. Jobs, however, saw far more and convinced his partner that they should start a company to make and sell the computers. Thus was born Apple Computer.

Diagnostic skills are the manager's ability to understand cause-and-effect relationships and to recognize the optimal solutions to problems.

Diagnostic Skills   Most successful managers also bring diagnostic skills to the organization. **Diagnostic skills** allow the manager to better understand cause-and-effect relationships and to recognize the optimal solution to problems. For example, Robert Goizueta, CEO of Coca-Cola, was concerned that the firm's stock price was not as high as he thought it should be. On closer analysis, he discovered the reason—the company was focusing too much attention on increasing sales without proper consideration of actual profits. He reoriented the firm's goals more toward enhancing returns to shareholders and, as a consequence, has achieved record stock prices. Goizueta used diagnostic skills to see what needed to be done.[9]

Of course, not every manager has an equal allotment of these four basic skills. Nor are equal allotments critical. As shown in Figure 2.2, for example, the optimal skills mix tends to vary with the manager's level in the organization. First-line managers generally need to depend more on their technical and interpersonal skills and less on their conceptual and diagnostic skills. Top managers tend to exhibit the reverse combination—a greater emphasis on conceptual and diagnostic skills and a somewhat lesser dependence on technical and interpersonal skills. Middle managers require a more even distribution of skills.

Managerial Challenges

Three important managerial challenges are workforce diversity, workplace issues and challenges, and downsizing.

Beyond its inherent pervasiveness in managerial work, organizational behavior has several implications for various managerial, organizational, and global challenges. From the managerial perspective, any number of critical issues might be discussed, but we focus on three in particular: workforce diversity, workplace issues and challenges, and downsizing.

Workforce Diversity

Workforce demographic variables such as age, gender, and ethnic composition are all changing.

From a wide variety of perspectives, workforce demographics are changing. These changes, in turn, are associated with age, gender, and ethnic composition. Figure 2.3 summarizes some changing workforce demographics.

8. Jennifer Reese, "America's Most Admired Corporations," *Fortune*, February 8, 1993, pp. 44–80.
9. Ibid.

FIGURE 2.2

Managerial Skills at Different Organizational Levels

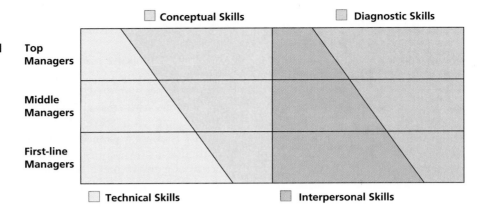

Age   The average age of workers in the United States is gradually increasing, partly because of declining birth rates and partly because people are living and working longer. Many organizations are finding retirees to be excellent part-time or temporary employees. McDonald's has hired hundreds of elderly workers in recent years. Apple Computer has used many retired workers for temporary assignments and projects. By hiring retirees, the organization gets the expertise of skilled workers and the individuals get extra income and an opportunity to continue to use their skills in a productive way.

Gender   An increasing number of women have entered the U.S. workforce. In 1950, only 34 percent of American women worked outside their homes; today almost two-thirds work part time or full time outside the home. Many occupations traditionally dominated by women—such as, nurses, teachers, and secretaries—continue to offer popular career opportunities for women. But women have also moved increasingly into occupations previously dominated by men, such as lawyers, physicians, and executives. Further, many blue-collar jobs are increasingly sought by women. On the other hand, more and more men are entering occupations previously dominated by women. For example, there are more male secretaries today than ever before.

Ethnic Composition   The ethnic composition of the workplace also is changing. One obvious change has been the increasing number of Hispanics and black Americans entering the workplace. Further, many of these individuals now hold executive positions. In addition, there has been a dramatic influx of immigrant workers in the last few years. Immigrants and refugees from Central America and Southeast Asia have entered the U.S. workforce in record numbers.

Clearly, then, along just about any dimension imaginable, the workforce is becoming more diverse. Workforce diversity enhances the effectiveness of most organizations, but it also provides special challenges for managers. We return to issues of workforce diversity in Chapter 20.

FIGURE 2.3

**Changing Demographics
in the U. S. Workforce**

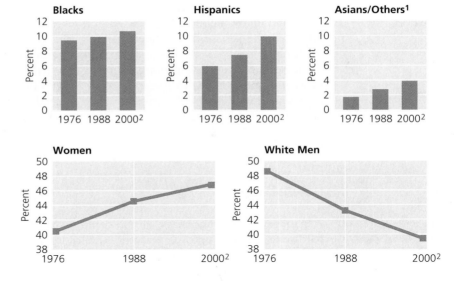

1. Including Native Americans, Alaskan natives, and Pacific Islanders
2. Projected
SOURCE: *The Wall Street Journal*, September 12, 1990, p. B1. Reprinted by permission of *THE WALL STREET JOURNAL*, © 1990 Dow Jones & Company, Inc. All Rights Reserved Worldwide.

Workplace Issues and Challenges

Employee privacy, employee rights, and unionization trends are important workplace challenges.

Another set of workplace issues and challenges has behavioral overtones. Three specific areas are employee privacy, employee rights, and unionization trends.

Employee Privacy   Employee privacy has become a major issue in many organizations in recent years. For example, some organizations have started to implement random drug tests. Background checks on prospective employees have become increasingly more comprehensive. And some firms have implemented extraordinary performance assessment devices, including random checks of telephone calls and frequency counts of keyboard strokes for word processing operators. Some people, however, believe that these and related activities are too intrusive and encroach too much into private lives. Thus, a manager in an organization that follows this trend needs to be sensitive to the resentment that these practices may create.[10]

Employee Rights   A related concern is employee rights. This issue actually spans a wide range of controversies. For example, issues have surfaced regarding the individual's right to smoke in the workplace. As more and more organizations limit or ban smoking, this issue will continue to be somewhat controversial. Broader controversies involve issues associated with job ownership and individual rights while at work. A popular (albeit not entirely correct) assumption about Japanese organizations is that their employees have lifetime job security. To the extent that U.S. firms adopt this practice, the question becomes one of due process and the right to appeal in instances of dismissal or reassignment.

10. "Is Your Boss Spying on You?" *Business Week*, January 5, 1990, pp. 74–75.

Unionization Trends Yet another managerial challenge is the general trend regarding union membership. For the past several years, union membership in the United States has steadily declined. Although most managers are likely to applaud this trend, organizations will carry the added burden of providing services to their employees that unions previously supplied. A strong balance between organizations and unions tends to free each from charges of exploitation. Without union representation, however, organizations will need to take extra precautions to ensure that workers are treated fairly. If not, union membership may well start to climb again. At the same time, unionism is emerging in unusual areas, including professional, technical, and white-collar fields.[11]

Downsizing

Downsizing is the process of purposely becoming smaller by reducing the size of the workforce or shedding divisions or businesses.

A managerial challenge that is all too common today is the trend for organizations to **downsize**—to purposely become smaller by reducing the size of their workforce or by shedding entire divisions or businesses. During the 1960s and 1970s, many U.S. firms dramatically added new operations and positions at all levels. Their sales were growing rapidly, and relatively little consideration had to be given to costs or expenses. As international competitiveness became more intense in the early 1980s, however, those same firms found that their costs had grown faster than their revenues. Thus, it was then necessary to cut back in a variety of areas, including payroll. From around the mid-1980s through the present, firms announcing the elimination of thousands of jobs have become commonplace. For example, General Motors and IBM announced recently that they would each be eliminating as many as 50,000 jobs during the next few years. Organizations going through such downsizing must be concerned about managing the effects of these cutbacks, not only for those who are being let go, but also for those who are surviving—often with a reduced level of job security.

Organizational Challenges

Important organizational challenges for managers include business strategy, ethics and social responsibility, and change.

Managers also face numerous challenges at an organizational level. The three issues most relevant to the domain of organizational behavior concern business strategy, ethics and social responsibility, and change.

Business Strategy

Business strategy is an outline of how a business intends to compete with other firms in the same industry.

A firm's **business strategy** focuses on how it intends to compete with other firms in the same industry. In general, most firms adopt one of three business strategies.[12] A firm using a *differentiation strategy* attempts to make its products or services at least appear to be different from others in the marketplace. For example, because Rolex has created the image that its watches are of higher quality and prestige than those offered by its competitors, it can charge a higher price.

11. "Unions May Be Poised to End Long Decline, Recover Some Clout," *Wall Street Journal*, August 28, 1987, pp. 1, 7.
12. Michael Porter, *Competitive Strategy* (New York: Free Press, 1980).

Alternatively, a firm that adopts a *cost leadership strategy* works aggressively to push its costs as low as possible. This allows the firm to charge a lower price for its products or services and thus gain more market share. The French firm Bic uses cost leadership to sell its low-price, disposable ball point pens. Finally, a *focus strategy* involves targeting products or services to meet the unique needs of a specific customer group. Fiesta Mart, a Houston-based supermarket, has prospered by targeting that city's large Hispanic population. Fiesta Mart customers can buy Mexican soft drinks, corn husks for wrapping tamales, and other ethnic products not readily available at other supermarkets.

A firm's managers must be cognizant of its business strategy when hiring employees. For example, if the business strategy calls for differentiation, the firm will need employees who are capable of producing high-quality products or services and projecting a differentiated image. On the other hand, a cost leadership strategy will dictate the need for people who can focus on cost cutting and who respond well to tight cost controls. And finally, a focus strategy will require people who clearly understand the target population being courted by the firm.

Ethics and Social Responsibility

Ethics are an individual's personal beliefs about what is right and wrong or good and bad. **Social responsibility** is the organization's obligation to protect or contribute to the social environment in which it functions.

Another organizational challenge that has taken on renewed importance relates to ethics and social responsibility. **Ethics** are an individual's beliefs about what is right and wrong or good and bad.[13] **Social responsibility**, meanwhile, is the organization's obligation to protect or contribute to the social environment in which it functions. Thus, whereas the two concepts are related, they are also distinct from each other.

Both ethics and social responsibility have taken on new importance in recent years. Scandals in organizations such as Drexel Burnham Lambert (stock market fraud), Beech-Nut (advertising chemically extended baby apple juice as 100 percent pure), and the Japanese firm Recruit (bribery of government officials) have made headlines around the world. From the social responsibility angle, increasing attention has been focused on pollution and business's obligation to help clean up our environment, business contributions to social causes, and so forth.[14] *The Ethical Dilemma* illustrates some of the complexities associated with ethics and social responsibility in organizations today.

Leadership, organization culture, and group norms—all important organizational behavior concepts—are relevant in managing these processes. For example, a recent brokerage scandal at Dean Witter Reynolds grew because individual brokers felt pressure from their colleagues to participate. The scandal at Beech-Nut was perpetuated because it started at the highest level of the organization. In contrast, during the Tylenol poisoning crisis in 1982, everyone at Johnson & Johnson knew exactly how to respond. Products were immediately recalled from store shelves, advertising was stopped, and informational briefings were scheduled—all without executive direction. Because employees knew the organizational culture so well, they knew how they would be expected to respond.[15]

13. Thomas M. Garrett and Richard J. Klonoski, *Business Ethics*, 3rd ed. (Englewood Cliffs, N.J.: Prentice-Hall, 1992).
14. Jerry W. Anderson, Jr., "Social Responsibility and the Corporation," *Business Horizons*, July–August 1986, pp. 22–27.
15. "At Johnson & Johnson, a Mistake Can Be a Badge of Honor," *Business Week*, September 26, 1988, pp. 126–128.

Ethical Dilemmas and Ice Cream

What goes around, comes around—or so they say. Several years ago, Ben Cohen and Jerry Greenfield founded an ice cream company called, simply enough, Ben & Jerry's. Ben & Jerry's ran into problems initially because they believed that Pillsbury-owned Häagen-Dazs was exerting pressure on its distributors to not carry their new ice cream. After eventually settling out of court, Ben & Jerry's went on to become an all-American success story, replete with old-time values and enormous profits.

Part of Ben & Jerry's charm has been its homespun approach to doing business. For example, Ben & Jerry's denotes a large percentage of its profits to social causes, especially to those with an environmental theme. And all employees of the firm share in the rewards, with a mandated narrow gap between the highest- and lowest-paid employees. Indeed, Ben & Jerry's has been the darling of all advocates of open-minded and enlightened management.

But now, critics are charging that Ben & Jerry's has forgotten its heritage. For example, several small ice cream start-up firms have charged that Ben & Jerry's has pressured its distributors to not carry the new entrants. The policy on wage differentials has also been changed so that higher-priced executive talent could be wooed. And critics also point out that while Cohen and Greenfield are millionaires, less than half a percent of the firm's stock has been transferred to the hands of employees.

Ben & Jerry's has also had some run-ins with the Federal Trade Commission. For example, the firm was recently charged with mislabeling some of its products as low fat when they actually had normal levels of fat content. And some skeptics point out that almost half of the Vermont firm's "homemade" ice cream is actually made in Indiana! Still, a few lapses aside, many observers agree that Ben & Jerry's is still managed in a highly ethical and responsible fashion. It's just hard to always stay on the high road.

SOURCES: "Cookies, Cream 'n' Controversy," *Newsweek*, July 5, 1993, p. 40; and "Food Firms Aim to Emulate Ben & Jerry's But Find Kitchen Hotter Than Expected," *Wall Street Journal*, March 21, 1990, p. B1.

Change

Another organizational challenge that managers must be prepared to address is change. Although organizations have always had to be concerned with managing change, the rapid and constant environmental change faced by businesses today has made change management even more critical. Simply, an organization that fails to monitor its environment and change to keep pace with that environment is doomed to failure.[16] But more and more managers are seeing change as an opportunity, not as a cause for alarm. Indeed, some managers think that if things get too placid in an organization, managers should shake things up to get everyone energized.[17] We discuss the management of organizational change in more detail in Chapter 18.

16. "Leaders of Corporate Change," *Fortune*, December 14, 1992, pp. 102–114.
17. Brian Dumaine, "Times Are Good? Create a Crisis," *Fortune*, June 28, 1993, pp. 123–130.

In downtown Riga, Lativia, an advertisement from Kellogg's urges people to eat Corn Flakes, claiming that "The world is having breakfast with us." Increasingly, with progressive globalization of the world economy, local manufacturers must contend with international competitors.

Competitive Challenges

Three important competitive challenges are global competition, quality and productivity, and the management of technology.

Organizations today also face myriad competitive challenges that they must address to survive and prosper. Three of the more important ones today are global competition, quality and productivity, and the management of technology.

Global Competition

The world economy is becoming increasingly global in character. But often people do not realize the true magnitude of this globalization trend nor the complexities it creates for managers. Consider, for example, the impact of international businesses on our daily lives. We wake to the sound of Panasonic alarm clocks made in Japan. For breakfast we drink milk from Carnation—a subsidiary of Nestlé, a Swiss firm—and coffee ground from Colombian beans. We dress in clothes sewn in Taiwan and drive in Japanese automobiles. Along the way, we stop and buy gas imported from the Middle East by Shell Oil, a Dutch firm. Of course, U.S. citizens are not alone in experiencing the effects of globalization. Indeed, people in other countries eat at McDonald's restaurants and snack on Mars candy bars and Coca-Cola soft drinks. They drive Fords, use IBM computers, and wear Levi jeans. They use Kodak film and fly on Boeing airplanes.

The globalization trend started in the immediate post-World War II years. The U.S. economy emerged strong and intact. U.S. businesses were the dominant suppliers worldwide in virtually all major industries. But war-torn Europe and the Far East rebuilt. Businesses there were forced to build new plants and other facilities, and their citizens turned to their work as a viable source of economic security. As a result, these economies grew in strength and each developed competitive advantages. And today those advantages are being exploited to their fullest.

The situation is further confounded by the rapid change that has characterized the international arena. In the early 1980s, the Eastern bloc countries (including East Germany) were economically stagnant, the Japanese and West German economies were dominant, many observers were writing off the United States, and countries like South Korea and Taiwan played only minor roles. By the early 1990s, however, much of the Eastern bloc countries had embraced capitalism and opened their markets, Japan was slowing down, the United States was coming back, Germany had unified, and South Korea and Taiwan had become powerhouses.

Managing in a global economy poses many different challenges and opportunities. For example, at a macro level, property ownership arrangements vary widely. So does the availability of natural resources and components of the infrastructure, as well as the role of government in business. But for our purposes, a very important consideration is how behavioral processes vary widely across cultural and national boundaries. Values, symbols, and beliefs differ sharply among cultures. Different work norms and the role work plays in a person's life, for example, influence patterns of both work-related behavior and attitudes toward work. They also affect the nature of supervisory relationships, decision-making styles and processes, and organizational configurations. Group and intergroup processes, responses to stress, and the nature of political behaviors also differ from culture to culture. We discuss these and other issues in more detail in Chapter 19.

Quality and Productivity

Quality is the total set of features and characteristics of a product or service that determine its ability to satisfy stated or implied needs.

Another competitive challenge that has attracted much attention is quality and productivity. **Quality** is the total set of features and characteristics of a product or service that define its ability to satisfy stated or implied needs.[18] Quality is an important issue for several reasons.[19] First, more and more organizations are using quality as a basis for competition. Ford, Chrysler, and Buick have launched major promotional campaigns in recent years stressing their products' improved quality, especially relative to Japanese competitors such as Honda and Toyota. Second, improving quality tends to increase productivity because making higher-quality products generally results in less waste and rework. Third, enhancing quality lowers costs. Whistler Corp. recently found that it was using 100 of its 250 employees to repair defective radar detectors that were built incorrectly the first time.[20]

Productivity is an indicator of how much an organization is creating relative to its inputs.

Quality is also important because of its relationship to productivity. Productivity has become a major issue for many organizations during the 1980s and 1990s. In a general sense, **productivity** is an indicator of how much an organization is creating relative to its inputs. For example, if Honda can produce a car for $11,000 while General Motors needs $13,000 to produce a comparable car, Honda is clearly more productive.

Although U.S. workers are the most productive in the world, productivity in other industrial countries, especially Japan and Germany, has grown much more

18. Ross Johnson and William O. Winchell, *Management and Quality* (Milwaukee: American Society for Quality Control, 1989).
19. "Quality," *Business Week*, November 30, 1992, pp. 66–75.
20. Joel Dreyfuss, "Victories in the Quality Crusade," *Fortune*, October 10, 1988, pp. 80–88.

rapidly than it has in the United States for the past several years. To counter this trend, experts have suggested numerous techniques and strategies. Many of these center around increased cooperation and participation on the part of workers. Ultimately, then, managers and workers will need to work in greater harmony and unity of purpose. The implications for organizational behavior are obvious: the more closely people work together, the more important it will be to understand behavioral processes and concepts.

Indeed, many of the things organizations can do to enhance the quality of their products and services depend on the people who work for them. Motivating employees to get involved in quality improvement efforts, increasing the level of participation throughout the organization, and rewarding people on the basis of contributions to quality are common suggestions—and all of them rely on human behavior.[21]

Technology

Technology is the mechanical and intellectual processes used to transform inputs into products and services.

A third major competitive challenge confronting managers today is the set of issues involving the management of technology. **Technology** is the mechanical and intellectual processes the organization uses to transform inputs (raw materials, parts, cash, facilities, and people) into products or services (computers, cars, pizza, and stock transactions). Historically, managing technology was essentially a reactive process. Whenever a supplier developed a new piece of equipment to replace an old one, the organization bought it and trained its workers how to use it.

In recent years, however, this pattern has changed. Computer-assisted manufacturing techniques, automation, and robotics have all transformed the workplace into a truly competitive arena. Firms that proactively manage their technology in creative and innovative ways gain notable competitive advantages over those that do not.

One reason for this trend is the newfound flexibility that recent technology has provided. For example, it used to be costly and time consuming to change an assembly from producing one product to producing another. Increasingly, however, organizations are learning to make such changes more routinely. And some automakers, like Ford, can actually produce different models of automobiles on the same line at the same time. The Japanese, however, set the pace in this area. For example, a division of Matsushita Electric Industrial Co. has developed technology to custom-make bicycles for individual customers. At a retail store, a customer is measured for size on a special frame, chooses colors and options, and so forth. Specifications are faxed to the plant, custom blueprints are prepared (by computer), and the bicycle is put into production. The firm can employ 11,231,862 variations on 18 models in 199 color patterns to accommodate any size person and deliver it in less than two weeks! (Actually, managers say they can do it in just a few days—the two-week delay is to heighten customer anticipation.)[22]

Computerized and automated technology like Matsushita's dramatically alters the relationship between people and the work that they do. Thus, organizations need to be sensitive to these changes and work to ensure that those most directly affected by a new technology play a meaningful role in developing it.

21. Patricia Sellers, "Companies That Serve You Best," *Fortune*, May 31, 1993, pp. 74–88.
22 . Susan Moffat, "Japan's New Personalized Products," *Fortune*, October 22, 1990, pp. 132–135.

Managing for Effectiveness

Managing for effectiveness involves balancing several individual-level, group-level, and organization-level outcomes.

A final set of issues we address in this chapter relates to the consequences of management. More specifically, what are the outcomes of different types of and approaches to management? As Figure 2.4 illustrates, three basic levels of outcomes determine organizational effectiveness: individual-, group-, and organization-level outcomes. *Developing Management Skills* provides some additional perspectives on the importance of these outcomes.

Individual-Level Outcomes

Several different outcomes at the individual level are important to managers. Given the focus of the field of organizational behavior, it should not be surprising that most of these outcomes are directly or indirectly addressed by various theories and models.

Individual Behaviors   First, several individual behaviors result from a person's participation in an organization. One important behavior is productivity. Productivity, as defined in terms of an individual, is an indicator of an employee's efficiency and is measured in terms of the products or services (or both) created per unit of input. For example, if Bill makes 100 units of a product in a day and Sara makes only 90 units in a day, then, assuming that the units are of the same quality and Bill and Sara make the same wages, Bill is more productive than Sara.

Performance, another important individual-level outcome variable, is a somewhat broader concept. It is made up of all work-related behaviors. For example, even though Bill is highly productive, he may also refuse to work overtime, express negative opinions about the organization at every opportunity, and do nothing unless it falls precisely within the boundaries of his job. Sara, on the other hand,

FIGURE 2.4

Managing for Effectiveness

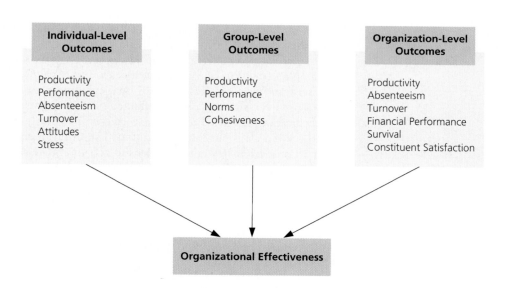

Individual-Level Outcomes	Group-Level Outcomes	Organization-Level Outcomes
Productivity	Productivity	Productivity
Performance	Performance	Absenteeism
Absenteeism	Norms	Turnover
Turnover	Cohesiveness	Financial Performance
Attitudes		Survival
Stress		Constituent Satisfaction

Organizational Effectiveness

Balancing Outcomes

Assume that you are the general manager of a medium-size manufacturing firm that makes camping equipment such as tents, stoves, and lanterns. When you took over the enterprise a few years ago, employees were being paid slightly more than the industry average. At the same time, the firm was so deeply in debt that it was bordering on bankruptcy.

You vowed to eliminate debt and restore the organization's financial health. In the years since, you have poured every available dollar the firm has generated into reducing debt. As part of your debt reduction program, you have also gradually cut back on wage increases for your workers. These additional funds have allowed you to cut debt even more than you originally expected. At the same time, however, average wages for your employees have gradually slid first to the industry average and now hover below that average by around 5 percent.

Today the firm is about one year away from being debt free. All of your extra funds are committed to paying off remaining debt. Unfortunately, your workers are threatening to strike unless they get an immediate pay increase. You face several difficult choices. The two most obvious alternatives are to borrow money to finance a wage increase or to call your workers' bluff and encourage them to be patient. Which would you do, and why?

may always be willing to work overtime, is a positive representative of the organization, and goes out of her way to make as many contributions to the organization as possible. Based on the full array of behaviors, then, we might conclude that Sara actually is the better performer.

Two other important individual-level behaviors are absenteeism and turnover. Absenteeism is a measure of attendance. Whereas virtually everyone misses work occasionally, some people miss far more than others. Some look for excuses to miss work and call in sick regularly just for some time off; others miss work only when absolutely necessary. Turnover occurs when a person leaves the organization. If the individual who leaves is a good performer or if the organization has invested heavily in training the person, turnover can be costly.

Individual Attitudes   Another set of individual-level outcomes influenced by managers consists of individual attitudes. (We discuss attitudes more fully in Chapter 3.) Levels of job satisfaction or dissatisfaction, organizational commitment, and organizational involvement are all important in organizational behavior.

Stress   Stress, discussed more fully in Chapter 9, is another important individual-level outcome variable. Given its costs, both personal and organizational, it should not be surprising that stress is becoming an increasingly important topic for both researchers in organizational behavior and practicing managers.

Group- and Team-Level Outcomes

Another set of outcomes exists at the group and team level. In general, some of these outcomes parallel the individual-level outcomes just discussed. For example, if an organization makes extensive use of work teams, team productivity and performance are important outcome variables. On the other hand, even if all the people in a group or team have the same or similar attitudes toward their jobs, the attitudes themselves are individual-level phenomena. Individuals, not groups, have attitudes.

But groups or teams also have unique outcomes that individuals do not share. For example, as we discuss in Chapter 11, groups develop norms that govern the behavior of individual group members. Groups also develop different levels of cohesiveness. Thus, managers need to assess both common and unique outcomes when considering individual- and group-level outcomes.

Organization-Level Outcomes

Finally, a set of outcome variables exists at the organization level. As before, some of these outcomes parallel those at the individual and group levels, but others are unique. For example, we can measure and compare organizational productivity. We can also develop organization-level indicators of absenteeism and turnover. But financial performance is generally assessed only at the organization level.

In terms of financial performance, organizations are commonly assessed on stock price, return on investment, growth rates, and the like. They are also evaluated in terms of their ability to survive and the extent to which they satisfy important constituents such as investors, government regulators, employees, and unions.

Clearly, then, the manager must balance different outcomes across all three levels of analysis. In many cases, these outcomes appear to contradict one another. For example, as illustrated earlier in *Developing Management Skills*, paying workers high salaries can enhance satisfaction and reduce turnover, but it also may detract from bottom-line performance. Thus, the manager must look at the full array of outcomes and attempt to balance them in an optimal fashion. The manager's ability to do this will be a major determinant of the organization's success.

Summary of Key Points

- By its very nature, management requires an understanding and appreciation of human behavior. Such an understanding and appreciation can help managers better understand those above and below them in the organization, those at the same level, those in other organizations, and themselves.
- The manager's job can be characterized in terms of four functions, three categories of roles, and four skills. The basic managerial functions are planning, organizing, leading, and controlling. Three of the roles are interpersonal, three are informational, and four are decision making. The four basic skills necessary for effective management are technical, interpersonal, conceptual, and diagnostic skills.
- Several managerial challenges confront managers. Workforce diversity addresses the changes in the age, gender, and ethnic composition in the organization. Other workplace challenges pertain to employee privacy, employee rights, and unionization trends. Downsizing is also an important managerial challenge today.

- Managers also face several important organizational challenges. Determining the most effective business strategy and matching people to that strategy is one important challenge. Ethics and social responsibility pose other important challenges. Finally, the management of change is also an important organizational challenge.
- Organizations must also meet competitive challenges if they are to succeed. Global competition is one of the most critical competitive challenges facing managers today. Product and service quality and productivity are also increasingly important in today's competitive world. Technology management is an additional major consideration.
- Managing for effectiveness involves the need to balance a variety of individual-level, group- and team-level, and organization-level outcome variables.

Discussion Questions

1. Is it possible for managers to worry too much about the behavior of their subordinates?
2. The text identifies four basic managerial functions. Based on your own experiences or observations, provide examples of each function.
3. Which managerial skill or skills do you think is one of your strengths? Which is one of your weaknesses? How might you improve the latter?
4. The text argues that we cannot understand organizations without understanding the behavior of the people within them. Do you agree or disagree with this assertion? Why?
5. Interview a local manager or business owner to find out his or her views on the importance of individual behavior to the success of the organization. Report your findings to the class.
6. What advice would you give managers to help them be better prepared to cope with changes in workforce demographics?
7. What limits, if any, should there be regarding an employee's rights to privacy at work?
8. Do you think that unions will continue to decline in importance or bounce back and start regaining lost membership? Why?
9. Of the three organizational challenges noted in the text, which do you think is most important? Which is least important? Give reasons for your answers.
10. Are there any businesses that have not been affected by globalization? Explain.
11. What individual-, group-, or organization-level outcome variables of consequence can you identify beyond those noted in the text?

EXPERIENTIAL EXERCISE

Purpose This exercise will help you develop a deeper and more complete appreciation for the complexities and nuances of managing individual behavior in organizational settings.

Format   You will first develop a scenario regarding a behavioral problem of your own choosing, along with a recommended course of action. You will then exchange scenarios with a classmate and compare recommendations.

Procedure   Select any single one of the managerial challenges (workforce diversity, workplace issues and challenges, or downsizing), organizational challenges (business strategy, ethics and social responsibility, or change), or competitive challenges (global competition, quality and productivity, or technology) discussed in this chapter. Working alone (perhaps as an outside-of-class assignment, if requested by your instructor), write a brief scenario (one page or less) describing a hypothetical organization facing that challenge. Your scenario should provide background about the firm, the specific challenge it is facing, and some detail about why that particular challenge is relevant.

On a separate page, recommend a course of action that a manager might take to address that challenge. For example, your challenge might be to cope with a new form of technology or to enhance quality. Your recommended action might be to form employee advisory groups to help implement the technology or to establish a new employee reward system to improve quality. Try to make the scenario you describe and the course of action you recommend as logically connected and as obviously linked as you possibly can. Also provide enough detail about the course of action so that your plan is readily apparent.

Next, exchange scenarios with one of your classmates. Without discussing it, read the other individual's scenario and develop your own recommended course of action for addressing that challenge. After you have finished, verbally summarize your recommendation(s) for your colleague and listen to his or her summary of recommendations for your scenario. Then exchange the written recommendations you prepared for your own scenarios and read them. Discuss similarities and differences between the two sets of recommendations. Explain the logic behind the recommendations you originally set forward, and listen carefully to the logic your colleague used to develop his or her own recommendations.

Follow-up Questions

1. Were the two sets of recommendations basically the same or basically different? Did the discussion alter your view of what should be done?
2. The contingency view, discussed in Chapter 1, would suggest that different courses of action might be equally effective. How likely is it that each of the two sets of recommendations you and your colleague developed might work?

CASE 2.1	U.S. Workers and Their Foreign Counterparts

A couple of years ago a top Japanese government official made headlines around the world by calling U.S. workers lazy and ridiculing their academic skills. Although many managers and workers in the United States were indignant—if not outraged—they were also at a loss as to how to defend themselves, except to argue that it just wasn't true.

In fact, the typical worker in the United States compares favorably with most other workers around the world. Much has been written about productivity levels in different countries. The fact is that although Japanese and German workers may be closing the gap, U.S. workers are still the most productive in the world.

For example, the average U.S. worker is 30 percent more productive than the average Japanese worker. Within the manufacturing sector, the average U.S. worker is 28 percent more productive than the average Japanese worker. And in many sectors of the economy—farming, construction, real estate, and insurance, to name a few—the average U.S. worker is more than 50 percent more productive than the average Japanese worker.

U.S. workers also outpace their international rivals in terms of workforce participation. For example, more than 66 percent of all U.S. citizens work outside the home, including 57 percent of the women. In Japan, workforce participation is 63 percent overall, with 49 percent of the country's women working outside the home. In Germany, only 55 of the total population works, with 43 percent of the German women employed outside the home.

U.S. workers also put in long hours. For example, the average U.S. worker spends 1,890 hours per year on the job. This represents a 15-percent increase in working hours since 1950. The Japanese do work more hours per year (an average of 2,173), but the Germans work fewer (an average of 1,668). Vacation days per year average 30 in Germany, only 12 in the United States, and 15.5 in Japan.

In terms of living standards, U.S. workers again measure up. Roughly the same percentage own houses and cars as their foreign counterparts, but the average size of U.S. workers' homes is far greater (more that 1,700 square feet, as compared to 1,250 in Germany and only 800 in Japan).

The criticisms about education also appear to be overstated. Whereas U.S. schools put far less emphasis on technical and vocational skills than do schools in Japan and Germany, a much higher percentage of the U.S. workforce has a high school education today than at any other time in history.

U.S. businesses provide far more opportunities for women and ethnic minorities than do Japan and Germany, and they are more progressive in terms of hiring the handicapped and addressing workforce diversity issues. They also provide more flexibility through part-time and temporary jobs, and usually provide better retirement provisions.

There are some trouble spots, however. One is that real income for many U.S. workers has actually declined, and the less educated have been the hardest hit. For example, workers with only a high school diploma saw their real earnings fall 15 percent during the 1980s. Other workers with higher levels of education did better, gaining 4 percent in real income during this same span. But workers in other countries did see bigger earnings gains.

Workers in the United States have also begun to change how they see their employers. Due in large measure to the recent trends in cutbacks and downsizing, many U.S. workers fear for their jobs. And most profess to have relatively little loyalty to their employers. More and more workers seem to identify with their profession or craft, as opposed to their employing organization.

Case Questions

1. What are the implications of the facts and statistics in this case for managers?
2. As a prospective manager, how might you take account of declining employee loyalty in your approach to supervising workers?
3. What is your own opinion of the average U.S. worker?

SOURCES: "Work-Force Study Finds Loyalty Is Weak, Divisions of Race and Gender Are Deep," *Wall Street Journal*, September 3, 1993, pp. B1, B2; and Myron Magnet, "The Truth About the American Worker," *Fortune*, May 4, 1992, pp. 48–65.

CASE 2.2   **Humanized Robots**

Helen Bowers was stumped. Sitting in her office at the plant, she pondered the same questions she had been facing for months: how to get her company's employees to work harder and produce more. No matter what she did, it didn't seem to help much.

Helen had inherited the business three years ago when her father, Jake Bowers, died unexpectedly.

Bowers Machine Parts, Inc., was founded four decades ago by Jake and had grown into a moderate-size corporation. Bowers makes replacement parts for large-scale manufacturing machines such as lathes and mills. The firm is headquartered in Kansas City and has three plants scattered throughout Missouri.

Although Helen grew up in the family business, she never understood her father's approach. Jake had treated his employees like part of his family. In Helen's view, however, he paid them more than he had to, asked their advice far more often than he should have, and spent too much time listening to their ideas and complaints. When Helen took over, she vowed to change how things were done and bring the firm into the twentieth century. In particular, she resolved to stop handling employees with kid gloves and to treat them like what they were: the hired help.

In addition to changing the way employees were treated, Helen had another goal for Bowers. She wanted to meet the challenge of international competition. Japanese firms had moved aggressively into the market for heavy industrial equipment. She saw this as both a threat and an opportunity. On the one hand, if she could get a toehold as a parts supplier to these firms, Bowers could grow rapidly. On the other, the lucrative parts market was also sure to attract more Japanese competitors. Helen had to make sure that Bowers could compete effectively with highly productive and profitable Japanese firms.

From the day Helen took over, she practiced a philosophy altogether different from her father's to achieve her goals. For one thing, she increased production quotas by 20 percent. She instructed her first-line supervisors to crack down on employees and eliminate all idle time. She also decided to shut down the company softball field her father had built. She thought the employees really didn't use it much, and she wanted the space for future expansion.

Helen also announced that future contributions to the firm's profit-sharing plan would be phased out. Employees were paid enough, she believed, and all profits were the rightful property of the owner—her. She had private plans to cut future pay increases to bring average wages down to where she thought they belonged. Finally, Helen also changed a number of operational procedures. In particular, she stopped asking other people for their advice. She reasoned that she was the boss and knew what was best. If she asked for advice and then didn't take it, it would only stir up resentment.

All in all, Helen thought, things should be going much better. Output should be up, and costs should be way down. This combination therefore should be resulting in much higher levels of productivity and profits.

But that's not what was happening. Whenever Helen walked through one of the plants, she sensed that people weren't doing their best. Performance reports indicated that output was only marginally higher than before but scrap rates had soared. Payroll costs indeed were lower, but other personnel costs were up. It seemed that turnover had increased substantially and training costs had gone up as a result.

In desperation, Helen finally had hired a consultant. After carefully researching the history of the organization and Helen's recent changes, the consultant made some remarkable suggestions. The bottom line, Helen felt, was that the consultant thought she should go back to that "humanistic nonsense" her father had used. No matter how she turned it, though, she just couldn't see the wisdom in this. People worked to make a buck and didn't want all that participation stuff.

Suddenly, Helen knew just what to do: she would announce that all employees who failed to increase their productivity by 10 percent would suffer an equal pay cut. She sighed in relief, feeling confident that she had finally figured out the answer.

Case Questions

1. How successful do you think Helen Bowers's new plan will be?
2. What challenges does Helen confront?
3. If you were Helen's consultant, what would you advise her to do?

CHAPTER 3

Foundations of Individual Behavior

OBJECTIVES

After studying this chapter, you should be able to:

Explain the psychological contracts, the person-job fit, and the nature of individual differences.

Describe the types and nature of physical and intellectual qualities among people in organizations.

Define personality and describe personality attributes that affect behavior in organizations.

Discuss attitudes in organizations and identify specific job-related attitudes that may affect behavior.

Describe perceptual processes and the role of attributions in organizations.

Explain how workplace behaviors can directly or indirectly influence organizational effectiveness.

Every individual has a unique set of values and priorities, and gets satisfaction from life in his or her own way.

Consider the following two persons. One is a casual, laid-back individual who prefers to work in public-sector organizations. In his mid-forties, he is relatively uninterested in money and instead likes to think that he is working for the good of society. He attended public school and while growing up, he never got into trouble. His current job is to provide quality training for workers at Anchor Advanced Products Inc., a plastics maker based in Morristown, Tennessee.

The other person is an intense entrepreneur who aggressively buys, restructures, and then sells businesses. He often lays off workers in the process, and has a reputation as a shrewd and tough-minded manager. While still a teenager, he smoked on the sly and forged letters to advance in the Boy Scouts. He went to private schools. Only in his mid-thirties, this person makes more than one million dollars a year and leads an extravagant, high-profile lifestyle.

These two individuals are as different as night and day. They are also brothers, Alex and Glenn Hutchins. Alex is the first individual described, and Glenn the second. Given the fundamental differences that have obviously characterized their lives, it should come as no surprise that they don't always get along very well. Each one sees the world and his brother in very different ways.

Alex, for example, finds Glenn's pursuit of financial gain repugnant and believes that leveraged buyouts of the sort his brother's firm specializes are a negative force in the U.S. economy. But Glenn thinks his firm is making positive contributions by making companies more efficient and competitive. Although they stay in touch because of family ties, their relationship is strained and distant.

But their paths recently crossed for the first time in a professional setting. Shortly after Alex accepted the training position at Anchor, he found out that the firm had recently been sold through a leveraged buyout managed by his brother's firm. His current view is that the debt absorbed by Anchor has put everyone there under greater pressure to boost productivity and enhance profitability. Thus, his opinion of Alex and his work is even stronger than before. Alex, meanwhile, says he empathizes with his brother but is simply trying to make Anchor more competitive while making an honest income for himself.[1]

A lex and Glenn Hutchins are alike in many ways. They are both male, they are both managers, and they both have families. But they are different in even more ways. They have different outlooks on life, want different things, and approach their work in very different ways. They have different personalities, different attitudes, and see the world in different ways. Although the differences between Alex and Glenn Hutchins are all the more dramatic because they are brothers, the same statements could actually be made about any two managers or workers selected from any organization in the world. Every person in an organization is fundamentally different from everyone else. Managers must recognize that these differences exist and attempt to understand them if they are to be successful.

1. "Two Brothers' Lives: Both White Collar, Yet Worlds Apart," *Wall Street Journal*, August 18, 1993, pp. A1, A4. Reprinted by permission of *Wall Street Journal*, © 1993 Dow Jones & Company, Inc. All Rights Reserved Worldwide.

This chapter describes several of the more important characteristics that differentiate people from one another in organizations. In the next section we investigate the psychological nature of people in organizations. We then note some of the physical and intellectual differences among individuals. The next section introduces the concept of personality and discusses several important personality attributes that can influence behavior in organizations. We then examine individual attitudes and their role in organizations. Basic perceptual processes are then discussed. Finally, we describe a number of basic individual behaviors that are important to organizations.

People in Organizations

As a starting point in understanding the behavior of people in organizational settings we must consider the basic nature of the individual-organization relationship. We must also gain an appreciation of the nature of individual differences.

Psychological Contracts

Whenever we buy a car or sell a house both buyer and seller sign a contract that specifies the terms of the agreement. A psychological contract is similar in some ways to a standard legal contract, but is less formal and well-defined. In particular, a **psychological contract** is the overall set of expectations held by an individual with respect to what he or she will contribute to the organization and what the organization, in return, will provide to the individual.[2] Thus, a psychological contract is not written on paper nor are all of its terms explicitly negotiated.

The essential nature of a psychological contract is illustrated in Figure 3.1. The individual makes a variety of **contributions** to the organization such as effort, skills, ability, time, and loyalty. These contributions presumably satisfy various needs and requirements of the organization. That is, because the organization may have hired the person because of her skills, the organization can reasonably expect that she will subsequently display those skills in the performance of her job.

A **psychological contract** is the overall set of expectations held by an individual with respect to what he or she will contribute to the organization and what the organization, in return, will provide to the individual.

An individual's **contributions** to the organization include such things as effort, skills, ability, time, and loyalty.

2. Denise M. Rousseau and Judi McLean Parks, "The Contracts of Individuals and Organizations," in Larry L. Cummings and Barry M. Staw (Eds.), *Research in Organizational Behavior*, Vol. 15 (Greenwich, Conn.: JAI Press, 1993), pp. 1–43.

FIGURE 3.1

The Psychological Contract

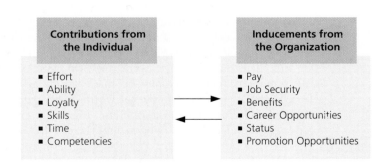

Organizations provide **inducements** to individuals in the form of tangible and intangible rewards.

In return for these contributions, the organization provides **inducements** to the individual. Some inducements, like pay and career opportunities, are tangible rewards. Others, like job security and status, are intangible. Just as the contributions available from the individual must satisfy needs of the organization, the inducements offered by the organization must serve the needs of the individual. That is, if a person accepts employment with an organization because he thinks he will earn an attractive salary and have an opportunity to advance, he will subsequently expect that those rewards will actually be forthcoming.

If both the individual and organization perceive that the psychological contract is fair and equitable, they will be satisfied with the relationship and are likely to continue it. On the other hand, if either party sees an imbalance or inequity in the contract it may initiate a change. For example, the individual may request a pay raise or promotion, decrease her contributed effort, or look for a better job elsewhere. The organization can also initiate change by requesting that the individual improve his skills through training, transferring him to another job, or terminating his employment altogether.

A basic challenge faced by the organization, then, is to manage psychological contracts. The organization must ensure that it is getting value from its employees. At the same time, it must also be sure that it is providing employees with appropriate inducements. If the organization is underpaying its employees for their contributions, for example, they may perform poorly or leave for better jobs elsewhere. On the other hand, if they are overpaid relative to their contributions, the organization is incurring unnecessary costs.

The Person-Job Fit

The **person-job fit** is the extent to which the contributions made by the individual match the inducements offered by the organization.

One specific aspect of managing psychological contracts is managing the person-job fit. The **person-job fit** is the extent to which the contributions made by the individual match the inducements offered by the organization. In theory, each employee has a specific set of needs that he wants fulfilled and a set of job-related behaviors and abilities to contribute. If the organization can take perfect advantage of those behaviors and abilities and exactly fulfill his needs, it will have achieved a perfect person-job fit.[3]

Of course, such a precise level of person-job fit is seldom achieved. One reason for this is that hiring procedures are imperfect. Managers can estimate employee skill levels when making hiring decisions and can improve them through training. But even simple performance dimensions are hard to measure objectively and validly. Another reason for imprecise person-job fits is that both people and organizations change. An individual who finds a new job stimulating and exciting may find the same job boring and monotonous after a few years of performing it. And when the organization adopts new technology it has changed the skills it needs from its employees. Still another reason for imprecision in the person-job fit is that each individual is unique. Measuring skills and performance is difficult enough. Assessing attitudes and personality is far more complex. Each of these individual differences serves to make matching individuals with jobs a difficult and complex process.

3. Jennifer A. Chatman, "Improving Interactional Organizational Research: A Model of Person-Organization Fit," *Academy of Management Review*, July 1989, pp. 333–349; and Charles A. O'Reilly III, Jennifer Chatman, and David F. Caldwell, "People and Organizational Culture: A Profile Comparison Approach to Assessing Person-Organization Fit," *Academy of Management Journal*, September 1991, pp. 487–516.

Individual Differences

Individual differences are personal attributes that vary from one person to another.

Every individual is unique in many different psychological, emotional, and behavioral ways. Each of these factors represents a potentially important individual difference. **Individual differences** are personal attributes that vary from one person to another. Individual differences may be physical, psychological, and emotional. Taken together, all of the individual differences that characterize any specific person serve to make that person unique from everyone else. Basic categories of individual differences include physical and intellectual differences, personality, attitudes, and perception. We discuss each of these more fully in the sections that follow. First, however, we need to also note the importance of the situation in assessing the behavior of individuals.

Are specific differences that characterize a given individual good or bad? Do they contribute to or detract from performance? The answer, of course, is that it depends on the circumstances. One person may be dissatisfied, withdrawn, and negative in one job setting but satisfied, outgoing, and positive in another. Working conditions, coworkers, and leadership are all important ingredients. Thus, whenever a manager attempts to assess or account for individual differences among her employees, she must also be sure to consider the situation in which behavior occurs. Attempting to consider both individual differences and contributions in relation to inducements and contexts, then, is a major challenge for managers as they attempt to establish effective psychological contracts with their employees and achieve optimal fits between people and jobs.

Physical and Intellectual Qualities

Physical differences among individuals are the most visible of all differences. They are also relatively easy to assess or document. Intellectual differences are somewhat more difficult to assess but are still relatively objective. Demographic differences among individuals are primarily physical, whereas differences in abilities, skills, and competencies involve both physical and intellectual properties. *Diversity in the Workplace* summarizes how successful organizations are capitalizing on diversity by hiring many different people such as the elderly and the handicapped.

Demographic differences are those differences associated with physical or biographical characteristics.

Demographic differences are those differences associated with physical or biographical characteristics. Basic demographic differences that exist in organizations include age, gender, race, and ethnic origin. Alex and Glenn Hutchins are different ages but are of the same gender, race, and ethnic origin. We cover these differences more fully in Chapter 20.

Individual ability, skill, and competency differences can involve physical or intellectual factors (or both), depending on the person and the task to be performed. **Abilities** are the capacities an individual has to perform well in one or more areas of activity, such as physical, mental, or interpersonal work.[4] General abilities can be applied to a variety of tasks. Individuals with numerical ability, for example, can be trained to apply this ability in a wide array of occupations, such

Abilities are the capacities an individual has to perform well in one or more areas of activity, such as physical, mental, or interpersonal work.

4. E. A. Fleishman, "On the Relation Between Abilities, Learning, and Human Performance," *American Psychologist*, Vol. 27, 1972, pp. 1018–1025.

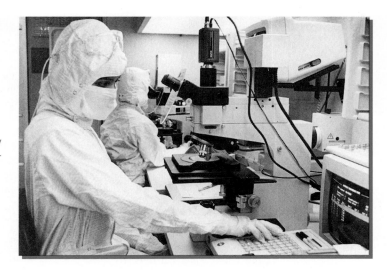

When an individual is hired, an unwritten psychological contract is made that he or she will contribute time and abilities to the organization, which will in turn reward him or her with pay and other inducements. This worker, wearing a dust-free "bunny suit," uses her highly specialized skills to test semiconductor disks for a Tustin, California, manufacturing facility.

as engineering, accounting, and computer science. Abilities develop from an individual's natural aptitudes and subsequent learning opportunities. Aptitudes are relatively enduring capacities for performing some activity effectively. Learning opportunities translate aptitudes into abilities through practice, experience, and formal training. Fixed aptitudes such as reaction time and finger dexterity tend to be less valuable to organizations than are aptitudes that can be developed through training, such as interpersonal or diagnostic abilities.

Individual **skills** are more task-specific than are abilities.

Individual **skills** are more task-specific than are abilities.[5] For example, an individual with the ability to work with numerical data who goes to school to learn about accounting develops a numerical skill specific to that field. Applying ability to a specialized area (for example, by passing the CPA exam) is a reflection of skill. Finally, **competencies** are refined skills that are honed by practice and experience and that enable the individual to develop a speciality.[6] For example, suppose that the accountant takes a position in the taxation department of a public accounting firm. As time passes, she develops more and more competency as a tax specialist. A colleague who specializes in auditing will have different competencies, although his similar abilities and skills would allow him to also develop competencies as a tax expert given training and time.

Competencies are refined skills that are honed by practice and experience and that enable the individual to develop a speciality.

Physical and mental abilities, which are an individual's primary productive capabilities, interact with social capability to determine an individual's ability to perform. Most organizations have a financial interest in enhancing the productive capabilities of all of their employees. Because experience plays such a major part in the development of abilities, skills, and competencies, these organizations try to structure and plan work experiences and training and development opportunities that help employees continue to develop throughout their careers.

5. Ward Edwards, "Discussion: Of Human Skills," *Organizational Behavior and Human Decision Processes*, Vol. 53, 1992, pp. 267–277.
6. Peter Warr and Mark Conner, "Job Competence and Cognition," in Barry M. Staw and Larry L. Cummings (Eds.), *Research in Organizational Behavior*, Vol. 14 (Greenwich, Conn.: JAI Press, 1992), pp. 91–127.

New Challenges in the Workplace

More and more organizations today are finding that they can capitalize on work-force diversity in many different ways. Each worker brings a variety of skills and abilities, and each is able to contribute to the firm in unique ways. By valuing that diversity and understanding how to capitalize on it, managers can enhance not only societal well-being but also the effectiveness of their firms.

Take older workers, for example. Some managers stereotype older workers as being slower and more resistant to change. But, in fact, some evidence suggests that just the opposite is true. Compared with younger workers, older workers are less accident prone, for example, draw from a broader experience base, and have learned many different skills during their work lives. And although they might not be as receptive to change as their younger colleagues, most older workers are perfectly comfortable with new procedures and methods as long as they understand why changes are necessary.

Physically challenged workers are also making ever-greater contributions to organizational effectiveness. Aided in part by recent federal legislation and in part by enlightened management practices, firms are realizing that although a person is not able to operate a conventional piece of equipment or perform a certain task because of physical limitations, he or she may be able to fully contribute in other ways. Indeed, some people's mental capabilities are enhanced by coping with physical limitations to the point where they can make superior contributions when given a chance.

Firms that don't get this message may lose out on attracting valuable people. For example, Don Dalton, paralyzed from the waist down, was unsuccessful in finding a challenging and satisfying job as a software programmer. Finally, he set up his own technology enhancement business in his garage. He first wrote software that allowed him to use voice commands to operate his computer. He then created for himself a work environment that fits his own abilities and limitations. His firm, Micro Overflow Corporation, recently passed the $1 million sales mark.

SOURCES: "Aided by Computers, Many of the Disabled Form Own Businesses," *Wall Street Journal*, October 8, 1993, pp. A1, A8; and Walter Kiechel III, "How to Manage Older Workers," *Fortune*, November 5, 1990, pp. 183–186.

Personality and Organizations

Personality is the relatively stable set of psychological attributes that distinguish one person from another.

If physical differences are relatively easy to observe and assess, personality differences are just the opposite. **Personality** is the relatively stable set of psychological attributes or traits that distinguish one person from another.[7] Understanding basic personality attributes is important because they affect people's behavior in organizational situations, as well as their perceptions of and attitudes toward the organization.[8]

7 . Lawrence Pervin, "Personality," in Mark Rosenzweig and Lyman Porter (Eds.), *Annual Review of Psychology*, Vol. 36 (Palo Alto, Calif.: Annual Reviews, 1985), pp. 83–114; and S. R. Maddi, *Personality Theories: A Comparative Analysis*, 4th ed. (Homewood, Ill.: Dorsey, 1980).

8. Lawrence Pervin, *Current Controversies and Issues In Personality*, 2nd ed. (New York: Wiley, 1984).

How Personalities Are Formed

The basic personalities of managers or employees are formed before they ever join an organization. Indeed, personality formation starts at birth and continues throughout adolescence. Hereditary characteristics (i.e., body shape and height) and the social (i.e., family and friends) and cultural (i.e., religion and values) context in which people grow up all interact to shape their basic personalities. As people grow into adulthood, their personalities become clearly defined and generally stable.

But a person's personality can still be changed as a result of organizational experiences. For example, suppose that a manager is subjected to prolonged periods of stress or conflict at work. As a result, he or she may become more withdrawn, anxious, and irritable. While removal of the stressful circumstances may eventually temper these characteristics, the individual's personality may also reflect permanent changes. From a more positive perspective, continued success, accomplishment, and advancement at work may cause an individual to become increasingly self-confident and outgoing. And situational influences can also affect personality in unexpected ways. For example, an industrial accident may cause someone to become a hero by risking her own life to save someone else. As a consequence, she may develop a new self-concept.

These types of extreme examples aside, managers should recognize that they can do little to change the basic personalities of their subordinates. Instead, they should work to understand the basic nature of their subordinates' personalities and how attributes of those personalities affect the subordinates' work behavior.

Personality Attributes at Work

Over the past few decades a considerable amount of research has been conducted to identify and further our understanding of personality attributes that are relevant to managers. Several of the more important attributes that have been identified and studied are listed and defined in Table 3.1.

Locus of control is the extent to which an individual believes that his or her behavior has a direct impact on the consequences of that behavior.[9] Some people, for example, believe that if they work hard they will succeed. They also believe that people who fail do so because they lack ability or motivation. Because these people believe that individuals are in control of their lives, they are said to have an *internal locus of control*. On the other hand, some people think that what happens to them is a result of fate, chance, luck, or the behavior of other people. For example, an employee who fails to get a promotion may attribute that failure to a politically motivated boss or just bad luck, rather than to her or his own lack of skills or poor performance record. Because these people think that forces beyond their control dictate what happens to them, they are said to have an *external locus of control*.

Self-efficacy is a related but subtly different personality characteristic. **Self-efficacy** is a person's beliefs about his or her capabilities to perform a task.[10]

Locus of control is the extent to which an individual believes that his or her behavior has a direct impact on the consequences of that behavior.

Self-efficacy is a person's beliefs about his or her capabilities to perform a task.

---

9. J. B. Rotter, "Generalized Expectancies for Internal vs. External Control of Reinforcement," *Psychological Monographs*, Vol. 80, 1966, pp. 1–28; and Bert De Brabander and Christopher Boone, "Sex Differences in Perceived Locus of Control," *The Journal of Social Psychology*, Vol. 130, 1990, pp. 271–276.
10. Marilyn E. Gist and Terence R. Mitchell, "Self-Efficacy: A Theoretical Analysis of Its Determinants and Malleability," *Academy of Management Review*, April 1992, pp. 183–211.

People with high self-efficacy believe that they are capable of performing well on a specific task, and people with low self-efficacy are more prone to doubt their ability to perform a specific task. Although self-assessments of ability contribute to self-efficacy, so too does the personality of the individual. Some people simply have more self-confidence than do others. This belief in their ability to perform a task effectively results in their being more self-assured and more able to focus their attention on performance.

Another important personality characteristic is authoritarianism. **Authoritarianism** is the extent to which an individual believes that power and status differences are appropriate within hierarchical social systems like organizations.[11] For example, a person who is highly authoritarian may accept directives or orders from someone with more authority purely because the other person is "the boss." Alternatively, while a person who is not highly authoritarian may still carry out appropriate and reasonable directives from the boss, he or she is also more likely to question things, express disagreement with the boss, and even to refuse to carry out orders if they are for some reason objectionable. A manager who is highly authoritarian may be relatively autocratic and demanding, and subordinates who are highly authoritarian will be more likely to accept this behavior from their leader. On the other hand, a manager who is less authoritarian may allow subordinates a bigger role in making decisions, and less authoritarian subordinates will respond positively to this behavior.[12]

Authoritarianism is the extent to which an individual believes that power and status differences are appropriate within hierarchical social systems like organizations.

11. T. W. Adorno, E. Frenkel-Brunswick, D. J. Levinson, and R. N. Sanford, *The Authoritarian Personality* (New York: Harper & Row, 1950).
12. "Who Becomes an Authoritarian?" *Psychology Today*, March 1989, pp. 66–70.

TABLE 3.1

Major Personality Attributes

Personality Attribute	Description
Locus of Control	The extent to which an individual believes that his or her behavior has a direct impact on the consequences of that behavior
Self-efficacy	A person's beliefs about his or her capabilities to perform a task
Machiavellianism	A personality attribute that results in behavior directed at gaining power and controlling the behavior of others
Self-esteem	The extent to which a person believes that he or she is a worthwhile and deserving individual
Risk Propensity	The degree to which an individual is willing to take chances and make risky decisions
Authoritarianism	The extent to which an individual believes that power and status differences are appropriate within hierarchial social systems like organizations
Dogmatism	Reflects the rigidity of a person's beliefs and his or her openness to other viewpoints

Dogmatism, another important personality attribute, refers to the rigidity of a person's beliefs and his or her openness to other viewpoints.[13] The popular terms for dogmatism are *close-minded* and *open-minded.* For example, suppose that a manager has such strong beliefs about how certain procedures should be carried out that she is unwilling to even listen to a new idea for doing them more efficiently. This person is close-minded, or highly dogmatic. Another manager in the same circumstances might be very receptive to listening to and trying new ideas. This manager can be seen as more open-minded, or less dogmatic. Dogmatism can be either beneficial or detrimental to organizations. Given the changing nature of organizations and their environments, individuals who are less dogmatic (that is, individuals who are open-minded) are more likely to be useful and productive organizational members.

Machiavellianism is another important personality trait. This concept is named after Niccolò Machiavelli, a sixteenth-century author. In his book entitled *The Prince*, Machiavelli explained how the nobility could more easily gain and use power. **Machiavellianism** is now used to describe behavior directed at gaining power and controlling the behavior of others. Research suggests that Machiavellianism is a personality trait that varies from person to person.[14] Individuals who are high on Machiavellianism tend to be rational and nonemotional, may be willing to lie to attain their personal goals, put little weight on loyalty and friendship, and enjoy manipulating others' behavior. Individuals who are low on Machiavellianism are more emotional, are less willing to lie to succeed, value loyalty and friendship highly, and get little personal pleasure from manipulating others.

Self-esteem is the extent to which a person believes that he or she is a worthwhile and deserving individual.[15] A person with high self-esteem is more likely to seek higher status jobs, be more confident in his or her ability to achieve higher

13. Edward Necka and Malgorzata Kubiak, "The Influence of Training in Metaphorical Thinking on Creativity and Level of Dogmatism," *Polish Psychological Bulletin*, Vol. 20, 1989, pp. 69–78.
14. R. Christie and F. L. Geis (Eds.), *Studies in Machiavellianism* (New York: Academic Press, 1970).
15. Jon L. Pierce, Donald G. Gardner, and Larry L. Cummings, "Organization-Based Self-Esteem: Construct Definition, Measurement, and Validation," *Academy of Management Journal*, Vol. 32, 1989, pp. 622–648.

These people are taking part in a re-enlistment ceremony in the United States Air Force. Individuals whose personalities mesh well with the ethic of the organization for which they work are more likely to be satisfied with their jobs, and consequently, to succeed at them.

levels of performance, and derive greater intrinsic satisfaction from his accomplishments. In contrast, a person with less self-esteem may be more content to remain in a lower-level job, be less confident of his or her ability, and focus more on extrinsic rewards.[16]

Risk propensity is the degree to which an individual is willing to take chances and make risky decisions.

Risk propensity is the degree to which an individual is willing to take chances and make risky decisions. A manager with a high risk propensity, for example, might be expected to experiment with new ideas and gamble on new products. She might also lead the organization in new and different directions. This manager might also be a catalyst for innovation. On the other hand, the same individual might also jeopardize the continued well-being of the organization if the risky decisions prove to be bad ones. A manager with low risk propensity might lead to a stagnant and overly conservative organization, or help the organization successfully weather turbulent and unpredictable times by maintaining stability and calm. Thus, the potential consequences of risk propensity to an organization are heavily dependent on that organization's environment.

Attitudes in Organizations

Another aspect of individuals in organizations is their attitudes. Attitudes are conceptually similar to, but also quite different from, personality attributes. We noted, for example, that personality attributes are shaped early in life and are difficult to change. Although some attitudes fit this description, other attitudes can be formed or changed quickly. We define **attitudes** as complexes of beliefs and feelings that people have about specific ideas, situations, or other people. Attitudes are important because they are the mechanism through which most people express their feelings. An employee's statement that he feels underpaid by the organization reflects his attitude about his pay. Similarly, when a manager says that she likes the new advertising campaign, she is expressing her attitude about the organization's marketing efforts.

Attitudes are complexes of beliefs and feelings that people have about specific ideas, situations, or other people.

How Attitudes Are Formed

Individual attitudes are formed in a variety of ways. The two dominant theoretical approaches to understanding attitude formation are the dispositional and situational approaches. Cognitive dissonance also affects attitudes. And once formed, attitudes may still be changed.

Dispositional View of Attitudes   Attitudes have historically been viewed as stable dispositions to behave toward objects in a certain way.[17] For any number of reasons, a person might decide that he or she does not like a particular political figure or a certain restaurant (a disposition). That person would then be expected to express consistently negative opinions of the candidate or restaurant and to maintain the consistent

16. Roy J. Blitzer, Colleen Petersen, and Linda Rogers, "How to Build Self-Esteem," *Training & Development*, February 1993, pp. 58–65.

17. Charles E. Kimble, *Social Psychology: Studying Human Interaction* (Dubuque, Iowa: Wm. C. Brown, 1990); and Frank E. Saal and Patrick A. Knight, *Industrial/Organizational Psychology* (Belmont, Calif.: Brooks/Cole, 1988).

and predictable intention of not voting for the political candidate or patronizing the restaurant. In the traditional dispositional view of attitudes, illustrated in Figure 3.2, attitudes contain three components: affect, cognition, and intention.

Affect refers to the individual's feelings toward something. In many ways, affect is similar to emotion—it is something over which we have little or no conscious control.[18] For example, most people react to words such as *love, hate, sex,* and *war* in a manner that reflects their feelings about what those words convey. Similarly, you may like one of your classes, dislike another, and be indifferent toward a third. If the class you dislike is an elective, you may not be particularly concerned. But if it is the first course in your chosen major, your affective reaction may cause you considerable anxiety.

Cognition is the knowledge a person presumes to have about something. You may believe that you like a class because the textbook is excellent, the class meets at your favorite time, the instructor is outstanding, and the workload is light. This "knowledge" may be true, partially true, or totally false. For example, you may intend to vote for a particular candidate because you think you know where the candidate stands on several issues. In reality, depending on the candidate's honesty and your understanding of his or her statements, the candidate's thinking on the issues may be exactly the same as yours, partly the same, or totally different. Cognitions are based on perceptions of truth and reality, and, as we note later, perceptions agree with reality to varying degrees.

18. Amy S. Wharton and Rebecca J. Erickson, "Managing Emotions on the Job and at Home: Understanding the Consequences of Multiple Emotional Roles," *Academy of Management Journal,* September 1993, pp. 457–486.

Affect refers to the individual's feelings toward something.

Cognition is the knowledge a person presumes to have about something.

FIGURE 3.2

The Dispositional View of Attitudes

Single Attitude About an Object

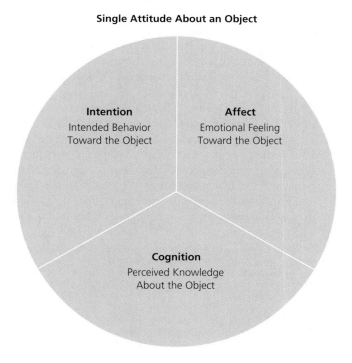

Intention
Intended Behavior
Toward the Object

Affect
Emotional Feeling
Toward the Object

Cognition
Perceived Knowledge
About the Object

Intention, as a component of an attitude, guides a person's behavior.

Intention guides a person's behavior. If you like your instructor, you may intend to take another class from him or her next semester. Intentions are not always translated into actual behavior, however. If the instructor's course next semester is scheduled for 8:00 A.M., you may decide that another instructor is just as good. Some attitudes, and their corresponding intentions, are much more central and important to an individual than others. You may intend to do one thing (take a particular class) but later alter your intentions because of a more important and central attitude (fondness for sleeping late).[19]

Situational View of Attitudes An alternative to the dispositional view of attitudes has been presented by Gerald Salancik and Jeffrey Pfeffer.[20] These scholars contend that research has not clearly demonstrated that attitudes are stable dispositions composed of precise components that are consistently reflected in individual responses. Instead, they argue, attitudes evolve from socially constructed realities. This approach suggests that the social context delivers information that shapes the individual's attitudes. By means of cues and guides, social information provides a specific prescription for socially acceptable attitudes and behaviors. Such information focuses attention on specific attributes of the setting (for example, the workplace), thus making behaviors and attitudes that dominate in that setting more salient (important to the individual). Figure 3.3 illustrates the situational view.

Suppose that a new employee joins a work group that has existed for some time. Very likely, the members of the group will quickly communicate to the newcomer how they feel about the boss and the reward system and how much effort the group thinks members should put out to perform a given task. As a result, the newcomer tends to adopt an attitude toward the boss and the reward system that is consistent with what she has been told to expect. She is also likely to perform at a level of effort acceptable to the group. The new employee's attitudes and behaviors, then, have been partly shaped by social information and its effects on the individual's perception of reality.

The situational view of attitudes is comparatively new, but it has proved interesting to researchers and managers alike. In general, most research provides at least partial support for this model, but the emerging opinion appears to be that attitudes are shaped by both objective attributes of the workplace and social information.[21]

Cognitive dissonance is the anxiety a person experiences when two sets of knowledge or perceptions are contradictory or incongruent.

Cognitive Dissonance **Cognitive dissonance** is the anxiety a person experiences when two sets of knowledge or perceptions are contradictory or incongruent. Cognitive dissonance also occurs when people behave in a fashion that is inconsistent with their attitudes.[22] For example, a person may realize that smoking and overeating are dangerous yet continue to do both. Because the attitudes and behaviors are not consistent with each other, the person probably will experience a certain amount of tension and discomfort and may engage in dissonance reduction, seeking ways to reduce the dissonance and the tension it causes. For example,

19. Bobby J. Calder and Paul H. Schurr, "Attitudinal Processes in Organizations," in Larry L. Cummings and Barry M. Staw (Eds.), *Research in Organizational Behavior*, Vol. 3 (Greenwich, Conn.: JAI Press, 1981), pp. 283–302.

20. Gerald Salancik and Jeffrey Pfeffer, "An Examination of Need-Satisfaction Models of Job Attitudes," *Administrative Science Quarterly*, Vol. 22, 1977, pp. 427–456; and Gerald Salancik and Jeffrey Pfeffer, "A Social Information Processing Approach to Job Attitudes and Task Design," *Administrative Science Quarterly*, Vol. 23, 1978, pp. 224–253.

21. Ricky W. Griffin, "Toward an Integrated Theory of Task Design," in Larry L. Cummings and Barry M. Staw (Eds.), *Research in Organizational Behavior*, Vol. 9 (Greenwich, Conn.: JAI Press, 1987), pp. 79–120.

22. Leon Festinger, *A Theory of Cognitive Dissonance* (Palo Alto, Calif.: Stanford University Press, 1957).

FIGURE 3.3

**The Situational View
of Attitudes**

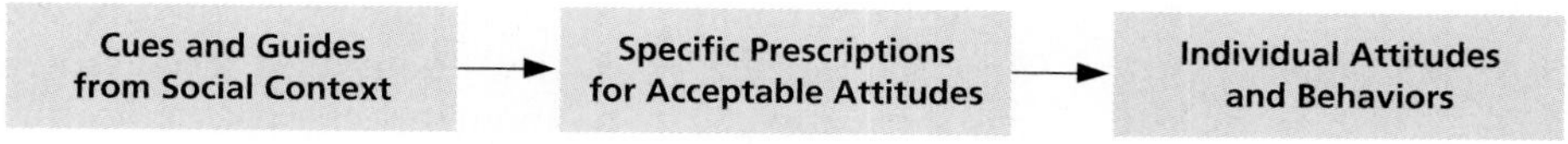

Cues and Guides from Social Context	→	Specific Prescriptions for Acceptable Attitudes	→	Individual Attitudes and Behaviors

the dissonance associated with overeating might be resolved by continually deciding to go on a diet "next week." In general, then, the person attempts to change the attitude, alter the behavior, or perceptually distort the circumstances to reduce tension and discomfort.

A classic study by Barry Staw provides a very insightful example of the processes of dissonance reduction.[23] The subjects in the study were male college students who joined the Reserve Officers Training Corps (ROTC) between 1969 and 1971. During that turbulent period, many male students joined the ROTC to avoid being drafted and sent to serve in Vietnam. The legally binding commitment to the ROTC involved on-campus military training while in college and a commission in the reserve forces after graduation. Just after this period, the Selective Service Administration instituted an annual lottery to determine who would be drafted. Each lottery number corresponded to a birthday: the lower the lottery number, the higher the odds of being drafted.

Staw assumed that ROTC students whose lottery numbers were high enough to keep them out of the draft would begin to experience cognitive dissonance because they had made a commitment that turned out to be unnecessary. He also predicted that those who received low numbers would experience less dissonance because their commitment continued to serve its intended purpose: to spare them active duty in the military. Staw asked a group of ROTC students to fill out questionnaires designed to measure their satisfaction with the ROTC program. As predicted, students with high lottery numbers—those who now had the least to gain by being in the program—indicated the most satisfaction. They apparently used satisfaction as a reason to justify their ROTC commitment given that it no longer served its original purpose.

Cognitive dissonance affects people in a variety of ways. We frequently encounter situations in which our attitudes conflict with our behaviors or with one another. Dissonance reduction is the way we deal with these feelings of discomfort and tension. In organizational settings, people contemplating leaving the organization may wonder why they continue to stay and work hard. As a result of this dissonance, they may conclude that the company is not so bad after all, that they have no immediate options elsewhere, or that they will leave "soon."

Attitude Change   As noted earlier, attitudes are not as stable as personality attributes. For example, attitudes may change as a result of new information. A manager may have a negative attitude about a new colleague because of his lack of job-related experience. After working with the new person for awhile, however, the manager may come to realize that he is actually very talented and subsequently develop a more positive attitude. Attitudes can also change as a result of changes in the object of the attitude. For example, if employees have a negative attitude about their pay because they feel underpaid, a big salary increase may result in more positive attitudes about their pay.

23. Barry M. Staw, "Attitudinal and Behavioral Consequences of Changing a Major Organizational Reward: A Natural Field Experiment," *Journal of Personality and Social Psychology*, Vol. 9, 1974, pp. 742–751.

Attitude change can also occur when the object of the attitude becomes less important or less relevant to the person. For example, suppose that an employee has a negative attitude about his company's health insurance. When his spouse gets a new job with an organization that has outstanding health insurance benefits, his attitude toward his own insurance may become more moderate simply because he no longer has to worry about it. Finally, as noted earlier, individuals may change their attitudes as a way of reducing cognitive dissonance.

Deeply rooted attitudes that have a long history are, of course, very difficult to change. For example, over a period of years Frank Lorenzo developed a reputation in the airline industry of being anti-union and for cutting wages and benefits. As a result, employees throughout the industry came to both dislike and distrust him. When he took over Eastern Airlines, its employees had such a strong attitude of distrust toward him that they could never agree to cooperate with any of his programs or ideas. Some of them actually cheered months later when Eastern went bankrupt, even though it was costing them their own jobs!

Important Work-Related Attitudes

People in an organization form attitudes about many different things. For example, employees are likely to have attitudes about their salary, promotion possibilities, their boss, employee benefits, the food in the company cafeteria, and the color of the company softball team uniforms. Of course, some of these attitudes are more important than others. Especially important attitudes are job satisfaction or dissatisfaction, organizational commitment, and job involvement.

Job satisfaction is an attitude that reflects the extent to which an individual is gratified by or fulfilled in his or her work.

Job Satisfaction   **Job satisfaction** is an attitude that reflects the extent to which an individual is gratified by or fulfilled in his or her work. Extensive research conducted on job satisfaction has indicated that personal factors such as an individual's needs and aspirations determine this attitude, along with group and organizational factors such as relationships with coworkers and supervisors and working conditions, work policies, and compensation.[24]

A satisfied employee also tends to be absent less often, to make positive contributions, and to stay with the organization.[25] In contrast, a dissatisfied employee may be absent more often, may experience stress that disrupts coworkers, and may be continually looking for another job. Contrary to what many managers believe, however, high levels of job satisfaction do not necessarily lead to higher levels of performance. One survey has also indicated that contrary to popular opinion, Japanese workers are less satisfied with their jobs than their counterparts in the United States.[26]

Organizational commitment is an attitude that reflects an individual's identification with and attachment to the organization.

Organizational Commitment and Job Involvement   Two other important work-related attitudes are organizational commitment and job involvement. **Organizational commitment** is an attitude that reflects an individual's identification with and attachment to the organization. A person with a high level of commitment is likely

24. Patricia C. Smith, L. M. Kendall, and Charles Hulin, *The Measurement of Satisfaction in Work and Behavior* (Chicago: Rand-McNally, 1969).
25. Cliff Hakim, "Boost Morale to Gain Productivity," *HR Magazine*, February 1993, pp. 46–53.
26. James R. Lincoln, "Employee Work Attitudes and Management Practice in the U.S. and Japan: Evidence From a Large Comparative Study," *California Management Review*, Fall 1989, pp. 89–106.

to see herself as a true member of the firm (for example, referring to the organization in personal terms like "we make high quality products"), to overlook minor sources of dissatisfaction with the firm, and to see herself remaining a member of the organization. In contrast, a person with less organizational commitment is more likely to see himself as an outsider (for example, referring to the organization in less personal terms like "they don't pay their employees very well"), to express more dissatisfaction about things, and to not see himself as a long-term member of the organization.[27] Research suggests that Japanese workers may be more committed to their organizations than are U.S. workers.[28]

Job involvement results in an individual's tendency to exceed the normal expectations associated with his or her job. An employee with little job involvement will see it as just something to do to earn a living. Thus, all of her motivation is extrinsic and she has little or no interest in learning how to perform the job better. On the other hand, a person with a lot of job involvement will derive intrinsic satisfaction from the job itself and will want to learn more and more about how to perform the job more effectively.

Richard Steers has demonstrated that these two attitudes strengthen with an individual's age, years with the organization, sense of job security, and participation in decision making.[29] Employees who feel committed to an organization and involved with their jobs have highly reliable habits, plan a long tenure with the organization, and muster more effort in performance. Although there are few definitive things that organizations can do to create or promote these attitudes, a few specific guidelines are available. For one thing, if the organization treats its employees fairly and provides reasonable rewards and job security, those employees will more likely be satisfied and committed. Allowing employees to have a say in how things are done can also promote all three attitudes. And designing jobs so that they are interesting and stimulating can enhance job involvement in particular.

Perception in Organizations

As noted earlier, an important element of an attitude is the individual's perception of the object about which the attitude is formed. **Perception** is the set of processes by which an individual becomes aware of and interprets information about the environment. If everyone perceived everything the same way, things would be a lot simpler (and a lot less exciting!). Of course, just the opposite is true: people perceive the same things in very different ways.[30] Moreover, people often assume that reality is objective, that we all perceive the same things in the same way. To test this idea, we could ask students at the Universities of Oklahoma and Texas to describe the most recent football game between their schools. The two quite conflicting stories we probably would hear arise primarily because of perception. The fans "saw" the same things but interpreted them in sharply contrasting ways. *The Ethical Dilemma* shows how one manager used perception to distort how people saw his company.

Job involvement results in an individual's tendency to exceed the normal expectations associated with his or her job.

Perception is the set of processes by which an individual becomes aware of and interprets information about the environment.

27. Frederick F. Reichheld, "Loyalty-Based Management," *Harvard Business Review*, March–April 1993, pp. 64–73.
28. Lincoln, "Employee Work Attitudes and Management Practice in the U.S. and Japan: Evidence From a Large Comparative Study."
29. Richard M. Steers, "Antecedents and Outcomes of Organizational Commitment," *Administrative Science Quarterly*, Vol. 22, 1977, pp. 46–56.
30. "One Man's Accident Is Shedding New Light on Human Perception," *Wall Street Journal*, September 30, 1993, pp. A1, A13.

Because perception plays a role in a variety of other workplace behaviors, managers need to have a general understanding of basic perceptual processes. As implied both here and in our definition, perception actually consists of several distinct processes. Moreover, in perceiving we receive information in many guises, from spoken words or visual images to movements and forms. Through the perceptual processes, the receiver assimilates the varied types of incoming information for the purpose of interpreting it.

Basic Perceptual Processes

Figure 3.4 shows two basic perceptual processes that are particularly relevant to managers—selective perception and stereotyping.

Selective perception is the process of screening out information with which we are uncomfortable or that contradicts our beliefs.

Selective Perception   **Selective perception** is the process of screening out information with which we are uncomfortable or that contradicts our beliefs. For example, suppose that a manager is exceptionally fond of a particular worker. The manager has a very positive attitude about the worker and thinks he is a top performer. One day the manager notices that the worker seems to be goofing off. Selective perception may cause the manager to quickly forget what she observed. Similarly, suppose that a manager has formed a very negative image of a particular worker. She thinks this worker is a poor performer and never does a good job. When she happens to observe an example of high performance from the worker, she, too, may not remember it for very long. In one sense, selective perception is beneficial because it allows us to disregard minor bits of information. Of course, this only holds true if our basic perception is accurate. If selective perception causes us to ignore important information, however, it can become quite detrimental.[31]

Stereotyping is the process of categorizing or labeling people on the basis of a single attribute or characteristic.

Stereotyping   **Stereotyping** is the process of categorizing or labeling people on the basis of a single attribute or characteristic. Common attributes from which people often stereotype are race and gender. Of course, stereotypes along these

31. Frank E. Saal and S. Craig Moore, "Perceptions of Promotion Fairness and Promotion Candidates' Qualifications," *Journal of Applied Psychology*, Vol. 78, 1993, pp. 105–110.

FIGURE 3.4

Basic Perceptual Processes

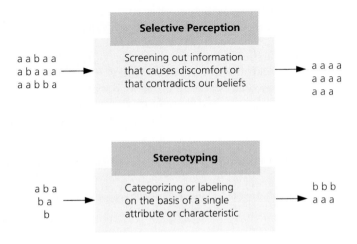

Reality Versus Perception

Federal regulations require that managers of publicly held corporations provide investors with realistic and accurate information about how well the organization is performing. Investors rely on the accuracy of that information when they decide whether to invest in a firm. Don Sheelen, former CEO of Regina Co., decided that investors might not like what he had to show them, so he showed them something altogether different.

Sheelen took over Regina in 1984. At the time, Regina was a small vacuum cleaner manufacturer. By 1988, Sheelen had more than tripled sales and reported record-breaking profits. Wall Street was convinced that Sheelen was a genius and that Regina was one of the hottest investments around. At each stockholders' meeting, Sheelen put on a better show than the year before, lavishly extolling the firm's potential. By 1988, the firm's stock price had risen from slightly more than $5 a share to $27.50 a share. As a result, Sheelen's own stake in the company sky-rocketed to almost $100 million.

Then things started to deteriorate. One of Regina's major new products, the Housekeeper vacuum cleaner, was beset by major quality problems. Thousands of vacuum cleaners were returned because they didn't work properly. Then Sheelen ordered one of his executives to alter the firm's financial reports to understate the number of Housekeepers that had been returned.

Sheelen also started altering other financial reports as well, overstating sales and overprojecting profits. He even attempted to demonstrate the superiority of the Housekeeper over a competing Hoover model for a group of analysts, but he didn't tell them that the model being demonstrated was "souped up" and was not available for sale to the public. Things still looked rosy for Regina.

Eventually, Regina's house of cards started to tumble. A member of the board of directors became troubled when Sheelen stopped reporting financial information at their meetings. After considerable pushing, Sheelen finally relented. The directors were astonished at what they saw. After the news was announced, Regina's stock price fell sharply and Sheelen himself was sent to jail. The final curtain came in the summer of 1990 when Regina was bought by Electrolux.

SOURCES: Amar Bhide and Howard H. Stevenson, "Why Be Honest If Honesty Doesn't Pay," *Harvard Business Review*, September–October 1990, pp. 121–129; Terence R. Mitchell and William G. Scott, "America's Problems and Needed Reforms: Confronting the Ethic of Personal Advantage," *Academy of Management Executive*, August 1990, pp. 23–35; and "How Don Sheelen Made a Mess That Regina Couldn't Clean Up," *Business Week*, February 12, 1990, pp. 46–50.

lines are inaccurate and can be harmful. For example, suppose that a human resource manager forms the stereotype that only women can perform certain tasks and that men are best suited for other tasks. To the extent that this affects the manager's hiring practices, he or she is (1) costing the organization valuable talent for both sets of jobs, (2) violating federal law, and (3) behaving unethically. On the other hand, certain forms of stereotyping can be useful and efficient. Suppose, for example, that a manager believes that communication skills are important for a particular job and that speech communication majors tend to have exceptionally good communication skills. As a result, whenever he interviews candidates for jobs he pays especially close attention to speech communication majors. To the extent that communication skills truly predict job performance and that majoring in speech communication does indeed provide those skills, this form of stereotyping can be beneficial.

Perception and Attribution

Attribution theory suggests that we observe behavior and then attribute causes to it.

Attribution theory, a relatively new addition to the field of organizational behavior, has extended our understanding of how perception affects behavior in organizations.[32] Fritz Heider and H. H. Kelley are the best-known contributors to attribution theory.[33] **Attribution theory** suggests that we observe behavior and then attribute causes to it. That is, we attempt to explain why people behave as they do. The process of attribution is based on perceptions of reality, and these perceptions may vary widely among individuals.

Figure 3.5 illustrates the basic attribution theory framework. To start the process, we observe behavior, either our own or someone else's. We then evaluate that behavior in terms of its degrees of consensus, consistency, and distinctiveness. *Consensus* is the extent to which other people in the same situation behave in the same way. *Consistency* is the degree to which the same person behaves in the same way at different times. *Distinctiveness* is the extent to which the same person behaves in the same way in other situations. As a result of various combinations of consensus, consistency, and distinctiveness, we form impressions or attributions as to the causes of behavior. We may believe the behavior is caused internally (by forces within the person) or externally (by forces in the person's environment)

For example, suppose that you observe that one of your subordinates is being rowdy, disrupting others' work and generally making a nuisance of himself. If you can understand the causes of this behavior, you may be able to change it. If the employee is the only one engaging in the disruptive behavior (low consensus), if he behaves like this several times each week (high consistency), and if you have seen him behave like this in other settings (low distinctiveness), a logical conclusion would be that internal factors are causing his behavior.

Suppose, however, that you observe a different pattern: everyone in the person's work group is rowdy (high consensus), and although the particular employee often is rowdy at work (high consistency), you have never seen him behave this way in other settings (high distinctiveness). This pattern indicates that something in the situation is causing the behavior, that is, that the causes of the behavior are external.

32. Mark J. Martinko and William L. Gardner, "The Leader/Member Attribution Process," *Academy of Management Review*, April 1987, pp. 235–249; and Jeffrey D. Ford, "The Effects of Causal Attributions on Decision Makers' Responses to Performance Downturns," *Academy of Management Review*, October 1985, pp. 770–786.
33. Fritz Heider, *The Psychology of Interpersonal Relations* (New York: Wiley, 1958); and H. H. Kelley, *Attribution in Social Interaction* (Morristown, N.J.: General Learning Press, 1971).

FIGURE 3.5

The Attribution Process

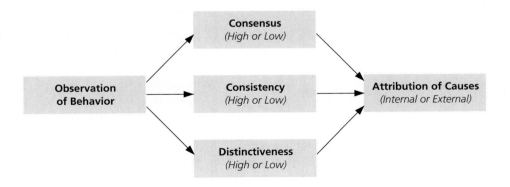

Types of Workplace Behavior

Now that we have looked closely at how individual differences—physical and intellectual differences, personality, attitudes, and perception—can influence behavior in organizations, let's turn our attention to what we mean by workplace behavior. **Workplace behavior** is a pattern of action by the members of an organization that directly or indirectly influences organizational effectiveness. One way to talk about workplace behavior is to describe its impact on performance and productivity, absenteeism and turnover, and organizational citizenship.

Workplace behavior is a pattern of action by the members of an organization that directly or indirectly influences organizational effectiveness.

Performance Behaviors

Performance behaviors are the total set of work-related behaviors that the organization expects the individual to display.

Performance behaviors are the total set of work-related behaviors that the organization expects the individual to display. Thus, they derive from the psychological contract. For some jobs, performance behaviors can be narrowly defined and easily measured. For example, an assembly line worker who sits by a moving conveyor and attaches parts to a product as it passes by has relatively few performance behaviors. He or she is expected to remain at the work station and correctly attach the parts. Performance can often be assessed quantitatively by counting the percentage of parts correctly attached.

For many other jobs, however, performance behaviors are more diverse and much more difficult to assess. For example, consider a research and development scientist at Merck. The scientist works in a lab trying to find new scientific breakthroughs that have commercial potential. The scientist must apply knowledge learned in graduate school with experience gained from previous research. Intuition and creativity are also important elements. And the desired breakthrough may take months or even years to accomplish. Organizations rely on a number of different methods for evaluating performance. The key, of course, is to match the evaluation mechanism with the job being performed.

Withdrawal Behaviors

Absenteeism occurs when an individual does not show up for work.

Another important type of work-related behavior is that which results in withdrawal—absenteeism and turnover. **Absenteeism** occurs when an individual does not show up for work. The cause may be legitimate (such as illness, jury duty, death in the family) or feigned (reported as legitimate but actually just an excuse to stay home). When an employee is absent, her or his work does not get done at all or a substitute must be hired to do it. In either case, the quantity or quality of actual output is likely to suffer. Obviously, some absenteeism is expected. The major concern of organizations is to minimize feigned absenteeism and reduce legitimate absences as much as possible. High absenteeism may be a symptom of other problems as well, such as job dissatisfaction and low morale.

Turnover occurs when people quit their jobs.

Turnover occurs when people quit their jobs. An organization usually incurs costs in replacing persons who have quit, but turnover that involves especially productive people is even more costly. Turnover seems to result from a number of factors including aspects of the job, the organization, the individual, the labor market, and family influences. In general, a poor person-job fit is also a likely cause of turnover.

Efforts to directly manage turnover are frequently fraught with difficulty, even in organizations that concentrate on rewarding good performers.[34] Of course, some turnover is inevitable and sometimes it may even be desirable. For example, if the organization is trying to cut costs by reducing its staff, having people voluntarily choose to leave is preferable to having to terminate them. And if the people who choose to leave are low performers or express high levels of job dissatisfaction, the organization may also benefit from turnover.

Organizational Citizenship

Organizational citizenship refers to the behavior of individuals who make a positive overall contribution to the organization.

Organizational citizenship refers to the behavior of individuals who make a positive overall contribution to the organization.[35] Consider, for example, an employee who does work that is acceptable in terms of both quantity and quality. However, she refuses to work overtime, she won't help newcomers learn the ropes, and she is generally unwilling to make any contribution to the organization beyond the strict performance of her job. Although this person may be seen as a good performer, she is not likely to be seen as a good organizational citizen.

Another employee may exhibit a comparable level of performance. In addition, however, he works late when the boss asks him to, he takes time to help newcomers learn their way around, and he is perceived as being helpful and committed to the organization's success. Whereas his level of performance may be seen as equal to that of the first worker, he is also likely to be seen as a better organizational citizen.

The determinant of organizational citizenship behaviors is likely to be a complex mosaic of individual, social, and organizational variables. For example, the personality, attitudes, and needs of the individual will have to be consistent with citizenship behaviors. Similarly, the social context, or work group, in which the individual works will need to facilitate and promote such behaviors (we discuss group dynamics in Chapter 11). And the organization itself, especially its culture, must be capable of promoting, recognizing, and rewarding these types of behaviors if they are to be maintained.[36] While the study of organizational citizenship is still in its infancy, preliminary research suggests that it may play a powerful role in organizational effectiveness.[37]

34. Robert P. Steel, W. H. Hendrix, and S. P. Balogh, "Confounding Effects of the Turnover Base Rate on Relations Between Time Lag and Turnover Study Outcomes: An Extension of Meta-analysis Finding and Conclusions," *Journal of Organizational Behavior*, May 1990, pp. 237–251.
35. See Dennis W. Organ and Mary Konovsky, "Cognitive Versus Affective Determinants of Organizational Citizenship Behavior," *Journal of Applied Psychology*, February 1989, pp. 157–164, for recent findings regarding this behavior.
36. Brian P. Niehoff and Robert H. Moorman, "Justice as a Mediator of the Relationship Between Methods of Monitoring and Organizational Citizenship Behavior," *Academy of Management Journal*, September 1993, pp. 527–556.
37. Organ and Konovsky, "Cognitive Versus Affective Determinants of Organizational Citizenship Behavior."

Summary of Key Points

- Understanding individuals in organizations is an important consideration for all managers. A basic framework that can be used to facilitate this understanding is the psychological contract—the set of expectations held by people with respect to what they will contribute to the organization and what they expect to get in return. Organizations strive to achieve an optimal person-job fit, but this process is complicated by the existence of individual differences.
- Some differences among people are physical and intellectual in nature. Physical differences include demographic differences like race, gender, and age. Differences in abilities, skills, and competencies may be physical, intellectual, or both.
- Personality is the relatively stable set of psychological and behavioral attributes that distinguish one person from another. Managers can do little to alter personality. Instead, they should strive to understand the effects of important personality attributes such as locus of control, self-efficacy, authoritarianism, dogmatism, Machiavellianism, self-esteem, and risk propensity.
- Attitudes are based on emotion, knowledge, and intended behavior, and they are influenced by social information. Whereas personality is relatively stable, some attitudes can be formed and changed easily. Others are more constant. Job satisfaction or dissatisfaction, organizational commitment, and job involvement are important work-related attitudes.
- Perception is the set of processes by which an individual becomes aware of and interprets information about the environment. Basic perceptual processes include selective perception and stereotyping. Perception and attribution are also closely related.
- Workplace behavior is a pattern of action by the members of an organization that directly or indirectly influences organizational effectiveness. Performance behaviors are the total set of work-related behaviors the organization expects the individual to display to fulfill the psychological contract. Basic withdrawal behaviors are absenteeism and turnover. Organizational citizenship refers to behavior that makes a positive overall contribution to the organization.

Discussion Questions

1. What is a psychological contract? Why is it important?
2. Identify examples of abilities and skills that are primarily physical. Identify others that are primarily intellectual. Finally, identify others that are both.
3. Sometimes people describe an individual as having "no personality." What is wrong with this statement? What does this statement actually mean?
4. Identify and describe five basic personality attributes.
5. What are the components of an individual's attitude?
6. Describe a circumstance or situation in which you formed a new attitude about something.
7. How does perception affect behavior?
8. What stereotypes do you form about people? Are they good or bad?
9. Identify and describe several important workplace behaviors.
10. As a manager, how would you go about trying to make someone a better organizational citizen?

Purpose   This exercise will give you insights into both the importance of personality in the workplace as well as some of the difficulties associated with assessing personality traits.

Format   You will first try to determine which personality traits are most relevant for different jobs. You will then write a series of questions that you think may help assess or measure those traits in prospective employees.

Procedure   First, read each of the following job descriptions:

Sales Representative   This position involves calling on existing customers to ensure that they continue to be happy with your firm's products. It also requires that the sales representative work to get customers to increase the quantity of your products they are buying as well as attract new customers. A sales representative must be aggressive but not pushy.

Office Manager   The office manager oversees the work of a staff of twenty secretaries, receptionists, and clerks. The manager hires them, trains them, evaluates their performance, and sets their pay. The manager also schedules working hours and, when necessary, disciplines or fires workers.

Warehouse Worker   Warehouse workers unload trucks and carry shipments to shelves for storage. They also pull orders for customers from shelves and take products for packing. The job requires that workers follow orders precisely; there is little room for autonomy or interaction with others during work.

Working alone, think of the single personality trait that you think is most necessary for a person to be able to effectively perform each of these three jobs. Next, write five questions that, when answered by a job applicant, will help you assess how that applicant scores on that particular trait. These questions should be of the type that can be answered on a five-point scale (i.e., strongly agree, agree, neither agree nor disagree, disagree, strongly disagree).

After you have completed writing your questions, exchange them with those of one of your classmates. Pretend that you are a job applicant. Provide honest and truthful answers to each question. After each of you has finished, discuss the traits each of you identified for each position and how well you think your classmate's questions actually measure those traits.

Follow-up Questions
1. How easy is it to measure personality?
2. How important do you believe it is for organizations to consider personality in hiring decisions?
3. Do perception and attitudes affect how people answer personality questions?

The rules of the game used to be simple and straightforward: U.S. workers were hired by big corporations and did what they were told by their bosses. In return, their income increased steadily and they knew that they could count on having their job for a long time. Now, however, things are different.

With relatively high levels of unemployment, for example, firms have realized that they don't have to keep pumping up wages to keep valuable workers. Current levels of unemployment are generally running more than 6 percent, so people are reluctant to leave their jobs as long as things don't get too bad. Moreover, recent trends in corporate cutbacks and downsizing programs have undermined worker confidence in job security.

Yet, many firms are expecting their employees to be more involved in planning their own work, making decisions, and contributing to bottom-line organizational performance. Work teams, participative management, and decentralization trends all carry the same implication: people at lower levels in the organization are expected to do more. Clearly, then, the sort of psychological contracts workers have with their employers today is far different from those of decades past.

Federal Express Corp. provides a good case in point. Just a few years ago, Federal Express dominated the market for overnight delivery services, and "Fed Ex-ing" was almost a generic term for shipping rush packages by courier. In 1983 the firm earned almost $24 in revenues on every package it delivered.

But competition in the overnight delivery business increased dramatically during the next several years. United Parcel Service, Airborne Express, and even the U.S. Postal Service began to take market share away from Federal Express. To fight back, the firm had little choice but to lower its prices. By 1993, Federal Express was earning only a little more than $13 in revenues on each package delivered, but its lower prices had increased the number of packages it was handling so that profits did not suffer much.

But some of the firm's continued profitability came from efficiency programs and cost-cutting plans. Moreover, many of the ideas for these programs came from Federal Express workers who had been organized into work teams. These teams took over much of their own supervision and set personal goals for boosting their contributions to the firm's overall level of effectiveness.

Interestingly, workers at Federal Express remain highly committed and loyal to the firm today, even though they haven't gotten many big raises lately. Part of their commitment stems from their getting a voice in how they do their jobs. And they simply draw pride from doing their jobs well.

Consider, for example, the case of Mark Horton. Horton is a Federal Express courier with a rural route 150 miles outside of Oklahoma City. Recently, his delivery truck broke down on a country road far from a repair shop. Undaunted, he strapped the eighteen packages he still had left to deliver onto his back, borrowed a bicycle, and finished his deliveries before 4:30.

How did Federal Express reward his efforts? The firm gave him a pin, a glass statue, an honorary dinner with other outstanding contributors, and some stock worth about $500. Not a bad reward at all—but a pay raise wasn't even discussed.

Of course, Federal Express is far from alone in these practices. More and more firms today are using one-time bonuses, plaques, theater or baseball tickets, and thank you notes from the boss in lieu of granting pay increases. This provides the firm with an avenue for expressing its appreciation while avoiding a spiralling payroll. Still, most employees are likely to tire of plaques and dinners and instead wish for a good, old-fashioned raise every once in awhile.

Case Questions

1. How are psychological contracts being changed today?
2. What roles do personality, attitudes, and perception play in the changes described in this case?
3. How would you assess Mark Horton's work-related behavior?

SOURCES: Jaclyn Fierman, "When Will You Get a Raise?" *Fortune*, July 12, 1993, pp. 34–36; "Federal Express to Offer Cheaper Overnight Delivery," *USA Today*, March 8, 1993, p. B2; and "Fedex: Europe Nearly Killed the Messenger," *Business Week*, May 25, 1992, pp. 124–126.

Susan Harrington continued to drum her fingers on her desk. She had a real problem and wasn't sure what to do next. She had a lot of confidence in Jack Reed, but she suspected that she was about the last person in the office who did. Perhaps if she ran through the entire story again in her mind she would see the solution.

Susan had been distribution manager for Clarkston Industries for almost twenty years. An early brush with the law and a short stay in prison had made her realize the importance of honesty and hard work. Henry Clarkston had given her a chance despite her record, and Susan had made the most of it. She now was one of the most respected managers in the company. Few people knew her background.

Susan had hired Jack Reed fresh out of prison six months ago. Susan understood how Jack felt when Jack tried to explain his past and asked for another chance. Susan decided to give him that chance, just as Henry Clarkston had given her a chance. Jack eagerly accepted a job on the loading docks and soon was able to load a truck as fast as anyone else in the crew.

Things had gone well at first. Everyone seemed to like Jack, and he made several new friends. Susan had been vaguely disturbed about two months ago, however, when another dock worker reported his wallet missing. She confronted Jack about this and was reassured when Jack understood her concern and earnestly but calmly asserted his innocence. Susan was especially relieved when the wallet was found a few days later.

Events of last week, however, had brewed serious trouble. First, a new personnel clerk came across records about Jack's past while updating employee files. Assuming the information was common knowledge, the clerk mentioned to several employees what a good thing it was to give ex-convicts like Jack a chance. The next day, someone in bookkeeping discovered money missing from petty cash. Another worker claimed to have seen Jack in the area around the office strongbox, which was open during working hours, earlier that same day.

Most people assumed that Jack was the thief. Even the worker whose wallet had been misplaced suggested that perhaps Jack indeed had stolen it but then returned it when questioned. Several employees had approached Susan and requested that Jack be fired. Meanwhile, when Susan had discussed the problem with Jack, Jack had been defensive and sullen and said little about the petty-cash situation other than to deny stealing the money.

To her dismay, Susan found that rethinking the story did little to solve her problem. Should she fire Jack? The evidence, of course, was purely circumstantial, yet everybody else seemed to see things quite clearly. Susan feared that if she did not fire Jack, she would lose everyone's trust and that some people might even begin to question her own motives.

Case Questions

1. Explain the events in this case in terms of perception and attitudes. Does personality play a role?

2. What should Susan do? Should she fire Jack, or give him another chance?

CHAPTER 4

Need-based Perspectives on Motivation

OBJECTIVES

After studying this chapter, you should be able to:

Define the concept of motivation and describe the basic motivational process.

Discuss the role of needs and motives in organizations.

Describe several historical perspectives on motivation.

Discuss three important need theories of motivation.

Discuss Herzberg's two-factor theory of motivation.

Identify and summarize three other important individual needs.

Describe parallels among the need theories.

For years managers in many businesses in the United States believed that they understood what most people seemed to want from their jobs—money, a nice title, job security, and plenty of opportunities for advancement. But just when they thought they had it all figured out, the rules seem to have changed.

The "baby boom" generation is the 76 million or so people born between 1946 and 1964. Many members of this group entered the job market as aggressive, career-oriented, individuals willing to put in long hours and make personal sacrifices in order to advance within the business. And most of them have now attained middle- or upper-level management positions within their organizations.

Their children, however, who have been called the "baby busters," often want altogether different things. Many of the 38 million baby busters, born between 1965 and 1975, appear to be much less aggressive than the previous generation. For example, they are more likely to turn down opportunities for overtime, refuse transfers to other cities even if it hurts their career, and leave work early enough to spend time with their families. They put a premium on life satis-

Many of the new generation of workers, the "baby busters," are placing a higher value on their overall quality of life than on their professional prestige. Intel's Aaron Evans is thinking about retiring already: "My idea of the good life is time to do things myself."

faction and strive to balance it against work-related demands.

A recent USA Today/CNN poll found that only 26 percent of the workers it surveyed wanted to hold a leadership position in their organizations. This contrasts with 41 percent of a similar group surveyed in 1986. Similarly, more than one-half of the more recent respondents indicated that their job was only something they did to earn money, with fewer than one-half saying that it was a meaningful part of their lives. In 1986, on the other hand, fewer than 40 percent said that they worked for only money. Clearly, then, the things that motivate people to work have changed.[1]

■■■■ People work for a wide variety of reasons. Some want money, some want challenge, and some want security. The things that each unique individual in an organization decides that he or she wants from work plays an instrumental role in determining motivation to work. As we see in this chapter, motivation is vital to all organizations and, hence, to their managers. Often the difference between highly effective organizations and less effective ones lies in the motivational profiles of their members. Thus, managers need to understand the nature of individual motivation, especially as it applies to work situations.

This is the first of three chapters that address employee motivation. Here we examine need-based perspectives on motivation. In Chapter 5, we explore process-based perspectives on motivation. Finally, in Chapter 6 we discuss learning-based perspectives on motivation.

1. "Busters Have Work Ethic of Their Own," *USA Today*, July 20, 1993, pp. 1B, 2B; Myron Magnet, "The Truth About the American Worker," *Fortune*, May 4, 1992, pp. 48–65; and Alan Deutschman, "What 25-Year-Olds Want," *Fortune*, August 27, 1990, pp. 42–50.

The Nature of Motivation

Motivation is the set of forces that cause people to behave in certain ways.[2] The student who stays up all night to ensure that his or her term paper is the best it can be, the salesperson who works on Saturdays to get ahead, and the doctor who makes follow-up phone calls to patients to check on their conditions are all motivated people. Of course, the student who avoids the term paper by spending the day at the beach, the salesperson who goes home early to escape a tedious sales call, and the doctor who skips follow-up calls to have more time for golf are also motivated. In both examples, these individuals are simply motivated to achieve different types of things. From the manager's viewpoint, the objective is to motivate people to behave in ways that are in the organization's best interest.[3]

The Importance of Motivation

One of the manager's primary tasks is to motivate people in the organization to perform at high levels. This means getting them to work hard, come to work regularly, and make positive contributions to the organization's mission. But job performance depends on ability and environment as well as on motivation. The relationship can be stated as follows:

$$P = f(M + A + E),$$

where P = performance, M = motivation, A = ability, and E = environment. To reach high levels of performance, an employee must want to do the job (motivation), be able to do the job (ability), and have the materials and equipment needed to do the job (environment). A deficiency in any one of these areas will hurt performance. A manager thus should strive to ensure that all three conditions are met.[4]

The Motivational Framework

To understand motivation we must start with the concepts of need deficiencies and goal-directed behaviors. Figure 4.1 shows the basic motivational framework we will use to organize our discussion.[5]

The starting point in the motivational process is a need. A **need** is anything an individual requires or wants. Motivated behavior usually begins when an individual experiences a deficiency in one or more important needs. Although satisfied needs may also serve to motivate behavior (for example, to maintain one's achieved standard of living), need deficiencies usually result in more intense feelings and behavioral changes. For example, if a person has not yet attained the standard of living he or she desires, this experienced need deficiency may serve to stimulate action on her part.

---

2. Richard M. Steers and Lyman W. Porter, *Motivation and Work Behavior*, 5th ed. (New York: McGraw-Hill, 1991), pp. 5–6. See also Frank J. Landy and Wendy S. Becker, "Motivation Theory Reconsidered," in Larry L. Cummings and Barry M. Staw (Eds.), *Research in Organizational Behavior*, Vol. 9 (Greenwich, Conn.: JAI Press, 1987), pp. 1–38.

3. Roland E. Kidwell, Jr., and Nathan Bennett, "Employee Propensity to Withhold Effort: A Conceptual Model to Intersect Three Avenues of Research," *Academy of Management Review*, July 1993, pp. 429–456.

4. Victor H. Vroom, *Work and Motivation* (New York: Wiley, 1964).

5. See Jack W. Brehm and Elizabeth A. Self, "The Intensity of Motivation," in Mark R. Rosenzweig and Lyman W. Porter (Eds.), *Annual Review of Psychology*, Vol. 40 (Palo Alto: Annual Reviews, Inc., 1989), pp. 109–132.

FIGURE 4.1

The Motivational Framework

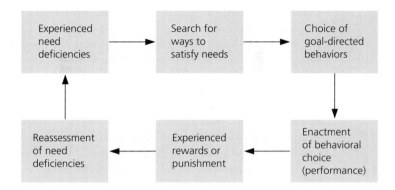

A need deficiency usually triggers a search for ways to satisfy it. Consider, for example, a person who feels her salary and position are deficient because she wants more income and because they do not reflect the importance to the organization of the work she does. She may believe that she has three options: to simply ask for a raise and a promotion, to work harder in the hope of earning a raise and a promotion, or to look for a new job with a higher salary and a more prestigious title.

Next comes a choice of goal-directed behaviors. While a person actually might pursue more than one option at the same time (such as both working harder while also looking for another job), most effort will likely be directed at only one option. In the next phase, the person actually enacts, or carries out, the behavior chosen to satisfy the need. For example, the person in our example may elect to work harder in hopes of earning a higher salary. At this point, she will likely begin putting in longer hours, working harder, and so forth. She will next experience either rewards or punishment as a result of this choice. She may perceive her situation to be punishing if she ends up earning no additional recognition and thus not getting a promotion or pay raise. Alternatively, she may be rewarded by actually getting the raise and promotion because of her higher performance.

Finally, the individual assesses the extent to which the achieved outcome fully addresses the original need deficiency. Suppose that the person wanted a 10 percent raise and a promotion to vice president. If she got both, she should be satisfied. On the other hand, if she got only a 7 percent raise and a promotion to assistant vice president, she will have to decide whether to keep trying, accept what she got, or choose one of the other options considered earlier. (Sometimes, of course, a need may go unsatisfied altogether despite the person's efforts.)

Needs and Motives in Organizations

Primary needs are things people require to sustain themselves.

Secondary needs are learned from the environment and culture in which the individual lives.

As just noted, a need is simply anything an individual requires or wants. Not surprisingly, then, most people have a large number of needs. These needs can be usefully grouped into two categories: primary versus secondary needs. **Primary needs** are things that people require to sustain themselves, such as food, water, and shelter. Thus, they are instinctive and physiologically based. **Secondary needs**, on the other hand, are more psychological in character and are learned from the environment and culture in which the individual lives. Examples of secondary needs are the needs for achievement, autonomy, power, order, affiliation, and understanding.

Secondary needs often seem to manifest themselves in organizational settings, so they are especially important to consider in an examination of motivated behavior. For example, if individuals are to be satisfied with the psychological contracts they have with their organization, the inducements offered by the organization must be consistent with their own unique needs. Offering a nice office and job security may not be sufficient if the individual is primarily seeking income and promotion opportunities. We noted in our opening incident some of the different needs that seem to motivate many younger workers today.

It is also important to note that people's needs will change with time. An individual may be satisfied with his compensation this year, but if he does not receive a raise for several years, he may begin to feel a need for more compensation. This means that from an organizational perspective programs designed to elicit certain behavior may lose their effectiveness as employees satisfy one set of needs and begin to identify another set of needs. Some firms are experimenting with flexible reward systems as a way to satisfy an array of different needs.

A **motive** represents the individual's reason for choosing one certain behavior from among several choices.

A **motive** represents the individual's reason for choosing one certain behavior from among several choices. Motives are derived from needs in that most behaviors are undertaken to satisfy one or more needs. For example, an individual may decide to have lunch to satisfy a need for food. She might choose to go to McDonald's because it's fast and convenient, Taco Bell because she's in the mood for Mexican food, or another spot simply because it's on the way to an afternoon business appointment. The reasons for each choice, then, reflect the individual's motive.

The linkages among needs, motives, and behavior are fairly simple and straightforward. A need serves as a stimulus for action. Motives are the channels through which the individual thinks the need can best be satisfied and thus reflect the specific behavioral choices enacted by the person. Finally, the manifestation of motives is actual behavior. For example, suppose that an employee wants to advance her career to gain income and prestige (needs). She decides to work harder and do higher quality work to impress her boss (motives). Thus, she works later each evening, comes into the office on Saturday, and pays more attention to detail as she strives for perfection (behaviors).

Motives can vary considerably in their degree of conscious deliberation and complexity. The simple decision of where to have lunch, for example, can be made quickly and without a great deal of thought. On the other hand, a major decision that affects the person's career or family may take much longer and involve many other considerations. *Diversity in the Workplace* discusses some fundamental differences in needs for different people.

Historical Perspectives on Motivation

Historical views on motivation, even though not always accurate, are of interest for several reasons. For one thing, they provide a foundation for contemporary thinking about motivation. For another, because they generally were based on common sense and intuition, an appreciation of their strengths and weaknesses can help managers gain useful insights into employee motivation in the workplace.

DIVERSITY IN THE WORKPLACE

Different Needs for Different People

Is should come as no surprise (especially after reading Chapter 3) that different people have different needs. Although each individual has a unique set of needs, however, similar patterns of needs are likely to typify people who share one or more diversity-related characteristic.

For example, employees who are married and have children are likely to need some degree of flexibility in their working arrangements, a benefit package attuned to family needs, and, increasingly, on-premise child care facilities. A single employee with fewer personal commitments, in contrast, may need less flexibility and a benefit package designed for individuals.

Older employees also have needs that are fundamentally different from those of younger workers. For example, they may be more interested in the intrinsic joys of work and less concerned about promotion. They may also be less willing to work long hours and may, in fact, prefer to work only part time.

Employees with physical handicaps will obviously have needs that differ from workers with no such handicaps. Special accommodations in facilities such as restrooms and workstations as well as in benefits are now legally required. But managers must recognize that apart from just the physical adjustments that must be made, the organization must be prepared to respond to other differences in basic needs as well.

Managers must also recognize that workers with different national and cultural backgrounds may have different needs. A worker from Japan, for example, may have a strong need to be accepted by the group and may be less interested in opportunities for individual recognition. Thus, a manager should not take a Japanese employee's unwillingness to seek a promotion as a sign that she or he does not want it. In the Japanese culture, self-promotion by individuals is frowned on—it is management's job to recognize and promote the right people.

SOURCES: Douglas T. Hall and Victoria A Parker, "The Role of Workplace Flexibility in Managing Diversity," *Organizational Dynamics*, Summer 1993, pp. 5–18; and Stephanie Overman, "Myths Hinder Hiring of Older Workers," *HR Magazine*, June 1993, pp. 51–56.

Early Views of Motivation

One early view of motivation was based on the concept of hedonism.

The earliest views on human motivation were dominated by the concept of hedonism: the idea that people seek pleasure and comfort and try to avoid pain and discomfort.[6] Although this view seems reasonable as far as it goes, there are many kinds of behavior that it cannot explain. For example, why do recreational athletes exert themselves willingly and regularly, whereas a hedonist prefers to relax? Why do people occasionally risk their lives for others in times of crisis? Why do volunteers give tirelessly of their own time to collect money for charitable causes?

The recognition that hedonism is an extremely limited—and often incorrect— view of human behavior prompted the emergence of other perspectives. William James, for one, argued that instinctive behavior and unconscious motivation are also important in human behavior.[7] Although many of James's ideas eventually were supplanted by other views, they helped reshape contemporary motivation theory.

6. Craig Pinder, *Work Motivation* (Glenview, Ill.: Scott, Foresman, 1984).
7. Ernest R. Hilgard and Richard C. Atkinson, *Introduction to Psychology*, 4th ed. (New York: Harcourt, Brace and World, 1967).

The Scientific Management Approach

As we note in Chapter 1, Frederick W. Taylor, the chief proponent of scientific management, assumed that employees are economically motivated and work so as to earn as much money as they can.[8] Taylor once used a pig-iron handler named Schmidt to illustrate the concepts of scientific management. Schmidt's job consisted of moving heavy pieces of iron from one pile to another. He appeared to be doing an adequate job and regularly met the standard of 12.5 tons per day. Taylor, however, believed Schmidt was strong enough to do much more. To test his ideas, Taylor designed a piece-rate pay system that would award Schmidt a fixed sum of money for each ton of iron he loaded. Then he had the following conversation with Schmidt and observed his work:

Taylor: Schmidt, are you a high-priced man?

Schmidt: Well, I don't know what you mean. [Several minutes of conversation ensued.]

Taylor: Well, if you are a high-priced man, you will do exactly as this man tells you tomorrow, from morning until night. When he tells you to pick up a pig and walk, you pick it up and walk, and when he tells you to sit down and rest, you sit down and rest. You do that right straight through the day. And what's more, no back talk. Do you understand that?

Schmidt started to work, and all day long and at regular intervals, was told by the man who stood over him with a watch, "Now pick up a pig and walk. Now sit down and rest. Now walk, now rest . . . ." He worked when he was told to work, and rested when he was told to rest. At half-past five in the afternoon, he had 47.5 tons loaded on the car. And he practically never failed to work at this pace and do the task that was set him during the three years that Taylor was at Bethlehem.[9]

Recent evidence suggests that Taylor may have fabricated the conversation just related; Schmidt himself may have been an invention.[10] If so, this willingness to fabricate shows just how strongly Taylor believed in his economic view of human motivation and in the need to spread the doctrine. But soon researchers recognized that scientific management theorists' assumptions about motivation could not explain complex human behavior. The next perspective on motivation to emerge in the management literature was the human relations movement.

The Human Relations Approach

The human relations view, which we also discussed in Chapter 1, arose from the Hawthorne studies.[11] This perspective suggested that people are motivated by things other than money—in particular that employees, as social beings, are motivated by and respond to the social environment at work. Favorable employee attitudes, such as job satisfaction, were presumed to result in increased employee performance. In Chapter 5, we explore this relationship in more detail. Here it is sufficient to say, as we did in Chapter 1, that the human relations viewpoint left most questions about human behavior unanswered. However, one of the primary

8. Frederick W. Taylor, *Principles of Scientific Management* (New York: Harper, 1911).

9. Ibid., pp. 46-47.

10. See Charles D. Wrege and Amedeo G. Perroni, "Taylor's Pig-Tale: A Historical Analysis of Frederick W. Taylor's Pig-Iron Experiment," *Academy of Management Journal*, March 1974, pp. 6–27.

11. Pinder, *Work Motivation*. See also Daniel Wren, *The Evolution of Management Thought*, 4th ed. (New York: Wiley, 1992).

theorists associated with this movement, Abraham Maslow, helped develop an important need theory of motivation.

Need Theories of Motivation

Need theories of motivation assume that need deficiencies cause behavior.

Need theories represent the starting point for most contemporary thought on motivation,[12] although these theories too attracted critics.[13] The basic premise of **need theories,** consistent with our motivation framework introduced earlier, is that human motivation is caused primarily by deficiencies in one or more important needs or need categories. Need theorists have attempted to identify and categorize the most salient needs, that is, those that are most important to people. The best-known need theories are the hierarchy of needs, manifest needs theory, and the ERG theory.

The Hierarchy of Needs

Maslow's hierarchy of needs theory assumes that human needs are arranged in a hierarchy of importance.

The most well-known need theory is the hierarchy of human needs developed by psychologist Abraham Maslow in the 1940s.[14] Influenced by the human relations school of thought, Maslow argued that human beings are "wanting" animals: they have innate desires to satisfy a given set of needs. Furthermore, Maslow believed these needs are arranged in a hierarchy of importance, with the most basic needs at the bottom, or foundation, of the hierarchy.

In the needs hierarchy, the categories of **deficiency needs** are physiological, security, and belongingness needs.

The needs hierarchy also identified two sets of **growth needs**: esteem and self-actualization needs.

Figure 4.2 depicts Maslow's hierarchy of needs. The three sets of needs at the bottom of the hierarchy are called **deficiency needs** because they must be satisfied for the individual to be fundamentally comfortable. The top two sets of needs are termed **growth needs** because they focus on personal growth and development.

12. Steers and Porter, *Motivation and Work Behavior.*
13. Gerald R. Salancik and Jeffrey Pfeffer, "An Examination of Need-Satisfaction Models of Job Attitudes," *Administrative Science Quarterly*, September 1977, pp. 427–456.
14. Abraham H. Maslow, "A Theory of Human Motivation," *Psychological Review*, Vol. 50, 1943, pp. 370–396; and Abraham H. Maslow, *Motivation and Personality* (New York: Harper & Row, 1954).

FIGURE 4.2

The Hierarchy of Needs

SOURCE: Adapted from Abraham H. Maslow, "A Theory of Human Motivation," *Psychological Review*, Vol. 50, 1943, pp. 374–396.

Beyond their physiological and security needs, human beings have belongingness needs. In an organizational setting, belongingness needs manifest themselves as a need for social acceptance by one's peers. This management training seminar helps to create feelings of belongingness among colleagues.

Physiological needs include the needs for food, sex, and air.

Security needs offer safety and security, as in adequate housing, clothing, and freedom from worry and anxiety.

Belongingness needs are the social needs that include the need for love and affection and the need to be accepted by peers.

Esteem needs encompass both the need for a positive self-image and the need to be respected by others.

Self-actualization needs involve realizing our full potential becoming all that we can be.

The most basic needs in the hierarchy are **physiological needs**. They include the needs for food, sex, and air. Next in the hierarchy are **security needs**, or things that offer safety and security, such as adequate housing and clothing and freedom from worry and anxiety. **Belongingness needs**, the third level in the hierarchy, are primarily social. Examples include the need for love and affection and the need to be accepted by peers. The fourth level, **esteem needs**, actually encompasses two slightly different kinds of needs: the need for a positive self-image and self-respect and the need to be respected by others. At the top of the hierarchy are **self-actualization needs**. These involve realizing our full potential and becoming all that we can be.

Beginning at the bottom of the hierarchy, according to Maslow, each need level must be satisfied before the level above it becomes important. Thus, once physiological needs have been satisfied their importance diminishes, and security needs emerge as the primary sources of motivation. This escalation up the hierarchy continues until the self-actualization needs become the primary motivators. Whenever a previously satisfied lower-level set of needs becomes deficient again, however, the individual returns to that level. For example, a person who loses his or her job is likely to stop worrying about self-actualization and begin to concentrate on finding another job to satisfy now deficient security needs.

In most organizational settings, physiological needs probably are the easiest to evaluate and to meet. Adequate wages, restrooms, ventilation, and comfortable temperatures and working conditions are examples of things that can satisfy this most basic level of needs.

Security needs in organizational settings can be satisfied by such things as job continuity (no layoffs), a grievance system (to protect against arbitrary supervisory actions), and an adequate insurance and retirement system (to guard against financial loss from illness and to ensure retirement income).

Most employees' belongingness needs are satisfied by family ties and group relationships both inside and outside the organization. In the workplace, for

Twenty-month-old Kristin Gavaza accompanies her mother, Charity Gavaza, to her office in Newport Beach, California. Workers must try to balance personal needs, such as spending time with their families, with gaining professional fulfillment. Every individual is motivated to a different extent by personal and professional factors.

example, people usually develop friendships that provide a basis for social interaction and can play a major role in satisfying social needs. Managers can enhance satisfaction of these needs by fostering a sense of group identity and interaction among employees. At the same time, managers can be sensitive to the probable effects (such as low performance and absenteeism) on employees of family problems or lack of acceptance by coworkers.

Esteem needs in the workplace are at least partially met by job titles, choice offices, merit pay increases, awards, and other forms of recognition. Of course, to be sources of long-term motivation, tangible rewards like these must be distributed equitably and be based on performance.

Self-actualization needs perhaps are the hardest to understand and the most difficult to satisfy. For example, assessing how many people really completely fulfill their full human potential is difficult. Indeed, most people who are doing well on Maslow's hierarchy will have satisfied his or her esteem needs and will be moving toward self-actualization. Working toward self-actualization may therefore be the ultimate goal for most people, as opposed to actually achieving it.

Maslow's needs hierarchy makes a certain amount of intuitive sense. Because it was the first motivation theory to be popularized, it is also one of the best known in management circles. Yet research has revealed a number of deficiencies in the theory: five levels of needs are not always present, the actual hierarchy of needs does not always conform to Maslow's model, and need structures are more unstable and variable than the theory would lead us to believe.[15] Thus, the theory's primary contribution seems to be in providing a general framework for categorizing needs.[16]

15. Mahmond A. Wahba and Lawrence G. Bridwell, "Maslow Reconsidered: A Review of Research on the Need Hierarchy Theory," *Organizational Behavior and Human Performance*, April 1976, pp. 212–240.
16. Howard S. Schwartz, "Maslow and Hierarchical Enactment of Organizational Reality," *Human Relations*, Vol. 36, No. 10, 1983, pp. 933–956.

Manifest Needs Theory

The **manifest needs theory** includes a wide variety of fundamental human needs.

Another interesting need framework is H. A. Murray's **manifest needs theory**. First presented by Murray in 1938,[17] the original theory identified a set of potentially important needs, but did so only at an abstract level. Its present conceptualization owes much to the work of J. W. Atkinson, who translated Murray's ideas and concepts into a more concrete, operational framework.[18]

Like Maslow's needs hierarchy concept, the manifest needs theory assumes that people have a set of needs that motivates behavior. The mechanisms by which needs operate, however, are somewhat more complex in this view than in Maslow's. Murray suggests that several categories of needs are important to most people and that any number of needs may operate in varying degrees at the same time. In other words, multiple needs motivate behavior simultaneously rather than in some preset order. Table 4.1 summarizes several of the needs that Murray perceived as most powerful.

Unlike Maslow, Murray did not arrange the needs he identified in any particular order of importance. (It is interesting to note that all of the manifest needs are learned needs. In other words, we are not born with any of them; we learn them as we grow.[19] In addition, Murray believed that each need has two components: direction and intensity. *Direction* refers to the person or object that is expected to satisfy the need. If you are hungry, getting to a local eating establishment may represent the direction of the need. *Intensity* represents the importance of the need. If you are very hungry, the need to get to a restaurant may be very great; if you are only moderately hungry, the intensity may be lower.

Appropriate environmental conditions are necessary for a need to become manifest. For example, if someone with a high need for power works in a job setting in which power is irrelevant, the need may remain latent—not yet influencing the person's behavior. But if conditions that increase the importance of power arise, the need for power may then manifest itself, and the employee will begin to work toward increasing his or her power. Little research has been done to evaluate Murray's theory. Some of the specific needs defined by Murray have been the subject of much research, however, as we discuss later in this chapter.

ERG Theory

The **ERG theory** represents an extension and refinement of the needs hierarchy theory.

The ERG theory describes **existence**, **relatedness**, and **growth needs**.

A third important need theory of motivation is the ERG theory, developed by Yale psychologist Clayton Alderfer.[20] In many respects, **ERG theory** extends and refines Maslow's needs hierarchy concept, although there are several important differences between the two. The *E*, *R*, and *G* stand for three basic need categories: existence, relatedness, and growth. **Existence needs**, perceived as necessary for basic human existence, roughly correspond to the physiological and security needs of Maslow's hierarchy. **Relatedness needs**, involving the need to relate to others, are similar to Maslow's belongingness and esteem needs. Finally, **growth needs** are analogous to Maslow's needs for self-esteem and self-actualization.

Like manifest needs, ERG theory suggests that more than one kind of need, for example, relatedness and growth needs, can motivate a person at the same time. A

17. H. A. Murray, *Explorations in Personality* (New York: Oxford University Press, 1938).
18. J. W. Atkinson, *An Introduction to Motivation* (Princeton, N.J.: Van Nostrand, 1964).
19. Ibid.
20. Clayton P. Alderfer, *Existence, Relatedness, and Growth* (New York: Free Press, 1972).

TABLE 4.1

Basic Manifest Needs

Need	Characteristics
Achievement	Individual aspires to accomplish difficult tasks; maintains high standards and is willing to work toward distant goals; responds positively to competition; willing to put forth effort to attain excellence.
Affiliation	Enjoys being with friends and people in general; accepts people readily; makes efforts to win friendships and maintain association with people.
Aggression	Enjoys combat and argument; easily annoyed; sometimes willing to hurt people to get his or her way; may seek to "get even" with people perceived as having harmed him or her.
Autonomy	Tries to break away from the restraints, confinement, or restrictions of any kind; enjoys being unattached, free, not tied to people, places, or obligations; may be rebellious when faced with restraints.
Exhibition	Wants to be the center of attention; enjoys having an audience; engages in behavior that wins the notice of others; may enjoy being dramatic or witty.
Impulsivity	Tends to act on the "spur of the moment" and without deliberation; gives vent readily to feelings and wishes; speaks freely; may be volatile in emotional expression.
Nurturance	Gives sympathy and comfort; assists others whenever possible, interested in caring for children, the disabled, or the infirm; offers a "helping hand" to those in need; readily performs favors for others.
Order	Concerned with keeping personal effects and surroundings neat and organized; dislikes clutter, confusion, lack or organization; interested in developing methods for keeping materials methodically organized.
Power	Attempts to control the environment and to influence or direct other people; expresses opinions forcefully; enjoys the role of leader and may assume it spontaneously.
Understanding	Wants to understand many areas of knowledge; values synthesis of ideas, verifiable generalization, logical thought, particularly when directed or satisfied intellectual curiosity.

SOURCE: Adapted from the *Personality Research Form Manual,* published by Research Psychologists Press, Inc., P.O. Box 984, Port Huron, Michigan 48060. Copyright © 1967, 1974, 1984, by Douglas N. Jackson. Used by permission.

The ERG theory suggests that if people become frustrated trying to satisfy one set of needs, they will regress to the previously satisfied set of needs.

more important difference from Maslow's hierarchy is that ERG theory includes a *frustration-regression component* and a *satisfaction-progression component* (see Figure 4.3). The satisfaction-progression process suggests that after satisfying one category of needs, a person progresses to the next level. On this point, the need hierarchy and ERG theory agree. The need hierarchy, however, assumed that the individual will remain at the next level until the needs at that level are satisfied. In

FIGURE 4.3

The ERG Theory

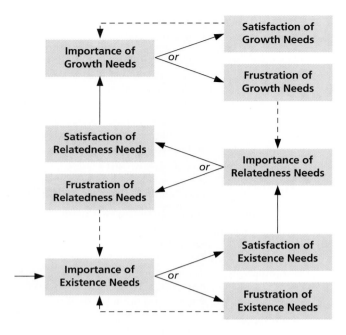

contrast, ERG theory argues that a person who is frustrated in trying to satisfy a higher level of needs eventually will regress to the preceding level.[21]

Suppose, for instance, a manager has satisfied her basic needs at the relatedness level and now is trying to satisfy her growth needs. For a variety of reasons, such as organizational constraints (i.e., few challenging jobs) and the absence of opportunities to advance, she is unable to satisfy those needs. According to ERG theory, frustration of her growth needs will cause the manager's relatedness needs to once again become dominate as motivators. The *Global Perspective* describes how frustration-regression processes are currently arising in Europe.

Because ERG theory is a fairly new addition to motivation literature, it has not been studied much. Preliminary evidence suggests, however, that ERG theory may be a more economical and powerful explanation of human motivation than either the needs hierarchy or manifest needs theory.[22]

The Dual-Structure Theory

Another important foundational theory of motivation is the dual-structure theory, which in many ways is similar to the need theories just discussed. This theory has played a major role in managerial thinking about motivation.

---

21. Ibid.
22. Clayton P. Alderfer, "An Empirical Test of a New Theory of Human Needs," *Organizational Behavior and Human Performance*, Vol. 4, 1969, pp. 142–175.

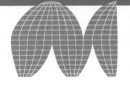

Changing International Needs

Just as the needs of workers in the United States are changing, so too are the needs of workers in other countries. In Europe, for example, many workers seem to be regressing back to existence needs. For years European firms provided solid salaries and ample benefits for their workers. These workers also enjoyed plenty of job security. As a result, many European workers enjoyed a nice lifestyle characterized by plenty of leisure time and opportunity for socializing.

More recently, however, many European firms have been cutting back their payrolls, eliminating benefits, and showing more willingness to lay off workers. As a result, many of their workers have started worrying more about their income and job security.

Changes have also been noted in Japan. Two common stereotypes exist about Japanese workers. The first is that they are workaholics, preferring to spend all their time at work. The second is that they all want the job security lifetime employment supposedly provides. In reality, both of these stereotypes are changing.

Consider Akiko Hara. Akiko spent two years working for a Japanese brokerage firm. She soon tired of working fifty-five hours each week, however, and decided to quit. She gave up bonuses, paid vacations, and job security in exchange for a part-time job paying half as much. Why? Because she wanted more out of life than just work. This pattern is emerging all across Japan. More and more Japanese workers are opting out of their equivalent of the rat race for a different lifestyle. Some seek part-time jobs only. Others work temporary jobs and take a break between assignments. Indeed, more than 12 percent of the Japanese workforce now falls into one of these two categories.

Japanese businesses, long accustomed to having a full complement of dedicated, full-time employees, are also having to adjust to this new trend. Nissan and Toyota, for example, use many part-time workers. The Fuji Bank has 1,500 part-time workers. Asahi Breweries uses 2,000 part-time sales representatives in addition to its 700-person regular staff. Clearly, then, worker needs are changing everywhere.

SOURCES: "Europe's Social Cushion Is Looking Rather Frayed," *Business Week*, July 5, 1993, p. 50; and "Japanese Workers Aren't All Workaholics," *Wall Street Journal*, May 8, 1989, p. A10.

Development of the Theory

The **dual-structure theory** identifies motivation factors, which affect satisfaction, and hygiene factors, which determine dissatisfaction.

Frederick Herzberg and his associates developed the **dual-structure theory** in the late 1950s and early 1960s.[23] Herzberg began by interviewing approximately two hundred accountants and engineers in Pittsburgh. He asked them to recall times when they felt especially satisfied and motivated by their jobs and times when they felt particularly dissatisfied and unmotivated. He then asked them to describe what caused the good and bad feelings. The responses to the questions were recorded by the interviewers and later subjected to content analysis. (In a content analysis, the words, phrases, and sentences used by respondents are analyzed and categorized according to their meanings.)

23. Frederick Herzberg, Bernard Mausner, and Barbara Snyderman, *The Motivation to Work* (New York: Wiley, 1959); and Frederick Herzberg, "One More Time: How Do You Motivate Employees?" *Harvard Business Review*, January–February 1968, pp. 53–62.

To his surprise, Herzberg found that entirely different sets of factors were associated with the two kinds of feelings about work. For example, a person who indicated "low pay" as a cause of dissatisfaction would not necessarily identify "high pay" as a cause of satisfaction and motivation. Instead, respondents associated entirely different causes, such as recognition or achievement, with satisfaction and motivation.

The findings led Herzberg to conclude that the traditional model of satisfaction and motivation was incorrect. As Figure 4.4 shows, job satisfaction had up until then been viewed as a single-structure construct, ranging from satisfaction to dissatisfaction. If this were the case, Herzberg reasoned, a single set of factors should influence movement back and forth along the continuum. But because his research had identified differential influences from two different sets of factors, Herzberg argued that two different dimensions must be involved. Thus, motivation was seen as a dual-structured phenomenon.

Figure 4.4 also illustrates the dual-structure concept that there is one dimension ranging from satisfaction to no satisfaction and another ranging from dissatisfaction to no dissatisfaction. Presumably the two dimensions must be associated with the two sets of factors identified in the initial interviews. Thus, this theory proposed that employees might be either satisfied or not satisfied and, at the same time, dissatisfied or not dissatisfied.[24]

24. Herzberg, Mausner, and Snyderman, *The Motivation to Work.*

FIGURE 4.4

The Dual-Structure Theory

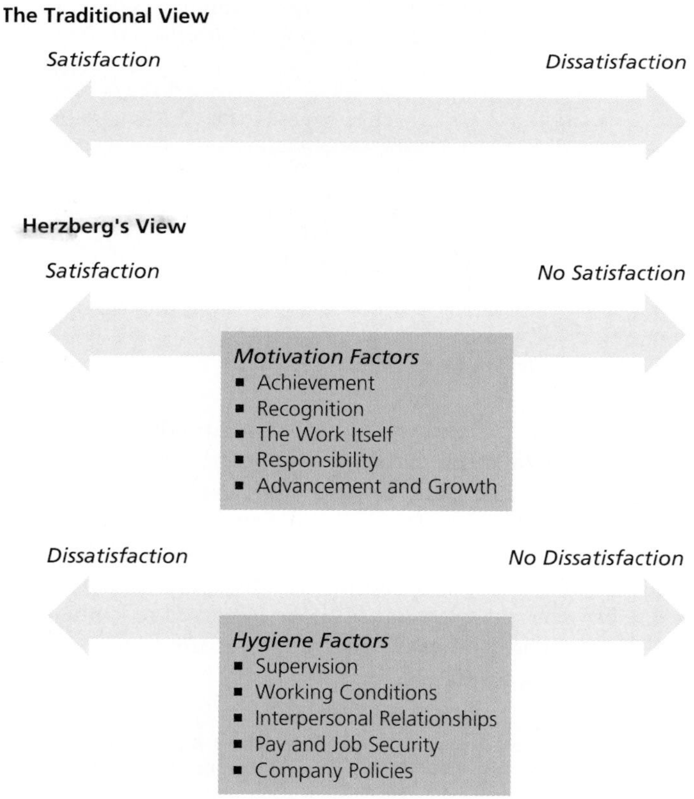

The Traditional View

Satisfaction ⟷ Dissatisfaction

Herzberg's View

Satisfaction ⟷ No Satisfaction

Motivation Factors
- Achievement
- Recognition
- The Work Itself
- Responsibility
- Advancement and Growth

Dissatisfaction ⟷ No Dissatisfaction

Hygiene Factors
- Supervision
- Working Conditions
- Interpersonal Relationships
- Pay and Job Security
- Company Policies

In addition, Figure 4.4 lists the primary factors identified in Herzberg's interviews. **Motivation factors**, such as achievement and recognition, were often cited by people in the original study as primary causes of satisfaction and motivation. When present in a job, these factors apparently could cause satisfaction and motivation; when they were absent, the result was feelings of no satisfaction as opposed to dissatisfaction.

The other set of factors, **hygiene factors**, came out in response to the question about dissatisfaction and lack of motivation. The respondents suggested that pay, job security, supervisors, and working conditions, if seen as inadequate, could lead to feelings of dissatisfaction. When these factors were considered acceptable, however, the person still was not necessarily satisfied; rather, she or he was simply not dissatisfied.[25]

To use the dual-structure theory in the workplace, Herzberg recommended a two-stage process. First, the manager should try to eliminate situations that cause dissatisfaction, which Herzberg assumed to be the more basic of the two dimensions. To reach this goal—achieving a state of no dissatisfaction—the manager presumably needs to attend to hygiene factors, such as ensuring that pay and job security are adequate and that working conditions are reasonable. According to the theory, once a state of no dissatisfaction exists, trying to further improve motivation through the hygiene factors is a waste of time. At that point, the motivation factors enter the picture. By increasing opportunities for achievement, recognition, responsibility, advancement, and growth, the manager can help subordinates feel satisfied and motivated.

Unlike many other theorists, Herzberg described quite explicitly how managers could apply his theory. In particular, he developed and described a technique called job enrichment for structuring employee tasks.[26] (We discuss job enrichment in Chapter 7.) Herzberg tailored this technique to his major motivation factors. This unusual attention to application may explain the widespread popularity of the dual-structure theory among practicing managers.

Evaluation of the Theory

Because it gained popularity so quickly, the dual-structure theory has been scientifically scrutinized more often than most other theories in the field of organizational behavior.[27] The results have been contradictory, to say the least. The initial study by Herzberg and his associates supported the basic premises of the theory, as did a few follow-up studies.[28] In general, studies that use the same methodology as Herzberg did (content analysis of recalled incidents) tend to support the theory.[29]

However, this methodology has itself come under attack. Studies that use other methods for measuring satisfaction and dissatisfaction frequently find results quite different from Herzberg's.[30]

Motivation factors are intrinsic to the work itself and include factors such as achievement and recognition.

Hygiene factors are extrinsic to the work itself and include factors like pay and job security.

25. Ibid.
26. Herzberg, "One More Time"; and Ricky W. Griffin, *Task Design: An Integrative Approach* (Glenview, Ill.: Scott, Foresman, 1982).
27. Pinder, *Work Motivation*.
28. Frederick Herzberg, *Work and the Nature of Man* (Cleveland: World, 1966); Valerie M. Bookman, "The Herzberg Controversy," *Personnel Psychology*, Summer 1971, pp. 155–189; and Benedict Grigaliunas and Frederick Herzberg, "Relevance in the Test of Motivation-Hygiene Theory," *Journal of Applied Psychology*, February 1971, pp. 73–79.
29. Pinder, *Work Motivation*.
30. Marvin Dunnette, John Campbell, and Milton Hakel, "Factors Contributing to Job Satisfaction and Job Dissatisfaction in Six Occupational Groups," *Organizational Behavior and Human Performance*, May 1967, pp. 143–174; and Charles L. Hulin and Patricia Smith, "An Empirical Investigation of Two Implications of the Two-Factor Theory of Job Satisfaction," *Journal of Applied Psychology*, October 1967, pp. 396–402.

If the theory is "method bound," as it appears to be, its validity is at best questionable. Several other criticisms have been directed against the theory. Critics say that the original sample of accountants and engineers may not represent the general working population. Furthermore, they maintain that the theory fails to account for individual differences. Also, subsequent research has found that a factor such as pay may bear on satisfaction in one sample and dissatisfaction in another, and research has found that the effect of a given factor depends on the individual's age and organizational level. Finally, say its critics, the theory does not define the relationship between satisfaction and motivation.[31]

It is not surprising, then, that the dual-structure theory is no longer held in high esteem by organizational behavior researchers.[32] Indeed, the field has since adopted far more complex and valid conceptualizations of motivation, most of which we discuss in Chapters 5 and 6. But because of its initial popularity and its specific guidance for application, the dual-structure theory merits a special place in the history of motivation research.

Other Important Needs

Each theory discussed thus far describes interrelated sets of important individual needs. Several other important needs have been identified. As noted earlier, J. W. Atkinson recently incorporated several of them into Murray's manifest needs framework. However, these needs have been studied most often as needs independent from these theories. The three most frequently cited are the needs for achievement, affiliation, and power.[33]

The Need for Achievement

The **need for achievement** is the desire to accomplish a task or goal more effectively than in the past.

The **need for achievement** is most frequently associated with the work of David McClelland;[34] it arises from an individual's desire to accomplish a goal or task more effectively than in the past. Need for achievement has been studied at both the individual and societal levels. At the individual level, the primary aim of research has been to pinpoint characteristics of high need achievers, the outcomes associated with high need achievement, and methods for increasing the need for achievement.

People with a high need for achievement tend to set moderately difficult goals, make moderately risky decisions, want immediate feedback, become preoccupied with their task, and assume personal responsibility.

Characteristics of High Need Achievers   High need achievers tend to set moderately difficult goals and to make moderately risky decisions. For example, when people playing ring toss are allowed to stand anywhere they want to, players with a low need for achievement tend to stand either so close to the target that there is no challenge or so far away that they have little chance of hitting the mark. High need achievers stand at a distance that offers challenge but also allows frequent success.

31. Nathan King, "A Clarification and Evaluation of the Two-Factor Theory of Job Satisfaction," *Psychological Bulletin*, July 1970, pp. 18–31. See also Dunnette, Campbell, and Hakel, "Factors Contributing to Job Satisfaction"; and R. J. House and L. Wigdor, "Herzberg's Dual-Factor Theory of Job Satisfaction and Motivation: A Review of the Evidence and a Criticism," *Personnel Psychology*, Summer 1967, pp. 369–389.
32. Pinder, *Work Motivation*.
33. Ibid.
34. David McClelland, *The Achieving Society* (Princeton, N.J.: Van Nostrand, 1961).

High need achievers also want immediate and specific feedback on their performance. They want to know how well they did something as quickly after finishing it as possible. For this reason, high need achievers frequently take jobs in sales, where they get almost immediate feedback from customers, and avoid jobs in areas such as research and development, where tangible progress is slower and feedback comes at longer intervals.

Preoccupation with their work is another characteristic of high need achievers. They think about it on their way to work, during lunch, and at home. They find putting their work aside difficult, and they become frustrated when they must stop working on a partly completed project.

Finally, high need achievers tend to assume personal responsibility for getting things done. They often volunteer for extra duties and find it difficult to delegate part of a job to someone else. Accordingly, they obtain a feeling of accomplishment when they have done more work than their peers without the assistance of others.

High need achievers are inclined to do well as individual entrepreneurs with little or no group reinforcement. Steven Jobs, the cofounder of both Apple Computer and NeXT, and Nolan Bushnell, a pioneer in electronic video games and founder of Atari, are both recognized as high need achievers, and each has done quite well for himself.

Consequences of Achievement   Although high need achievers tend to be successful, they often do not achieve top management posts. The most common explanation is that high need for achievement helps people advance quickly through the ranks, but the traits associated with the need often conflict with the requirements of high-level management positions. Because of the amount of work they are expected to do, top executives must be able to delegate tasks to others, they seldom receive immediate feedback, and they often must make decisions that are either more or less risky than a high need achiever would be comfortable with.[35]

Learning Achievement   McClelland estimated that only around 10 percent of the population of the United States has a high need for achievement. Nevertheless, he argued that proper training could greatly boost an individual's need for achievement.[36] The training program developed by McClelland and his associates tries to teach trainees to think like high need achievers, increase personal feedback to trainees about themselves, and develop a group esprit de corps that supports high effort and success. In sum, the trainers work to create a group feeling that will reinforce the characteristics of high need achievers.

Achievement and Economic Development   McClelland also conducted research on the need for achievement at the societal level. He believed that a nation's level of economic prosperity correlates with its citizens' need for achievement.[37] The higher the percentage of a country's population that has a high need for achievement, the stronger and more prosperous that nation's economy; conversely, the

35. Michael J. Stahl, "Achievement, Power, and Managerial Motivation: Selecting Managerial Talent with the Job Choice Exercise," *Personnel Psychology*, Winter 1983, pp. 775–790.
36. David McClelland, "Achievement Motivation Can Be Learned," *Harvard Business Review*, November–December 1965, pp. 6–24. See also Robert L. Helmreich, Linda L. Sawin, and Alan L. Carsrud, "The Honeymoon Effect in Job Performance: Temporal Increases in the Predictive Power of Achievement Motivation," *Journal of Applied Psychology*, May 1986, pp. 185–188.
37. McClelland, *The Achieving Society*.

lower the percentage, the weaker the economy. The reason for this correlation is that high need achievers tend toward entrepreneurial success. Hence, one would expect a country with many high need achievers to have a high level of business activity and economic stimulation.

The Need for Affiliation

The **need for affiliation** is the need for human companionship.

Individuals also experience the **need for affiliation**, that is, the need for human companionship.[38] Little research has been done on the need for affiliation, but researchers recognize several ways in which people with a high need for affiliation differ from those with a lower need. Individuals with a high need tend to want reassurance and approval from others and usually are genuinely concerned about others' feelings. They are likely to act and think as they believe others want them to, especially those with whom they strongly identify and desire friendship. As we might expect, people with a strong need for affiliation most often work in jobs with a lot of interpersonal contact, such as sales and teaching positions.

The Need for Power

The **need for power** is the desire to control the resources in one's environment.

A third major individual need is the **need for power**, that is, the desire to control one's environment, including financial, material, information, and human resources.[39] People vary greatly along this dimension. Some spend time and energy seeking power; others avoid power if at all possible. People with a high need for power can be successful managers if three conditions are met. First, they must seek power for the betterment of the organization rather than for their own interests. Second, they must have a fairly low need for affiliation (fulfilling a personal need for power may well alienate others in the workplace). Third, they need plenty of self-control so that they can curb their desire for power when it threatens to interfere with effective organizational or interpersonal relationships.[40]

Integrating the Need-based Perspectives

Although each of the various need-based approaches to motivation is unique, all can be integrated across several common areas.

In this chapter we examine several views of individual motives and needs. Despite their differences, the theories intersect at several points.[41] Both the needs hierarchy and the ERG theory, for instance, determine a hierarchy of needs, whereas the dual-structure theory proposes two discrete continua for two need categories. The individual needs identified by each of the three theories are actually strikingly similar. Figure 4.5 illustrates the major likenesses among them.

38. Stanley Schachter, *The Psychology of Affiliation* (Stanford, Calif.: Stanford University Press, 1959).
39. David McClelland and David H. Burnham, "Power Is the Great Motivator," *Harvard Business Review*, March–April 1976, pp. 100–110.
40. Pinder, *Work Motivation*; and McClelland and Burnham, "Power Is the Great Motivator."
41. For one recent approach to integrating needs, see Russell Cropanzano, Keith James, and Maryalice Citera, "A Goal Hierarchy Model of Personality, Motivation, and Leadership," in Larry L. Cummings and Barry M. Staw (Eds.), *Research in Organizational Behavior*, Vol. 15 (Greenwich, Conn.: JAI Press, 1993), pp. 267–322.

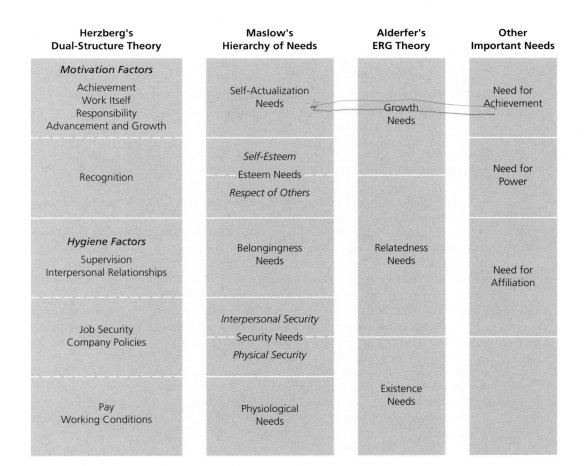

Herzberg's Dual-Structure Theory	Maslow's Hierarchy of Needs	Alderfer's ERG Theory	Other Important Needs
Motivation Factors Achievement Work Itself Responsibility Advancement and Growth	Self-Actualization Needs	Growth Needs	Need for Achievement
Recognition	*Self-Esteem* Esteem Needs *Respect of Others*		Need for Power
Hygiene Factors Supervision Interpersonal Relationships	Belongingness Needs	Relatedness Needs	Need for Affiliation
Job Security Company Policies	*Interpersonal Security* Security Needs *Physical Security*		
Pay Working Conditions	Physiological Needs	Existence Needs	

FIGURE 4.5

Parallels Among the Need-based Perspectives on Motivation

The hygiene factors described by the dual-structure theory correspond highly with the lower three levels of the needs hierarchy. In particular, pay and working conditions correspond to physiological needs, job security and company policies correspond to security needs, and supervision and interpersonal relations correspond to belongingness needs. Meanwhile, the dual-structure motivation factors parallel the top two levels of the needs hierarchy. Recognition, for example, is comparable to esteem; achievement, the work itself, responsibility, and advancement and growth might all be categorized as part of the self-actualization process.

There are also clear similarities between Maslow's needs hierarchy and the ERG theory. The existence needs in the ERG theory correspond to the physiological and physical security needs in the hierarchy perspective. The relatedness needs overlap with the interpersonal security needs, the belongingness needs, and the need for respect from others in the need hierarchy. Finally, the growth needs correspond to Maslow's self-esteem and self-actualization needs.

The independent individual needs we discussed can also be correlated with the need theories. The need for affiliation clearly is analogous to relatedness needs in the ERG theory, belongingness needs in the needs hierarchy, and interpersonal relations in the dual-structure theory. The need for power overlaps with the ERG theory's relatedness and growth needs; the need for achievement parallels ERG's growth needs and the needs hierarchy's self-actualization needs.

Unfortunately, despite the many conceptual similarities among the need theories that have emerged over the years, the theories share an inherent weakness.[42] For example, they do an adequate job of describing the factors that motivate behavior, but they tell us very little about the actual processes of motivation.[43] Even if two people are obviously motivated by interpersonal needs, they may pursue quite different paths to satisfy those needs. In Chapter 5, we describe several theories that try to solve that piece of the motivation puzzle.

Summary of Key Points

- Motivation is the set of forces that cause people to behave in various ways. Motivation starts with a need. People search for ways to satisfy their needs and then behave accordingly. Their performance of this behavior results in rewards or punishment. To varying degrees, a favorable outcome may satisfy the original need.
- A need is anything an individual requires or wants. Primary needs are things that people require to sustain themselves, such as food, water, and shelter. Secondary needs are more psychological in character and are learned from the environment and culture in which the individual lives. A motive represents the individual's reason for choosing one certain behavior from among several choices.
- The earliest view of motivation was based on the concept of hedonism, the idea that people seek pleasure and comfort and seek to avoid pain and discomfort. Scientific management extended this view by asserting that money is the primary human motivator in the workplace. The human relations view suggested that social factors are primary motivators.
- According to Abraham Maslow, human needs are arranged in a hierarchy of importance, from physiological to security to belongingness to esteem and, finally, to self-actualization. The manifest needs theory includes many work-related needs that may operate simultaneously. The ERG theory is a refinement of Maslow's original hierarchy that also includes the frustration-regression component.
- In Herzberg's dual-structure theory, satisfaction and dissatisfaction are two distinct dimensions instead of opposite ends of the same dimension. Motivation factors are presumed to affect satisfaction and hygiene factors to affect dissatisfaction. Herzberg's theory is well known among managers but has several deficiencies.
- Other important individual needs include the needs for achievement, affiliation, and power. These needs are part of Murray's theory but have been more widely studied in isolation.

Discussion Questions

1. Is it possible for someone to be unmotivated, or is all behavior motivated?
2. Is it useful to characterize motivation in terms of a deficiency? Why or why not? Is it possible to characterize motivation in terms of excess? If so, how?

42. Salancik and Pfeffer, "An Examination of Need-Satisfaction Models of Job Attitudes."
43. Pinder, *Work Motivation*.

3. When has your level of performance been directly affected by motivation? By your ability? By the environment?

4. What are the similarities between the views of human motivation taken by the scientific management theorists and those taken by the human relations theorists? How do they differ?

5. Identify examples from your own experience that support, and others that refute, Maslow's hierarchy of needs theory.

6. Which do you think has the greatest value: the hierarchy of needs theory, the manifest needs theory, or the ERG model? Explain.

7. Do you agree or disagree with the basic assumptions of Herzberg's dual-structure theory? Why?

8. Which of the need theories discussed in the chapter has the most practical value for managers? Which one has the least practical value?

9. How do you evaluate yourself in terms of your needs for achievement, affiliation, and power?

10. Do you agree or disagree with the assertion that the need for achievement can be learned? Do you think it might be easier to learn it as a young child or as an adult?

11. What other important needs might emerge as topics for managerial consideration in the future?

EXPERIENTIAL EXERCISE

Purpose   In this exercise, you will apply the theories discussed in the chapter to your own needs and motives.

Format   First, you will develop a list of things you want from life. Then you will categorize them according to one of the theories in the chapter. Next, you will discuss your results with a small group of classmates.

Procedure   Prepare a list of approximately fifteen things that you want from life. These can be very specific (such as a new car) or very general (such as a feeling of accomplishment in school). Try to include some things that you want right now and other things that you want later in life. Next, choose the one motivational theory discussed in this chapter that best fits your set of needs. Classify each item from your "wish list" in terms of the need or needs it might satisfy.

Your instructor will then divide the class into groups of three. Spend a few minutes in the group discussing each person's list and its classification according to needs.

After the small-group discussions, your instructor will reconvene the entire class. Discussion should center on the extent to which each theory can serve as a useful framework for classifying individual needs. Students who found that their needs could be neatly categorized or those who found little correlation between their needs and the theories are especially encouraged to share their results.

Follow-up Questions

1. As a result of this exercise, do you now place more or less trust in the need theories as viable management tools?
2. Could a manager use some form of this exercise in an organizational setting to enhance employee motivation?

<table>
<tr><td>C A S E   4 . 1</td><td>Motivation at Amway</td></tr>
</table>

Richard DeVos and Jay Van Andel lead one of the most unusual organizations in the world, Amway Corporation. DeVos and Andel founded Amway in Van Andel's Michigan basement in 1959. Their first product was Frisk, an organic biodegradable multipurpose liquid cleaner (since renamed LOC, for Liquid Organic Cleaner). A variety of other products soon followed, including several other household cleaning products and numerous different personal grooming products.

DeVos and Van Andel decided from the very beginning not to sell their products through traditional retail channels. Instead, they chose to use a direct distribution strategy. They started by enlisting other individuals to sell Amway products to their own friends, neighbors, and coworkers. DeVos and Van Andel sold their products to these individuals at a hefty discount. Those people then sold the products at a preset retail price, keeping the difference for their own personal profit.

Sales grew quickly, and DeVos and Van Andel began to investigate ways to expand their business. They decided to allow each of their individual distributors to recruit other distributors. Amway would continue to sell products to the original distributors. Those distributors would likewise continue to sell those products themselves, but would also sell them to the new distributors as well. The new distributors would then sell the products to their own friends, family, and coworkers. Profits would be distributed between the company itself, the original distributor, and the secondary distributor.

Under this scheme, if each distributor recruited three new distributors, and each of those distributors recruited three new distributors, and so on until there were ten levels of distribution, when the distribution channel reached ten levels the original distributor would have 88,572 individuals working in his or her sales organization. Moreover, if each of those distributors sold $1,000 worth of products, the sales organization under the original distributor would have sales of almost $89 million.

Today Amway has around 500,000 distributors in the United States, around 500,000 in Japan, and hundreds of thousands more in Canada, Germany, Mexico, Korea, and several others countries scattered around the world. About one-half of all these distributors leave the organization each year but are replaced by other eager entrepreneurs.

How much does the typical Amway distributor make? Perhaps a bit surprisingly, not much. The average Amway distributor only sells around $1,700 worth of products each year. After deducting her or his costs, barely $1,000 in profits remain. Only a few major distributors make large amounts of money. For example, one distributor in North Carolina has more than 100,000 distributors in his sales organization and nets over $410 million a year. But again, this is the exception, not the rule.

So why do people join forces with Amway in the first place? The answer lies in the firm's complex set of incentives. For example, Amway hires only people who share the beliefs of its founders—people who tend to be deeply religious, patriotic, and strong believers in the free enterprise system. Although no promises are made to newcomers, they are widely exposed to success stories about Amway distributors who have made fortunes.

Even people who do not expect to get rich develop fond feelings about Amway. They get to be their own boss, for example, setting their own hours and working as much—or as little—as they want. They are also drawn to the almost evangelical fervor espoused by the firm. Major distributors, for example, hold rallies under large tents. Amway distributors come to the rallies to recite the pledge of allegiance, hear about new success stories, learn about new products, and sing "God Bless America."

Amway has confronted its share of controversy over the years. For example, the Canadian government accused the firm of running a pyramid scheme and some overzealous Amway distributors were accused of spreading damaging rumors about its rival, Procter & Gamble. Although these setbacks may hurt sales and recruiting for a short time, however, Amway has always been able to bounce back stronger than ever.

Case Questions

1. Why do people join the Amway organization?
2. Which needs do most Amway distributors satisfy through their association with the firm?
3. Do you know anyone who is or has been associated with Amway? If so, why did they enlist? How do they feel about the organization today?

SOURCES: "The Power of Positive Inspiration," *Forbes*, December 9, 1991, pp. 244–250; "From Soap to Stocks," *Barron's*, May 31, 1993, pp. 28, 29; and "Ruthless Capitalists Need Not Apply," *Canadian Business*, July 1993, pp. 110–111.

C A S E   4 . 2   **More Than a Paycheck**

Lemuel Greene was a trainer for National Home Manufacturers, a large builder of prefabricated homes. National Home had hired Greene fresh from graduate school with a master's degree in English. At first, the company put him to work writing and revising company brochures and helping with the most important correspondence at the senior level. But soon both Greene and senior management officials began to notice how well he worked with executives on their writing, how he made them feel more confident about it, and how, after working with an executive on a report, that executive often was much more eager to take on the next writing task.

So National Home moved Greene into its prestigious training department. The company's trainers worked with thousands of supervisors, managers, and executives, helping them learn everything from a new computer language to time management skills to how to get the most out of the workers on the plant floor, many of whom were unmotivated high school dropouts. Soon Greene was spending all his time giving short seminars on executive writing as well as coaching his students to perfect their memos and letters.

Greene's move into training meant a big increase in salary, and when he started working exclusively with the company's top brass, it seemed he got a bonus every month. Greene's supervisor, Mirela Albert, knew he was making more than many executives who had been with the company three times as long, and probably twice as much as any of his graduate school classmates who concentrated in English. Yet in her biweekly meetings with him, she could tell that Greene wasn't happy.

When Albert asked him about it, Greene replied that he was in a bit of a rut, he had to keep saying the same things over and over in his seminars, and business memos weren't as interesting as the literature he had been trained on. But then, after trailing off for a moment, he blurted out, "They don't need me!" The fact that the memos filtering down through the company were now flawlessly polished, or that the annual report was 20 percent shorter yet said everything it needed to, didn't fulfill Greene's desire to be needed.

The next week, Greene came to Albert with a proposal: what if he started holding classes for some of the floor workers, many of whom had no future within or outside the company because they could write nothing but their own names? Albert took the idea to her superiors. They told her that they wouldn't oppose it, but Greene couldn't possibly keep drawing such a high salary if he worked with people whose contribution to the company was compensated at $4 an hour.

Greene agreed to a reduced salary and began offering English classes on the factory floor, billed by management (who hoped to avoid a wage hike that year) as an added benefit of the job. At first only two or three workers showed up—and they, Greene believed, only wanted an excuse to get away from the nailing guns for awhile. But gradually word got around that Greene was serious about what he was doing and didn't treat the workers like kids in a remedial class.

At the end of the year, Greene got a bonus from a new source: the vice president in charge of production. Although Greene's course took workers off the job for a couple of hours a week, productivity actually had improved since his course began, employee turnover had dropped, and, for the first time in more than a year, some of the floor workers had begun to apply for supervisory positions. Greene was pleased with the bonus, but when Albert saw him grinning as he walked around the building, she knew he wasn't thinking about his bank account.

Case Questions

1. What need theories would explain Lemuel Greene's unhappiness despite his high income level?
2. Greene seems to have drifted into being a teacher. Given his needs and motivations, do you think teaching is an appropriate profession for him?

Process-based Perspectives on Motivation

OBJECTIVES

After studying this chapter, you should be able to:

Describe the equity theory of motivation.

Describe the expectancy theory of motivation.

Describe the goal setting theory of motivation.

Discuss participation, empowerment, and motivation.

Relate attribution theory to motivation.

Integrate the process-based perspectives on motivation.

Whirlpool engineers show off an ozone-friendly refrigerator created for a national contest to design energy-efficient appliances. This refrigerator was the product of three years of all-out effort on the part of the team of engineers.

A group of employees at Whirlpool recently participated in an unusual contest. They worked numerous seventy-hour weeks, experienced frequent setbacks and frustration, and endured unbearable deadlines and unrealistic expectations. What were they working for? An opportunity for their employer to reap a windfall of $30 million.

The contest was sponsored by the Natural Resources Defense Council (NRDC). First announced in 1990, the purpose of the contest was to motivate appliance makers to create new energy-efficient and environmentally friendly refrigerators. The winning firm would receive a rebate from the NRDC for each refrigerator sold using the new technology—potentially worth as much as $30 million.

Whirlpool executives wanted very much to win the contest. They believed that winning would not only make the firm more competitive, but that it would also bring favorable publicity as well. The only question remaining was how to go about competing for the big prize.

Whirlpool executives created a team of highly motivated and talented engineers. Named to head up the group were a manager named Vincent Anderson and an engineer named Bob Ho. Anderson and Ho then chose all the other members of the group. Relying on their own personal instincts and brief interviews with various potential candidates, Anderson and Ho chose five more persons to join them. For the next three years the group labored mightily to beat the competition. Their potential reward? Pride and a sense of satisfaction.

Of course, other manufacturers also had their own teams of engineers working on the contest. Whirlpool and Frigidaire breathed sighs of relief when the two of them were named as semifinalists in the summer of 1993. But each remained on the edge of its seat awaiting news of the final victor. And on June 29, 1993, the results were announced: Whirlpool took the big prize![1]

■ ■ ■ ■ **M**anagers at Whirlpool were able to get a group of their employees to put forth their maximum effort for a sustained period of time—and all for the good of the organization. How did they accomplish this feat? By tapping into the full and complex mosaic of employee motivation. Coercing employees to perform the way that Anderson, Ho, and the others did would have been fruitless. Instead, fortunately, Whirlpool created conditions under which employees might choose to work hard and in the best interests of the firm.

In Chapter 4, we introduced a number of basic motivational concepts and theories drawn from need-based perspectives. For a motivational framework to have value, however, it must capture the full range of complexity that typifies human

1. "The Great Refrigerator Race," *Business Week*, July 5, 1993, pp. 78–81; "How to Listen to Consumers," *Fortune*, January 11, 1993, pp. 77–79; and "Whirlpool Wins Prizes of $30 Million to Build Efficient Refrigerator," *Wall Street Journal*, June 30, 1993, p. B4.

behavior. Basic need theories are limited in this respect; thus, the field of organizational behavior has turned to more sophisticated conceptualizations of motivation to understand its causes in work settings.[2]

The general distinction between the basic approaches introduced in Chapter 4 and the more advanced theories discussed in this chapter and the next rests on the difference between content and process. The need-based perspectives reflect a content perspective in that they attempt to describe what factor or factors motivate behavior; that is, they try to list specific things that motivate behavior. The more sophisticated process-based perspectives, introduced in this chapter, focus on the ways in which motivated behavior occurs; in other words, they explain how people go about satisfying their needs.[3] Process-based perspectives also describe how people choose among behavioral alternatives.

We begin this chapter by discussing the equity theory of motivation. Then we turn to perhaps the most complete motivational framework of all, the expectancy theory of motivation. Goal-setting theory, participation and empowerment, and attribution theory are then described in detail. (In Chapter 6 we examine more fully the consequences of motivation from the learning-based perspective.)

> The process-based perspectives on motivation focus on how motivated behavior occurs in an effort to satisfy needs.

The Equity Theory of Motivation

> Equity theory focuses on people's desire to perceive equity and avoid inequity.
>
> Equity is the belief that we are being treated fairly in relation to others, and inequity is the belief that we are being treated unfairly in relation to others.

The **equity theory** of motivation is based on the relatively simple premise that people in organizations want to be treated fairly.[4] The theory defines **equity** as the belief that we are being treated fairly in relation to others and **inequity** as the belief that we are being treated unfairly in relation to others.

Equity theory is just one of several theoretical formulations derived from social comparison processes.[5] Social comparisons involve evaluating our own situation in the context of others' situations. In this chapter, we focus mainly on equity theory because it is the most highly developed of the social comparison conceptualizations and the one that applies most directly to the work motivation of people in organizations.

Forming Equity Perceptions

People use a four-step process to form equity perceptions. Putting this in an organizational context, the individual first evaluates how she or he is being treated by the organization. Next, the individual evaluates how a "comparison-other" is being treated. The comparison-other might be a person in the same work group,

---

2. For a review see Ruth Kanfer, "Motivation Theory and Industrial and Organizational Psychology," in Marvin D. Dunnette and Leaetta M. Hough (Eds.), *Handbook of Industrial and Organizational Psychology*, Vol. 1 (Palo Alto, Calif.: Consulting Psychologists Press, Inc., 1990), pp. 75–170.

3. John P. Campbell, Marvin D. Dunnette, Edward E. Lawler, and Karl E. Weick, *Managerial Behavior, Performance, and Effectiveness* (New York: McGraw-Hill, 1970).

4. J. Stacey Adams, "Toward an Understanding of Inequity," *Journal of Abnormal and Social Psychology*, November 1963, pp. 422–436. See also Richard T. Mowday, "Equity Theory Predictions of Behavior in Organizations," in Richard M. Steers and Lyman W. Porter (Eds.), *Motivation and Work Behavior*, 4th ed. (New York: McGraw-Hill, 1987), pp. 89–110.

5. Paul S. Goodman, "Social Comparison Processes in Organizations," in Barry M. Staw and Gerald R. Salancik (Eds.), *New Directions in Organizational Behavior* (Chicago: St. Clair, 1977), pp. 97–131.

Part 2   Individual Processes in Organizations

someone in another part of the organization, or even a composite of several people scattered throughout the organization. After evaluating the treatment of self and other, the individual compares the respective situations. As a consequence of this comparison, the individual experiences either equity or inequity. Depending on the strength of this feeling, the person may choose to pursue one or more of the alternatives discussed in the next section.

People form perceptions of equity or inequity by comparing what they give to the organization (inputs) relative to what they get back (outcomes) and how this ratio compares with those of others.

Equity theory casts the equity comparison process in terms of input-to-outcome ratios. Inputs are an individual's contributions to the organization, such as education, experience, effort, and loyalty. Outcomes are what he or she receives in return, such as pay, recognition, social relationships, and intrinsic rewards. Thus, this part of the equity process is essentially a personal assessment of one's psychological contract. A person's assessment of inputs and outcomes for both self and other are based partly on objective data (for example, the person's own salary) and partly on perceptions (such as the comparison-other's level of recognition). The equity comparison thus takes the following form:

$$\frac{\text{Outcome (self)}}{\text{Input (self)}} \qquad \text{compared to} \qquad \frac{\text{Outcome (other)}}{\text{Input (other)}}$$

If the two sides of this psychological equation are in balance, the person experiences a feeling of equity. But if the two sides do not balance, a feeling of inequity results. We should stress, however, that a perception of equity does not require that the perceived outcomes and inputs be equal; rather, only that their ratios be the same. A person may believe that his comparison-other deserves to make more money because she works harder, thus making her higher outcome-input ratio acceptable. Only if the other person's outcomes seem disproportionate to her inputs will the comparison provoke a perception of inequity.

Responses to Perceptions of Equity and Inequity

As a result of perceptions of equity or inequity, people can choose a variety of responses in an effort to maintain equity or reduce perceived inequity.

Figure 5.1 summarizes the results of an equity comparison. A perception of equity generally motivates the person to maintain the status quo. She or he will continue to provide the same level of input to the organization, at least as long as her or his outcomes do not change and the inputs and outcomes of the comparison-other also do not change. A person who perceives inequity, however, is motivated to reduce it: the greater the inequity, the stronger the level of motivation.

People use six common methods to reduce inequity.[6] First, we may change our own inputs. Thus, a person may put more or less effort into the job, depending on which way the inequity lies, as a way of altering her own ratio. If she believes that she is being under-rewarded, she may decrease her effort, and vice versa.

Second, we may change our own outcomes. This might include demanding a pay raise, seeking additional avenues for growth and development, or even stealing. Or it might involve altering our perceptions of the value of our current outcomes.

A third, more complex response is to alter our perceptions of ourselves. After perceiving an inequity, for example, a person may change the original self-assessment and thus decide that he is really contributing less but receiving more than he originally believed.

6. J. Stacey Adams, "Inequity in Social Exchange," in L. Berkowitz (Ed.), *Advances in Experimental Social Psychology*, Vol. 2 (New York: Academic Press, 1965), pp. 267–299.

FIGURE 5.1

Responses to Perceptions of Equity and Inequity

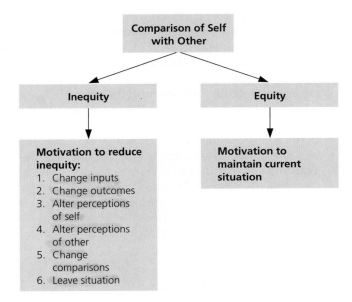

Fourth, we may alter our perception of the other's inputs, outcomes, or both. For example, a person who feels under-rewarded may conclude that his comparison-other must actually be working more hours than it originally appeared.

Fifth, we may change the object of comparison. A person may conclude, for instance, that the current comparison-other is the boss's personal favorite, is unusually lucky, or has special skills and abilities. Another person thus would provide a more valid basis for comparison.

As a last resort, we may simply leave the situation. Transferring to another department or quitting altogether may seem to be the only way to reduce inequity. *Developing Management Skills* provides you with some additional insights into the equity process.

Evaluation and Implications

Equity theory has been the subject of much research. Most studies have been somewhat narrowly focused, however, and have examined only one ratio: pay (hourly and piece-rate) versus the quality or quantity of worker output given over-payment and underpayment.[7] Findings support the predictions of equity theory quite consistently, especially when workers feel underpaid. When people experience inequity while paid on a piece-rate basis, they tend to reduce their inputs by decreasing quality and to increase their outcomes by producing more units of work. When a person paid by the hour experiences inequity, the theory predicts an increase in quality and quantity if the person feels overpaid and a decrease in quality and quantity if the person feels underpaid. Research evidence provides stronger

7. Craig Pinder, *Work Motivation* (Glenview, Ill.: Scott, Foresman, 1984).

Coping with Inequity

Almost everyone has experienced a feeling of unfairness or inequity at some time in their life, perhaps at work, in a family situation, or in a classroom. But regardless of the situation, when it happens the consequences are often the same: a sense of frustration and perhaps anger, and a desire to eliminate the inequity so that fair play can again reign.

Try to recall the most extreme feeling of inequity you have ever experienced. Write down on a piece of paper a brief discussion of the context for the inequity—where you were, what you were doing, and so forth. Then write down all the things you were contributing and all the things you were getting back from the situation.

Next, try to recall if the inequity was an absolute feeling—based on its own merits alone—or a comparative one—in relation to someone else. If it involved someone else, write down the things the other person was contributing and getting back. Finally, write down specifically why you felt inequity.

Exchange notes with a classmate. After reading and reflecting on your classmate's scenario, try to think of the most and least effective ways he or she could have reduced the inequity. Meanwhile, your classmate will be doing the same thing with your description. Now discuss with your classmate what you each think the other should have done, and what you each actually did. Looking back, did you handle the situation in the best way? Would you do things differently if you could?

support for responses to underpayment than for responses to overpayment, but overall, most studies appear to uphold the basic premises of the theory.[8]

One interesting new twist on equity theory suggests that some people are more sensitive than others to perceptions of inequity. That is, some individuals pay more attention to their relative standing in the organization through their equity-based comparisons. Other people, however, focus more on their own situation without regard to the situation of others.[9]

For managers, the most important implication of equity theory relates to organizational rewards and reward systems. Because "formal" organizational rewards (such as pay and task assignments) are more easily observed than are "informal" rewards (such as intrinsic satisfaction and feelings of accomplishment), they often are at the center of a person's equity perceptions. Social comparisons clearly are a powerful factor in the workplace.

Equity theory offers managers three messages. First, everyone in the organization needs to understand the basis for rewards. If people are to be rewarded more for high-quality work than for quantity of work, that fact needs to be clearly

8. Richard A. Cosier and Dan R. Dalton, "Equity Theory and Time: A Reformulation," *Academy of Management Review*, April 1983, pp. 311–319. See also Jerald Greenberg, "Cognitive Reevaluation of Outcomes in Response to Underpayment Inequity," *Academy of Management Journal*, March 1989, pp. 174–184.

9. Richard C. Huseman, John D. Hatfield, and Edward W. Miles, "A New Perspective on Equity Theory: The Equity Sensitivity Construct," *Academy of Management Review*, October 1987, pp. 222–234. See also Wesley C. King, Jr., Edward W. Miles, and D. David Day, "A Test and Refinement of the Equity Sensitivity Construct," *Journal of Organizational Behavior*, Vol. 14, 1993, pp. 301–317.

communicated to everyone. Second, people tend to take a multifaceted view of their rewards; they perceive and experience a variety of rewards, some tangible and others intangible. Finally, people base their actions on their perceptions of reality. If two people make exactly the same salary but each thinks the other makes more, each will base his or her experience of equity on the perception rather than on reality. Hence, even if a manager knows that two employees are being fairly rewarded, the employees themselves may not necessarily agree.

The Expectancy Theory of Motivation

Expectancy theory is a complex, more encompassing model of motivation than equity theory. Over the years since its original formulation, the theory's scope and complexity have continued to grow.

The Basic Expectancy Model

The basic expectancy theory model emerged from the work of Edward Tolman and Kurt Lewin.[10] Victor Vroom, however, is generally credited with first applying the theory to the motivation of individuals in the workplace.[11] The theory attempts to determine how individuals choose among alternative behaviors. The basic premise of **expectancy theory** is that motivation depends on how much we want something and how likely we think we are to get it. The following simple example illustrates this premise.

Expectancy theory suggests that people are motivated by how much they want something and how likely they think they are to get it.

Suppose that a recent college graduate is looking for her first managerial job. While scanning the want ads, she sees that Exxon is seeking a new executive vice president to oversee its foreign operations. The starting salary is $600,000. The student would love the job, but she does not bother to apply because she recognizes that she has no chance of getting it. Continuing on, she sees a position that involves scraping bubble gum from underneath desks in college classroom buildings. The starting salary is $4 an hour, and no experience is necessary. Again, however, the student is unlikely to apply; even though she thinks that she could get the job, she does not want it.

Then she comes across an advertisement for a management training position with a large company. No experience is necessary, the primary requirement is a college degree, and the starting salary is $25,000. She will probably apply for this position because (1) she wants it and (2) she thinks that she has a reasonable chance of getting it. (Of course, this simple example understates the true complexity of most choices. Job-seeking students may have strong geographic preferences, have other job opportunities, and also be considering graduate school. Most decisions, in fact, are quite complex.)

Figure 5.2 summarizes the basic expectancy model. The model's general components are effort (the result of motivated behavior), performance, and outcomes.

10. Edward C. Tolman, *Purposive Behavior in Animals* (New York: Appleton-Century-Crofts, 1932); and Kurt Lewin, *The Conceptual Representation and the Measurement of Psychological Forces* (Durham, N.C.: Duke University Press, 1938).
11. Victor Vroom, *Work and Motivation* (New York: Wiley, 1964).

FIGURE 5.2

**The Expectancy Theory
of Motivation**

(Note that performance is considered a joint function of effort, environment, and ability; this is consistent with our discussion in Chapter 4.) Expectancy theory emphasizes the linkages among these elements, which are described in terms of expectancies and valences.

The **effort-to-performance expectancy** is the individual's perception of the probability that effort will lead to performance.

Effort-to-Performance Expectancy The **effort-to-performance expectancy** is an individual's perceived probability that effort will lead to performance. If a person believes that his or her effort will lead to higher performance, this expectancy is very strong—perhaps approaching a probability of 1.0—where 1.0 equals absolute certainty that the outcome will occur. A person who believes that her or his performance will be the same no matter how much effort is made, has a low expectancy—close to 0—where 0 means that there is no probability that the outcome will occur. The person who thinks that there is a moderate relationship between his or her effort and subsequent performance has an expectancy somewhere between 1.0 and 0.

The **performance-to-outcome expectancy** is the individual's perception of the probability that performance will lead to certain outcomes.

Performance-to-Outcome Expectancy The **performance-to-outcome expectancy** is an individual's perceived probability that performance will lead to certain outcomes. If a person thinks a high performer is certain to get a pay raise, this expectancy is close to 1.0. At the other extreme, a person who believes that raises are entirely independent of performance has an expectancy close to 0. Finally, a person who thinks that performance has some bearing on the prospects for a pay raise, has an expectancy somewhere between 1.0 and 0. In a work setting, several performance-to-outcome expectancies are relevant because, as Figure 5.2 shows, several outcomes might logically result from performance. Each outcome will have its own expectancy.

An **outcome** is anything that might result from performance.

The **valence** of an outcome refers to how attractive or unattractive an outcome is to a particular individual.

Outcomes and Valences An **outcome** is anything that might potentially result from performance. High-level performance conceivably might produce a pay raise, a promotion, recognition from the boss, fatigue, stress, and less time to rest. The **valence** of an outcome is the relative attractiveness or unattractiveness of that outcome to the person. Pay raises, promotions, and recognition might all have positive valences, whereas fatigue, stress, and less time to rest might all have negative valences.

People vary in the strength of their outcome valences. Work-related stress may be a major negative factor for one person but only a slight annoyance for another. Similarly, a pay increase may have a strong positive valence for someone desperately in need of money, a slight positive valence for someone interested mostly in getting a promotion, and even a negative valence for someone in an unfavorable tax position!

The basic expectancy framework suggests that three conditions must be met before motivated behavior will occur. First, the effort-to-performance expectancy must be well above zero. That is, the individual must have a reasonable expectation that an exertion of effort will produce high levels of performance. Second, the performance-to-outcome expectancies also must be well above zero. Thus, the person must believe that performance may realistically result in valued outcomes. And third, the sum of all the valences for the potential outcomes relevant to the person must be positive. One or more valences may be negative so long as the positives outweigh the negatives. For example, stress and fatigue may have moderately negative valences, but if pay, promotion, and recognition have very high positive valences, the overall valence of the set of outcomes associated with performance will still be positive.

Conceptually, the valences of all relevant outcomes and the corresponding pattern of expectancies are assumed to interact in an almost mathematical fashion to determine the level of motivation. Most people do assess likelihoods of and preferences for various consequences of behavior, but they seldom approach them in such a calculating manner.

The Porter-Lawler Extension

The Porter-Lawler extension of expectancy theory suggests that a high performance level, if followed by equitable rewards, may lead to increased satisfaction.

The presentation of expectancy theory in the 1960s placed it in the mainstream of contemporary motivation theory. Since then, the model has been refined and extended many times. Most modifications have focused on the identifying and measuring outcomes and expectancies. An exception is the variation of expectancy theory developed by Lyman W. Porter and Edward E. Lawler. These researchers used expectancy theory to develop a novel view of the relationship between employee satisfaction and performance.[12] Although the conventional wisdom was that satisfaction leads to performance, Porter and Lawler argued the reverse: if rewards are adequate, high levels of performance may lead to satisfaction.

The Porter-Lawler extension appears in Figure 5.3. Some of its features are quite different from the original formulation of expectancy theory. For example, the extended model includes abilities, traits, and role perceptions. At the beginning of the motivational cycle, effort is a function of the value of the potential reward for the employee (its valence) and the perceived effort-reward probability (an expectancy). Effort then combines with abilities, traits, and role perceptions to determine actual performance.

Performance results in two kinds of rewards. *Intrinsic rewards* are intangible—a feeling of accomplishment, a sense of achievement, and so forth. *Extrinsic rewards* are tangible outcomes such as pay and promotion. The individual judges the value of his or her performance to the organization and uses social comparison processes to form an impression of the equity of the rewards received. If the rewards are regarded as equitable, the employee feels satisfied. In subsequent cycles, satisfaction with rewards influences the value of the rewards anticipated, and actual performance following effort influences future perceived effort-reward probabilities.

12. Lyman W. Porter and Edward E. Lawler, *Managerial Attitudes and Performance* (Homewood, Ill.: Dorsey Press, 1968).

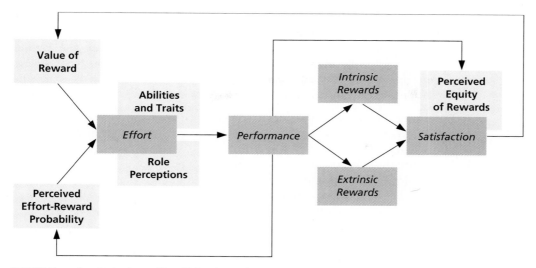

SOURCE: Figure from Porter, Lyman W. and Edward E. Lawler, *Managerial Attitudes and Performance*, copyright © 1968 by Richard D. Irwin, Inc. Used with permission.

FIGURE 5.3

The Porter-Lawler Extension of Expectancy Theory

Evaluation and Implications

Expectancy theory has been tested by many different researchers in a variety of settings and using a variety of methods.[13] As noted earlier, the complexity of the theory has been both a blessing and a curse.[14] Nowhere is this double-edged quality more apparent than in the research undertaken to evaluate the theory.

Several studies have supported various parts of the theory. For example, both kinds of expectancy and valence have been found to be associated with effort and performance in the workplace.[15] Research has also confirmed expectancy theory's claims that people will not engage in motivated behavior unless they (1) value the expected rewards, (2) believe their efforts will lead to performance, and (3) believe their performance will result in the desired rewards.[16]

Expectancy theory is so complicated, however, that researchers have found it quite difficult to test.[17] In particular, the measures of various parts of the model may lack validity, and the procedures for investigating relationships among the variables often have been less scientific than researchers would like. Moreover, people are seldom as rational and objective in choosing behaviors as expectancy theory implies. Still, the logic of the model, combined with the consistent, albeit modest, research support for it, suggests that the theory has much to offer.[18]

13. See Terence R. Mitchell, "Expectancy Models of Job Satisfaction, Occupational Preference, and Effort: A Theoretical, Methodological, and Empirical Appraisal," *Psychological Bulletin*, Vol. 81, 1974, pp. 1096–1112; and John P. Campbell and Robert D. Pritchard, "Motivation Theory in Industrial and Organizational Psychology," in Marvin D. Dunnette (Ed.), *Handbook of Industrial and Organizational Psychology* (Chicago: Rand McNally, 1976), pp. 63–130, for reviews.
14. Pinder, *Work Motivation*.
15. Ibid.
16. Campbell and Pritchard, "Motivation Theory in Industrial and Organizational Psychology."
17. Pinder, *Work Motivation*.
18. Ibid.

Because expectancy theory is so complex, it is difficult to apply directly in the workplace. A manager would need to figure out what rewards each employee wants and how valuable those rewards are to each individual, measure the various expectancies, and finally adjust the relationships to create motivation. Nevertheless, expectancy theory offers several important and relevant guidelines for the practicing manager. Some of the more fundamental guidelines include:

1. Determine the primary outcomes each employee wants.
2. Decide what levels and kinds of performance are needed to meet organizational goals.
3. Make sure the desired levels of performance are possible.
4. Link desired outcomes and desired performance.
5. Analyze the situation for conflicting expectancies.
6. Make sure the rewards are large enough.
7. Make sure the overall system is equitable for everyone.[19]

The Goal Setting Theory of Motivation

Whereas the expectancy theory of motivation remains the most complete (and complex) model of motivation, other models focusing on specific aspects of the motivation process have also proven useful. The goal setting theory, in particular, has helped managers learn new ways to enhance employee motivation. From a motivational perspective, a **goal** is a desirable objective to be achieved.

A **goal** is a desirable objective to be achieved.

In most organizational settings, goals are used for two purposes. First, they are a useful framework for managing motivation. Managers and employees can set goals for themselves and then work toward those goals. Second, goals are an effective control device. Control is the management activity directed at monitoring how well the organization is performing. Thus, if the organization's goal is to increase sales by 10 percent, a manager can use individual goals to help attain the overall goal. Further, comparing people's short-term performances with their goals can be an effective way to monitor the organization's long-run performance.

Social learning theory perhaps best describes the role and importance of goal setting in organizations.[20] This perspective suggests that the extent to which people achieve their goals results in feelings of pride or shame for performance. In other words, a person who achieves a goal will be proud of having done so, whereas a person who fails to achieve a goal will feel shame and personal disappointment. The degree of pride or shame a person experiences is affected by the belief that he or she can or cannot function at the desired level of performance. This belief is called self-efficacy. A sense of **self-efficacy** is the belief that we can still accomplish our goals even if we have failed to do so in the past.

Self-efficacy is the belief that we can still accomplish our goals even if we have failed to do so in the past.

19. David A. Nadler and Edward E. Lawler, "Motivation: A Diagnostic Approach," in J. Richard Hackman, Edward E. Lawler, and Lyman W. Porter (Eds.), *Perspectives on Behavior in Organizations*, 2nd ed. (New York: McGraw-Hill, 1983), pp. 67–78.
20. A. Bandura, *Social Learning Theory* (Englewood Cliffs, N.J.: Prentice-Hall, 1977).

This Pratt and Whitney employee inspects his work on a jet engine, to ensure it is of the best quality. When employees take pride in their work and strive to do the best job possible, it shows that they are committed to the goals they have set out to reach.

The Goal Setting Theory

Social learning theory provides insights into why and how goals can serve to motivate behavior. It also helps us understand how different people cope with failing to reach their goals. But the research of Edwin Locke and his associates most decisively showed the utility of goal setting theory in a motivational context.[21]

The goal setting theory of motivation assumes that behavior is a result of conscious goals and intentions. Therefore, by setting goals for people in the organization, a manager should be able to influence their behavior. Given this premise, the challenge is to develop a thorough understanding of the processes by which people set goals and then work to reach them. In the original version of goal setting theory, two specific goal characteristics—goal difficulty and goal specificity—were presumed to shape performance.

Goal Difficulty   **Goal difficulty** is the extent to which a goal is challenging and requires effort. If people work to achieve goals, we can reasonably assume that they will work harder to achieve more difficult goals. But a goal must not be so difficult that it is unattainable. If a new manager asks her sales force to increase sales by 300 percent, the group may become disillusioned. A more realistic but still difficult goal—perhaps a 50 percent increase—would be a better incentive.

Reinforcement also fosters motivation toward difficult goals. A person who is rewarded for achieving a difficult goal will be more inclined to strive toward the next

Goal difficulty is the extent to which a goal is challenging and requires effort.

21. See Edwin A. Locke, "Toward a Theory of Task Performance and Incentives," *Organizational Behavior and Human Performance*, Vol. 3, 1968, pp. 157–189.

difficult goal than will someone who has received no reward after reaching the first goal. A substantial body of research supports the importance of goal difficulty.[22] In one study, for example, managers at Weyerhaeuser set difficult goals for truck drivers hauling loads of timber from cutting sites to wood yards. Over a nine-month period, the drivers increased the quantity of wood they delivered by an amount that would have required $250,000 worth of new trucks at the previous per-truck average load.[23]

Goal Specificity   **Goal specificity** refers to the clarity and precision of the goal. A goal of "increasing productivity" is not very specific; a goal of "increasing productivity by 3 percent in the next six months" is quite specific. Some goals, such as those pertaining to costs, output, profitability, and growth are readily specified. Other goals, however, such as those dealing with employee job satisfaction, morale, company image and reputation, and ethics and social responsibility may be much harder to state in specific terms.

Like difficulty, specificity has also been shown to be consistently related to performance.[24] The previously cited study of timber truck drivers, for example, also examined goal specificity. The initial loads that the truck drivers were carrying were found to be 60 percent of the maximum weight each truck could haul. The managers set a new goal for drivers of 94 percent, which the drivers were soon able to reach. The goal thus was quite specific as well as difficult.

Because his theory attracted so much widespread interest and support from researchers and managers alike, Locke, together with Gary Latham, eventually proposed an expanded model of the goal setting process.[25] The expanded model, shown in Figure 5.4, attempts to capture more fully the complexities of goal setting in organizations.

22. Gary P. Latham and Gary Yukl, "A Review of Research on the Application of Goal Setting in Organizations," *Academy of Management Journal*, Vol. 18, 1975, pp. 824–845.
23. Gary P. Latham and J. J. Baldes, "The Practical Significance of Locke's Theory of Goal Setting," *Journal of Applied Psychology*, Vol. 60, 1975, pp. 187–191.
24. Latham and Yukl, "A Review of Research on the Application of Goal Setting in Organizations."
25. Edwin A. Locke and Gary P. Latham, *A Theory of Goal Setting and Task Performance* (Englewood Cliffs, N.J.: Prentice-Hall, Inc., 1990).

FIGURE 5.4

The Expanded Goal Setting Theory of Motivation

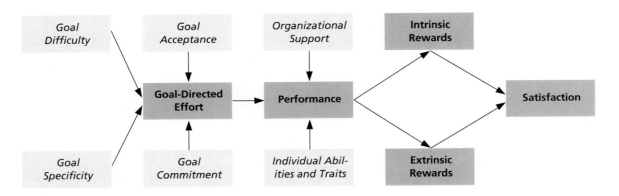

SOURCE: Reprinted, by permission of publisher, from *Organized Dynamics*, Autumn/1979. © 1979. American Management Association, New York. All rights reserved.

Part 2   Individual Processes in Organizations

Goal acceptance is the extent to which a person adopts a goal as his or her own.

Goal commitment is the extent to which a person is personally interested in reaching a goal.

The expanded theory argues that goal-directed effort is a function of four goal attributes: difficulty and specificity, as already discussed, and acceptance and commitment. **Goal acceptance** is the extent to which a person adopts a goal as his or her own. **Goal commitment** is the extent to which she or he is personally interested in reaching the goal. The manager who vows to take whatever steps are necessary to cut costs by 10 percent has made a commitment to achieve the goal. Factors that can foster goal acceptance and commitment include participating in the goal setting process, making goals challenging but realistic, and believing that goal achievement will lead to valued rewards.[26]

Actual performance is then presumed to be determined by the interaction of goal directed effort, organizational support, and individual abilities and traits. Organizational support is whatever the organization does to help or hinder performance. Positive support might mean making adequate personnel and a sufficient supply of raw materials available; negative support might mean failing to fix damaged equipment. Individual abilities and traits are the skills and other personal characteristics necessary for doing a job. As a result of performance, a person receives various intrinsic and extrinsic rewards, which in turn influence satisfaction. Note that the latter stages of this model are quite similar to the Porter and Lawler expectancy model discussed earlier.

Broader Perspectives on Goal Setting

Management by objectives (MBO) is a collaborative goal setting process during which organizational goals cascade down throughout the organization.

Goal setting is also undertaken in some organizations from the somewhat broader perspective of **management by objectives**, or **MBO**. Figure 5.5 illustrates the basic MBO process.[27] MBO is essentially a collaborative goal setting process through which organizational goals systematically cascade down through the organization. Our discussion describes the steps in a general way; many organizations, however, have adopted MBO to suit their own purposes.

The starting point in a successful MBO program is top management support. Top managers must stand behind the program and take the first step by establishing overall goals for the organization.[28] After initial organizational goals are set by these top managers, supervisors and subordinates throughout the organization collaborate in setting goals. First, the organizational goals are communicated to everyone. Then each manager meets with each subordinate. During this meeting, the manager explains the unit goals to the subordinate and the two determine together how the subordinate can most effectively contribute to those goals. The manager acts as a counselor and helps ensure that the subordinate develops goals that are verifiable. For example, a goal of "cutting costs by 5 percent" is verifiable, whereas a goal of "doing my best" is not. Finally, manager and subordinate ensure that the subordinate has the resources needed to reach his or her goals. The entire process spirals downward as each subordinate meets with his or her own subordinates to develop their goals. Thus, as we noted earlier, the initial goals set at the top cascade down through the entire organization.

26. Mark E. Tubbs, "Commitment as a Moderator of the Goal-Performance Relation: A Case for Clearer Construct Definition," *Journal of Applied Psychology*, Vol. 78, 1993, pp. 86–97.
27. See Stephen J. Carroll and Henry L. Tosi, *Management by Objectives* (New York: Macmillan, 1973).
28. Robert Rodgers, John E. Hunter, and Deborah L. Rogers, "Influence of Top Management Commitment on Management Program Success," *Journal of Applied Psychology*, Vol. 78, 1993, pp. 151–155.

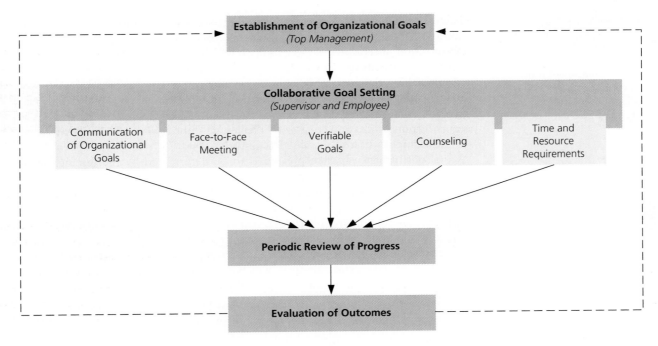

Establishment of Organizational Goals
(Top Management)

Collaborative Goal Setting
(Supervisor and Employee)

Communication of Organizational Goals

Face-to-Face Meeting

Verifiable Goals

Counseling

Time and Resource Requirements

Periodic Review of Progress

Evaluation of Outcomes

SOURCE: Adapted from Ricky W. Griffin, *Management*, 4th ed. (Boston: Houghton Mifflin, 1993), p. 242. Adapted by permission.

FIGURE 5.5

The MBO Process

During the time frame set for goal attainment (usually one year), the manager periodically meets with each subordinate again to check progress. The manager may, for example, need to modify goals in light of new information, provide additional resources, or take other action. At the end of the specified time period, managers hold a final evaluation meeting with each subordinate. At this meeting, manager and subordinate assess how well goals were met and discuss why. This meeting often serves as the annual performance review as well, determining salary adjustments and other rewards based on reaching goals. Finally, this meeting may also serve as the initial goal setting meeting for the next year's cycle.

Evaluation and Implications

Goal setting theory itself has been widely tested in a variety of settings.[29] Research has demonstrated fairly consistently that goal difficulty and specificity are closely associated with performance. Other elements of the theory, such as acceptance and commitment, have been studied less frequently. A few studies have shown the importance of acceptance and commitment, but little is currently known about how people accept and become committed to goals.

Researchers have argued that goal setting theory is not really a theory but simply an effective motivational technique. The goal setting process may also be a narrow and unnecessarily rigid view of employee behavior. Some important aspects of

29. Locke and Latham, *A Theory of Goal Setting and Task Performance.*

behavior cannot be quantified easily, and goal setting may focus too much attention on the short run at the expense of long-term considerations. Despite these objections, however, goal setting appears to be a useful approach to motivation.

From a different perspective, MBO is a very popular technique. Alcoa, Tenneco, Black & Decker, General Foods, and Du Pont, for example, have used it extensively. MBO's popularity stems in part from the approach's many strengths. For one thing, MBO clearly has the potential to motivate employees because it helps implement goal setting theory on a systematic basis throughout the organization. It also clarifies the basis for rewards, and it can spur communication. Performance appraisals are easier and more clear cut under MBO. Further, managers can use the system for control purposes.

However, there are also pitfalls in using MBO. Sometimes top managers do not really participate; that is, the goals essentially start in the middle of the organization and may not reflect the real goals of top management, and those who do participate may become cynical. That is, they interpret the lack of participation by top management as a sign that the goals are not important, and therefore view their own involvement as a waste of time. There is also a tendency to overemphasize quantitative goals to enhance verifiability. An MBO system also requires a great deal of paperwork and record keeping because every goal must be documented. Finally, some managers do not really let subordinates participate in goal setting but, instead, assign goals and order subordinates to accept them.

On balance, MBO is often an effective and useful system for managing goal setting in organizations. Research suggests that it can actually do many of the things its advocates claim, but it must also be handled carefully. In particular, most organizations need to tailor it to their own unique circumstances. Properly used, MBO can be an effective approach to managing an organization's reward system. It requires, however, individual, one-on-one interactions between each supervisor and each individual employee. These one-on-one interactions can often be difficult situations.

Participation, Empowerment, and Motivation

Participation is the process of giving employees a voice in making decisions about their own work.

Empowerment is the process of enabling workers to set their own work goals, make decisions, and solve problems within their sphere of responsibility and authority.

Participative management and empowerment also represent important process-based perspectives on employee motivation. **Participation** is the process of giving employees a voice in making decisions about their own work. **Empowerment** is the process of enabling workers to set their own work goals, make decisions, and solve problems within their sphere of responsibility and authority. Empowerment is a somewhat broader concept that promotes participation in a wide variety of areas, including but not limited to work itself, work context, and work environment. A historical perspective is necessary to fully understand participative management and empowerment.

Early Perspectives on Participation and Empowerment

The human relations movement in vogue from the 1930s through the 1950s (see Chapter 1) assumed that employees who are happy and satisfied will work harder. This movement stimulated general interest in worker participation in various organ-

Worker Participation at Toyota

For years Toyota has been one of the most effective automobile manufacturers in the world. The Japanese-based company is a market leader everywhere it sells cars, has earned profits consistently, and has a solid reputation for quality. Like its domestic competitors Nissan, Honda, and others, Toyota prospered by involving employees in running its plants and in making decisions. Quality circles and work teams have long been an established part of the work scene at Toyota.

During a worldwide auto slump in the 1980s, however, Toyota made one of its few mistakes. Looking for ways to boost productivity and control costs, and anticipating a projected labor shortage, the firm began to aggressively replace workers with robots and to rely ever heavily on automation. Unfortunately, these measures did not help, and Toyota's profits continued to slide.

Then Mikio Kitano entered the picture. Kitano had been assigned to Toyota's U.S. operations during the firm's automation frenzy. In 1990 he was named director of production engineering and brought back to Japan. During one of his early plant tours he saw the radical increase in automation. After a bit of investigation and conversations with hundreds of workers, he made the decision to back off from robotics and go back to the way things were during Toyota's earlier, more profitable years.

First, he eliminated robots from complicated jobs. He then identified several areas where the work processes could be simplified—and thus performed more easily and with less cost. He also reaffirmed the company's commitment to work participation. Toyota's employee involvement program had come to a halt during Kitano's stint abroad, but he began moving it forward once again. For example, he increased the use of work teams in Toyota by 20 percent during his first year back on the job. While it's still too early to see the total effects of Kitano's work, most experts believe that he has gotten Toyota back on the winning track.

SOURCES: "The Factory Guru Tinkering with Toyota," *Business Week*, May 17, 1993, pp. 95–97; and "Toyota Retooled," *Business Week*, April 4, 1994, pp. 54–57.

izational activities. The hope was that if employees were given the opportunity to participate in decision making concerning their work environment, they would be satisfied, and satisfaction supposedly would result in improved performance. But managers tended to see employee participation merely as a way to increase satisfaction, not as a source of potentially valuable input. Eventually, managers began to recognize that employee input was useful in itself, apart from its presumed effect on satisfaction. That is, they came to see employees as valued human resources that can contribute to organizational effectiveness.[30] The *Global Perspective* shows how Toyota is using participation and empowerment to boost productivity.

The role of participation and empowerment in motivation can be expressed in terms of both the need-based perspectives discussed in Chapter 4 and the expectancy theory. Employees who participate in decision making may be more

30. Raymond E. Miles, "Conflicting Elements in Managerial Ideologies," *Industrial Relations*, October 1964, pp. 77–91.

A team of workers at the Toyota factory in Samut Prakan, Thailand, makes final adjustments to a car. By encouraging workers to make their own decisions, Toyota has boosted its productivity and made this automobile factory the most successful in Thailand.

committed to executing decisions properly. Furthermore, the successful process of making a decision, executing it, and then seeing the positive consequences can help satisfy one's need for achievement, provide recognition and responsibility, and enhance self-esteem. Simply being asked to participate in organizational decision making also may enhance an employee's self-esteem. In addition, participation should help clarify expectancies; that is, by participating in decision making, employees may better understand the linkage between their performance and the rewards they want most.

Areas of Participation

At one level, employees can participate in addressing questions and making decisions about their own jobs. Instead of just telling them how to do their jobs, for example, managers can ask employees to make their own decisions about how to do them. Based on their own expertise and experience with their tasks, workers might be able to improve their own productivity. In many situations, they might also be well qualified to make decisions in areas such as what materials and tools to use.

Management might also let workers make decisions about administrative matters, such as work schedules. If jobs are relatively independent of one another, employees might decide when to change shifts, take breaks, go to lunch, and so forth. A work group or team might also be able to schedule vacations and days off for all of its members. Furthermore, employees are increasingly being asked to participate in broader issues of product quality. Such participation has become a hallmark of successful Japanese and other international firms, and many U.S. companies have followed suit.[31]

31. See Putai Jin, "Work Motivation and Productivity in Voluntarily Formed Work Teams: A Field Study in China," *Organizational Behavior and Human Decision Processes*, Vol. 54, 1993, pp. 133–155, for an interesting example.

Techniques and Issues in Empowerment

Organizations have experimented with a variety of techniques and philosophies for promoting participation and empowerment for their employees. Simple techniques such as suggestion boxes and question-and-answer meetings allow a certain degree of participation, for example. More recently, managers have investigated integrative participation techniques. One of the best known integrative techniques is quality circles. **Quality circles** (**QCs**) usually are defined as small groups of volunteers who meet regularly to identify, analyze, and solve quality and related problems that pertain to their work.[32] Quality circles became popular in the United States in the early 1980s. Widely used in Japan, they were presumed to have played a role in that country's rapid economic and technological growth.

Quality circles (**QCs**) are groups of volunteer employees who meet regularly to identify and propose solutions to quality and related problems in the organization.

Several steps are involved in creating successful quality circles. The first step is to seek volunteers. Recruitment usually stresses the circle's potential to help the organization and influence its future. The participants, of course, must be true volunteers; participation through coercion probably will have more negative than positive consequences. QCs usually have eight to ten members drawn from the same work area or related areas so that they have a common frame of reference. A circle's membership ordinarily is fixed, although people may be added or dropped as appropriate. The circle members usually receive some form of problem-solving training to help them address work problems. Training may be provided only at the outset or as an ongoing process.

Quality circle meetings are almost always held on company premises and on company time. One meeting a week is standard, with each meeting lasting about one hour, but variation exists from company to company. During meetings the circle members identify, analyze, and solve quality problems in their areas of responsibility. Problems range from eliminating vandalism to reducing defects in a particular production process. Since U.S. firms learned of the success of quality circles in Japan, many have adopted them, including Westinghouse, Hewlett-Packard, Texas Instruments, Eastman Kodak, and Procter & Gamble.

Many firms report positive results from quality circles, although little research has assessed their effectiveness. One recent study found the disappointing result that although quality circles were effective for awhile, their contributions eventually began to diminish.[33] Many organizations have more recently broadened their perspectives on participation and empowerment. The work team, discussed more completely in Chapter 7, is one currently used widespread method for empowering workers.

Regardless of the specific technique or method used, however, empowerment will only enhance organizational effectiveness if certain conditions exist. First, the organization must be sincere in its efforts to spread power and autonomy to lower levels of the organization. Token efforts to promote participation in only a few areas are not likely to succeed. Second, the organization must be committed to maintaining participation and empowerment. Workers will be resentful if they are given more control, only to later have it reduced or taken away altogether. Third, the organization must be systematic and patient in its efforts to empower workers. Turning over too much control too quickly can spell disaster. And finally, the

32. G. Munchus, "Employer-Employee Based Quality Circles in Japan: Human Resource Implications for American Firms," *Academy of Management Review*, April 1983, pp. 255–261.

33. Ricky W. Griffin, "A Longitudinal Assessment of the Consequences of Quality Circles in an Industrial Setting," *Academy of Management Journal*, June 1988, pp. 338–358.

organization must be prepared to increase its commitment to training. Employees being given more freedom in how they work will quite likely need additional training to help them exercise that freedom most effectively.

Attribution Theory and Motivation

The attribution theory of employee motivation suggests that employees observe their own behavior, attribute external or internal interpretations to it, and shape future motivated behavior accordingly.

In Chapter 3, we discussed the role of attribution in perception. We should also note the motivational implications of attribution theory.[34] According to the attribution view of employee motivation, a person observes his or her behavior through the processes of self-perception. On the basis of these perceptions, the individual decides whether her or his behavior is a response primarily to external or to internal factors. Through this attribution of causes, the individual decides whether he or she is basically extrinsically or intrinsically motivated and develops a preferred pattern of future incentives. A person who believes that he is extrinsically motivated will seek extrinsic rewards, such as pay or status symbols, as future incentives. One who feels that she is intrinsically motivated will look more for intrinsic incentives in the future.

Although relatively little work has been done on attribution theory's applications to motivation, there have been some intriguing findings. For example, Deci reasoned that paying an intrinsically motivated person on an incentive basis (that is, providing extrinsic rewards) would make him or her become more extrinsically motivated and less intrinsically motivated. Deci's research has indicated that if people are paid to do something they already like to do (are intrinsically motivated), their level of "liking" diminishes. Furthermore, if the pay is later withheld, their level of effort also diminishes. Thus, attributional processes appear to play a meaningful role in employee motivation in the workplace.[35]

Integrating the Process-based Perspectives

Because the process-based perspectives on employee motivation are so disparate, drawing the same sorts of clear comparisons that Figure 4.5 showed for the need-based perspectives is difficult. Nevertheless, several consistent lines of reasoning can be identified within the process-based perspectives.[36] Figure 5.6 represents an integrated view of the basic processes embedded in the equity, expectancy, and goal setting theories of motivation.[37]

The figure suggests that goal difficulty, specificity, acceptance, and commitment all lead to goal-directed effort. More general types of effort also result from a person's

34. H. H. Kelley, *Attribution in Social Interaction* (Morristown, N.J.: General Learning Press, 1971).
35. See E. L. Deci, "Effects of Externally Mediated Rewards on Intrinsic Motivation," *Journal of Applied Psychology*, Vol. 18, 1971, pp. 105–115. See also Paul C. Jordan, "Effects of an Extrinsic Reward on Intrinsic Motivation: A Field Experiment," *Academy of Management Journal*, June 1986, pp. 405–412.
36. See Anthony J. Mento, Edwin A. Locke, and Howard J. Klein, "Relationship of Goal Level to Valence and Instrumentality," *Journal of Applied Psychology*, Vol. 77, 1992, pp. 395–405, for one interesting example.
37. See Kanfer, "Motivation Theory and Industrial and Organizational Psychology," for a look at other integrated perspectives.

FIGURE 5.6

Integrating the Process-based Perspectives on Motivation

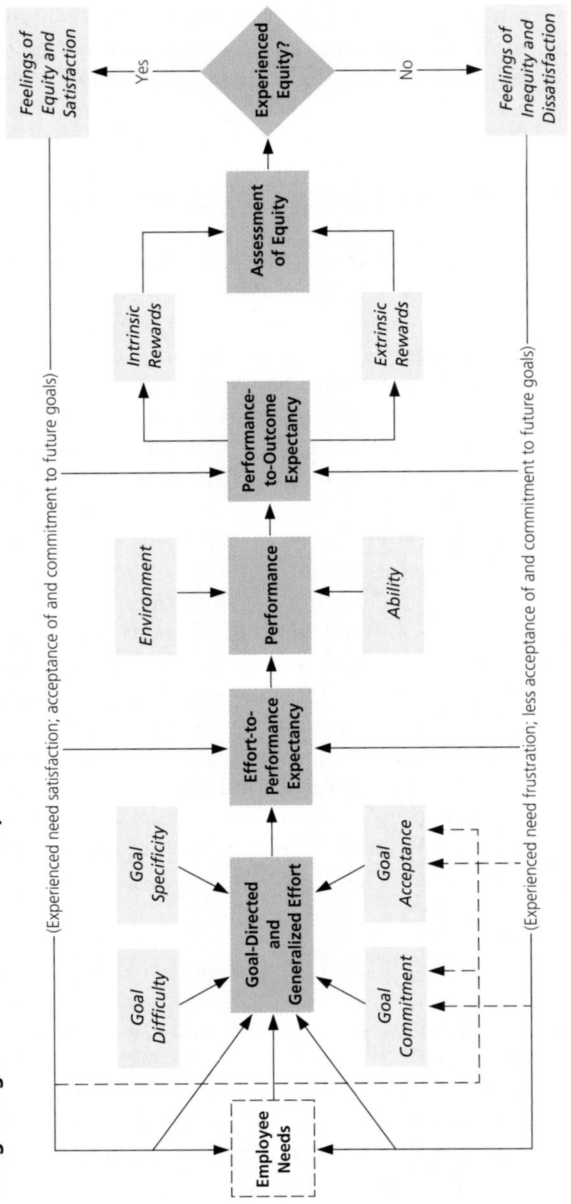

beliefs as to how he or she can satisfy various individual needs. The effort-to-performance expectancy mediates the relationship between both goal-directed effort and generalized effort and potential performance and combine with environmental factors and individual abilities to produce a given level of performance. Performance-to-outcome expectancies then mediate between performance and various intrinsic and extrinsic rewards (outcomes).

After the individual actually experiences both types of rewards, she or he then assesses them through the equity comparison processes described earlier. If the rewards are perceived to be equitable, the employee will be motivated to maintain the status quo, will experience need satisfaction, and will likely be more accepting of and committed to future goals. In addition, the effort-to-performance and performance-to-outcome expectancies will be strengthened. On the other hand, if rewards are perceived to be inequitable, in addition to the responses to inequity described earlier, the individual will not experience need satisfaction and will be less accepting of and committed to goals. In addition, effort-to-performance and performance-to-outcome expectancies will be weakened.

Summary of Key Points

- The equity theory of motivation assumes that people want to be treated fairly. It hypothesizes that people compare their own input-to-outcome ratio in the organization to the ratio of a comparison-other. If they believe that their treatment has been relatively inequitable, they take steps to reduce the inequity.
- Expectancy theory, a somewhat more complicated model, follows from the assumption that people are motivated to work toward a goal if they want it and think that they have a reasonable chance of achieving it. The effort-to-performance expectancy is the belief that effort will lead to performance. The performance-to-outcome expectancy is the belief that performance will lead to certain outcomes. Valence is the desirability to the individual of the various possible outcomes of performance.
- The Porter-Lawler extension of expectancy theory provides useful insights into the relationship between satisfaction and performance. This model suggests that performance may lead to a variety of intrinsic and extrinsic rewards. When perceived as equitable, these rewards lead to satisfaction.
- Goal setting provides a useful and meaningful way to motivate employees toward the achievement of various goals. If goals are specific and moderately difficult and if employees accept and are committed to those goals, they are more likely to work toward them. MBO is a generalized method of using goal setting throughout an organization in a systematic and organized fashion.
- Participative management and empowerment can help improve employee motivation in many business settings. Quality circles have received much attention in recent years as a potentially useful way to increase employee participation. Organizations that want to empower their employees need to understand a variety of issues as they go about promoting participation.
- Attribution theory also has been applied to employee motivation. The theory suggests that employees perceive their behavior as stemming from either external or internal causes and are motivated by rewards that correspond to the causes of their behavior. The process-based perspectives can be integrated in a variety of different ways.

Discussion Questions

1. Besides the need-based versus process-based distinctions, are there any basic differences between the motivation theories discussed in Chapters 4 and 5?
2. Have you ever experienced inequity in a job or a class? How did it affect you?
3. What might be some managerial implications of equity theory beyond those discussed in the chapter?
4. Do you think that expectancy theory is too complex for direct use in organizational settings? Why or why not?
5. Do you agree or disagree with the relationships between performance and satisfaction suggested by Porter and Lawler? Cite examples that both support and refute the model.
6. Critique the goal setting theory of motivation. Specifically, what do you see as its strength and weakness?
7. Develop a framework whereby an instructor could use goal setting in running a class such as this one.
8. What are the motivational consequences of participative management—specifically, quality circles—from the frame of reference of another theory or theories?
9. What motivational problems might result from an organization's attempt to set up quality circles?
10. Cite personal examples of attribution processes and motivation.

EXPERIENTIAL EXERCISE

Purpose This exercise will help you recognize both the potential value and the complexity of expectancy theory.

Format Working alone, you will be asked to identify the various aspects of expectancy theory that are pertinent to your class. You will then share your thoughts and results with some of your classmates.

Procedure Considering your class as a workplace and your effort in the class as a surrogate for a job, do the following:

1. Identify six or seven outcomes that might happen as a result of good performance in your class (for example, a good grade or a recommendation from your instructor). Your list must include at least one undesirable outcome (for example, a loss of free time).
2. Using a value of 10 for "extremely desirable," −10 for "extremely undesirable," and 0 for "complete neutrality," assign a valence to each outcome. In other words, the valence you assign to each outcome should be somewhere between 10 and −10, inclusive.
3. Assume that you are a high performer. On that basis, estimate the probability of each potential outcome. Express this probability as a percentage.

4. Multiply each valence by its associated probability, and sum the results. This total is your overall valence for high performance.
5. Assess the probability that if you exert effort, you will be a high performer. Express the probability as a percentage.
6. Multiply this probability by the overall valence for high performance calculated in step 4. This score reflects your motivational force—that is, your motivation to exert high effort.

Now form groups of three or four. Compare your scores on motivational force. Discuss why some scores differ widely. Also, note whether any group members had similar force scores but different combinations of factors leading to those scores.

Follow-up Questions

1. What does the exercise tell you about the strengths and limitations of expectancy theory?
2. Would this exercise be useful for a manager to run with a group of subordinates? Why or why not?

| CASE 5.1 | **Worthington's Approach Pays Off—For Workers and Management** |

Unlike many U.S. companies these days, Worthington Industries hasn't really struggled much lately. Worthington, based in Columbus, Ohio, has increased its earnings 250 percent over the last ten years and posts an average return on equity of more than 17 percent. Financial analysts project continued optimism for the firm for at least the next several years.

Worthington operates in a real nuts-and-bolts manufacturing industry. The firm processes steel, makes railcar castings, and molds plastics. Worthington operates thirty plants, mostly in the east and northeastern regions of the United States. The company was founded in 1955 by John H. McConnell, who still serves as its chairman.

How has McConnell led Worthington to such sustained strong performance? He gives most of the credit to the way he treats his employees. McConnell's own first job was as a machine operator in a heavily unionized automobile factory. One day a union official chewed him out because he finished his daily quota in five hours, instead of stretching the work out so as to take all day.

A few years later when he started Worthington,

McConnell knew that he had to do things differently. He recalled from his personal experiences in the auto industry that when management and unions were working for different things, both often suffered. His goal at Worthington was to create a work environment wherein people would find it in their own interests to work for the good of the company.

He started by eliminating time clocks and plant supervisors. He believed that this would show his workers that he trusted them and did not feel a need to monitor or control them. McConnell also gave his workers a great deal of autonomy. They can refuse to accept a shipment of materials, for example, if they believe that it does not meet their standards.

McConnell also decided to pay all his workers a salary, rather than a wage, and promised never to lay them off during bad times. Because the steel industry is cyclical, workers accustomed to frequent layoffs found this promise to be particularly attractive. McConnell has kept his promise, too—no Worthington employee has been laid off because business was slack.

McConnell also decided to tie a substantial portion of his workers' income to their performance and to the performance of the firm. The base pay workers earn is relatively low. But each worker also receives cash bonuses tied to his or her own performance, as well as profit sharing tied to the firm's overall profitability. Workers can also participate in a stock purchase program that McConnell put in place several years ago.

To illustrate how the plan works, consider a typical Worthington production employee during 1993. This average individual will earn $11,200 in cash bonuses on top of her or his base salary. In addition, the employee will also receive between $1,200 and $3,000 more in deferred profit sharing. If the employee has been with the company for more than twenty years, he or she likely has around $380,000 in a profit-sharing account. More than 4,000 Worthington employees have also chosen to participate in the firm's stock purchase plan. All told, employees own more than $200 million in Worthington stock, with an average individual value of around $45,000.

Worthington employees also have opportunity for advancement. McConnell only hires outside managers when the firm needs some specialized form of

expertise not available internally. The firm's current president started as an operating employee, as did five of the company's nine vice presidents.

Has Worthington's approach paid off? McConnell believes it has. Absenteeism hovers around 1.5 percent, half the industry average. And the firm's steel processing sales per employee averages around $445,000, second in the industry only to Steel Technologies Inc., which uses a similar approach to manage its workers. It's easy to see, then, why things look so good for Worthington Industries.

Case Questions

1. Which theory of motivation best explains why employees at Worthington perform so well?
2. What future motivation-related problems might Worthington have to address to maintain its performance?

SOURCES: "'You Have to Trust the Work Force,'" *Forbes*, July 19, 1993, pp. 78-81; and "Worthington Will Build a Thin-Slab Minimill," *Iron Age*, August 1993, p. 10.

| CASE 5.2 | **Equity in Academia** |

When the last student left Melinda Wilkerson's office at 5:30 P.M., the young English professor just sat, too exhausted to move. Her desk was piled high with student papers, journals, and recommendation forms. "There goes my weekend," she thought to herself, knowing that reading and commenting on the thirty journals alone would take up all of Saturday. She liked reading the journals, getting a glimpse of how her students were reacting to the novels and poems she had them read, watching them grow and change. But recently, as she picked up another journal from the bottomless pile or greeted another student with a smile, she often wondered whether it was all worth it.

Wilkerson had had such a moment about an hour earlier, when Ron Agua, whose office was across the hall, had waved to her as he walked past her door.

"I'm off to the Rat," he announced. "Come join us if you ever get free." For a moment Wilkerson had stared blankly at the student before her, pondering the scene at the Rathskeller, the university's most popular restaurant and meeting place. Agua would be there with four or five of the department's senior members, including Alice Bordy, the department chair. All would be glad to have her join them . . . if only she didn't have so much work.

At the start of her first year as an assistant professor, Wilkerson had accepted her overwhelming workload as part of the territory. Her paycheck was smaller and her hours longer than she had expected, but Agua and the other two new faculty members seemed to be suffering under the same burdens.

But now, in her second semester, Wilkerson was beginning to feel that things weren't right. While the stream of students knocking on her door persisted, she noticed that Agua was spending less time talking and more time at his word processor than he had the first semester. When asked, Agua told her he had reduced his course load because of his extra work on the department's hiring and library committees. He seemed surprised when Wilkerson admitted that she didn't know there was such a thing as a course reduction.

As the semester progressed, Wilkerson realized that there was a lot she didn't know about the way the department functioned. Agua would disappear once a week or so to give talks to groups around the state and then would turn those talks into papers for scholarly journals—something Wilkerson didn't dream of having time to do. She and Agua were still good friends, but she began to see differences in their approaches. "I cut down my office hours this semester," he told her one day. "With all those students around all the time, I just never had a chance to get my work done."

Wilkerson had pondered that statement for a few weeks. She thought that dealing with students was "getting work done." But when salaries for the following year were announced, she realized what Agua meant. He would be making almost $1,000 more than she; the human resources committee viewed his committee work as a valuable asset to the department, his talks around the state already had earned him notoriety, and his three upcoming publications clearly put him ahead of the other first-year professors.

Wilkerson was confused. Agua hadn't done anything sneaky or immoral—in fact, everything he did was admirable, things she would have liked to do. His trips to the Rat gave him the inside scoop on what to do and whom to talk to, but she couldn't blame him

for that either. She could have done exactly the same thing. They worked equally hard, she thought. Yet Agua already was the highly paid star, whereas she was just another overworked instructor.

As she began piling all the books, papers, and journals into her bag, Wilkerson thought about what she could do. She could quit and go somewhere else where she might be more appreciated, but jobs were hard to find and she suspected that the same thing might happen there. She could charge sex discrimination and demand to be paid as much as Agua, but that would be unfair to him and she didn't really feel discriminated against for being a woman. The university simply didn't value what she did with her time as highly as they valued what Agua did with his.

Putting on her coat, Wilkerson spotted a piece of paper that had dropped out of one of the journals. She picked it up and saw it was a note from Wendy Martin, one of her freshman students. "Professor Wilkerson," it read, "I just wanted to thank you for taking the time to talk to me last week. I really needed to talk to someone experienced about it, and all my other professors are men, and I just couldn't have talked to them. You helped me a whole lot."

Sighing, Wilkerson folded the note, put it in her bag, and closed her office door. Suddenly the pile of journals and the $1,000 didn't seem so important.

Case Questions

1. What do you think Melinda Wilkerson will do? Is she satisfied with the way she is being treated?

2. Explain the behaviors of Wilkerson and Agua using the motivation theories in this chapter.

C H A P T E R

Learning-based Perspectives on Motivation

OBJECTIVES

After studying this chapter, you should be able to:

Define learning and discuss both the traditional and contemporary views of learning.

Describe reinforcement theory and learning.

Identify and discuss several related aspects of learning.

Describe organizational behavior modification from the standpoint of learning and motivation.

Discuss social learning in organizations.

Concerned about the excessive turnover rate at the IRS, managers created a new system that more directly links employee performance with rewards. IRS workers now have a clearer understanding of how to achieve their career goals, and turnover has fallen by more than eight percent.

One of the most critical agencies of the U.S. federal government is the Internal Revenue Service, or IRS. The IRS is responsible for interpreting U.S. tax law, setting all tax regulations within the context of that law, and collecting taxes from individuals and businesses. With over 100,000 employees, the IRS is one of the government's biggest organizations.

Like any government or business organization, the IRS has its share of management issues and problems that must continually be addressed. One of the IRS's most recent management problems was turnover. In particular, a few years ago managers recognized that turnover had slowly increased until it was approaching 28 percent. This unacceptably high rate of turnover was resulting in excessive replacement and training costs and was also adversely affecting morale among those employees who stayed in their jobs.

A task force was appointed and spent several months investigating the problem. The task force decided that the biggest cause of turnover in the organization was that employees did not see any connection between their work and the rewards they received. That is, employees believed that they would receive the same rewards, regardless of whether they worked hard or did just enough to get by.

After reviewing the report, managers at the IRS developed a new reward system that more clearly linked performance and rewards (especially promotions). Specifically, formal mechanisms were created that allow employees to specify the kind of career path they want to pursue within the organization. Their managers then help employees set goals that enable them to have the highest likelihood of achieving the career they want. Actual performance appraisals are then used to continually assess how well they are doing in relation to their career goals.

It took approximately six years to plan and fully implement the new system. The results so far, however, are quite promising. In particular, turnover has dropped to less than 20 percent. In addition, productivity has improved and the number of complaints filed by employees has dropped significantly.[1]

■ ■ ■ ■ The IRS has the same motivational problems as any organization, such as attracting good employees, developing them into productive contributors, and retaining their services. Its new strategy linking career development with performance has helped the organization significantly lower its turnover rates. Employees now see a clear link between their behavior (performance) and its consequences (career advancement).

In our last two chapters we examined first the needs and motives that motivate behavior (in Chapter 4) and then the process used by people that results in certain behavioral choices (in Chapter 5). In this chapter, the last of three devoted to

1. Deena Harkins, Zandy Leibowitz, and Stephen Forrer, "How the IRS Finds and Keeps Good Employees," *Training & Development*, April 1993, pp. 76–78; and *The United States Budget for 1993* (Washington; U.S. Prints Office), p. 806.

employee motivation, we look more closely at the consequences of the behavioral choices made by people in organizations. As we will see, learning is the cornerstone of how the consequences of behavior affect future behavior. We start by examining the nature of learning. We then introduce and discuss reinforcement theory, the basis of learning in organizations. Several related aspects of learning are then described. Organizational behavior modification, a specific motivational strategy based on learning theory, is then discussed. Finally, we describe social learning in organizations.

The Nature of Learning

Most people have a general sense of what learning means.[2] People also, however, have many misconceptions about this basic human process. In this section we define learning, summarize traditional and contemporary views of learning, and briefly examine learning in organizations.

Definition of Learning

Learning is a relatively permanent change in behavior or behavioral potential based on direct or indirect experience.

Learning is a relatively permanent change in behavior or behavioral potential that results from direct or indirect experience.[3] Given both the complexities and importance of human learning in organizations, however, we should carefully examine each component of this definition in more detail.

First, note that learning involves change of some sort or another. After we have learned, we are somehow different from who we were before—for better or worse. Employees at Ford, for example, learn new job skills, new ideas, and how to be more productive. Unfortunately, other employees in some organizations may also learn how to steal, how to cheat, and how to avoid work.

Second, changes brought about by learning tend to be relatively long lasting. Thus, a student who memorizes material for an exam and promptly forgets it after the test has not really learned anything. Likewise, Ford workers who get less done at the end of the day than in the morning have not learned to work more slowly; they are simply tired. In contrast, if we really learn something, like the Pledge of Allegiance or how to ride a bicycle, we can easily perform the task again and again, even if long periods of time elapse without our thinking about it.

Third, learning affects behavior or behavioral potential. Because we cannot read minds, of course, we must often depend on observation to see how much learning has occurred. If a word processing operator who keyboarded seventy words a minute before taking a new training course can now keyboard eighty-five words a minute, we can infer that learning has occurred. Other kinds of learning are harder to discern. Suppose that an employee who has always arrived at work on time sees the boss scold some workers who came in late. The punctual worker now has an added incentive to be on time every day. Even though actual behavior has not been altered, learning has taken place because potential behavior—the likelihood of being tardy—has been reduced.

2. See Fred Kofman and Peter M. Senges, "Communities of Commitment: The Heart of Learning Organizations," *Organizational Dynamics*, Autumn 1993, pp. 5–23, for a discussion of various perspectives on learning in organizations.
3. S. H. Hulse, J. Deese, and H. Egeth, *The Psychology of Learning*, 7th ed. (New York: McGraw-Hill, 1992). See also Gib Akins, "Varieties of Organizational Learning," *Organizational Dynamics*, Autumn 1987, pp. 36–48.

Finally, the changes brought about by learning result from direct or indirect experience. The word processing operator probably sat and practiced at a real keyboard during the training session (an example of direct experience). But the punctual employee learned about punishment for tardiness only by observing what the boss said to coworkers; nothing was done or said to him or her directly. This is learning through indirect experience. We should also distinguish between experience and simple physical maturation. Most adults can easily lift a twenty-pound sack of potatoes and a five-year-old cannot. This is so not because of experience and resultant learning but because physical maturation has simply made the adult stronger.

The Traditional View: Classical Conditioning

Classical conditioning is a simple form of learning that links a conditioned response with an unconditioned stimulus.

To understand contemporary thinking on learning, we first need to be aware of its historical roots. By far the most influential historical approach to learning is classical conditioning as described by Ivan Pavlov.[4] **Classical conditioning** is a simple form of learning in which a conditioned response is linked with an unconditioned stimulus. Figure 6.1 illustrates how classical conditioning works.

Pavlov's theory was based on a famous series of experiments with dogs. Pavlov knew that if he gave meat to the dogs, they would salivate. The meat was an unconditioned, or a natural, stimulus, and the salivation an unconditioned, or a reflexive, response. This link is shown as step 1 in Figure 6.1. Next, Pavlov rang a bell at the same time he presented meat. Before that, the dogs did not associate the ringing of the bell with eating, so the bell alone brought no response. But by ringing the bell while presenting the meat, Pavlov established a relationship between the two stimuli in the minds of the dogs. Step 2 in the figure shows this linkage. Eventually, the dogs associated eating with the sound of the bell so completely that they would salivate whenever the bell was rung, even if no meat was forthcoming (step 3). The bell had become a conditioned stimulus able to call up the newly conditioned, or learned, response.

4. Ivan P. Pavlov, *Conditional Reflexes* (New York: Oxford University Press, 1927).

FIGURE 6.1

Classical Conditioning

Step 1

| Unconditioned Stimulus (Manager delivers bad news to subordinates) | → | Unconditioned Response (Subordinates feel dejected and unhappy) |

Step 2

| Conditioned Stimulus (Manager wears blue suit) | | |
| Unconditioned Stimulus (Manager delivers bad news to subordinates) | → | Response (Subordinates feel dejected and unhappy) |

Step 3

| Conditioned Stimulus (Manager wears blue suit) | → | Conditioned Response (Subordinates feel dejected and unhappy) |

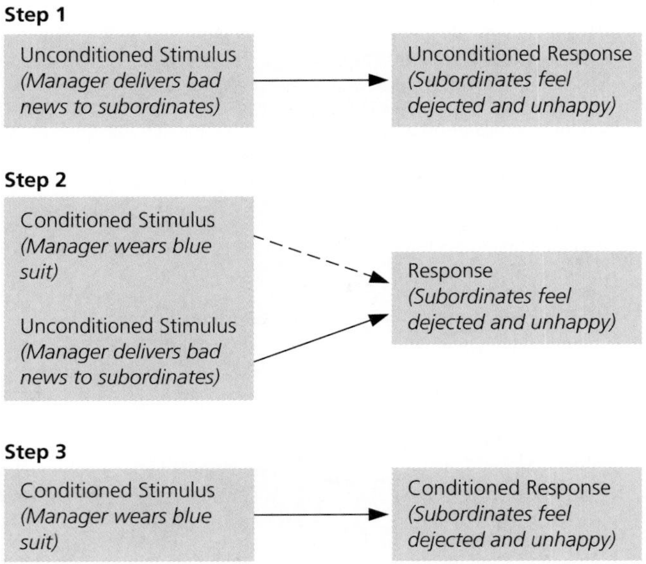

Figure 6.1 shows a simple organizational example of classical conditioning. In reality, however, simple forms of this conditioning seldom occur among human beings. Learning theorists soon recognized that although classical conditioning offered some interesting insights into the learning process, it explained human learning inadequately. For one thing, classical conditioning relies on simple cause-and-effect relationships between one stimulus and one response; it cannot explain more complex forms of learned behavior that typify human beings. For another, classical conditioning ignores the concept of choice; it assumes that behavior is reflexive, or involuntary. Therefore, this perspective cannot explain situations in which people consciously and rationally choose one course of action among many. Because of these shortcomings of classical conditioning, theorists eventually developed other approaches that seemed more useful in explaining the processes associated with complex learning.

The Contemporary View: Learning as a Cognitive Process

Learning is a cognitive process that involves conscious and active behavior.

Although contemporary learning theory is not tied to a single theory or model, it generally views learning as a cognitive process; that is, it assumes people are conscious, active participants in how they learn.[5] Figure 6.2 illustrates some underpinnings of the cognitive view of learning.[6]

First, in the cognitive view, people draw on their experiences and use past learning as a basis for present behavior. These experiences represent presumed knowledge, or cognitions. For example, an employee faced with a choice of job assignments will use previous experiences in deciding which one to accept. Second, people make choices about their behavior. The employee recognizes her two alternatives and chooses one. Third, people recognize the consequences of their choices. Thus, when the employee finds the job assignment rewarding and fulfilling, she will recognize that the choice was a good one and will understand why. Finally, people evaluate those consequences and add them to prior learning, which affects future choices. Faced with similar job choices next year, the employee very likely will choose one as similar as possible to the earlier one.[7]

5. Hulse, Deese, and Egeth, *The Psychology of Learning*. For recent perspectives, see also Douglas F. Cellar and Gerald V. Barrett, "Script Processing and Intrinsic Motivation: The Cognitive Sets Underlying Cognitive Labels," *Organizational Behavior and Human Decision Processes*, August 1987, pp. 115–135; and Max H. Bazerman and John S. Carroll, "Negotiator Cognition," in L. L. Cummings and Barry M. Staw (Eds.), *Research in Organizational Behavior*, Vol. 9 (Greenwich, Conn.: JAI Press, 1987), pp. 247–288.
6. See Robert Wood and Albert Bandura, "Social Cognitive Theory of Organizational Management," *Academy of Management Review*, July 1989, pp. 361–384.
7. Harry Binswanger, "Volition as Cognitive Self-Regulation," *Organizational Behavior and Human Decision Processes*, Vol. 50, 1991, pp. 154–178.

FIGURE 6.2

Learning as a Cognitive Process

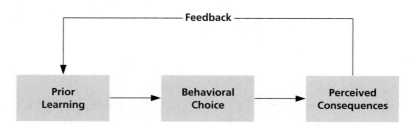

According to contemporary learning theory, learning is a cognitive process; that is, people use their past experiences when making behavioral choices. Volunteers from General Electric, who are allied with the National Society of Black Engineers, tutor minority high school students in the hopes that a positive experience with learning will make college a more attractive and more feasible option for the students.

As implied earlier, several perspectives on learning take a cognitive view. Perhaps foremost among them is reinforcement theory. In any event, this approach is most relevant to understanding human learning processes in organizational settings. Before discussing reinforcement theory, however, we should first establish the organizational context of learning.

Learning in Organizations

Most people associate learning with formal education and with school in particular. Whereas this association is quite logical, we should also note the pervasive extent to which learning also occurs in organizations.[8]

From a simple orientation perspective, for example, newcomers to an organization learn when to come to work, how to dress, whom to ask for assistance, where to park, how to apply for annual leave, when to expect a paycheck, and how to file an insurance claim. From a performance perspective, employees learn how to do their jobs more effectively, what is expected of them in the way of performance outcomes, and what it takes to get rewarded. From a social perspective, employees learn how to get along with their colleagues, which behaviors are acceptable and which are unacceptable, and the norms of the group. From a political perspective, employees learn how to get along with their bosses, whom to avoid, and whom to trust. And from a career perspective, employees learn how to get ahead, how to get promotions, which job assignments to seek and which to avoid, and the like. Clearly, then, much of organizational life and the behavior of individuals within organizations are influenced by learning and learning processes.

8. Edgar H. Schein, "On Dialogue, Culture, and Organizational Learning," *Organizational Dynamics*, Autumn 1993, pp. 40–51.

Reinforcement Theory and Learning

Reinforcement theory is based on the idea that behavior is a function of its consequences.

Reinforcement theory, also called operant conditioning, is generally associated with the work of B. F. Skinner.[9] In its simplest form, **reinforcement theory** suggests that behavior is a function of its consequences.[10] Thus, behavior that results in pleasant consequences is more likely to be repeated, and behavior that results in unpleasant consequences is less likely to be repeated.

Reinforcement theory further suggests that in any given situation, people will explore a variety of possible behaviors. Future behavioral choices are affected by the consequences of earlier behaviors. Cognitions, as already noted, also play an important role. Thus, rather than assuming a mechanical stimulus-response linkage suggested by the traditional classical view of learning, contemporary theorists believe that people consciously explore different behaviors and systematically choose those that result in the most desirable outcomes.

Suppose that a new employee at Monsanto in St. Louis wants to learn the best way to get along with his boss. At first, the employee is very friendly and informal, but the boss responds by acting aloof and, at times, annoyed. Because the boss does not react positively, the employee is unlikely to continue this behavior. In fact, the employee starts acting more formal and professional and finds the boss much more receptive to this posture. In all likelihood, the employee will continue this new set of behaviors because they result in positive consequences.

Types of Reinforcement in Organizations

Reinforcement is the consequences of behavior.

The consequences of behavior are called **reinforcement**. Managers can use various kinds of reinforcement to affect employee behavior. There are four basic forms of reinforcement: positive reinforcement, avoidance, extinction, and punishment. Which form a manager should use depends on the situation. Figure 6.3 summarizes the concepts underlying the four basic kinds of reinforcement.

Positive reinforcement is a reward or other desirable consequence that a person achieves after exhibiting behavior.

Positive Reinforcement

Positive reinforcement is perhaps the most familiar part of reinforcement theory to people outside the fields of psychology and organizational behavior. **Positive reinforcement** is a reward or other desirable consequence that follows behavior. A compliment from the boss after completing a difficult job and a salary increase following a period of high performance are examples of positive reinforcement. In general, CEO compensation should be positive reinforcement for effectively managing the organization. At Corning's ceramics factory in Virginia, workers receive bonuses for pulling blemished materials from assembly lines before they go into more expensive stages of production.[11]

The general effect of providing positive reinforcement after behavior is to maintain or increase the frequency of that behavior.[12] Managers might define "desirable" employee behavior as hard work, punctuality, conscientiousness, and loyalty

9. B. F. Skinner, *Science and Human Behavior* (New York: Macmillan, 1953); and B. F. Skinner, *Beyond Freedom and Dignity* (New York: Knopf, 1972).
10. Fred Luthans and Robert Kreitner, *Organizational Behavior Modification and Beyond* (Glenview, Ill.: Scott, Foresman, 1985).
11. "Workers: Risks and Rewards," *Time*, April 15, 1991, pp. 42–43.
12. Luthans and Kreitner, *Organizational Modification and Beyond*.

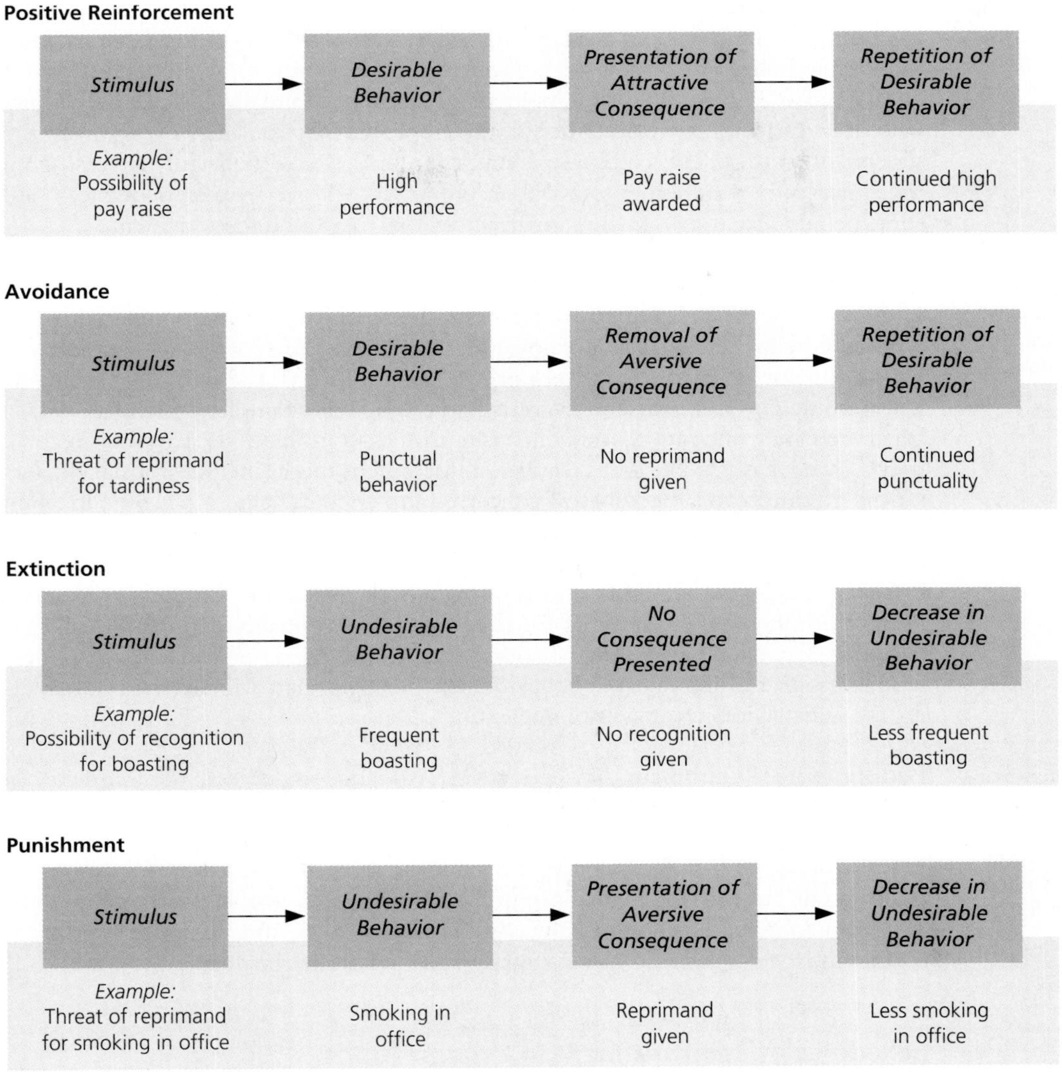

Positive Reinforcement

Stimulus	→	Desirable Behavior	→	Presentation of Attractive Consequence	→	Repetition of Desirable Behavior
Example: Possibility of pay raise		High performance		Pay raise awarded		Continued high performance

Avoidance

Stimulus	→	Desirable Behavior	→	Removal of Aversive Consequence	→	Repetition of Desirable Behavior
Example: Threat of reprimand for tardiness		Punctual behavior		No reprimand given		Continued punctuality

Extinction

Stimulus	→	Undesirable Behavior	→	No Consequence Presented	→	Decrease in Undesirable Behavior
Example: Possibility of recognition for boasting		Frequent boasting		No recognition given		Less frequent boasting

Punishment

Stimulus	→	Undesirable Behavior	→	Presentation of Aversive Consequence	→	Decrease in Undesirable Behavior
Example: Threat of reprimand for smoking in office		Smoking in office		Reprimand given		Less smoking in office

FIGURE 6.3

Kinds of Reinforcement

and commitment to the organization. When employees exhibit these behaviors, the manager may reward them with pay increases, praise, some kind of formal recognition, promotions, and the like. In terms of reinforcement theory, the rewards are intended to ensure the same type of behavior in the future. Of course, different people work for different reasons. To be useful as positive reinforcement, rewards should therefore be tailored to the needs of the individual. In addition, a reward should be directly linked with the desirable behavior, and the individual should have ample opportunity to achieve the reinforcement. For example, a person who gets a raise in salary after a period of high performance should be made aware explicitly that the raise was given because of the performance. Likewise, the level of performance needed to get the raise should not be set so high as to be impossible to reach.

Avoidance, or negative reinforcement, is the opportunity to avoid or escape from an unpleasant circumstance after exhibiting behavior.

Avoidance   **Avoidance**, also known as *negative reinforcement*, is another means of increasing the frequency of desirable behavior. Rather than receiving a reward after a desirable behavior, the person is given the opportunity to avoid an unpleasant consequence. For example, an employee's boss may habitually criticize individuals who dress casually. To avoid criticism, the employee may routinely dress to suit the supervisor's tastes. The employee is engaging in desirable behavior (at least from the supervisor's viewpoint) to avoid an unpleasant, or aversive, consequence. And some people accept low-paying, unattractive jobs to avoid unemployment.

Extinction decreases the frequency of behavior by eliminating a reward or desirable consequence that follows that behavior.

Extinction   Whereas positive reinforcement and avoidance increase the frequency of desirable behavior, **extinction** decreases the frequency of undesirable behavior, especially behavior that was previously rewarded. In other words, if rewards are withdrawn for behaviors that were previously reinforced, the behaviors probably will become less frequent and eventually die out. For example, a manager with a small staff may encourage frequent visits from subordinates as a way to keep in touch with what is going on. Positive reinforcement might include cordial conversation, attention to subordinates' concerns, and encouragement to come in again soon. As the staff grows, however, the manager may find that such unstructured conversations now make it difficult to get her own job done. She then might brush off casual conversation and reward only to-the-point "business" conversations. Withdrawing the rewards for casual chatting probably will extinguish that behavior. We should also note, of course, that if managers, inadvertently or otherwise, cease to reward valuable behaviors such as good performance and punctuality, those behaviors too may become extinct.[13]

Punishment is an unpleasant, or aversive, consequence that results from behavior. Schedules of reinforcement indicate when or how often managers should reinforce certain behaviors.

Punishment   Punishment, like extinction, also tends to decrease the frequency of undesirable behaviors. **Punishment** is an unpleasant, or aversive, consequence of undesirable behavior. In the workplace, undesirable behavior might include slacking off, being late, stealing, or arguing unnecessarily with the boss. Examples of punishment are verbal or written reprimands, pay cuts, loss of privileges, layoffs, and termination. Punishment is by nature controversial, and therefore we discuss arguments for and against it in a separate section later in the chapter.

Schedules of Reinforcement in Organizations

Schedules of reinforcement indicate when or how often managers should reinforce certain behaviors.

Should the manager try to reinforce every instance of desirable behavior, or is applying reinforcement according to some plan or schedule more effective? Generally, that depends on the situation. Table 6.1 summarizes five basic schedules of reinforcement that managers can use.[14]

With **continuous reinforcement**, behavior is rewarded every time it occurs.

Continuous Reinforcement   **Continuous reinforcement** rewards behavior every time it occurs. Continuous reinforcement is very effective in increasing the frequency of a desirable behavior, especially in the early stages of learning. When reinforcement is withdrawn, however, extinction sets in very quickly. The schedule poses serious practical difficulties as well: the manager must monitor every behavior

13. Ibid.
14. Ibid.

Second-year tax accountants at Peat, Marwick and Main learn new software for tax preparation at the company's educational facility in Montvale, New Jersey. While at the facility, they are given eight hours of intensive computer training, receiving continuous reinforcement as they learn.

of an employee and provide effective reinforcement. This schedule, then, is seldom worth much to managers. Offering partial reinforcement according to one of the other four schedules is much more typical.

Fixed-interval reinforcement provides reinforcement on a fixed time schedule.

Fixed-Interval Reinforcement **Fixed-interval reinforcement** means providing reinforcement on a predetermined, constant schedule. The Friday afternoon paycheck is a good example of a fixed-interval reinforcement. Unfortunately, in many

TABLE 6.1

Schedules of Reinforcement

Schedule of Reinforcement	Nature of Reinforcement
Continuous	Behavior is reinforced every time it occurs.
Fixed-Interval	Behavior is reinforced according to some predetermined, constant schedule based on time.
Variable-Interval	Behavior is reinforced after periods of time, but the time span varies from one time to the next.
Fixed-Ratio	Behavior is reinforced according to the number of behaviors exhibited, with the number or behaviors needed to gain reinforcement held constant.
Variable-Ratio	Behavior is reinforced according to the number of behaviors exhibited, but the number of behaviors needed to gain reinforcement varies from one time to the next.

situations the fixed-interval schedule will not necessarily maintain high performance levels. If employees know the boss will drop by to check on them every day at 1:00 P.M., they are likely to be working hard at that time, hoping to gain praise and recognition or to avoid the boss's wrath. But at other times of the day, the employees probably will not work as hard because they have learned that reinforcement is unlikely except during the daily visit.

Variable-interval reinforcement varies the amount of time between reinforcement.

Variable-Interval Reinforcement **Variable-interval reinforcement** also uses time as the basis for applying reinforcement, but it varies the interval between reinforcements. This schedule is inappropriate for paying wages, but it can work well for other types of positive reinforcement, such as praise and recognition, and for avoidance. Consider again the group of employees just described. Suppose that instead of coming by at exactly 1:00 P.M. every day, the boss visits at a different time each day: 9:30 A.M. on Monday, 2:00 P.M. on Tuesday, 11:00 A.M. on Wednesday, and so on. The following week, the times change. Because the employees do not know just when to expect the boss, they probably will work fairly hard until her visit. Afterward, they may drop back to lower levels because they have learned that she will not be back until the next day.

Fixed-Ratio Reinforcement The fixed- and variable-ratio schedules gear reinforcement to the number of desirable or undesirable behaviors rather than to blocks of time. With **fixed-ratio reinforcement**, the number of behaviors needed to obtain reinforcement is constant. Assume that a work group enters its cumulative performance totals into the office computer every hour. The manager of the group uses the computer to monitor its activities. He might adopt a practice of dropping by to praise the group every time it reaches a performance level of 500 units. Thus, if the group does this three times on Monday, he stops by each time; if it reaches the mark only once on Tuesday, he stops by only once. The fixed-ratio schedule can be fairly effective in maintaining desirable behavior. Employees tend to develop a feel for what it takes to be reinforced and work hard to keep up their performance.

Fixed-ratio reinforcement provides reinforcement after a fixed number of behaviors.

Variable-ratio reinforcement varies the number of behaviors between reinforcement.

Variable-Ratio Reinforcement With **variable-ratio reinforcement**, the number of behaviors required for reinforcement varies over time. An employee performing under a variable-ratio schedule is motivated to work hard because each successful behavior increases the probability that the next one will result in reinforcement. With this schedule, the exact number of behaviors needed to obtain reinforcement is not crucial; what is important is that the intervals between reinforcement not be so long that the worker gets discouraged and stops trying. The supervisor in the fixed-ratio example could reinforce his work group after it reaches performance levels of 325, 525, 450, 600, and so on. A variable-ratio schedule can be quite effective, but it is difficult and cumbersome to use when formal organizational rewards, such as pay increases and promotions, are the reinforcers. A fixed-interval system is the best way to administer these rewards.

In summary, relying on any given schedule for all rewards is difficult or impractical. Instead, the manager should use the schedule best suited to the reinforcement being used and try to link outcomes with behaviors according to the needs of the organization and its employees. The *Global Perspective* describes how different types and schedules of reinforcement are altering the way Japanese employees see their jobs.

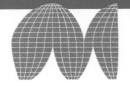
New Forms of Reinforcement in Japan

Traditionally, the Japanese worker went to work for a big company and remained loyal and dedicated to that firm for his or her entire career. Japanese firms require that their employees work long hours, but provide partial compensation for this by offering reasonably strong job security.

But in recent years things have begun to change. Some Japanese workers are rejecting the traditional employment model and instead are opting for part-time or temporary work. Many of them find that although they make less money under this arrangement, they are happier and more fulfilled with their lives. This allows them to avoid what they perceive to be the drudgery and routine of traditional forms of work.

Japanese firms are also benefitting from this trend. As in the United States, many Japanese firms have needed to cut their workforces in recent years. Part-time and temporary workers have given these firms the flexibility to add workers when demand is high without staffing positions with permanent workers.

But in a society that values group harmony above individual achievement, the potential exists for labor problems in the future. Permanent workers, for example, are rewarded for long-term commitment and service, perform a wide array of functions (some of them almost trivial), and expect nothing special in return (other than salary and security). But part-time and temporary workers are more motivated by immediate gratification, are more likely to do only what their job description entails, and expect specific and prompt recognition and reward for their efforts.

SOURCES: "Japanese Workers Aren't All Workaholics," *Wall Street Journal*, May 8, 1989, p. A10; "Farewell Japanese Fast Track," *Business Week*, December 10, 1990, pp. 192–200; and "Just as U.S. Firms Try Japanese Management, Honda Is Centralizing," *Wall Street Journal*, April 11, 1990, pp. A1, A10.

Related Aspects of Learning in Organizations

Several additional aspects of learning affect on individual behavior in organizations. Among them are stimulus generalization, stimulus discrimination, the arguments for and against punishment, and other managerial implications of learning.

Stimulus Generalization

Stimulus generalization is the process of recognizing the same or similar stimuli in different settings.

Stimulus generalization refers to how people recognize the same or similar stimuli in different settings.[15] In other words, it is the process by which they can generalize a contingent reinforcement from one setting to another. Figure 6.4 illustrates a simple example of the process. After an initial stimulus-response-consequence sequence, a person learns the behaviors likely to produce some kind of reinforcement. Later, when presented with a similar stimulus in different surroundings, he or she knows that the same response is likely to elicit a similar consequence.

Consider a plant manager for General Electric who has a history of effective troubleshooting. Over the years he has been assigned to several plants, each with a

15. W. R. Nord, "Beyond the Teaching Machine: The Neglected Area of Operant Conditioning in the Theory and Practice of Management," *Organizational Behavior and Human Performance*, Vol. 4, 1969, pp. 375–401.

FIGURE 6.4

**Stimulus Generalization
and Discrimination**

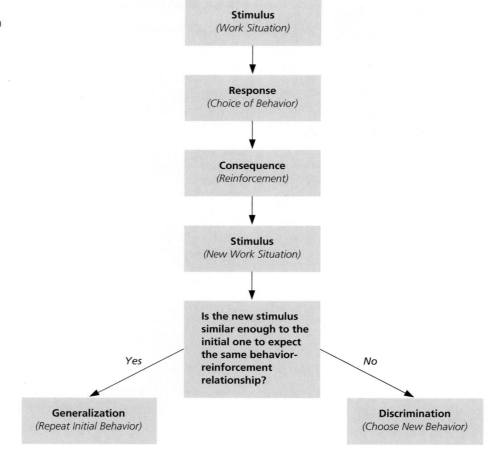

serious operating problem. After successfully addressing the difficulties, he has always received an extended vacation, a bonus, and a boost in his base salary. He has learned the basic contingencies, or requirements, of reinforcement for his job: the stimulus is the assignment, the response is correcting problems, and the consequences are several positive reinforcers. When the manager gets his next assignment, he probably will generalize from his past experiences. Even though he will be in a different plant with different problems and employees, he will know what is expected of him and understand what it takes to be rewarded.

Stimulus Discrimination

Stimulus discrimination is the process of recognizing differences among stimuli.

Stimulus discrimination is the ability to recognize differences among stimuli.[16] This process is also shown in Figure 6.4. As in stimulus generalization, the person learns the basic stimulus-response-consequence sequence for one stimulus. When

16. Ibid.

confronted with a new stimulus, however, he or she can discriminate between the two stimuli and respond differently.

Suppose that the troubleshooting plant manager is assigned to a plant that is running smoothly. His routine response to new situations has always been to identify and solve problems, but he now must discriminate between his new situation and his earlier ones. He then will also recognize that he needs a different set of behaviors, or responses, to meet performance expectations and receive positive reinforcement.

Punishment

Earlier we defined punishment as an unpleasant, or aversive, consequence after an individual engages in undesirable behavior. Thus, any unpleasant consequence that follows behavior can be called punishment.[17] A punishment that is structured, official, and organizationally sanctioned is called discipline. When a boss yells at an employee who has dropped a bottle of solvent, punishment has taken place. If the boss formally reprimands the worker and puts a written account of the reprimand in the employee's personnel folder, this action represents an attempt at discipline. To be effective, discipline must be perceived as punishing, but in fact it may not always be seen as such. For example, a subordinate planning to quit in the near future might find the supervisor's written reprimand amusing.

Although punishment is common in organizations, many managers and researchers question its practical value for influencing employee behavior. They argue that punishment cannot be effective unless employee behavior is continually observed. Punishment is likely to only suppress behavior temporarily rather than permanently extinguish it, and the side effects of punishment, such as hostility and anger, may outweigh any potential benefits. Furthermore, undesirable behavior often can be changed through extinction or environmental engineering. For example, if two employees who frequently must interact are constantly arguing with each other, stopping the bickering may be possible without punishing. The manager might alter their environment by having them deal with each other through a neutral third party.

In some situations, however, punishment may be an appropriate tool for altering behavior. Many of life's unpleasantries teach us what to do by means of punishment. Falling off a bike, drinking too much, or going out in the rain without an umbrella all lead to punishing consequences (getting bruised, suffering a hangover, and getting wet), and we often learn to change our behavior as a result. Furthermore, certain types of undesirable behavior may have far-reaching negative effects if they go unpunished. For instance, an employee who sexually harasses a coworker, a clerk who steals money from the petty-cash account, and an executive who engages in illegal stock transactions all deserve punishment.

When punishment is needed, how is it most effectively meted out and how can its negative consequences be reduced? First, punishment should be applied before the undesirable behavior has been strongly reinforced. Thus, punishment should work better the second time an employee is late rather than the tenth time. Second the punishment should immediately follow the undesirable behavior to emphasize the connection between the behavior and the consequence in the person's mind. Third, punishment should focus on the behavior, not on the person; thus, it

17. See Richard Arvey and John M. Ivancevich, "Punishment in Organizations: A Review, Propositions, and Research Suggestions," *Academy of Management Review*, April 1980, pp. 123–132 for a review of the literature on punishment.

should be impersonal, consistent across time, and impartial. Finally, the punishment should have as much informational value as possible. The employee should know exactly what he or she did to warrant the punishment, the reason why punishment follows such an action, and the consequences of repeating the behavior.

Managerial Implications of Learning

Learning is closely related to employee training and performance evaluation and rewards.

Learning also carries with it a number of other managerial implications as well. Chief among these are training and performance evaluation and rewards.

Learning and Training   Learning is the major goal of employee training. Many organizations devote vast resources to training and development to expand the skills and abilities of their employees. Andrew Grove, president of Intel Corp., heartily believes in the importance of employee training. Intel's employees spend from 2 to 4 percent of their time in the classroom. Much of this training, handled by Intel's own managers, focuses on how employees can benefit the organization while enhancing their own rewards.[18] Likewise, Motorola currently spends more than $120 million a year on employee training.[19] *The Ethical Dilemma* discusses some of the issues and controversies associated with ethics training.

Learning and Performance Evaluation and Rewards   Learning also ties in with organizational practices in the performance evaluation and reward system. Performance evaluation refers to how managers assess the work behavior of individuals and groups; rewards are the positive reinforcements (salary, promotion, public recognition) companies give for desirable behavior.[20] We discuss performance evaluation and rewards in Chapter 8.

Other Implications   In addition to motivation, performance evaluation and rewards, and training, still other implications can be drawn from learning theory. First, learning theory can explain certain forms of managerial behavior toward subordinates. Suppose that a manager always delivers bad news to subordinates in a certain way. If the subordinates receive the news graciously and constructively, they are giving the manager positive reinforcement. Thus, the manager probably will use the same mode of delivery in the future. Second, many aspects of the learning process underscore the manager's role as a teacher and the subordinate's role as a learner. Finally, learning processes clearly influence the day-to-day interactions, both official and casual, among people in organizations. Almost everything we do in response to others, for example, has reinforcing consequences for them.

Organizational Behavior Modification

As already noted, learning theory has considerable relevance to managers and to organizations in many different areas. Another major organizational application of

---

18. Andrew S. Grove, "Why Training Is the Boss's Job," *Fortune*, January 23, 1984, pp. 93–96.
19. Ronald Henkoff, "Companies That Train Best," *Fortune*, March 22, 1993, pp. 62–75.
20. See Gary P. Latham, "Job Performance and Appraisal," in Cary Cooper and Ivan Robertson (Eds.), *International Review of Industrial and Organizational Psychology*, Vol. 1 (London: Wiley, 1986), pp. 117–0156, for a recent review.

Can Ethics Be Taught?

Training a secretary to use new word processing software is relatively simple. Similarly, teaching a machinist to operate a new piece of equipment is straightforward. But how do you teach ethics? This is a problem with which many universities and businesses in the United States are grappling.

For example, a few years ago a former Harvard student led a campaign to raise $30 million for the Harvard Business School. The gift was dedicated to teaching ethics. Professors and administrators viewed this gift as a mixed blessing—having extra resources was nice, but could ethics really be taught?

Although no one really knows how effectively the Harvard program is working, ethics has become an integral part of its business curriculum. Among the initiatives are the following: (1) all MBA students at Harvard take a nine-session non-credit course on ethics, (2) faculty are encouraged to integrate ethical issues into their courses, (3) the school offers three different ethics electives, and (4) all students write an essay about how they dealt with an ethical issue or problem.

Businesses are also doing many different things in an effort to teach their employees to behave more ethically. Codes of conduct are now common, for instance, and most management development programs have at least one module devoted to ethics. Some firms, like Mobil and Monsanto, have required that all managers undergo ethics training.

Still, many skeptics remain unconvinced. A frequent criticism levied at ethics courses and programs is that ethics reflect individual values and cannot really be taught. They also charge that little is done to evaluate the effectiveness of ethics instruction. On the other hand, advocates argue that training can help sensitize people to better recognize ethical situations and provide at least some guidance in how to deal with those situations.

SOURCES: "Can Ethics Be Taught? Harvard Gives It the Old College Try," *Business Week*, April 6, 1992, p. 34; and Kenneth Labich, "The New Crisis in Business Ethics," *Fortune*, April 20, 1992, pp. 167–176.

learning theory is organizational behavior modification (OB Mod.). OB Mod. represents a major motivational theory that guides managers in their application of reinforcement theory to guide the behaviors of subordinates.

Behavior Modification in Organizations

Organizational behavior modification, or **OB Mod.**, is the application of reinforcement theory to organizational settings.

Organizational behavior modification, or **OB Mod.**, is the application of reinforcement theory to people in organizational settings.[21] As we saw earlier, reinforcement theory suggests that we can increase the frequency of desirable behaviors by linking those behaviors with positive consequences and decrease undesirable behaviors by linking them with negative consequences. OB Mod. characteristically uses positive reinforcement to encourage desirable behaviors in employees. Figure 6.5 illustrates the basic steps in OB Mod.

21. Fred Luthans and Robert Kreitner, *Organizational Behavior Modification* (Glenview, Ill.: Scott, Foresman, 1975); and Luthans and Kreitner, *Organizational Behavior Modification and Beyond*.

FIGURE 6.5

Steps in Organizational Behavior Modification

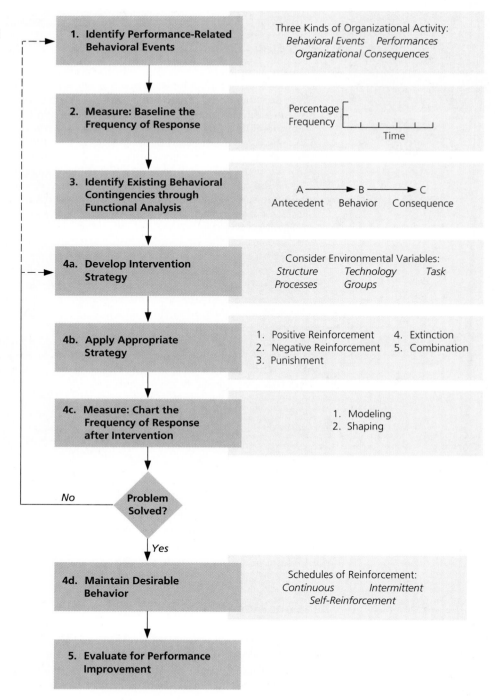

1. **Identify Performance-Related Behavioral Events**

   Three Kinds of Organizational Activity:
   Behavioral Events   Performances
   Organizational Consequences

2. **Measure: Baseline the Frequency of Response**

   Percentage Frequency
   Time

3. **Identify Existing Behavioral Contingencies through Functional Analysis**

   A ⟶ B ⟶ C
   Antecedent   Behavior   Consequence

4a. **Develop Intervention Strategy**

   Consider Environmental Variables:
   Structure   Technology   Task
   Processes   Groups

4b. **Apply Appropriate Strategy**

   1. Positive Reinforcement   4. Extinction
   2. Negative Reinforcement   5. Combination
   3. Punishment

4c. **Measure: Chart the Frequency of Response after Intervention**

   1. Modeling
   2. Shaping

Problem Solved?

No / Yes

4d. **Maintain Desirable Behavior**

   Schedules of Reinforcement:
   Continuous   Intermittent
   Self-Reinforcement

5. **Evaluate for Performance Improvement**

SOURCE: Reprinted, by permission of the publisher, from *Personnel*, July–August 1974. © 1974. American Management Association, New York. All rights reserved.

The first step is to identify performance-related behavioral events; that is, desirable and undesirable behaviors. For example, a manager of an electronics store might decide that the most important behavior for salespeople working on commission is to greet customers warmly and show them the exact merchandise they came in to see. Note in Figure 6.5 that three kinds of organizational activity are associated with this behavior: the behavioral event itself, the performance that results, and the organizational consequences that befall the individual.

Next, the manager measures baseline performance—the existing level of performance for each individual. This usually is stated in terms of a percentage frequency across different time intervals. For example, the electronics store manager may observe that a particular salesperson currently is greeting around 40 percent of the customers each day as desired.

The third step is to identify the existing behavioral contingencies, or consequences, of performance; that is, what happens now to employees who perform at various levels? If an employee works hard, does he or she get a reward or just get tired? For example, the electronics store manager may observe that when customers are greeted warmly and assisted competently, they buy something 40 percent of the time, whereas customers who are not properly greeted and assisted make a purchase only 20 percent of the time. Thus, the salesperson earns both gratification from the sales and higher commissions.

At this point, the manager develops and applies an appropriate intervention strategy. In other words, some contextual or environmental variable that may affect the performance-reward linkage—structure, process, technology, groups, or the task—is changed with the goal of making high-level performance more rewarding. Various kinds of positive reinforcement are used to guide employee behavior in desired directions. The electronics store manager might offer a sales commission plan whereby salespeople earn a percentage of the dollar amount taken in by each sale. The manager might also compliment salespeople who give appropriate greetings and ignore those who do not. The reinforcement helps shape the behavior of salespeople. In addition, an individual salesperson who does not get reinforced may model the behavior of more successful salespersons.

After the intervention step, the manager again measures performance to determine whether the desired effect has been achieved. If not, the manager must redesign the intervention strategy or repeat the entire process. For instance, if the salespeople in the electronics store are still not greeting customers properly, the manager may need to look for other forms of positive reinforcement—perhaps a higher-percentage commission.

If performance has increased, the manager must try to maintain the desirable behavior through some schedule of positive reinforcement. For example, higher commissions might be granted for every other sale or for sales over a certain dollar amount. (As we saw earlier, a reinforcement schedule defines the interval at which reinforcement will be given.)

Finally, the manager looks for improvements in individual employees' behavior. Here the emphasis is on offering meaningful longer-term rewards, such as promotions and salary adjustments, to sustain ongoing efforts to improve performance.[22]

---

22. Luthans and Kreitner, *Organizational Behavior Modification and Beyond.*

The Effectiveness of OB Mod.

Unlike expectancy theory, OB Mod. is relatively simple. As a result, it has been used by many types of organizations, with varying levels of success.[23] A program at Emery Air Freight prompted much of the initial enthusiasm for OB Mod., and other success stories also have caught the attention of practicing managers.[24] For example, B. F. Goodrich increased productivity more than 300 percent and Weyerhaeuser increased productivity by at least 8 percent in three different work groups.[25] These results suggest that OB Mod. is a valuable method for improving employee motivation in many situations.

OB Mod. also has certain drawbacks. First, not all applications have worked. For example, a program at Standard Oil of Ohio was discontinued because it failed to meet its objectives; another program at Michigan Bell was only modestly successful. Further, managers frequently have only limited means for providing meaningful reinforcement for their employees. In addition, some have argued that OB Mod. is manipulative because it tries to suppress individual freedom of behavioral choice. Much of the research testing OB Mod. has gone on in laboratories and thus is hard to generalize to the real world. And even if OB Mod. works for awhile, the impact of the positive reinforcement may wane once the novelty has worn off, and employees may come to view it as a routine part of the compensation system.[26]

The Ethics of OB Mod.

Although OB Mod. has considerable potential for enhancing motivated behavior in organizations, it is not without its critics. One major concern that some observers have raised about OB Mod. relates to ethical issues that surround its use. The primary ethical argument against OB Mod. is that its use has the potential to compromise individual freedom of choice. Managers may tend to select reinforcement contingencies that have advantages for the organization, with little or no regard for what is best for the individual employee. Thus, workers may be rewarded for working hard, producing high-quality products, and so forth. But behaviors promoting their personal growth and development or the reduction of their personal experienced levels of stress may go unrewarded.

An element of manipulation is also involved in OB Mod. Indeed, its very purpose is to shape the behaviors of others. Thus, rather than giving employees an array of behaviors from which to choose, managers may instead continually funnel employee efforts through an increasingly narrow array of behavioral options such that they eventually have little choice but to select the limited set of behaviors approved of by managers.

These ethical issues are, of course, real concerns that should not be ignored. At the same time, other methods and approaches used by managers may have the same goals of shaping the behavior of others. Thus, OB Mod. is not really unique

23. W. Clay Hamner and Ellen P. Hamner, "Organizational Behavior Modification on the Bottom Line," *Organizational Dynamics*, Spring 1976, pp. 3–21.
24. "At Emery Air Freight: Positive Reinforcement Boosts Performance," *Organizational Dynamics*, Winter 1973, pp. 41–50; and Hamner and Hamner, "Organizational Behavior Modification on the Bottom Line."
25. Hamner and Hamner, "Organizational Behavior Modification on the Bottom Line."
26. Edwin Locke, "The Myths of Behavior Mod in Organizations," *Academy of Management Review*, Vol. 2, 1977, pp. 543–553.

in its potential for misuse or misrepresentation. Importantly, managers must recognize and not abuse their ability to alter subordinate behavior and employees must maintain control of their own work environment to the point where they are fully cognizant of the behavioral choices they are making.

Social Learning in Organizations

Social learning occurs when people observe the behaviors of others, recognize its consequences, and alter their own behavior as a result.

In recent years, managers and researchers have also begun to recognize the power of social learning.[27] **Social learning** occurs when people observe the behaviors of others, recognize its consequences, and alter their own behavior as a result.[28] For example, a person can learn to do a new job by observing others or by watching videotapes. And recall the earlier example in which an employee learned to avoid being late by seeing the boss reprimand fellow workers. Each of these examples is a form of social learning. Thus, social learning theory suggests that individual behavior is determined by a person's cognitions and social environment.[29] More specifically, people are presumed to learn behaviors and attitudes at least partly in response to what others expect of them.

Several conditions must be met to produce an appropriate environment for social learning. First, the behavior being observed and imitated must be relatively simple. Although we can learn to push three or four buttons to set specifications on a machine or to turn on a computer by watching someone else, we probably cannot learn a complicated sequence of operations for the machine or how to run software on the computer without also practicing the various steps ourselves.

Second, social learning usually involves observed and imitated behavior that is concrete, not intellectual. We can learn by watching others how to respond to the different behaviors of a particular manager or how to assemble a few component parts into a final assembled product. But we probably cannot learn through simple observation how to write computer software, how to write complicated text, how to conceptualize, or how to think abstractly.

Finally, for social learning to occur we must possess the physical ability needed to imitate the behavior that we observe. Most of us can watch televised baseball games or tennis matches every weekend but still cannot hit a curve ball like Barry Bonds or execute a backhand like Steffi Graf.

Social learning affects organizational behavior in a variety of ways.[30] Indeed, many of the behaviors we exhibit in our daily work lives are learned from others. Suppose that a new employee joins an existing work group. She already has some basis for knowing how to behave (i.e., education and previous experience). The group provides a set of very specific cues, however, that help the employee see how she needs to tailor her behavior to fit the specific situation she is now in. The group may indicate how the organization expects its members to dress, how people are "supposed" to feel about the boss, and so forth. Hence, the employee

27. Robert Wood and Albert Bandura, "Social Cognitive Theory of Organizational Management," *Academy of Management Review*, Vol. 13, 1989, pp. 361–384.
28. H. M. Weiss, "Subordinate Imitation of Supervisory Behavior: The Role of Modeling in Organizational Socialization," *Organizational Behavior and Human Performance*, Vol. 19, 1977, pp. 89–105.
29. Albert Bandura, *Principles of Behavior Modification* (New York: Holt, 1969). See also Henry P. Sims, Jr., and Dennis Gioia, *The Thinking Organization* (San Francisco: Jossey-Bass, 1986).
30. For an interesting example, see Robert F. Morrison and Thomas M. Brantner, "What Enhances or Inhibits Learning a New Job? A Basic Career Issue," *Journal of Applied Psychology*, Vol. 77, pp. 926–940.

learns how to behave in the new situation partly in response to what she already knows and partly in response to what others suggest and demonstrate.

Summary of Key Points

- Learning represents the third part of the motivational cycle for employees in organizations. Their needs stimulate them to select various behaviors to achieve need satisfaction. A variety of motivational processes determine how they go about trying to satisfy those needs. Learning provides the consequences of those choices and shapes the behaviors they will select in the future.
- Learning is a relatively permanent change in behavior or behavioral potential that results from direct or indirect experience. The traditional view of learning, classical conditioning, focuses on conditioned and unconditioned stimuli and responses. The contemporary view, however, suggests that learning is a cognitive process involving individual choice.
- Reinforcement theory is the learning perspective most relevant to managers and organizations. The basic types of reinforcement are positive reinforcement, avoidance, extinction, and punishment. Schedules of reinforcement include continuous, fixed-interval, variable-interval, fixed-ratio, and variable-ratio.
- Important related aspects of learning in organizations include stimulus generalization (seeing the similarities in reinforcement contingencies in different settings), stimulus discrimination (seeing the differences in reinforcement contingencies in different situations), and punishment. Learning also has implications for training, performance evaluation and rewards, and other areas.
- Organizational behavior modification, or OB Mod., is the application of reinforcement principles and concepts to organizational settings. Using a variety of reinforcers and reinforcement contingencies, several organizations have achieved impressive motivational improvements through OB Mod. Managers should also be aware of ethical concerns about OB Mod.
- Social learning occurs when people observe the behaviors of others, recognize its consequences, and alter their own behavior as a result. Social learning is increasingly being seen as an important component of organizational behavior.

Discussion Questions

1. Describe how the need-based perspectives (Chapter 4), the process-based perspectives (Chapter 5), and the learning-based perspectives (Chapter 6) work together to explain employee motivation at work.
2. Identify five things you have truly learned recently. How have these things changed your behavior?
3. Have you ever experienced classical conditioning? If so, what were the circumstances?
4. Think of occasions on which you experienced each of the four types of reinforcement.
5. Identify the five types of reinforcement that you receive most often. On what schedule is each made available to you?

6. Think of times when you have experienced stimulus generalization and discrimination. What were the circumstances for each?
7. What are your personal views of punishment? How do your views differ from those presented in this chapter?
8. The OB Mod. theory of motivation seems more application based than the equity or expectancy theories. It is also rather narrow in scope. What are the advantages and disadvantages of a theory that has these characteristics?
9. What are some ways your instructor might use OB Mod. in the classroom to shape your behavior? Are there ways you can shape your instructor's behavior with some of the same techniques?
10. Have you ever experienced social learning? What were the circumstances?

EXPERIENTIAL EXERCISE

Purpose   This exercise will give you insights into the problems and mechanisms of providing reinforcement to people in organizations.

Format   Your instructor will divide the class into groups of three. Each group will develop a reinforcement system that the instructor might use to reinforce student behavior in the classroom.

Procedure   First, working with your teammates, develop a list of desirable and undesirable behaviors that students might potentially exhibit in the classroom. For example, responding to questions from the instructor might be a desirable behavior, and whispering to one's neighbor while the instructor is talking might be an undesirable behavior.

Next, identify various kinds of reinforcement that your instructor might use to increase the frequency of the desirable behaviors and decrease the occurrence of the undesirable behaviors. Most of these should be rewards (i.e., positive reinforcement), but a few might also rely on avoidance, punishment, or extinction.

Next, develop appropriate schedules for the various kinds of reinforcement. Your instructor will then select a few groups at random to present their systems to the rest of the class. (A variation might have a member from a group role-play the instructor using the reinforcement system developed by his or her group.)

Follow-up Questions

1. How useful do you think your system would actually be if your instructor used it?
2. How much easier or more difficult would it be to do the same exercise in a work setting?

Du Pont is the largest chemical producer in the United States. In reality, though, the firm is much more than just a chemical operation. Its five core business groups include fibers, polymers, resins, petroleum, and a set of diversified businesses ranging from electronics to sporting goods. Among its more well-known brand names are Conoco, Dacron, Lucite, Lycra, Mylar, Remington, and Teflon.

Like all businesses, Du Pont is always looking for new ways to become more efficient, more productive, and thus more profitable. A few years ago the firm implemented a dramatically different type of reward system in one of its business groups, the fibers business. The aim of the new system was to more directly connect actual performance on the job with subsequent rewards. That is, Du Pont wanted to use positive reinforcement to promote higher productivity.

Whereas most executive salaries include a base pay component with additional bonus incentives, Du Pont's plan included every employee in the fibers group. The plan was to be phased in over five years. At the end of that five-year period, fibers group employees were to be at a salary level 6 percent below that of their colleagues in other Du Pont businesses.

But the fibers group employees would have opportunities to make up the difference through bonuses tied to group performance. In addition, they could actually earn more than their counterparts in other Du Pont business groups by exceeding their group performance goals.

The plan began with management's setting an annual business profitability goal. If the fibers group earned profits of less than 80 percent of its goal, no employees in the group would earn a bonus. That is, each would receive normal compensation (set 6 percent below that of other Du Pont employees), but nothing more.

On the other hand, if 80 percent of the goal was achieved, all employees would receive a 3 percent bonus. As actual profits came closer to reaching the goal, bonuses also increased as well. If the goal was precisely met, all employees would get a 6 percent bonus, putting them on equal footing with all other Du Pont workers.

But as actual profits began to exceed profit goals, bonuses would also go up beyond the 6 percent level

as well. The upper level was set at an actual profit level of 150 percent of the profit goal. At this level of performance, each member of the group would receive a bonus of 18 percent, putting her or his income 12 percent above that of comparable Du Pont employees in other business groups.

Managers were optimistic that this plan would enhance motivation among all fibers group employees as well as allow the organization to maintain flexibility in its reward system. Because base salaries would drop 6 percent, the firm would save $36 million per year. If profits were lower than expected, these cost savings could help cushion the blow. But if profits were strong, the firm could afford the extra expense while sharing some of its bounty with its employees.

Unfortunately, things did not work out as Du Pont had hoped. At first, everyone was enthusiastic about the plan. The firm reported that many employees were aggressively looking for ways to cut costs, boost output, and help the firm be more profitable. One manager noted that his secretary had started routing him through smaller airports to save on travel costs. Another indicated that mailroom employees questioned the necessity for a large (and costly) mailing that the firm was doing.

But two years after the plan went into effect, it was dropped. The reason? In the first year the group had made its profit goal and everyone received a bonus. But in year two it became apparent that the fibers group would fall far short of its profit goal. As employees began to assess how this was going to affect their total compensation, reality set in and they started to revolt.

At first, Du Pont decided to give each employee the option of staying with the program or moving back to the traditional reward system. Managers quickly realized, however, that most people were opting out of the program altogether. They then decided to just scrap the whole thing and re-adopt their original conventional system.

Case Questions

1. Why do you think Du Pont's positive reinforcement plan didn't work?

2. Could the system have been better designed so as to achieve the results Du Pont wanted?

3. What other forms of positive reinforcement might have worked with Du Pont's system?

SOURCES: Gary Hoover, Alta Campbell, and Patrick J. Spain (Eds.), *Hoover's Handbook of American Business 1993* (Austin, Tex.: The Reference Press, 1992), p. 259; "Du Pont Will Start Pay-Incentive Plan for All Fibers Business Workers in '89," *Wall Street Journal*, October 6, 1988, p. A4; and "Paying Workers to Meet Goals Spreads but Gauging Performance Proves Tough," *Wall Street Journal*, September 10, 1991, pp. B1, B8.

C A S E 6 . 2	**A Tale of Two Factories**

Stuart and Sheila Youngblood are twins. All their lives they have tried to maintain their own individuality. For example, they rebelled against dressing alike when they were young and intentionally pursued different interests as they were growing up. Later, they purposefully chose to attend different colleges—and even adopted different majors.

But each is struck by how similar their careers have turned out to be. Stuart went to work for a medium-size manufacturing firm after graduation and today is a plant manager for the company's largest production facility. Sheila went to graduate school and worked for a big international firm for awhile. But recently she accepted an offer to manage a plant for a growing Midwest manufacturing concern. The plants that Stuart and Sheila manage are both nonunionized, employ about the same number of people, use similar technology, and are located only about twenty miles apart.

During a recent Thanksgiving holiday family celebration at their parents' home, the Youngbloods talked about this coincidence and compared notes on their respective problems and opportunities. Each is facing some of the same problems, but each has elected to pursue different methods of solving them.

Stuart's plant has been facing problems of declining productivity and increased absenteeism and turnover. His boss has told him that he had complete freedom to do whatever he wanted to solve the problems. After consulting with his top human resource manager, Stuart has decided to implement an incentive program. His program has three components.

First, he is implementing a plant-wide reward system designed to boost productivity. For each 1 percent increase in total plant productivity (increased output per unit of input, decreased input per unit of output, or some combination of the two), he is paying back one-third of the dollar value of the increase into an employee bonus pool. At the end of the year this pool will be divided evenly among all operating employees in the plant.

The second part of his program focuses on absenteeism. Most people who are absent call in sick (each worker gets twelve sick days per year). Stuart has installed a plan whereby workers get paid time-and-a-half for all their unused sick days at the end of the year. He has also implemented a weekly attendance-incentive program. Every day each worker gets to draw a playing card from a large deck. At the end of the week, the person with the best poker hand gets an extra hour off for lunch (but you must have five cards to play!).

Finally, he has also implemented a program intended to lower turnover. Each worker in the plant now receives a seniority bonus at the end of the year. The longer a person stays with the company, the larger his or her end-of-the-year bonus. Moreover, any employee who leaves before the end of the year forfeits that year's bonus altogether.

Sheila listened intently while Stuart explained his plan. Her plant was experiencing some of the same problems. The plant's productivity, while not great, was no worse than at other plants the company owned. But employee tardiness, absenteeism, and turnover were major problems. Indeed, Sheila had been hired specifically because upper management thought she could provide some solutions.

Sheila had decided to implement harsh measures. First, she was implementing new controls for ensuring that people were at work on time. In the past, any worker could have a friend or coworker punch his or her time card. Under Sheila's system, though, employees had to punch their own time card and then turn it in to a supervisor.

Any time an employee was late for work, a note was placed in that person's personnel file. Three late reports within six months were now grounds for dismissal. There also was a new mandate that if you were too sick to work, then you were sick enough to need to see a doctor. Thus, employees who were sick are now required to bring a note from their doctor verifying their illness and validating their absence from work.

Although Sheila felt confident that these measures would cut tardiness and absenteeism, she was less sure of how to tackle turnover. She had briefly thought about announcing that anyone caught looking for another job would be immediately terminated. On reflection, however, she had decided that this was impractical and too costly to enforce. She listened with interest to Stuart's description of his program, but did not believe that it would work in her plant. Nevertheless, Stuart and Sheila resolved to keep each other informed as to how well their respective plans were working.

Case Questions

1. Analyze Stuart and Sheila's programs from the standpoint of reinforcement theory. What are the advantages and disadvantages of each program?
2. Which plan do you think will prove to be most effective? Why?

CHAPTER 7

Designing Jobs for Individuals and Teams

OBJECTIVES

After studying this chapter, you should be able to:

Summarize the historical development of job design and evaluate early approaches to job design.

Discuss and evaluate the job characteristics approach to job design.

Summarize the role of social information in job design.

Describe how jobs can be designed for teams.

Discuss work teams in organizations.

Identify and summarize related aspects of job design.

By making the jobs its employees perform more efficient, GTE has been able to cut its costs and raise its revenues.

GTE Corporation has been going through a major overhaul of all its business operations. As a starting point, the firm looked at ways to make single jobs that its workers perform more efficient and productive. Consider, for example, how GTE changed the jobs of its repair clerks.

Before the changes, repair clerks took calls about repair service that customers needed. The details were written down and passed to a technician who tested lines and switches until the problem was identified and corrected. On rare occasions—about one-half of 1 percent of the time—repairs could actually be made while the customer was still on the line. The primary performance criterion for repair clerks was how fast they took calls.

GTE decided that it wanted more problems solved while the customer was on the line. Managers believed that this would improve both service quality and efficiency. The first step was to move basic testing and switching equipment to the desks of the repair clerks. The job title of the clerks was changed to "front-end technician," and each one received training in how to perform testing that would solve many basic problems.

Performance measures were also changed. Instead of focusing on how fast calls were taken, GTE now concentrates on the number of problems that are solved by the front-end technicians without having to be passed on to others. So far, under the new system around 30 percent of all problems are being solved by the front-end technicians while the customer is on the line. GTE's goal is for this level to eventually exceed 70 percent.

Similar changes are being made in other jobs as well. By linking sales and billing with repair services, for example, GTE has boosted productivity in one department by more than 20 percent. Although GTE is still several years away from completing its overhaul, virtually all of its initial efforts have paid off handsomely. Indeed, the firm hopes to cut its total costs by 10 percent while simultaneously increasing its revenues by 15 percent—all by changing the way its employees perform their jobs.[1]

G TE has rediscovered a basic challenge of management that deals with the way people work. One of the fundamental elements of managing an organization is structuring jobs for people to perform. The key to success is to create jobs that optimize the organization's needs for productivity and efficiency while simultaneously motivating and satisfying the employees who perform those jobs. As people and organizations change, and as we continue to learn more about management, it is important to occasionally look back at those jobs and make whatever changes might be necessary to improve them.[2]

1. Thomas A. Stewart, "Reengineering: The Hot New Managing Tool," *Fortune*, August 23, 1993, pp. 40–48; and Walter Kiechel III, "How We Will Work in the Year 2000," *Fortune*, May 17, 1993, pp. 38–52.
2. Ricky W. Griffin and Gary C. McMahan, "Motivation Through Job Design," in Jerald Greenberg (Ed.), *Organizational Behavior: State of the Science* (New York: Lawrence Erlbaum and Associates, 1994).

This chapter is about how people see and respond to their jobs. It also addresses how managers can deal with these perceptions and responses for the benefit of both the organization and the employees. We start with a discussion of historical approaches to job design. Then we discuss a major perspective on job design, the job characteristics approach. Next, we describe how social information affects job design. We also examine how jobs can be designed for teams and look at the use of work teams in organizations. Then we identify related perspectives on job design.

Historical Approaches to Job Design

Job design evolved first toward greater specialization and more recently away from extreme levels of specialization.

To understand job design, we must first trace how approaches to work have evolved. At first, the trend was toward increasing specialization and standardization of jobs. Eventually, however, this trend slowed and reversed. In this section, we examine the reasons for this developmental pattern and the dominant approaches to job design that emerged along the way.

The Evolution of Job Design

Although formal theories of job design are a fairly recent development, the actual need to design work has a long history. The construction of the pyramids in ancient Egypt, for example, was founded on job specialization: grouping jobs together by function. The ancient Romans devoted much attention to designing jobs in the production sector.

More recently, in the mid-1800s (the general craft stage), many families made and produced all the things they needed, including food. General craft jobs came about as individuals ceased or reduced their own food production, invested their labor in the production of other necessities such as clothing and furniture, and traded or bartered these items for food and goods. Over time, people's work became increasingly specialized. For example, the general craft of clothing production splintered into specialized craft jobs such as weaving, tailoring, and sewing. This evolution toward specialization accelerated as the Industrial Revolution swept Europe in the 1700s and 1800s and followed in similar form in the United States in the later 1800s.

Eventually, the trend toward specialization became a subject of formal study. The two most influential students of specialization were Adam Smith and Charles Babbage. Smith, an eighteenth-century Scottish economist, originated the phrase *division of labor* in his classic book *An Inquiry into the Nature and Causes of the Wealth of Nations*, published in 1776.[3] The book tells the story of a group of pin makers who specialized their jobs so that they could produce many more pins per person in a day than each could have made by working alone. In Smith's time, pin making, like most other production work, was still an individual job. One person would perform all tasks: drawing out a strip of wire, clipping it to the proper length, sharpening one end, attaching a head to the other end, and polishing the

3. Adam Smith, *An Inquiry into the Nature and Causes of the Wealth of Nations* (New York: Modern Library, 1937). Originally published in 1776.

finished pin. With specialization, one person did nothing but draw out wire, another did the clipping, and so on. Smith attributed the dramatic increases in output to factors such as increased dexterity owing to practice, decreased time changing from one production operation to another, and the development of specialized equipment and machinery. The basic principles described in *The Wealth of Nations* provided the foundation for the assembly line.

Charles Babbage wrote *On the Economy of Machinery and Manufactures* in 1832.[4] Extending Smith's work, Babbage cited several additional advantages of job specialization: relatively little time was needed to learn specialized jobs, waste decreased, workers needed to make fewer tool and equipment changes, and workers' skills improved through frequent repetition of tasks.

As the Industrial Revolution spread to the United States, job specialization proliferated throughout industry. Although it began in the mid-1880s, job specialization reached its peak with the development of scientific management in the early 1900s.

Job Specialization

Job specialization, as advocated by scientific management, involves studying jobs, breaking them down into small component parts, and standardizing how they should be performed.

The chief proponent of **job specialization**, Frederick W. Taylor, argued that jobs should be scientifically studied, broken down into their smallest component tasks, and then standardized across all workers doing the jobs.[5] (Recall our discussion of scientific management in Chapter 1.) Taylor's view was consistent with the premises of the division of labor as discussed by Smith and Babbage. In practice, job specialization generally brought most, if not all, of the advantages its advocates claimed. Specialization paved the way for large-scale assembly lines and was at least partly responsible for the dramatic gains in output U.S. industry achieved for several decades after the turn of the century.

Job specialization can also promote monotony and boredom.

On the surface, job specialization appears to be a rational and apparently efficient way to structure jobs. In practice, however, it can cause problems for the people who perform those jobs. Foremost among the problems is the extreme monotony of highly specialized tasks. Consider the job of assembling toasters. A person who does the entire assembly may find the job complex and challenging, but such a process may also be inefficient. If the job is specialized so that the worker simply inserts a heating coil into the toaster as it passes along on an assembly line, the process may be efficient, but it is unlikely to interest or challenge the worker. A worker numbed by boredom and monotony may be less motivated to work hard and more inclined to do poor quality work or to complain about the job. For these reasons, managers began to search for job design alternatives to specialization. One of the primary catalysts for this search was a famous study of jobs in the automobile industry.

In 1952, Walker and Guest published a study of Detroit automobile workers.[6] The purpose of the study was to assess how satisfied the workers were with various aspects of their jobs. The workers indicated that they were reasonably satisfied with their pay, working conditions, and the quality of their supervision. However, they expressed extreme dissatisfaction with the actual work they did. During that era, automobile plants were excessively noisy, the moving assembly line dictated a

4. Charles Babbage, *On the Economy of Machinery and Manufactures* (London: Charles Knight, 1832).
5. Frederick W. Taylor, *The Principles of Scientific Management* (New York: Harper & Row, 1911).
6. C. R. Walker and R. Guest, *The Man on the Assembly Line* (Cambridge, Mass.: Harvard University Press, 1952).

Optimizing Job Specialization

An important element in job design for managers is to find the optimal level of job specialization. Highly specialized jobs have the potential to be performed with high levels of efficiency but may prove to be boring and monotonous. Too little specialization, however, can cause inefficiency and ambiguity. Thus, optimizing job specialization is an important process.

Select a job with which you have some familiarity. It might be a job you currently hold or have performed in the past. Alternatively, you might also select a job you see performed regularly (i.e., a sales clerk in a local specialty shop where you buy clothes, the gas station attendant where you buy gas).

Analyze the job you have selected and identify as many specific and discrete tasks within that job as possible. (For example, the sales clerk's job may involve waiting on customers, returning unpurchased garments from dressing rooms to the sales floor, ringing up purchases, folding and wrapping garments for customers, and restocking shelves from inventory.)

Now, break down the overall job into as many highly specialized jobs as possible. (For example, a retail store might employ different people to perform each of the specific tasks identified above.) Where would you draw the line in order to optimize specialization? That is, would it actually be best to have different people perform each highly specialized task, would it be best to have a single person perform all the tasks (as is currently the case), or would it be best to package sets of tasks together and have a few different workers perform each set of tasks?

rigid, and grueling pace, and jobs were highly specialized and standardized. The workers complained about six facets of their jobs: the mechanical pacing by an assembly line, repetitiveness, low skill requirements, involvement with only a portion of the total production cycle, limited social interaction with others in the workplace, and no control over the tools and techniques used in the job. These sources of dissatisfaction were a consequence of the job design prescriptions of scientific management. Thus, managers began to recognize that job specialization might lead to efficiency but eventually—and if carried too far—too much specialization would also have a number of negative consequences. *Developing Management Skills* provides some insights into the nature of job specialization.

Early Alternatives to Job Specialization

In response to Walker and Guest's findings, as well as to other reported problems with job specialization and a general desire to explore ways to create less monotonous jobs, managers formulated two alternative approaches: job rotation and job enlargement.

Job Rotation   **Job rotation** involves systematically shifting workers from one job to another to sustain their motivation and interest. Figure 7.1 contrasts job rotation and job specialization. Under specialization, each job is broken down into small tasks. For example, assembling pens for distribution might involve four discrete tasks: testing the ink cartridge, inserting the cartridge into the barrel of the

Job rotation is the systematic movement of workers from one job to another in an attempt to minimize monotony and boredom.

pen, screwing the cap onto the barrel, and inserting the assembled pen into a box. Then individual workers are assigned to perform each of these four tasks.

When job rotation is introduced, the tasks themselves stay the same. As Figure 7.1 shows, however, the workers who perform them are systematically rotated across the various tasks. Jones, for example, starts out with task 1 (testing ink cartridges). On a regular basis, perhaps weekly or monthly, she is systematically rotated to task 2, to task 3, to task 4, and back to task 1. Gonzalez, who starts out on task 2 (inserting cartridges into barrels), rotates ahead of Jones to tasks 3, 4, 1, and back to 2.

Numerous firms have used job rotation, including American Cyanamid, Baker Hughes, Ford, and Prudential Insurance. However, job rotation did not entirely live up to expectations.[7] The problem was, again, narrowly defined, routine jobs. If a rotation cycle takes workers through the same old jobs, the workers simply experience several routine and boring jobs instead of just one. Although a worker may begin each job shift with modest renewed interest, the effect usually is short-lived.

Rotation may also decrease efficiency. The practice clearly sacrifices the proficiency and expertise that grow from specialization. At the same time, job rotation is an effective training technique because a worker rotated through a variety of

7. Ricky W. Griffin, *Task Design: An Integrative Approach* (Glenview, Ill.: Scott, Foresman, 1982).

FIGURE 7.1
Job Specialization, Rotation, and Enlargement

Job Specialization

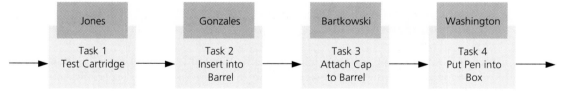

Job Rotation

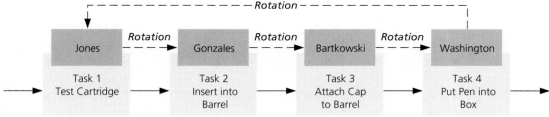

Job Enlargement

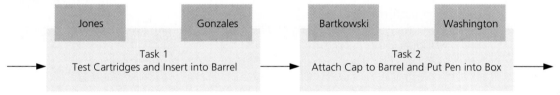

related jobs acquires a larger set of job skills. Thus, there is increased flexibility in transferring workers to new jobs. Many U.S. firms now use job rotation for training, but few rely on it to enhance employee motivation.

Job Enlargement   **Job enlargement**, or horizontal job loading, means that the worker's job is expanded to include tasks previously performed by other workers. This process is also illustrated in Figure 7.1. Before enlargement, workers perform a narrowly defined, specialized task; afterward, they have a "larger" task to do. Thus, after enlargement Jones and the other workers each do "bigger" tasks than they did previously. Thus, assembling the pens has been redefined as two tasks rather than four. Jones and Gonzalez do the first task, while Bartkowski and Washington do the other. The logic behind this change is that the increased number of tasks will reduce monotony and boredom.

> **Job enlargement** involves giving workers more tasks to perform.

Maytag was one of the first companies to use job enlargement.[8] In the assembly of washing machine water pumps, for example, jobs done sequentially by six workers at a conveyor belt were modified so that each worker completed an entire pump alone. (Note that this step brings job design back full-circle to the pre-specialization production of pins, as described by Adam Smith.) Other organizations that have implemented job enlargement included AT&T, the U.S. Civil Service, and Colonial Life Insurance Co.

Unfortunately, job enlargement often fails to have the desired effects. Generally, if the entire production sequence consists of simple, easy-to-master tasks, merely doing more of them does not meaningfully change the worker's job. If the task of putting two bolts on a piece of machinery is "enlarged" to putting on three bolts and connecting two wires, the monotony of the original job essentially remains.

Job Enrichment

Job rotation and job enlargement seemed promising but eventually disappointed managers looking for answers to the ill effects of extreme specialization. They failed partly because they were intuitive, narrow approaches rather than fully developed, theory-driven methods. As a result, a new, more complex approach to task design—job enrichment—emerged in the late 1950s.

> **Job enrichment** means giving workers more tasks to perform and more control over how to perform those tasks.

Job enrichment is based on the dual-structure theory of motivation, as discussed in Chapter 4. That theory proposed that employees could be motivated by positive job-related experiences such as feelings of achievement, responsibility, and recognition. To this end, it suggests vertical job loading—not only adding more tasks to a job, as in horizontal loading, but also giving the employee more control over those tasks. Vertical job loading was presumed to enrich a job in six ways:

1. *Accountability.* Workers should be held responsible for their performance.
2. *Achievement.* Workers should believe that they are doing something worthwhile.
3. *Feedback.* Workers should receive direct and clear information about their performance.
4. *Work pace.* To the extent possible, workers should be able to set their own work pace.

8. H. Conant and M. Kilbridge, "An Interdisciplinary Analysis of Job Enlargement: Technology, Cost, Behavioral Implications," *Industrial and Labor Relations Review*, Vol. 18, No. 7, 1965, pp. 377–395.

TABLE 7.1

Principles of Vertical Job Loading

Principle	Motivators Involved
A. Removing some controls while retaining accountability	Responsibility and personal achievement
B. Increasing the accountability of individuals for their own work	Responsibility and recognition
C. Giving a person a complete natural unit of work (module, division, area and so on)	Responsibility, achievement, and recognition
D. Granting additional authority to an employee in his activity; job freedom	Responsibility, achievement, and recognition
E. Making periodic reports directly available to the worker himself rather than to the supervisor	Internal recognition
F. Introducing new and more difficult tasks not previously handled	Growth and learning
G. Assigning individuals specific or specialized tasks, enabling them to become experts	Responsibility, growth, and advancement

SOURCE: Reprinted by permission of *Harvard Business Review*. An exhibit from "One More Time: How Do You Motivate Employees?" by Frederick Herzberg (September–October 1987). Copyright © 1987 by the President and Fellows of Harvard College; all rights reserved.

5. *Control over resources.* If possible, workers should have control over the resources used in their jobs.

6. *Personal growth and development.* Workers should have the opportunity to learn new skills.[9]

Table 7.1 outlines how these characteristics can potentially be added to a job. Job enrichment programs have been reported at various companies including AT&T, Texas Instruments, IBM, and General Foods. To see how job enrichment operates, we describe two of these programs in more detail.

An experiment at AT&T involved a group of eight typists who were responsible for preparing service orders. Managers believed that turnover in the group was too high and performance was too low. Analysis revealed several deficiencies in the work. The typists worked in relative isolation, and any service representative could ask any typist to type work orders. As a result, they believed that they had little client contact or responsibility, and they received scant feedback on their job performance. The job enrichment program focused on creating a typing team. Each member of the team was paired with a service representative, and the tasks were restructured: ten discrete steps were replaced with three more complex ones. In addition, the typists received specific feedback on performance, and their job titles

9. Frederick Herzberg, "One More Time: How Do You Motivate Employees?" *Harvard Business Review*, January–February 1968, pp. 53–62; and Frederick Herzberg, "The Wise Old Turk," *Harvard Business Review*, September–October 1974, pp. 70–80.

were changed to reflect their greater responsibility and status. As a result of these changes, the number of orders delivered on time increased from 27 to 90 percent, accuracy improved, and turnover dropped significantly.[10]

Texas Instruments used job enrichment to improve janitorial jobs. The company gave janitors more control over their schedules and let them sequence their own cleaning jobs and purchase their own supplies. The outcome? Turnover dropped, cleanliness improved, and the company reported estimated cost savings of approximately $103,000.[11]

At the same time, we should note that many job enrichment programs have failed. Some companies have found job enrichment to be cost ineffective, and others believe that it simply does not produce the expected results.[12] Several programs at Prudential Insurance, for example, were abandoned because managers believed that they were benefiting neither employees nor the firm. Several reasons for this pattern have been offered.

Some of the criticism is associated with the dual structure theory of motivation, on which job enrichment is based. In Chapter 4, we reviewed the major objections: the theory confuses employee satisfaction with motivation, is fraught with methodological flaws, ignores situational factors, and is not convincingly supported by research.[13]

Thus, there are still many unanswered questions about the usefulness of job enrichment. Other specific criticisms of job enrichment include the following:

1. Many reports of the success of job enrichment programs have been evangelical in nature; that is, the authors of these studies overstate the potential benefits of job enrichment and minimize its pitfalls.
2. Evaluations of job enrichment programs often have been methodologically flawed. Many studies have been poorly designed, making the results subject to alternative explanations.
3. Few failures have been reported in the literature, although some job enrichment programs have probably not achieved their goals. Without information about these failures, developing a full understanding of job enrichment is difficult.
4. Situational factors seldom have been assessed. Some situations probably are more favorable to job enrichment efforts than others. Unfortunately, we have not developed an understanding of the factors that lead to success or failure.
5. Economic data pertaining to the effectiveness of job enrichment are rare. Because job enrichment often is an expensive proposition, managers need a carefully developed procedure for evaluating the technique's costs and benefits. Such procedures have not been developed.[14]

Because of these and other problems, job enrichment recently has fallen into disfavor among managers. Yet some valuable aspects of the concept can be salvaged. The efforts of managers and academic theorists ultimately have led to more

10. R. N. Ford, "Job Enrichment Lessons from AT&T," *Harvard Business Review*, January–February 1973, pp. 96–106.
11. E. D. Weed, "Job Enrichment 'Cleans Up' at Texas Instruments," in J. R. Maher (Ed.), *New Perspectives in Job Enrichment* (New York: Van Nostrand, 1971).
12. Griffin and McMahan, "Motivation Through Job Design," and Griffin, *Task Design*.
13. Robert J. House and L. Wigdor, "Herzberg's Dual-Factor Theory of Job Satisfaction and Motivation: A Review of the Evidence and a Criticism," *Personnel Psychology*, Vol. 20, 1967, pp. 369–389.
14. J. Richard Hackman, "On the Coming Demise of Job Enrichment," in E. L. Cass and F. G. Zimmer (Eds.), *Man and Work in Society* (New York: Van Nostrand, 1975).

Through re-designing jobs, this team at Bell Atlantic managed to reduce the time the company needed to hook up customers to long-distance carriers from sixteen days to a few hours, thus regaining the company's competitive edge.

complex and sophisticated viewpoints. Many of these advances are evident in the job characteristics approach, which we consider next.

The Job Characteristics Approach

The **job characteristics approach** focuses on the motivational attributes of jobs.

The **job characteristics approach** evolved from work on the motivational attributes of jobs (such as autonomy and feedback), was expanded to include explicit consideration of individual differences in employee responses to a job, and eventually was codified in the Job Characteristics Theory.[15] The job characteristics approach dominated thinking about job design in the 1970s and 1980s.

Job Characteristics

The job characteristics approach began with the pioneering work of Turner and Lawrence, who conducted a large-scale project in the mid 1960s to assess employee responses to different kinds of jobs.[16] Turner and Lawrence believed that

15. J. Richard Hackman and Greg Oldham, "Motivation Through the Design of Work: Test of a Theory," *Organizational Behavior and Human Performance*, Vol. 16, 1976, pp. 250–279. See also Michael A. Campion and Paul W. Thayer, "Job Design: Approaches, Outcomes, and Trade-Offs," *Organizational Dynamics*, Winter 1987, pp. 66–78.
16. A. N. Turner and P .R. Lawrence, *Industrial Jobs and the Worker* (Boston: Harvard School of Business, 1965).

workers would prefer complex, challenging tasks to monotonous, boring ones. They predicted that job complexity would be associated with employee satisfaction and attendance. Tasks were described in terms of six job characteristics assumed to be desirable motivational properties of jobs: (1) variety, (2) autonomy, (3) required social interaction, (4) opportunities for social interaction, (5) knowledge and skill requirements, and (6) responsibility. Thus, a worker whose job was rated high on all six characteristics would be expected to have relatively high levels of satisfaction and attendance. If the job rated low on all attributes, the job holder would be expected to be less satisfied and more frequently absent.

These predictions were tested on 470 employees holding forty-seven different jobs in several manufacturing plants. Field observations and interviews were used to measure the relevant variables. Measures of the six job characteristics were combined into a single measure of task complexity, which then was compared with measures of satisfaction and attendance. The results confirmed the predicted relationship between task complexity and attendance but showed no relationship between task complexity and satisfaction.

Because of this second unexpected finding, Turner and Lawrence looked at their data more closely. They discovered a positive relationship between task complexity and the satisfaction of workers from factories in small towns but not workers in larger towns. To explain this pattern, the researchers concluded that the workers in larger communities had a variety of nonwork interests and consequently were less involved in and motivated by their work. The workers in smaller towns, on the other hand, had fewer nonwork interests and, therefore, were more responsive to the positive features of their jobs.

This explanation was tenuous at best, but we must consider that the original study had not been designed to assess individual differences. Recall that the implicit assumption of the study had been that everyone would respond to job conditions in the same way. Examining the results from the perspective of individual differences, on the other hand, would have allowed for the possibility of variations in people's reactions. Hence, the explanations were necessarily imprecise and speculative. The chief value of the unexpected findings was to highlight the potential role of individual differences in the workplace.

Job Design and Individual Differences

Individual differences may affect how workers perceive and respond to their jobs.

Among the first researchers to explore the role of individual differences among job holders were Hulin and Blood.[17] As a starting point, they developed a more precise explanation of Turner and Lawrence's findings, arguing that rural-urban differences actually reflected adherence to middle-class work norms such as the Protestant work ethic. They theorized that people governed by the work ethic would be highly motivated by challenging, complex jobs, whereas people who believed less strongly in the work ethic would be less interested and motivated by the same kind of job. The Protestant work ethic was also assumed to be more prevalent in rural settings. A preliminary study of this explanation provided reasonable but not total support for it.[18]

17. Charles L. Hulin and Milton R. Blood, "Job Enlargement, Individual Differences, and Worker Responses," *Psychological Bulletin*, Vol. 69, 1968, pp. 41–55; and Milton R. Blood and Charles L. Hulin, "Alienation, Environmental Characteristics, and Worker Responses," *Journal of Applied Psychology*, Vol. 51, 1967, pp. 284–290.
18. Blood and Hulin, "Alienation, Environmental Characteristics, and Worker Responses."

In light of this mixed evidence, other researchers also tried to develop ways of understanding individual differences.[19] Foremost among these efforts was the work of Hackman and Lawler. They suggested that psychological or motivational characteristics are what really matter in how people react to jobs.[20] Specifically, they borrowed from the need-based perspectives on motivation. They reasoned that people motivated by higher-order needs, such as the needs for self-actualization and personal growth and development, would be enthused by complex, challenging jobs, whereas those with weak higher-order needs would be less motivated by such jobs. The initial test of this idea was promising enough to encourage the development of another formal theory of job design—the Job Characteristic Theory.[21]

The Job Characteristics Theory

Working with Greg Oldham, Hackman used the findings from the test of the individual-differences interpretation to develop the Job Characteristics Theory. Figure 7.2 shows the basic features of this important theory.[22]

At the core of the **Job Characteristics Theory** are what Hackman and Oldham termed *critical psychological states*. These states are presumed to determine the extent to which characteristics of the job enhance employee responses to that task. The three critical psychological states are as follows:

1. *Experienced meaningfulness of the work.* The degree to which the individual experiences the job as generally meaningful, valuable, and worthwhile.
2. *Experienced responsibility for work outcomes.* The degree to which individuals feel personally accountable and responsible for the results of their work.
3. *Knowledge of results.* The degree to which individuals continuously understand how effectively they are performing the job.[23]

If employees experience these states at a sufficiently high level, they are likely to feel good about themselves and to respond favorably to their jobs. Hackman and Oldham suggest that the three critical psychological states are triggered by five characteristics of the job, or *core job dimensions*:

1. *Skill variety.* The degree to which the job requires a variety of activities that involve different skills and talents.
2. *Task identity.* The degree to which the job requires completion of a "whole" and identifiable piece of work, that is, a job that has a beginning and an end with a tangible outcome.
3. *Task significance.* The degree to which the job affects the lives or work of other people, both in the immediate organization and in the external environment.
4. *Autonomy.* The degree to which the job allows the individual substantial freedom, independence, and discretion to schedule the work and determine the procedures for carrying it out.

The **Job Characteristics Theory** identifies three critical psychological states: experienced meaningfulness of the work, experienced responsibility for work outcomes, and knowledge of results.

The Job Characteristics Theory identifies five core job dimensions: skill variety, task identity, task significance, autonomy, and feedback.

19. Griffin, *Task Design.*
20. J. Richard Hackman and Edward E. Lawler, "Employee Reactions to Job Characteristics," *Journal of Applied Psychology*, Vol. 55, 1971, pp. 259–286.
21. Ibid.
22. Hackman and Oldham, "Motivation Through the Design of Work"; and J. Richard Hackman and Greg Oldham, *Work Redesign* (Reading, Mass.: Addison-Wesley, 1980).
23. Hackman and Oldham, "Motivation Through the Design of Work," pp. 256–257.

FIGURE 7.2

The Job
Characteristics Theory

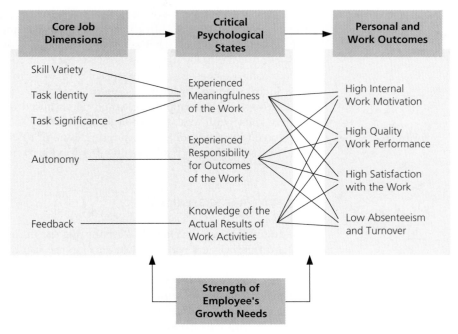

SOURCE: J. R. Hackman and G. R. Oldham, "Motivation Through the Design of Work: Test of a Theory." *Organizational Behavior and Human Performance*, Vol. 16, 1976, pp. 250–279. Copyright ©1976 by Academic Press, Inc. Used with permission of the publisher and author.

5. *Feedback.* The degree to which the job activities give the individual direct and clear information about the effectiveness of his or her performance.

Figure 7.2 shows how the core job dimensions stimulate the psychological states. Skill variety, task identity, and task significance are expected to affect the person's experienced meaningfulness of the work; autonomy is expected to influence the experienced responsibility for outcomes of the work; and feedback contributes to knowledge of the actual results of work activities. The critical psychological states then determine a variety of personal and work outcomes: high internal work motivation (i.e., intrinsic motivation), high-quality work performance, high satisfaction with the work, and low absenteeism and turnover. Finally, the strength of the employee's growth needs is expected to influence the effects of other elements of the theory. Hackman and Lawler's earlier findings suggested that the effects would be very strong in people whose higher-order needs are strong and weak in people whose higher-order needs are weak.

The Job Characteristics Theory is tested with the **Job Diagnostic Survey**, or **JDS**.

To test the Job Characteristics Theory, Hackman and Oldham developed the **Job Diagnostic Survey**, or **JDS**.[24] This questionnaire measures employee perceptions of job characteristics, various psychological states, personal and work outcomes, and strength of growth needs. Figure 7.3 illustrates the use of data obtained from the JDS. The graph on the left summarizes the level of each of the five job characteristics for two hypothetical jobs. Job A clearly has higher levels of each of the five character-

24. J. Richard Hackman and Greg Oldham, "Development of the Job Diagnostic Survey," *Journal of Applied Psychology*, Vol. 60, 1975, pp. 159–170.

FIGURE 7.3

JDS Profile of "Good"
and "Bad" Jobs

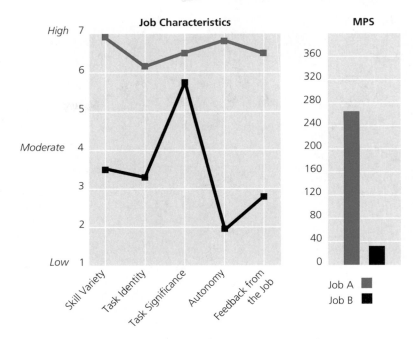

SOURCE: J. R. Hackman, "Work Design, " in J. R. Hackman and J. I. Suttle (Eds.), *Improving Life at Work: Behavioral Science Approaches to Organizational Change* (Santa Monica, Calif.: Goodyear, 1977), p. 135. Used by permission.

istics than job B. The chart on the right shows each job's **motivating potential score,** or **MPS,** which is calculated according to the following formula:

The JDS provides a **motivating potential score,** or **MPS,** for jobs.

$$\text{MPS} = \frac{(\text{Variety} + \text{Identity} + \text{Significance})}{3} \times \text{Autonomy} \times \text{Feedback}$$

The MPS provides a summary index of a job's overall potential for motivating employees. Thus, the JDS can be used to identify jobs in the organization with high and low motivating potential. Jobs with a low MPS index are candidates for redesign to improve their potential for motivating job holders.

Hackman has also developed a general set of guidelines to help managers implement the theory; these are shown as implementing concepts in Figure 7.4.[25] Managers can do things such as combine existing tasks into more complex ones, form natural work units (that is, group similar tasks), establish direct relationships between workers and clients, increase worker autonomy through vertical job loading, and open feedback channels. Theoretically, such actions should enhance the MPS of each task. Using these guidelines, sometimes in adapted form, several organizations have successfully implemented job design changes. Among them are 3M, Volvo, AT&T, Xerox, Texas Instruments, and Motorola.[26]

25. J. Richard Hackman, "Work Design," in J. Richard Hackman and J. L. Suttle (Eds.), *Improving Life at Work: Behavioral Science Approaches to Organizational Change* (Santa Monica, Calif.: Goodyear, 1977).
26. Griffin, *Task Design.*

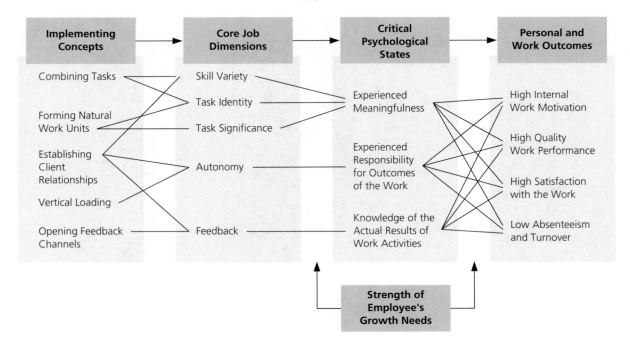

Implementing Concepts	Core Job Dimensions	Critical Psychological States	Personal and Work Outcomes

Combining Tasks

Forming Natural Work Units

Establishing Client Relationships

Vertical Loading

Opening Feedback Channels

Skill Variety

Task Identity

Task Significance

Autonomy

Feedback

Experienced Meaningfulness

Experienced Responsibility for Outcomes of the Work

Knowledge of the Actual Results of Work Activities

High Internal Work Motivation

High Quality Work Performance

High Satisfaction with the Work

Low Absenteeism and Turnover

Strength of Employee's Growth Needs

SOURCE: J. R. Hackman, G. R. Oldham, R. Oldham, R. Janson, and K. Purdy, "A New Stage for Job Enrichment." Copyright ©1975 by The Regents of the University of California. Reprinted from the *California Management Review*: Vol. 17, No. 4. By permission of The Regents.

FIGURE 7.4

Implementing the Job Characteristics Theory

Much research has been devoted to this approach to job design.[27] This research generally has supported the Job Characteristics Theory, although actual job performance has seldom been found to correlate with job characteristics.[28] Several apparent weaknesses in the theory also have come to light. First, the JDS is not always as valid and reliable as it should be.[29] Further, the role of individual differences frequently has not been supported by research. Finally, implementation guidelines are not specific and managers usually must modify at least part of the theory to use them.[30] Still, the theory remains a viable and popular perspective on studying and changing jobs.[31]

27. Griffin, *Task Design*. See also Karlene H. Roberts and William Glick, "The Job Characteristics Approach to Task Design: A Critical Review," *Journal of Applied Psychology*, Vol. 66, 1981, pp. 193–217; and Ricky W. Griffin, "Toward an Integrated Theory of Task Design," in Larry L. Cummings and Barry M. Staw (Eds.), *Research in Organizational Behavior*, Vol. 9 (Greenwich, Conn.: JAI Press, 1987), pp. 79–120.

28. Ricky W. Griffin, M. Ann Welsh, and Gregory Moorhead, "Perceived Task Characteristics and Employee Performance: A Literature Review," *Academy of Management Review*, October 1981, pp. 655–664.

29. John L. Cordery and Peter P. Sevastos, "Responses to the Original and Revised Job Diagnostic Survey: Is Education a Factor in Responses to Negatively Worded Items?" *Journal of Applied Psychology*, Vol. 78, 1993, pp. 141–143.

30. Roberts and Glick, "The Job Characteristics Approach to Task Design."

31. For recent examples, see Donald J. Campbell, "Task Complexity: A Review and Analysis," *Academy of Management Review*, January 1988, pp. 40–52; Donald G. Gardner, "Task Complexity Effects on Non-Task–Related Movements: A Test of Activation Theory," *Organizational Behavior and Human Decision Processes*, Vol. 45, 1990, pp. 209–231; and Barry M. Staw and Richard D. Boettger, "Task Revision: A Neglected Form of Work Performance," *Academy of Management Journal*, September 1990, pp. 534–559.

Social Information and Jobs

A relatively new perspective on job design that provides additional insight into how people perceive their jobs considers the role of social information in the workplace. Salancik and Pfeffer raised this issue after analyzing the literature from which the job characteristics approach to job design has grown.[32] The basic purpose of their analysis was to assess need-based perspectives on motivation. In addition, however, they expanded their analysis to address job design. They question the validity of two basic assumptions of the job characteristics approach: (1) that people have basic and stable needs that can be satisfied, at least partially, by their job; and (2) that jobs have stable and objective characteristics that people perceive and respond to consistently and predictably. They claim, for example, that people probably do not think of their jobs in terms of dimensions such as variety and autonomy. Only when a questionnaire inquires about the variety and autonomy of their jobs do those dimensions come to mind. They also point to potential flaws in earlier approaches to job design, such as measurement deficiencies.[33]

The **social information processing model** of job design suggests that individual needs, task perceptions, and reactions are socially constructed realities.

Salancik and Pfeffer developed the **social information processing model**, which suggests that individual needs, task perceptions, and reactions are a result of socially constructed realities. In other words, social information in the workplace shapes the individual's perception of the job and responses to it. For example, if a newcomer to the organization is told, "You're really going to like it here because everybody gets along so well," the newcomer assumes that the job should be evaluated in terms of social interactions and that those interactions are satisfactory. But if the message is, "You won't like it here because the boss is lousy and the pay is worse," the newcomer may think that the job's most important aspects are interactions with the boss and pay and that both areas are deficient.[33]

Figure 7.5 shows the complete social information processing model. Basically, the model suggests that commitment, rationalization (self-interpretation of behavior), and information saliency (importance) are defined through a variety of processes. These processes include the following:

1. *Choice.* The freedom to choose different behaviors.
2. *Revocability.* The ability to change behaviors.
3. *Publicness.* The degree of visibility to others.
4. *Explicitness.* The ability to be clear and obvious.
5. *Social norms and expectations.* The knowledge of what others expect from someone.
6. *External priming.* The receiving of cues from others.

Attributional and enactment processes then combine with social reality construction processes to influence task environmental characteristics (perceptions), attitudes and needs, and, indirectly, behaviors.

32. Gerald Salancik and Jeffrey Pfeffer, "An Examination of Need-Satisfaction Models of Job Attitudes," *Administrative Science Quarterly*, Vol. 22, 1977, pp. 427–456; and Gerald Salancik and Jeffrey Pfeffer, "A Social Information Processing Approach to Job Attitudes and Task Design," *Administrative Science Quarterly*, Vol. 23, 1978, pp. 224–253.
33. Salancik and Pfeffer, "A Social Information Processing Approach."

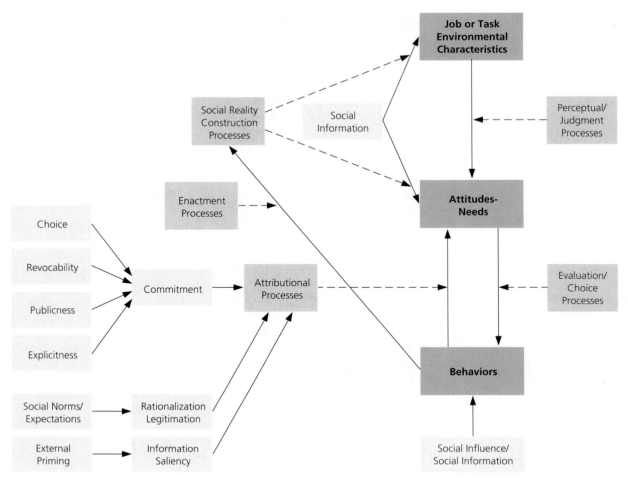

Key
————— Relationships Among Concepts
— — — Processes That Mediate Relationships Among Constructs

FIGURE 7.5

The Social Information Processing Model of Job Design

To date, the social information processing model has gotten mixed support from empirical research.[34] Laboratory experiments and field studies often have found that social information influences task perceptions and attitudes, but they also have shown the importance of job characteristics.[35] The findings suggest that task perceptions may be a joint function of objective task properties and social

34. Joe Thomas and Ricky W. Griffin, "The Social Information Processing Model of Task Design: A Review of the Literature," *Academy of Management Review*, October 1983, pp. 672–682. See also Griffin, "Toward an Integrated Theory of Task Design."
35. Charles A. O'Reilly and D. F. Caldwell, "Informational Influence as a Determinant of Perceived Task Characteristics and Job Satisfaction," *Journal of Applied Psychology*, Vol. 64, 1979, pp. 157–165; and Ricky W. Griffin, "Objective and Social Sources of Information in Task Redesign: A Field Experiment," *Administrative Science Quarterly*, June 1983, pp. 184–200.

This American Airlines ground crew prepares for a plane's departure at the San Jose, California, airport. Some jobs are designed for teams, creating a degree of autonomy for the team. This group is responsible for a set of tasks, but is able to decide itself how to perform them, and who will perform which parts of the task.

information.[36] For example, positive social information and a well-designed task may produce more favorable evaluations by job holders than either information or task properties alone would produce. Conversely, negative information and a poorly designed task may produce more negative reactions than either social information or job properties would by themselves. In situations where social information and task conditions do not reinforce each other, they may cancel each other out, as when negative social information may diminish the positive effects of a well-designed task. Similarly, positive information may at least partly offset the negative consequences of a poorly designed task. At present, debate is considerable as to which of the three views—the job characteristics model, the social information processing model, or a model combining both—is correct.

Designing Jobs for Teams

Increasingly, many jobs are being designed for groups rather than for individuals.

The job design perspectives we have discussed to this point have focused almost exclusively on individual jobs. Many situations, however, call for designing jobs for groups or teams. Considering a group-based approach to job design may be appropriate under either of two circumstances. First, some jobs are simply better

36. Griffin, "Objective and Social Sources of Information in Task Redesign." See also Griffin, "Toward an Integrated Theory of Task Design," and Donald J. Campbell, "Task Complexity: A Review and Analysis," *Academy of Management Review*, January 1988, pp. 40–52.

suited to a team than to an individual.[37] For example, it may be more efficient for British Airways to use a team to service a Boeing 747 than to assign the job to a set of individuals. Second, a group-based job design might be best when the organization wants to use teams as a mechanism for enhancing individual motivation. One early form of this approach is autonomous work groups.

Autonomous work groups are sometimes used as a basis for group job design.

In **autonomous work groups**, jobs are structured for groups rather than for individuals. The group itself is then given considerable discretion in scheduling, individual work assignments, and other matters that traditionally have been management prerogatives—even to the extent of hiring new members and determining members' pay increases.

Several organizations have used autonomous work groups. For example, Westinghouse, General Foods, and Volvo have enjoyed considerable success with these approaches. An autonomous work group at Volvo's Kalmar plant has its own inventory area, toilets, changing rooms, and so on. The intended effect is to make workers feel as though they work in a small machine shop rather than in a huge factory. Each group is responsible for a complete set of tasks, such as wiring or upholstery. The group itself decides who will perform each task and can control the speed at which incoming cars enter its work area. The group thus functions fairly autonomously. Unfortunately, while autonomous work groups often result in higher quality products, they are also more costly when compared to traditional assembly line techniques. Indeed, Volvo recently announced that it would soon close the Kalmar plant.

Groups are used as a basis for designing jobs in other situations as well. For example, committees are essentially work groups with a task to perform. Although the task may be to draft a report or make a recommendation, it nevertheless can become quite salient to the group members, and as a result they may come to see it as an important part of their job. Quality circles can also be viewed as a group-based approach to getting work done. Thus, in each instance where these or other kinds of groups are the work unit, the manager must recognize the basis for using a group task design and arrange things accordingly.

Work Teams in Organizations

Although autonomous work groups and committees represent important group-based approaches to job design, another group-based approach has attracted considerable attention recently. This approach makes use of **cross-functional work teams**. Such teams, which comprise representatives from different functional areas of the organization, work together on various projects and activities.[38]

Cross-functional work teams comprise representatives from different functional areas of the organization and work together on various projects and activities.

Federal Express is making extensive use of cross-functional teams. The firm has organized its 1,000 clerical workers into teams of between 5 and 10 members each. One team was credited with cutting service errors (incorrect billing, lost packages, etc.) by 13 percent in one year alone. Another discovered a glitch in the firm's billing system that was costing Federal Express more than $2 million per year. Other firms that are adopting this approach include General Mills, 3M, Aetna Life & Casualty, and Chaparral Steel.

37. Richard Saavedra, P. Christopher Earley, and Linn Van Dyne, "Complex Interdependence in Task-Performing Groups," *Journal of Applied Psychology*, Vol. 78, 1993, pp. 61–72.
38. Brian Dumaine, "Who Needs a Boss?" *Fortune*, May 7, 1990, pp. 52–60.

The entire approach to managing teams is derived from Japanese experiences. To create a team the organization selects representatives from appropriate departments (such as finance, marketing, and production) and assigns them to a particular project, such as introducing a new product. To generate the maximum effectiveness of teams, the organization needs to achieve an integration of structurally defined groups in interaction with a well-defined culture based on cooperation and trust between labor and management. In many ways, the cross-functional teams adopted by Federal Express and similar organizations are the beginning of this approach in that they foster a group-based work environment.

A good example of the effectiveness of the Japanese approach is the Toyota–General Motors joint venture in California, New United Motor Manufacturing Inc. (NUMMI). The facility was originally opened and operated by GM, but was shut down in 1982 because of very bad quality problems and abysmal labor relations. GM later entered into a joint venture with Toyota, and the plant was reopened under Japanese management. The new management team trained each of the plant's 2,500 workers in group harmony, trust, and cooperation. The organization developed a team-based approach to work in conjunction with a new culture based on participation and cooperation. The result? The plant now makes higher-quality Chevrolets and Toyotas than any other GM plant and some Toyota plants in Japan.[39] (NUMMI is featured in Case 7.1 at the end of this chapter.)

Related Aspects of Job Design

Three other issues pertaining to job design that are not tied to any particular theory are employee work schedules, automation and robotics, and worker flexibility. (Another issue, the use of temporary workers, is explored in *The Ethical Dilemma*.)

Work Schedules

Alternative work schedules such as the compressed workweek, flexible work schedules (flextime), and job sharing often are used in organizations.

Employee work schedules are not related to job design in the strictest sense, but they are a direct point of contact between the employee and the job. Managers have been seeking new work scheduling methods that improve employees' work-related experiences and at the same time improve attendance, motivation, and attitudes. Three alternative approaches to work scheduling are the compressed workweek, flexible work schedules, and job sharing.

An employee following a **compressed workweek** schedule works a full forty-hour week in fewer than the traditional five days.

Compressed Workweek An employee following a **compressed workweek** schedule works a full forty-hour week in fewer than the traditional five days. Most typically, this schedule involves working ten hours a day for four days, leaving an extra day off. Another alternative is for employees to work slightly less than ten hours a day but to complete the forty hours by lunch time on Friday. Organizations that have used the compressed workweek include John Hancock, Atlantic Richfield, and R. J. Reynolds. Research has found little evidence, however, that a compressed workweek improves motivation or attendance.[40]

39. "Hands Across the Workplace," *Time*, December 26, 1988, pp. 14–17.
40. A. R. Cohen and H. Gadon, *Alternative Work Schedules: Integrating Individual and Organizational Needs* (Reading, Mass.: Addison-Wesley, 1978).

Temporary Workers in Organizations

More and more organizations today are turning to temporary workers instead of hiring new permanent employees. Indeed, it may come as a surprise to many people that the largest private employer in the United States today is Manpower Inc., a temporary employment agency with 560,000 people on its payroll.

Using temporary workers appeals to organizations for a variety of reasons. For one thing, they pay few, if any, benefits to temporary workers. For another, they can add and eliminate workers as their business needs dictate, without having to go through rigorous selection processes or enduring the pain of terminating people. And some members of the temporary workforce prefer this arrangement because it provides them with variety and offers them the flexibility of choosing when they work.

But for many members of the so-called disposable workforce, the trend toward more and more temporary jobs is anything but exciting. For example, many experience insecurity, knowing that they may or may not have a job the next day. And because the different jobs they hold pay different wages, they have difficulty budgeting for their personal expenses. The temporary agencies that employ them provide basic benefits, but they are usually not comparable to those provided by businesses to permanent workers. And finally, many temporary workers argue that they miss the sense of belonging and importance that goes along with a permanent job.

Clearly, then, both employers and employees must carefully weigh the pros and cons of temporary workers. Organizations gain flexibility and lower costs, but may sacrifice loyalty and team unity. Likewise, the employees, themselves, get employment, variety, and flexibility, but give up security and group membership.

SOURCES: "Disposable Workers," *Time*, March 29, 1993, pp. 43–47; and "The Tempting of America," *Time*, March 29, 1993, pp. 40–41.

Flexible Work Schedules Flexible work schedules, or flextime, may be more promising. Flextime gives employees some control over their working hours and thus, from a task design point of view, contributes to employee autonomy. Research evidence suggests that flextime may be an effective motivational strategy. With **flexible work schedules**, or **flextime**, the workday is broken down into two categories: flexible time and core time. All employees must be at their workstations during core time, but they can choose their own schedules during flexible time. Thus, if core time is late morning and early afternoon, one employee may choose to start work early in the morning and leave in midafternoon, another to start in the late morning and work until late afternoon, and still another to start early in the morning, take a long lunch break, and work until late afternoon. Organizations that have used this method include Control Data Corp., Metropolitan Life Insurance Co., and the U.S. government.

Job Sharing In **job sharing**, two part-time employees share one full-time job. One person may perform the job from 8:00 A.M. to noon and the other from 1:00 P.M. to 5:00 P.M. Job sharing may be desirable for people who want to work only part-time or when job markets are tight. For its part, the organization can accommodate the preferences of a broader range of employees and may benefit from the

With **flexible work schedules**, or **flextime**, the workday is broken down into two categories: flexible time and core time. All employees must be at their workstations during core time, but they choose their own schedules during flexible time.

In **job sharing**, two part-time employees share one full-time job.

talents of more people. Although job sharing has not been scientifically evaluated, it appears to be a useful alternative to traditional work scheduling. Another work scheduling variation is an increasing movement toward permanent part-time, or contingent, workers. Organizations often do not have to pay benefits to part-time workers and can use them to easily cut back or expand the workforce as needed.

Automation and Robotics

Automation and robotics are changing the way many jobs are designed.

Industry's growing reliance on automation and robotics has a variety of implications for job design, some positive and others perhaps negative.[41] In general, these relate to the potential changes that automation and robotics may bring to existing jobs. For example, automation may eliminate many boring, routine, and hazardous jobs from the workplace, theoretically allowing workers to move into more interesting and challenging jobs.[42] But automation may also dehumanize jobs. Witness the many grocery stores that are adopting optiscan technology that reads prices from printed bar codes as the checkout clerk passes products over a screen. The clerk may now be more efficient, but he or she also has much less to do. Some newer units even have audio capabilities: they call out the prices, the total bill, and the customer's change and even say, "Thank you"! Required only to pass items over the scanner, the clerk becomes merely an adjunct to the technology.

Worker Flexibility

Worker flexibility is becoming a popular method of designing jobs. In some ways, it represents a new approach to job rotation.

Still another emerging perspective on job design is the notion of flexible workers. In some ways, this approach is a refinement of the job rotation model described earlier. Its basic idea is that organizations can enhance their effectiveness by training workers to perform a number of different jobs. Employees generally receive a pay increase when they master each new job. The organization can then transfer employees around to different jobs as needed.

Lechmere department stores in Florida have been very successful using flexible workers. One employee may learn to unload trucks, operate a checkout computer, and sell sporting goods. The firm benefits because it can reassign employees as needed to get different things done. Also, employees seem to like the system.[43]

The flexible-worker approach and simple job rotation differ in three basic ways. First, people get transferred across completely different jobs rather than across narrow tasks within the same job. Second, they receive a financial incentive for becoming more flexible. Finally, the rotation itself often is spontaneous and exciting, whereas in simple job rotation the changes are mechanical and routinized. All things considered, the concept of the flexible worker is likely to become increasingly popular.

41. Hackman, "Work Design"; Griffin, *Task Design*; and Hackman and Oldham, *Work Redesign*.
42. Toby D. Wall, Paul R. Jackson, and Keith Davids, "Operator Work Design and Robotics System Performance: A Serendipitous Field Study," *Journal of Applied Psychology*, Vol. 77, 1992, pp. 353–362.
43. Norm Alster, "What Flexible Workers Can Do," *Fortune*, February 13, 1989, pp. 62–66.

Summary of Key Points

- Until the 1950s, historical trends showed a general movement toward increasingly specialized jobs. Since then, there has been a consistent move away from extreme specialization. Two early alternatives to specialization were job rotation and job enlargement. Job enrichment stimulated considerable interest in job design.
- The Job Characteristics Theory grew out of the early work on job enrichment. One basic premise of this theory is that jobs can be described in terms of a specific set of motivational characteristics. Another is that managers should work to enhance the presence of those motivational characteristics in jobs but should also take individual differences into account.
- Advocates of the social information processing view question some basic premises of the job characteristics approach. Social information processing theorists argue that neither employee needs nor task perceptions are stable, consistently predictable properties; rather, they are socially constructed realities. Today the emerging opinion is that employees' task perceptions and attitudes are jointly determined by objective task properties and social information.
- Sometimes jobs are more appropriately designed for groups than for individuals. Many tasks can be effectively performed by groups. Autonomous work groups and work teams also are widely used.
- Cross-functional work teams are increasingly used by organizations as a way to structure jobs. By using representatives from different functional areas as part of the same team, organizations can improve efficiency and find new and creative solutions to problems.
- There are also several related issues that pertain to job design. Compressed workweeks, flexible work schedules, and job sharing are scheduling innovations. Automation and robotics also have implications for job design. Worker flexibility is still another increasingly important approach.

Discussion Questions

1. What are the primary advantages and disadvantages of job specialization? Were they the same in the early days of mass production?
2. When might job enlargement be especially effective and especially ineffective? What about job rotation?
3. Are there any trends today that suggest a return to job specialization?
4. What are the strengths and weaknesses of job enrichment? When might it be useful?
5. Do you agree or disagree with the idea that individual differences affect how people respond to their jobs? Explain.
6. What are the primary similarities and differences between job enrichment and the Job Characteristics Theory?
7. Can you recall any instances in which social information affected how you perceived or felt about something?
8. What alternative work schedules besides those discussed in the chapter can you think of?
9. How do automation and robotics make work easier? How do they make it more difficult?
10. What other job design alternatives can you envision emerging in the future?

Purpose   This exercise will help you assess the processes involved in redesigning jobs.

Format   Working in small groups, you will diagnose an existing job in terms of its motivating potential, analyze its motivating potential in comparison to other jobs, suggest ways to redesign it, and then assess the effects of your redesign suggestions on other elements in the workplace.

Procedure   Your instructor will divide the class into groups of three or four people each. In assessing the characteristics of jobs, use a scale value of 1 ("very little") to 7 ("very high").

1. Using the scale values, assign scores on each core job dimension used in the Job Characteristics Theory (see page xxx) to the following jobs: secretary, professor, food server, auto mechanic, lawyer, short-order cook, department store clerk, construction worker, and newspaper reporter.
2. Calculate the motivating potential score (MPS) (see page yyy) for each job, and rank-order them from highest to lowest.
3. Your instructor will now assign your group one of the jobs from the list. Discuss how you might reasonably go about enriching the job.
4. Calculate the new MPS score for the redesigned job, and check its new position in the rank-ordering.
5. Discuss the feasibility of your redesign suggestions. In particular, look at how your recommended changes might necessitate organizational change such as changes in other jobs, the reward system, and the selection criteria used in hiring people for the job.
6. Briefly discuss your observations with the rest of the class.

Follow-up Questions

1. How might the social information processing model have explained some of your own perceptions in this exercise?
2. Are some jobs simply impossible to redesign?

CASE 7.1   **NUMMI: A New Look at Job Specialization**

The conventional wisdom among management experts today is that high levels of job specialization and standardization result in jobs that are boring, monotonous, and routine. These conditions, in turn, presumably lead to lower levels of productivity and satisfaction and higher levels of absenteeism and turnover. But in at least one California factory, evidence suggests that the conventional wisdom may need revisiting.

Just outside Fremont, California, sits one of General Motors's greatest failures—and one of its biggest successes. The Fremont plant was opened by General Motors in 1963 to manufacture GM trucks and the Chevrolet Malibu and Century. Following

---

the prescriptions of scientific management, industrial engineers specialized and standardized every single manufacturing job in the plant. Moreover, management saw its goal as ensuring that workers tightly adhered to their job descriptions and met their productivity quotas.

And as the human relationists might have predicted, productivity and other key indicators of performance effectiveness were all quite poor. For example, worker productivity at Fremont was the lowest of any GM plant. The plant also quickly developed a reputation for turning out poor quality products. Absenteeism ran so high that the plant employed 20 percent more workers than it needed just to make sure that enough workers would be present on any given day to staff the assembly lines.

After several unsuccessful efforts to turn things around at Fremont, GM gradually began to cut back on its investment in the plant. Finally, in early 1982, GM closed the doors at Fremont and announced that all its production would be transferred to other factories.

During this same period, GM had been in discussions with Toyota regarding possible joint ventures. GM wanted to learn more about Toyota's manufacturing methods and management style, and Toyota needed production capability in the United States and wanted to learn more about the U.S. supply and distribution systems. In early 1983 the two firms agreed to reopen the Fremont plant under the nickname of NUMMI (for New United Motor Manufacturing Inc.). The agreement stipulated that Fremont would make both Toyota and Chevrolet products. Toyota would handle product design, engineering, production, and day-to-day management of the plant; GM would handle marketing and sales.

Although Toyota initially did not want the United Auto Workers union at NUMMI, it soon found that it had no choice. The UAW was the legal bargaining representative of the plant. In addition, GM feared a union backlash if it tried to set up NUMMI as a nonunion operation. Over a twenty-month period, NUMMI hired 2,200 hourly workers, 85 percent of whom had previously worked at the plant when it was a GM operation.

Toyota insisted that as many remnants as possible of the "old days" be eliminated—reserved parking for managers and the executive dining room, for example. But Toyota also insisted on training the workers in Japanese work methods. Team leaders and managers, for example, spent three weeks in Japan training at a Toyota plant there.

The foundation at NUMMI was trust, agreement, and shared goals and values. Workers were made to feel appreciated and valued. Managers worked hard to eliminate the "us-versus-them" mentality that had pervaded the old Fremont organization. Instead, workers and managers work together for their own mutual benefit (job security, productivity, and so forth).

A major part of this way of doing business was allowing workers to design their own jobs. Somewhat surprising, the jobs they created for themselves were every bit as specialized and standardized as had been their former jobs. They also decided that they should work harder. For example, under the previous work arrangements the average employee had work to do about 45 seconds out of every 60. But under the new system, they work almost 57 seconds out of every 60. The difference is that they created the jobs themselves, work with less control and supervision, and can change the system if they decide it needs to be changed.

How have things gone so far? Productivity at Fremont is the highest at any GM plant, the quality of its products rivals that achieved in Toyota's Japanese factories, and absenteeism is down to less than 3 percent per day. Clearly, then, the impact of job specialization is not as simple and direct as managers once believed.

Case Questions

1. Why does job specialization work so well now, but did not work previously?

2. What other explanations besides participation might account for the results achieved at Fremont?

3. Why don't more firms follow the NUMMI model?

SOURCES: Paul S. Adler, "Time-and-Motion Regained," *Harvard Business Review*, January–February 1993, pp. 97–108; and "Toyota Retooled," *Business Week*, April 4, 1994, pp. 54–57.

Standard Decoy Co. in Witchell, Maine, has been making traditional wooden hunting decoys since 1927. Cyrus Witchell began the business by carving a couple of ducks a day by hand. Demand and competition have long since driven the company to use modern machinery and assembly line techniques, turning out two hundred ducks daily even on the slowest days.

When Stewart Alcorn, Cyrus Witchell's grandson, took over the business, he knew things needed to change. Output hadn't fallen, and the company was surviving financially despite competition from what he called "plastic ducks" from the Far East. But Alcorn noticed that productivity per worker had stayed the same for ten years, even during the period since the company bought the latest equipment. While touring the plant, he noticed many employees yawning and found himself doing the same. No one quit. No one complained. They all gave him a smile when he walked by. But no one seemed excited with the work.

Alcorn decided to take a survey. He appointed a respected worker at each step in the production process to ask each of his or her coworkers questions and to fill in the response sheets. One conclusion emerged from the survey: the "fine-tuners," as Alcorn thought of them, were the most content. That is, those who used fine tools and brushes to get the duck's heads, expressions, and feathers just right seemed to most enjoy their work. In contrast, the people who planed and cut the wood into blocks, rough-cut the body shapes, spray-painted the body color, and applied the varnish were all pretty bored.

Alcorn had heard about a technique called "job rotation," and decided to try it out. He gave all workers a taste of the "fun" jobs. He asked for volunteers to exchange jobs for one morning a week. The fine-tuners were skeptical, and the other workers were only slightly more enthusiastic. The whole program turned out a disaster. Even with guidance, the planers and spray-painters could not master the higher-precision techniques, and the fine-tuners seemed willing to give them only limited assistance. After one trial week, Alcorn gave up.

During lunch break that Friday, Alcorn was wandering around outside the plant bemoaning his failure. Then he noticed one of the rough-cutters, Al Price, whittling at something with an ordinary pocket knife. It turned out to be a block of wood that he had cut incorrectly and normally would have thrown in the scrap heap. But as Price said, "It kind of looked like a duck, in an odd way," and he had started whittling on it in spare moments.

Alcorn liked what he saw and asked Price if he would be willing to sell him the duck when he got through with it. Price looked surprised, but he agreed. The following week, Alcorn noticed that Price had finished the whittling and was getting one of the fine-tuners to help him paint the duck in a way that made it look even odder. When it was finished, Alcorn offered it to one of his regular customers, who took a look at it, said, "You've got hand made?" and asked if he could order a gross.

By the middle of the next month, Alcorn's "Odd Ducks" program was in full swing. Workers were held responsible for producing their usual number of conventional ducks, but they were allowed to use company tools and materials any time they wanted to work on their own projects. There were no quotas or expectations for the Odd Ducks. Some employees worked on one for weeks; others collaborated and produced one or two a day. Some wouldn't sell their ducks but crafted them to practice their skills and brought them home to display on their mantles. Those who would sell kept half the selling price. That price usually did not amount to more than their regular hourly wage, but no one seemed to care about the precise amount of income.

The response to the Odd Duck program was so great that Alcorn put up a bulletin board titled "Odd Letters," where he posted appreciative notes from customers. Most of these customers, it seemed, had no interest in hunting but just liked to have the ducks around. And when Alcorn learned that some of his customers were in turn selling the ducks as "Cyrus Witchell's Olde Time Odd Ducks," he did not complain.

Case Questions

1. How did the "Odd Ducks" program enrich the jobs at Standard Decoy?

2. What motivated workers to participate in making the Odd Ducks?

C H A P T E R

8

Performance Measurement and Rewards

OBJECTIVES

After studying this chapter, you should be able to:

Discuss the purposes and basics of performance management and measurement.

Describe the contribution of performance management to total quality management.

Discuss reward systems in organizations, including their roles, purposes, and types of reward systems.

Summarize issues regarding the management of reward systems.

For its successes in quality improvement, the Wallace Company won the Baldrige Award in 1990. Wallace's new employee performance enhancement system was integral to the company's overall improvement. The system was centered around employee-supervisor discussions of job functions that helped to increase employee satisfaction and productivity.

The Wallace Company won the Malcolm Baldrige National Quality Award in 1990. A major distributor of pipes, valves, and fittings for the chemical and oil industries, Wallace was in the middle of a major industry downturn in the 1980s. The decision to make a marked improvement in quality throughout the company was taken in response to industry demands for improved quality and service as well as for survival. Its quality improvement plan included statistical process control of inventory levels, delivery schedules, returned goods, and other critical factors; improved communication and training; and reorienting the culture of the organization toward total quality improvement—areas typically addressed in quality improvement programs.

One of the most interesting features of the quality improvement effort was in the performance management system. Management replaced the old system with a performance enhancement program, which was designed to help the employee identify how performance can be improved, rather than focus on what the employee did wrong in the past. Employees fill out a form on which they evaluate how well they perform each job function and the importance of each job function. Supervisors also fill out the same form for each employee. The completed forms are analyzed by computer, which also develops a profile of job functions, importance, and the differences between how the employee and the supervisor rated the job function and its importance.

The employee then schedules a meeting with the supervisor to discuss their different perceptions. They also discuss the job functions and ways to improve performance. Thus, the focus of the process is on nonthreatening discussions of the job functions, the job's quality and production factors, and how the employee can contribute to them.

The performance enhancement program was only part of the comprehensive quality program at Wallace. However, it was an important part. In addition to winning the Malcolm Baldrige National Quality Award, in the five-year period from 1985 to 1989, absenteeism was cut in half, employee turnover declined 60 percent, and sales per employee increased significantly.[1]

■ ■ ■ ■ "Let's be frank: Most managers hate conducting performance appraisals."[2] Managers use many different excuses to avoid formally appraising the performance of employees who work for them. The most common excuses are: "It takes too much time," "The form we use is bad" and "I'm not qualified to judge others," "No one does it to me," and "It's so painful." The integrated

1. Richard Blackburn and Benson Rosen, "Total Quality and Human Resources Management: Lessons Learned from Baldrige Award-Winning Companies," *Academy of Management Executive*, August 1993, pp. 49–66; and Robert C. Hill and Sara M. Freedman, "Managing the Quality Process: Lessons from a Baldrige Award Winner: A Conversation with John W. Wallace, Chief Executive Officer of The Wallace Company," *Academy of Management Executive*, February 1992, pp. 76–88.
2. Walter Kiechel III,"How to Appraise Performance," *Fortune*, October 12, 1987, pp. 239–240.

American middle-management fast food executives learn Japanese-style leadership and management at a thirteen-day basic training seminar in Malibu, California. This particular program is centered around the ideals of teamwork, obedience, and strenuous work that have led Japanese companies to success.

performance enhancement program at the Wallace Company is intended to work with other quality improvement efforts within the company and, therefore, to make the system easier to use and more meaningful for managers. Management hopes to eliminate the typical statements that supervisors make about doing performance appraisals.

To some employees, performance appraisal is an annual ordeal in which "the boss tries to explain to me why I'm not getting a raise." Other employees look forward to their performance appraisals as opportunities to examine their work and career prospects. At the management level, some line managers dread the performance appraisal system forced on them by the human resource department because of the paperwork required. Top management, in contrast, may view performance appraisal as the most important part of human resource management. Executives, however, are just as likely to avoid formal appraisal as are lower-level managers.[3] Performance management systems that are typically associated with quality improvement efforts, such as those at Wallace, are designed to focus on helping employees improve the quality of their performance and be less of a fearful event.

We begin this chapter by examining the nature of performance management and measurement. Then we discuss in more detail how a good performance management system contributes to total quality management. Next, we turn to reward systems and their role in motivation. We identify important types of rewards and explore perspectives on managing reward systems.

Performance measurement, or performance appraisal, is the process by which a manager (1) evaluates an employee's work behaviors by measurement and comparison with previously established standards, (2) records the results, and (3) communicates the results to the employee.

The Nature of Performance Management and Measurement

Performance measurement, or performance appraisal, is the process by which a manager (1) evaluates an employee's work behaviors by measurement and comparison with previously established standards, (2) records the results, and (3) communicates the results to the employee. A **performance management system (PMS)**

3. Clinton O. Longenecker and Dennis A. Gioia, "The Executive Appraisal Paradox," *Academy of Management Executive*, May 1992, pp. 18–28.

A performance management system (PMS) comprises the organizational processes and activities involved in performance measurement.

comprises the organizational processes and activities involved in performance measurement, as shown in Figure 8.1. Performance measurement involves a manager and an employee, whereas the PMS includes the organizational processes and activities that support the activity. The timing and frequency of evaluations, determination of who appraises whom, measurement procedures, storage and distribution of information, methods of recording the evaluations, and the organization's total quality management program are all aspects of the performance management system. Performance measurement has been called one of the most powerful and important tools for managing human resources in an organization.[4]

Purposes of Performance Measurement

The most basic purpose of performance measurement is to provide information about work behaviors that can be used for feedback, reward allocation, training and development, and personnel planning.

Performance measurement may serve as many as twenty different purposes,[5] but the most basic is to provide information about work behaviors. The end product of performance measurement is information. This information can be used as a basis for feedback, reward allocation, training and development, and human resource planning. All these uses can benefit both the employee and the organization if the performance management system is functioning properly.

Feedback tells the employee where she or he stands in the eyes of the organization. Measurements, of course, are also used to decide and justify reward allocations. Performance evaluations may be used as a starting point for discussions on training, development, and improvement. Finally, the data produced by the performance management system can be used to prepare personnel needs forecasts and management succession plans and to guide human resource activities such as recruiting, training, and development programs. Performance appraisal information can indicate that an employee is ready for promotion or that he or she needs additional training to gain experience in another area of company operations. It may also show that an individual does not have the skills for a certain job and that another person should be recruited to fill that particular role.

FIGURE 8.1

Performance Management System

4. Charles J. Fombrun and Robert L. Laud, "Strategic Issues in Performance Appraisal: Theory and Practice," *Personnel*, November–December 1983, pp. 23–31.
5. H. John Bernardin and Richard W. Beatty, *Performance Appraisal: Assessing Human Behavior at Work* (Boston: Kent, 1984).

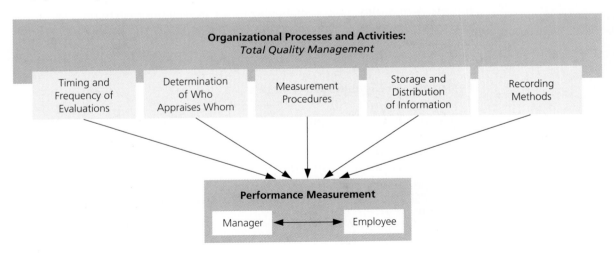

FIGURE 8.2

Purposes of Performance Measurement

Basic Purpose of Performance Measurement: Provide Information about Work Performance	
Judgment of Past Performance	*Development of Future Performance*
Provide a basis for reward allocation Provide a basis for promotions, transfers, layoffs, and so on Identify high-potential employees Validate selection procedures Evaluate previous training programs	Foster work improvement Identify training and development opportunities Develop ways to overcome obstacles and performance barriers Establish supervisor-employee agreement on expectations

Job performance feedback is the primary use of measurement information. Other purposes of performance measurement can be grouped into two broad categories, judgmental and developmental, as shown in Figure 8.2.

Performance measurement with a judgmental orientation focuses on past performance and is concerned mainly with the measurement and comparison of performance and with the uses of the information generated.[6] Judgmental performance appraisals often are used in part to control employee behaviors. The organization rewards desired behaviors with wage raises, promotions, and entrance into high-potential employee development programs and punishes undesirable behaviors with transfers and layoffs, denial of wage increases, and demotions. Performance measurement can provide the necessary documentation for the termination of employees.[7] Performance measurement with a judgmental orientation also provides valuable feedback on the effectiveness of the organization's selection procedures and training programs.

Performance measurement with a developmental orientation focuses on future performance and uses information resulting from evaluations for performance improvement. If improved future performance is the intent of the measurement process, as in quality improvement efforts, the manager may focus on goals or targets for the employee, elimination of obstacles or problems that hinder performance, and future training needs.

Performance Measurement Basics

Employee appraisals are common in every type of organization. How they are done, however, differs across organizations. There are many issues to decide regarding how to conduct an appraisal. Two of the most important issues are who does the appraisal and the frequency of the appraisal.

Margin notes:

Performance measurement with a judgmental orientation focuses on past performance and is concerned mainly with the measurement and comparison of performance and with the uses of the information generated.

Performance measurement with a developmental orientation focuses on future performance and uses information resulting from evaluations or performance improvement.

Two important issues are who does the appraisal and the frequency of the appraisal.

6. L. Cummings and Donald P. Schwab, *Performance in Organizations: Determinants and Appraisal* (Glenview, Ill.: Scott, Foresman, 1973).
7. Kenneth R. Gilberg, "Employee Terminations: Risky Business," *Personnel Administrator,* March 1987, pp. 40–46.

In most measurement systems, the employee's primary evaluator is the supervisor.

The Appraiser   In most measurement systems, the employee's primary evaluator is his or her supervisor.[8] Many other people who observe or are affected by the employee, however, can contribute to the process. These potential raters include managers of other work units, first-level supervisors, second-level supervisors, staff personnel, peers (people at the same level within the organization, but with whom the employee—the ratee—does not work), subordinates, clients or customers, coworkers (people with whom the ratee works either directly or indirectly in the organization), and other employees (people in the organization who are neither peers nor coworkers).

Measurement problems often arise if the supervisor has less than full knowledge of the employee's performance. For example, the supervisor may have little first-hand knowledge of the performance of an employee who works alone outside the company premises, such as a salesperson who makes solo calls on clients or a maintenance person who handles equipment problems in the field. Similar problems may arise when the supervisor has a limited understanding of the technical knowledge involved in an employee's job.

One solution to these problems is a multiple-rater system that incorporates the ratings of several people who have experience with the performance of the employee being rated. Another possible solution is to use the employee as an evaluator. Although they may not actually do so, most employees can evaluate themselves in an unbiased manner.[9] Self-appraisal may be appropriate for evaluating and comparing a given employee's performance in different categories, such as performance quality, interpersonal skills, and team leadership, and it can be quite useful for development and performance improvement. One method of involving employees more in the measurement process is to have the employee and the supervisor work together to do the appraisal. Los Alamos National Laboratory and the Wallace Company are two organizations that use systems that involve both the manager and the employee.[10]

Whoever performs the evaluation must be properly trained. Training usually is designed to reduce rating errors by increasing the rater's observation and categorization skills.[11] In training sessions, raters typically are given examples of different performance levels and methods of recording observations, such as diary keeping. Employees usually perceive performance appraisals as fair if raters are trained and use some form of diary to record actual events.[12]

Frequency of the Appraisal   Regardless of the employee's level of performance, the type of task, or the employee's need for information regarding her or his performance, the organization usually conducts performance appraisals regularly, typically once a year. Conducting performance appraisals annually is convenient for organizational purposes such as record keeping and predictability. Some organizations conduct appraisals semiannually.

8. Richard I. Henderson, *Performance Appraisal* (Reston, Va.: Reston, 1984).
9. P. A. Mabe and S. G. West, "Validity of Self-Evaluation of Ability: A Review and Meta Analysis," *Journal of Applied Psychology*, June 1982, pp. 280–296.
10. Kenneth E. Apt and David W. Watkins, "What One Laboratory Has Learned about Performance Appraisal," *Research Technology Management*, July–August 1989, pp. 22–28; and Hill and Freedman, "Managing the Quality Process: Lessons from a Baldrige Award Winner."
11. Bernardin and Beatty, *Performance Appraisal*.
12. Jerald Greenberg, "Determinants of Perceived Fairness of Performance Evaluations," *Journal of Applied Psychology*, May 1986, pp. 340–342.

Recently some concern has arisen that rigidly established intervals may be inappropriate for all organizations. Three primary issues surround the timing of performance appraisals. First, the task or job cycle time may suggest more frequent performance appraisals; that is, when the employee has finished a distinct unit of work. Second, the organization may need information regarding employee performance for record keeping on a particular project or unit. Third, certain employees may need to have job performance information at more frequent intervals. Several systems for monitoring employee performance on an "as-needed" basis have been proposed as an alternative to the traditional annual system.[13]

Performance Management and Total Quality Management

Total quality management is based on the fact that what is measured is what gets done.

Total quality management (TQM) is a fundamental change in an organization's culture that involves a focus on the customer, an environment of trust and openness, the formation of work teams, breaking down of internal organizational barriers, team leadership coaching, shared powers, and continuous improvement.

Performance management and total quality management are inseparable. One of the basic tenets of total quality management is that improvement only comes in that which is measured.[14] In this section we briefly review total quality management as it incorporates the principles of performance management.

Total quality management (TQM) is a fundamental change in the organization's culture to one that includes a focus on the customer, an environment of trust and openness, formation of work teams, breaking down of internal organizational barriers, team leadership and coaching, shared power, and continuous improvement.[15] The quality culture has to be communicated throughout the organization, involving employees at all levels. Jobs must be redesigned, and all employees must receive significant retraining. Finally, progress toward quality must be measured and rewarded throughout the organization. One company that measures and rewards progress toward diversity goals is Colgate-Palmolive, described in *Diversity in the Workplace*.

All Malcolm Baldrige National Quality Award winners have incorporated quality dimensions into their performance management systems.[16] Table 8.1 summarizes the ways that TQM is reflected in the performance management system.

13. Donald B. Fedor and M. Ronald Buckley, "Issues Surrounding the Need for More Frequent Monitoring of Individual Performance in Organizations," *Public Personnel Management*, Winter 1988, pp. 435–442.
14. Richard J. Schonberger, "Is Strategy Strategic? Impact of Total Quality Management on Strategy," *Academy of Management Executive*, August 1992, pp. 80–87.
15. Pauline N. Brody, "Introduction to Total Quality Management: A Report of Proceedings from the Xerox Quality Forum II," August 1990.
16. Blackburn and Rosen, "Toward Quality and Human Resources Management."

TABLE 8.1

TQM in Performance Management

Ways TQM Is Reflected in the Performance Management System

- Incorporates quality dimensions into the review process
- Uses data from customers, peers, and self-assessment
- Changes the focus from performance to future development
- Focuses on continuous improvement
- Uses team measurement and review

Colgate-Palmolive Uses the Pay System to Encourage Diversity

Colgate-Palmolive is known for having one of the most comprehensive and integrative diversity programs in the United States. In fact, Ann Morrison, president of the New Leaders Institute and noted expert on getting ahead in corporations, lists Colgate-Palmolive as one of sixteen model organizations in managing diversity. Morrison suggests the inclusion of diversity in performance evaluations and in promotion and criteria as two of her top-ten diversity practices. Colgate-Palmolive goes even further by linking pay to progress in meeting diversity goals in the company.

In its Executive Incentive Compensation Plan, about 550 managers in the United States are responsible for making improvement in diversity goals. In the compensation plan, about two-thirds of the bonus is based on meeting financial targets, and one-third is based on individual goals, some of which are the diversity goals.

Managers at Colgate-Palmolive claim that the linking of pay to meeting diversity goals is only a very small part of the diversity program. In fact, they suggest that by itself, it would probably have little effect. Linking pay and diversity goals adds more importance to the overall diversity program, however, because diversity is now measurable and part of the bonus is dependent on it. It is a very tangible way to communicate to managers that diversity is important to Colgate-Palmolive. Colgate-Palmolive seems to realize that what gets measured is what gets done.

SOURCES: "Diversity," *Training and Development*, April 1993, pp. 39–43; and Stephenie Overman, "A Measure of Success," *HR Magazine*, December 1992, pp. 38–40.

Employees are rated on how well they meet customer needs, quality of work, problem solving, and team contributions. In many cases, old-style performance evaluations that focused on past behaviors have been discarded and replaced with newer systems that emphasize planning for future improvements and solving performance problems, as was done at the Wallace Company. Performance management in a TQM setting may also include performance reviews of teams, not just individuals. In addition, because providing customer service is so important to TQM, some performance management systems include input from customers. Companies such as Cadillac and Federal Express routinely include input from peers in the review process.

The founder of the TQM philosophy, W. Edwards Deming, called for the elimination of numerical productivity and work-standard type goals because they focused management's attention on short-run targets and away from satisfying the customer. Instead, he proposed that employee, team, and organizational goals focus on continuous improvement in quality, customer service, decreased product development time, skill upgrading, reduced machine setup time, and increased machine run time.

The performance management systems that organizations use vary greatly in their methods and in their effectiveness. Some are successful, and some are not; some are constantly being changed in a search for improvements. Four factors are crucial to success in incorporating the principles of TQM into the performance management system: commitment to objectives, job analysis, the performance plan, and performance measurement.

Commitment to Objectives

A successful performance management system is based on a strong commitment from the entire organization, especially top management, toward quality improvement.

Successfully incorporating the principles of TQM into the performance management system depends on a strong commitment from the entire organization, especially top management, toward quality improvement. This commitment is made manifest in the objectives of the system. Top management must know what they want the PMS to accomplish and communicate their objectives to those responsible for developing and managing the system, as well as to all employees covered by the system. Clear objectives and strong organizational commitment to quality improvement give supervisors confidence that the time and effort they devote to performance management is worthwhile and gives employees more interest in using the performance review to change behaviors and improve performance. Clearly stated objectives also allow managers to monitor the program, evaluate it periodically, and make any necessary adjustments.[17]

Job Analysis

Job analysis is the process of systematically collecting information about specific jobs for use in developing a performance measurement system, in writing job or position descriptions, and in establishing equitable pay systems.

The second factor in incorporating TQM into an effective PMS is a sound job analysis system that provides comprehensive and accurate descriptions of all jobs in the organization.[18] **Job analysis** is the process of systematically gathering information about specific jobs for use in developing a performance measurement system, in writing job or position descriptions, and in developing equitable pay systems. If an employee's job performance is to be evaluated fairly, the job must be precisely and clearly defined.[19]

Job analysis information can be gathered in various ways and by various people including the employee, a specialist in the human resource department, or an outside consultant. It is of utmost importance to know the purpose of gathering the information because particular performance measurement methods require specific types of information from the job analysis. Therefore, the job analysis method must match the uses for the information. Some methods of job analysis can be very time consuming and expensive; others can be simple and inexpensive. The organization must be certain that the information gained from the analysis will be important enough and used often enough to justify the expense.

There are several job analysis methods, including critical incident, functional job analysis, and job inventory techniques. The best method for an organization, however, is the one that provides information appropriate for the PMS and is the most practical for the situation. Because the job analysis method used is a major determinant of the structure of the pay system that results, managers must be careful to select the proper job analysis techniques.

---

17. See Marshall Whitmire, "Program Evaluation of a Medical Center Performance Appraisal System" (unpublished doctoral dissertation, Arizona State University, 1985), for a discussion of the importance of setting objectives for the PMS.
18. See Henderson, *Performance Appraisal*, and Bernardin and Beatty, *Performance Appraisal*, for more detailed discussions of job analysis.
19. See Patricia S. Eyres, "Assessment: Legally Defensible Performance Appraisal Systems," *Personnel Journal*, July 1989, pp. 58–62, and Ronald G. Wells, "Guidelines for Effective and Defensible Performance Appraisal Systems," *Personnel Journal*, October 1982, pp. 776–782, for good discussions of the importance of well-defined job analysis and performance standards in performance appraisals.

Performance Plan

A **performance plan** is an understanding between an employee and manager of what and how the job is to be done so that both parties know what is expected and how success is defined and measured.

Closely tied to the job analysis is the performance plan. A **performance plan** is an understanding between an employee and manager of what and how the job is to be done so that both parties know what is expected and how success is defined and measured.[20] In TQM terms, a performance plan defines the areas of improvement that an employee is striving for. It defines the goals and standards for improvement in quality or skills. A performance plan can help clarify mutual expectations, serve as the basis for periodic reviews, and reduce arguments, conflicts, and grievances.

Human resource professionals suggest several guidelines for using performance plans. First, performance plans should never promise more than can reasonably be delivered. That is, employee and manager should be realistic about what can be expected from the employee. Second, the performance plan should be based on what the organization deems to be important. Improvements in quality, response time, or cycle time are popular areas for improvement in TQM. Finally, performance plans should cover broad areas of responsibility so they keep the employee focused on the major parts of the job and not on something that is of little importance.[21]

Performance Measurement

The courts and Equal Employment Opportunity guidelines have recommended that performance measurements be based on job-related criteria.

The cornerstone of TQM and a good performance management system is the method by which performance is measured. Detailed descriptions of the many different methods for measuring performance is beyond the scope of this book and may be more appropriately covered in a course in human resource management or performance appraisal. In this section, however, we present a few general comments about how performance can be measured. The measurement method provides the information managers use in making decisions regarding salary adjustment, promotion, transfer, training, and discipline. The courts and Equal Employment Opportunity guidelines have recommended that performance measurements be based on job-related criteria rather than on some other factor such as friendship, age, gender, religion, or national origin.[22] Determining exactly what is being measured with some systems is often difficult. Some systems focus on the measurement of specific behaviors or performance outcomes, whereas others emphasize the measurement of personality traits, such as leadership ability, enthusiasm, or ability to work with others.

In addition, the measurement systems used in performance appraisals must be valid, reliable, and free of bias to provide useful information for the decision maker. They must not produce ratings that are consistently too lenient or severe or that bunch up in the middle, and they must be free of perceptual and timing errors.

Organizations use many different appraisal techniques that differ according to whether they evaluate employees individually or in comparison with others. Individual performance measurement methods vary greatly and have advantages and disadvantages. Some of the most popular individual methods are graphic rating

20. Jerry Eisen, "Performance Plans Help Define Goals, Objectives, and Standards," *Human Resources Update*, April 1993, p. 1.
21. Ibid
22. Leonard Berger, "Promise of Criterion-Referenced Performance Appraisal (CRPA)," *Review of Public Personnel Administration*, Vol. 3, 1983, pp. 21–32.

scales, checklists, essays or diaries, behaviorally anchored rating scales, forced choice systems, and management by objectives. These systems are easy to use and familiar to most managers. However, the major problems common to all individual methods are the tendency to rate most individuals about the same and the inability to discriminate among variable levels of performance.

Comparative methods evaluate two or more employees by comparing them to each other on various performance dimensions. In general, these methods were developed to eliminate the tendency to rate most individuals about the same and to provide information useful for reward allocation decisions. The most popular comparative methods are ranking, forced distribution, paired comparisons, and the use of multiple raters in making comparisons. Comparative methods, however, are more difficult to use, are unfamiliar to many managers, and may require sophisticated development procedures and a computerized analytical system to extract usable information.

Reward Systems in Organizations

The **reward system** consists of all organizational components—including people, processes, rules and procedures, and decision-making activities—involved in the allocation of compensation and benefits to employees in exchange for their contributions to the organization.

Employees contribute many resources to the organization: time, effort, knowledge, skills, creativity, and energy.

Tangible compensation consists of rewards that have a definite value. **Intangible compensation** refers to rewards whose value is less easily defined.

The reward system is an important tool that managers can use to channel employee motivation in desired ways. The **reward system** consists of all organizational components—including people, processes, rules and procedures, and decision-making activities–involved in the allocation of compensation and benefits to employees in exchange for their contributions to the organization. As we examine organizational reward systems, it is important to keep in mind their relationship to employee motivation, perception, and learning (covered in Chapters 3 through 6). In short, reward systems in an organizational context cannot be studied apart from their effects on individuals.[23]

The organizational reward system and the performance measurement system are the major links in the exchange process between individual employees and the organization. Employees contribute many resources to the organization: time, effort, knowledge, skills, creativity, and energy. In turn, the organization rewards its employees with both tangible and intangible compensation. **Tangible compensation** consists of rewards that have a definite value, such as pay, pension plans, life and health insurance, and vacations. **Intangible compensation** refers to rewards whose value is less easily defined, such as status symbols, opportunities to be creative, and self-esteem. Figure 8.3 illustrates this transaction process.

As is typical of most areas in the field of organizational behavior, the transaction process is dynamic rather than static. If either party feels the transaction is not equitable, the parties may attempt to reach agreement on an equitable relationship or they may terminate the relationship. Nor does the transaction relationship exist in a vacuum. Both parties are at least somewhat aware of the transactions between employees and other organizations. For instance, workers whose employment depends on open negotiation, such as union members, some public school teachers, or government workers, actual salaries or hourly wages are well known. Others

23. Edward E. Lawler, *Pay and Organization Development* (Reading, Mass.: Addison-Wesley, 1981); Edward E. Lawler, "The Design of Effective Reward Systems," in Jay W. Lorsch (Ed.), *Handbook of Organizational Behavior* (Englewood Cliffs, N.J.: Prentice-Hall, 1987), pp. 255–271; and Jeffrey Pfeffer and Alison Davis-Blake, "Understanding Organizational Wage Structures," *Academy of Management Journal*, Vol. 30, 1987, pp. 437–455.

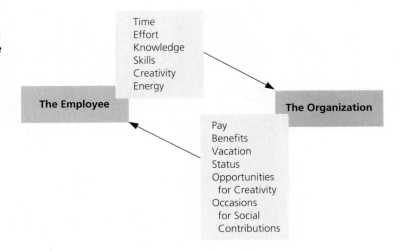

FIGURE 8.3

The Transaction Between
the Organization and the
Individual

may openly discuss wages or salaries with coworkers and friends. Because an organization's reward system is the one part of the transaction process that the organization can control, the system must be properly designed and carefully managed.

Roles, Purposes, and Meanings of Rewards

The purposes of the reward system are to attract, retain, and motivate qualified employees, based on three issues: the concept of fairness and equality of rewards, the importance of each employee's contribution to the organization, and the status of the external labor market.

In most organizations the purpose of the reward system is to attract, retain, and motivate qualified employees.[24] Compensation philosophy centers on three issues: the concept of fairness and equality of rewards, the importance of each employee's contribution to the organization, and the status of the external labor market.

The organization's compensation structure must be equitable and consistent to ensure equality of treatment and compliance with the law. In addition, compensation should be a fair reward for the individual's contributions to the organization, although in most cases these contributions are difficult, if not impossible, to measure objectively. Given this limitation, managers should be as fair and equitable as possible. Finally, the system must be competitive in the external labor market for the organization to attract and retain competent workers in appropriate fields.

Beyond these broad considerations, an organization must develop its philosophy of compensation based on its own conditions and needs, and this philosophy must be defined and built into the actual reward system. For example, the compensation philosophy of Lincoln Electric Co. is that all employees should receive compensation in accordance with their accomplishments and should share in the profits they helped create.[25] As a result, Lincoln employees earn about twice as much as similar workers at other companies, yet labor costs per sales dollar at Lincoln are well below industry averages.

24. Douglas B. Gehrman, "Beyond Today's Compensation and Performance Appraisal Systems," *Personnel Administrator*, March 1984, pp. 21–33; and Jeffrey Kerr and John W. Slocum, Jr., "Managing Corporate Culture through Reward Systems," *Academy of Management Executive*, Vol. 1, No. 2, May 1987, pp. 99–108.
25. James F. Lincoln, *A New Approach to Industrial Economics* (New York: Devin-Adair, 1961), reprinted in Arthur A. Thompson, Jr., and A. J. Strickland III, *Strategic Management: Concepts and Cases*, 3rd ed. (Plano, Tex.: Business Publications, 1984), p. 948.

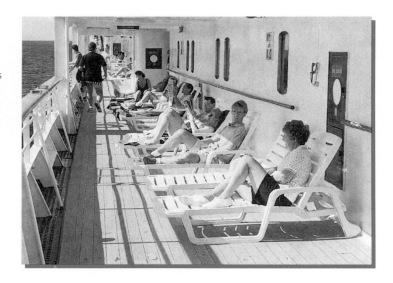

A well-developed compensation philosophy articulates the purpose of the system and provides a framework for making compensation decisions. It can serve as a point of stability in changing economic, technological, and labor market conditions. In addition, a clearly stated philosophy can give the system credibility among those most affected by it—the employees. The organization needs to decide what types of behaviors or performance it wants to encourage with a reward system because what is rewarded tends to recur. Possible behaviors include performance, longevity, attendance, loyalty, contributions to the "bottom line," responsibility, and conformity.

Performance measurement assesses these behaviors, but the choice of which behaviors to reward is a function of the compensation system. A reward system must also take into account volatile economic issues such as inflation, market conditions, technology, and labor union activities.

It is also important for the organization to recognize that organizational rewards have many meanings for employees. Intrinsic and extrinsic rewards carry both surface and symbolic value. The **surface value** of a reward to an employee is the meaning it has at an objective level. A salary increase of 5 percent, for example means that an individual has 5 percent more spending power than before, whereas a promotion, on the surface, means new duties and responsibilities. Rewards also carry **symbolic value**. Consider what frequently happens when a professional football or basketball team signs a top college prospect for a large salary. The new player often feels enormous pressure to live up to the salary, and veteran players may argue that their pay should be increased to keep the salary structure in balance. Rewards convey to people how much they are valued by the organization, as well as their importance relative to others. Consider again a 5 percent salary increase. If the recipient later finds out that everyone else got 3 percent or less, he or she will feel vitally important to the organization, someone whose contributions are recognized and valued. On the other hand, if everyone else got at least 8 percent, the person probably will believe the organization places little value on his

The **surface value** of a reward to an employee is the meaning it has at an objective level.

Rewards also carry **symbolic value**; these rewards convey to people how much they are valued by the organization.

or her contributions. In short, then, managers need to tune in to the many meanings rewards can convey—not only the surface messages but the symbolic messages as well.[26]

Types of Rewards

Most organizations use several different types of rewards. The most commonly used rewards are money (wages, salary, commission), incentive systems, benefits, perquisites, and awards. The rewards are combined in a compensation package.

Money For most people, the most important organizational reward is money. Obviously, money is important because of the things it can buy, but, as we just noted, it can also symbolize an employee's worth. A recent study found that out of 730 executives (2 for each of the 365 largest U.S. corporations), 467 reported income of more than $1 million in 1992.[27] Clearly, monetary rewards play an important role in organizations. The rapid increases in executive pay has been the subject of much debate over the past several years. *The Ethical Dilemma* discusses the issues of executive pay.

The student of organizational behavior must understand the importance of money as a type of compensation. Employee compensation is a major cost of doing business—as much as 50 to 60 percent in many organizations. Pay is considered a major source of employee dissatisfaction.[28] As the most tangible part of the transaction relationship between the organization and the individual, it also can be used as an instrument of change within the organization. For example, salary adjustments might consciously be used to signal who is more valuable and who is less valuable to the organization or to clarify norms as to what is expected and what will be rewarded in the future.

To verify the competitiveness of its pay scales, an organization can also conduct a survey of pay at other companies in the same industry or use data from surveys conducted by groups such as the Bureau of Labor Statistics, the American Management Association, or the Administrative Management Society. Other issues of concern in the design of a pay system include the number of pay grades and the number of steps within each grade; the minimum, midpoint, and maximum pay levels for each grade and for the organization as a whole; the amount of overlap between grades; the way in which an employee moves from one step or grade to the next; and the effect on the pay system of changes in external conditions (for example, labor supply and demand or inflation).[29]

Incentive Systems Incentive systems usually promise additional money for certain types of performance. Examples of incentive programs include the following:

26. See Richard T. Mowday, "Equity Theory Predictions of Behavior in Organizations," in Richard M. Steers and Lyman W. Porter (Eds.), *Motivation and Work Behavior*, 4th ed. (New York: McGraw-Hill, 1987), pp. 89–110; and Rabindra N. Kanungo and Jon Hartwick, "An Alternative to the Intrinsic-Extrinsic Dichotomy of Work Rewards," *Journal of Management*, Vol. 13, Winter 1987, pp. 751–766.
27. "Executive Pay: The Party Ain't Over Yet," *Business Week*, April 26, 1993, pp. 56–79.
28. See Lawler, *Pay and Organization Development*, for a more detailed discussion of organizational pay issues.
29. See Richard I. Henderson, *Performance Appraisal* (Reston, Va.: Reston, 1984), for more information on the design of pay structures.

Executive Pay: Too High and Out of Control? Or Justly Deserved?

Executive pay has continued to go up significantly even though experts have been calling for reform for several years. Experts have noted that because of inflation and other factors, the average salaries of hourly workers, teachers, and engineers have risen at a rate of about 30 percent each decade since the 1960s. Executive pay also rose at about that rate until the 1980s, when executive pay increased by more than 400 percent. Estimates are that the CEOs of the top U.S. corporations average approximately $2 million per year in total compensation (salary, bonus, and long-term compensation), while the average hourly worker earns about $25,000 per year and the average teacher earns about $34,000 per year. The loudest cries come from stockholders who get very little return for their investment and the workers of companies who get either laid off or no pay raises when the executives get large pay raises.

One explanation for this phenomenon is that executive pay is usually set by a special compensation committee of the board of directors of the company. A common practice is to have several members of this committee be chief executive officers of other companies. It is no surprise that a committee of CEOs is likely to recommend that one of their counterparts, especially one who appointed them to the board, be very highly paid. Another reason for the extremely large increases has been the nature of long-term incentive options awarded to executives. Although, in theory, these seem like good methods of tying pay to performance, closer examination has revealed that many of the conditions that had to be met for the stock options to be awarded were too easy and virtually guaranteed to be easily met.

SOURCES: "Executive Pay: Compensation at the Top Is Out of Control. Here's How to Reform It," *Business Week*, March 30, 1992, pp. 52–58; Geoffrey Colvin, "How to Pay the CEO Right," *Fortune*, April 6, 1992, pp. 60–69; "What, Me Overpaid? CEO's Fight Back," *Business Week*, May 4, 1992, pp. 142–148; and "Executive Pay: The Party Ain't Over Yet," *Business Week*, April 26, 1993, pp. 55–79.

1. *Piecework programs.* Tie a worker's earnings to the number of units produced.
2. *Gain-sharing programs.* Grant additional earnings to employees or work groups for cost-reduction efforts or ideas.
3. *Commission programs.* Provide sales personnel with earnings based on the number of units they sell.
4. *Bonus systems.* Provide management personnel with lump sums from a special bonus pool based on the financial performance of the organization or a unit of the organization.
5. *Long-term compensation.* Provides management personnel with substantial additional income based on stock price performance, earnings per share, or return on equity.
6. *Merit pay plans.* Base raises on the employee's performance as determined by objectively measured productivity or by the results of a performance appraisal
7. *Profit-sharing plans.* Distribute a percentage of the organization's profits to all employees at a predetermined rate.
8. *Employee stock option plans.* Typically set aside a block of stock in the company for employees to purchase at a reduced rate, with the expectation that employees who own part of the company are more committed to it and work harder to increase the value of their stock.

Plans oriented mainly toward individual employees may cause increased competition for the rewards and some possibly disruptive behaviors, such as sabotaging a coworker's performance, sacrificing quality for quantity, or fighting over customers. A group incentive plan, on the other hand, requires that employees trust one another and work together. Of course, incentive systems have advantages and disadvantages. Long-term compensation for executives is particularly controversial because of the large sums of money involved and the basis for the payments.[30] The successful implementation of an incentive program depends on the history and traditions of the organization; the nature of the organization's products or services; current political, economic, and legal conditions; and employee needs and perceptions about the system.

Benefits Another major component of the compensation package is the employee benefits plan. Benefits often are called *indirect compensation.* Typical benefits provided by organizations include the following:

1. *Payment for time not worked, both on and off the job.* On-the-job free time includes lunch periods, rest periods, coffee breaks, wash-up times, and get-ready time. Off-the-job time not worked includes vacations, sick leaves, holidays, and personal days.
2. *Social security contributions.* The employer contributes half the money paid into the system established under the Federal Insurance Contributions Act (FICA). The employee pays the other half, making a total of approximately $3,045 per year for the average employee. The employee receives social security income when she or he retires.
3. *Unemployment compensation.* People who have lost their jobs or are temporarily laid off get a percentage of their wages from the state. Funds come from payments by companies as regulated by state laws.
4. *Disability and workers' compensation benefits.* Employers contribute funds to assist workers who are ill or injured and cannot work owing to occupational injury or ailment. These benefits are regulated by federal and state laws.
5. *Life and health insurance programs.* Most organizations offer insurance at a cost far below what individuals would pay to buy insurance by themselves.
6. *Pension plans.* Most organizations offer plans to provide supplementary income to employees after they retire. These company-paid or joint employee-and-company-paid programs are meant to supplement social security.

A company's social security, unemployment, and workers' compensation contributions are set by law. But how much to contribute for other kinds of benefits is up to each company. Some organizations contribute more to the cost of these benefits than others do. Some companies pay the entire cost; others pay a percentage of the cost of certain benefits, such as health insurance, and bear the entire cost of others. Offering benefits beyond wages became a standard component of compensation during World War II as a way of increasing employee compensation when wage controls were in effect. Since then, competition for employees and employee demands (expressed, for instance, in union bargaining) have caused companies to increase these benefits. In many organizations, benefits now account for 30 to 40 percent of payroll.

30. "Is the Top Brass Overpaid? Six Big Guns Sound Off," *Business Week*, March 30, 1992, pp. 56–57.

Benefits are becoming a larger burden on organizations in the United States than on organizations in other countries.

The burden of providing employee benefits is growing heavier for firms in the United States than it is for organizations in other countries. For example, Chrysler Corp. now spends about $700 per car on health benefits for its workers, whereas foreign car manufacturers spend only about $200 per car.[31] Although these benefit costs could be reduced, employers do not know what the ramifications of cuts would be in terms of employee morale, motivation, turnover, and recruiting. Benefits therefore are a major concern for businesses, and some are trying to reduce the costs of indirect compensation. The motivational power of benefits is unknown; however, weak or poorly designed benefit packages have been shown to cause employee dissatisfaction.

Perquisites are means of compensation in the form of special privileges associated with employees of relatively high rank in the organization.

Perquisites **Perquisites,** which are means of compensation in the form of special privileges, are an aspect of the exchange relationship that has received little theoretical consideration but much legal attention and media coverage. For years, the top executives of many organizations were allowed privileges such as unlimited use of the company airplane, motor home, vacation home, and executive dining room. Eventually, the Internal Revenue Service ruled that some "perks" constitute a form of income and thus can be taxed. The IRS decision has substantially changed the nature of these benefits, but they have not entirely disappeared, nor are they likely to. More than anything else, perquisites seem to add to the status of their recipients and thus serve to increase job satisfaction and reduce turnover.

Awards In many companies, employees receive awards for everything from seniority to perfect attendance, from zero defects (quality work) to cost reduction suggestions. Award programs can be costly in the time required to run them and in money if cash awards are given.

Award systems can improve performance under the right conditions. In one medium-size manufacturing company, careless work habits were pushing up the costs of scrap and rework (the cost of scrapping defective parts or reworking them to meet standards). Management instituted a zero-defects program to recognize employees who did perfect or near perfect work. The first month, two workers in shipping caused only one defect in more than 2,000 parts handled. Division management called a meeting in the lunchroom and recognized each worker with a plaque and a ribbon. The next month, the same two workers had two defects and there was no award. The following month, the two workers had zero defects and, once again top management called a meeting to give out plaques and ribbons. Elsewhere in the plant, defects, scrap, and rework decreased dramatically as workers evidently sought recognition for quality work. What worked in this particular plant may or may not work in others. The effects of award programs can be explained by reinforcement theory (Chapter 6) or the various need theories (Chapter 4).

Managing Reward Systems

Much of our discussion on reward systems has focused on general issues. As Table 8.2 shows, however, the organization must address other issues in the development of organizational reward systems. The organization must consider its ability to pay employees at certain levels, economic and labor market conditions, and the

31. "Employee Benefits for a Changing Work Force," *Business Week,* November 5, 1990, pp. 31–40.

TABLE 8.2

Issues to Consider
in Developing Reward
Systems

Issue	Important Examples
Pay Secrecy	■ Open, closed, partial ■ Link with performance appraisal ■ Equity perceptions
Employee Participation	■ By human resource department ■ By joint employee/management committee
Flexible System	■ Cafeteria-style benefits ■ Annual lump sum or monthly bonus ■ Salary versus benefits
Ability to Pay	■ Organization's financial performance ■ Expected future earnings
Economic and Labor Market Factors	■ Inflation rate ■ Industry pay standards ■ Unemployment rate
Impact on Organizational Performance	■ Increase in costs ■ Impact on performance

impact of the pay system on organizational financial performance. In addition, the organization must consider the issues of reward system flexibility, the degree of employee participation in the reward system, and pay secrecy.

Flexible Reward Systems

A **flexible reward system** allows employees to choose the combination of benefits that best suits their needs.

Flexible, or cafeteria-style, reward systems are a recent and increasingly popular variation on the standard compensation system.[32] A **flexible reward system** allows employees to choose the combination of benefits that best suits their needs. For example, younger workers starting a family may prefer additional maternity or paternity benefits or a family medical plan that pays 100 percent, whereas a worker nearing retirement may want to maximize pension benefits. Organizations even get more for their benefits dollars by using the flexible approach. Flexible systems generally require more administrative time and effort to develop and maintain than the standard approach, but the benefits of the flexible approach seem to outweigh these costs. In fact, most companies save enough money to pay back the initial investment in a few years.[33]

32. See Dale Gifford, "The Status of Flexible Compensation," *Personnel Administrator*, May 1984, pp. 19–25, for more information on flexible compensation systems.
33. Lance D. Tane and Michael E. Treacy, "Benefits That Bend with Employees' Needs," *Nation's Business*, April 1984, pp. 80–82; Henderson, *Performance Appraisal*; and "Benefits Are Getting More Flexible–But Caveat Emptor," *Business Week*, September 8, 1986, pp. 64–66.

Some organizations are starting to apply the flexible approach to pay. For example, employees sometimes have the option of taking an annual salary increase in one lump sum rather than in monthly increments. General Electric recently implemented such a system for some of its managers.[34] Although lump-sum payments necessitate special provisions for taxes and for payback if the employee quits during the year the raise was given, this alternative lets the employee lay hands on the full amount of the increase at one time, possibly resulting in a greater motivational impact. In a totally flexible reward system, employees are able to trade off salary increases for benefits increases, and vice versa.

Participative Pay Systems

In keeping with the current trend toward worker involvement in organizational decision making, employee participation in the pay process is also increasing. A **participative pay system** may involve the employee in the system's design, administration, or both. A pay system can be designed by staff members of the organization's human resource department, a committee of managers in the organization, an outside consultant, the employees, or a combination of these sources. Organizations that have used a joint management-employee task force to design the compensation system generally have succeeded in designing and implementing a plan that managers could use and employees believed in.[35]

Employee participation in administering the pay system is a natural extension of having employees participate in its design. Examples of companies that have involved employees in the administration of the pay system include Romac Industries, where employees vote on the pay of other employees; Graphic Controls Corp., where each manager's pay is determined by a group of peers; and the Friedman-Jacobs Co., where employees set their own wages based on their perceptions of their performance.[36] Allowing individuals and work groups to set their own salaries may not be appropriate for all organizations, but it can be successful in organizations characterized by a climate of trust, joint problem solving, and a participative management style.

Pay Secrecy

A policy of open salary information means that the exact salary amounts for employees are public knowledge. State governments, for instance, make public the salary of everyone on their payrolls. Complete secrecy means that no information is available to employees regarding other employees' salaries, average or percentage raises, or salary ranges. The National Labor Relations Board recently upheld an earlier ruling that an employer's starting or enforcing a rule that forbids employees' discussing their salaries "constitutes interference, restraint, and coercion of protected employee rights

---

34. "How'd You Like a Big Fat Bonus—But No Raise?" *Business Week*, November 3, 1986, pp. 30–31.
35. Lawler, *Pay and Organization Development*, pp. 101–111. See also Jack C. Horn, "Bigger Pay for Better Work," *Psychology Today*, July 1987, pp. 54–57.
36. See Lawler, *Pay and Organization Development*, pp. 109–110.

under the National Labor Relations Act."[37] Although a few organizations have a completely public or a completely secret system, most are somewhere in the middle.

Diverse issues surround the question of secret versus open pay.[38] Some workers believe their pay is their business and no one else's; others prefer knowing exactly where they stand in relation to other employees. (The latter is a concrete example of an equity perception issue.) In an open pay system, managers must be able to defend the pay differences to those who are paid less. From a motivational point of view, an open system may clarify the relationship between pay and performance for all concerned. Moreover, research evidence suggests that in a secret system, employees tend to overestimate coworkers' pay, which can cause motivational problems.[39] In light of these considerations, many organizations have elected a compromise solution: a partially open system that lets employees know the salary range of jobs and average increases within each range.

Summary of Key Points

- Performance measurement, or performance appraisal, is the process by which work behaviors are measured and compared with established standards and the results recorded and communicated. Its purposes are to evaluate employees' work performance and to provide information for organizational uses such as compensation, personnel planning, and employee training and development. Two primary issues of performance appraisal are who does the appraisal and at what frequency should the appraisal be done.
- The measurement of performance and total quality management are inseparable. Total quality management is a fundamental change in the organization's culture to one that includes a focus on the customer, an environment of trust and openness, formation of work teams, breaking down of internal organizational barriers, team leadership and coaching, shared power, and continuous improvement. The essential elements for success of TQM are commitment to objectives, job analysis, the performance plan, and measurement of performance.
- Performance can be measured through individual assessment methods (graphic rating scales, checklists, essays or diaries, behaviorally anchored rating scales, forced choice, and management by objectives); comparative techniques (ranking, forced distribution, and paired comparison); and new approaches that use multiple raters and comparative methods. Each method has advantages and disadvantages.
- Another major aspect of managing people in organizations is the reward system. The purpose of the reward system is to attract, retain, and motivate qualified employees and to maintain a pay structure that is internally equitable and externally competitive. Rewards have both surface and symbolic value.
- Rewards take the form of money, incentive systems, benefits, perquisites, and awards. Factors such as motivational impact, cost, and fit with the organizational system must be considered when designing or analyzing a reward system. Other issues related to reward systems are the flexibility of reward systems (or cafeteria-style benefits), employee participation in the pay system, and secrecy of the pay system.

37. Jerry Eisen, "Rule Against Salary Discussion Big No-No," *Human Resources Update,* April 1993, p. 1.
38. See Lawler, *Pay and Organization Development,* pp. 43–50, for more discussion of the secret versus open pay system.
39. Ibid.

Discussion Questions

1. Why are employees not simply left alone to do their jobs? Why, instead do they have their performance measured and evaluated all the time?
2. In what ways is your performance as a student evaluated?
3. How can you as a student apply total quality management to your job as a student?
4. If you were the manager of a work group, which type of performance measurement method would you use? Why?
5. As a student in this class, what "rewards" do you receive in exchange for your time and effort? What are the rewards for the professor who teaches this class? How do your contributions and rewards differ from those of some other student in the class?
6. Do you expect to obtain the rewards you discussed in question 5 on the basis of your intelligence, your hard work, the number of hours you spend in the library, your height, your good looks, your work experience, or some other personal factor?
7. What does Herzberg's dual-structure theory of motivation (discussed in an earlier chapter) tell us about rewarding employees at work?
8. What does expectancy theory of motivation (discussed in an earlier chapter) tell us about rewarding employees at work?
9. Often institutions in the federal and state governments give the same percentage pay raise to all of their employees. What do you think is the effect of this type of pay raise on employee motivation?
10. If you were analyzing your university from the TQM point of view, how would you suggest that the TQM effort bring together, or integrate, performance measurement, performance management, and the university reward system?

EXPERIENTIAL EXERCISE

Purpose   The purpose of this exercise is to illustrate how compensation can be used to affect employee motivation.

Format   You will be asked to review eight managers and make salary adjustments for each.

Procedure   Following are your notes on the performance of eight managers who work for you. You (either individually or as a group, depending on how your instructor chooses to do the exercise) have to make salary increase recommendations for eight managers who have just completed their first year with the company and are now to be considered for their first annual raise. Keep in mind that you may be setting precedents and that you need to keep salary costs down. Your company, however, has no formal restrictions on the kind of raises you can give. Indicate the sizes of the raise that you would like to give each manager by writing a percentage next to each of their names.

Your instructor might alter the situation in one of several ways. One way is to assume that all of the eight managers entered the company at the same salary, say $30,000, which gives a total salary expense of $240,000. If upper management has allowed a salary raise pool of 10 percent of the current salary expenses, then you as the manager have $24,000 to give out as raises. In this variation, students are able to deal with actual dollar amounts rather than just percentages for the raises. Another interesting variation is to assume that all of the managers entered the company at different salaries, averaging $30,000. (The instructor can create many interesting possibilities for how these salaries might vary.) Then, the students can suggest salaries for the different managers.

_____ % *Abraham McGowan*. Abe is not, as far as you can tell, a good performer. You have checked your view with others and they also do not feel that he is effective. However, you happen to know that he has one of the toughest work groups to manage. His subordinates have low skill levels and the work is dirty and hard. If you lose him you are not sure whom you could find to replace him.

_____ % *Benjy Berger*. Benjy is single and seems to live the life of a carefree bachelor. In general, you feel that his job performance is not up to par, and some of his "goofs" are well known to his fellow employees.

_____ % *Clyde Clod*. Although you consider Clyde to be one of your best subordinates, it is quite apparent that other people do not consider him to be an effective manager. Clyde has married a rich wife, and as far as you know he does not need additional money.

_____ % *David Doodle*. You happen to know from your personal relationship with "Doodles" that he badly needs more money because of certain personal problems he is having. As far as you are concerned, he also happens to be one of the best of your subordinates. For some reason your enthusiasm for him is not shared by your other subordinates and you have heard them make joking remarks about his performance.

_____ % *Ellie Ellesberg*. Ellie has been very successful so far in the tasks she has undertaken. You are particularly impressed by this because she has a hard job. She needs money more than many of the other people, and you are sure that they also respect her because of her good performance.

_____ % *Fred Foster*. Fred has turned out to be a very pleasant surprise to you. He has done an excellent job and it is generally accepted among the others that he is one of the best people. This surprises you because he is often frivolous and does not seem to care very much about money and promotion.

_____ % *Greta Goslow*. Your opinion is that Greta just is not cutting the mustard. Surprisingly enough, however, when you check with others to see how they feel about her, you discover that her work is very highly regarded. You also know that she badly needs a raise. She was just recently widowed and is finding it extremely difficult to support the house and her young family of four.

_____ % *Harry Hummer*. You know Harry personally and he just seems to squander his money continually. He has a fairly easy job assignment and your own view is that he does not do it particularly well. You are, therefore, quite surprised to find that several of the other new managers think that he is the best of the new group.

After you have made the assignments for the eight people, you will have a chance to discuss them either in groups or in the larger class discussion.

Follow-up Questions

1. Is there a clear difference between the highest and lowest performer? Why or why not?
2. Did you notice the differences in the types of information that you had available to make the raise decisions? How did you utilize the different sources of information?
3. In what ways did your assignment of raises reflect different views of motivation?

SOURCE: Adaptation of "Motivation Through Compensation" by Douglas T. Hall from the *Instructor's Manual for Experiences in Management and Organizational Behavior*, by Edward E. Lawler, III. Copyright © 1975 by John Wiley and Sons, Inc. Reprinted by permission of Edward E. Lawler, III.

| CASE 8.1 | **Innovative Pay at General Electric's Plant in Puerto Rico** |

General Electric Co. is the fifth largest industrial corporation in the U.S. It has 274 manufacturing plants in 26 countries. It is large, old, and the subject of much public scrutiny. Its chief executive officer, John F. (Jack) Welch, is often quoted, interviewed, and reported on in the popular and business press. According to a survey, in 1992 Welch was the thirteenth highest-paid chief executive in the United States, making a total of almost $18 million ($3.5 million in salary and bonuses and approximately $14.5 million in long-term compensation.)

Because of Welch's high salary, the importance of increasing employee productivity, and the downsizing of the company, pay practices and increasing productivity are major issues throughout the company. Many of the divisions are relatively autonomous in how they do business in manufacturing, marketing, and even human resource practices. For example, its new plant in Bayamon, Puerto Rico (part of the capacitor and power protection division), has only three layers of employees: 172 hourly workers, 15 salaried employees, no supervisors, and no staff. In effect, it is an organization with no supervisors or middle managers. Employees, who work in one of the traditional functional areas, are also organized into ten-person teams, each team responsible for a major area of the plant, such as shipping, receiving, and assembly. The teams meet every week. The salaried employees serve as advisors to these functional area teams. Employees rotate from one functional area into others every six months and thus learn different jobs throughout the plant as well as how the different products and the plant work together.

One of the most innovative aspects of this work-training program is that employees receive a $0.25 per hour pay increase at each rotation. Additional pay increases are awarded for taking classes in English and other business-related subjects. In addition, employees are awarded bonuses of up to $225 each quarter for plantwide performance and attendance. This innovative training and pay system, along with the lack of supervision and employee/team management, is credited with increasing the productivity of the plant to more than 20 percent that of other similar plants in the company, and further productivity increases are expected.

Case Questions

1. Of what importance is the difference between the pay of the chief executive officer, Jack Welch, and the self-managed hourly workers in the Puerto Rican plant?
2. Describe the difference between pay for training and pay for performance in terms of their impact on performance.

SOURCES: James C. Hyatt, "GE Boosted Welch's Incentives in 1992," *Wall Street Journal*, March 11, 1993, p. B12; "Executive Pay: The Party Ain't Over Yet," *Business Week*, April 26, 1993, pp. 56–79; "The Search for the Organization of Tomorrow," *Fortune*, May 18, 1992, pp. 92–98; and Gary Hoover, Alta Campbell, and Patrick J. Spain, *Hoover's Handbook of American Business 1993*, The Reference Press, p. 291.

Andy Davis was proud of his restaurant, The Golden Bow. Its location was perfect, its decor tasteful, its clientele generous and distinguished. When he first took over the business a year ago, Davis had worried that the local labor shortage might make it difficult to hire good workers. But he had made some contacts at a local college and hired a group of servers who worked well with customers and with one another. The only problem he still had not solved was the dishwasher.

At first Davis felt lucky when he found Eddie Munz, a local high school dropout who had some experience washing dishes. Davis could not afford to pay a dishwasher more than $4 an hour, but Eddie did not seem to mind that. Moreover, Eddie seemed to get the dishes clean. But he was so slow! Davis originally thought Eddie just was not quick about anything, but he changed his mind as he observed his behavior in the kitchen. Eddie loved to talk to the cooks, often turning his back on the dishes for minutes at a time to chitchat. He also nibbled desserts off of dirty plates and sprayed the servers with water whenever they got near him. The kitchen was always a mess, and so many dishes would pile up that often two hours after closing time, when everything else was ready for the next day, Eddie would still be scraping and squirting and talking. Davis began to wonder if there was a method to Eddie's madness: he was getting paid by the hour, so why should he work faster? But Davis did not like having a constantly sloppy kitchen, so he determined to have a talk with Eddie.

Davis figured out what Eddie had been making on his reasonably efficient nights—$28—and then met with Eddie and made him a proposal. First he asked Eddie how soon he thought he could finish after the last customer left. Eddie said an hour and a quarter.

When Davis asked if he would be interested in getting off forty-five minutes earlier than he had been, Eddie seemed excited. And when he offered to pay Eddie the $28 for a complete job every night, regardless of when he finished, Eddie could hardly contain himself. It turned out he did not like to work until 2:00 A.M., but he needed every dollar he could get.

The next week, a new chalkboard appeared next to the kitchen door leading out to the dining room. On top it read, "Eddie's Goal for a Record Time." By the end of the first week, Davis printed on the bottom "1." Davis began inspecting the dishes more often than usual, but he found no decrease in the quality of Eddie's work. So on Sunday, he said to Eddie, "Let's try for an hour."

A month later, the board read "42 minutes." The situation in the kitchen had changed radically. The former "Eddie the Slob" had become "Eddie the Perfectionist." His area spotless, he was often waiting when someone came from the dining room with a stack of dirty plates, and he took it as a personal affront if anyone found a spot on a plate he had washed. Instead of complaining about Eddie squirting them, the servers kidded him about what a worker he had become, and they stacked the plates and separated the silver to help him break his record. And the first time Eddie got done at 12:42, they all went out for an hour on the town together.

Case Questions

1. What did Davis do to change Eddie's behavior?
2. Which elements of total quality management and performance management did Davis use?
3. Could Davis have used a different system of rewards to get the same results from Eddie?

CHAPTER 9

Managing Stress and Interpersonal Conflict

OUTLINE

OBJECTIVES

After studying this chapter, you should be able to:

Discuss the nature of work stress.

Identify and discuss several causes of stress.

Identify and describe several consequences of stress.

Explain ways to manage stress.

Describe the nature of conflict in organizations.

The Sharpe family of Peoria, Illinois, prays before a meal. Jim Sharpe, a United Auto Workers union steward, was forced to put his home up for sale as a result of the drawn out strike against his employer, Caterpillar.

It seemed to be a typical battle between labor and management: the powerful United Auto Workers (UAW) against Caterpillar Inc., the world's largest builder of earthmoving and construction equipment. The UAW wanted to use the contract they negotiated with Deere, the farm equipment manufacturer, as a pattern for the Caterpillar contract. Caterpillar, on the other hand, claimed that its business was substantially different from Deere's because it ships more than half of its equipment overseas, and therefore a totally different contract was needed. Initially, in 1991, the UAW struck two Caterpillar plants employing 2,400 workers. Caterpillar retaliated with a lockout of 5,650 workers at other plants. In mid-1992, approximately half of the union workers were on the job, while thousands were outside the gates walking the picket lines.

Caught in the middle of this dispute were the workers. Richard Owens, an eighteen-year veteran with five children, was locked out and demanded the union drop the pattern idea and bargain with the company. Paul Branan had been laid off from another company in the area and was trying to get a job at $17 an hour to replace one of the more than 12,600 striking Caterpillar workers: He faced the prospect of retaliation from his neighbors. Jim Sharpe, a union representative, was selling his house because of the conflict. The local public had mixed reactions because so many people were affected. Unemployment was high—about 9 percent.

In April 1992, the 5½-month strike ended as workers went back to work when the company threatened to replace the striking workers. Negotiations continued as workers worked without a contract. Feelings among the company, the union, and the local citizens were quite volatile. Conflict between the company and the union was causing thousands of people to experience significant work, family, and lifestyle stress.[1]

C ompanies can be a major source of stress in the lives of their employees, as well as in the everyday lives of the local citizens. Organizations and the people who work in them experience constant pressure to produce more with better quality and with less input. Workers want to keep their jobs and be good citizens, while maintaining their self-respect. To meet increasing competitive pressures around the world, companies must seek to improve productivity and quality, while lowering costs. Conflict, stress, burnout, turnover, and other unpleasant side effects inevitably occur.

In this chapter, we examine a number of insights into stress and conflict in the workplace. First, we explore the nature of stress and describe Type A and Type B personality profiles, which is an approach to understanding why some people are more prone to stress than others. Next, we identify and discuss a number of causes of stress. Then, we consider the potential consequences of stress. In addition, we

1. "Now Playing in Peoria," *Fortune*, July 12, 1993, pp. 11-12; "The Cat and the Mice," *Newsweek*, April 20, 1992, p. 56; and Gary Slutsker, "Cat Claws Back," *Forbes*, February 17, 1992, p. 46.

highlight several things people and organizations can do to effectively manage stress at work. Finally, we discuss the nature of conflict in organization.

The Nature of Stress

Many people think that they understand stress. In reality, stress is complex and often misunderstood. To learn how job stress truly works, we must first define stress and then relate it to the individual in the workplace.

Stress Defined

Stress has been defined in many ways, but most definitions say that stress is caused by a stimulus, that the stimulus can be either physical or psychological, and that the individual responds to the stimulus in some way.[2] Here, then, we define **stress** as a person's adaptive response to a stimulus that places excessive psychological or physical demands on him or her.

Stress is a person's adaptive response to a stimulus that places excessive psychological or physical demands on that person.

Given the underlying complexities of this definition, we need to examine its components carefully. First is the notion of adaptation. As we discuss shortly, people adapt to stressful circumstances in any of several ways. Second is the role of the stimulus. This stimulus, generally called a *stressor*, is anything that induces stress. Third, stressors can be either psychological or physical. Finally, the demands placed on the individual by the stressor must be excessive for stress to result. Of course, what is excessive for one person may be perfectly tolerable for another. Simply, a person must perceive the demands as excessive or stress will not result.

Stress and the Individual

Much of what we know about stress today can be traced to the pioneering work of Dr. Hans Selye.[3] Selye identified what he called the general adaptation syndrome and the concepts of eustress and distress.

General Adaptation Syndrome   Figure 9.1 graphically shows the **general adaptation syndrome (GAS)**. According to this view, each of us has a normal level of resistance to stressful events. Some of us can tolerate a great deal of stress and others much less, but we all have a basic threshold at which stress starts to affect us.

The **general adaptation syndrome (GAS)** identifies three stages of response to a stressor: alarm, resistance, and exhaustion.

The GAS begins when a person first encounters a stressor. The first stage is called alarm. At this point, the person may react with some degree of panic and wonder how to cope. The individual may also have to resolve whether to "fight-or-flee": can I deal with this, or should I run away? For example, suppose that a manager is assigned a lengthy report to write overnight. Her first reaction may be, "How will I ever get this done by tomorrow?"

2. See James C. Quick and Jonathan D. Quick, *Organizational Stress and Preventive Management* (New York: McGraw-Hill, 1984), for a review.
3. Hans Selye, *The Stress of Life* (New York: McGraw-Hill, 1976).

FIGURE 9.1

The General Adaptation Syndrome (GAS)

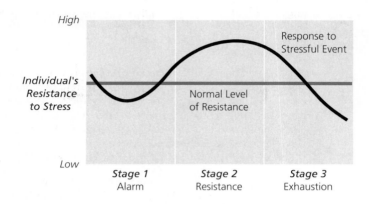

If the stressor is too extreme, the person may simply be unable to cope with it. Most of the time, however, the individual gathers his or her strength (physical or emotional) and resists the negative effects of the stressor. The manager with the long report to write may calm down, call home to say she is working late, roll up her sleeves, order out for dinner, and get to work. Thus, at stage 2 of the GAS, the person is resisting the effects of the stressor.

Often, the resistance phase ends the GAS. If the manager completes the report earlier than she expected, she may drop it in her briefcase, smile to herself, and head home tired but happy. On the other hand, prolonged exposure to a stressor without resolution may bring on stage 3 of the GAS: exhaustion. At this stage, the person literally gives up and can no longer fight the stressor. The manager may fall asleep at her desk at 3 A.M. and fail to finish the report.

Distress and Eustress   Selye also pointed out that the sources of stress need not be bad.[4] For example, receiving a bonus and then deciding what to do with the money can be stressful. So can getting a promotion, gaining recognition, getting married, and similar "good" things. Selye called this type of stress **eustress**. As we see later, eustress can lead to a number of positive outcomes for the individual.

Of course, stress can also be negative. Called **distress,** negative stress is what most people think of when they hear the word *stress*. Excessive pressure, unreasonable demands on our time, and bad news all fall into this category. As the term suggests, this form of stress generally results in negative consequences for the individual.

For purposes of simplicity, we continue to use the simple term *stress*. Throughout our discussion, however, remember that stress can be either good or bad. It can motivate and stimulate us, or it can lead to any number of dangerous side effects.

Individual Differences   Noting the effects of individual differences on stress is also important. We already noted that people differ in their normal levels of resistance to stressors. Differences may include factors such as cultural differences, gender, and personal characteristics.

Cultural differences are important in determining how stress affects people. For example, research by Cary Cooper suggests that U.S. executives may experience less stress than executives in many other countries, including Japan and Brazil. In

Eustress is the pleasurable stress that accompanies positive events.

Distress is the unpleasant stress that accompanies negative events.

4. Ibid.

Type A or Type B?

This test will help you develop insights into your own tendencies toward Type A or Type B behavior patterns. Answer the questions honestly and accurately about either your job or your school, whichever requires the most time each week. Then calculate your score according to the instructions that follow the questions. Discuss your results with a classmate. Critique each other's answers and see if you can help each other develop a strategy for reducing Type A tendencies.

Choose from the following responses to answer the questions below:

a. Almost always true   c. Seldom true
b. Usually true   d. Never true

1. I do not like to wait for other people to complete their work before I can proceed with mine.
2. I hate to wait in most lines.
3. People tell me that I tend to get irritated too easily.
4. Whenever possible I try to make activities competitive.
5. I have a tendency to rush into work that needs to be done before knowing the procedure I will use to complete the job.
6. Even when I go on vacation, I usually take some work along.
7. When I make a mistake, it is usually because I have rushed into the job before completely planning it through.
8. I feel guilty for taking time off from work.
9. People tell me I have a bad temper when it comes to competitive situations.
10. I tend to lose my temper when I am under a lot of pressure at work.
11. Whenever possible, I will attempt to complete two or more tasks at once.
12. I tend to race against the clock.
13. I have no patience for lateness.
14. I catch myself rushing when there is no need.

Individual differences affect how people respond to stressors.

addition, the major causes of stress differ in various countries. In Germany, for example, the major cause of stress is time pressure and deadlines. In South Africa, the major cause of stress is long hours on the job. In Sweden, the major cause of stress is the encroachment of work on private lives.[5]

Still other research suggests that women are perhaps more prone to experience the psychological effects of stress, whereas men may report more physical effects.[6] Finally, some studies suggest that people who see themselves as complex individuals are better able to handle stress than are people who view themselves as relatively simple.[7] We should add, however, that the study of individual differences in stress is still in its infancy. It is, therefore, premature to draw rigid conclusions about how different types of people handle stress.

5. Carol Kleiman, from *The Chicago Tribune*, March 31, 1988.
6. Todd D. Jick and Linda F. Mitz, "Sex Differences in Work Stress," *Academy of Management Review*, October 1985, pp. 408–420; and Debra L. Nelson and James C. Quick, "Professional Women: Are Distress and Disease Inevitable?" *Academy of Management Review*, April 1985, pp. 206–218.
7. "Complex Characters Handle Stress Better," *Psychology Today*, October 1987, p. 26.

Type A and Type B Personality Profiles

As we noted earlier, not everyone responds to stress in the same way. In fact, virtually every aspect of stress, from what triggers it to its consequences, can vary from person to person. One line of thinking about systematic differences among people is in terms of Type A and Type B personality profiles.

The Type A and Type B profiles were first observed by two cardiologists, Meyer Friedman and Ray Rosenman.[8] The idea started when a worker repairing the upholstery on their waiting room chairs noted that many of the chairs were worn only on the front. This suggested to the two cardiologists that many heart patients were anxious and had a hard time sitting still.

Using this observation as a starting point, and based on their own clinical practice, Friedman and Rosenman concluded that their patients exhibited two very different types of behavior patterns. Their research led them to conclude that the differences were personality based.

Type A people are extremely competitive, are highly committed to work, and have a strong sense of time urgency.

The **Type A** individual is extremely competitive, is very devoted to work, and has a strong sense of time urgency. Moreover, this individual is likely to be aggressive, impatient, and highly work oriented. He or she has a lot of drive and wants to accomplish as much as possible in as short a time as possible.

Type B people are less competitive, are less committed to work, and have a weaker sense of time urgency.

The **Type B** person, in contrast, is less competitive, is less devoted to work, and has a weaker sense of time urgency. This person feels less conflict with either people or time and has a more balanced, relaxed approach to life. She or he has more confidence and is able to work at a constant pace. Finally, the Type B person is not necessarily any more or less successful than the Type A individual.

Friedman and Rosenman point out that people are not purely Type A or Type B; instead, people tend toward one or the other type. For example, an individual might exhibit marked Type A characteristics much of the time but still be able to relax once in awhile and even occasionally forget about time.

Early research by Friedman and Rosenman on the Type A and Type B profile differences yielded some alarming findings. In particular, the researchers argued that Type A persons were much more likely to experience coronary heart disease than were Type B persons.[9] In recent years, however, follow-up research by other scientists suggests that the relationship between Type A behavior and the risk of coronary heart disease is not as straightforward as once believed.[10]

Although the reasons are unclear, recent findings suggest that persons with Type A traits are much more complex than originally believed. They not only exhibit the traits noted earlier, but they are also likely to be depressed and hostile. Any one or a combination of these feelings can lead to heart problems. Moreover, different approaches to measuring Type A tendencies have yielded different results.

Finally, in one study that found Type A persons to actually be less susceptible to heart problems than Type B persons, the researchers nevertheless offered an explanation consistent with earlier thinking: because persons who show Type A behavior are compulsive, they seek treatment earlier and are more likely to follow their doctors' orders![11] *Developing Management Skills* will help you gain insights into your own mix of Type A and Type B tendencies.

---

8. Meyer Friedman and Ray H. Rosenman, *Type A Behavior and Your Heart* (New York: Knopf, 1974).
9. Ibid.
10. Joshua Fischman, "Type A on Trial," *Psychology Today*, February 1987, pp. 42–50.
11. "Prognosis for the 'Type A' Personality Improves in a New Heart Disease Study," *Wall Street Journal*, January 14, 1988, p. 27.

Common Causes of Stress

Many things can cause stress. Figure 9.2 shows two broad categories: organizational stressors and life stressors. It also shows three categories of stress consequences: individual consequences, organizational consequences, and burnout.

Organizational Stressors

Basic **organizational stressors** include task demands, physical demands, role demands, and interpersonal demands.

Task demands are stressors associated with the specific job a person performs.

Organizational stressors are various factors in the workplace that can cause stress. Four general sets of organizational stressors are task demands, physical demands, role demands, and interpersonal demands.[12]

Task Demands **Task demands** are stressors associated with the specific job a person performs. Some occupations are by nature more stressful than others. The jobs of a surgeon, air traffic controller, and professional football coach obviously are more stressful than those of a hospital orderly, airplane baggage loader, and football team equipment manager.

12. Selye, *The Stress of Life*. See also Stephan J. Motowidlo, John S. Packard, and Michael R. Manning, "Occupational Stress: Its Causes and Consequences for Job Performance," *Journal of Applied Psychology*, Vol. 71, 1986, pp. 618–629.

FIGURE 9.2

Causes and
Consequences of Stress

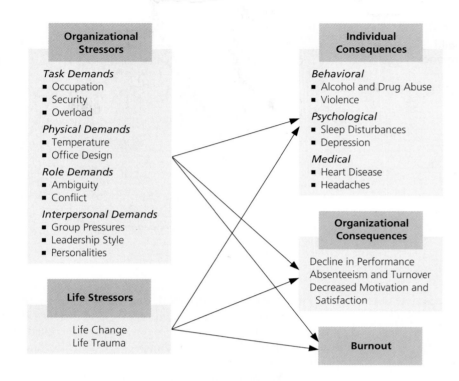

Organizational Stressors	Individual Consequences
Task Demands	**Behavioral**
▪ Occupation	▪ Alcohol and Drug Abuse
▪ Security	▪ Violence
▪ Overload	**Psychological**
Physical Demands	▪ Sleep Disturbances
▪ Temperature	▪ Depression
▪ Office Design	**Medical**
Role Demands	▪ Heart Disease
▪ Ambiguity	▪ Headaches
▪ Conflict	

Interpersonal Demands
▪ Group Pressures
▪ Leadership Style
▪ Personalities

Organizational Consequences

Decline in Performance
Absenteeism and Turnover
Decreased Motivation and
Satisfaction

Life Stressors

Life Change
Life Trauma

Burnout

SOURCE: Adapted from James C. Quick and Jonathan D. Quick, *Organizational Stress and Preventive Management*, McGraw-Hill, 1984, pp. 19, 44, and 76. Reprinted with permission of McGraw-Hill, Inc.

Beyond specific task-related pressures, other task demands may pose physical threats to a person's health. These conditions exist in occupations such as coal mining and toxic waste handling. Indeed, one recent survey placed the jobs of a miner and a police officer among the ten most stressful jobs in U.S. industry.[13]

Security is another task demand that can cause stress. Someone in a relatively secure job is not likely to worry unduly about losing that position. On the other hand, if job security is threatened stress can increase dramatically. For example, stress generally increases throughout an organization during a period of layoffs or immediately after a merger with another firm. Such a phenomenon has been observed at a number of organizations, including AT&T, Safeway, and Digital Equipment.[14]

Yet another task demand stressor is overload. Overload occurs when a person simply has more work to do than he or she can handle. The overload can be either quantitative (the individual has too many tasks to perform or too little time in which to perform them) or qualitative (the person may believe that she or he lacks the ability to do the job). *The Ethical Dilemma* describes how some employees of Food Lion believe that too much is expected of them at work.

We should also note that the opposite of overload may also be undesirable. As Figure 9.3 shows, low task demands can result in boredom and apathy just as overload can cause tension and anxiety. Thus, a moderate degree of workload-related stress is optimal because it leads to high levels of energy and motivation.

13. "Stress on the Job," *Newsweek*, April 25, 1988, pp. 40–45.
14. "Corporate Mergers Take a Toll on Employees in Lost Jobs and Family Strain," *Wall Street Journal*, September 9, 1986, p. 1.

FIGURE 9.3

Workload, Stress, and Performance

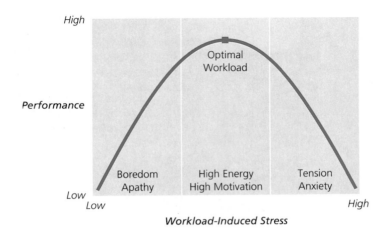

Physical Demands **Physical demands** relate to the setting of the job. One important element is temperature. Working outdoors in extreme temperatures can result in stress, as can an improperly heated or cooled office. Strenuous labor such as loading heavy cargo or lifting packages can also cause stress.

Office design can also be a source of stress. A poorly designed office can make it difficult for people to have privacy or promote too much or too little social interaction. Too much interaction may distract a person from his or her task, whereas too little may lead to boredom or loneliness. Likewise, poor lighting, inadequate work surfaces, and the like can create stress.[15]

Role Demands **Role demands** also can be stressful to people in organizations. A **role** is the part an individual plays in the organization or work group. As such, it has formal (i.e., job-related and explicit) requirements as well as informal (i.e., social and implicit) requirements. People in an organization or work group expect a person in a particular role to act in certain ways. They transmit these expectations formally and informally. The individual perceives the role expectations with varying levels of accuracy, and then enacts his or her role. When "errors" creep into the role episode, however, either role ambiguity or role conflict can result. Role expectations can also lead to overload, which can have negative consequences such as stress.[16]

Role ambiguity occurs when a person is uncertain as to the exact nature of a particular role. Inadequate job descriptions, vague instructions from a supervisor, or unclear cues from coworkers can all result in role ambiguity and perceived stress. Another possible disruption is **role conflict**, which arises when demands of or messages about roles are essentially clear but also somewhat contradict one another. **Interrole conflict** occurs when a person experiences conflict among two or more roles. A part-time student who is told by an instructor that there will be an exam tomorrow and is also told by his boss that he has to work late tonight will experience interrole conflict and increased stress.

Physical demands relate to the setting of the job.

Role demands relate to the **role** or part an individual plays in the organization or work group.

Role ambiguity occurs when a person is uncertain as to the exact nature of a particular role.

Role conflict arises when demands of or messages about roles are essentially clear but also somewhat contradict one another.

15. Robert I. Sutton and Anat Rafaeli, "Characteristics of Work Stations as Potential Occupational Stressors," *Academy of Management Journal,* June 1987, pp. 260-276.
16. Daniel Katz and Robert L. Kahn, *The Social Psychology of Organizations,* 2nd ed. (New York: Wiley, 1978).

Food Lion Keeps the Pressure on Employees

Food Lion Inc. is one of the fastest-growing grocery chains in the United States. In 1991, the firm had total sales of $6.4 billion, up from $2.4 billion in 1986. Food Lion expanded into Texas, increased the number of stores to more than 1,000, and plans to invade Maryland, Arkansas, and Louisiana.

The firm has achieved this remarkable growth pattern through relentless cost control, centralized distribution and buying, and efficiency measures. The firm's net profit margins are 3 percent compared to the industry average of 1 percent. Some critics charge, however, that Food Lion employees are paying a substantial price for its growth.

Each Food Lion store manager is allocated a certain number of labor hours each week based on projected sales for the week, the number of items scanned at cash registers the previous week, and what each department should do in forty hours per week. The manager has to live within this budget. As a result, employees complain of unrelenting pressure and little slack. For example, baggers are taught to fill bags with two hands, and stockers are expected to reload shelves at the rate of fifty cases per hour.

Some workers have complained that they work sixty to seventy hours per week, with no overtime pay, to meet the schedule. One meat department manager recently quit because of the pressure. He noted that in his previous job with Kroger, he supervised three other meat cutters. At Food Lion, he was expected to do the same volume of work with only a single part-time assistant.

Managers also are under tremendous pressure. If they use up their labor hours, they have to pitch in themselves to get the work done. A store manager who also recently quit complained that she could never satisfy her supervisor regardless of the number of hours she worked each week. Toward the end of her time with the firm, she was averaging one hundred hours of work per week.

SOURCES: "Food Lion: Still Stalking in Tough Times," *Business Week*, June 22, 1992, p. 70; Thomas A. Stewart, "Do You Push Your People Too Hard?" *Fortune*, October 22, 1990, pp. 121–128; "Much More Than a Day's Work—For Just a Day's Pay," *Business Week*, September 23, 1991, p. 40; and Claire Poole, "Stalking Bigger Game," *Forbes*, April 1, 1991, pp. 73–74.

Interrole conflict occurs when a person experiences conflict among two or more roles.

Intrarole conflict arises when a person gets contradictory messages from different people in the same role.

Intrarole conflict arises when a person gets contradictory messages from different people in the same role. Suppose one of your subordinates tells you that another subordinate is loafing and needs to be told to work harder. The second subordinate, meanwhile, expresses concern that the first is working too hard and needs to be told to ease up before she collapses from exhaustion. It will take astute investigation to find out which set of messages is more accurate.

Another example of intrarole conflict occurs in the role of the supermarket cashier. The cashier receives role expectations from three sources: management, coworkers, and customers. Role theory generally would suggest that the managers and coworkers have the dominant impact on behaviors. In the case of supermarket cashiers, however, the dominant role sender is the steady stream of customers. Furthermore, the demands of the customers often conflict with managerial or organizational rules and instructions and produce stress.[17]

17. Anat Rafaeli, "When Cashiers Meet Customers: An Analysis of the Role of Supermarket Cashiers," *Academy of Management Journal*, Vol. 32, 1989, pp. 245–273.

In **intrasender conflict,** the same person sends contradictory messages to the recipient.

Person-role conflict results if there is some basic incongruence between the person and his or her job.

In **intrasender conflict**, the same person sends contradictory messages to the recipient. Suppose that a worker tells her boss right before Christmas that she would appreciate chances to earn extra money but then refuses the first offer of overtime. The manager will be uncertain as to her true preferences.

Finally, **person-role conflict** can result if there is some basic incongruence between the person and his or her job. An active supporter of Greenpeace who also works for Exxon might have experienced person-role conflict during the follow-up to the oil spill in Prince William Sound in 1989, as might people who are pressured to do illegal or unethical things or something distasteful like firing a favorite employee.

Thus, the role a person plays is made up of the expectations that the group or the organization has for the person filling a particular role. The way an employee perceives and acts out his or her role often plays a major part in the stress experienced by the individual.[18]

Interpersonal demands are stressors associated with the individuals on the job.

Interpersonal Demands A final set of organizational stressors consists of three **interpersonal demands**, stressors associated with the individuals on the job. Group pressures include pressure to restrict output and pressure to conform to the group's norms. For instance, as we have noted before, a work group commonly arrives at an informal agreement about how much each member will produce. Individuals who produce much more or much less than this level may be pressured by the group to get back in line. An individual who feels a strong need to vary from the group's expectations (perhaps to get a pay raise or promotion) will experience a great deal of stress, especially if acceptance by the group also is important to him or her.

Leadership style also may cause stress. Suppose that an employee needs a great deal of social support from his leader. The leader, however, is quite brusque and shows no concern or compassion for him. This employee will likely feel stressed. Similarly, assume that an employee feels a strong need to participate in decision making and to be active in all aspects of management. Her boss is very autocratic and refuses to consult subordinates about anything. Once again stress is likely to result.[19] Finally, conflicting personalities and behaviors may cause stress. Conflict can occur when two or more people must work together even though their personalities, attitudes, and behaviors differ. For example, a person with an internal locus of control—that is, someone who always wants to control how things turn out—might get frustrated working with a person with an external locus of control—that is, someone who likes to wait and just let things happen. Likewise, a smoker and a nonsmoker who are assigned adjacent offices obviously will experience stress.[20]

Life Stressors

Common **life stressors** generally are categorized in terms of life change and life trauma.

Stress in organizational settings also can be influenced by events that take place outside the organization. **Life stressors** generally are categorized in terms of life change and life trauma.[21]

18. See Edward R. Kemery, Arthur G. Bedeian, Kevin W. Mossholder, and John Touliatos, "Outcomes of Role Stress: A Multisample Constructive Replication," *Academy of Management Journal*, June 1985, pp. 363–375, for an examination of the effects of role demands.
19. See Gary M. Kaufman and Terry A. Beehr, "Interactions Between Job Stressors and Social Support: Some Counterintuitive Results," *Journal of Applied Psychology*, Vol. 71, 1986, pp. 522–526, for an interesting study in this area.
20. David R. Frew and Nealia S. Bruning, "Perceived Organizational Characteristics and Personality Measures as Predictors of Stress/Strain in the Work Place," *Academy of Management Journal*, December 1987, pp. 633–646.
21. Quick and Quick, *Organizational Stress and Preventive Management.*

Life change is any meaningful change in a person's personal or work situation.

Life Change   Thomas Holmes and Richard Rahe first developed and popularized the notion of life change as a source of stress.[22] **Life change** is any meaningful change in a person's personal or work situation. Holmes and Rahe reasoned that major changes in a person's life can lead to stress and eventually to disease. Table 9.1 summarizes their findings on major life change events. Note that several of these events relate directly (fired at work, retirement) or indirectly (change in residence) to work.

Individual consequences of stress can be behavioral, psychological, or medical.

Each event's point value supposedly reflects the event's effect on the individual. At one extreme, a spouse's death, assumed to be the most traumatic event considered, is assigned a point value of 100. At the other extreme, minor violations of the law carry only 11 points. The points themselves represent life change units, or LCUs. Note also that the list includes negative events (divorce and trouble with boss) as well as positive ones (marriage and vacation).

Holmes and Rahe argued that a person can handle a certain threshold of LCUs, but beyond that level problems can set in. In particular, they suggest that people who encounter more than 150 LCUs in a given year will experience a decline in their health the following year. A score of between 150 and 300 LCUs supposedly carries a 50 percent chance of major illness, while the chance of major illness is said to increase to 70 percent if the number of LCUs exceeds 300.

These ideas offer some insight into the potential impact of stress and underscore our limitations in coping with stressful events. Although research on Holmes and Rahe's proposals has provided only mixed support, an avenue that does seem promising, however, is based on the notion of hardiness.

The *hardiness* approach suggests that some people have what are termed *hardier* personalities than do others. People with hardy personalities have an internal locus of control, are strongly committed to the activities in their lives, and view change as an opportunity for advancement and growth. Such people are seen as less likely to suffer illness if they experience high levels of LCUs, whereas people with low hardiness may be more susceptible to the predicted effects of high LCUs.[23]

A **life trauma** is any upheaval in an individual's life that alters his or her attitudes, emotions, or behaviors.

Life Trauma   Approaching individual stress in terms of life trauma is similar to using the notion of life change. The life trauma approach, however, has a narrower, more direct, and shorter-term focus than the life change approach. A **life trauma** is any upheaval in an individual's life that alters his or her attitudes, emotions, or behaviors.

To illustrate, according to the life change view, a divorce adds to a person's potential for health problems in the following year. At the same time, obviously, the person will also experience emotional turmoil during the actual divorce process itself. This turmoil, the focus of the term *life trauma*, clearly will cause stress, much of which may spill over into the workplace.[24]

Major life traumas that may cause stress include marital problems, family difficulties, and health problems initially unrelated to stress. For example, suppose that a person learns she has developed arthritis that will limit her favorite activity, skiing. Her dismay over the news may translate into stress at work.

22. Thomas H. Holmes and Richard H. Rahe, "The Social Readjustment Rating Scale," *Journal of Psychosomatic Research*, Vol. 11, 1967, pp. 213–218.
23. Susan C. Kobasa, "Stressful Life Events, Personality, and Health: An Inquiry into Hardiness," *Journal of Personality and Social Psychology*, January 1979, pp. 1–11; and Susan C. Kobasa, S. R. Maddi, and S. Kahn, "Hardiness and Health: A Prospective Study," *Journal of Personality and Social Psychology*, January 1982, pp. 168–177.
24. Evelyn J. Bromet, Mary A. Dew, David K. Parkinson, and Herbert C. Schulberg, "Predictive Effects of Occupational and Marital Stress on the Mental Health of a Male Workforce," *Journal of Organizational Behavior*, Vol. 9, 1988, pp. 1–13.

Rank	Life Event	Mean Value	Rank	Life Event	Mean Value
1	Death of spouse	100	23	Son or daughter leaving home	29
2	Divorce	73	24	Trouble with in-laws	29
3	Marital separation	65	25	Outstanding personal achievement	28
4	Jail term	63	26	Spouse beginning or starting work	26
5	Death of close family member	63	27	Beginning or ending school	26
6	Personal injury or illness	53	28	Change in living conditions	25
7	Marriage	50	29	Revision of personal habits	24
8	Fired at work	47	30	Trouble with boss	23
9	Marital reconciliation	45	31	Change in work hours or conditions	20
10	Retirement	45	32	Change in residence	20
11	Change in health of family member	44	33	Change in schools	20
12	Pregnancy	40	34	Change in recreation	19
13	Sex difficulties	39	35	Change in church activities	19
14	Gain of new family member	39	36	Change in social activities	18
15	Business readjustment	39	37	Mortgage or loan less than $10,000*	17
16	Change in financial state	38	38	Change in sleeping habits	16
17	Death of close family friend	37	39	Change in the number of family get-togethers	15
18	Change to different line of work	36	40	Change in eating habits	15
19	Change in number of arguments with spouse	35	41	Vacation	13
20	Mortgage over $10,000*	31	42	Christmas	12
21	Foreclosure of mortgage or loan	30	43	Minor violations of the law	11
22	Change in responsibilities of work	29			

The amount of life stress that a person has experienced in a given period of time, say one year, is measured by the total number of life change units (LCUs). These units result from the addition of the values (shown in the righthand column) associated with events that the person has experienced during the target time period.

*With inflation, the value of mortgage that produces stress may be nearer to $100,000; however, no research confirms this figure.

SOURCE: Reprinted with permission from Journal of Psychosomatic Research, Vol. 11, Thomas H. Holmes and Richard H. Rahe, "The Social Adjustment Rating Scale," Copyright 1967, Elsevier Science Ltd., Pergamon Imprint, Oxford, England.

TABLE 9.1

Life Changes and Life Change Units

Consequences of Stress

A number of consequences can result from stress. As we already noted, if the stress is positive, the result may be more energy, enthusiasm, and motivation. Of more concern, of course, are the negative consequences of stress. Referring to Figure 9.2, three sets of consequences that can result from stress are individual consequences, organizational consequences, and burnout.[25]

We should first note that many of the factors listed are obviously interrelated. For example, alcohol abuse is shown as an individual consequence. Yet alcohol abuse by an employee is also of consequence to the organization. An employee who drinks on the job may perform poorly and create a hazard for others. If the

25. Quick and Quick, *Organizational Stress and Preventive Management*. See also John M. Ivancevich and Michael T. Matteson, *Stress and Work: A Managerial Perspective* (Glenview, Ill.: Scott, Foresman, 1980).

category for a consequence seems somewhat arbitrary, be aware that each consequence is categorized according to its primary constituent.

Individual Consequences

Individual consequences of stress, then, are those outcomes that mainly affect the individual. The organization also may suffer, either directly or indirectly, but it is the individual who pays the real price. Three categories of individual consequences of stress are behavioral, psychological, and medical.

Behavioral Consequences   Behavioral consequences of stress are responses that may harm the person under stress or others. One such behavior is smoking. Research has clearly documented that people who smoke tend to smoke more when they experience stress. There is also evidence that alcohol and drug abuse are linked to stress, although this relationship is less documented.[26] Other possible behavioral consequences are accident proneness, violence, and appetite disorders.

Psychological Consequences   Psychological consequences of stress relate to an individual's mental health and well-being. When people experience too much stress at work, they may become depressed or sleep too much or not enough. Stress may also lead to family problems and sexual difficulties.[27]

Medical Consequences   The medical consequences of stress affect a person's physical well-being. Heart disease and stroke, among other illnesses, have been linked to stress. Other common medical problems resulting from too much stress include headaches, backaches, ulcers and related stomach and intestinal disorders, and skin conditions such as acne and hives.[28]

Organizational Consequences

Organizational consequences of stress can involve performance decline, withdrawal, or unfavorable changes in attitudes.

Clearly, any of the individual consequences just discussed can also affect the organization. Still other effects of stress have even more direct consequences for organizations. These include decline in performance, withdrawal, and negative changes in attitudes.

Performance   One clear organizational consequence of too much stress is a decline in performance. For operating workers, a decline can translate into poor-quality work or a drop in productivity. For managers, it can mean faulty decision making or disruptions in working relationships as people become irritable and hard to get along with.

Withdrawal   Withdrawal behaviors also can result from stress. For the organization, the two most important forms of withdrawal behavior are absenteeism and quitting. People who are having a hard time coping with stress in their jobs are more likely to call in sick or consider leaving the organization for good. Other,

26. Quick and Quick, *Organizational Stress and Preventive Management.*
27. Ibid.
28. Ibid.

more subtle forms of withdrawal also can result from stress. A manager may start missing deadlines or taking longer lunch breaks. An employee may withdraw psychologically by ceasing to care about the organization and the job.[29]

Attitudes   Another direct organizational consequence of employee stress relates to attitudes. As we just noted, job satisfaction, morale, and organizational commitment can all suffer, along with motivation to perform at high levels. As a result, people may be more prone to complain about unimportant things, do only enough work to get by, and so forth.

Burnout

Burnout is a general feeling of exhaustion that develops when an individual simultaneously experiences too much pressure and too few sources of satisfaction.

A final consequence of stress has implications for both people and organizations. **Burnout** is a general feeling of exhaustion that develops when an individual simultaneously experiences too much pressure and too few sources of satisfaction.[30]

Burnout generally develops in a predictable way.[31] First, people with high aspirations and strong motivation to get things done are prime candidates for burnout under certain conditions. They are especially vulnerable when the organization suppresses or limits their initiative while constantly demanding that they serve the organization's own ends.

In such a situation, the individual is likely to put too much of himself or herself into the job. In other words, the person may well keep trying to accomplish his or her own agenda while simultaneously trying to fulfill the organization's expectations. The most likely effects of this situation are prolonged stress, fatigue, frustration, and helplessness under the burden of overwhelming demands. The person literally exhausts his or her aspirations and motivation, much as a candle burns itself out. Loss of self-confidence and psychological withdrawal follow. Ultimately, burnout results. At this point, the individual may start dreading going to work in the morning, put in longer hours but get less accomplished than before, and generally display mental and physical exhaustion.

Managing Stress in the Workplace

Given that stress is widespread and so potentially disruptive in organizations, people and organizations should be concerned about how to manage it more effectively. And, in fact, they are. Many strategies have been developed to help manage stress in the workplace. As shown in Figure 9.4 some are strategies for individuals, and others are geared toward organizations.[32]

29. Quick and Quick, *Organizational Stress and Preventive Management.* See also "Stress: The Test Americans Are Failing," *Business Week,* April 18, 1988, pp. 74–76.
30. Leonard Moss, *Management Stress* (Reading, Mass.: Addison-Wesley, 1981).
31. See Susan E. Jackson, Richard L. Schwab, and Randall S. Schuler, "Toward an Understanding of the Burnout Phenomenon," *Journal of Applied Psychology,* Vol. 71, 1986, pp. 630–640; and Daniel W. Russell, Elizabeth Altmaier, and Dawn Van Velzen, "Job-Related Stress, Social Support, and Burnout among Classroom Teachers," *Journal of Applied Psychology,* Vol. 72, 1987, pp. 269–274.
32. Quick and Quick, *Organizational Stress and Preventive Management.*

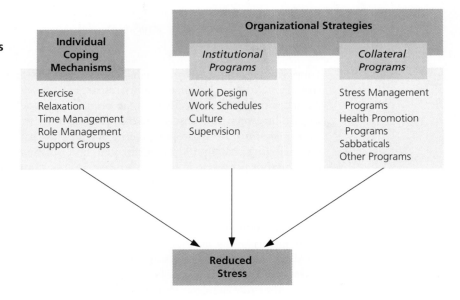

Individual Coping Strategies

Individual strategies for managing stress include exercise, relaxation, time management, role management, and support groups.

Many strategies for helping individuals manage stress have been proposed. Five of the most popular strategies are exercise, relaxation, time management, role management, and support groups.

Exercise   One method by which individuals can manage their stress is through exercise. People who exercise regularly are known to be less likely to have heart attacks than inactive people are. More directly, research has suggested that people who exercise regularly feel less tension and stress, are more self-confident, and show greater optimism. People who do not exercise regularly feel more stress and are more likely to be depressed.[33] Many U.S. executives are exercising as a way to help them cope with stress. Lawrence Perlman, chief executive officer of Control Data Corporation, gets up at 5:30 every morning and runs three to seven miles. He and other top managers claim that regular exercise helps them feel better and allows them to cope with the demands of the workday.[34]

Relaxation   A related method individuals can use to manage stress is relaxation. We noted at the beginning of the chapter that coping with stress requires adaptation. Proper relaxation is an effective way to adapt.

Relaxation can take many forms. One way to relax is to take regular vacations. A recent study found that people's attitudes toward a variety of workplace characteristics improved significantly after a vacation.[35] People can also relax while on the job. For example, experts have recommended that people take regular rest breaks

33. C. Folkins, "Effects of Physical Training on Mood," *Journal of Clinical Psychology*, April 1976, pp. 385–390.
34. Fay Rice, "How Execs Get Fit," *Fortune*, October 22, 1990, pp. 144–152; Brian O'Reilly, "New Truths about Staying Healthy," *Fortune*, September 25, 1989, pp. 57–66; and Marjory Roberts and T. George Harris, "Wellness at Work," *Psychology Today*, May 1989, pp. 54–56.
35. John W. Lounsbury and Linda L. Hoopes, "A Vacation from Work: Changes in Work and Nonwork Outcomes," *Journal of Applied Psychology*, Vol. 71, 1986, pp. 392–401.

during their normal workday. A popular way of resting is to sit quietly with closed eyes for ten minutes every afternoon. (Of course, having an alarm clock handy might also be necessary!)

Time Management Time management is often recommended for managing stress. The idea is that many daily pressures can be eased or eliminated if a person manages time more effectively. One popular approach to time management is to make a list every morning of the things to be done that day. Then group the items on the list into three categories: critical activities that must be performed, important activities that should be performed, and optional or trivial things that can be delegated or postponed. Then, of course, do the things on the list in their order of importance. This strategy helps people get more of the important things done every day and also encourages delegating less important activities to others.

Role Management Somewhat related to time management is the idea of role management, in which an individual actively works to avoid overload, ambiguity, and conflict. For example, a person who does not know what is expected should not sit and worry about it. Instead, he or she should ask for clarification from the boss.

Another role management strategy is to learn to say "no." As simple as saying it might sound, a lot of people create problems for themselves by always saying "yes." Besides working in their regular jobs, they agree to serve on committees, volunteer for extra duties, and accept extra assignments. Sometimes, of course, we have no choice but to accept an extra obligation (if our boss tells us to complete a new project, we most likely will have to do it). Many times, however, saying "no" is a viable option.[36]

Support Groups A final method for managing stress is to develop and maintain support groups. A support group is simply a group of family members or friends with whom a person can spend time. Going out after work with a couple of coworkers to a basketball game, for example, can help relieve the stress that builds up during the day. Supportive family and friends can help people diffuse normal stress on an ongoing basis.

Support groups can be particularly useful during times of crisis. For example, suppose that an employee has just learned that she did not get the promotion she has been working toward for months. Having good friends to lean on—be it to talk to or to yell at—may help her tremendously.[37]

Organizational Coping Strategies

Organizational strategies for helping people cope with stress include institutional programs and collateral programs.

Increasingly, organizations are realizing that they should be involved in managing their employees' stress. There are two different rationales for this view. One is that because the organization is at least partly responsible for creating the stress, it should help relieve it. The other is that workers experiencing lower levels of harmful stress will be able to function more effectively. Two basic organizational strategies for helping employees manage stress are institutional programs and collateral programs. Figure 9.4 shows common organizational methods in these categories.

36. "Eight Ways to Help You Reduce the Stress in Your Life," *Business Week Careers*, November 1986, p. 78.
37. Daniel C. Ganster, Marcelline R. Fusilier, and Bronston T. Mayes, "Role of Social Support in the Experiences of Stress at Work," *Journal of Applied Psychology*, Vol. 71, 1986, pp. 102–110.

Beyond encouraging a lower-stress environment in the workplace itself, one way an organization can help its employees cope with stress is by instituting collateral programs such as health promotion programs. Here, Honda employees do aerobics as part of one such program.

Institutional Programs *Institutional programs* for managing stress are undertaken through established organizational mechanisms.[38] For example, properly designed jobs (discussed in Chapter 7) and work schedules can help ease stress. Shift work in particular can cause major stress for employees, as they constantly have to adjust their sleep and relaxation patterns. Thus, the design of work and work schedules should be a focus of organizational efforts to reduce stress.[39]

The organization's culture (covered in Chapter 17) also can be used to help manage stress. In some organizations, for example, there is a strong norm against taking time off or going on vacation. In the long run, such norms can cause major stress. Thus, the organization should strive to foster a culture that reinforces a healthy mix of work and nonwork activities.

Finally, supervision can play an important role in managing stress. If made aware of their potential for assigning stressful amounts of work, supervisors can do a better job of keeping workloads reasonable.

Collateral Programs In addition to their institutional efforts aimed at reducing stress, many organizations are turning to collateral programs. A *collateral stress program* is an organizational program specifically created to help employees manage stress. Organizations have adopted stress management programs, health promotion programs, sabbaticals, and other kinds of programs for this purpose.

Table 9.2 summarizes several examples of stress management programs organizations have adopted. More and more companies are developing their own programs or adopting existing programs of this type.[40]

Table 9.2 also gives examples of firms that have employee fitness programs. These programs attack stress indirectly by encouraging employees to exercise. On the negative side, this kind of effort costs considerably more because the firm must invest in physical facilities. Still, more and more companies are exploring this option.[41]

38. Randall S. Schuler and Susan E. Jackson, "Managing Stress through PHRM Practices: An Uncertainty Interpretation," in K. Rowland and G. Ferris (Eds.), *Research in Personnel and Human Resources Management*, Vol. 4 (Greenwich, Conn.: JAI Press, 1986), pp. 183–224.
39. Quick and Quick, *Organizational Stress and Preventive Management*.
40. Ibid.
41. Richard A. Wolfe, David O. Ulrich, and Donald F. Parker, "Employee Health Management Programs: Review, Critique, and Research Agenda," *Journal of Management*, Winter 1987, pp. 603–615.

TABLE 9.2

Representative Approaches to Stress Management in Organizations

Examples of Stress Management Programs	Examples of Stress Management Programs
■ IBM, Hewlett-Packard, and the U.S. Air Force have sponsored seminars on the value of humor in helping minimize workplace stress.	■ L. L. Bean maintains three different health and fitness centers for its employees. The centers are open from 6 A.M. to 6 P.M. every day.
■ Lockheed and First Nationwide Bank have sponsored screening programs to help employees detect signs of hypertension and training programs to help cope with it.	■ Tenneco has a comprehensive health maintenance facility adjacent to its headquarters building in Houston. In addition to physical conditioning opportunities, the center sponsors numerous workshops and seminars on health maintenance. Membership is free to all employees.
■ Chevron provides training sessions to educate employees about AIDS and smoking.	■ Saatchi & Saatchi, a New York–based advertising firm, has an elaborate gymnasium available for its employees to use.
■ Intel and Apple offer sabbaticals to executives to help them avoid burnout.	■ Westinghouse has started constructing employee fitness centers in all of its facilities. The centers are available at no charge to all employees and their families.
■ Cambridge Research Lab in Boston offers workers a class in the Oriental art of tai to help them cope with stress.	

SOURCES: Faye Rice, "How Execs Get Fit," *Fortune*, October 22, 1990, pp. 144–152; Marjory Roberts and T. George Harris, "Wellness at Work," *Psychology Today*, May 1989, pp. 50–54; Brian Dumaine, "Cool Cures for Burnout," *Fortune*, June 20, 1988, pp. 78–84; and "A Cure for Stress," *Newsweek*, October 12, 1987, pp. 64–65.

Finally, organizations try to help employees cope with stress through other kinds of programs. For example, existing career development programs, like that at General Electric, are used for this purpose. Other companies use programs promoting everything from humor to massage as antidotes for stress.[42] Of course, little or no research supports some of the claims made by advocates of these programs. Thus, managers must take steps to ensure that any organizational effort to help employees cope with stress is at least reasonably effective.

Conflict in Organizations

Conflict is disagreement among parties. It has both positive and negative characteristics.

One cause of stress in organizations is conflict. In its simplest form, **conflict** is disagreement among parties. When two persons or groups disagree over major issues, conflict is often the result. Conflict can occur among individuals or among groups. Often it is generated by political behavior or battles over limited resources. In particular, it frequently occurs when a person or a group believes that its attempts to achieve its goal are being blocked by another person or group. For example, conflict may arise over financial resources, the number of authorized positions in work

42. "A Cure for Stress?" *Newsweek*, October 12, 1987, pp. 64–65.

groups, or the number of microcomputers to be purchased for departments. Conflict may also result from anticipating trouble: a person may behave antagonistically toward another person that she or he expects to pose obstacles to goal achievement.[43]

Although conflict often is considered harmful and thus something to avoid, it can also have some benefits. A total absence of conflict can lead to apathy and lethargy. A moderate degree of focused conflict, on the other hand, can stimulate new ideas, promote healthy competition, and energize behavior. In some organizations, especially profit-oriented ones, many managers believe conflict to be dysfunctional. On the other hand, managers in not-for-profit organizations view conflict as beneficial and conducive to higher quality decision making.[44]

The Nature of Conflict

Figure 9.5 illustrates the basic nature of organizational conflict. When groups strive for the same goal, hold little or no antagonism toward one another, and behave according to rules and procedures, competition is the most likely outcome. In contrast, conflict is likely when one group's goals jeopardize the others', there is open antagonism among the groups, and few rules and procedures regulate their behavior. When this happens, the goals become extremely important, the antagonism increases, rules and procedures are violated, and conflict occurs.[45] We have more to say about competition later in this section.

Reactions to Conflict

Interactions between people and groups depend on the importance of the issues and the compatibility of the goals.

The most common reactions to conflict are avoidance, accommodation, competition, collaboration, and compromise.[46] Whenever conflict occurs it is really the people who are in conflict. In many cases, however, people are acting as representatives of the groups to which they belong. In effect they work together, representing their group as they strive to do their part in helping the group achieve its goals. Thus, whether the conflict is between people acting as individuals or people acting as representatives of groups, the five types of interactions can be analyzed in terms of relationships among the goals of the people or the groups they represent.

Reactions to conflict can be differentiated according to their importance to the attainment of each party's goals and the degree of compatibility among the groups' goals, as shown in Figure 9.6. The importance of the interaction to the goal attainment of each party ranges from very high to very low. The degree of **goal compatibility** is the extent to which the goals can be achieved simultaneously. In other words, the goals are compatible if one party can accomplish its goals without preventing the other from accomplishing its goals. The goals are incompatible if the accomplishment of one party's goals prohibits the other from accomplishing its goals. The degree of goal compatibility can vary from very incompatible to very compatible. At the midpoint of each continuum, goals are

Goal compatibility is the extent to which the goals of more than one person or group can be achieved at the same time.

43. See Stephen P. Robbins, *Managing Organizational Conflict* (Englewood Cliffs, N.J.: Prentice-Hall, 1974), for a classic review.
44. Charles R. Schwenk, "Conflict in Organizational Decision Making: An Exploratory Study of Its Effects in For-Profit and Not-for-Profit Organizations," *Management Science*, April 1990.
45. Robbins, *Managing Organizational Conflict*.
46. Kenneth Thomas, "Conflict and Conflict Management," in Marvin Dunnette (Ed.), *Handbook of Industrial and Organizational Psychology* (Chicago: Rand McNally, 1976), pp. 889–935.

FIGURE 9.5

Conflict-Competition Relationship

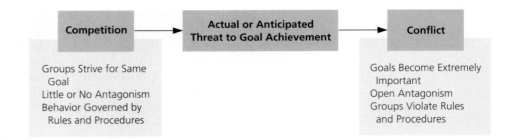

neither very important nor very unimportant and neither very incompatible nor very compatible.

Avoidance occurs when the interacting parties' goals are incompatible and the interaction is relatively unimportant to the attainment of the goals.

Avoidance   **Avoidance** occurs when an interaction is relatively unimportant to either party's goals and the goals are incompatible, as in the bottom left-hand corner of Figure 9.6. Because the parties to the conflict are not striving toward compatible goals and the issues in question seem unimportant, the parties simply try to avoid interacting with one another. For example, one state agency simply ignores another agency's requests for information. The requesting agency then practices its own form of avoidance by not following up on the requests.

Accommodation occurs when the parties' goals are compatible but the interaction is relatively unimportant to their attainment.

Accommodation   **Accommodation** occurs when the goals are compatible but the interactions are not considered important to overall goal attainment, as in the bottom right-hand corner of Figure 9.6. Interactions of this type may involve discussions that center on how the parties can accomplish their interdependent tasks with the least expenditure of time and effort. This type of interaction tends to be very friendly.[47]

Competition occurs when the goals are incompatible and the interactions are important to the attainment of goals.

Competition   **Competition** occurs when the goals are incompatible and the interactions are important to the attainment of each party's goals, as in the top left-hand corner of Figure 9.6. If all parties are striving for a goal but only one can reach its goal, the parties will be in competition. As we noted earlier, if a competitive situation gets out of control, as when there is open antagonism and no rules or procedures to follow, then competition can result in conflict. Thus, the types of interactions, conflict and competition, can interact. Sometimes conflict can be changed to competition if the parties agree to rules to guide the interaction and conflicting parties agree to not be hostile toward each other. On the other hand, a competitive situation can result in conflict if the interaction gets out of control.

In one freight warehouse and storage firm, the first, second, and third shifts each sought to win a weekly prize by posting the highest productivity record. Workers on the winning shift received recognition in the company newspaper. Because the issue was important to each group and the interests of the groups were incompatible, the result was competition.

The competition among the shifts encouraged each shift to produce more per week, which increased the company's output and eventually improved its overall welfare (and thus the welfare of each group). Both the company and the groups

47. Robert R. Blake, Herbert A. Shepard, and Jane S. Mouton, *Managing Intergroup Conflict in Industry* (Houston: Gulf, 1964).

FIGURE 9.6

Five Types of Reactions to Conflict

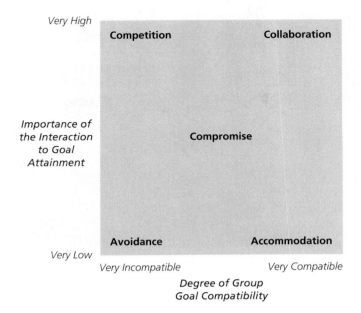

SOURCE: Adapted from Kenneth Thomas, "Conflict and Conflict Management," in Marvin Dunnette (Ed.), *Handbook of Industrial and Organizational Psychology* (Chicago: Rand McNally, 1976), pp. 889–935. Reprinted by permission.

benefitted from the competition because it fostered innovative and creative work methods, which further boosted productivity. After about three months, however, the competition got out of control. The competition among the groups led to poorer overall performance when the groups started to sabotage other shifts and inflate records. Under these conditions, the competition changed to open conflict and resulted in actual decreases in work performance.[48]

Collaboration occurs when the interaction is very important to goal attainment and the goals are compatible.

Collaboration **Collaboration** occurs when the interaction is very important to goal attainment and the goals are compatible, as in the top right-hand corner of Figure 9.6. At first glance, this may seem to be a simple interaction in which the parties participate jointly in activities to accomplish goals after agreeing on the goals and their importance. In many situations, however, agreeing on goals, their importance, and especially the means for achieving them is no easy matter. In a collaborative interaction, goals may differ but be compatible. Parties to a conflict may initially have difficulty working out the ways in which all can achieve their goals. Because the interactions are important to goal attainment, however, the parties are willing to continue to work together to achieve the goals. Collaborative relationships can lead to new and innovative ideas and solutions to any differences among the parties.[49]

Compromise occurs when the interaction is moderately important to the attainment of goals and the goals are neither completely compatible nor completely incompatible.

Compromise **Compromise** occurs when the interactions are moderately important to goal attainment and the goals are neither completely compatible nor completely incompatible. In a compromise situation, parties interact with others striving to achieve goals, but they may not aggressively pursue goal attainment in either a competitive or collaborative manner because the interactions are not that

48. Alfie Kohn, "How to Succeed Without Even Vying," *Psychology Today*, September 1986, pp. 22–28.
49. Andrew S. Grove, "How to Make Confrontation Work for You," *Fortune*, July 23, 1984, pp. 73–75.

One of the central responsibilities of leaders is to participate in conflict resolution. Managers must often intervene before a conflict disrupts their organization or squanders too much time. At the General Motors Plant in Arlington, Texas, city and state leaders resolve a conflict, announcing that a plant will be kept open, in response to protests at an earlier planning meeting to shut it down.

important to goal attainment. On the other hand, the parties may not avoid one another or be accommodating because the interactions are somewhat important. Often each gives up something, but because the interactions are only moderately important, they do not regret what they have given up.

Contract negotiations between union and management are an example of compromise. Each side brings numerous issues of varying importance to the bargaining table. Through rounds of offers and counteroffers, the two sides give and take on the issues. The complexity of such negotiations is increasing as negotiations spread to multiple plants in different countries. Agreements between management and labor in a Ford plant in the United States may be unacceptable to both parties in Canada.[50] Weeks of negotiations ending in numerous compromises usually result in a contract agreement between the union and management.

In summary, interactions between people or groups can result in several types of reactions to the conflict. If the goals of the parties are very compatible, the parties may engage in mutually supportive interactions, that is, collaboration or accommodation. If the goals are very incompatible, each may attempt to foster its own success at the expense of the others, engaging in competition or avoidance.

Managing Conflict

Depending on the circumstances, a manager may need to either resolve or stimulate conflict.

Conflict resolution is necessary when a potentially harmful conflict situation exists.

Given the potentially disruptive effects of conflict and the multiple reactions to conflict that can occur, managers need to be sensitive to how it can be managed. When a potentially harmful conflict situation exists, a manager needs to engage in **conflict resolution**. As Figure 9.7 shows, conflict needs to be resolved when it causes major disruptions in the organization and absorbs time and effort that could be used more productively. In addition, conflict needs to be resolved when its focus is on the group's internal goals rather than on the organizational goals. We describe the principal conflict-handling strategies later in this section.

50. "Ford of Canada Reaches Tentative Pact with Union Similar to Chrysler Contract," *Wall Street Journal*, October 2, 1987, p. 5; and "What's Throwing a Wrench into Britain's Assembly Lines?" *Business Week*, February 29, 1988, p. 4.

FIGURE 9.7

**Conflict Management
Alternatives**

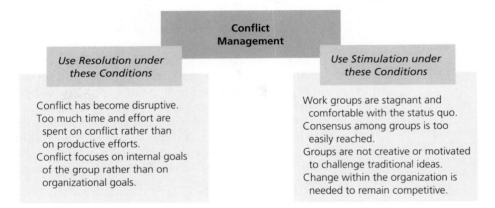

Conflict Management	
Use Resolution under these Conditions	*Use Stimulation under these Conditions*
Conflict has become disruptive. Too much time and effort are spent on conflict rather than on productive efforts. Conflict focuses on internal goals of the group rather than on organizational goals.	Work groups are stagnant and comfortable with the status quo. Consensus among groups is too easily reached. Groups are not creative or motivated to challenge traditional ideas. Change within the organization is needed to remain competitive.

Conflict stimulation is the creation and constructive use of conflict by a manager.

Remember, however, that sometimes a manager should be concerned about the absence of conflict. An absence of conflict may indicate that the organization is stagnant and employees are content with the status quo. It may also suggest that work groups are not motivated to challenge traditional and well-accepted ideas.[51] **Conflict stimulation** is the creation and constructive use of conflict by a manager.[52] Its purpose is to bring about situations where differences of opinion are exposed for examination by all. For example, if competing organizations are making notable changes in products, markets, or technologies, a manager may need to stimulate innovation and creativity by challenging the status quo. Stimulating conflict may provide employees with the motivation and opportunity to reveal differences of opinion that they previously kept to themselves. When all parties to the conflict are interested enough in an issue to be somewhat antagonistic toward other groups, they often expose their hidden doubts or opinions. This, in turn, allows the parties to get to the heart of the matter and often to develop unique solutions to the problem. Indeed, the interactions may lead the groups to recognize that a problem in fact exists. Conflict, then, can be a catalyst for creativity and change in an organization.

Several methods for stimulating conflict under controlled conditions are available.[53] These include altering the physical location of groups to stimulate more interaction, forcing more resource sharing, and implementing other changes in relationships among groups. In addition, training programs can be used to increase employee awareness of potential problems in group decision making and group interactions. Adopting the role of "devil's advocate" in discussion sessions is another method of stimulating conflict among groups. In this role, a manager challenges the prevailing consensus of opinion to ensure that all alternatives have been critically appraised and analyzed. Although the devil's advocate role often is unpopular, it is a good way to stimulate constructive conflict.

Of course, too much conflict is also a concern. If conflict becomes excessive or destructive, the manager needs to adopt a strategy for reducing or resolving it. Managers should first attempt to determine the source of the conflict. Is it due to differences in goals, perceptions of the difficulty of goal attainment, or the impor-

51. Irving Janis, *Groupthink*, 2nd ed. (Boston: Houghton Mifflin, 1982).
52. Robbins, *Managing Organizational Conflict*.
53. Ibid.

tance of the goals to the conflicting parties? Then the manager can attempt to move the conflicting parties into one of the five types of reactions to conflict, depending on the nature of the conflicting parties. To foster collaboration, trying to help people see that their goals are really not as different as they seem to be might be appropriate. One way to do this is to help groups view their goals as part of a superordinate goal to which the goals of both conflicting parties can contribute. A **superordinate goal** is a goal of the overall organization and is more important to the well-being of the organization and its members than the more specific goals of the conflicting parties. If the goals are not really that important and very incompatible, the manager may need to develop ways to help the conflicting parties avoid each other. Similarly, accommodation, competition, or compromise might be appropriate for the conflicting parties.

A **superordinate goal** is an organizational goal that is more important to the well-being of the organization and its members than the more specific goals of the interacting parties.

Summary of Key Points

- Stress is a person's adaptive response to a stimulus that places excessive psychological or physical demands on that person. According to the general adaptation syndrome, the three stages of response to stress are alarm, resistance, and exhaustion. Two important forms of stress are eustress and distress. People differ in their response to stress in part because of their personalities. Type A personalities are more competitive and time driven than Type B personalities. Initial evidence suggested that Type A persons are more susceptible to coronary heart disease than Type B persons, but recent findings provide less support.
- Stress can be caused by many factors. Major organizational stressors are task demands, physical demands, role demands, and interpersonal demands. Life stressors include life change and life trauma.
- Stress has many consequences. Individual consequences can be behavioral, psychological, and medical problems. Organizational consequences can affect performance and attitudes or cause withdrawal. Burnout is another possibility.
- Primary individual mechanisms for managing stress are exercise, relaxation, time management, role management, and support groups. Organizations use both institutional and collateral programs to help employees manage stress.
- Conflict is a disagreement between parties and a common cause of stress in organizations. Five types of reactions to conflict are avoidance, accommodation, competition, collaboration, and compromise. The types of reactions are determined by the compatibility of goals and the importance of the interaction to group goal attainment. Managers should recognize that conflict can be beneficial as well as harmful.

Discussion Questions

1. Describe one or two recent times when stress had both good and bad consequences for you.
2. Describe a time when you successfully avoided stage 3 of the GAS and another time when you got to stage 3.

3. What are the major stressors for a student?
4. Is an organizational stressor or a life stressor likely to be more powerful?
5. What consequences are students most likely to suffer as a result of too much stress?
6. Do you agree with the assertion that a certain degree of stress is necessary to induce high energy and motivation?
7. What can be done to prevent burnout? If someone you know is suffering burnout, how would you advise that person to recover from it?
8. Do you consider yourself to have a Type A or a Type B personality? Why?
9. Can a person who has a Type A personality change? If so, how?
10. Do you practice any of the stress reduction methods discussed in the text? Which one(s)? Are there others that you use?
11. Do you agree or disagree with the assertion that conflict can be both good and bad? Cite examples of both cases.

EXPERIENTIAL EXERCISE

Purpose   This exercise is intended to help you develop a better understanding of how stress affects you. It will also help you recognize your level of stress on the job or in school.

Format   Following is a set of questions about your job. If you do not work, respond to the questions in terms of your role as a student.

Procedure   Take the following test, figure your score, and then see if your stress level is normal, beginning to be a problem, or dangerous. Answer the statements by putting a number in front of each:

- 1 if the statement is seldom true.
- 2 if the statement is sometimes true.
- 3 if the statement is mostly true.

_____ 1. Even over minor problems, I lose my temper and do embarrassing things, like yell or kick a garbage can.

_____ 2. I hear every piece of information or question as criticism of my work.

_____ 3. I take criticism of my work as a personal attack.

_____ 4. My emotions seem flat whether I'm told good news or bad news about my performance.

_____ 5. Sunday nights are the worst time of the week.

_____ 6. To avoid going to work I'll even call in sick when I'm feeling fine.

_____ 7. I feel powerless to lighten my work load or schedule, even though I've always got far too much to do.

_____ 8. I respond irritably to any request from coworkers.

_____ 9. On the job and off, I get highly emotional over minor accidents, like typographical errors or spilled coffee.

_____10. I tell people about sports or hobbies that I'd like to do but say I never have time because of the hours I spend at work.

_____11. I work overtime consistently, yet I never feel caught up.

_____12. My health is running down; I often have headaches, backaches, and stomachaches.

_____13. If I even eat lunch, I do it at my desk while working.

_____14. I see time as my enemy.

_____15. I can't tell the difference between work and play; it all feels like one more thing to be done.

_____16. Everything I do feels like a drain on my energy.

_____17. I feel like I want to pull the covers over my head and hide.

_____18. I feel off-center or distracted—I do things like walk into mirrored pillars in department stores and excuse myself.

_____19. I blame my family—because of them, I have to stay in this job and location.

_____20. I have ruined my relationship with coworkers whom I feel I compete against.

Scoring Add up the points you wrote beside the questions. Interpret your score as follows:

- 20–29: You have normal amounts of stress.
- 30–49: Stress is becoming a problem. You should try to identify its source and manage it.
- 50–60: Stress is at dangerous levels. Seek help or it could result in worse symptoms, such as alcoholism or illness.

Follow-up Questions

1. How valid do you think your score is?
2. Is it possible to anticipate stress ahead of time and plan ways to help manage it?

SOURCE: From *USA Today*, June 16, 1987. Copyright 1987, *USA Today*. Excerpted with permission.

CASE 9.1   U.S. Bank Overworking Employees—Like Everyone Else?

Like many companies, U.S. Bank is expecting more from its employees—or so it seems. Employees are putting in extra-long days working well into the evening most nights, and coming in on weekends and holidays. Employees knew that their work would increase after a recent merger for a while, but they have been surprised that the extra work required to get the job done has become permanent. In the human resource department, for example, six people are expected to do the work of the seventy that used to be in the department.

Employees at U.S. Bank are not alone in experiencing increased pressure to do more work. The rash of companies that are downsizing to meet foreign competition, reduce costs, or just survive is increasing. Rarely do these companies also mandate reduced performance or establish a cutback in production or services offered. Usually, the surviving employees are expected to pick up the slack and maintain the same or higher levels of production and service. Rather than complain, the surviving employees may be afraid that they, too, may lose their job, and they, therefore, agree to the increased work and try to find ways to get it all done. Most often, this means working longer hours per day and more days per week. One manager who went into work on a holiday counted ninety employees who had already signed in to work on their day off.

Getting it all done may mean a cutback in quality or quantity of production, skipping the least important tasks, working longer hours each day, taking more work home at night, and coming in on weekends and holidays to catch up. Obviously, the increase in hours means a decrease in time to do other things, such as enjoying time with the family, recreation, and pursuing hobbies. The increase in work and the decrease in relaxing time may also lead to accumulated increases in stress levels and lower productivity, service, quality, and personal well-being. Some workers are complaining that all they do is work and commute, which leaves little time to raise the children and develop strong family relationships.

U.S. Bank has tried to make it worth the effort for its employees. Rather than work harder and longer for the same pay, U.S. Bank established a new 401(k) pension plan that is tied to the company's profits. The idea is to show employees that their extra work to help the company improve can pay off financially for them. But the continued extra work and pressure to do more are having a measurable effect on employees at U.S. Bank. The bank's employee assistance program, which offers counseling to employees, reports that counselors are seeing more employees who are having trouble coping with their jobs. They may be making more money, but the extra work and pressure seem to be taking its toll.

Case Questions

1. Discuss the factors that are causing stress for the employees at U.S. Bank.

2. Discuss the results of the stress experienced by employees at U.S. Bank.

3. What are managers in companies that are pushing for more productivity and performance from their employees to do to avoid the inevitable pressure and stress on employees?

SOURCES: Fisher, Anne B., *Fortune*, © 1992 Time Inc. All rights reserved. Additional source: Joe Asher, "U.S. Bancorp Managers Sing Same Tune", *ABA Banking Journal*, August 1991, p. 50.

CASE 9.2	**Stress Takes Its Toll**

Larry Field had a lot of fun in high school. He was a fairly good student, especially in math, he worked harder than most of his friends, and somehow he ended up going steady with Alice Shiflette, class valedictorian. He worked summers for a local surveyor, William Loude, and when he graduated Mr. Loude offered him a job as number-three man on one of his survey crews. The pay was not very high, but Field already was good at the work, and he believed that all he needed was a steady job to boost his confidence sufficiently to ask Alice to marry him. Once he did, the sequence of events that followed unfolded rapidly. He started work in June, he and Alice were married in October, Alice took a job as a secretary in a local company that made business forms, and a year later they had their first child.

The baby came as something of a shock to Field. He had come to enjoy the independence his own paycheck afforded him every week. Food and rent took up most of it, but he still enjoyed playing basketball a few nights a week with his high school buddies and spending Sunday afternoons on the softball field. When the baby came, however, Field's brow began to furrow a bit. He was only twenty years old, and he still was not making much money. He asked Mr. Loude for a raise and got it—his first.

Two months later, one of the crew chiefs quit just when Mr. Loude's crews had more work than they

---

could handle. Mr. Loude hated to turn down work, so he made Larry Field into a crew chief, giving his crew some of the old instruments that were not good enough for the precision work of the top crews, and assigned him the easy title surveys in town. Because it meant a jump in salary, Field had no choice but to accept the crew chief position. But it scared him. He had never been very ambitious or curious, so he had paid little attention to the training of his former crew chief. He knew how to run the instruments—the basics, anyway—but every morning he woke up terrified that he would be sent on a job that he could not handle.

During his first few months as a crew chief, Field began doing things that his wife thought he had outgrown. He frequently talked so fast that he would stumble over his own words, stammer, turn red in the face, and have to start all over again. He began smoking too, something he had not done since they had started dating. He told his two crew members that smoking kept his hands from shaking when he was working on an instrument. Neither of them smoked, and when Field began lighting up in the truck while they were waiting for the rain to stop, they would become resentful and complain that he had no right to ruin their lungs too.

Field found it particularly hard to adjust to being "boss," especially because one of his workers was get-ting an engineering degree at night school and both crew members were the same age as he. He felt sure that Alfonso Reyes, the scholar, would take over his position in no time. He kept feeling that Alfonso was looking over his shoulder and began snapping any time they worked close together.

Things were getting tense at home, too. Alice had to give up her full-time day job to take care of the baby, so she had started working nights. They hardly ever saw each other, and it seemed as though her only topic of conversation was how they should move to California or Alaska, where she had heard that survey-ors were paid five times what Field made. Field knew his wife was dissatisfied with her work and believed her intelligence was being wasted, but he did not know what he could do about it. He was disconcerted when he realized that drinking and worrying about the next day at work while sitting at home with the baby at night had become a pattern.

Case Questions

1. What signs of stress was Larry Field exhibiting?
2. How was Larry Field trying to cope with his stress? Can you suggest more effective methods?

Decision Making, Creativity, and Innovation

OBJECTIVES

After studying this chapter, you should be able to:

Discuss the importance of decision making in organizations.

Describe several ways of making decisions in organizations.

Discuss escalation of commitment and ethics in decision making.

Summarize creativity and innovation in decision making.

Marriott Corporation is among the largest hotel chains in the world. The firm is also a major supplier of food and services management to business, health care, and education through a variety of concessions operations. After experiencing a major growth spurt during the 1980s, Marriott hit a series of roadblocks in the early 1990s. Three forces combined to halt Marriott's growth: a collapsing real estate market, an oversupply of hotel space, and a recession that slowed business travel.

To address these problems, Marriott executives made not one but two critical decisions. The first was to split the firm into two new ones. One company, Marriott International, retains control of the company's profitable hotel operations. The other, Host Marriott, handles the firm's concessions operations and assumes almost all of its debt. Announcement of this plan prompted a surge in the company's stock price. But angry bondholders filed a lawsuit to block the action because their bond holdings would be assigned to the debt-laden Host Marriott operation, thereby depressing their value considerably.

In response to a halt in growth in the early 1990's, Marriott Corporation made the decisive move of splitting its successful hotel business from its less profitable concessions operations. These guests are checking into the New York City Marriott Marquis, one of the 752 hotels owned by the chain in 1993.

The other decision made by Marriott represents a major departure for the firm because of the risk it entails. Marriott has previously followed a strategy of building its own new hotels, selling them to investors, and then managing them for a hefty royalty fee. This strategy was relatively low risk because the firm usually had a hotel sold and a management contract negotiated before it ever started construction. And the firm retained control over quality and other operating standards.

But now the company has started franchising—allowing other firms to use the Marriott name on properties that Marriott itself does not control. Although this approach allows for faster expansion with less capital investment, it also carries with it higher risk. If a given franchised operation fails to live up to Marriott's reputation, for example, the firm suffers. So far, at least, Marriott has avoided this problem by only accepting proven and reliable franchisees who share the company's goals and agree to uphold its quality standards.[1]

■ ■ ■ ■ Marriott's recent actions reflect a fundamental part of the management process in any organization—making decisions. Indeed, some experts believe that decision making is the most basic of all management activities. Some decisions, like those just described, represent major events that will have a dramatic impact on a firm's future growth, its profits, and even its survival. Others, such as deciding on the colors of the firm's new letterhead or when to reorder office supplies, will likely have much less impact. But all decisions are important, and thus we need to understand the processes and methods through which decisions are made.

1. "Know When to Change the Game," *Fortune*, June 28, 1993, pp. 101–102; and "Marriott Unloads Some Baggage," *Business Week*, October 19, 1992, p. 34.

This chapter explores decision making in detail. We start by examining the nature of decision making. Next, we describe several different approaches to understanding the decision-making process. We then identify and discuss two related behavioral aspects of decision making. Finally, we conclude by discussing creativity and innovation as issues in organizations that play a major role in decision making.

The Nature of Decision Making

Decision making is the process of choosing one alternative from among several.

Managers' decisions usually are guided by a goal.

Decision making is choosing one alternative from several. In football, for example, the quarterback can run any of perhaps a hundred plays. With the goal of scoring a touchdown always in mind, he chooses the play that seems to promise the best outcome. His choice is based on his understanding of the game situation, the likelihood of various outcomes, and his preference for each outcome.

Figure 10.1 shows the basic elements of decision making. A decision maker's actions are guided by a goal. Each of several alternative courses of action is linked with various outcomes. Information is available regarding the alternatives, the likelihood that each outcome will occur, and the value of each outcome relative to the goal. On the basis of his or her evaluation of the information, the decision maker chooses one alternative.

Decisions made in organizations can be classified according to frequency and information conditions. In a decision-making context, *frequency* describes how often a particular decision recurs, and *information conditions* describe how much information about the predictability of various outcomes is available.

FIGURE 10.1

**Elements of
Decision Making**

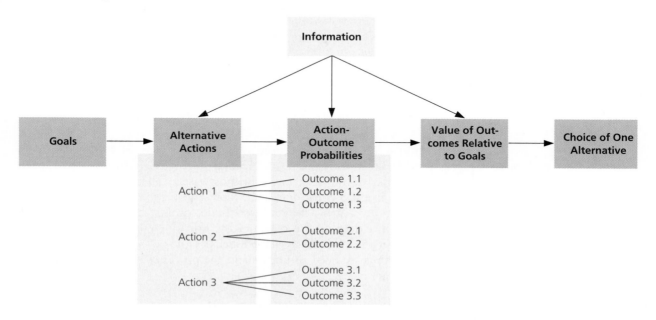

Types of Decisions

A **programmed decision** is a decision that recurs often enough for a decision rule to be developed.

A **decision rule** is a statement that tells a decision maker which alternative to choose based on the characteristics of the decision situation.

The frequency of recurrence determines whether a decision is programmed or nonprogrammed. A **programmed decision** recurs often enough for a decision rule to be developed. A **decision rule** tells decision makers which alternative to choose once they have information about the decision situation. Whenever the situation is encountered, the appropriate decision rule is used. Programmed decisions usually are highly structured; that is, the goals are clear and well known, the decision making procedure is already established, and the sources and channels of information are clearly defined.[2]

Airlines use established procedures when a piece of equipment breaks down and cannot be used on a particular flight. Passengers may not view the issue as a programmed decision because they experience this situation relatively infrequently. But to the airlines, equipment problems that render a plane unfit for service arise regularly. Each airline has its own clear-cut set of procedures to use in the event of an equipment problem. Depending on the nature of the problem and other circumstances (such as the number of passengers booked and the next scheduled flight for the same destination), a given flight may be delayed, cancelled, or continued on a different plane.

A **nonprogrammed decision** is a decision that recurs infrequently and for which there is no previously established decision rule.

Problem solving is a form of decision making in which the issue is unique and requires development and evaluation of alternatives without the aid of a programmed decision rule.

All problems require a decision, but not all decisions require problem solving.

When a problem or decision situation has not been encountered before, however, the decision maker cannot rely on previously established decision rules. Such a decision is called a **nonprogrammed decision**, and it requires problem solving. **Problem solving** is a special form of decision making in which the issue is unique—alternatives are developed and evaluated without the aid of a decision rule. Nonprogrammed decisions are poorly structured because information is ambiguous, there is no clear procedure for making the decision, and the goals often are vague.[3] Marriott's two decisions were both nonprogrammed decisions.

Table 10.1 summarizes the characteristics of programmed and nonprogrammed decisions. Note that programmed decisions are more common at the lower levels of the organization, whereas a primary responsibility of top management is to make the difficult, nonprogrammed decisions that determine the long-term effectiveness of the organization. By definition, the strategy decisions for which top management is responsible are poorly structured and nonroutine and have far-reaching consequences.[4] Programmed decisions, then, can be made according to previously tested rules and procedures. Nonprogrammed decisions generally require the decision maker to exercise judgment and creativity.[5] In other words, all problems require a decision, but not all decisions require problem solving.

Information Required for Decision Making

Decisions are made to bring about desired outcomes, but the available information about those outcomes varies. The range of available information can be repre-

2. Herbert Simon, *The New Science of Management Decision* (New York: Harper & Row, 1960), p. 1.
3. Simon, *The New Science of Management Decision*.
4. Nandini Rajagopalan, Abdul M. A. Rasheed, and Deepak K. Datta, "Strategic Decision Processes: Critical Review and Future Directions," *Journal of Management*, Vol. 19, No. 2, pp. 349–384.
5. See Bernard M. Bass, *Organizational Decision Making* (Homewood, Ill.: Irwin, 1983), pp. 13–15, for a discussion of poorly structured and well-structured problems.

TABLE 10.1

Characteristics
of Programmed
and Nonprogrammed
Decisions

Characteristics	Programmed Decisions	Nonprogrammed Decisions
Type of Decision	Well structured	Poorly structured
Frequency	Repetitive and routine	New and unusual
Goals	Clear, specific	Vague
Information	Readily available	Not available, unclear channels
Consequences	Minor	Major
Organizational Level	Lower levels	Upper levels
Time for Solution	Short	Relatively long
Basis for Solution	Decision rules, set procedures	Judgment and creativity

Certainty is a condition where the outcome of each alternative is known.

Risk is a condition where the decision maker does not know with certainty what the outcome of a given action will be, but has enough information to estimate the probabilities of occurrence of various outcomes.

sented as a continuum whose endpoints represent complete certainty, at which point all alternative outcomes are known, and complete uncertainty, at which point alternative outcomes are unknown. At every point on the continuum, except the point representing complete certainty, or course, risk is involved.

Different information conditions present different challenges to the decision maker.[6] For example, suppose that Nintendo's marketing manager is trying to determine whether to launch an expensive promotional effort for a new video game (see Figure 10.2). For simplicity, assume that there are only two alternatives: to promote the game or not to promote it. Under a condition of **certainty**, the manager knows the outcomes of each alternative. If the new game is promoted heavily, the company will realize a $1 million profit. Without promotion, the company will realize only a $200,000 profit. Here the decision is simple: promote the game.

Under a condition of **risk**, the decision maker cannot know with certainty what the outcome of a given action will be but has enough information to estimate the probabilities of occurrence of various outcomes. Thus, working from information gathered by the market research department, the marketing manager in our example can estimate the likelihood of each outcome in a risk situation. In this case, the alternatives are defined by the size of the market. The probability for a large video game market is 0.6, and the probability for a small market is 0.4. The manager can calculate the expected value of the promotional effort based on these probabilities and the expected profits associated with each. To find the expected value of an alternative, the manager multiplies each outcome's value by the probability of its occurrence. The sum of these calculations for all possible outcomes represents that alternative's expected value. In this case, the expected value of alternative 1—to promote the new game—is as follows:

6. See George P. Huber, *Managerial Decision Making* (Glenview, Ill.: Scott, Foresman, 1980) pp. 90–115, for a discussion of decision making under conditions of certainty, risk, and uncertainty.

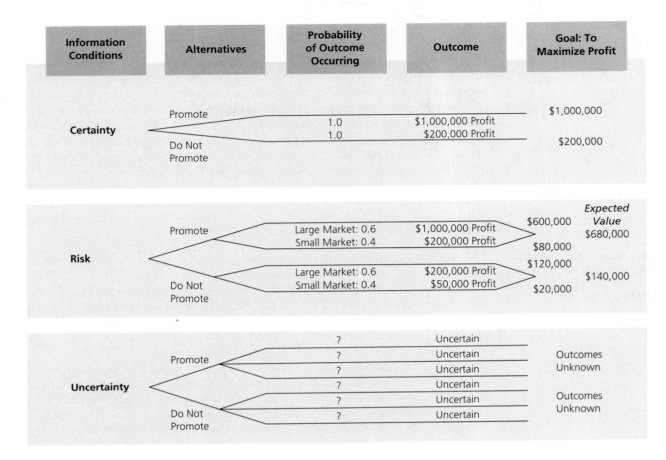

Information Conditions	Alternatives	Probability of Outcome Occurring	Outcome	Goal: To Maximize Profit
Certainty	Promote	1.0	$1,000,000 Profit	$1,000,000
	Do Not Promote	1.0	$200,000 Profit	$200,000
Risk	Promote	Large Market: 0.6 Small Market: 0.4	$1,000,000 Profit $200,000 Profit	$600,000 $80,000 *Expected Value* $680,000
	Do Not Promote	Large Market: 0.6 Small Market: 0.4	$200,000 Profit $50,000 Profit	$120,000 $20,000 $140,000
Uncertainty	Promote	? ? ?	Uncertain Uncertain Uncertain	Outcomes Unknown
	Do Not Promote	? ? ?	Uncertain Uncertain Uncertain	Outcomes Unknown

FIGURE 10.2

Alternative Outcomes Under Different Information Conditions

$$0.6 \times \$1,000,000 = \$600,000$$
$$+ \ 0.4 \times \$ \ \ 200,000 = \$ \ \ 80,000$$
$$\text{Expected value of alternative 1} = \$680,000$$

The expected value of alternative 2 (shown in Figure 10.2) is $140,000. The marketing manager should choose the first alternative because its expected value is higher. The manager should recognize, however, that although the numbers look convincing, they are based on incomplete information and are only estimates of probability.

The decision maker who lacks enough information to estimate the probability of outcomes (or perhaps even to identify the outcomes at all) faces a condition of **uncertainty**.[7] Nintendo's marketing manager might face this situation if sales of video games had recently collapsed and it was not clear whether the precipitous drop was temporary or permanent or when information to clarify the situation would be available. Under such circumstances, the decision maker may wait for more information to reduce uncertainty or rely on judgment, experience, and intuition to make the decision.

Uncertainty occurs when a decision maker lacks enough information to estimate the probability of outcomes.

7. See Bass, *Organizational Decision Making*, pp. 83–89, for a discussion of uncertainty.

The Decision-Making Process

Several approaches to decision making offer insights into the process by which managers arrive at their decisions. The rational approach is appealing because of its logic and economy. Yet these very qualities raise questions about this approach because actual decision making often is not a wholly rational process. The behavioral approach, meanwhile, attempts to account for the limits on rationality in decision making. The practical approach to decision making combines features of the rational and behavioral approaches. Finally, the personal approach focuses on the decision-making processes individuals use in difficult situations.

The Rational Approach

The **rational decision-making approach** assumes that managers follow a systematic, step-by-step process. It further assumes that the organization is economically based and managed by decision makers who are entirely objective and have complete information.[8] Figure 10.3 identifies the steps of the process, starting with a statement of a goal and running logically through the process until the best decision is made, implemented, and controlled.

> The **rational decision-making approach** is a systematic, step-by-step process for making decisions.

Statement of Situational Goal   The rational decision-making process begins with the statement of a situational goal, or desired end state. The goal of a marketing department, for example, may be to obtain a certain market share by the end of the year. (Some models of decision making do not start with a goal. We include it because it is the standard used to determine whether there is a decision to be made.)

Identification of the Problem   The purpose of problem identification is to gather information that bears on the goal. If there is a discrepancy between the goal and the actual state, action may be needed. In the marketing example, the group may gather information about the company's actual market share and compare it with the desired market share. A difference between the two represents a problem that necessitates a decision. Reliable information is very important in this step. Inaccurate information can lead to an unnecessary decision or no decision when one is required.

> Determination of the decision type means deciding whether a decision is to be programmed or nonprogrammed.

Determination of Decision Type   Next, the decision makers must determine if the problem represents a programmed or a nonprogrammed decision. If a programmed decision is needed, the appropriate decision rule is invoked, and the process moves on to the choice among alternatives. A programmed marketing decision may be called for if analysis reveals that competitors are outspending the company on print advertising. Because creating and buying space for print advertising is a well-established function of the marketing group, it requires only a programmed decision.

Although it may seem simple to diagnose a situation as programmed, apply a decision rule, and arrive at a solution, mistakes can still occur. Choosing the

8. See Bass, *Organizational Decision Making*, pp. 27–31, on the economic theory of the firm.

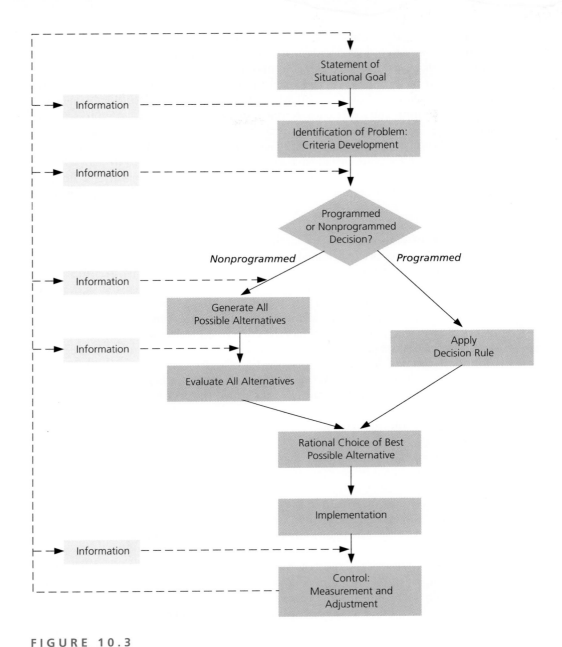

FIGURE 10.3
The Rational Decision-Making Process

wrong decision rule or assuming that the problem calls for a programmed decision when a nonprogrammed decision actually is required can result in unacceptable decisions. The same caution applies to the determination that a nonprogrammed decision is called for. If the situation is wrongly diagnosed, the decision maker wastes time and resources seeking a new solution to an old problem or "reinventing the wheel."

Generation of Alternatives   If decision makers have determined that a problem needs a nonprogrammed decision, the next step is to generate alternatives. The rational process assumes that decision makers will generate all possible alternative solutions to the problem. Because even simple business problems can have scores of possible solutions, however, this assumption is unrealistic. Decision makers may rely on education and experience as well as knowledge of the situation to generate alternatives. In addition, they may seek information from other people such as peers, subordinates, and supervisors. Decision makers may analyze the symptoms of the problem for clues or fall back on intuition or judgment to develop alternative solutions.[9] If Nintendo's marketing department determines that a nonprogrammed decision is required, it will need to generate alternatives for increasing market share.

Evaluation of Alternatives   Evaluation involves the assessment of all possible alternatives against predetermined decision criteria. The ultimate decision criterion is, "Will this alternative bring us nearer to the goal?" The decision maker must examine each alternative for evidence that it will reduce the discrepancy between the desired state and the actual state. The evaluation process usually includes (1) a description of the anticipated outcomes (benefits) of each alternative, (2) an evaluation of the anticipated costs of each alternative, and (3) an estimation of the uncertainties and risks associated with each alternative.[10] For most decisions, the decision maker does not have perfect information regarding the outcomes of all alternatives. At one extreme, as shown earlier in Figure 10.2, outcomes may be known with certainty; at the other, the decision maker has no information whatsoever and the outcomes are entirely uncertain. But risk is the most common situation.

Choice of an Alternative   Whether the decision is programmed or nonprogrammed, the choice of an alternative is usually the most crucial step in the decision-making process. Choice consists of selecting the alternative with the highest possible payoff, based on the benefits, costs, risks, and uncertainties of all alternatives. In the Nintendo game promotion example, the decision maker evaluated the two alternatives by calculating their expected values. Following the rational approach, the manager would choose the one with the largest expected value.

Even in the rational approach, however, difficulties can arise in choosing an alternative. First, when two or more alternatives have equal payoffs, the decision maker must obtain more information or use some other criterion to make the choice. Second, when no single alternative will accomplish the objective, some combination of two or three alternatives may have to be implemented. Finally, if no alternative or combination of alternatives will solve the problem, the decision maker must obtain more information, generate more alternatives, or change the goals.[11]

An important part of the choice phase is the consideration of **contingency plans**—alternative actions that can be taken if the primary course of action is

Contingency plans are alternative actions to take if the primary course of action is unexpectedly disrupted or rendered inappropriate.

9. "'90s Style Brainstorming," *Forbes ASAP*, October 25, 1993, pp. 44–61.
10. Milan Zeleny, "Descriptive Decision Making and Its Application," *Applications of Management Science*, Vol. 1, 1981, pp. 327–388; and Henry Mintzberg, Duru Raisinghani, and André Thoret, "The Structure of 'Unstructured' Decision Processes," *Administrative Science Quarterly*, June 1976, pp. 246–275.
11. See E. Frank Harrison, *The Managerial Decision Making Process*, 2nd ed. (Boston: Houghton Mifflin, 1981), pp. 41–43, for more on choice processes.

unexpectedly disrupted or rendered inappropriate.[12] Planning for contingencies is part of the transition between choosing the preferred alternative and implementing it. In developing contingency plans, the decision maker usually asks questions such as, "What if something unexpected happens during the implementation of this alternative?"; "If the economy goes into a recession, will the choice of this alternative ruin the company?"; and "How can we alter this plan if the economy suddenly rebounds and begins to grow?"

Implementation   Implementation puts the decision into action. It uses the commitment and motivation of those who participated in the decision-making process (and may actually bolster individual commitment and motivation). To be successful, implementation requires the proper use of resources and good management skills. After the decision to promote the new Nintendo game heavily, for example, the marketing manager must implement the decision by assigning the project to a work group or task force. The success of this team depends on the leadership, the reward structure, the communications system, and the group dynamics. Sometimes the decision maker begins to doubt a choice already made. This doubt is called *post-decision dissonance* or *cognitive dissonance*.[13] To reduce the tension created by the dissonance, the decision maker may seek to rationalize the decision further with new information.

> Cognitive dissonance is the anxiety a person experiences when two sets of knowledge or perceptions are contradictory or incongruent.

Control: Measurement and Adjustment   In the final stage of the rational decision-making process, the outcomes of the decision are measured and compared with the desired goal. If a discrepancy remains, the decision maker may restart the decision-making process by setting a new goal (or reiterating the existing one). The decision maker, unsatisfied with the previous decision, may modify the subsequent decision-making process to avoid another mistake. Changes can be made to any part of the process, as Figure 10.3 illustrates by the arrows leading from the control step to each of the other steps. Decision making therefore is a dynamic, self-correcting, and ongoing process in organizations.

Suppose that a marketing department implements a new print advertising campaign. After implementation, it will constantly monitor market research data and compare its new market share to the desired market share. If the advertising has the desired effect, no changes will be made in the promotion campaign. If, however, the data indicate no change in the market share, additional decisions and implementation of a contingency plan may be necessary. For example, when Nissan introduced its luxury car line Infiniti, it relied on a zen-like series of ads that featured images of rocks, plants, and water—but no images of the car. At the same time, Toyota was featuring pictures of its new luxury car line, Lexus, and quickly established itself in the market. When Infiniti managers realized their mistake, they quickly pulled the old ads and started running new ones centered around images of their car.[14]

12. Donald C. Hambrick and David Lei, "Toward an Empirical Prioritization of Contingency Variables for Business Strategy," *Academy of Management Journal*, December 1985, pp. 763–788; and Ari Ginsberg and N. Ventrakaman, "Contingency Perspectives of Organizational Strategy: A Critical Review of the Empirical Research," *Academy of Management Review*, July 1985, pp. 412–434.
13. Leon Festinger, *A Theory of Cognitive Dissonance* (Palo Alto, Calif.: Stanford University Press, 1957).
14. Patricia Sellers, "The Dumbest Marketing Ploys," *Fortune*, October 5, 1992, pp. 88–94.

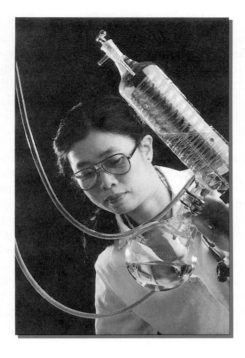

An example of someone using a rational approach to decision making, this scientist at a Union Carbide lab follows a step-by-step process to support a hypothesis. She will conduct experiments methodically until she produces the desired reaction.

Strengths and Weaknesses of the Rational Approach   The rational approach has several strengths. It forces the decision maker to consider a decision in a logical, sequential manner, and the in-depth analysis of alternatives enables the decision maker to choose on the basis of information rather than emotion or social pressure. The rigid assumptions of this approach often are unrealistic, however.[15] The amount of information available to managers usually is limited by either time or cost constraints, and most decision makers have limited ability to process information about the alternatives. In addition, not all alternatives lend themselves to quantification that allows for easy comparison. Finally, because they cannot predict the future, decision makers will not likely know all possible outcomes.[16]

The Behavioral Approach

Whereas the rational approach assumes that managers operate with logic and rationality, the behavioral approach acknowledges the role and importance of human behavior in the decision-making process. In particular, a crucial assumption of the behavioral approach is that decision makers operate with **bounded rationality** rather than with the perfect rationality assumed by the rational approach. The assumption rests on the argument that although individuals seek the best solution to a problem, the demands of processing all information bearing on the problem, generating all possible solutions, and choosing the single best solution are beyond the capabilities of most decision makers. Thus, individuals will accept less than ideal solutions based on a process that is neither exhaustive nor entirely rational.

Bounded rationality is the assumption that decision makers cannot deal with all possible aspects and information about the problem and all alternatives and therefore choose to tackle some meaningful subset of it.

15. See Harrison, *The Managerial Decision Making Process*, pp. 53–57, for more on the advantages and disadvantages of the rational approach.
16. See Paul C. Nutt, "The Formulation Processes and Tactics Used in Organizational Decision Making," *Organization Science*, Vol. 4, No. 2, 1993, pp. 226–236.

Part 3   Enhancing Performance in Organizations

Decision makers operating with bounded rationality limit inputs and base decisions on judgment and personal biases as well as on logic.[17]

The **behavioral approach** is characterized by (1) the use of procedures and rules of thumb, (2) suboptimizing, and (3) satisficing. Uncertainty in decision making can initially be reduced by reliance on procedures and rules of thumb. If, for example, increasing print advertising has increased a company's market share in the past, the linkage may be used by company employees as a rule of thumb in decision making. When the previous month's market share drops below a certain level, the company might increase its print advertising expenditures by 25 percent during the following month.

Suboptimizing is knowingly accepting less than the best possible outcome. Frequently, optimizing a particular decision in a real-world situation is not feasible, given organizational constraints. To avoid unintended negative effects on other departments, product lines, or decisions, the decision maker often must suboptimize.[18] An automobile manufacturer, for example, can cut costs dramatically and increase efficiency if it schedules the production of one model at a time. Thus, the production group's optimal decision is single-model scheduling. But the marketing group, seeking to optimize its sales goals by offering a wide variety of models, may demand the opposite production schedule: short runs of entirely different models. The groups in the middle, design and scheduling, may suboptimize the benefits the production and marketing groups are seeking by planning long runs of slightly different models. This is the practice of the large auto manufacturers, such as General Motors and Ford, which make several body styles in numerous models on the same production line.

The final feature of the behavioral approach is **satisficing**: examining alternatives only until a solution that meets minimal requirements is found and then ceasing to look for a better one.[19] The search for alternatives usually is a sequential process guided by procedures and rules of thumb based on previous experiences with similar problems. When the first minimally acceptable choice is encountered, the search often ends. The resulting choice may narrow the discrepancy between the desired and the actual states, but it is not likely to be the optimal solution. As the process is repeated, incremental improvements will slowly reduce the discrepancy between the actual and desired states.

The Practical Approach

Because of the unrealistic demands of the rational approach and the limited, short-run orientation of the behavioral approach, neither is entirely satisfactory. The worthwhile features of each, however, can be combined into a **practical approach** to decision making, shown in Figure 10.4. Although the steps in this process are the same as in the rational approach, the conditions recognized by the behavioral approach are added to provide a more realistic process. For example, the practical approach suggests that rather than generating all alternatives, the decision maker

The **behavioral approach** uses rules of thumb, suboptimizing, and satisficing in making decisions.

Suboptimizing is knowingly accepting less than the best possible outcome to avoid unintended negative effects on other aspects of the organization.

Satisficing is examining alternatives only until a solution that meets minimal requirements is found.

The **practical approach** to decision making combines the steps of the rational approach with the conditions in the behavioral approach to create a more realistic process for making decisions in organizations.

17. See James G. March and Herbert A. Simon, *Organizations* (New York: Wiley, 1958), for more on the concept of bounded rationality.
18. Herbert A. Simon, *Administrative Behavior: A Study of Decision Making Processes in Administrative Organizations*, 3rd ed. (New York: Free Press, 1976).
19. Richard M. Cyert and James G. March, *A Behavioral Theory of the Firm* (Englewood Cliffs, N.J.: Prentice-Hall, 1963), p. 113; and Simon, *Administrative Behavior*.

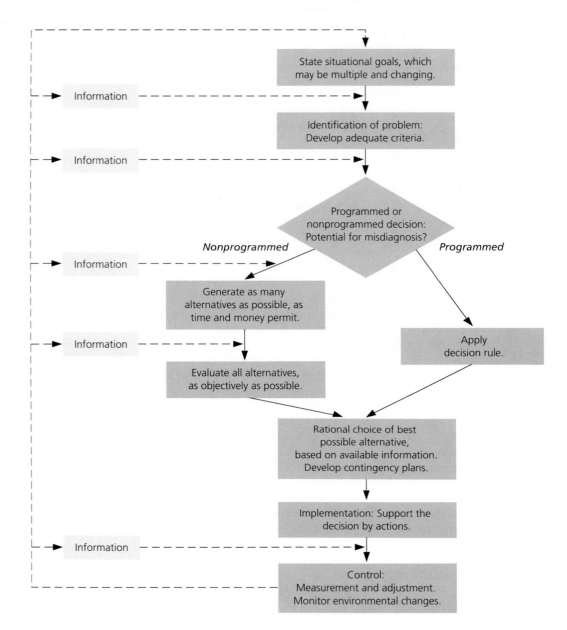

State situational goals, which
may be multiple and changing.

Information

Identification of problem:
Develop adequate criteria.

Information

Programmed or
nonprogrammed decision:
Potential for misdiagnosis?

Nonprogrammed   *Programmed*

Information

Generate as many
alternatives as possible, as
time and money permit.

Apply
decision rule.

Information

Evaluate all alternatives,
as objectively as possible.

Rational choice of best
possible alternative,
based on available information.
Develop contingency plans.

Implementation: Support the
decision by actions.

Information

Control:
Measurement and adjustment.
Monitor environmental changes.

FIGURE 10.4

**Practical Approach to
Decision Making with
Behavioral Guidelines**

should try to go beyond rules of thumb and satisficing limitations and generate as many alternatives as time, money, and other practicalities of the situation allow. In this synthesis of the two approaches, the rational approach provides an analytical-framework for making decisions, whereas the behavioral approach provides a moderating influence.

In practice, decision makers use some hybrid of the rational, behavioral, and practical approaches to making the tough day-to-day decisions in running organizations. Some decision makers use a methodical process of gathering all available information, developing and evaluating alternatives, and seeking advice from knowledgeable people before making a decision. Others fly from one decision to another, making seemingly hasty decisions, and barking out orders to subordinates. The second group seems to not use much information or a rational approach to making decisions. Recent research, however, has shown that managers who make decisions very quickly probably are using just as much, or more, information and generating and evaluating as many alternatives as slower, more methodical decision makers.[20] *Developing Management Skills* helps provide some experience in using these different approaches to making decisions.

The Conflict Model

Although the models just described have provided important insight into decision making, they do not fully explain the processes people engage in when they are nervous, worried, and agitated over making a decision that has major implications for them, their organization, or their families. In short, they still do not reflect the conditions under which many decisions are made. One attempt to provide a more realistic view of individual decision making is the model presented by Irving Janis and Leon Mann.[21] The Janis-Mann process, called the **conflict model**, is based on research in social psychology and individual decision processes. The model has five basic characteristics:

> The **conflict model** is a very personal approach to decision making because it deals with the personal conflicts that people experience in particularly difficult decision situations.

1. It applies only to important life decisions—marriage, schooling, career, major organizational decisions—that commit the individual or the organization to a certain course of action after the decision.
2. It recognizes that procrastination and rationalization are mechanisms by which people avoid making difficult decisions and coping with its associated stress.
3. It explicitly acknowledges that some decisions probably will be wrong and that the fear of making an unsound decision can be a deterrent to making any decision at all.

> **Self-reactions** are comparisons of alternatives with internalized moral standards.

4. It provides for **self-reactions**—comparisons of alternatives with internalized moral standards. Internalized moral standards guide decision making as much as economic and social outcomes do. A proposed course of action may offer many economic and social rewards, but if it violates the decision maker's moral convictions, it is unlikely to be chosen.
5. It recognizes that at times the decision maker is ambivalent about alternative courses of action; in such circumstances, making a wholehearted commitment to a single choice is very difficult. Major life decisions seldom allow compromise, however; usually they are either/or decisions that require commitment to one course of action.

The Janis-Mann conflict model of decision making is shown in Figure 10.5. A concrete example will help explain each step. Our hypothetical individual is Richard, a thirty-year-old engineer, with a working wife and two young children. Richard has been employed at a large manufacturing company for eight years. He keeps abreast of his career situation through visits with peers at work and in other companies, feedback from his manager and others regarding his work and future with the firm, the alumni magazine from his university, and other sources.

20. Kathleen M. Eisenhardt, "Making Fast Strategic Decisions in High-Velocity Environments," *Academy of Management Journal*, September 1989, pp. 543–576.
21. Irving L. Janis and Leon Mann, *Decision Making: A Psychological Analysis of Conflict, Choice, and Commitment* (New York: Free Press, 1977).

At work one morning, Richard learns that he has been passed over for a promotion for the second time in a year. He investigates the information, which can be considered negative feedback, and confirms it. As a result, he seeks out other information regarding his career at the company, the prospect of changing employers, and the possibility of going back to graduate school to get an MBA. At the same time, he asks himself, "Are the risks serious if I do not make a change?"

FIGURE 10.5

The Janis-Mann Conflict Model of Decision Making

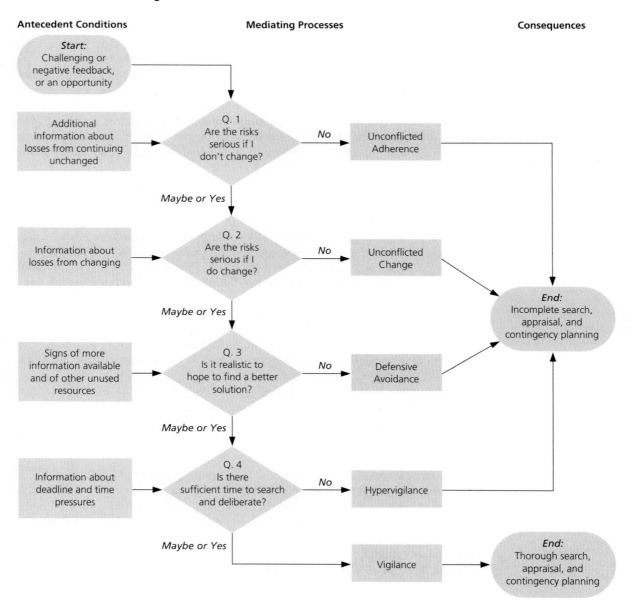

SOURCE: Reprinted with permission of The Free Press, an imprint of Simon & Schuster, Inc. from *Decision Making: A Psychological Analysis of Conflict, Choice, and Commitment* by Irving L. Janis and Leon Mann. Copyright © 1977 by The Free Press.

Rational Versus Practical Approaches to Decision Making

Managers need to recognize and understand the different models that they use to make decisions. They also need to understand the extent to which they are predisposed to be relatively autocratic or relatively participative in making decisions. To develop your skills in these areas, perform the following activity.

First, assume that you are the manager of a firm that is rapidly growing. Recent sales figures strongly suggest the need for a new plant to produce more of your firm's products. Important decisions include where the plant is to be built and how large it should be (for example, a small and less-expensive plant to meet current needs that can be expanded in the future versus a large and more expensive plant that might have excess capacity today but may meet long-term needs better).

Using the rational approach diagrammed in Figure 10.3, trace through the process the manager might use to make this decision. Note the kinds of information that might be required and the extent to which other people might need to be involved in making the decision at each point.

Next, go back and look at various steps in the process where behavioral processes might intervene and affect the overall process. Will bounded rationality come into play? How about satisficing?

Finally, use the practical approach shown in Figure 10.4 and trace through the process again. Again note where other input may be needed. Try to identify places in the process where the rational and practical approaches are likely to result in the same outcome and places where differences are most likely to occur.

Unconflicted adherence means continuing with activities if doing so does not entail serious risks.

If the answer is no, Richard will continue his present activities. In the model's terms, this option is called **unconflicted adherence**. If the answer is yes or maybe, Richard will move to the next question in the model.

The second step asks, "Are the risks serious if I do change?" If Richard goes on to this step, he will gather information about potential losses from making a change. He may, for example, find out whether he would lose health insurance and pension benefits if he changed jobs or went back to graduate school. If he believes that changing presents no serious risks, Richard will make the change, called an **unconflicted change**. Otherwise, he will move on to the next step.

Unconflicted change involves making changes in present activities if doing so presents no serious risks.

But suppose Richard has determined that the risks are serious whether he makes a change or not. He believes he must make a change because he will not be promoted further in his present company, yet serious risks are associated with making a change—perhaps loss of benefits, uncertain promotion opportunities in another company, and lost income from going to graduate school for two years. In the third step, Richard wonders, "Is it realistic to hope to find a better solution?" He continues to look for information that can help him make the decision. If the answer to this third question is negative, Richard may give up the hope of finding anything better and opt for what Janis and Mann call **defensive avoidance**; that is, he will make no change and avoid any further contact with the issue. A positive response, however, will move Richard to the next step.

Defensive avoidance means making no changes in present activities and avoiding any further contact with associated issues because there appears to be no hope of finding a better solution.

Here the decision maker, who now recognizes the serious risks involved yet expects to find a solution, asks, "Is there sufficient time to search and deliberate?" Richard now asks himself how quickly he needs to make a change. If he believes that he has little time to deliberate, perhaps because of his age, he will experience

---

Hypervigilance is frantic, superficial pursuit of some satisfying strategy. **Vigilant information processing** involves thoroughly investigating all possible alternatives, weighing their costs and benefits before making a decision, and developing contingency plans.

what Janis and Mann call **hypervigilance**. In this state, he may suffer severe psychological stress and engage in frantic, superficial pursuit of some satisfying strategy. (This might also be called panic!) If, on the other hand, Richard believes that he has two to three years to consider various alternatives, he will undertake **vigilant information processing**, in which he will thoroughly investigate all possible alternatives, weigh their costs and benefits before making a choice, and develop contingency plans.

Negative answers to the questions in the conflict model lead to responses of unconflicted adherence, unconflicted change, defensive avoidance, and hypervigilance. All are coping strategies that result in incomplete search, appraisal, and contingency planning. A decision maker who gives the same answer to all the questions will always engage in the same coping strategy. If the answers change as the situation changes, however, the individual's coping strategies may change as well. The decision maker who answers positively to each of the four questions is led to vigilant information processing, a process similar to that outlined in the rational decision making model. The decision maker objectively analyzes the problem and all alternatives, thoroughly searches for information, carefully evaluates the consequences of all alternatives, and diligently plans for implementation and contingencies.

Related Behavioral Aspects of Decision Making

Although the behavioral, practical, and conflict approaches to decision making each have behavioral components, we still have two additional behavioral aspects of decision making to consider. These are escalation of commitment and ethics.

Escalation of Commitment

Escalation of commitment is the tendency to persist in an ineffective course of action when evidence reveals that the project cannot succeed.

Sometimes people continue to try to implement a decision despite clear and convincing evidence that substantial problems exist. **Escalation of commitment** refers to the tendency to persist in an ineffective course of action when evidence indicates that the project is doomed to failure. A good example is the decision by the government of British Columbia to hold EXPO' 86 in Vancouver. Originally, the organizers expected the project to break even financially, so the province would not have to increase taxes to pay for it. As work progressed, expenses clearly were far greater than had been projected. But organizers considered it too late to call off the event, despite the huge losses that obviously would occur. Eventually, the province conducted a $300 million lottery to try to cover the costs.[22] Similar examples abound in stockmarket investments, in political and military situations, and in organizations developing any type of new project.

Barry Staw has suggested several possible reasons for escalation of commitment.[23] Some projects require much front-end investment and offer little return until the end, so the investor must stay in all the way to get any payoff. These "all

22. Jerry Ross and Barry M. Staw, "Expo' 86: An Escalation Prototype," *Administrative Science Quarterly*, June 1986, pp. 274–297.
23. Barry M. Staw, "Escalation of Commitment to a Course of Action," *Academy of Management Review*, October 1981, pp. 577–587.

or nothing" projects require unflagging commitment. Furthermore, investors or project leaders often become so ego involved with their project that their self-identities are totally wrapped up in it.[24] Failure or cancellation seems to threaten their reason for existence. Therefore, they continue to push the project as potentially successful despite strong evidence to the contrary. Other times, the social structure, group norms, and group cohesiveness support a project so strongly that cancellation is impossible. Organizational inertia also may force an organization to maintain a failing project. Thus, escalation of commitment is a phenomenon that has a strong foundation.

"Throwing good money after bad" is the popular way of saying that even if a decision is going bad, one stays committed to it because one has invested so much in it.

How can an individual or organization recognize that a project needs to be stopped before it results in "throwing good money after bad?" Several suggestions have been made; some are easy to put to use, and others are more difficult. Having good information about a project is always a first step to prevent the escalation problem. Usually it is possible to schedule regular sessions to discuss the project, its progress, the assumptions on which it originally was based, the current validity of these assumptions, and any problems with the project. An objective review is necessary to maintain control.

Some organizations have begun to make separate teams responsible for the development and implementation of a project to reduce ego involvement. Often the people who initiate a project are those who know the most about it, however, and their expertise can be valuable in the implementation process. Staw suggests that a general strategy for avoiding the escalation problem is to try to create an "experimenting organization" in which every program and project is reviewed regularly and managers are evaluated on their contribution to the total organization rather than to specific projects.[25] The decision by Congress to scrap the Supercollider project in Texas in 1993 represented an effort to avoid escalation to a decision that had already cost almost twice its original budgeted amount.

Ethics and Decision Making

As we noted in Chapter 2, *ethics* are a person's beliefs about what is right and wrong behavior. Ethical behavior conforms to generally accepted social norms, whereas unethical behavior does not conform to generally accepted social norms. Although some decisions made by managers have little or nothing to do with their own personal ethics, many other decisions are, in fact, influenced by the manager's own ethics. For example, decisions involving such disparate issues as hiring and firing employees, negotiating with customers and suppliers, setting wages and assigning tasks, and maintaining one's expense account are all subject to ethical influences.

In general, ethical dilemmas for managers may center around direct personal gain, indirect personal gain, or simple personal preferences. Consider, for example, a top executive contemplating a decision about a potential takeover. His or her stock-option package may result in enormous personal gain if the decision goes one way, even though stockholders may benefit more if the decision goes the other way. An indirect personal gain may result from a certain decision that does not directly add value to a manager's personal worth but does serve to enhance

24. Joel Brockner, Robert Houser, Gregg Birnbaum, Kathy Lloyd, Janet Deitcher, Sinaia Nathanson, and Jeffrey Z. Rubin, "Escalation of Commitment to an Ineffective Course of Action: The Effect of Feedback Having Negative Implications for Self-Identity," *Administrative Science Quarterly*, March 1986, pp. 109–126.
25. Barry M. Staw and Jerry Ross, "Good Money after Bad," *Psychology Today*, February 1988, pp. 30–33.

A film production crew holds a brainstorming meeting at Parsons School of Design in New York City. The crew hopes to be able to come up with an innovative and appropriate way to handle the technical demands of the film while complementing its content matter.

her or his career. Or the manager may face a choice for relocating a company facility where one of the options is closest to his or her residence.

Whenever managers make decisions, they should carefully and deliberately consider the ethical context of that decision. The goal, of course, is for the manager to make the decision that is in the best interest of the firm, as opposed to the best interest of the manager. To accomplish this requires personal honesty and integrity. Managers also find that discussing potential ethical dilemmas with colleagues is helpful. Others can often provide an objective view of a situation that may help a manager unintentionally avoid making an unethical decision.

Creativity and Innovation in Decision Making

Creativity and innovation are important concepts related to decision making. Each is a unique concept in its own way, but each also plays a major role in how decisions get made. **Creativity** is the process of developing original and imaginative views of situations. **Innovation**, on the other hand, is the process of creating and doing new things that are introduced into the marketplace as products, processes, or services.

Creativity and Decision Making

Creativity is an important part of decision making in organizations. Without creativity, managers would be greatly constrained in making decisions. Moreover,

Creativity is the process of developing original and imaginative views of situations.

Innovation is the process of creating and doing new things that are introduced into the marketplace as products, processes, or services.

organizations would never change, and their employees would stagnate.[26] The *Global Perspective* outlines how some Japanese companies are attempting to become more creative.

The Creative Individual   Individual creativity is a core requirement for managers whose aim is to make important and meaningful decisions. Numerous researchers have focused their efforts on attempting to describe the common attributes of creative individuals. These attributes generally fall into three categories: background experiences, personality traits, and cognitive abilities.[27]

Experiences are the events that people live through during childhood and young adulthood. Researchers have noticed that many creative individuals were raised in an environment in which creativity was valued.[28] Mozart was raised in a family of musicians and began composing and performing music at age six. Pierre and Marie Curie, great scientists in their own right, also raised a daughter, Irene, who won the Nobel Prize in chemistry. People with very different background experiences than these, however, are also creative. The African American abolitionist and writer Frederick Douglass was born into slavery in Tuckahoe, Maryland, with very limited opportunities for education. Nonetheless, Douglass became one of the most influential figures of his era. His powerful oratory and creative thinking helped lead to the Emancipation Proclamation, which ended slavery in the United States.

A variety of personality traits have been linked with individual creativity. The personality traits shared by most creative people are broad interests, an attraction to complexity, high levels of energy, independence and autonomy, strong self-confidence, and a strong belief that one is, in fact, creative.[29] Individuals who have these personality characteristics are more likely to be creative than people who do not have them.

Cognitive abilities are an individual's power to think intelligently and to effectively analyze situations and data.

Cognitive abilities are an individual's power to think intelligently and to effectively analyze situations and data. Research suggests that intelligence may be a precondition for individual creativity, which means that while most creative people are highly intelligent, not all intelligent people necessarily are creative. Creativity is also linked with the ability to think divergently and convergently. *Divergent thinking* is a skill that allows people to see differences between situations, phenomena, or events. *Convergent thinking* is a skill that allows people to see similarities between situations, phenomena, or events. Creative people are generally very skilled at both divergent and convergent thinking.

Some of the decisions made by Lee Iaccoca after he assumed the presidency of Chrysler illustrate the interplay between divergent and convergent thinking. When he joined Chrysler, the company was losing millions of dollars, laying off employees, and

---

26. Joseph V. Anderson, "Weirder than Fiction: The Reality and Myths of Creativity," *The Academy of Management Executive*, Vol. 6, No. 4, pp. 40–49.

27. See Richard W. Woodman, John E. Sawyer, and Ricky W. Griffin, "Toward a Theory of Organizational Creativity," *Academy of Management Review*, April 1993, pp. 293–321.

28. The study of the impact of background characteristics on creativity has a long tradition, stemming from the work of F. Galton, *Hereditary Genius* (London: Macmillan, 1869). More recent work on background and creativity can be found in C. E. Schaefer and A. Anastasi, "A Biographical Inventory for Identifying Creativity in Adolescent Boys," *Journal of Applied Psychology*, 1968, pp. 42–48; D. K. Simonton, "Biographical Typicality, Eminence, and Achievement Styles," *Journal of Creative Behavior*, 1986, pp. 14–22; and B. Singh, "Role of Personality versus Biographical Factors in Creativity," *Psychological Studies*, 1986, pp. 90–92. This entire approach to understanding creativity has been criticized by F. B. Barron and D. M. Harrington, "Creativity, Intelligence, and Personality," *Annual Review of Psychology*, 1981, pp. 439–476.

29. See Barron and Harrington, "Creativity, Intelligence, and Personality," and Richard Woodman and Lyle Schoenfeldt, "An Interactionist Model of Creative Behavior," *Journal of Creative Behavior*, 1990, pp. 10–20, for summaries of this personality trait literature.

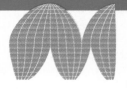
Creativity in Japan

Rightly or wrongly, the Japanese carry with them certain stereotypes about their creativity. Specifically, the prevailing opinion is that the Japanese are not particularly creative. Their emphasis on group harmony tends to stifle individual initiative and leads people to spend more time doing what's good for the group than what they might prefer to do as individuals.

In the marketplace, Japanese firms are renowned for taking technology developed in other countries (the creative part of development) and then exploiting it for their own benefit. For example, the technology used to produce videocassette recorders, compact discs, and many other contemporary electronics products was developed outside of Japan, but Japanese firms took that technology, developed and refined it, and are now among the world market leaders in virtually every category.

In recent years, however, Japanese managers have realized that their relative lack of creativity may be a liability. Their future growth may depend more on developing their own new ideas and technological breakthroughs. Thus, some are taking steps to learn to be more creative. For example, Omron Corporation, a firm that makes electronic control devices, has started a monthly training program for its middle managers. The program focuses on helping those managers develop their creative thinking skills.

Fuji Photo Film, Shimizu Corporation (Japan's largest construction company), and Shiseido (Japan's largest cosmetics firm) are among just a few of the hundreds of Japanese firms that are, for the first time, trying to teach their employees to think and make decisions creatively.

How well will it work? Only time will tell. But managers in the rest of the world should remember how they and their colleagues disregarded Japan's early efforts after World War II to become an industrial force. If the Japanese can have just a portion of that level of success in its efforts to spur creativity, the stereotypes may well be shattered.

SOURCES: Emily Thornton, "Japan's Struggle to Be Creative," *Fortune*, April 19, 1993, pp. 129–134; "Exercise in Fun Takes Advantage of Reengineering,", *Journal of Direct Marketing*, Winter 1994, pp. 79–82; and "The Enigma of Japanese Advertising," *The Economist*, August 14, 1993, pp. 59–60.

on the verge of bankruptcy. Once the organization was stabilized financially with the help of government loans, Iaccoca turned to improving the products available to potential Chrysler customers. The first task was to catalog what a range of different customers might want in a car in terms of size, performance, cost, and styling. Describing these diverse and sometimes contradictory customer needs is an example of divergent thinking. One of Iaccoca's insights was that it might be possible to meet all these different customer needs by manufacturing different versions of one basic automobile design. This design became known as the "K-car." Finding a common solution to numerous problems was the result of using convergent thinking.[30]

The Creative Process   Although creative people often report that ideas seem to come to them "in a flash," individual creative activity actually tends to progress through a series of stages.[31] Figure 10.6 summarizes the major stages of the

30. Lee Iacocca (with William Novak), *Iacocca: An Autobiography* (New York: Bantam, 1984).
31. See Thomas V. Busse and Richard S. Mansfield, "Theories of the Creative Process: A Review and a Perspective," *Journal of Creative Behavior*, 1980, pp. 91–103, for a discussion of this and other models of the creative process.

FIGURE 10.6

The Creative Process

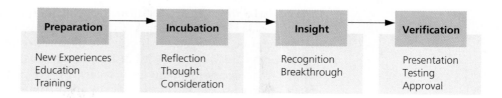

Creativity is not spontaneous; it involves preparation, incubation, insight, and verification.

creative process. Although not all creative activity has to follow these four stages, much of it does.

The first step in the creative process is preparation. Preparation involves more than just sitting around waiting for something to happen; it is an active process that may require strenuous effort. Many writers, for example, travel extensively, seeking new experiences and talking to a variety of people. Education and training also are necessary for much creative work. An opera singer trains under a voice coach, a scientist spends long hours in a lab, and an actor takes drama classes; all are preparing for creative activities. Creative decision makers study the issues surrounding a decision and participate extensively in group meetings where new ideas and alternative points of view abound, such as in brainstorming meetings.

Incubation, the next step in the process, is a time for (often subconscious) reflection, thought, and consideration. During this stage, a person shifts direct attention away from involvement in the problem, perhaps by literally "sleeping on it," socializing with friends, or participating in some recreational activity such as hiking or mountain climbing. Meanwhile, ideas pertaining to the central issue are maturing and new ideas may be formulating in the person's mind. The desired outcome is something new: a novel idea, decision, or performance. Whatever form this burst of creativity takes, it is usually referred to as insight.

Insight is the breakthrough achieved as a result of preparation and incubation. Suppose a manager has been told by her boss that she must fire one of two important employees because of budget cuts. The manager wants to find a way to retain both employees. She prepares by analyzing all the budget information that she can find and looking over the performance record of each employee. Then she goes to a movie with a friend to think things over. At some point—perhaps during intermission, over dessert after the movie, or while driving to work the next day—she suddenly recognizes a strategy for keeping both subordinates. This recognition is insight.

The last stage of the creative process is *verification*: determining whether an insight is valid. The manager just described, for example, may need to present her idea to her boss. If the boss approves the idea, and thus verifies it, it can be implemented. If the idea is not accepted, however, the manager may have to continue to search for new ideas and strategies. Similarly, scientists must test their breakthroughs in the laboratory and authors must submit their work to editors for approval. Each of these checks represents a form of verification. Many verification systems have flaws, however. Kevin Costner took his script for *Dances with Wolves* to several movie studios before he found one willing to produce the film.

Innovation and Decision Making

We earlier noted the connection between creativity, innovation, and decision making. In organizations, innovation involves every aspect of managing technology, from research through development, manufacturing, and marketing. One of the organization's biggest challenges is to bring creative technology to the needs of the marketplace in the most cost-effective manner possible.[32]

Many risks are associated with being an innovative company. The most basic is the risk that decisions about new technology or innovation will backfire. As research proceeds and engineers and scientists continue to develop new ideas or solutions to problems, there is always the possibility that the innovation will fail to perform. For this reason, organizations commit considerable resources to testing new innovations.[33] A second risk is the possibility that a competitor will make decisions enabling them to get a new innovation to the market first. The marketplace has become a breeding ground for continuous innovation. Motorola, for example, is striving to build a company in which customer needs shape new-product development without crippling the firm's technological leadership in its basic products.

Types of Innovation   Innovation can be either radical, systems, or incremental. *Radical innovation* represents a major breakthrough that changes or creates whole industries. Examples include xerography (which was invented by Chester Carlson in 1935 and became the hallmark of Xerox Corp.), steam engines, and the internal combustion engine (which paved the way for today's automobile industry). *Systems innovation* creates a new functionality by assembling parts in new ways. For example, the gasoline engine began as a radical innovation and became a systems innovation when it was combined with bicycle and carriage technology to create automobiles. *Incremental innovation* continues the technical improvement and extends the applications of radical and systems innovations. There are many more incremental innovations than there are radical and systems innovations. In fact, several incremental innovations often are necessary to make radical and systems innovations work properly. Incremental innovations force organizations to continuously improve their products and keep abreast or ahead of the competition.

New Ventures   New ventures based on innovations require entrepreneurship, or good leadership, to make the new idea work. The profile of the entrepreneur typically includes the need for achievement, a desire to assume responsibility, a willingness to take risks, and a focus on concrete results. Entrepreneurship can occur inside or outside large organizations. Outside entrepreneurship requires all of the complex aspects of the innovation process. Inside entrepreneurship also requires entrepreneurial activity within a system that usually discourages chaotic activity.

Large organizations typically do not facilitate or promote entrepreneurial types of activities. Thus, for a large organization to continue to be innovative and develop new ventures, it must encourage entrepreneurial activity within the organization. This form of activity, often called **intrapreneurship**, usually is most effective when it is a part of everyday life in the organization and occurs throughout the organization rather than in the research and development department alone.

Intrapreneurship is entrepreneurial activity that takes place within the context of a large organization.

Corporate Research   The most common aspect of developing innovation in the traditional organization takes the form of corporate research, or research and development. Corporate research usually is set up to support existing businesses, provide

---

32. Watts S. Humphrey, *Managing for Innovation: Leading Technical People* (Englewood Cliffs, N.J., Prentice-Hall, 1987).
33. Laurie K. Lewis and David R. Seibold, "Innovation Modification During Intraorganizational Adoption," *The Academy of Management Executive*, Vol. 10, No. 2, pp. 322–354.

incremental innovations in the organization's businesses, and explore potential new technology bases. Often it is established in a laboratory either on the site of the main corporate facility or some distance away from normal operations.

Corporate researchers are responsible for keeping the company's products and processes technologically advanced. Product life cycles vary a great deal depending on the rate at which a product becomes obsolete and whether substitutes for the product are developed. Obviously, if a product becomes either obsolete or substitutable, the profits from its sales will decrease. The job of corporate research is to prevent this from happening by keeping the company's products current.

Summary of Key Points

- Decision making is the process of choosing one alternative from several. The basic elements of decision making include a goal, alternative courses of action, potential outcomes of the alternatives (each with its own value relative to the goal), and a choice of one alternative based on evaluation of the outcomes. Information is available regarding the alternatives, outcomes, and values.
- Programmed decisions are well-structured, recurring decisions made according to set decision rules. Nonprogrammed decisions involve nonroutine, poorly structured situations with unclear sources of information; they cannot be made according to existing decision rules. Decision making may also be classified according to the information available. The classifications—certainty, risk, and uncertainty—reflect the amount of information available regarding the outcomes of alternatives.
- Decision making may be viewed as a completely rational process in which goals are established, a problem is identified, alternatives are generated and evaluated, a choice is made and implemented, and control is exercised. The behavioral model provides another view of the decision-making process. It is characterized by the use of procedures and rules of thumb, suboptimizing, and satisficing. The rational and behavioral views can be combined into a practical model. The Janis-Mann conflict model recognizes the personal anxiety individuals face when they must make highly consequential decisions.
- Two related behavior aspects of decision making are escalation of commitment and ethics. Escalation of commitment to an ineffective course of action occurs in many decision situations. It may be caused by psychological, social, ego, and organizational factors. Ethics also play an important role in many managerial decisions.
- Creativity is the process of developing original and imaginative views of situations. The steps in the creative process are preparation, incubation, insight, and verification. Decision making also plays an important role in how effectively an organization manages innovation.

Discussion Questions

1. Some have argued that people, not organizations, make decisions and that the study of "organizational" decision making therefore is pointless. Do you agree with this argument? Why or why not?

2. What information did you use in deciding to enter the school you now attend?
3. When your alarm goes off each morning, you have a decision to make: whether to get up and go to school or work or stay in bed and sleep longer. Is this a programmed or nonprogrammed decision? Why?
4. Describe at least three points in the decision-making process at which information plays an important role.
5. How does the role of information in the rational model of decision making differ from the role of information in the behavioral model?
6. Why does it make sense to discuss several different models of decision making?
7. Can you think of a time when you satisfied when making a decision? Have you ever suboptimized?
8. Describe a situation in which you experienced escalation of commitment to an ineffective course of action. What did you do about it? Do you wish you had handled it differently? Why or why not?
9. Do you consider yourself to be a creative person? Why or why not? What role has your creativity played in making decisions?
10. Why do some organizations seem to be so much more innovative than others?

EXPERIENTIAL EXERCISE

Purpose This exercise will allow you to make decisions and help you understand the difference between programmed and nonprogrammed decisions. You will also learn how decision making by an individual differs from decision making by a group.

Format You will be asked to make decisions both individually and as a member of a group.

Procedure Following is a list of typical organizational decisions. Your task is to determine whether they are programmed or nonprogrammed. Number your paper, and write P for programmed or N for nonprogrammed next to each number.

Next, your instructor will divide the class into groups of four to seven. All groups should have approximately the same number of members. Your task as a group is to make the decisions that you just made as individuals. In arriving at your decisions, do not use techniques such as voting or negotiating ("OK, I'll give in on this one if you'll give in on that one"). The group should discuss the difference between programmed and nonprogrammed decisions and each decision situation until all members at least partly agree with the decision.

Decision List

1. Hiring a specialist for the research staff in a highly technical field
2. Assigning workers to daily tasks
3. Determining the size of the dividend to be paid to shareholders in the ninth consecutive year of strong earnings growth
4. Deciding whether to officially excuse an employee's absence for medical reasons

5. Selecting the location for another branch of a 150-branch bank in a large city
6. Approving the appointment of a new law school graduate to the corporate legal staff
7. Making the annual assignment of graduate assistants to the faculty
8. Approving the request of an employee to attend a local seminar in his or her special area of expertise
9. Selecting the appropriate outlets for print advertisements for a new college textbook
10. Determining the location for a new fast-food restaurant in a small but growing town on the major interstate highway between two very large metropolitan areas

Follow-up Questions

1. To what extent did group members disagree about which decisions were programmed and which were nonprogrammed?
2. What primary factors did the group discuss in making each decision?
3. Were there any differences between the members' individual lists and the group lists? If so, discuss the reasons for the differences.

CASE 10.1   **Crisis Decision Making at Pepsico**

It's every manager's worst nightmare—reading the morning paper or watching the evening news and seeing one of your firm's products linked with a customer's death or serious injury. It happened to managers at Johnson & Johnson when Tylenol capsules laced with cyanide killed eight persons. It happened to managers at Jack-in-the-Box when they learned that tainted meat used to prepare hamburgers at their restaurants had poisoned 300 people, killing at least one of them. And it happened to managers at Pepsico when they learned that people had reported finding syringes in Pepsi cans.

Many of the decisions that managers make on a day-to-day basis can be carefully processed and the alternatives deliberately weighed. There is seldom any great urgency, for instance, in identifying a new plant location, selecting a new supplier, or choosing a new advertising campaign. But during a crisis, managers must respond immediately and make the best decisions for the long-term benefit of their firm.

During the Tylenol crisis several years ago, managers at Johnson & Johnson won praise for their immediate actions and candid answers to questions. They kept everyone fully informed as to what was going on and pulled all products from retailers' shelves immediately. In contrast, when the Exxon tanker *Valdez* ran aground off the coast of Alaska and dumped thousands of gallons of oil into the water, the firm's CEO was roundly criticized for delaying any action and for dodging questions for days.

In the summer of 1993, Craig Weatherup, CEO of Pepsi-Cola North America, was mowing his back yard when he was summoned to the telephone. On the line was David Kessler, commissioner of the Food and Drug Administration. Kessler's news was ominous—someone had reported finding a syringe in a can of Pepsi. Weatherup knew that he had to prepare for quick action. Besides the matter of public health, Pepsi-Cola has been in a long-standing war with rival Coca-Cola for market share. Any loss in market share to Coke might be difficult, if not impossible, to recover. Thus, Weatherup had to take the right actions, and take them quickly.

In consultation with Kessler from the FDA, Weatherup quickly outlined Pepsi-Cola's strategy. Kessler wanted to avoid public panic and get to the bottom of things. Both individuals believed that the claims about syringes were false. Because of the manner in

---

which beverages are canned, someone tampering with them is almost impossible. Thus, Kessler also wanted to make sure that people understood the legal penalties for making false claims about product tampering.

Weatherup, meanwhile, wanted to get the matter solved and put to rest as soon as possible so as to not further damage the product's image. Meanwhile, other claims about syringes began pouring in from across the country. Within two weeks, more than fifty such claims had been made.

Over the course of the next few days Weatherup made a series of critical decisions as the crisis unfolded. The first decision was to not recall Pepsi-Cola products from retailers' shelves. For one thing, Weatherup did not believe that the syringes were really in the cans to begin with. And even if they were, all consumers had to do was to pour the soda into a glass rather than drink it from the can.

Next, he had his staff prepare video footage showing the details of the canning process. The purpose of the video was to demonstrate how difficult it would be for someone to tamper with the product during the canning process. He made this footage available to every news agency who requested information about the crisis.

Finally, and some say most importantly, he made the decision that he himself would be the firm's spokesperson during the crisis. Although some advisors worried that Weatherup's unassuming, no-nonsense style might not be as well received as that of someone more skilled in public relations, he believed that he was best pre-

pared to answer questions and that those questions should be answered by the person at the top.

Thus, he appeared on the "MacNeil/Lehrer Newshour," "Larry King Live," "Nightline," and other programs. During this same time, the FDA arrested a man in Pennsylvania for making up a story about a syringe in a Pepsi can. This allowed Weatherup and Kessler, during a "Nightline" appearance, to discuss the penalties for false claims about product tampering.

Soon, more arrests followed. All told, more than twenty persons were arrested for making false tampering claims. In all likelihood, one person started it all, hoping to extract a payoff or settlement from the firm. As the story spread, other people had the same idea and began making similar claims. Eventually, no evidence was found to support any claims about syringes being in Pepsi cans. The firm did not suffer any great damage, and Weatherup won kudos for his straightforward and aggressive handling of the situation.

Case Questions

1. What types of decisions did Weatherup make? What information did he have as he made them?
2. Which decision-making process did he use?
3. What were the ethical issues involved in making the decisions at Pepsico?

SOURCES: "The Right Moves, Baby," *Business Week*, July 5, 1993, pp. 30–31; "Punching Out a Hoax," *Sales & Marketing Management*, October 1993, p. 12; "Boxed in at Jack in the Box," *Business Week*, February 15, 1993, p. 40.

| C A S E   1 0 . 2 | **A Big Step for Peak Electronics** |

Lynda Murray, chief executive officer of Peak Electronics Corp., faced a difficult decision. Her company was a leader in making parts for standard cassette players and recorders. Murray had watched with some misgivings as digital technology hit the market in the form of digital audio tape (DAT), and she had to decide whether to lead Peak into the digital age. Even though digital tape players were encountering legal hurdles in the U.S. market, they were starting to take hold

in Japan and Europe. Was the United States—and Peak—ready for them?

Murray had plenty of help in making the decision. First she met with the company's marketing division. Everyone had an opinion. Some predicted that every audio component would be digital by the turn of the century; others believed the popularity of even compact disc players was already waning. Everyone agreed that they needed time to conduct surveys, gather data, and find out what products the public really wanted and how much they would be willing to pay for them.

The people in research and development had a different approach. They were tired of making small improvements in a mature and perfected product. They had been reading technical material about digital tape, and they saw it as an exciting new technology that would give an innovative company a chance to make it big. Time was of the essence, they insisted. If Peak was to become an important supplier of parts for the new decks, it had to have the components ready. Delay would be fatal to the product.

A meeting of the vice presidents produced a scenario with which Murray was all too familiar. Years ago these executives had discovered that they could not out-argue one another in these meetings, but they had faith in their staffs' abilities to succeed where they had failed. Before Murray even walked into the room, she knew what their recommendation would be: to create a committee of representatives from each division and let them thoroughly investigate all aspects of the decision. Such an approach had worked before, but Murray was not sure it was right this time.

Desperate to make the decision and get it out of her mind, Murray mentioned it to her fifteen-year-old son, who, it turned out, knew everything about digital tape. In fact, he told her, one of his friends—the rich one—had been holding off on buying a new tape deck so that he would be on the cutting edge of digital recording. "It's gotta happen, Mom," her son said. "People want it."

Intellectually, Murray believed that he was right. The past thirty years had shown that Americans had an insatiable appetite for electronic gadgets and marvels. Quadraphonic sound and early analog videodiscs were the only exceptions she could think of to the rule that if someone invented an improved way of reproducing images or sound, someone else would want to buy it.

But intuitively, Murray was not so sure. She had a bad feeling about the new technology. She believed the record companies, which had lost the battle to tape manufacturers, might get together with compact disc makers and audio equipment manufacturers to stop the digital technology from entering the U.S. market. So far, no U.S. company had invested substantially in the technology, so no one had an interest in funding the legal battle to remove the barriers to the new machines.

Exhausted, Murray went to bed. She hoped that somehow her subconscious mind would sort out all the important factors and she would wake up knowing the right decision.

Case Questions

1. What sources of information and opinion about the new technology seem most reliable? Which would you ignore?
2. If you were Murray, what would your next step be?

Group Dynamics

OBJECTIVES

After studying this chapter, you should be able to:

Define the term *group* and discuss why the study of groups is important in managing organizations.

Describe the differences between formal and informal groups in organizations.

Trace the stages of group development from initial introduction to a mature stage of productivity and control.

Summarize the major factors affecting group performance.

Discuss group decision making.

Identify the important dimensions of intergroup dynamics.

Discuss the factors that managers must consider in managing groups in organizations.

Like the Xerox Corporation, Eastman Kodak has created a multifunctional coordinating group, called the "Zebras," that operates across departments to greatly improved the company's efficiency.

Companies everywhere are learning new ways of doing things, restructuring to serve the customer better, and creating adaptive organizations organized around processes. Nowhere is this more evident than at Xerox Corp. Chief executive officer Paul Allaire claims that employee creativity and innovation are essential to regaining the global marketplace and has restructured Xerox from a function-oriented, staff-driven firm to one that is innovative and responsive to the market.

The cornerstone of the new structure and culture is flexible teams. Teams are created to solve existing problems and are then disbanded as members go on to other teams to solve new problems. For example, Xerox has always been able to ship a copier to a customer faster than its competitors. When it discovered that customers were less interested in the fastest delivery and were more interested in knowing the exact date a new copier would arrive, with assistance in installation, service, and accurate billing, Xerox created a multifunctional team to solve the problems. The team, which included people from accounting, distribution, and sales, found that in the traditional functional organization chart paperwork would get lost and there was little communication between departments. Each department would do its job and pass it along to the next department. The team developed a manufacturing and distribution process that gave the customers what they wanted. Now, a coordinating group also cuts across horizontal lines in the organization chart and coordinates the flow of copiers through manufacturing to the customer, saving more than $200 million per year in inventory costs.[1]

Organizations use groups—groups such as the Zebras at Eastman Kodak, the multifunctional team at Xerox, a football team, an engineering work group, and a group of nurses working the night shift at a local hospital—to get their work done. In this chapter we first define group and summarize the importance of groups in organizations. Then we describe different types of groups and discuss the stages groups go through as they develop from newly formed groups to mature, high-performing units. Next, we identify four important factors in group performance. Then we discuss group decision making and problem solving. Finally, we move to a discussion of how groups interact with each other in organizations, and we summarize the important elements in managing groups in organizations.

Figure 11.1 presents a three-phase model of group dynamics. The first phase includes the type of group and the reasons for group formation. The second phase encompasses a four-step process of group development and the four primary group performance factors. The final phase includes a mature group that is productive and adaptive. The model also shows that mature groups make decisions

1. Robert Howard, David A. Nadler, and Marc S. Gerstein, "The CEO as Organizational Architect: An Interview with Xerox's Paul Allaire," *Harvard Business Review*, September–October 1992, pp. 106–122; Brian Dumaine, "The Bureaucracy Busters," *Fortune*, June 17, 1991, pp. 36–50; and Thomas A. Stewart, "The Search for the Organization of Tomorrow," *Fortune*, May 18, 1992, pp. 92–98.

FIGURE 11.1

**A General Model
of Group Dynamics**

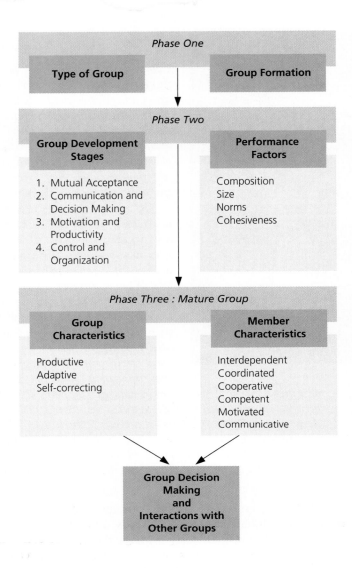

and engage in interactions with other groups. This model serves as the framework for our discussion of groups in this chapter.

Overview of Groups and Group Dynamics

Work groups consist of people who are trying to make a living for themselves and their families. The work group often is the primary source of social identity for employees and can affect their performance at work as well as their relationships outside the organization.[2] A group in an organization often takes on a life of its own that transcends the individual members.

2. Blake E. Ashforth and Fred Mael, "Social Identity Theory and the Organization," *Academy of Management Review*, January 1989, pp. 20–39.

Definition of Group

Definitions of the term *group* are as abundant as the research on groups. Groups can be defined in terms of perceptions, motivation, organization, interdependencies, and interactions.[3] Marvin Shaw offers a simple and comprehensive definition: a **group** is two or more persons who interact with one another in such a manner that each person influences and is influenced by each other person.[4] The concept of interaction is essential to this definition. Two people who are physically near each other are not a group unless they interact and have some influence on each other. Coworkers may work side by side on related tasks, but if they do not interact they are not a group. The presence of others may influence the performance of a group: an audience may stimulate the performance of actors, or an evaluator may inhibit the employee's behavior.[5] Neither the audience nor the evaluator can be considered part of the group, however, unless interaction occurs.

Although groups have goals, note that our definition makes no mention of a group goal or the motivations of group members. This omission implies that members of a group may identify little or not at all with the group's goal. People can be a part of a group and enjoy the benefits of group membership without wanting to pursue any group goal. Members can get their needs satisfied just by being members. Of course, the quality of the interactions and the group's performance may be affected by the members' lack of interest in the group goal. But a goal does exist even if it is secondary to certain group members.

Our definition of group also suggests a limit on group size. A collection of people so large that its members cannot interact with and influence one another does not meet this definition. And in reality, the dynamics of large assemblies of people usually differ significantly from those of small groups. Our focus in this chapter is on small groups in which the members interact with and influence one another.

The Importance of Studying Groups

We cannot study behavior in organizations without attempting to understand the behavior of people in group settings. Groups are everywhere in our society. Most people belong to several groups—a family, bowling team, church group, fraternity or sorority, or work group at the office.[6] Some groups are formally established in a work or social organization; others are more loosely knit associations of people.

To understand the behavior of people in organizations, we must understand the forces that affect individuals as well as the ways individuals affect the organization. The behavior of individuals both affects and is affected by the group. The accomplishments of groups are strongly influenced by the behavior of their individual members. For example, adding one key all-star player to a basketball team may make the difference between having a bad season and winning a league championship. At the same time, a group has a profound effect on the behaviors of its

3. Marvin E. Shaw, *Group Dynamics: The Psychology of Small Group Behavior*, 3rd ed. (New York: McGraw-Hill, 1981).
4. Ibid., p. 11.
5. Gerald R. Ferris and Kendrith M. Rowland, "Social Facilitation Effects on Behavioral and Perceptual Task Performance Measures: Implications for Work Behavior," *Group and Organization Studies*, December 1983, pp. 421–438; and Jeff Meer, "Loafing Through a Tough Job," *Psychology Today*, January 1985, p. 72.
6. J. Paul Sorrels and Bettye Myers, "Comparison of Group and Family Dynamics," *Human Relations*, May 1983, pp. 477–490.

members.[7] In the 1987 strike involving NFL football players, some players crossed the picket line but others who needed the money did not because they feared reprisal from striking players.[8] Thus, the behavior of many individuals was affected by factors within the group. We discuss this further in the section on group norms. From a managerial perspective, the work group is the primary means by which managers coordinate individuals' behavior to achieve organizational goals. Managers direct the activities of individuals, but they also direct and coordinate interactions within groups. For example, the manager's efforts to boost salespersons' performance has been shown to have both individual and group effects.[9] Therefore, the manager must pay attention to both the individual and the group in trying to increase employee performance. Because the behavior of individuals is essential to the group's success or failure, the manager must be aware of individual needs and interpersonal dynamics to manage groups effectively and efficiently.

Group Formation

People join or form groups because they expect that certain personal needs will be satisfied.

Groups are formed to satisfy both organizational and individual needs. Groups are formed in organizations because managers expect that organizational tasks can be better completed and coordinated if people work together in work groups. Individuals join groups to satisfy a need. An employee may join a work group to get or keep a job. Individuals may form an informal group or join an existing one for many purposes: attraction to people in the group, its activities (such as playing bridge, running marathons, or gardening), or its goals. People may also join a group because they want companionship or they want to be identified as a member of the group. In any case, people join groups for personal need satisfaction. In other words, they expect that they will get something in return for their membership in the group.

Understanding why a group forms is important in studying individual behavior in groups. Suppose that people join a bridge group primarily for social contact. If a more competitive player substitutes one evening for a regular player, she or he joins the group (temporarily) with a different goal in mind. The substitute may be annoyed when the game slows down or stops altogether because the other players are absorbed in a discussion. The regular members, on the other hand, may be irritated when the substitute interrupts the discussion and rebukes his or her partner for faulty technique. Someone who wants to resolve the resulting conflict will need to understand why each person joined the group. The inconsistencies in behavior arise because each member seeks the satisfaction of a different need. Settling the dispute may require that the regulars and the substitute be more tolerant of each other's behavior, at least for the rest of the evening. Even then, however, the substitute player may not be invited back the next time a regular member cannot attend.

Thus, understanding why people join groups sheds light on apparent inconsistencies in behavior and the tensions likely to result from them. Such an

7. Alfred W. Clark and Robert J. Powell, "Changing Drivers' Attitudes Through Peer Group Decision," *Human Relations*, February 1984, pp. 155–162.
8. See Bill Saporito, "The Life of a Scab," *Fortune*, October 26, 1987, pp. 91-94; and Jill Lieber, "A Test of Loyalty," *Sports Illustrated*, October 5, 1987, pp. 41–43.
9. Francis J. Yammarino and Alan J. Dubinsky, "Salesperson Performance and Managerially Controllable Factors: An Investigation of Individual and Work Group Effects," *Journal of Management*, Vol. 16, 1990, pp. 87–106.

TABLE 11.1

Classification Scheme for Types of Groups

	Relatively Permanent	Relatively Temporary
Formal	Command groups	Task groups
	Quality assurance department	Pope's Special Council on Finances
	Cost accounting group	Task force on new-product quality
Informal	Friendship groups	Interest groups
	Friends who do many activities together (attend the theater, play games, travel)	Bowling group Women's network

understanding will enable us to better manage certain kinds of conflict that arise in groups in organizations.

Types of Groups

Our first task in understanding group processes is to develop a typology of groups that provides insight into their dynamics. Groups may be loosely categorized according to their degrees of formalization (formal or informal) and permanence (relatively permanent or relatively temporary). Table 11.1 shows this classification scheme.

Formal Groups

Formal groups are formed by the organization to do its work and usually are included in the organization chart.

A **command group,** or functional group, is a relatively permanent, formal group with functional reporting relationships.

A **task group** is a relatively temporary, formal group established to do a specific task.

Formal groups are established by the organization to do its work and usually are included in the organization chart. Formal groups include the **command** (or functional) **group,** which is relatively permanent and characterized by functional reporting relationships, and the **task group,** which is created to perform a specific task and is relatively temporary. In business organizations, most employees work in command groups, typically specified on an official organization chart. The size, shape, and organization of a company's command groups can vary considerably.

Typical command groups in organizations include the quality assurance department, the industrial engineering department, the cost accounting department, and the personnel department. Other types of command groups include work teams organized according to the Japanese style of management, in which subsections of manufacturing and assembly processes are assigned to a team of workers. The team members decide among themselves who will do each task.

Teams are becoming widespread in automobile manufacturing. General Motors is organizing its highly automated assembly lines into work teams of between five and twenty workers.[10] Although participative teams are becoming more popular in

10. "Detroit vs. the UAW: At Odds over Teamwork," *Business Week*, August 24, 1987, pp. 54–55.

organizations, command groups, whether entire departments or sophisticated work teams, are the dominant type of work group in organizations. Federal Express organized its clerical workers into teams that manage themselves.[11]

Task, or special-project, groups are usually temporary. Task groups often are established to solve a particular problem. Once a task group solves the problem or makes recommendations, it is usually dissolved. While serving in a task group, people typically remain members of their command groups, or functional departments, and continue to carry out the normal duties of their jobs. If the task group requires a great deal of time and effort, the members' command group duties may be temporarily reduced. Task groups exist in organizations around the world. For example, in 1981 the Pope established a special task force of cardinals to study the financial condition of the Vatican and develop new ways to raise money.[12]

Informal Groups

Informal groups are established by their members.

A **friendship group** is relatively permanent and informal and draws its benefits from the social relationships among its members.

An **interest group** is relatively temporary and informal and is organized around a common activity or interest of its members.

Whereas formal groups are established by an organization, **informal groups** are formed by their members. They consist of the friendship group, which is relatively permanent, and the interest group, which may be shorter lived. A **friendship group** arises from friendly relationships among members and the enjoyment they get from being together. An **interest group** is organized around a common activity or interest, although friendships may develop among members.

Good examples of interest groups are the networks of working women that developed during the 1980s. Many of these groups began as informal social gatherings of women who wanted to meet with other women working in male-dominated organizations, but they soon developed into interest groups whose benefits went far beyond the initial social purposes. The networks became information systems for counseling, job placement, and management training. Some networks eventually were established as formal, permanent associations; some remained informal groups based more on social relationships than on any specific interest; and others were dissolved. These groups may be partly responsible for the past decade's dramatic increase in the percentage of women in managerial and administrative jobs.[13]

Stages of Group Development

Groups are not static. Instead, they typically develop through a four-stage process: (1) mutual acceptance, (2) communication and decision making, (3) motivation and productivity, and (4) control and organization.[14] The stages and the activities that typify them are shown in Figure 11.2. We treat the stages as separate and distinct. Because their activities overlap, however, pinpointing exactly when a group moves from one stage to another is difficult.

11. Brian Dumaine, "Who Needs a Boss?" *Fortune*, May 7, 1990, pp. 52–60.
12. Shawn Tully, "The Vatican's Finances," *Fortune*, December 21, 1987, pp. 28–40.
13. "Women at Work," *Business Week*, January 28, 1985, pp. 80–85.
14. Bernard M. Bass and Edward C. Ryterband, *Organizational Psychology*, 2nd ed. (Boston: Allyn and Bacon, 1979), pp. 252–254.

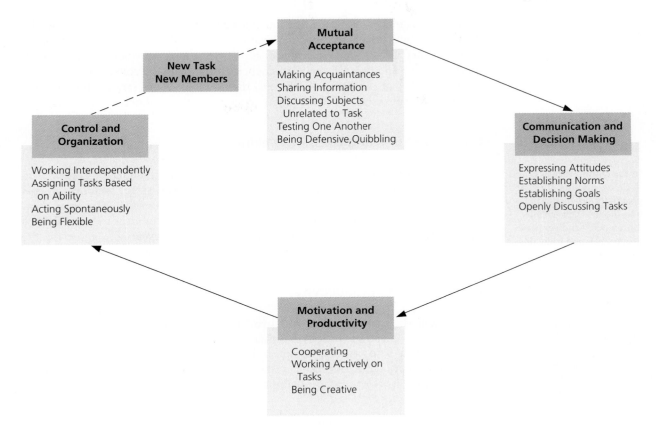

FIGURE 11.2
Stages of Group Development

Mutual Acceptance

The **mutual acceptance stage** of group development is characterized by members sharing information about themselves and getting to know each other.

In the **mutual acceptance stage** of group development, members get to know one another by sharing information about themselves. They often test one another's opinions by discussing subjects that have little to do with the group, such as the weather, sports, or recent events within the organization. Some aspects of the group's task, such as its formal objectives, may also be discussed at this stage. Such discussion probably will not be very productive, however, because the members are unfamiliar with each other and do not know how to evaluate one another's comments. If the members do happen to know one another already, this stage may be brief; it is unlikely to be skipped altogether because the group and its purpose are new. Besides, there are likely to be a few members whom the others do not know well or at all.[15]

As the members get to know one another, discussion may turn to more sensitive issues, such as the organization's politics or recent controversial decisions. In this way, the participants explore one another's reactions, knowledge, and expertise. From the

15. John P. Wanous, Arnon E. Reichers, and S. D. Malik, "Organizational Socialization and Group Development: Toward an Integrative Perspective," *Academy of Management Review*, October 1984, pp. 670–683.

discussion, members may learn each other's views on a variety of issues, how similar their beliefs and values are, and the extent to which they can trust one another. Members may discuss their expectations about the group's activities in terms of their previous group and organizational experience.[16] Eventually, the conversation will turn to the business of the group. When this discussion becomes serious, the group is moving to the next stage of development, communication and decision making.

Communication and Decision Making

In the **communication and decision-making stage** of group development, members discuss their feelings more openly and agree on group goals and individual roles in the group.

Once group members have begun to accept one another, the group progresses to the **communication and decision-making stage**. In this stage, members discuss their feelings and opinions more openly than in the previous stage. They may show more tolerance for opposing viewpoints and explore different ideas to bring about a reasonable solution or decision. Members discuss and eventually agree on the group's goals. Then they are assigned roles and tasks to accomplish the goals.

Motivation and Productivity

In the **motivation and productivity stage** of group development, members cooperate, help each other, and work toward task accomplishment.

In the next stage, **motivation and productivity**, emphasis shifts from personal concerns and viewpoints to activities that will benefit the group. Members cooperate and actively help others accomplish their goals. The members are highly motivated and may carry out their tasks creatively. In this stage, the group is accomplishing its work and is moving toward the final stage of development.

Control and Organization

In the **control and organization stage** of group development—now a mature group—members work together and are flexible, adaptive, and self-correcting.

In the final stage, **control and organization**, the group works effectively toward accomplishing its goals. Tasks are assigned by mutual agreement and according to ability. In a mature group, the members' activities are relatively spontaneous and flexible, rather than subject to rigid structural restraints. Mature groups evaluate their activities and potential outcomes and take corrective actions if necessary. The characteristics of flexibility, spontaneity, and self-correction are very important if the group is to remain productive over an extended period.

Not all groups go through all four stages. Some groups disband before reaching the final stage. Others fail to complete a stage before moving on to the next one.[17] Rather than spend the time necessary to get to know one another and build trust, for example, a group may cut short the first stage of development because of pressure from its leader, from deadlines, or from an outside threat (such as the boss). If members are forced into activities typical of a later stage while the work of an earlier stage remains incomplete, they are likely to become frustrated: the group will not develop completely and will be less productive than it could be.[18] Group productivity depends on successful development at each stage. A group that evolves fully through

16. Susan Long, "Early Integration in Groups: A Group to Join and a Group to Create," *Human Relations*, April 1984, pp. 311–332.
17. Wanous, Reichers, and Malik, "Organizational Socialization and Group Development."
18. Steven L. Obert, "Developmental Patterns of Organizational Task Groups: A Preliminary Study," *Human Relations*, January 1983, pp. 37–52.

the four stages of development will become a mature, effective group.[19] Its members will be interdependent, coordinated, cooperative, competent at their jobs, motivated to do them, and in active communication with one another.[20]

Finally, as working conditions and relationships change, either through a change in membership or when a task is completed and a new task is begun, groups may need to reexperience one or more of the stages of development to maintain cohesiveness and productivity characteristic of a well-developed group. The San Francisco Forty-Niners, for example, returned from the NFL strike of 1987 to an uncomfortable and apprehension-filled period. Their coach, Bill Walsh, conducted rigorous practices but also allowed time for players to get together to air their feelings. Slowly team unity returned, and players began joking and socializing again as they prepared for the rest of the 1987 season.[21] Their redevelopment as a mature group resulted in Super Bowl victories in 1989 and 1990.

Although these stages are not separate and distinct in all groups, many groups have made fairly predictable transitions in activities at about the midpoint of the time period available for task completion.[22] A group may begin with its own distinctive approach to the problem and maintain it until about halfway through the allotted time period. A midpoint transition is often accompanied by a burst of concentrated activity, reexamination of assumptions, dropping old patterns of activity, adopting new perspectives of the work, and making dramatic progress. During stage two, the new patterns of activity may be maintained from the midpoint until close to the end of the time period allotted for the activity. Another transition may occur just before the deadline. At this transition, groups often go into the completion stage, launching a final burst of activity to finish the job.

Group Performance Factors

Group performance factors—composition, size, norms, and cohesiveness—affect the success of the group in fulfilling its goals.

The performance of any group is affected by several factors other than the reasons for its formation and the stages of its development. In a high-performing group, a group synergy often develops in which the group's performance is more than the sum of the individual contributions of its members. Several additional factors may account for this accelerated performance.[23] The four basic **group performance factors** are composition, size, norms, and cohesiveness.

Composition

Group composition refers to the degree of similarity or difference in the characteristics of the members on factors important to the group's work.

The composition of a group plays an important role in determining group productivity.[24] **Group composition** is most often described in terms of the homogeneity or heterogeneity of the members. A group is homogeneous if the members are similar in one or several ways that are critical to the work of the

19. Bass and Ryterband, *Organizational Psychology*, pp. 252–254.
20. Bernard M. Bass, "The Leaderless Group Discussion," *Psychological Bulletin*, September 1954, pp. 465–492.
21. Jill Lieber, "Time to Heal the Wounds," *Sports Illustrated*, November 2, 1987, pp. 86–91.
22. Connie J. G. Gersick, "Marking Time: Predictable Transitions in Task Groups," *Academy of Management Journal*, vol. 32, 1989, pp. 274–309.
23. James H. Davis, *Group Performance* (Reading, Mass.: Addison-Wesley, 1964), pp. 82–86.
24. Shaw, *Group Dynamics*.

group, such as age, work experience, education, technical specialty, or cultural background. The members in heterogeneous groups, differ in one or more ways that are critical to the work of the group. Homogeneous groups often are created when people are assigned to command groups based on a similar technical specialty. Although the people who work in such command groups may differ on some factors, such as age or work experience, they are homogeneous in terms of a critical work performance variable: technical specialty. Special focus groups or task forces are often created because of their composition to address diversity issues. Examples of this are discussed in *Diversity in the Workplace*.

Much research has explored the relationship between a group's composition and its productivity. The group's heterogeneity in terms of age and tenure with the group have been shown to be related to turnover;[25] that is, groups with members of different ages and experiences with the group tend to experience frequent changes in membership. Table 11.2 summarizes task variables that make a homogeneous or heterogeneous group more effective than its counterpart. A homogeneous group is likely to be more productive in situations in which the group task is simple, cooperation is necessary, the group tasks are sequential, or quick action is required.

A heterogeneous group is more likely to be productive when the task is complex, requires a collective effort (that is, each member does a different task and the sum of these efforts constitutes the group output), and demands creativity or when speed is less important than thorough deliberations. For example, a group asked to generate ideas for marketing a new product probably needs to be heterogeneous to develop as many different ideas as possible.

The link between group composition and type of task is explained by the interactions typical of homogeneous and heterogeneous groups. A homogeneous group tends to have less conflict, fewer differences of opinion, smoother communication, and more interaction. A task that requires cooperation and speed therefore makes a homogeneous group more desirable. If, however, the task requires complex analysis of information and creativity to arrive at the best possible solution, a heterogeneous group may be more appropriate because it generates a wide range of viewpoints. More discussion and more conflict are likely, both of which can enhance the group's decision making.

Group composition often becomes especially important when organizations create joint ventures with companies from other countries and form other types of

---

25. Charles A. O'Reilly III, David F. Caldwell, and William P. Barnett, "Work Group Demography, Social Integration, and Turnover," *Administrative Science Quarterly*, Vol. 34, March 1989, pp. 21–37.

TABLE 11.2

Task Variables and Group Composition

A homogeneous group is more useful for:	A heterogeneous group is more useful for:
Simple tasks	Complex tasks
Sequential tasks	Collective tasks
Cooperation required	Creativity required
Speed required	Speed not important

SOURCE: Based on discussion in Bernard M. Bass and Edward C. Ryterband, *Organizational Psychology*, 2nd ed. (Boston: Allyn and Bacon, 1979). Reprinted by permission.

U S West and Levi Strauss Use Diversity Groups

Many companies are finding that groups are the key to creating the multicultural organization necessary for success in the next century. Two types of groups have become popular: special focus groups and diversity task forces.

Special focus groups concentrate on the needs of members who usually represent a single minority or special set of employees. Groups may be formed of Hispanic Americans or Native Americans, or further broken down into professional and minority groups, such as differently abled engineers. Diversity task forces, on the other hand, usually comprise people representing a broad cross-section of minority groups, organizational levels, and functional areas. Diversity task forces are usually able to provide a broader perspective to organizational diversity issues because of their heterogeneous composition.

U S West's special focus groups include eight Employee Resource Groups (ERG) made up of people who have special interests, such as Native Americans, veterans, gays and lesbians, and differently abled workers. The ERGs provide a way for special workers to have a collective voice for their concerns and social support. The Native American ERG recently expressed their concern that most Native Americans were in the occupational trades rather than management. The company has begun to address this issue by altering training, promotion, and hiring processes. Now all ERGs help the company with succession planning by providing lists of candidates who they think are ready for advancement. In addition, representatives of the ERGs meet monthly with the vice president of human resources to discuss their concerns.

The diversity task force at Levi Strauss & Co. is a Diversity Council that is made up of two members of every group. The Diversity Council assists in the support of informal networks of employees and meets regularly with the company's executive committee. The Diversity Council is only part of its $5 million annual expenditure for comprehensive training to increase all employees' awareness of the importance of workforce diversity and increase their management skills. Although U S West and Levi Strauss approach the issue in different ways, both are using employee groups extensively to promote the management of diversity within their organizations.

SOURCES: Shari Caudron, "U S WEST Finds Strength in Diversity," Personnel Journal, March 1992, pp. 40–44; Lawrence M. Baytos, "Launching Successful Diversity Initiatives," HR Magazine, March 1992, pp. 91–97; and "Diverse by Design," Business Week, October 23, 1992, p. 72.

---

international alliances. Joint ventures have become common in the automobile and electronics industries. For example, managers from the United States tend to exhibit individualistic behaviors in a group setting, whereas managers from the People's Republic of China tend to exhibit more collectivistic behaviors.[26] Thus, when these two different types of managers work together in a group, as they might in some type of joint venture, the managers must be trained to be cautious and understanding in their interactions and the types of behaviors that they exhibit.

26. P. Christopher Earley, "Social Loafing and Collectivism: A Comparison of the United States and the People's Republic of China," *Administrative Science Quarterly*, 1989, pp. 565–581.

Size

Group size refers to the number of members of the group and affects the number of resources available to perform the task.

A group can have as few as two members or as many members as can interact and influence one another. **Group size** can have an important effect on performance. A group with many members has more resources available and may be able to complete a large number of relatively independent tasks. Among groups established to generate ideas, those with more members tend to produce more ideas, although the rate of increase in the number of ideas diminishes rapidly as the group grows.[27] Beyond a certain point, the greater complexity of interactions and communication may make it more difficult for a large group to achieve agreement.

Interactions and communication are much more likely to be formalized in larger groups. Large groups tend to set agendas for meetings and to follow a protocol or parliamentary procedure to control discussion. As a result, some time that otherwise might be available for task accomplishment is taken up in administrative duties such as organizing and structuring the interactions and communications within the group. Also, the large size may inhibit participation of some people [28] and increase absenteeism[29] because so many people are trying to contribute. If repeated attempts to contribute or participate are thwarted by the sheer number of similar efforts by other members, some people may give up trying to make a meaningful contribution and may even stop coming to group meetings. Furthermore, large groups may present more opportunities for interpersonal attraction, leading to more social interactions and fewer task interactions. How much of a problem this becomes depends on the nature of the task and the characteristics of the people involved.

Norms

A **group norm** is a standard against which the appropriateness of a behavior is measured.

A **group norm** is a standard against which the appropriateness of a behavior is judged.[30] Thus, a norm is the expected behavior or behavioral pattern in a certain situation. Group norms usually are established during the second stage of group development (communication and decision making) and carried forward into the maturity stage.[31] People often have expectations about the behavior of others. By providing a basis for predicting others' behaviors, norms enable people to formulate response behaviors. Without norms, the activities within a group would be chaotic.

Norms result from the combination of members' personality characteristics, the situation, the task, and the historical traditions of the group. Lack of conformity to group norms may result in verbal abuse, physical threats, ostracism, or ejection from the group. Group norms are enforced, however, only for actions that are important to group members.[32] For example, if the office norm is for employees to wear suits to convey a professional image to clients, a staff member who wears blue jeans and a sweatshirt violates the group norm and will hear

27. Shaw, *Group Dynamics*, pp. 173–177.
28. Davis, *Group Performance*, p. 73.
29. Steven E. Markham, Fred Dansereau, Jr., and Joseph A. Alutto, "Group Size and Absenteeism Rates: A Longitudinal Analysis," *Academy of Management Journal*, December 1982, pp. 921–927.
30. Davis, *Group Performance*, p. 82.
31. Bass and Ryterband, *Organizational Psychology*, pp. 252–254.
32. Shaw, *Group Dynamics*, pp. 280–293.

about it quickly. But if the norm is that dress is unimportant because little contact with clients occurs in the office, someone wearing blue jeans may not even be noticed.

Norms serve four purposes:

1. *Norms help the group survive.* Groups tend to reject deviant behavior that does not contribute to accomplishing group goals or to the survival of the group if it is threatened. Accordingly, a successful group that is not under threat may be more tolerant of deviant behavior.
2. *Norms simplify and make more predictable the behaviors expected of group members.* Norms mean that members do not have to analyze each behavior and decide on a response. Members can anticipate the actions of others on the basis of group norms, usually resulting in increased productivity and goal attainment.
3. *Norms help the group avoid embarrassing situations.* Group members often want to avoid damaging other members' self-images and are likely to avoid certain subjects that might hurt a member's feelings.
4. *Norms express the central values of the group and identify the group to others.* Certain clothes, mannerisms, or behaviors in particular situations may be a rallying point for members and may signify to others the nature of the group.[33]

Norms usually regulate the behavior of group members rather than their thoughts or feelings.[34] Members thus may believe one thing but do another to maintain membership in a group. For example, during the Iran-Contra affair from 1985 to 1987, there were several meetings in which the president and aides, such as Lt. Col. Oliver North, National Security Advisor Robert McFarlane, and Central Intelligence Agency directory William Casey, discussed the sale of arms to Iran in exchange for American hostages.[35] Secretary of State George P. Schultz and Secretary of Defense Caspar W. Weinberger were known to be against the sale of arms to Iran, even indirectly through Israel. The president and others strongly favored such arms sales and were eager to achieve the release of American hostages held in Iran. Thus, Schultz and Weinberger did not attend meetings in which further arms sales were authorized.[36] Although whether they were excluded by the members or excluded themselves by not attending is not clear, norms clearly affected the meetings and outcomes. From the group's perspective, the norms were to approve the arms transfer. Anyone who continued to argue against the transfer would not be in the group. Thus, Schultz and Weinberger knew that they were in the minority and were making it uncomfortable for the president. If they wanted to maintain their valued membership in the president's cabinet as heads of two of the most powerful agencies of the executive branch, they knew that they should not continue to cause trouble. Thus, the group norms regarding how presidential advisors are supposed to act may have led them to decide not to attend.

33. Daniel C. Feldman, "The Development and Enforcement of Group Norms," *Academy of Management Review,* January 1984, pp. 47–53.
34. J. Richard Hackman, "Group Influences on Individuals," in Marvin D. Dunnette (Ed.), *Handbook of Industrial and Organizational Psychology* (Chicago: Rand McNally, 1976), pp. 1455–1525.
35. John Tower, Edmund Muskie, and Brent Skowcroft, *The Tower Commission Report* (New York: Joint publication of Bantam Books and Times Books, 1987); and *Taking the Stand: The Testimony of Lieutenant Colonel Oliver L. North* (New York: Pocket Books, 1987).
36. Tower, Muskie, and Skowcroft, *The Tower Commission Report*, pp. 37–38.

Cohesiveness

Group cohesiveness is the motivation of members to remain in the group.

Group cohesiveness results from "all forces acting on the members to remain in the group."[37] The forces that create cohesiveness are attraction to the group, resistance to leaving the group, and the motivation to remain a member of the group.[38] As shown in Figure 11.3, group cohesiveness is related to many aspects of group dynamics that we have already discussed—maturity, homogeneity, and manageable size.

Figure 11.3 also shows that group cohesiveness can be increased by competition or by the presence of an external threat.[39] Either factor can serve as a clearly defined goal that focuses members' attention on their task and increases their willingness to work together. The threat of NFL teams' using replacement players for those on strike had the immediate effect of unifying the players against the owners. The players became more cohesive and vowed more strongly than ever to hold out.[40] Similarly, in the Iran-Contra affair, the inner group (Casey, North, McFarlane, and Vice Admiral Poindexter) became a cohesive group owing to the need for secrecy and threats of exposure by Congress and the media.[41]

Finally, successfully reaching goals often increases the cohesiveness of a group because people are proud to be identified with a winner and to be thought of as competent and successful. This may be one reason for the popular phrase, "Success breeds success." A group that is successful may become more cohesive and possibly even more successful. One example is the initial success of the design group at

37. L. Festinger, "Informal Social Communication," *Psychological Review*, September 1950, p. 274.
38. William E. Piper, Myriam Marrache, Renee Lacroix, Astrid M. Richardson, and Barry D. Jones, "Cohesion as a Basic Bond in Groups," *Human Relations*, February 1983, pp. 93–108.
39. Davis, *Group Performance*, pp. 78–81.
40. Paul Zimmerman, "When Push Came to Shove," *Sports Illustrated*, October 5, 1987, pp. 38–43.
41. Tower, Muskie, and Skowcroft, *The Tower Commission Report,* and *Taking the Stand.*

FIGURE 11.3

Factors That Affect Group Cohesiveness and Consequences of Group Cohesiveness

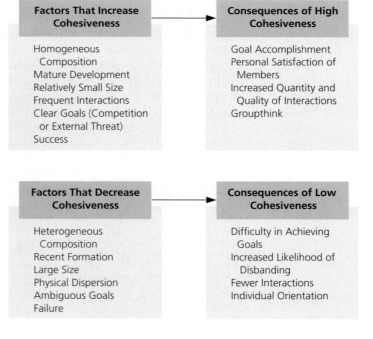

Factors That Increase Cohesiveness	Consequences of High Cohesiveness
Homogeneous Composition	Goal Accomplishment
Mature Development	Personal Satisfaction of Members
Relatively Small Size	Increased Quantity and Quality of Interactions
Frequent Interactions	Groupthink
Clear Goals (Competition or External Threat)	
Success	

Factors That Decrease Cohesiveness	Consequences of Low Cohesiveness
Heterogeneous Composition	Difficulty in Achieving Goals
Recent Formation	Increased Likelihood of Disbanding
Large Size	Fewer Interactions
Physical Dispersion	Individual Orientation
Ambiguous Goals	
Failure	

Cohesive groups have much higher rates of productivity than non-cohesive groups. At the Hallmark Company, a new cross-departmental team works together on a card. Previously, each stage of production was carried out by an individual who had little contact with the other project participants. Hallmark expects this new system to reduce its new-product development time by half.

Apple Computer in its creation of the Macintosh personal computer. The members worked and partied together and became quite cohesive. (Of course, other factors can get in the way of continued success, such as personal differences and egos and the lure of more individual success in other activities.)

Research on group performance factors has focused on the relationship between cohesiveness and group productivity. Highly cohesive groups appear to be more effective at achieving the goals of the group than groups low in cohesiveness, especially in research and development groups in U.S. companies.[42] However, highly cohesive groups will not necessarily be more productive in an organizational sense than groups with low cohesiveness. As Figure 11.4 illustrates, when a group's goals are compatible with the organization's, a cohesive group probably will be more productive than one that is not cohesive. In other words, if a highly cohesive group has the goal of contributing to the good of the organization, it is very likely to be productive in organizational terms. But if such a group decides on a goal that has little to do with the business of the organization, it probably will achieve its own goal, even at the expense of any organizational goal. In a recent study of group characteristics and productivity, group cohesiveness was the only factor that was consistently related to high performance for research and development engineers and technicians.[43]

Cohesiveness may also be a primary factor in the development of certain problems for some decision-making groups. An example is groupthink, which occurs when a group's overriding concern is a unanimous decision rather than the critical analysis of alternatives.[44] In the next section we discuss groupthink in detail. These

42. Robert T. Keller, "Predictors of the Performance of Project Groups in R&D Organizations," *Academy of Management Journal*, December 1986, pp. 715–726.
43. Ibid.
44. Irving L. Janis, *Groupthink*, 2nd ed. (Boston: Houghton Mifflin, 1982), p. 9.

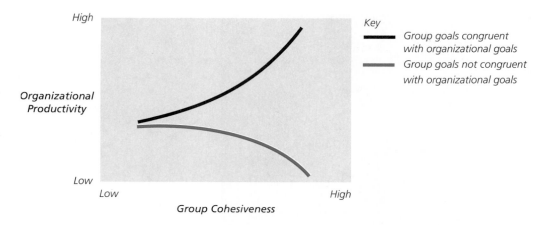

FIGURE 11.4

Group Cohesiveness, Goals, and Productivity

problems, together with the evidence regarding group cohesiveness and productivity, mean that a manager must carefully weigh the pros and cons of fostering highly cohesive groups.

Group Decision Making

People in organizations work in a variety of groups—formal and informal, permanent and temporary. Most of these groups make decisions that affect the welfare of the organization and the people in it. Here we discuss several issues surrounding how groups make decisions: group polarization, groupthink, group participation in decision making, and group problem solving.

Group Polarization

Members' attitudes and opinions with respect to an issue or a solution may change during the group discussion. Some studies of this tendency have showed the change to be a fairly consistent movement toward a more risky solution, called risky shift.[45] Other studies and analyses have revealed that the group-induced shift is not always toward more risk; the group is just as likely to move toward a more conservative view.[46] Generally, **group polarization** occurs when the average of the group members' post-discussion attitudes tends to be more extreme than average pre-discussion attitudes.[47]

Group polarization is the tendency for a group's average post-discussion attitudes to be more extreme than its average pre-discussion attitudes.

45. James A. F. Stoner, "Risky and Cautious Shifts in Group Decisions: The Influence of Widely Held Values," *Journal of Experimental Social Psychology*, October 1968, pp. 442–459; and M. A. Wallach, N. Kogan, and D. J. Bem, "Group Influence on Individual Risk Taking," *Journal of Abnormal and Social Psychology*, August 1962, pp. 75–86.
46. Dorwin Cartwright, "Risk Taking by Individuals and Groups: An Assessment of Research Employing Choice Dilemmas," *Journal of Personality and Social Psychology*, December 1971, pp. 361–378.
47. S. Moscovici and M. Zavalloni, "The Group as a Polarizer of Attitudes," *Journal of Personality and Social Psychology*, June 1969, pp. 125–135.

Several features of group discussion contribute to polarization.[48] When individuals discover in group discussion that others share their opinions, they may feel more strongly about their opinions, resulting in a more extreme view. Persuasive arguments also can encourage polarization. If members who strongly support a particular position are able to express themselves cogently in the discussion, less avid supporters of the position may become convinced that it is correct. In addition, members may believe that because the group is deciding, they are not individually responsible for the decision or its outcomes. This diffusion of responsibility may enable them to accept and support a decision more radical than those they would make as individuals.

Polarization can profoundly affect group decision making. If group members are known to lean toward a particular decision before a discussion, it may be expected that their post-decision position will be even more extreme. Understanding this phenomenon may be useful for one who seeks to group members' decisions.

Groupthink

Groupthink is a mode of thinking that occurs when members of a group are deeply involved in a cohesive in-group and desire for unanimity offsets their motivation to appraise alternative courses of action.

Although highly cohesive groups often are very successful at accomplishing their goals, such groups can have serious difficulties as well. One problem is groupthink. **Groupthink,** according to Irving L. Janis, is "a mode of thinking that people engage in when they are deeply involved in a cohesive in-group, when the members' strivings for unanimity override their motivation to realistically appraise alternative courses of action."[49] When groupthink occurs, the group unknowingly makes unanimity rather than the best decision its goal. Groupthink can occur in decision making within organizations.

Group Characteristics   Figure 11.5 outlines the groupthink process. The group characteristics that foster the development of groupthink are cohesiveness, the leader's promotion of his or her preferred solution, and insulation of the group from experts' opinions. Group cohesiveness was defined earlier in this chapter as the forces acting on members to remain in the group. When members strongly wish to maintain their membership in the group, they may tend to agree with what seems to be the prevailing mood of the group, even if they personally may have some doubts. When the leader makes known her or his preferences regarding the solution, members may unwillingly go along in order to maintain their membership. Insulation of the group from the opinions of experts means that the group ignores or may not have access to ideas, suggestions, and advice from people outside the group who could help. Thus, when these three characteristics exist, groupthink is likely to occur. In addition, the figure shows that the likelihood of groupthink increases when two other conditions also exist: time pressure to reach a solution and a leader who displays a distinctively closed style. When the group is under time pressure to reach a solution, members feel a strong need to respond faster through seeking agreement and not properly evaluating all alternatives. A closed style displayed by the leader means that the leader does not encourage dissent among the members and, in fact, may discourage disagreement, thereby fostering unanimity among the members when they do not really agree. This type of

48. See Shaw, *Group Dynamics,* pp. 68–76, for further discussion of group polarization.
49. Janis, *Groupthink,* p. 9.

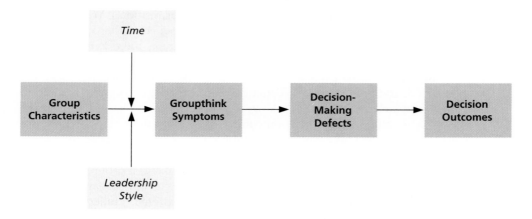

SOURCE: Gregory Moorhead, Richard Ference, and Chris P. Neck, "Group Decision Fiascoes Continue: Space Shuttle Challenger and a Revised Groupthink Framework", *Human Relations*, Vol. 44, 1991, pp. 539–550.

FIGURE 11.5

The Groupthink Process

style may occur whether or not the leader states his or her preferred solution to the problem. These last two moderating conditions were prominent in the analysis of the disaster associated with the explosion of the space shuttle Challenger in 1986.[50]

Symptoms of Groupthink   A group in which groupthink has taken hold exhibits eight well-defined symptoms:

1. *An illusion of invulnerability*, shared by most or all members, that creates excessive optimism and encourages extreme risk taking.
2. *Collective efforts to rationalize to discount warnings* that might lead members to reconsider assumptions before recommitting themselves to past policy decisions.
3. *An unquestioned belief in the group's inherent morality*, inclining members to ignore the ethical and moral consequences of their decisions.
4. *Stereotyped views of "enemy" leaders as too evil* to warrant genuine attempts to negotiate or as too weak or stupid to counter whatever risky attempts are made to defeat their purposes.
5. *Direct pressure on a member who expresses strong arguments against any of the group's stereotypes, illusions, or commitments*, making clear that such dissent is contrary to what is expected of loyal members.
6. *Self-censorship of deviations from the apparent group consensus*, reflecting each member's inclination to minimize the importance of his or her doubts and counterarguments.
7. *A shared illusion of unanimity* (resulting partly from self-censorship of deviations, augmented by the false assumption that silence means consent).

50. Gregory Moorhead, Richard Ference, and Chris P. Neck, "Group Decision Fiascoes Continue: Space Shuttle Challenger and a Revised Groupthink Framework, *Human Relations*, Vol. 44, 1991, pp. 539–550.

8. *The emergence of self-appointed mindguards*, members who protect the group from adverse information that might shatter their shared complacency about the effectiveness and morality of their decisions.[51]

Janis contends that the group involved in the Watergate cover-up—Richard Nixon, H. R. Haldeman, John Ehrlichman, and John Dean—may have been a victim of groupthink. Evidence of most of the groupthink symptoms can be found in the unedited transcripts of the group's deliberations.[52]

Decision-making Defects and Decision Quality   When groupthink dominates group deliberations, the likelihood that the decision-making defects will occur increases. The group is less likely to survey a full range of alternatives and may focus on only a few (often one or two). In discussing a preferred alternative, the group may fail to examine it for nonobvious risks and drawbacks. Even when new information is obtained, the group may not reexamine previously rejected alternatives for nonobvious gains or some means of reducing apparent costs. The group may reject expert opinions that run counter to its own views and may choose to consider only information that supports its preferred solution. The decision to launch the space shuttle Challenger in January 1986 may have been a product of groupthink because, due to the increased time pressure to make a decision and the leaders' style, negative information was ignored by the group that made the decision.[53] Finally, the group may not consider any potential setbacks or counter-moves by competing groups and therefore may fail to develop contingency plans. Note that Janis contends that these six defects may arise from other common problems as well: fatigue, prejudice, inaccurate information, information overload, and ignorance.[54]

Defects in decision making do not always lead to bad outcomes or defeats. Even if its own decision-making processes are flawed, one side can win a battle because of the poor decisions made by the other side's leaders. Nevertheless, decisions produced by defective processes have a lower probability of success.

Although the arguments for the existence of groupthink are convincing, the hypothesis has not been subjected to rigorous empirical examination. Research supports parts of the model but leaves some questions unanswered.[55]

Prevention of Groupthink   Several suggestions have been offered to help managers reduce the probability of groupthink in group decision making.[56] Summarized in Table 11.3, these prescriptions fall into four categories depending on whether they apply to the leader, the organization, the individual, or the process. All are designed to facilitate the critical evaluation of alternatives and discourage the single-minded pursuit of unanimity.

51. Irving L. Janis, *Victims of Groupthink* (Boston: Houghton Mifflin, 1972), pp. 197–198.
52. Janis, *Groupthink*.
53. Moorhead, Ference, and Neck, "Group Decision Fiascoes Continue: Space Shuttle Challenger and a Revised Groupthink Framework," pp. 539-550.
54. Janis, *Groupthink*, pp. 193-197; and Gregory Moorhead, "Groupthink: Hypothesis in Need of Testing," *Group and Organization Studies*, December 1982, pp. 429–444.
55. Gregory Moorhead and John R. Montanari, "Empirical Analysis of the Groupthink Phenomenon," *Human Relations*, May 1986, pp. 399–410; and John R. Montanari and Gregory Moorhead, "Development of the Groupthink Assessment Inventory," *Educational and Psychological Measurement*, Vol. 49, Spring 1989, pp. 209–219.
56. Janis, *Groupthink*.

TABLE 11.3

Prescriptions for Prevention of Groupthink

A. **Leader prescriptions**
1. Assign everyone the role of critical evaluator.
2. Be impartial; do not state preferences.
3. Assign the devil's advocate role to at least one group member.
4. Use outside experts to challenge the group.
5. Be open to dissenting points of view.

B. **Organizational prescriptions**
1. Set up several independent groups to study the same issue.
2. Train managers and group leaders in group think prevention techniques.

C. **Individual prescriptions**
1. Be a critical thinker.
2. Discuss group deliberations with a trusted outsider; report back to the group.

D. **Process prescriptions**
1. Periodically break the group into subgroups to discuss the issues.
2. Take time to study external factors.
3. Hold second-chance meetings to rethink issues before making a commitment.

Participation in Decision Making

Participation in decision making is an important part of managing motivation, leadership, organization structure, and decision-making processes.

A major issue in group decision making is the degree to which employees should participate in the process. Early management theories, such as those of the scientific management school, advocated a clear separation between the duties of managers and workers: management was to make the decisions, and employees were to implement them.[57] Other approaches have urged that employees be allowed to

57. Frederick W. Taylor, *The Principles of Scientific Management* (New York: Harper & Row, 1911).

This worker is responsible for ensuring minimal quality variation in Alcoa wire harnesses. She is responsible for deciding whether or not the harnesses, which bundle a car's entire electrical system into 700 wires, meet Alcoa's performance standards. Many employees find it gratifying to participate in decision making on the job.

Electromation Inc. Finds That Its Teams May Be Illegal

Electromation Inc., a small (200 employees) electrical parts manufacturer in Elkhart, Indiana, was suffering huge losses in 1988. To cut costs, it discontinued an attendance bonus program and eliminated a wage increase. As might be expected, employees objected. Management responded by setting up several committees of up to six workers and one or two managers to discuss compensation, absenteeism, and other work issues and to channel feedback up to company management.

This situation is typical of many companies across the United States that established worker teams to improve quality, reduce costs, and resolve other work-related issues. The problem is that in 1990, a committee of the National Labor Relations Board (NLRB) ruled that the committees were illegal under the Wagner Act of 1935. Later in 1992, the full Board agreed. Now both sides are filing briefs and appeals, which will probably lead to arguments before the Supreme Court in the mid 1990s.

So does that mean that all worker teams are illegal? Probably not, although employers such as Motorola, General Mills, Corning, and Du Pont that utilize teams extensively are a bit nervous. The Wagner Act expressly forbids employers from dominating, interfering with, or contributing to the formation of any organization of any kind or any employee representation committee that exists for the purpose of dealing with employers concerning grievances, wages, hours of employment, or conditions of work. Electromation's teams were set up by management to discuss absenteeism, pay, and conditions of work. Workers on the committees were representing other workers and communicating to top management. As far as the NLRB is concerned, this is the primary function of labor unions, which are protected by federal law. This situation has raised a number of ethical questions. Do all worker-management teams fulfill this same role? Why does management encourage the development of worker teams? Is it manipulation of workers to get more work out of them? Does management set up worker teams to avert unions in the workplace?

SOURCES: Bob Smith, "Employee Committee or Labor Union?" *Management Review*, April 1993, pp. 54–57; "Teamsters Versus Teams," *Training and Development*, March 1993, pp. 9–10; "Putting a Damper on That Old Team Spirit," *Business Week*, May 4, 1992, p. 60; and "Are Work Teams Illegal?" *Fortune*, January 13, 1992, p. 14.

participate in decisions to increase their ego involvement, motivation, and satisfaction.[58] Numerous research studies have shown that whereas employees who seek responsibility and challenge on the job may find participation in the decision-making process both motivating and enriching, other employees may regard such participation as a waste of time and a management imposition.[59] In addition, there is some indication that some types of employee teams may be illegal, as discussed in *The Ethical Dilemma*.

Whether employee participation in decision making is appropriate depends on the situation. The Vroom-Yetton-Jago model of leadership (discussed in Chapter

58. Rensis Likert, *New Patterns of Management* (New York: McGraw-Hill, 1961); and Chris Argyris, *Personality and Organization* (New York: Harper & Row, 1957).
59. N. C. Morse and E. Reimer, "The Experimental Change of a Major Organizational Variable," *Journal of Abnormal and Social Psychology*, January 1956, pp. 120–129; and Lester Coch and John R. P. French, "Overcoming Resistance to Change," *Human Relations*, Vol. 1, 1948, pp. 512–532.

12) is one popular approach to determining the appropriate degree of employee participation.[60] The model includes decision styles that vary from autocratic (the leader alone makes the decision) to democratic (the group makes the decision, with each member having an equal say). The choice of style rests on eight considerations that concern the characteristics of the situation and the subordinates.

Participation in decision making is also related to organizational structure. For example, in a decentralized organization, some decision-making authority is delegated throughout the organizational hierarchy. The more decentralized the organization, then, the more its employees tend to participate in decision making. Regardless of whether one views participation in decision making as a topic of leadership, organization structure, or motivation, it remains an important aspect of organizations that continues to occupy managers and organizational scholars.[61]

Group Problem Solving

A typical interacting group may have difficulty with any of several steps in the decision-making process. One common problem arises in the alternative generation phase: the search may be arbitrarily ended before all plausible alternatives have been identified. Several types of group interactions can have this effect. If members immediately express their reactions to the alternatives as they are first proposed, potential contributors may begin to censor their ideas to avoid embarrassing criticism from the group. Less-confident group members, intimidated by members who have more experience, higher status, or more power, also may censor their ideas for fear of embarrassment or punishment. In addition, the group leader may limit idea generation by enforcing requirements concerning time, appropriateness, cost, feasibility, and the like.

To improve the alternative generation process, managers may employ any of three techniques—brainstorming, the nominal group technique, or the Delphi technique—to stimulate the group's problem-solving capabilities.

Brainstorming is a technique used in the alternative generation phase of decision making that assists in development of numerous alternative courses of action.

Brainstorming   **Brainstorming,** a technique made popular in the 1950s, is most often used in the idea generation phase of decision making and is intended to solve problems that are new to the organization and have major consequences. In brainstorming, the group convenes specifically to generate alternatives. The members present ideas and clarify them with brief explanations. Each idea is recorded in full view of all members, usually on a flip chart. To avoid self-censoring, no attempts to evaluate the ideas are allowed. Group members are encouraged to offer any ideas that occur to them, even those that seem too risky or impossible to implement. (The absence of such ideas, in fact, is evidence that the group members are engaging in self-censorship.) In a subsequent session, after the ideas have been recorded and distributed to members for review, the alternatives are evaluated.

The intent of brainstorming is to produce totally new ideas and solutions by stimulating the creativity of group members and encouraging them to build on

60. Victor H. Vroom and Arthur G. Jago, *The New Leadership* (Englewood Cliffs, N.J.: Prentice-Hall, 1988).
61. See Carrie R. Leana, Edwin A. Locke, and David M. Schweiger, "Fact and Fiction in Analyzing Research on Participative Decision Making: A Critique of Cotton, Vollrath, Froggatt, Lengnick-Hall, and Jennings," *Academy of Management Review*, January 1990, pp. 137–146, and John L. Cotton, David A. Vollrath, Mark L. Lengnick-Hall, and Mark L. Froggatt, "Fact: The Form of Participation Does Matter—A Rebuttal to Leana, Locke, and Schweiger," *Academy of Management Review*, January 1990, pp. 147–153.

the contributions of others. Brainstorming does not provide the resolution to the problem, an evaluation scheme, or the decision itself. Instead, it produces a list of alternatives that is more innovative and comprehensive than one developed by the typical interacting group.

The Nominal Group Technique   The **nominal group technique (NGT)** offers another means of improving group decision making. Whereas brainstorming is used primarily for alternative generation, NGT may be employed in other phases of decision making, such as identifying the problem and appropriate criteria for evaluating alternatives. In NGT, a group of individuals convenes to address an issue. The issue is described to the group, and each individual writes a list of ideas; no discussion among the members is permitted. Following the five- to ten-minute idea generation period, individual members take turns reporting their ideas, one at a time, to the group. The ideas are recorded on a flip chart, and members are encouraged to add to the list by building on the ideas of others. After all ideas have been presented, the members may discuss them and continue to build on them or proceed to the next phase. This part of the NGT process can also be carried out without a face-to-face meeting—for example, by mail, telephone, or computer. A meeting, however, helps members develop a group feeling and puts interpersonal pressure on the members to do their best in developing their lists.[62]

After the discussion, members privately vote on or rank the ideas or report their preferences in some other agreed-on way. Reporting is private to reduce any feelings of intimidation. After voting, the group may discuss the results and continue to generate and discuss ideas. The generation-discussion-vote cycle can continue until an appropriate decision is reached.

The nominal group technique has two principal advantages. It helps overcome the negative effects of power and status differences among group members, and it can be used in the problem exploration, alternative generation, and evaluation phases of decision making. Its primary disadvantage lies in its structured nature, which may limit creativity.

The Delphi Technique   The **Delphi technique** originally was developed by Rand Corp. as a method of systematically gathering the judgments of experts for use in developing forecasts. It is designed for groups that do not meet face to face. For instance, the product development manager of a major toy manufacturer might use the Delphi technique to probe the views of industry experts to forecast developments in the dynamic toy market.

The manager who desires the input of a group is the central figure in the process. After recruiting participants, the manager develops a questionnaire for them to complete. The questionnaire is relatively simple in that it contains straightforward questions that deal with the issue, trends in the area, new technological developments, and other factors in which the manager is interested. The manager summarizes the responses and reports back to the experts with another questionnaire. This cycle may be repeated as many times as necessary to generate the information the manager needs.

The Delphi technique is useful when experts are physically dispersed, anonymity is desired, or the participants are known to have difficulty communicating with one

---

62. See Bernard M. Bass, *Organizational Decision Making* (Homewood, Ill: Irwin, 1983), pp. 162–163, for further discussion of the nominal group technique.

another because of extreme differences of opinion.[63] This method also avoids the intimidation problems that may exist in decision-making groups. On the other hand, the technique eliminates the often fruitful results of direct interaction among group members.

Intergroup Dynamics

Interactions among groups are based on the characteristics of the interacting groups, the organizational context within which the groups operate, and the task and situational bases of the interactions.

A group's contribution to an organization depends on its interactions with other groups as well as on its own productivity. Many organizations are increasing their use of cross-functional teams to address complex and increasingly important organizational issues. The result has been a heightened emphasis on the teams' interactions with other groups. Groups that actively interact with other groups by asking questions, initiating joint programs, and sharing their team's achievements usually are the most productive.

Interactions are the essential to understanding intergroup dynamics. The orientation of the groups toward their goals takes place within a highly complex set of conditions that determine the relationship among the groups. The most important of these factors are presented in the model of intergroup dynamics in Figure 11.6. The model emphasizes three primary factors that influence intergroup interactions: group characteristics, organizational factors, and task and situational bases of interaction.

First, we must understand the major characteristics of the interacting groups. Each group brings to the interaction its own unique features. As individuals become a part of a group, they tend to identify so strongly with the group that their views of other groups become biased, and harmonious relationships may be difficult to achieve.[64] Furthermore, because the individuals who make up each group contribute to the group processes, the groups' norms, size, composition, and cohesiveness all affect the interactions with other groups. Thus, understanding the individuals in the group and the important characteristics of the group can help managers monitor intergroup interactions.

Second, the organizational setting within which the groups interact can have a powerful influence on intergroup interactions. The organization's structure, rules and procedures, decision-making processes, and goals and reward systems all influence interactions. For example, organizations in which frequent interactions occur and strong ties among groups exist usually are characterized as low-conflict organizations.[65]

Five factors that determine the nature of group interactions are location, resources, time and goal interdependence, task uncertainty, and task interdependence.

Third, the task and situational bases of interactions focus on the working relationships among the interacting groups and on the reasons for the interactions. As Figure 11.6 shows, five factors affect intergroup interactions: location, resources, time and goal interdependence, task uncertainty, and task interdependence. These factors both create the interactions and determine their characteristics, such as the

63. See George P. Huber, *Managerial Decision Making* (Glenview, Ill: Scott, Foresman, 1980), pp. 205–212, for more details on the Delphi technique.
64. Blake E. Ashforth and Fred Mael, "Social Identity Theory and the Organization," *Academy of Management Review*, January 1989, pp. 20–39.
65. Reed E. Nelson, "The Strength of Strong Ties: Social Networks and Intergroup Conflict in Organizations," *Academy of Management Journal*, June 1989, pp. 377–401; and "Now That It's Cruising, Can Ford Keep Its Foot to the Gas?" *Business Week*, February 11, 1985, pp. 48–52.

FIGURE 11.6

**Factors That Influence
Intergroup Interactions**

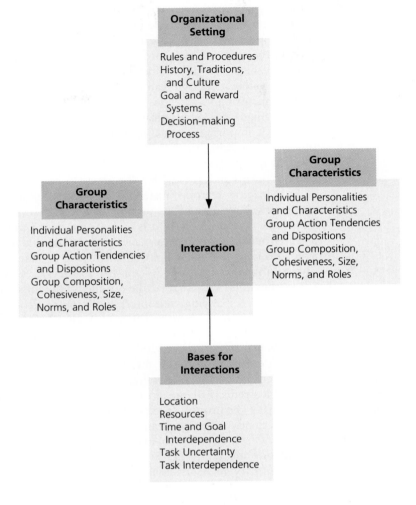

**Organizational
Setting**

Rules and Procedures
History, Traditions,
  and Culture
Goal and Reward
  Systems
Decision-making
  Process

**Group
Characteristics**

Individual Personalities
  and Characteristics
Group Action Tendencies
  and Dispositions
Group Composition,
  Cohesiveness, Size,
  Norms, and Roles

**Group
Characteristics**

Individual Personalities
  and Characteristics
Group Action Tendencies
  and Dispositions
Group Composition,
  Cohesiveness, Size,
  Norms, and Roles

Interaction

**Bases for
Interactions**

Location
Resources
Time and Goal
  Interdependence
Task Uncertainty
Task Interdependence

frequency of interaction, the volume of information exchange among groups, and the type of coordination the groups need to interact and function. For example, if two groups will heavily depend on each other to perform a task about which much uncertainty exists, they will need a great deal of information from each other to define and perform the task.

Managing Group and Intergroup Dynamics in Organizations

Managing groups in organizations is difficult. Managers must know what types of groups—command or task, formal or informal—exist in the organization. If a certain command group is very large, there will probably be several informal subgroups to be managed. A manager might want to take advantage of existing informal groups, "formalizing" some of them into command or task groups based on a subset of the tasks to be performed. Other informal groups may need to be broken up to make task assignment easier. In assigning tasks to people and subgroups, the manager must also consider individual motivations for joining groups, as well as the composition of groups.

Quite often, a manager can help ensure that a group develops into a productive unit by nurturing its activities in each stage of development. Helpful steps include encouraging open communication and trust among the members, stimulating discussion of important issues, providing task-relevant information at appropriate times, and assisting in the analysis of external factors, such as competition and external threats and opportunities. Managers might also encourage the development of norms and roles within the group to help out in development.

In managing a group, managers must consider the goals of the people in the group as well as those of the group as a whole. Developing a reward structure that lets people reach their own goals by working toward those of the group can result in a very productive group. A manager may also be able to influence some factors that affect group cohesiveness. For example, trying to stimulate competition, provoke an external threat to the group, establish a goal-setting system, or employ participative approaches might help harness the productive potential of high cohesiveness.

Strategies for dealing with interactions among groups must be carefully chosen, following thorough examination and analysis of the groups, their goals, their unique characteristics, and the organizational setting in which the interactions occur. Managers can use a variety of strategies to increase the efficiency of intergroup interactions. Some of the most common mechanisms for altering the way that groups interact is to encourage interacting groups to focus on a superordinate goal, which reflects the goals of the larger organization rather than the more specific goals of the groups. In other situations, management might want to add linking roles to help differing groups understand the differences between them. Finally, management may need to make changes in reporting relationships, decision-making priorities, and rules and procedures to properly manage group interactions.

In summary, managers must be aware of the organizational and social implications of their attempts to manage people in groups in organizations. Groups affect the behavior of people and, individual efforts, when aggregated to the group level, are the source of group performance. As prevalent as groups are in our society, managers must strive to improve their understanding of people in the groups to which they belong.

Managers can change the ways groups interact by altering the physical arrangements, changing the resource distribution, stressing a superordinate goal, training employees to manage group interactions more effectively, and changing the structure of the organization.

Summary of Key Points

- A group is two or more persons who interact so as to influence one another. Studying groups is important because groups are everywhere in our society, they can profoundly affect individual behavior, and the behavior of individuals in a group is essential to the group's success or failure. The work group is the primary means by which managers coordinate individual behavior to achieve organizational goals. Group formation depends on the expectation that a need will be satisfied as a result of membership.
- Groups may be differentiated on the bases of degree of formality and relative permanence. The two types of formal groups are command and task groups.

Friendship and interest groups are the two types of informal groups. Command groups are relatively permanent work groups established by the organization and usually are specified on an organization chart. Task groups, although also established by the organization, are relatively temporary and exist only until the specific task is accomplished. In friendship groups, the affiliation among members arises from close social relationships and the enjoyment that comes from being together. The common bond in interest groups is the activity in which the members engage.

■ Groups develop in four stages: mutual acceptance, communication and decision making, motivation and productivity, and control and organization. Although the stages are sequential, they may overlap. A group that does not fully develop within each stage will not fully mature as a group, resulting in lower group performance.

■ Four additional factors affect group performance: composition, size, norms, and cohesiveness. The homogeneity of the people in the group affects the interactions that occur and the productivity of the group. The effect of increasing the size of the group depends on the nature of the tasks and the people in the group. Norms, which help people function and relate to one another in predictable and efficient ways, serve four purposes: they facilitate group survival, simplify and make more predictable the behaviors of group members, help the group avoid embarrassing situations, and express the central values of the group and identify the group to others. Group cohesiveness is the result of all forces that act on members to keep them in the group (or the tendency of the group to stay together).

■ Group decision making involves problems as well as benefits. One possible problem is group polarization, the shift of members' attitudes and opinions to a more extreme position after group discussion. Another difficulty is groupthink, a mode of thinking in which the striving for unanimity overrides the critical appraisal of alternatives. Yet another concern involves employee participation in decision making. The appropriate degree of participation depends on the characteristics of the situation.

■ A model of intergroup dynamics assumes that group interactions reflect certain needs for interaction, occur within a specific organizational setting, and occur among unique groups. The five bases of intergroup interactions determine the characteristics of the interactions including frequency, the volume of information exchanged, and the type of coordination the groups need to interact and function. Interactions among work groups involve some of the most complex relationships in organizations. They are based on five factors: location, resources, time and goal interdependence, task uncertainty, and task interdependence.

■ Managers must also be aware of the many factors that affect group performance and understand the people as well as the group issues. This includes understanding why groups form, how the develop over time, what the characteristics are of a high-performance group, and strategies for managing the interactions among groups.

Discussion Questions

1. Why is it useful for a manager to be familiar with the concepts of group behavior? Why is it useful for an employee to be familiar with these concepts?

2. Our definition of a group is somewhat broad. Would you classify each of the following collections of people as a group or as something else? Explain why.

   a. 70,000 people at a football game
   b. Students taking this course
   c. People in an elevator
   d. People on an escalator
   e. Employees of IBM
   f. Employees of your local college bookstore

3. List four groups to which you belong. Identify each as formal or informal.
4. For each group you listed in question 3, describe the reasons for its formation. Why did you join each group? Why might others have decided to join each group?
5. In which stage of development is each of the four groups listed in question 3? Did any group move too quickly through any of the stages? Explain.
6. Analyze the composition of two of the groups to which you belong. How are they similar in composition? How do they differ?
7. Are any of the groups to which you belong too large or too small to get its work done? If so, what can the leader or the members do to alleviate the problem?
8. List two norms of two of the groups to which you belong. How are these norms enforced?
9. Discuss the following statement: "Group cohesiveness is the good, warm feeling we get from working in groups and is something that all group leaders should strive to develop in the groups they lead."
10. How are group polarization and groupthink similar? How do they differ?
11. Consider one of the groups to which you belong and describe the interactions that group has with another group.

EXPERIENTIAL EXERCISE

Purpose This exercise demonstrates the benefits a group can bring to accomplishing a task.

Format You will be asked to do the same task both individually and as part of a group.

Procedure **Part 1:** You will need a pen or pencil and an 8 ½" × 11" sheet of paper. Working alone, do the following:

1. Write the letters of the alphabet in a vertical column down the left-hand side of the paper: A–Z.
2. Your instructor will randomly select a sentence from any written document and read out loud the first twenty-six letters in that sentence. Write these letters in a vertical column immediately to the right of the alphabet column. Everyone should have identical sets of 26 two-letter combinations.
3. Working alone, think of a famous person whose initials correspond to each pair of letters, and write the name next to the letters, for example, "MT Mark Twain." You

will have ten minutes. Only one name per set is allowed. One point is awarded for each legitimate name, so the maximum score is 26 points.

4. After time expires, exchange your paper with another member of the class and score each other's work. Disputes about the legitimacy of names will be settled by the instructor. Keep your score for use later in the exercise.

Part 2: Your instructor will divide the class into groups of five to ten. All groups should have approximately the same number of members. Each group now follows the procedure given in part 1. Again write the letters of the alphabet down the left-hand side of the sheet of paper, this time in reverse order: Z–A. Your instructor will dictate a new set of letters for the second column. The time limit and scoring procedure are the same. The only difference is that the groups will generate the names.

Part 3: Each team identifies the group member who came up with the most names. The instructor places these "best" students into one group. Then all groups repeat part 2, but this time the letters from the reading will be in the first column and the alphabet letters will be in the second column.

Part 4: Each team calculates the average individual score of its members on part 1 and compares it with the team score from parts 2 and 3. Your instructor will put the average individual score and team scores for each group on the board.

Follow-up Questions

1. Do the average individual scores and the team scores differ? What are the reasons for the difference, if any?
2. Although the team scores in this exercise usually are higher than the average individual scores, under what conditions might individual averages exceed group scores?

SOURCE: Adapted from John E. Jones and J. William Pfeiffer (Eds.), *The 1979 Annual Handbook for Group Facilitators* (San Diego, Calif.: University Associates, 1979), pp. 19–20. Copyright © 1979 by Pfeiffer & Company, San Diego, CA. Used with permission.

CASE 11.1   **Eastman Kodak's Zebras Do It as a Team**

Pressure for improvement in operating results for Eastman Kodak is coming from many different sources. In 1993, Eastman Kodak's chief executive officer, Kay Whitmore, was told by its board and by the California Public Employees Retirement System to turn the company around and start making money. In 1993 Kodak had net profits of $1.1 billion on total revenues of $20.2 billion. Its disc camera made fuzzy pictures, and its copiers and printers were losing money; its drug and chemicals business made money, but not much. Eastman Kodak has already cut management levels by two and eliminated more than 2,000 jobs in administration and research and development. It was trying desperately to get into the electronic picture business, but its bread and butter remained the photography business. And even that is being threatened by low-cost film makers who were selling a thirty-six print roll of color film for $2 less than Kodak's.

The one bright spot was its black-and-white film manufacturing operation. Back in the late 1980s the black-and-white operation was running 15 percent over cost and always late in filling orders, sometimes as much as forty-two days. The operation usually scored near the bottom in Kodak's morale surveys. Black-and-white film is used in medical technology, high-technology information gathering (spy satellites), and printing, amounting to more than 7,000 different products worth more than $2 billion per year. With that much at stake, losses piling up, and morale sinking, beginning in 1989 the black-and-white group discarded the traditional vertical hierarchy and adopted a horizontal organization, creating a twenty-five member leadership team and other teams in charge of each major product stream.

The traditional manufacturing functional approach in the black-and-white operation was changed to a team-flow process. Teams of employees were responsible for the flow of materials through the process. Old-style departments were eliminated and replaced with cross-functional teams responsible for streams, or flows, of product. Employees call themselves Zebras, and the black-and-white theme is all over the place in signs, clothes, zebra heads, and furnishings. Special Zebra teams were put in charge of each product stream for the hundreds of products for the Health Sciences Division.

The results were amazing. By 1992, the Zebra group was 15 percent *under* the cost budget, rather than over;

response time was down to twenty days; and employees were smiling again. Zebra team members were proud of their work, their product stream, and themselves. In other words, morale was up. Zebras can change the flow as needs dictate because the flow belongs to them. There is significant ownership in the total process. Eastman Kodak's challenge may now lie in how to use streams and flows in their other businesses.

Case Questions

1. Describe each of the group performance factors that seem to be in place to make the Zebra teams work.
2. How do you think the intergroup interactions changed with the initiation of the Zebra teams?

SOURCES: "Higher Rewards in Lowered Goals," *Business Week*, March 8, 1993, pp. 75–78; Thomas A. Stewart, "The Search for the Organization of Tomorrow," *Fortune*, May 18, 1992, pp. 92–98; Carol J. Loomis, "The Battle to Shape Up Kodak," *Fortune*, May 31, 1993, pp. 62–63; and Joan E. Rigdon, "Whitmore Gets Weak Backing From 2 Holders," *Wall Street Journal*, May 6, 1993, p. C11.

CASE 11.2	A Multicultural Task Force

Jose has been appointed the chairperson of a task force to design the primary product line for a new joint venture between companies from Japan, the United States, and South America. The new joint venture company will make, sell and service pet caskets (coffins) for the burial of beloved pets, mostly dogs and cats. One month earlier, each company had assigned personnel to the team:

■ From the Japanese company, Furuay Masahiko from Yokohama, assistant to the president of the Japanese company; Hamada Isao from Tokyo, the director of marketing from its technology group; and Noto Takeshi from Tokyo, the assistant director of its financial management department.

■ From the United States company, Thomas Boone from Chicago, the top purchasing manager from its lumber and forest lands group; Richard Maret from Buffalo, the co-director of the company's information systems group; and Billy Bob "Tex" Johnson from Arizona, the former CEO, now retired and a consultant for the company.

■ From the South American company, Mariana Preus from Argentina, the head of product design for that company's specialty animal products group; Hector Bonilla from Mexico City, an expert in automated systems design for wood products; and Mauricio Gomes, a representative of the Chilean subsidiary that will be in charge of design and construction for the plant which will be located in Chile to take advantage of the vast forest there.

These members were chosen for their expertise in the various areas and were taking valuable time away from their normal assignments to participate in the joint venture.

The group came together for its first meeting at 10:00 A. M. today. Jose started the meeting by reviewing the history of the development of the joint venture and how the three company presidents had decided to create it. Then Jose reviewed the market for the new pet coffins. He stressed that the committee was to design a product to meet increasing demand for it around the world and an increasingly competitive marketplace created by the entry of many low-cost suppliers. He then opened the meeting for comments and suggestions.

Mariana Preus spoke first: "In my opinion, the current designs that we have in production are good as is. They are top-notch designs, using the latest technology for processing. They use the best woods available and they should sell great. I don't see why we have to design a whole new product line." Noto Takeshi agreed and urged the committee to recommend that the current designs were good enough and should be immediately incorporated into the plans for the new manufacturing plant. Jose interrupted the discussion: "Look, the council of presidents put this joint venture together to completely revolutionize the product and its manufacture based on solid evidence and industry data. We are to redesign the product and its manufacturing systems. That is our job, so let's get started." Jose knew that the presidents had considered using existing designs but had rejected the idea because the designs were too old and not easily manufacturable at costs low enough to make a significant impact on the market. He told the group this and reminded them that the purpose of the committee was to design a new product.

The members then began discussing possible new design elements, but the discussion always returned to the benefits of using the existing designs. Finally, Tex spoke up: "I think we ought to do what Mariana suggested earlier. It makes no sense to me to design new caskets when the existing designs are good enough to do the job." The others nodded their heads in agreement. Jose again reminded them of the purpose of the group and said such a recommendation would not be well received by the council of presidents. Nevertheless, the group insisted that Jose write a memo to the council of presidents with the recommendation to use existing designs and to begin immediately to design the plant and the manufacturing system. The meeting adjourned and the members headed to the golf course at 10:45 A.M.

Jose returned to his computer and started to write the memo, but he knew it would anger the presidents. He hoped that he would not be held responsible for the actions of the group committee, even though he was its chairperson. He wondered what had gone wrong and what he could have done to prevent it.

Case Questions

1. Which characteristics of group behavior discussed in the chapter can you identify in this case?
2. How did the diverse nature of the group affect the committee's actions?
3. If you were in Jose's position, what would you have done differently? What would you do now?

CHAPTER

12

Leadership Models and Concepts

OBJECTIVES

After studying this chapter, you should be able to:

Describe the general nature of leadership and outline a framework for categorizing leadership models and concepts.

Summarize the trait and behavioral approaches to leadership.

Describe the LPC theory of leadership.

Explain the path-goal theory of leadership.

Describe the Vroom-Yetton-Jago model of leadership.

Summarize the leader-member exchange model and the life cycle theory of leadership.

Contemporary CEOs must be innovative leaders who can steer their companies through changes and toward success, as well as talented managers who are capable of regulating all company activities.

There's an old axiom in sports that coaches get too much credit when their teams win and too much blame when they lose. Some experts argue that the same holds true for leaders of big corporations. Today's CEO is expected to be an exemplary manager, charting an organization's competitive strategy while simultaneously controlling costs and boosting profits. But the CEO is also expected to be a strong leader, providing bold vision and leading the organization in a unified and effective manner. And when the organization does not perform, it's often the CEO who gets the heat. Recent events at Eli Lilly and Company provide interesting insights into the expectations placed on today's leaders.

Eli Lilly is one of the world's largest pharmaceutical makers, with operations in 28 countries; its products are sold in more than 110 countries. Lilly's annual sales are around $6 billion. For decades Eli Lilly has been a tradition-bound, centralized firm. Its top managers have routinely practiced autocratic decision making and kept tight control over all organizational activities. Managers followed well-understood rules about how they should dress and how they should behave. For example, all executives at the firm wore conservative suits at all times and interacted with lower-level managers in a distant and formal manner.

In 1991, Lilly's CEO, Richard Wood, retired and his hand-picked successor, Vaughn Bryson, took over. At the time, Eli Lilly was struggling because of increased competition, a dearth of new products under development, and the impending expiration of a number of major patents. Bryson knew from the beginning that he faced formidable challenges. But what he may not have known was how difficult it would be to untie his own hands to face those challenges.

Bryson decided that if Lilly were to regain its competitive edge, the firm needed to become more decentralized, to empower middle managers, and to increase its responsiveness to its competitive environment. And he sought to imbue the organization with his own style of leadership. In contrast to Wood and other top managers at Lilly, Bryson believed in informality, openness, and participation. He delegated decision making to others, mingled with lower-level managers, and generally attempted to lead by example rather than by decree.

Unfortunately, others at Eli Lilly did not agree with Bryson's approach to running the firm. After only twenty months on the job, he was asked to retire in mid-1993. Although the firm's board of directors argued that the decision was based on Bryson's performance, many industry experts contended that he had not been given enough time to turn the firm around and that the decision was based on differences in style more than on substance.[1]

1. "Eli Lilly 'Under Serious Pressure'," *USA Today*, June 29, 1993, p. 4B; "Bad Chemistry Fuels Many CEO Departures," *USA Today*, June 29, 1993, p. 1B; and "Lilly Looks for a Shot of Adrenaline," *Business Week*, November 23, 1992, pp. 70–75.

Both Richard Wood and Vaughn Bryson were managers. Opinion differs, however, as to whether either of them was an effective leader. One thing is clear, however: the two executives had different views of how a manager should lead an organization. Wood believed that to be a leader, a person needed to remain aloof, formal, and autocratic. Bryson, on the other hand, thought a leader should be part of the group, informal, and participative. These dramatic differences in beliefs and style opened up a void between the two that could only end with one of them leaving the organization.

Today's executives are expected to be both able managers and strong leaders. Although most experts believe that they understand the basic ideas underlying effective management, leadership is a much more elusive phenomenon. Indeed, the mystique of leadership is one of the most widely debated, studied, and sought-after commodities of organizational life.[2] Managers talk about the characteristics that make an effective leader, and organizational scientists have extensively researched the same issue. Unfortunately, neither group has definitively answered the many questions concerning leadership.

In some organizations, leaders have no meaningful effect. In others, leaders make the difference between enormous success and overwhelming failure. Some leaders are effective in one organization but not in others. Other leaders succeed no matter where they are.[3] Despite hundreds of studies on leadership, researchers have found no simple way to account for these inconsistencies. Why, then, should we study leadership? First, leadership is of great practical importance to organizations. Second, researchers have isolated and verified some variables that influence leadership effectiveness.[4]

We begin this chapter, the first of two devoted to leadership, with a discussion of the nature of leadership, including a definition of the concept and a framework of leadership perspectives. Then we turn to historical views of leadership, focusing on the trait and behavioral approaches. Next, we examine three leadership theories that have formed the basis for most leadership research: the LPC theory developed by Fiedler, the path-goal theory, and the Vroom-Yetton-Jago model. We conclude by describing two other contemporary models of leadership. In our next chapter we explore other elements of leadership, focusing more specifically on influence processes in organizations.

The Nature of Leadership

Management and leadership are distinct elements. Management involves formal position power, whereas leadership relies on social influence processes.

Before we define leadership, we need to make some important distinctions. First, management and leadership are not the same thing.[5] Management relies on formal position power to influence people, whereas leadership stems from social influence processes. The chief of staff of a large hospital is clearly a manager by virtue of the position itself. At the same time, this person may not be respected or trusted by others

2. Bernard M. Bass, *Bass and Stogdill's Handbook of Leadership*, 3rd ed. (Riverside, N.J.: Free Press, 1990). See also James R. Meindl and Sanford B. Ehrlich, "The Romance of Leadership and the Evaluation of Organizational Performance," *Academy of Management Review*, January 1987, pp. 91–109.
3. William G. Pagonis, "The Work of the Leader," *Harvard Business Review*, November–December 1992, pp. 118–126.
4. Ralph M. Stogdill, *Handbook of Leadership* (New York: Free Press, 1974). See also Bass, *Bass and Stogdill's Handbook of Leadership*.
5. Abraham Zaleznik, "Managers and Leaders: Are They Different?" *Harvard Business Review*, March–April 1992, pp. 126–135.

and may have to rely solely on authority vested in the position to get people to do things. But an emergency room nurse with no formal authority may be quite effective at taking charge of a chaotic situation and directing others in how to deal with specific patient problems. Others in the emergency room may respond because they trust the nurse's judgment and have confidence in the nurse's decision-making skills.

The head of pediatrics, supervising a staff of twenty other doctors, nurses, and attendants, may also enjoy their complete respect, confidence, and trust. They take his advice and follow his orders without question, and often go far beyond the job's requirements to help carry out the unit's mission. Thus, being a manager does not ensure that a person is also a leader—any given manager may or may not also be a leader. Similarly, a leadership position can also be formal—someone appointed to head a group—or informal—one who emerges from the ranks of the group according to a consensus of the members. The chief of staff just described is a manager but not a leader. Meanwhile, the emergency room nurse is a leader but not a manager. And the head of pediatrics is both.

A Definition of Leadership

Leadership is both a process and a property. As a process, leadership involves the use of noncoercive influence. As a property, leadership is the set of characteristics attributed to someone who is perceived to use influence successfully.

Experts have proposed many definitions of leadership, but none has won wide acceptance.[6] We define **leadership** in terms of both process and property. As a process, leadership is the use of noncoercive influence to direct and coordinate the activities of group members toward goal accomplishment. As a property, leadership is the set of characteristics attributed to those who are perceived to use such influence successfully.[7] From an organizational viewpoint, leadership is vital because it has such a powerful influence on individual and group behavior. Moreover, because the goal toward which the group directs its efforts is the desired goal of the leader, it may or may not mesh with organizational goals.[8]

Leadership involves neither force nor coercion. A manager who relies solely on force and formal authority to direct the behavior of subordinates is not exercising leadership.[9] Thus, as noted earlier, a manager or supervisor may or may not also be a leader. It is also important to note that the set of characteristics that may be attributed to a leader may well be characteristics that the individual really possesses. On the other hand, however, they may also only be ones that he or she is merely perceived to possess.

A Framework of Leadership Perspectives

Leadership theory is based on a variety of different perspectives. One useful framework for organizing the predominant leadership perspectives differentiates models and approaches to leadership along two dimensions: focus and approach.[10]

6. See Gary Yukl and David D. Van Fleet, "Theory and Research on Leadership in Organizations," in M. D. Dunnette and L. M. Hough (Eds.), *Handbook of Industrial and Organizational Psychology*, Vol. 3 (Palo Alto, Calif.: Consulting Psychologists Press, Inc., 1992), pp. 148–197.

7. Arthur G. Jago, "Leadership: Perspectives in Theory and Research," *Management Science*, March 1982, pp. 315–336.

8. John W. Gardner, *On Leadership* (New York: The Free Press, 1990).

9. Jay A. Conger, "Leadership: The Art of Empowering Others," *Academy of Management Executive*, August 1989, pp. 17–24.

10. Jago, "Leadership: Perspectives in Theory and Research."

Focus refers to whether leadership is viewed as a set of traits (trait perspective) or as a set of behaviors (behavioral perspective). Those working from the trait perspective see leadership primarily in terms of relatively stable and enduring individual characteristics that separate leaders from nonleaders. In other words, leaders are believed to have certain innate characteristics that are important for leader effectiveness.[11] On the other hand, the behavioral perspective focuses on observable leader behaviors—the actions of the leader—rather than on inherent, unobservable traits.[12]

The second dimension of this framework is *approach*. The approach dimension is concerned with whether a particular theory or model of leadership takes a universal or a contingency perspective. The universal perspective assumes that there is "one best way" to lead, that effective leadership always conforms to this ideal, and that effective leadership in one situation or organization will also be effective in a different situation or organization. The contingency perspective assumes that the situation in which leadership is exercised is crucial. Because effective leadership depends on the situation, leadership is contingent on situational factors.

When combined, the two dimensions of focus and approach yield the four perspectives on leadership shown in Table 12.1. From a Type I perspective, leadership is a set of traits possessed by the effective leader in any group or organizational context. Early research on leadership, referred to as trait theories, took this perspective. From a Type II viewpoint, leadership is a set of behaviors displayed by the effective leader, again in any group or organizational setting. The Michigan and Ohio State studies, which we describe shortly, were based on this perspective. The Type III perspective assumes that leadership traits vary with the situation. Fiedler's LPC model represents this view. Leadership from a Type IV perspective is a set of behaviors that are contingent on the situation. The path-goal theory and the Vroom-Yetton-Jago model illustrate this perspective.

> Some leadership approaches focus on traits, whereas others focus on behaviors.

> Some leadership approaches take a universal perspective; others use a contingency perspective.

11. Gary A. Yukl, *Leadership in Organizations*, 3rd ed. (Englewood Cliffs, N.J.: Prentice-Hall, 1994).
12. Ibid.

TABLE 12.1
A Framework of Leadership Perspectives

		Approach	
		Universal	**Contingent**
Focus	**Leader Traits**	Type I Trait theories	Type III Fiedler's LPC model
	Leader Behaviors	Type II Michigan studies Ohio State studies	Type IV Path-goal theory Vroom-Yetta-Jago model

SOURCE: Arthur G. Jago, "Leadership Perspectives in Theory and Research," *Management Science*, Vol. 22, 1982, p. 316. Used by permission.

Early Approaches to Leadership

Although leaders and leadership have profoundly influenced the course of human events, careful scientific study began only about a century ago. That early study suggested that the specific abilities needed by leaders varied across situations.[13] Early in this century, however, emphasis on the situation was replaced with studies of the traits, or personal characteristics, of leaders. Later, research shifted again to examine actual leader behaviors.

Trait Approaches to Leadership

The **trait approach** to leadership attempted to identify stable and enduring traits that differentiated effective leaders from nonleaders.

Many early leadership researchers believed that leaders such as Lincoln, Napoleon, Hitler, and Gandhi had some unique set of qualities, or traits, that distinguished them from their peers and were presumed relatively stable and enduring. Following this **trait approach**, these researchers focused on identifying leadership traits, developing techniques for measuring them, and using the techniques to select leaders.[14]

Hundreds of studies guided by this research agenda were conducted during the first several decades of this century. The earliest writers believed that important leadership traits might include intelligence, dominance, self-confidence, energy, activity, and task-relevant knowledge. The results of ensuing studies gave rise to a long list of additional traits. Unfortunately, the list quickly became so long that its practical value was dubious. In addition, the results of many studies were inconsistent. For example, some writers found that effective leaders tended to be taller than ineffective leaders, whereas others came to the opposite conclusion. Some even suggested leadership traits based on body shape, astrological sign, or handwriting characteristics. The trait approach also had a major theoretical problem: it could neither specify nor prove how presumed leadership traits are connected to leadership per se.[15] For these and other reasons, the trait approach was all but abandoned several decades ago.

In recent years, however, there has been renewed interest in the trait approach to leadership. For example, some researchers have sought to introduce a limited set of traits back into the leadership literature. These traits include drive, motivation, honesty and integrity, self-confidence, cognitive ability, knowledge of the business, and charisma (which is discussed in Chapter 13).[16] Although it is too early to really know whether these traits have validity from a leadership perspective, a serious and scientific assessment of appropriate traits may further our understanding of the leadership phenomenon. *Diversity in the Workplace* also shows how some organizations are dealing with demographic traits of both leaders and their subordinates in new types of training programs.

13. David D. Van Fleet and Gary A. Yukl, "A Century of Leadership Research, in D. A. Wren and J. A. Pearce II (Eds.), *Papers Dedicated to the Development of Modern Management*. (Chicago: The Academy of Management, 1986), pp. 12–23.

14. Bass, *Bass and Stogdill's Handbook of Leadership*.

15. See Walter Kiechel III, "Beauty and the Managerial Beast," *Fortune*, November 10, 1986, pp. 201–203, for an interesting discussion of leadership traits.

16. Shelly A. Kirkpatrick and Edwin A. Locke, "Leadership: Do Traits Matter?" *The Academy of Management Executive*, May 1991, pp. 48–60.

DIVERSITY IN THE WORKPLACE

Developing Diverse Leaders

It's no secret that organizations are becoming more and more diverse. And to help cope with this diversity, many firms are providing diversity training to help everyone form new understandings about others in the workplace. Increasingly, this training is aimed at developing new and better leaders for tomorrow's business challenges. Surprisingly, public utilities are at the forefront of diversity leadership training.

For example, the Public Service Company of New Mexico recently implemented an organization-wide diversity training program. Although every manager in the organization participated in diversity training, special additional training modules were created for women and minorities. These modules were designed to help those individuals better understand leadership roles and how they could most effectively play those roles. A similar program has been used at the Public Service Company of Colorado.

California has been even more aggressive in this regard. For example, Southern California Edison set a specific goal of increasing the presence of women and minorities among the ranks of managers. Although these groups were already represented among managers, the organization believed that there were not enough of them. A comprehensive training and development program was implemented specifically for women and minorities with the objective of better preparing them for upper management leadership positions. This program focused on developing new skills among the participants and accelerating their promotions into management positions. So far, the program has been a big success, with the number of women and minorities holding management positions increasing by almost 100 percent since the inception of the new training program in 1990.

Sources: L. Joseph Semien, "Opening the Utility Door for Women and Minorities," *Public Utilities Fortnightly*, July 5, 1990, pp. 29–31; Marlene G. Fine, Fern L. Johnson, and M. Sallyanne Ryan, "Cultural Diversity in the Workplace," *Public Personnel Management*, Fall 1990, pp. 305–319; and Stephenie Overman, "Managing the Diverse Work Force," *HR Magazine*, April 1991, pp. 32–36.

Behavioral Approaches to Leadership

The **behavioral approach** to leadership tried to identify behaviors that differentiated effective leaders from non-leaders.

In the late 1940s, most researchers began to shift away from the trait approach and to look at leadership as an observable process or activity. The goal of the so-called **behavioral approach** was to determine what behaviors are associated with effective leadership. The researchers assumed that the behaviors of effective leaders differed somehow from the behaviors of less-effective leaders and that the behaviors of effective leaders would be the same across all situations. The behavioral approach to the study of leadership included the Michigan studies, the Ohio State studies, and the Leadership Grid.

The **Michigan leadership studies** defined job-centered and employee-centered leadership as opposite ends of a single leadership dimension.

The Michigan Studies The **Michigan leadership studies** include a program of research on leadership behavior conducted at the University of Michigan.[17] The goal of this work was to determine the pattern of leadership behavior that results in effective group performance. From interviews with supervisors and subordinates of

17. Rensis Likert, *New Patterns of Management* (New York: McGraw-Hill, 1961).

high- and low-productivity groups in several organizations, the researchers collected and analyzed descriptions of supervisory behavior to determine how effective supervisors differed from ineffective ones. Two basic forms of leader behavior were identified—job-centered and employee-centered—as shown in the top portion of Figure 12.1.

The leader who exhibits *job-centered leader behavior* pays close attention to the work of subordinates, explains work procedures, and is interested mainly in performance. The leader's main concern is efficient completion of the task. The leader who engages in *employee-centered leader behavior*, meanwhile, attempts to build effective work groups with high performance goals.[18] The leader's main concern is with high performance, but that was to be accomplished by paying attention to the human aspects of the group. These two styles of leader behavior were presumed to be at opposite ends of a single dimension. Thus, Likert and his associates suggested that any given leader could exhibit either job-centered or employee-centered leader behavior, but not both at the same time. Moreover, they suggested that employee-centered behavior was more likely to result in effective group performance than was job-centered leader behavior.

The **Ohio State leadership studies** defined leader consideration and initiating-structure behaviors as independent dimensions of leadership.

The Ohio State Studies The **Ohio State leadership studies** were conducted about the same time as the Michigan studies (in the late 1940s and early 1950s).[19] During this program of research, behavioral scientists at Ohio State University developed a questionnaire, which they administered in both military and industrial settings, to assess subordinates' perceptions of their leaders' behavior.[20] The Ohio State studies identified several forms of leader behavior but tended to focus on the two most important ones: consideration and initiating structure.

18. Likert, *New Patterns of Management*.
19. Edwin Fleishman, E. F. Harris, and H. E. Burtt, *Leadership and Supervision in Industry* (Columbus, Ohio: Bureau of Educational Research, Ohio State University, 1955).
20. Ibid.

FIGURE 12.1

Early Behavioral Approaches to Leadership

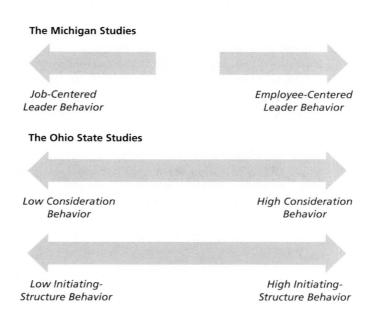

The Michigan Studies

Job-Centered Leader Behavior   Employee-Centered Leader Behavior

The Ohio State Studies

Low Consideration Behavior   High Consideration Behavior

Low Initiating-Structure Behavior   High Initiating-Structure Behavior

At 44, Carol Bartz is chairman and CEO of Autodesk, a California software maker. Effective leaders like Bartz tend to be characterized by their engagement in employee-centered leader behavior and their ability to balance consideration behavior with initiating-structure behavior according to the demands of a situation.

When engaging in *consideration behavior*, the leader is concerned with the subordinates' feelings and respects subordinates' ideas. The leader-subordinate relationship is characterized by mutual trust, respect, and two-way communication. When using *initiating-structure behavior*, on the other hand, the leader clearly defines the leader-subordinate roles so that subordinates know what is expected of them. The leader also establishes channels of communication and determines the methods for accomplishing the group's task.

Unlike the employee-centered and job-centered leader behaviors, consideration and initiating structure were not thought to be located on the same behavioral dimension. Instead, as shown in the bottom portion of Figure 12.1, researchers saw them as independent dimensions of the leader's behavioral repertoire. As a result, a leader could exhibit high initiating structure and low consideration or low initiating structure and high consideration. A leader could also exhibit high or low levels of each behavior simultaneously. For example, a leader may clearly define subordinate's roles and expectations but exhibit little concern for their feelings. Alternatively, she or he may be concerned about subordinate's feelings but fail to define roles and expectations clearly. Finally, the leader may do both or neither. The researchers believed that the most effective leaders would be those who exhibited both forms of behavior simultaneously.

The Ohio State researchers also investigated the stability of leader behaviors over time. They found that a given individual's leadership pattern appeared to

21. See Edwin A. Fleishman, "Twenty Years of Consideration and Structure," in Edwin A. Fleishman and James G. Hunt (Eds.), *Current Developments in the Study of Leadership* (Carbondale, Ill.: Southern Illinois University Press, 1973), pp. 1–40.

change little as long as the situation remained fairly constant.[21] They also looked at the combinations of initiating-structure and consideration behaviors that were related to effectiveness. At first, they believed that leaders who exhibit high levels of both behaviors would be most effective. An early study at International Harvester (now Navistar International Corporation), however, found that employees of supervisors who ranked high on initiating structure were higher performers but also expressed lower levels of satisfaction. Conversely, employees of supervisors who ranked high on consideration had lower performance ratings but also had fewer absences from work.[22] Later research, however, showed that these conclusions were misleading because the studies did not consider all the important variables. In other words, the situational context limits the extent to which consistent and uniform relationships exist between leader behaviors and subordinate responses. As a result, there are no simple answers to what constitutes effective leader behavior because leader effectiveness will vary from one situation to another.

The **Leadership Grid**® evaluates leader behavior along two dimensions, concern for production and concern for people. It suggests that effective leadership styles include high levels of both behaviors.

The Leadership Grid   The **Leadership Grid**® was developed as a framework for portraying types of leadership behavior and their various potential combinations.[23] Developed primarily as a consulting tool to apply the Ohio State findings, the grid consists of two dimensions. The first dimension is *concern for production*. A manager's concern for production is rated along a nine-point scale, where 9 represents high concern and 1 indicates low concern. A manager who has high concern for production is task oriented and focuses on getting results, or accomplishing the mission. The second dimension is *concern for people*, also rated on a nine-point scale, with 9 for high and 1 for low. As might be expected, a manager who has a high concern for people avoids conflict and strives for friendly relations with subordinates.

These two dimensions are combined and integrated to form a 9-by-9 grid. As a result, the grid identifies an array of possible leader behavior combinations. The developers of the grid suggest that the 9,9 position (in the upper right-hand corner of the grid) is the most effective leadership style; that is, a manager who has a high concern for both people and production simultaneously will be the most effective leader. Their prescription, while based on their experiences as consultants to firms such as Gulf Oil (now a part of Chevron) and Exxon and on anecdotal evidence from managers who have used the grid, has been shown to be less than optimal in many situations.[24]

The Michigan, Ohio State, and grid behavioral models attracted considerable attention from managers and behavioral scientists. Unfortunately, later research on each model revealed important weaknesses—for example, they were not always supported by research and they were found to be ineffective in some settings.[25] The behavioral approaches were valuable and important because they identified several fundamental leader behaviors that are still used in most leadership theories

22. Fleishman, Harris, and Burtt, *Leadership and Supervision in Industry*.
23. See Robert R. Blake and Anne Adams McCanse, *Leadership Dilemmas–Grid Solutions* (Houston: Gulf, 1991); and Robert R. Blake and Jane S. Mouton, *The Managerial Grid* (Houston: Gulf, 1964).
24. See P. C. Nystrom, "Managers and the Hi-Hi Leader Myth," *Academy of Management Journal*, 1978, Vol. 21, pp. 325–331; and L. L. Larson, J. G. Hunt, and R. N. Osborn, "The Great Hi-Hi Leader Behavior Myth: A Lesson From Occam's Razor," *Academy of Management Journal*, 1976, Vol. 19, pp. 628–641.
25. See Yukl, *Leadership in Organizations*.

today. Moreover, they also moved leadership research from the narrow trait theory approach. Given the exploratory nature of both the Michigan and Ohio State studies, they have provided researchers with several basic insights into basic leadership processes. In trying to precisely specify a set of leader behaviors effective in all situations, however, the studies overlooked the enormous complexities of individual behavior in organizational settings.

In the end, their most basic shortcoming was that they failed to meet their primary goal—to identify universal leader-behavior/follower-response patterns and relationships. Managers and behavioral scientists thus realized that still different approaches were needed to accommodate the complexities of leadership. Consequently, they began to focus on contingency theories to better explain leadership and its consequences. These theories assume that appropriate leader behavior will vary across settings. Their focus is on how to better understand how different situations call for different forms of leadership. The three major contingency theories are discussed next, beginning with the LPC theory.

The LPC Theory of Leadership

The **LPC theory of leadership** suggests that a leader's effectiveness depends on the situation.

The **LPC theory of leadership,** developed by Fred Fiedler, marked a return of leadership theory to a recognition of the importance of the group and situation on leadership. The LPC theory attempts to explain and reconcile both the leader's personality and the complexities of the situation.[26] (This theory was originally called the "contingency theory of leadership." Because this label has come to have generic connotations, however, new labels are being used to avoid confusion. The letters "LPC" stand for "least preferred coworker," a concept we explain later in this section). The LPC theory contends that a leader's effectiveness depends on the situation and, as a result, some leaders may be effective in one situation or organization but not in another. The theory also explains why this discrepancy may occur and identifies leader-situation matches that should result in effective performance.

Task Versus Relationship Motivation

Fiedler and his associates maintained that leadership effectiveness depends on the match between the leader's personality and the situation. Fiedler devised a special term to describe a leader's basic personality trait: task versus relationship motivation. He also conceptualized the situational context in terms of its favorableness for the leader, ranging from highly favorable to highly unfavorable.

Fiedler identified two forms of leader behavior thought to reflect the leader's personality: task motivation and relationship motivation.

In some respects, task versus relationship motivation resembles the basic concepts identified in the behavioral approaches. *Task motivation* parallels job-centered and initiating-structure leader behavior, and *relationship motivation* is similar to employee-centered and consideration leader behavior. A major difference, however, is that Fiedler viewed task versus relationship motivation as a personality trait that is basically constant for any given person.

26. See Fred E. Fiedler, *A Theory of Leadership Effectiveness* (New York: McGraw-Hill, 1967).

In Fiedler's theory, leader behavior is measured with an instrument called the least preferred coworker scale, or LPC.

The degree of task or relationship motivation present in a given leader is measured by the least preferred coworker scale (LPC).[27] The LPC instructions ask respondents (leaders) to think of all the persons with whom they have worked and to then select their least preferred coworker. Respondents then describe this least preferred coworker by marking a series of sixteen scales anchored at each end by a positive or negative quality or attribute. For example, three of the items Fiedler uses in the LPC are:

Pleasant	8	7	6	5	4	3	2	1	Unpleasant
Inefficient	1	2	3	4	5	6	7	8	Efficient
Unfriendly	1	2	3	4	5	6	7	8	Friendly

The higher numbers on the scales are associated with a positive evaluation of the least preferred coworker. (Note that the higher scale numbers are associated with the more favorable term and that some items reverse both the terms and the scale values. The latter feature forces the respondent to read the scales more carefully and to provide more valid answers.) Respondents who describe their least preferred coworker in consistently positive terms receive a high LPC score, whereas those who use consistently negative terms receive a low LPC score.

Fiedler assumed that a respondent's descriptions say more about the respondent herself or himself than about the least preferred coworker. He believed, for example, that everyone's least preferred coworker is likely to be equally "unpleasant" and that differences in descriptions actually reflect differences in a personality trait among the respondents. Fiedler contended that high-LPC leaders are basically more concerned with interpersonal relations, whereas low-LPC leaders are more concerned with task-relevant problems. Not surprisingly, controversy has always surrounded the LPC scale. Researchers have offered several interpretations of the LPC score, arguing that it may be an index of behavior, personality, or some other unknown factor.[28] Indeed, the LPC measure—and its interpretation—has long been one of the most debated and argued aspects of this theory.

Situational Favorableness

In Fiedler's theory, situational favorableness is determined by leader-member relations, task structure, and leader position power.

Fiedler also identified three factors that determine the favorableness of the situation. In decreasing order of influence, these factors are leader-member relations, task structure, and leader position power.

Leader-member relations refers to the personal relationship that exists between subordinates and their leader. It is based on the extent to which subordinates trust, respect, and have confidence in their leader, and vice versa. A high degree of mutual trust, respect, and confidence obviously indicates good leader-member relations, and a low degree indicates poor leader-member relations.

Task structure has four components. Goal-path multiplicity is the number of ways that the job can be performed. Decision verifiability refers to how well the

27. Fred E. Fiedler, "The Effects of Leadership Training and Experience: A Contingency Model Interpretation," *Administrative Science Quarterly*, Vol. 17, No. 4 (December 1972), p. 455. Used by permission of Administrative Science Quarterly. Copyright © 1972 Cornell University. All rights reserved.
28. See Chester A. Schriesheim, B. D. Bannister, and W. H. Money, "Psychometric Properties of the LPC Scale: An Extension of Rice's Review," *Academy of Management Review*, April 1979, pp. 287–294.

job provides feedback on results. Decision specificity is the degree to which a task has an optimal solution or outcome. Goal clarity refers to how clearly the requirements of the job are stated.

Tasks that have low multiplicity and high verifiability, specificity, and clarity are considered structured. Jobs of this type are routine, easily understood, and unambiguous. As a result, contingency theory presumes structured tasks to be more favorable because the leader need not be closely involved in defining activities and can devote time to other matters. On the other hand, tasks that have high multiplicity and low verifiability, specificity, and clarity are unstructured—nonroutine, ambiguous, complex, and presumed to be more unfavorable because the leader must play a major role in guiding and directing the activities of subordinates.

Leader position power is the power inherent in the leader's role itself. If the leader has the power to assign work, reward and punish employees, and recommend them for promotion, position power is high and favorable. If, however, the leader must have job assignments approved by someone else, does not give rewards and punishment, and has no voice in promotions, position power is low and unfavorable; that is, many decisions are beyond the leader's control.

Leader Motivation and Situational Favorableness   Fiedler and his associates conducted numerous studies examining the relationships among leader motivation, situational favorableness, and group performance. Table 12.2 summarizes the results of these studies.

To begin interpreting the results, let's first examine the situational favorableness dimensions shown in the table. The various combinations of these three dimensions result in eight different situations. These situations, in turn, define a continuum ranging from very favorable to very unfavorable situations from the leader's perspective. The table also identifies the leadership approach that is supposed to achieve high group performance in each of the eight situations. A task-oriented leader is appropriate for very favorable as well as very unfavorable situations. For example, the LPC theory predicts that if leader-member relations are poor, the task is unstructured, and leader position power is low, a task-oriented leader will be effective. It also predicts that a task-oriented leader will be effective if leader-member relations are good, the task is structured, and leader position power is

According to Fiedler, a task-oriented leader is appropriate for a very favorable or a very unfavorable situation. Person-oriented behavior is predicted to work best when the situation is moderately favorable or unfavorable.

TABLE 12.2

The LPC Theory of Leadership

Leader Member Relations	Good				Poor			
Task Structure	Structured		Unstructured		Structured		Unstructured	
Position Power	High	Low	High	Low	High	Low	High	Low
Situational Favorableness	Very favorable				Moderately favorable		Very unfavorable	
Recommended Leader Behavior	Task-oriented behavior				Person-oriented behavior		Task-oriented behavior	

high. Finally, for situations of intermediate favorability, the theory suggests that a person-oriented leader will be most likely to get high group performance.

Leader-Situation Match   What happens if a person-oriented leader faces a very favorable or very unfavorable situation or a task-oriented leader faces a situation of intermediate favorability? Fiedler refers to these leader-situation combinations as mismatches. A basic premise of his theory is that leadership behavior is a personality trait. Thus, the mismatched leader cannot adapt to the situation and achieve effectiveness. Fiedler contends that when a leader's style and the situation do not match, the only available course of action is to change the situation through "job engineering."[29]

Fiedler suggests that if a person-oriented leader ends up in a situation that is very unfavorable, the manager should attempt to improve matters by spending more time with subordinates to improve leader-member relations and by laying down rules and procedures to provide more task structure. Fiedler and his associates have also developed a widely used training program for supervisors on how to assess situational favorability and change the situation to achieve a better match.[30] Weyerhaeuser and Boeing are among the firms that have experimented with Fiedler's training program.

Evaluation and Implications

The validity of Fiedler's LPC theory has been heatedly debated because of the inconsistency of the research results. Apparent shortcomings of the theory are that the LPC measure lacks validity, the theory is not always supported by research, and Fiedler's assumptions about the inflexibility of leader behavior are unrealistic.[31] The theory itself, however, does represent an important contribution because it returned the field to a study of the situation and gave explicit consideration to the organizational context and its role in effective leadership.

The Path-Goal Theory of Leadership

Another important contingency approach to leadership is the path-goal theory. Developed in the 1970s by Martin Evans and Robert House, the path-goal theory focuses on the situation and leader behaviors rather than on fixed traits of the leader.[32] The path-goal theory thus allows for the possibility of adapting leadership to the situation.

29. See Fred E. Fiedler, "Engineering the Job to Fit the Manager," *Harvard Business Review*, September–October 1965, pp. 115–122.
30. See Fred E. Fiedler, Martin M. Chemers, and Linda Mahar, *Improving Leadership Effectiveness: The Leader Match Concept* (New York: Wiley, 1976).
31. See Schriesheim, Bannister, and Money, "Psychometric Properties of the LPC Scale"; George Graen, K. M. Alvares, J. B. Orris, and J. A. Martella, "Contingency Model of Leadership Effectiveness: Antecedent and Evidential Results," *Psychological Bulletin*, October 1970, pp. 285–296; and J. Timothy McMahon, "The Contingency Theory: Logic and Method Revisited," *Personnel Psychology*, Winter 1972, pp. 697–711. See also Lawrence H. Peters, Darrell D. Hartke, and John T. Pohlmann, "Fiedler's Contingency Theory of Leadership: An Application of the Meta-Analysis Procedures of Schmidt and Hunter," *Psychological Bulletin*, April 1985, pp. 274–285.
32. See Martin G. Evans, "The Effects of Supervisory Behavior on the Path-Goal Relationship," *Organizational Behavior and Human Performance*, May 1970, pp. 277–298; Robert J. House, "A Path-Goal Theory of Leadership Effectiveness," *Administrative Science Quarterly*, September 1971, pp. 321–339; and Robert J. House and Terence R. Mitchell, "Path-Goal Theory of Leadership," *Journal of Contemporary Business*, Autumn 1974, pp. 81–98.

At a Microsoft Corp. office, an employee is given instructions by her leader. One way in which a leader might influence an employee's performance, according to the path-goal theory, is by clarifying what path of actions, if performed effectively, will lead him or her toward his or her desired goals.

Basic Premises

The path-goal theory has its roots in the expectancy theory of motivation discussed in Chapter 5. Recall that expectancy theory says that a person's attitudes and behaviors can be predicted from two interrelated factors: the degree to which the person believes job performance will lead to various outcomes (expectancy) and the value of those outcomes (valences) to the individual. The **path-goal theory of leadership** argues that subordinates are motivated by their leader to the extent that the behaviors of that leader influence their expectancies. In other words, the leader affects subordinates' performance by clarifying the behaviors (paths) that will lead to desired rewards (goals). Ideally, of course, getting a reward in an organization depends on effective performance. Path-goal theory also suggests that a leader may behave in different ways in different situations.

The **path-goal theory of leadership** suggests that effective leaders clarify the paths (behaviors) that will lead to desired rewards (goals).

The path-goal theory proposes four kinds of leader behavior: directive, supportive, participative, and achievement-oriented.

Leader Behaviors   As Figure 12.2 shows, path-goal theory identifies four kinds of leader behavior: directive, supportive, participative, and achievement-oriented. With *directive leadership*, the leader lets subordinates know what is expected of them, gives specific guidance as to how to accomplish tasks, schedules work to be done, and maintains definitive standards of performance for subordinates. A leader exhibiting *supportive leadership* is friendly and shows concern for subordinates' status, well-being, and needs. With *participative leadership*, the leader consults with subordinates about issues and takes their suggestions into account before making a decision. Finally, *achievement-oriented leadership* involves setting challenging goals, expecting subordinates to perform at their highest level, and showing strong confidence that subordinates will put forth effort and accomplish the goals.[33] Unlike Fiedler's contingency theory, path-goal theory assumes that leaders can change their

33. See House and Mitchell, "Path-Goal Theory of Leadership."

FIGURE 12.2

The Path-Goal Theory
of Leadership

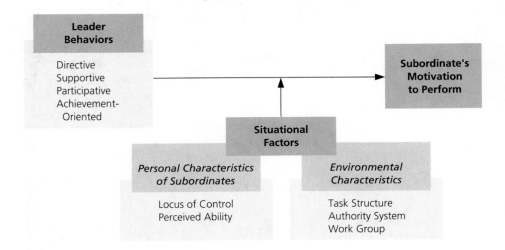

behavior and exhibit any or all of these leadership styles. The theory also predicts that the appropriate combination of leadership styles depends on situational factors.

Situational Factors   The path-goal theory proposes two types of situational factors that influence how leader behavior relates to subordinate satisfaction: the personal characteristics of the subordinates and the characteristics of the environment (see Figure 12.2). Two important personal characteristics of subordinates are locus of control and perceived ability. Locus of control, discussed in Chapter 3, refers to the extent to which individuals believe that what happens to them results from their own behavior or from external causes. Research indicates that individuals who attribute outcomes to their own behavior may be more satisfied with a participative leader (because they believe that their own efforts can make a difference), whereas individuals who attribute outcomes to external causes may respond more favorably to a directive leader (because they think that their own actions are of little consequence).[34] Perceived ability refers to how people view their ability with respect to the task. Employees who rate their own ability relatively high are less likely to feel a need for directive leadership (because they think they know how to do the job), whereas those who perceive their own ability to be relatively low may prefer directive leadership (because they think they need someone to show them how to do the job).

Important environmental characteristics are task structure, the formal authority system, and the primary work group. The path-goal theory proposes that leader behavior will motivate subordinates if it helps them cope with environmental uncertainty created by those factors. In some cases, however, certain forms of leadership will be redundant, decreasing subordinate satisfaction. For example, when task structure is high, directive leadership is less necessary and therefore less effective; similarly, if the work group gives the individual plenty of social support, a supportive leader will not be especially attractive. Thus, the extent to which leader behavior matches the people and environment in the situation is presumed to influence subordinates' motivation to perform.

The path-goal theory suggests that appropriate leader behavior depends on several personal characteristics of subordinates and characteristics of the environment.

Important personal characteristics included in path-goal theory are locus of control and perceived ability.

Important environmental characteristics included in path-goal theory are task structure, the formal authority system, and the primary work group.

34. See Terence R. Mitchell, "Motivation and Participation: An Integration," *Academy of Management Journal*, June 1973, pp. 160–179.

Evaluation and Implications

The path-goal theory was designed to provide a general framework for understanding how leader behavior and situational factors influence subordinate attitudes and behaviors. But the intention of the path-goal theorists was to stimulate research on the theory's major propositions, not to offer definitive answers. Researchers hoped that a more fully developed, formal theory of leadership would emerge from continued study. Further work actually has supported the theory's major predictions, but it has not validated the entire model.[35] Moreover, many of the theory's predictions remain overly general and have not been fully refined and tested.

The Vroom-Yetton-Jago Model of Leadership

The **Vroom-Yetton-Jago** model of leadership attempts to prescribe how much participation subordinates should be allowed in making decisions.

The third major contemporary theory of leadership is the **Vroom-Yetton-Jago model**, first proposed by Victor Vroom and Philip Yetton and later revised and expanded by Vroom and Arthur Jago.[36] Like the path-goal theory, the model attempts to prescribe a leadership style appropriate to a given situation. It also assumes that the same leader may display different leadership styles. But the Vroom-Yetton-Jago model concerns itself with only a single aspect of leader behavior: subordinate participation in decision making. The goals of the model are to protect the quality of the decision while ensuring acceptance of the decision by subordinates.

Basic Premises

In the Vroom-Yetton-Jago model, the leader assesses critical problem attributes and then adopts one of five basic levels of participation.

The Vroom-Yetton-Jago model assumes that the degree to which subordinates should be encouraged to participate in decision making depends on the characteristics of the situation. In other words, no one decision-making process is best for all situations. After evaluating each of the problem attributes (characteristics of the problem or decision), the leader determines an appropriate decision style that specifies the amount of subordinate participation.

Vroom and Jago's expansion of the original model requires the use of a decision tree.[37] The manager assesses the situation in terms of several variables. During the assessment, the manager provides yes or no answers to a series of questions. These answers guide the manager through the paths of the decision tree to a recommended course of action. There are actually four trees: two for group-level decisions and two for individual-level decisions. One of each is for use when time is of the utmost importance and the other for when time is less important and the manager wants instead to develop the subordinates' decision-making abilities.

The decision tree for time-driven group problems is shown in Figure 12.3. The problem attributes (situational variables) are arranged along the top of the decision

35. See Yukl, *Leadership in Organizations*.
36. See Victor H. Vroom and Philip H. Yetton, *Leadership and Decision Making* (Pittsburgh: University of Pittsburgh Press, 1973); and Victor H. Vroom and Arthur G. Jago, *The New Leadership* (Englewood Cliffs, N.J.: Prentice-Hall, 1988).
37. Vroom and Jago, *The New Leadership*.

tree and, as just noted, are expressed as questions. To use the model, the decision maker starts at the left-hand side of the diagram and asks the first question. For instance, the manager first decides whether the problem involves a quality requirement—that is, are there quality differences in the alternatives, and do they matter? The answer determines the path to the second node on the decision tree, and the

FIGURE 12.3

The Vroom-Yetton-Jago Model (Time-Driven Group Problems)

QR	*Quality Requirement:*	How important is the technical quality of this decision?
CR	*Commitment Requirement:*	How important is subordinate commitment to the decision?
LI	*Leader's Information:*	Do you have sufficient information to make a high-quality decision?
ST	*Problem Structure:*	Is the problem well structured?
CP	*Commitment Probability:*	If you were to make the decision by yourself, is it reasonably certain that your subordinate(s) would be committed to the decision?
GC	*Goal Congruence:*	Do subordinates share the organizational goals to be attained in solving this problem?
CO	*Subordinate Conflict:*	Is conflict among subordinates over preferred solutions likely?
SI	*Subordinate Information:*	Do subordinates have sufficient information to make a high-quality decision?

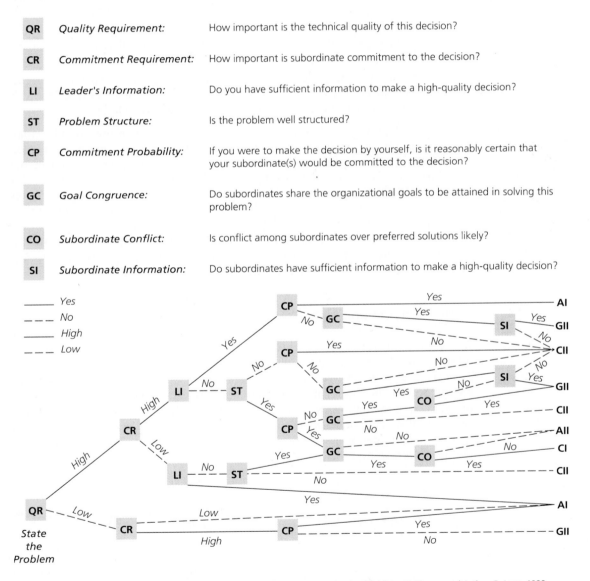

SOURCE: Reprinted from *The New Leadership: Managing Participation in Organizations* by Victor H. Vroom and Arthur G. Jago, 1988, Englewood Cliffs, N.J.: Prentice-Hall. Copyright 1987 by V. H. Vroom and A. G. Jago. Used with permission of the authors.

manager asks the question pertaining to that attribute. This process continues until the manager reaches a terminal node. In this way, the manager identifies an effective decision-making style for the situation.

The various decision styles reflected at the ends of the tree branches represent different levels of subordinate participation, which the manager should attempt to adopt in a given situation. The five styles are defined as follows:

AI: The manager makes the decision alone.

AII: The manager asks for information from subordinates but makes the decision alone. Subordinates may or may not be informed about the situation.

CI: The manager shares the situation with individual subordinates and asks for information and evaluation. Subordinates do not meet as a group, and the manager alone makes the decision.

CII: The manager and subordinates meet as a group to discuss the situation, but the manager makes the decision.

GII: The manager and subordinates meet as a group to discuss the situation, and the group makes the decision. (The original model included a GI style, but it was dropped because it was indistinguishable from this GII style.)[38]

The complete Vroom-Yetton-Jago model today is even more complex than Vroom and Yetton's earlier version. The other three trees, for example, include still different situational attributes and decision styles. Moreover, several of the questions now allow more than a simple yes or no answer. To compensate for this difficulty, Vroom and Jago have developed computer software to help managers assess a particular situation accurately and quickly and then make an appropriate decision regarding employee participation.[39] Many firms, including Halliburton Company, Litton Industries, and Borland International, have provided their managers with training in how to use the Vroom-Yetton-Jago model. *Developing Management Skills* provides some practice for you in using the model.

Evaluation and Implications

Because the expanded Vroom-Yetton-Jago model is relatively new, it has not been fully scientifically tested. The original model attracted a great deal of attention, however, and generally was supported by research.[40] For example, some research has supported the idea that individuals who make decisions consistent with the predictions of the model are more effective than those who make decisions inconsistent with it. The model therefore appears to be a tool that managers can apply with some confidence in deciding how much subordinates should participate in the decision-making process.

---

38. Reprinted from *Leadership and Decision Making*, by Victor H. Vroom and Philip W. Yetton, by permission of the University of Pittsburgh Press. ©1973 by University of Pittsburgh Press.

39. Vroom and Jago, *The New Leadership*.

40. See Madeline E. Heilman, Harvey A. Hornstein, Jack H. Cage, and Judith K. Herschlag, "Reactions to Prescribed Leader Behavior as a Function of Role Perspective: The Case of the Vroom-Yetton Model," *Journal of Applied Psychology*, February 1984, pp. 50–60; and R. H. George Field, "A Test of the Vroom-Yetton Normative Model of Leadership," *Journal of Applied Psychology*, February 1982, pp. 523–532.

Applying the Vroom-Yetton-Jago Model

You are the southwestern United States branch manager of an international manufacturing and sales organization. The firm's management team is looking for ways to increase efficiency. As one part of this effort, the company recently installed an integrated computer network linking sales representatives, customer service employees, and other sales support staff. Sales were supposed to increase and sales expenses to drop as a result.

But exactly the opposite has occurred: sales have dropped a bit, and expenses are up. You have personally inspected the new system and believe that the hardware is fine. You believe that the software linking the various computers, however, is less than ideal.

The subordinates you have quizzed about the system, on the other hand, think that the entire system is fine. They attribute the problems to a number of factors, including inadequate training in how to use the system, a lack of incentives for using it, and generally poor morale. Whatever the reasons given, each subordinate questioned exhibited strong feelings about the computer network.

Your boss has just called you and expressed concern about the problems. He has indicated that he has confidence in your ability to solve the problem and will leave it in your hands. However, he wants a report on how you plan to proceed within one week.

First, think of how much participation you would normally be inclined to allow your subordinates in making this decision. Next, apply the Vroom-Yetton-Jago model to the problem and see what it suggests regarding the optimal level of participation. Compare your normal approach to the recommended solution.

Other Contemporary Approaches to Leadership

Because leadership is such an important area, managers and researchers continue to study it. As a result new ideas, theories, and perspectives are continuously being developed. Two of the more well known ones are the leader-member exchange model and the life cycle theory.

The Leader-Member Exchange Model

The **leader-member exchange (LMX) model** of leadership stresses that leaders develop unique working relationships with each of their subordinates.

The **leader-member exchange (LMX) model** of leadership, conceived by George Graen and Fred Dansereau, stresses the importance of variable relationships between supervisors and each of their subordinates.[41] Each superior-subordinate pair is referred to as a *vertical dyad*. The model differs from earlier approaches in that it focuses on the differential relationship leaders often establish with different subordinates. Figure 12.4 shows the basic concepts of the leader-member exchange theory.

41. George Graen and J. F. Cashman, "A Role-Making Model of Leadership in Formal Organizations: A Developmental Approach," in J. G. Hunt and L. L. Larson (Eds.), *Leadership Frontiers* (Kent, Ohio: Kent State University Press, 1975), pp. 143–165; and Fred Dansereau, George Graen, and W. J. Haga, "A Vertical Dyad Linkage Approach to Leadership within Formal Organizations: A Longitudinal Investigation of the Role-Making Process," *Organizational Behavior and Human Performance*, Vol. 15, 1975, pp. 46–78.

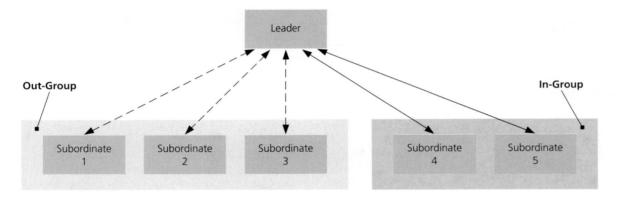

FIGURE 12.4

The Leader-Member Exchange (LMX)

The model suggests that supervisors establish a special relationship with a small number of trusted subordinates referred to as the in-group. The in-group usually receives special duties requiring responsibility and autonomy and may also receive special privileges. Subordinates who are not a part of this group are called the out-group, and they receive less of the supervisor's time and attention. Note in the figure that the leader has a dyadic, or one-to-one, relationship with each of the five subordinates.

Early in his or her interaction with a given subordinate, the supervisor initiates either an in-group or out-group relationship. How a leader selects members of the in-group is not clear, but the decision may be based on personal compatibility and subordinates' competence. Research has confirmed the existence of in-groups and out-groups. In addition, studies generally have found the in-group members to have a higher level of performance and satisfaction than out-group members.[42]

The Life Cycle Theory

The **life cycle theory** of leadership identifies different combinations of leadership presumed to work best with different levels of organizational maturity on the part of followers.

Another popular perspective among practicing managers is the **life cycle theory**. Like the grid discussed earlier, the life cycle theory was developed as a consulting tool. This theory is based on the notion that appropriate leader behavior depends on the "maturity" of the leader's followers.[43] In this instance, maturity refers to the subordinate's degree of motivation, competence, experience, and interest in accepting responsibility. Figure 12.5 shows the basic life cycle model.

The model suggests that as follower maturity increases from low to high, the leader needs to move gradually from much task-oriented behavior to little task-

42. See Robert P. Vecchio and Bruce C. Gobdel, "The Vertical-Dyad Linkage Model of Leadership: Problems and Prospects," *Organizational Behavior and Human Performance*, Vol. 34, 1984, pp. 5–20. See also Dennis Duchon, Stephen G. Green, and Thomas D. Taber, "Vertical Dyad Linkage: A Longitudinal Assessment of Antecedents, Measures, and Consequences," *Journal of Applied Psychology*, Vol. 71, 1986, pp. 56–60; and Kenneth J. Dunegan, Dennis Duchon, and Mary Uhl-Bien, "Examining the Link Between Leader-Member Exchange and Subordinate Performance: The Role of Task Analyzability and Variety as Moderators," *Academy of Management Journal*, March 1992, pp. 59–76.

43. Paul Hersey and Kenneth H. Blanchard, *Management of Organizational Behavior: Utilizing Human Resources*, 3rd ed. (Englewood Cliffs, N.J.: Prentice-Hall, 1977).

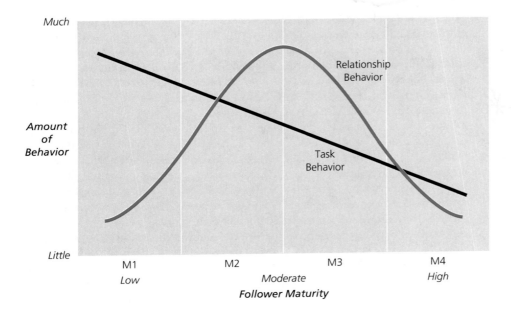

Much

Amount
of
Behavior

Little

Relationship
Behavior

Task
Behavior

| M1 | M2 | M3 | M4 |
| Low | Moderate | | High |

Follower Maturity

SOURCE: P. Hersey and K. Blanchard, *Management of Organizational Behavior: Utilizing Human Resources 3/e.* ©
1977, p. 165. Adapted by permission of Prentice-Hall, Inc., Englewood Cliffs, N.J.

FIGURE 12.5

**The Life Cycle Theory
of Leadership**

oriented behavior. At the same time, person-oriented behavior (labeled relationship behavior in the figure) should start at little, rise at a moderate rate, and then
decline again. The life cycle theory has much appeal for managers. It has been
shown, however, to be logically inconsistent and has not been been supported by
careful, scientific research. Thus, although it may look good, managers should be
cautious about adopting it too mechanistically.[44]

Summary of Key Points

- Leadership is both a process and a property. Leadership as a process is the use of
  noncoercive influence to direct and coordinate the activities of group members
  toward goal accomplishment. As a property, leadership is the set of characteristics attributed to those who are perceived to use such influence successfully.
  Leadership theories are concerned with either leader traits or leader behaviors
  and approach the concept from either a universal or a contingency perspective.
- Early leadership research attempted primarily to identify important traits of leaders.
  The weaknesses of the trait approach prompted researchers to examine leader
  behaviors to identify universally applicable forms of leadership behavior. However,
  some behavioral scientists are developing a renewed interest in leadership traits.

44. See Claude L. Graeff, "The Situation Leadership Theory: A Critical Review," *Academy of Management Review,*
1983, Vol. 8, pp. 285–296.

- The Michigan studies defined two kinds of leader behavior: job-centered and employee-centered. These behaviors were viewed as points on a single continuum. At about the same time, studies at Ohio State University recognized consideration and initiating-structure behaviors as the most important of several leader behaviors. These behaviors were viewed as separate dimensions. The Leadership Grid® suggested that the most effective leaders are those who have a high concern for both people and production.

- Newer contingency theories of leadership attempt to identify appropriate leadership styles on the basis of the situation. Fiedler's LPC theory stated that leadership effectiveness depends on a match between the leader's style (viewed as a trait of the leader) and the favorableness of the situation. Situation favorableness, in turn, is determined by leader-member relations, task structure, and leader position power. Leader behavior is presumed to reflect a constant personality trait and therefore cannot easily be changed.

- The path-goal theory focuses on appropriate leader behavior for various situations. The path-goal theory suggests that directive, supportive, participative, or achievement-oriented leader behavior may be appropriate depending on the personal characteristics of subordinates and the characteristics of the environment. Unlike the LPC theory, this view presumes that leaders can alter their behavior to best fit the situation.

- The Vroom-Yetton-Jago model suggests appropriate decision-making styles based on situation characteristics. The Vroom-Yetton-Jago theory essentially is a model for deciding how much subordinates should participate in the decision-making process. The model is designed to protect the quality of the decision and ensure decision acceptance by subordinates. Managers ask questions about their situation and follow a series of paths through a decision tree that subsequently prescribes for them how much they should involve subordinates in a particular decision.

- Two recent perspectives that are not rooted in traditional leadership theories are the leader-member exchange (LMX) model and the life cycle theory. The leader-member exchange model focuses on specific relationships between a leader and individual subordinates. The life cycle theory acknowledges that leader behavior toward a particular group needs to change over time as the group becomes more mature.

Discussion Questions

1. How would you define leadership? Compare and contrast your definition with the one given in this chapter.
2. Cite examples of managers who are not leaders and leaders who are not managers. What makes them one and not the other? Also, cite examples of both formal and informal leaders.
3. What traits do you think characterize successful leaders? Do you think that the trait approach has validity?
4. What other forms of leader behavior besides those cited in the chapter can you identify?
5. Critique Fiedler's LPC theory. Are other elements of the situation important? Do you think Fiedler's assertion about the inflexibility of leader behavior makes sense? Why or why not?

6. Do you agree or disagree with Fiedler's assertion that leadership motivation is basically a personality trait? Why?

7. Compare and contrast the LPC and path-goal theories of leadership. What are the strengths and weaknesses of each?

8. Of the three major leadership theories—the LPC theory, the path-goal theory, and the Vroom-Yetton-Jago model—which is the most comprehensive? Which is the narrowest? Which has the most practical value?

9. How realistic do you think it is for managers to attempt to use the Vroom-Yetton-Jago model as prescribed? Explain.

10. Which of the two contemporary theories of leadership do you believe holds the most promise? Why?

11. Could either of the two contemporary perspectives be integrated with any of the three major theories of leadership? If so, how?

EXPERIENTIAL EXERCISE

Purpose   This exercise will help you better understand the behaviors of successful and unsuccessful leaders.

Format   You will be asked to identify contemporary examples of successful and unsuccessful leaders and then to describe how these leaders differ.

Procedure
1. In small groups, identify recent examples of individuals in important positions who could be thought of as leaders. To begin with, you might go to the library and find brief biographies, case studies, or articles about various leaders. Sources might include periodicals such as *Fortune, Business Week,* and *Forbes;* biographies of famous and infamous personalities such as Vince Lombardi, Adolf Hitler, and Abraham Lincoln; or popular-press books about contemporary leaders like General Norman Schwarzkopf or Lee Iacocca. Or, watch the national or local news for reports on political, business, or sports leaders.

2. Choose two leaders who most people would consider very successful and two who would be deemed unsuccessful.

3. Identify similarities and differences between the two successful leaders and between the two unsuccessful leaders.

4. Identify similarities and differences between the two successful and the two unsuccessful leaders.

5. Relate the successes and failures to at least one theory or perspective discussed in the chapter.

6. Select one group member to report your findings to the rest of the class.

Follow-up Questions

1. What role does luck play in leadership?

2. Are there factors about the leaders you researched that might have predicted their success or failure before they achieved leadership roles?

3. What are some criteria of successful leadership?

The U.S. banking industry has been beset by one crisis after another. International competition, deregulation, and scandal have combined to bring some of the largest and most prosperous banks in the United States to their knees, and many of them have disappeared altogether. New York–based Citicorp is among the survivors. Today the firm ranks as the largest bank corporation in the United States and one of the largest in the world.

But Citicorp did hit some rough spots along the way. In the late 1980s, for example, the bank underestimated problems in its loan portfolios and came perilously close to falling below FDIC guidelines for financial solvency. And critics believe that even after executives recognized this problem they were too slow to deal with it. But recognize it they eventually did and have since taken major steps to turn things around.

In contrast to many of its domestic competitors, Citicorp has maintained reasonable financial health by concentrating on its foreign operations. While many U.S. banks were fighting each other for market share, Citicorp focused on international banking, establishing branches and building networks in almost 100 countries. While the United States remains Citicorp's most important market, the firm is also strong throughout Europe and Asia.

One factor in Citicorp's success has been the continuity in leadership provided by John Reed. Reed became CEO of Citicorp in 1984 at the relatively young age of forty-four, and now, more than ten years later, is still at the helm. Reed's presence has provided a calming and stabilizing influence throughout the firm, and he has demonstrated a clear ability to change his leadership approach as the bank and its environment have changed.

During the 1980s, Reed used primarily a hands-off approach to running Citicorp. His predecessor, Walter Wriston, was a legend in U.S. banking. Under his leadership, for example, Citicorp invented the certificate of deposit, became the first large-scale bank holding corporation, and was among the first to install automatic teller machines. When Reed took over, he knew better than to shake things up. Instead, he allowed things to go on as they had been and assumed the role of a laissez-faire overseer.

Citicorp's on-going strategy when Reed took over was focused on revenue growth. Thus, the firm concentrated on entering new markets, attracting new customers, and increasing income. Unfortunately, firms that use this strategy are sometimes prone to ignoring costs. Simply stated, if next month's income increases enough, this month's expenses don't seem to matter. But when next month's income becomes stable—or begins to drop—dramatic jumps in this month's expenses spell trouble. And this is exactly what happened to Citicorp in the late 1980s.

When the international economy turned sour, Citicorp's revenue growth began to level off. But poorly performing loan portfolios, bad debts on real estate, and high operating costs continued to eat away at the firm's resources. As Citicorp began to attract the attention of the FDIC in 1990, Reed knew that he needed to take charge and make changes.

Over the next few years, he implemented a far-ranging program of cost cutting and expense controls. For example, executive expense accounts were cut, and the firm began to systematically study areas in operations that were inefficient, where cost savings could be achieved, or both. Reed also brought in some new executives to help turn things around. These executives replaced others who could not, in Reed's opinion, change their approach to doing business.

At the same time, he decided to flatten Citicorp's structure by eliminating several layers of management. He reasoned that, in addition to saving money, this step would make Citicorp more responsive to its competitors and to its environment and eliminate much of the bureaucracy that had characterized the firm during simpler and more stable times. But he also more clearly defined a set of decisions for which he would accept personal responsibility. To date, Reed's efforts appear to be paying off. Citicorp seems to have its loan problems under control, is effectively managing its costs, and has been given new operating freedom by the FDIC. And Reed has emerged with a new image—that of a leader capable of making hard choices and getting the job done.

Case Questions

1. Characterize John Reed's leadership style.

2. Relate Reed's approach to leadership to the various theories, models, and concepts discussed in this chapter.
3. Go to the library and find out how Citicorp is doing today.

SOURCES: Carol J. Loomis, "The Reed That Citicorp Leans On," *Fortune*, July 12, 1993, pp. 90–93; "Citicorp Hires Ex-Kodak Aide for Senior Post," *Wall Street Journal*, July 20, 1993, pp. A3, A6; and "When Machines Screw Up," *Forbes*, June 7, 1993, pp. 110–111.

CASE 12.2   Right Boss, Wrong Company

Betty Kesmer was continuously on top of things. In school, she had always been at the top of her class. When she went to work for her uncle's shoe business, Fancy Footwear Inc., she had been singled out as the most productive employee and the one with the best attendance. The company was so impressed with her that it sent her to get an M.B.A. to groom her for a top management position. In school again, and with three years of practical experience to draw on, Kesmer had gobbled up every idea put in front of her, relating many of them to her work at Fancy Footwear. When Kesmer graduated at the top of her class, she returned to Fancy Footwear. To no one's surprise, when the head of the company's largest division took advantage of the firm's early retirement plan, Kesmer was given his position.

Kesmer knew the pitfalls of being suddenly catapulted to a leadership position, and she was determined to avoid them. In business school, she had read cases about family businesses that fell apart when a young family member took over with an iron fist, barking out orders, cutting personnel, and destroying morale. Kesmer knew a lot about participative management, and she was not going to be labeled an arrogant know-it-all.

Kesmer's predecessor, Max Worthy, had run the division from an office at the top of the building, far above the factory floor. Two or three times a day, Worthy would summon a messenger or a secretary from the offices on the second floor and send a memo out to one or another group of workers. But as Kesmer saw it, Worthy was mostly an absentee autocrat, making all the decisions from above and spending most of his time at extended lunches with his friends from the Elks Club.

Kesmer's first move was to change all that. She set up her office on the second floor. From her always-open doorway she could see down onto the factory floor, and as she sat behind her desk she could spot anyone walking by in the hall. She never ate lunch herself but spent the time from 11 to 2 down on the floor, walking around, talking, and organizing groups. The workers, many of whom had twenty years of seniority at the plant, seemed surprised by this new policy and reluctant to volunteer for any groups. But in fairly short order, Kesmer established a worker productivity group, a "Suggestion of the Week" committee, an environmental group, a worker award group, and a management relations group. Each group held two meetings a week, one without and one with Kesmer. She encouraged each group to set up goals in its particular focus area and develop plans for reaching those goals. She promised any support that was within her power to give.

The group work was agonizingly slow at first. But Kesmer had been well trained as a facilitator, and she soon took on that role in their meetings, writing down ideas on a big board, organizing them, and later communicating them in notices to other employees. She got everyone to call her "Betty" and set herself the task of learning all their names. By the end of the first month, Fancy Footwear was stirred up.

But as it turned out, that was the last thing most employees wanted. The truth finally hit Kesmer when the entire management relations committee resigned at the start of their fourth meeting. "I'm sorry, Ms. Kesmer," one of them said. "We're good at making shoes, but not at this management stuff. A lot of us are heading toward retirement. We don't want to be supervisors."

Astonished, Kesmer went to talk to the workers with whom she believed she had built good relations. Yes, they reluctantly told her, all these changes did make them uneasy. They liked her, and they didn't want to complain. But given the choice, they would rather go back to the way Mr. Worthy had run things. They never saw Mr. Worthy much, but he never got in their hair. He did his work, whatever that was, and they did theirs. "After you've been in a place doing one thing for so long," one worker concluded, "the last thing you want to do is learn a new way of doing it."

Case Questions

1. What factors should have alerted Kesmer to the problems that eventually came up at Fancy Footwear?
2. Could Kesmer have instituted her changes without eliciting a negative reaction from the workers? If so, how?

CHAPTER 13

Leadership and Influence Processes

OBJECTIVES

After studying this chapter, you should be able to:

Discuss influence and relate it to leadership in organizations.

Identify and describe two influence-based approaches
to leadership.

Describe the nature of power, identify and discuss various
types of power, and explain how to use different kinds
of power.

Discuss politics and political behavior and their role
in organizations.

Describe impression management and how people use it to
influence others.

Identify and discuss leadership substitutes in organizations.

The fresh perspective of a new employee can be invaluable to a firm in need of restructuring. However, it is important that new employees be able to work within the existing corporate culture. The preservation of harmony in the workplace and the satisfaction of existing employees must at times take precedence over the introduction of radical ideas.

As part of CEO John Reed's efforts to restore Citicorp to financial health (see Case 12.1), he has brought in several top executives from other firms. One of the most publicized managers to join Reed at Citicorp is Christopher J. Steffen. Steffen is a well-traveled executive with a reputation for hard-nosed cost-cutting and a penchant for attracting the spotlight.

Steffen's career began at Hyatt, where he developed a strong reputation for his financial skills. He left Hyatt in 1980 and took a position at Allied Tube & Conduit. Allied's former CEO says that he and Steffen never got along and that Steffen left after only eleven weeks. He also charges that Steffen made major organizational changes without consulting the CEO and introduced ideas at board meetings that he had not discussed with the CEO in advance.

Steffen's next stop was Chrysler, where he was given a lot of credit for the firm's effective cost-cutting program. He had a difficult relationship with Chrysler's chief financial officer, Steve Miller, but because the firm's culture tolerated conflict, the two managed to work together with minimal harm to the company. Still, after several years he left when it became apparent that he was not going to be promoted.

Steffen then took a top executive position with Honeywell while the firm was in the midst of a major restructuring. He quickly helped crystallize the firm's plans, sketching out several major steps one night on two restaurant napkins. When he later had the napkins framed and hung in his office, it stirred resentment among his colleagues who thought that he was taking too much credit for work they had already done.

After another failed bid for promotion, Steffen left Honeywell in 1993 and took a high-profile job at Eastman Kodak, yet another firm in the midst of restructuring. And like at Honeywell, he also quickly angered some Kodak executives who thought that he was taking too much credit for plans they had formulated before he ever arrived. This time, though, Steffen's tenure was short-lived. He shocked the firm by resigning after only eleven (again) weeks. Steffen charged that managers at Kodak were not serious about changing the way they did business and that his approach would work better elsewhere.

Even though Steffen maintained that he had not had any conversations with Reed about a position at Citicorp before submitting his resignation to Kodak, he was nevertheless hired so quickly that it made some observers skeptical. Because of the frequency with which he has changed jobs and the trail of complaints about his taking credit for other people's ideas, some managers at Citicorp greeted his hiring with a marked lack of enthusiasm. But Reed believes that he can make an important contribution to Citicorp's continued effectiveness.[1]

1. "Is Chris Steffen Too Tough for His Own Good?" *Business Week*, June 7, 1993, pp. 80–82; and Carol J. Loomis, "The Reed That Citicorp Leans On," *Fortune*, July 12, 1993, pp. 90–93.

■■■■ Christopher Steffen has clearly held a number of leadership positions in a variety of organizations. But is he himself truly a leader? He also has had vast amounts of power and has used that power for a variety of purposes. Although some people might argue that his efforts have generally helped the organization where he was working, others might claim that his uses of power were excessive and did more harm than good. Like most managers in any organization, Steffen also quite likely has engaged in political behavior to further his own aims. Regardless of attributions made about his goals or behaviors, Steffen has consistently influenced others around him. As we see, leadership, influence, and power are usually intertwined.

This chapter explores a variety of leadership concepts from an influence perspective. We first revisit the role of influence in leadership. We then introduce and discuss two contemporary influence-based perspectives on leadership—transformational leadership and charismatic leadership. Next we describe power and political behavior in organizations, influence-based phenomenon which may or may not directly involve leadership. Impression management, a related but distinct concept, is then introduced and explored. Finally, we discuss how substitutes for leadership can function in organizations.

Leadership as Influence

Recall that in Chapter 12 we defined leadership (from a process perspective) as the use of noncoercive influence to direct and coordinate the activities of group members toward goal accomplishment. We then described a number of leadership models and theories based variously on leadership traits, behaviors, and contingencies. Unfortunately, most of these models and theories essentially ignore the influence component of leadership. That is, they tend to focus on the characteristics of the leader (traits, behaviors, or both) and the responses from followers (satisfaction, performance, or both, for instance) with little regard for how influence is actually exercised by the leader in an effort to bring about the desired responses from followers.

But influence should actually be seen as the cornerstone of the process. Regardless of the leader's traits or behaviors, leadership only matters if influence actually occurs. That is, how effectively a person affects the behavior of others through influence ultimately determines whether she or he is really a leader. No one can truly be a leader without the ability to influence others. And if someone does have the ability to influence others, he or she has the clear potential to become a leader.[2]

Influence is the ability to affect the perceptions, attitudes, or behaviors of others.

Influence can be thought of as the ability to affect the perceptions, attitudes, or behaviors of others.[3] If a person can make another person recognize that her working conditions are more hazardous than she currently believes them to be (change in perceptions), influence has occurred. Likewise, if an individual can convince someone else that the organization is a much better place to work than he cur-

---

2. See Bernard Keys and Thomas Case, "How to Become an Influential Manager," *The Academy of Management Executive*, November 1990, pp. 38–51.
3. Robert W. Allen and Lyman W. Porter (Eds.), *Organizational Influence Processes* (Glenview, Ill.: Scott, Foresman, 1983).

rently believes it to be (change in attitude), influence has occurred. And if some-one can get someone else to work harder or to file a grievance against the boss (change in behavior), influence has occurred. Note, too, that influence can be enacted in ways that are beneficial or harmful.[4] Someone can be influenced into helping clean up a city park on the weekend as part of a community service pro-gram, for example, or influenced to use or sell drugs.

Influence-based Approaches to Leadership

In recent years influence has become a meaningful component of many leadership models and concepts. The two contemporary approaches to leadership discussed in this section, for example, are each tied directly or indirectly to influence. These approaches are transformational leadership and charismatic leadership.

Transformational Leadership

Transformational leadership, a relative newcomer to the leadership literature, focuses on the basic distinction between leading for change and leading for stabil-ity.[5] According to this viewpoint, much of what a leader does occurs in terms of normal and routine work-related transactions—assigning work, evaluating perfor-mance, making decisions, and so forth. Occasionally, however, the leader has to initiate and manage major change, such as manage a merger, create a work group, or define the organization's culture. Leader behaviors relating to normal, work-related activities involve transactional leadership; initiating and managing change entails transformational leadership.

In particular, **transformational leadership** is the set of abilities that allow the leader to recognize the need for change, to create a vision to guide that change, and to execute the change effectively. Only a leader with tremendous influence can hope to perform these functions successfully. The *Global Perspective* summarizes how a prominent French manager is leading his organization through a number of major changes. Some experts believe that leadership for change is such a vital organizational function that even successful firms need to change regularly to avoid complacency and stagnation.[6]

Some leaders are able to adopt either transformational or transactional perspec-tives, depending on their circumstances. Others are able to be one or the other but not both. Some might argue that Christopher Steffen is a great transactional leader because of his financial acumen and ability to effectively manage firms through restructuring. At the same time, his transformational skills may be suspect because of his difficulties working with others and engendering team spirit. Stanley Gault, on the other hand, is quite successful as a transformational leader.

Transformational leader-ship is the set of abilities that allow the leader to recognize the need for change, to create a vision to guide that change, and to execute that change effectively.

4. Gary Yukl and J. Bruce Tracey, "Consequences of Influence Tactics Used with Subordinates, Peers, and the Boss," *Journal of Applied Psychology*, Vol. 77, No. 4, 1992, pp. 525–535.
5. See James MacGregor Burns, *Leadership* (New York: Harper & Row, 1978), and Karl W. Kuhnert and Philip Lewis, "Transactional and Transformational Leadership: A Constructive/Developmental Analysis," *Academy of Management Review*, October 1987, pp. 648–657.
6. See Brian Dumaine, "Times Are Good? Create a Crisis," *Fortune*, June 28 1993, pp. 123–130.

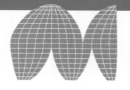
Transformational Leadership at Elf Sanofi

Elf Sanofi, a leading drug company, is a division of the French government-owned giant Elf Aquitaine. For decades the firm had been content to manufacture and sell a stable of proprietary, generic, and over-the-counter drugs. A few years ago, however, a new CEO came on board and shook things up.

Jean-Francois Dehecq was hired to do precisely that. Government officials recognized that if Elf Sanofi was going to become sufficiently profitable to be privatized, it would need a major overhaul in its business practices. They hired Dehecq because he had a reputation for transforming slow-growth, staid firms into aggressive and fast-growing ones.

The first thing Dehecq did was to increase the firm's commitment to research and development. He knew that new product development was critical in the pharmaceutical industry and felt that Elf was lagging behind in that area. More importantly, he also began to push for aggressive international expansion.

One of the first actions taken by Dehecq was structuring a strategic alliance with Sterling Winthrop, a division of Eastman Kodak. The two firms combined a significant portion of their pharmaceutical operations into a new enterprise they called Sanofi Winthrop. The idea was that Elf could provide leadership in Europe, while Sterling was a force in the U.S. market. Dehecq also led a move to expand aggressively to other parts of the world. For example, Elf now has major operations in China and Russia.

Dehecq also wants to expand Elf beyond the drug industry. One recent step in this direction was the acquisition of Yves Saint Laurent, a purveyor of fashions and fragrances. Although some observers criticized this move, Dehecq maintains that he has only started to make changes at Elf Sanofi.

SOURCES: "'We Had to Be Different,'" *Forbes*, August 16, 1993, pp. 60–63; and Alan Chai, Alta Campbell, and Patrick J. Spain (Eds.), *Hoover's Handbook of World Business 1993* (Austin, Tex.: The Reference Press, 1992), pp. 214–215.

When he took over Rubbermaid several years ago, he transformed the firm into one of the most innovative and fastest growing companies in the United States. After moving to Goodyear, he enjoyed similar successes by transforming the venerable tire maker into a highly profitable and fast-growing competitor in the world tire market.[7]

Charismatic Leadership

Charismatic leadership assumes that charisma is an individual characteristic of a leader.

The concept of **charismatic leadership**, like the trait theories discussed in Chapter 12, assumes that charisma is an individual characteristic of the leader. **Charisma** is a form of interpersonal attraction that inspires support and acceptance. All else equal, then, someone with charisma is more likely to be able to influence others than is someone without charisma. For example, a highly charismatic supervisor will be more successful in influencing subordinate behavior than a supervisor who

7. "Leaders of Corporate Change," *Fortune*, December 14, 1992, pp. 104–114.

Charisma is a form of interpersonal attraction that inspires support and acceptance from others.

lacks charisma. Thus, influence is again a fundamental element of this perspective.

Robert House first proposed a theory of charismatic leadership in 1977 based on research findings from a variety of social science disciplines.[8] His theory suggests that charismatic leaders are likely to have a lot of self-confidence, a firm conviction in their beliefs and ideals, and a strong need to influence people. They also tend to communicate high expectations about follower performance and express confidence in followers. Donald Trump is an excellent example of a charismatic leader. Even though he has made his share of mistakes and generally is perceived as only an "average" manager, many people view him as larger than life.[9]

Figure 13.1 portrays the three elements of charismatic leadership in organizations that most experts acknowledge today.[10] The first involves envisioning: the leader needs to be able to articulate a compelling vision of the future, set high expectations, and model behaviors consistent with meeting those expectations. Next, the charismatic leader must be able to energize others through a demonstration of personal excitement, personal confidence, and patterns of success. And finally, the charismatic leader enables others by supporting them, by empathizing with them, and by expressing confidence in them.

Charismatic leadership ideas are quite popular among managers today and are the subject of numerous books and articles. Unfortunately, few studies have specifically attempted to test the meaning and impact of charismatic leadership. Additionally, lingering ethical issues about charismatic leadership, however, trouble some people. *The Ethical Dilemma* summarizes these concerns about ethical and unethical charismatic leaders.

8. See Robert J. House, "A 1976 Theory of Charismatic Leadership," in J. G. Hunt and L. L. Larson (Eds.), *Leadership: The Cutting Edge* (Carbondale, Ill.: Southern Illinois University Press, 1977), pp. 189–207. See also Jay A. Conger and Rabindra N. Kanungo, "Toward a Behavioral Theory of Charismatic Leadership in Organizational Settings," *Academy of Management Review*, October 1987, pp. 637–647.
9. Stratford P. Sherman, "Donald Trump Just Won't Die," *Fortune*, August 13, 1990, pp. 75–79.
10. David A. Nadler and Michael L. Tushman, "Beyond the Charismatic Leader: Leadership and Organizational Change," *California Management Review*, Winter 1990, pp. 77–97.

FIGURE 13.1

The Charismatic Leader

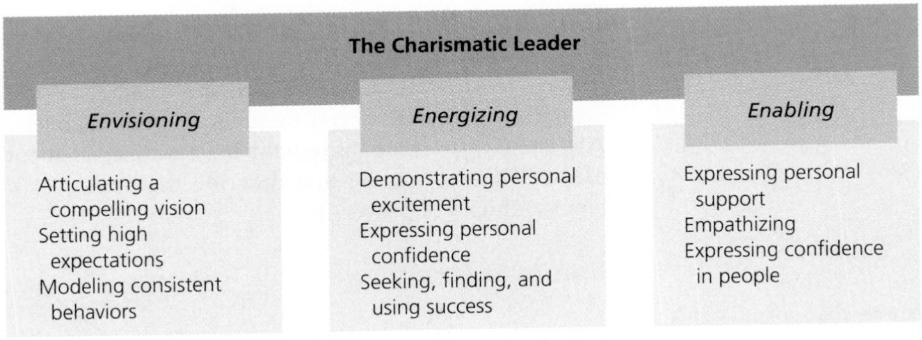

SOURCE: David A. Nadler and Michael L. Tushman, "Beyond the Charismatic Leader: Leadership and Organizational Change," *California Management Review*, Winter 1990, pp. 70–97.

Ethics and Charisma

Even if they don't agree with his politics, people agree that Ronald Reagan has charisma. Charisma also played a role in the success of Martin Luther King, Franklin Delano Roosevelt, Mary Kay Ash, and Lee Iacocca. On the other hand, Adolph Hitler, John DeLorean, and David Koresh also had charisma. Jane Howell and Bruce Avolio recently discussed ethical aspects of charismatic leadership. As shown in the following table, unethical charismatic leaders work for their own gain and pay little regard to their subordinates. But ethical charismatic leaders are much more concerned with the total organization and the welfare of those who follow them.

Unethical Charismatic Leader	Ethical Charismatic Leader
Uses power only for personal gain or impact	Uses power to serve others
Promotes own personal vision	Aligns vision with followers' needs and aspirations
Censures critical or opposing views	Considers and learns from criticism
Demands own decisions be accepted without question	Stimulates followers to think independently and to question the leader's view
Engages in one-way communication	Encourages open, two-way communication
Is insensitive to followers' needs	Coaches, develops, and supports followers; shares recognition with others
Relies on convenient external moral standards to satisfy self-interests	Relies on internal moral standards to satisfy organizational and societal interests

SOURCE: Jane Howell and Bruce Avolio, "The Ethics of Charismatic Leadership: Submission or Liberation?" *The Academy of Management Executive*, February 1992, p. 45. Copyright © 1992. Used with permission.

Power in Organizations

Influence is also closely related to the concept of power. Power is one of the most significant forces that can exist in an organization. Moreover, power can be an extremely important ingredient in organizational success—or organizational failure. In this section we first describe the nature of power. Then we examine the types and uses of power.

Nature of Power

Power is the potential ability of a person or group to exercise control over another person or group.

Power has been defined dozens of different ways so, not surprisingly, there is no one generally accepted definition. Drawing from the common meanings of the term, we define **power** as the potential ability of a person or group to exercise

Since becoming CEO of Warnaco in 1986, Linda Wachner has cut its debt by 40 percent, doubled operating cash flow, made the company public and herself America's most successful businesswoman. Wachner's rise to power is a product of her hard work, her high expectations for herself and for her employees, and her dedication to her motto, "Do it now."

control over another person or group.[11] Power is distinguished from influence by its reliance on control. Thus, power might be thought of as an extreme form of influence.

One obvious aspect of our definition is that it expresses power in terms of potential; that is, we may be able to control others but may choose not to exercise that control. Nevertheless, simply having the potential may be sufficient to influence others in some settings. We should also note that power may reside in individuals (such as managers and informal leaders), in formal groups (such as departments and committees), and in informal groups (such as a clique of influential people). Finally, we should note the direct linkage between power and influence. If a person can convince another person to change his or her opinion on some issue, to engage in or refrain from some behavior, or to view circumstances in a certain way, that person has exercised influence—and used power.

Considerable differences of opinion exist about how thoroughly power pervades organizations. Some people argue that virtually all interpersonal relations are influenced by power, whereas others believe that power is confined only to certain situations. Whatever the case, power undoubtedly is a pervasive part of organizational life. It affects decisions ranging from the choice of strategies to the color of the new office carpeting. It makes or breaks careers. And it enhances or limits organizational effectiveness.

Types of Power in Organizations

Within the broad framework of our definition, there obviously are many types of power. These types usually are described in terms of bases of power and position power versus personal power.

11. For reviews of the meaning of power, see Henry Mintzberg, *Power in and around Organizations* (Englewood Cliffs, N.J.: Prentice-Hall, 1983); Jeffrey Pfeffer, *Power in Organizations* (Marshfield, Mass.: Pitman Publishing, 1981); John Kenneth Galbraith, *The Anatomy of Power* (Boston: Houghton Mifflin, 1983); and Gary A. Yukl, *Leadership in Organizations*, 3rd ed. (Englewood Cliffs, N.J.: Prentice-Hall, 1994).

Five general bases of power can exist in organizations.

Bases of Power The most widely used and recognized analysis of the bases of power is the framework developed by John R. P. French and Bertram Raven.[12] French and Raven identified five general bases of power in organizational settings: legitimate, reward, coercive, expert, and referent power.

Legitimate power is power that is granted by virtue of one's position in the organization.

Legitimate power, which is essentially authority, is granted by virtue of one's position in the organization. A manager has legitimate power over her subordinates, over their subordinates, and so on. The organization specifies that it is legitimate for the designated individual to direct the activities of others. The bounds of this legitimacy are defined partly by the formal nature of the position involved and partly by informal norms and traditions. For example, it was once commonplace for managers to expect their secretaries not only to perform work-related activities such as typing and filing but to run personal errands like picking up laundry and buying gifts. In highly centralized, mechanistic, and bureaucratic organizations such as the military, the legitimate power inherent in each position is closely specified, widely known, and strictly followed. In more organic organizations, such as research and development labs, the lines of legitimate power often are blurry. Employees may work for more than one boss at the same time, and leaders and followers may be on a nearly equal footing.

Reward power is the extent to which a person controls rewards that another person values.

Reward power is the extent to which a person controls rewards that are valued by another. The most obvious examples of organizational rewards are pay, promotions, and work assignments. If a manager has almost total control over the pay his subordinates receive, can make recommendations about promotions, and has considerable discretion to make job assignments, he has a high level of reward power. Reward power can extend beyond material rewards. As we noted in our discussions of motivation theory in Chapters 4 through 6, people work for a variety of reasons that include more than just pay. For instance, some people may be motivated primarily by a desire for recognition and acceptance. To the extent that a manager's praise and acknowledgment satisfy those needs, that manager has an additional form of reward power.

Coercive power is the extent to which a person has the ability to punish or physically or psychologically harm someone else.

Coercive power exists when someone has the ability to punish or physically or psychologically harm another person. For example, some managers berate subordinates in front of others, belittling their efforts and generally making their lives miserable. Certain forms of coercion may be subtle. In some organizations, a particular division may be notorious as a resting place for people who have no future with the company. Threatening to transfer someone to a dead-end branch or some other undesirable location thus is a form of coercion. Clearly, the more negative the sanctions a person can bring to bear on others, the stronger is her or his coercive power. At the same time, coercive power is used at considerable cost: employee resentment and hostility are often a result of its use.

Expert power is the extent to which a person controls information that is valuable to someone else.

Control over expertise or, more precisely, over information is another source of power. For example, to the extent that an inventory manager has information that a sales representative needs, the inventory manager has **expert power** over the sales representative. The more important the information and the fewer the alternative sources for getting it, the greater the power. Expert power can reside in many niches in an organization; it transcends positions and jobs. Although legitimate, reward, and coercive power may not always correspond exactly to formal

12. John R. P. French and Bertram Raven, "The Bases of Social Power," in Darwin Cartwright (Ed.), *Studies in Social Power* (Ann Arbor, Mich.: University of Michigan Press, 1959), pp. 150–167. See also Philip M. Podsakoff and Chester A. Schriesheim, "Field Studies of French and Raven's Bases of Power: Critique, Reanalysis, and Suggestions for Future Research," *Psychological Bulletin*, Vol. 97, 1985, pp. 387–411.

authority, they often do. Expert power, on the other hand, may be much less in keeping with formal authority. Upper-level managers usually decide on the organization's strategic agenda. But individuals at lower levels in the organization may have the expertise those managers need to do this task. A research scientist may have crucial information about a technical breakthrough of great importance to the organization and its strategic decisions. Or an assistant may take on so many of the boss's routine and mundane activities that the manager loses track of such details and comes to depend on the assistant to keep things running smoothly. In still other situations, lower-level participants are given power as a way to take advantage of their expertise.

Referent power is power through identification. If José is highly respected by Adam, José has referent power over Adam. Like expert power, referent power does not always correlate with formal organizational authority. In some ways, referent power is similar to the concept of charisma in that it often involves trust, similarity, acceptance, affection, willingness to follow, and emotional involvement. Referent power usually surfaces as imitation. For example, suppose that a new department manager is the youngest person in the organization to have reached that rank. Further, employees widely believe that she is being groomed for the highest levels of the company. Other people in the department may begin to imitate her, thinking that they too may be able to advance. They may begin dressing like her, working the same hours, and trying to pick up as many work-related pointers from her as possible.

Position Versus Personal Power   The French and Raven framework is only one approach to examining the origins of organizational power. Another approach categorizes power in organizations as one of two types: position power or personal power.

Position power resides in the position, regardless of the person holding the job. Thus, legitimate, reward, and some aspects of coercive and expert power can all contribute to position power. Position power thus is similar to authority. In creating a position, the organization simultaneously establishes a sphere of power for the person filling that position. He or she generally will have the power to direct the activities of subordinates in performing their jobs, control some of their potential rewards, and have a say in their punishment and discipline. There are, however, limits to a manager's position power. A manager cannot order or control activities that fall outside his or her sphere of power, for instance, and direct a subordinate to commit crimes, perform personal services, or take on tasks that clearly are not part of the subordinate's job.

Personal power resides in the person, regardless of his or her position in the organization. Thus, the primary bases of personal power are referent and some traces of expert, coercive, and reward power. Charisma may also contribute to personal power. Someone usually exercises personal power through rational persuasion or by playing on followers' identification with him or her. An individual with personal power often can inspire greater loyalty and dedication in followers than someone who has only position power. The stronger influence stems from the fact that the followers are acting more from choice than from necessity (as dictated, for example, by their organizational responsibilities) and thus will respond more readily to requests and appeals. Of course, the influence of a leader who relies only on personal power also is limited because followers may freely decide not to accept his or her directives or orders.

Referent power exists when one person wants to be like or imitates someone else.

Position power resides in the position, regardless of who is filling that position.

Personal power resides in the person, regardless of the position being filled.

In Chapter 12, we noted the distinction between formal and informal leaders. These two concepts are also related to position and personal power. A formal leader will have, at a minimum, position power, and an informal leader will have some measure of personal power. Just as a person may be both a formal and an informal leader, he or she can have both position and personal power simultaneously. Indeed, such a combination usually has the greatest potential influence on the actions of others. Figure 13.2 illustrates how personal and position power can interact to determine how much overall power a person has in a particular situation. An individual with both personal and position power will have the strongest overall power. Likewise, an individual with neither personal nor position power will have the weakest overall power. Finally, when either personal or position power is high but the other is low, the individual will have a moderate level of overall power.

The Uses of Power in Organizations

Power can be used in many ways in an organization. Gary Yukl has presented a useful perspective for understanding how power may be wielded.[13] His perspective has two closely related components. The first relates power bases, requests from individuals possessing power, and probable outcomes in the form of prescriptions for the manager. Table 13.1 indicates the three outcomes that potentially result when a leader tries to exert power.[14] These outcomes depend on the leader's base of power, how that base is operationalized, and the subordinate's individual characteristics (for example, personality traits or past interactions with the leader).

Commitment probably will result from the attempt to exercise power if the subordinate accepts and identifies with the leader. Such an employee will be highly motivated by requests that seem important to the leader. For example, a leader might explain that a new piece of software will greatly benefit the organization if developed as soon as possible. A committed subordinate will work just as hard as the leader to complete the project, even if that means working overtime. Sam

Attempts to use power can result in commitment, compliance, or resistance.

13. Yukl, *Leadership in Organizations*, Chapter 2.
14. See also Thomas A. Stewart, "New Ways to Exercise Power," *Fortune*, November 6, 1969, pp. 52–64.

FIGURE 13.2

Position Power and Personal Power

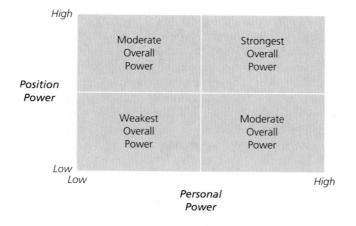

TABLE 13.1

Uses and Outcomes of Power

Source of Leader Influence	Type of Outcome		
	Commitment	**Compliance**	**Resistance**
Referent Power	*Likely*	*Possible*	*Possible*
	If request is believed to be important to leader	If request is perceived to be unimportant to leader	If request is for something that will bring harm to leader
Expert Power	*Likely*	*Possible*	*Possible*
	If request is persuasive and subordinates share leader's task goals	If request is persuasive but subordinates are apathetic about leader's task goals	If leader is arrogant and insulting, or subordinates oppose task goals
Legitimate Power	*Possible*	*Likely*	*Possible*
	If request is polite and very appropriate	If request or order is seen as legitimate	If arrogant demands are made or request does not appear proper
Reward Power	*Possible*	*Likely*	*Possible*
	If used in a subtle, very personal way	If used in a mechanical, impersonal way	If used in a manipulative, arrogant way
Coercive Power	*Very unlikely*	*Possible*	*Likely*
		If used in a helpful, nonpunitive way	If used in a hostile or manipulative way

SOURCE: Table adapted by Gary A. Yukl from information in John R. P. French, Jr., and Bertram Raven, "The Bases of Social Power," in *Studies in Social Power*, Dorwin P. Cartwright, ed. (Ann Arbor, Mich.: Institute for Social Research, the University of Michigan, 1959), pp. 150–167. Data used by permission of the Institute for Social Research.

Walton once asked all Wal-Mart employees to start greeting customers with a smile and an offer to help. Because Wal-Mart employees generally were motivated and loyal, most of them accepted his request. Compliance means the subordinate is willing to carry out the leader's wishes as long as doing so will not require extra effort and energy. Thus, the subordinate may work at a reasonable pace but refuse to work overtime, insisting that the job will still be there tomorrow. Many ordinary requests from a boss and the subsequent responses of subordinates fit this description. *Resistance* occurs when the subordinate fights the leader's wishes. A resistant subordinate may even deliberately neglect the project to ensure that it is not done as the leader wants. When Frank Lorenzo ran Continental Airlines, some employees occasionally disobeyed his mandates as a form of protest against his leadership of the firm.

Table 13.2 goes on to suggest ways that leaders can use and enhance various kinds of power in the most effective way. By *effective*, we mean using power that is

TABLE 13.2

Guidelines for Using Power

Basis of Power	Guidelines for Use
Referent Power	Treat subordinates fairly
	Defend subordinates' interests
	Be sensitive to subordinates' needs, feelings
	Select subordinates similar to oneself
	Engage in role modeling
Expert Power	Promote image of expertise
	Maintain credibility
	Act confident and decisive
	Keep informed
	Recognize employee concerns
	Avoid threatening subordinates' self-esteem
Legitimate Power	Be cordial and polite
	Be confident
	Be clear and follow up to verify understanding
	Make sure request is appropriate
	Explain reasons for request
	Follow proper channels
	Exercise power regularly
	Enforce compliance
	Be sensitive to subordinates' concerns
Reward Power	Verify compliance
	Make feasible, reasonable requests
	Make only ethical, proper requests
	Offer rewards desired by subordinates
	Offer only credible rewards
Coercive Power	Inform subordinates of rules and penalties
	Warn before punishing
	Administer punishment consistently and uniformly
	Understand the situation before acting
	Maintain credibility
	Fit punishment to the infraction
	Punish in private

SOURCE: Reprinted from Gary A. Yukl, *Leadership in Organization*, 2nd ed., © 1989, pp. 44–49. Reprinted by permission of Prentice-Hall, Inc., Englewood Cliffs, N.J.

most likely to engender commitment or, at the least, compliance, and least likely to engender resistance. For example, with a somewhat mechanistic approach, managers may enhance their referent power by choosing subordinates with backgrounds similar to their own. They might, for instance, build a referent power base by hiring several subordinates who went to the same college they did. A more subtle way to exercise referent power is through role modeling: the leader behaves as she or he wants subordinates to behave. As noted earlier, because subordinates relate to and identify with a leader with referent power, they may subsequently attempt to emulate that person's behavior.[15]

15. French and Raven, "The Bases of Social Power."

In using expert power, managers can subtly make others aware of their education, experience, and accomplishments. To maintain credibility, a leader should not pretend to know things that he or she really does not know. A leader whose pretensions are exposed will rapidly lose expert power. A confident and decisive leader demonstrates a firm grasp of situations and takes charge when circumstances dictate. Managers should also keep themselves informed about developments related to tasks, valuable to the organization, and relevant to their expertise. A leader who recognizes employee concerns works to understand the underlying nature of these issues and takes appropriate steps to reassure subordinates. For example, if employees feel threatened by rumors that they will lose office space after an impending move, the leader might ask them about this concern and then find out just how much office space will be available and tell the subordinates. Finally, to avoid threatening the self-esteem of subordinates, a leader should be careful not to flaunt expertise or behave like a know-it-all.

In general, a leader exercises legitimate power by formally requesting that subordinates do something. The leader should be especially careful to make requests diplomatically if the subordinate is sensitive about his or her relationship with the leader. This might be the case, for example, if the subordinate is older or more experienced than the leader. But although the request should be polite, it should be made confidently. The leader is in charge and needs to convey his or her command of the situation. The request should also be clear. Thus, the leader may need to follow up to ascertain that the subordinate has understood it properly. To ensure that a request is seen as appropriate and legitimate to the situation, the leader may need to explain the reasons for it. Often subordinates do not understand the rationale behind a request and consequently are unenthusiastic about it. Following proper channels when dealing with subordinates is also important. Suppose that a manager has asked a subordinate to spend his day finishing an important report. Later, while the manager is out of the office, her boss comes by and asks the subordinate to drop that project and work on something else. The subordinate will then be in the awkward position of having to choose which of two higher-ranking individuals to obey. Exercising authority regularly will reinforce its presence and legitimacy in the eyes of subordinates. Compliance with legitimate power should be the norm because if employees resist a request, the leader's power base may diminish. Finally, the leader exerting legitimate power should attempt to be responsive to subordinates' problems and concerns in the same ways we outlined for using expert power.

Reward power is, in some respects, the easiest base of power to use. Verifying compliance simply means that the leader should find out whether subordinates have carried out his or her request before giving rewards; otherwise, subordinates may not recognize a performance-reward linkage. The request to be rewarded must be both reasonable and feasible because even the promise of a reward will not motivate a subordinate who thinks a request should not be or cannot be carried out. The same can be said for a request that seems improper or unethical. Among other things, such a request suggests that the reward must not be perceived as a bribe or other shady offering. Finally, if the leader promises a reward that subordinates know she or he cannot actually deliver, or if they have little use for a reward the manager can deliver, they will not be motivated to carry out the request. Further, they may grow skeptical of the leader's ability to deliver rewards that are worth something to them.

Coercion is certainly the most difficult form of power to exercise. Because coercive power is likely to cause resentment and to erode referent power, it should be used infrequently, if at all. Compliance is about all one can expect from using coercive power—and that only if the power is used in a helpful, nonpunitive way; that is, if the sanction is mild and fits the situation and if the subordinate learns from it. In most cases, resistance is the most likely outcome, especially if coercive power is used in a hostile or manipulative way. The first guideline for using coercive power—that subordinates should be fully informed about rules and the penalties for violating them—will prevent accidental violations of a rule, which pose an unpalatable dilemma for a leader. Overlooking an infraction on the grounds of ignorance may undermine the rule or the leader's legitimate power, but carrying out the punishment probably will create resentment. As an example of providing reasonable warning before inflicting punishment, the first violation of a rule may simply be met by a warning about the consequences of another violation. Of course, a serious infraction such as theft or violence warrants immediate and severe punishment. The disciplinary action needs to be administered consistently and uniformly because doing so will show that punishment is both impartial and clearly linked to the infraction. Leaders should obtain complete information about what has happened before they punish because punishing the wrong person or administering uncalled-for punishment can stir great resentment among subordinates. Credibility must be maintained because a leader who continually makes threats but fails to carry them out will lose both respect and power. Similarly, if the leader uses threats that subordinates know are beyond his or her ability, the attempted use of power will be fruitless. Obviously, too, the severity of the punishment generally should match the seriousness of the infraction. Finally, punishing someone in front of others adds humiliation to the penalty, which reflects poorly on the leader and makes those who must watch and listen uncomfortable as well.

Politics and Political Behavior

Organizational politics are activities carried out by people to acquire, enhance, and use power and other resources to obtain their desired outcomes.

A concept closely related to power in organizational settings is politics, or political behavior. Pfeffer has defined **organizational politics** as activities people perform to acquire, enhance, and use power and other resources to obtain their preferred outcomes in a situation where uncertainty or disagreement exists.[16] Thus political behavior is the general means by which people attempt to obtain and use power. Put simply, the goal of such behavior is to get one's own way about things.

The Pervasiveness of Political Behavior

Organizational politics are pervasive in most organizations.

A classic survey provides some interesting insights into how managers perceive political behavior in their organizations.[17] Roughly one-third of the 428 managers who responded believed that political behavior influenced salary decisions in their organizations, whereas 28 percent believed that it affected hiring decisions. Three-fourths of the respondents also believed that political behavior is more prevalent at higher levels of the organization than at lower levels. More than one-half believed that politics are unfair, unhealthy, and irrational but also acknowledged that suc-

16. Pfeffer, *Power in Organizations*.
17. Victor Murray and Jeffrey Gandz, "Games Executives Play: Politics at Work," *Business Horizons*, December 1980, pp. 11–23. See also Jeffrey Gandz and Victor Murray, "The Experience of Workplace Politics," *Academy of Management Journal*, June 1980, pp. 237–251.

cessful executives must be good politicians and that behaving politically is necessary to get ahead. The survey results suggest that managers see political behavior as an undesirable but unavoidable facet of organizational life.[18]

Politics often is viewed as synonymous with dirty tricks or back stabbing and therefore as something distasteful and best left to others. But the results of the survey just described demonstrate that political behavior in organizations, like power, is pervasive. Thus, rather than ignoring or trying to eliminate political behavior, managers might more fruitfully consider when and how organizational politics can be used constructively.

Figure 13.3 presents an interesting model of the ethics of organizational poli -

18. See Stefanie Ann Lenway and Kathleen Rehbein, "Leaders, Followers, and Free Riders: An Empirical Test of Variation in Corporate Political Involvement," *Academy of Management Journal*, December 1991, pp. 893–905.
19. Gerald F. Cavanaugh, Dennis J. Moberg, and Manuel Velasquez, "The Ethics of Organizational Politics," *Academy of Management Review*, July 1981, pp. 363–374.

FIGURE 13.3

A Model of Ethical Political Behavior

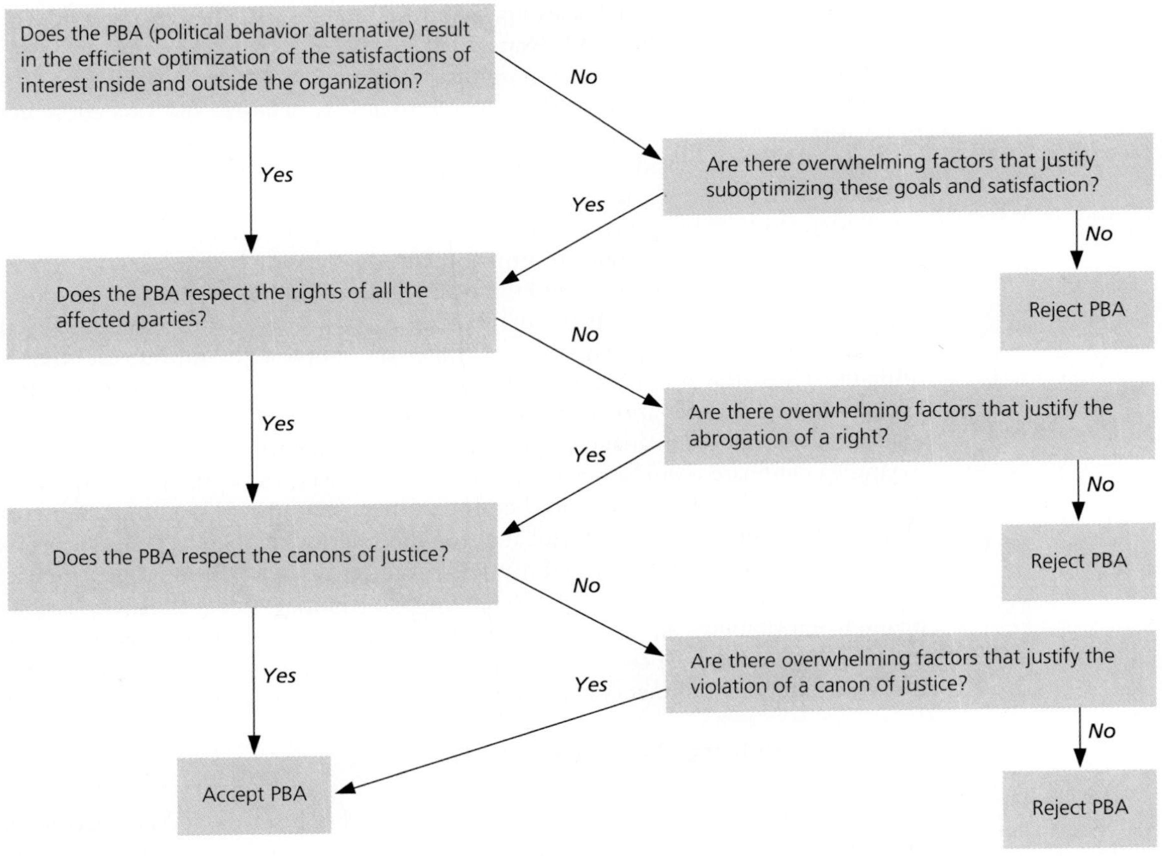

SOURCE: Gerald F. Cavanaugh, Dennis J. Moberg, and Manuel Velasquez, "The Ethics of Organizational Politics," *Academy of Management Review*, July 1981, p. 368. Used by permission.

tics.[19] In the model, a political behavior alternative (PBA) is a given course of action, largely political in character, in a particular situation. The model considers political behavior ethical and appropriate under two conditions: (1) if it respects the rights of all affected parties and (2) if it adheres to the canons of justice (that is, a common-sense judgment of what is fair and equitable). Even if the political behavior does not meet these tests, it may be ethical and appropriate under certain circumstances. For example, politics may play a part in the choice of employees to let go during a recessionary period of cutbacks. In all cases where nonpolitical alternatives exist, however, the model recommends the rejection of political behavior that abrogates rights or justice.

To illustrate how the model works, consider Susan Jackson and Bill Thompson, two assistant professors of English literature. University regulations stipulate that only one of the assistant professors may be tenured; the other must be let go. Both Susan and Bill submit their credentials for review. By most objective criteria, such as number of publications and teaching evaluations, the two faculty members' qualifications are roughly the same. Because he fears termination, Bill begins an active political campaign to support a tenure decision favoring him. He continually reminds the tenured faculty of his intangible contributions, such as his friendship with influential campus administrators. Susan, on the other hand, decides to say nothing and let her qualifications speak for themselves. The department ultimately votes to tenure Bill and let Susan go.

Was Bill's behavior ethical? Assuming that his comments about himself were accurate and that he said nothing to disparage Susan, his behavior did not affect her rights; that is, she had an equal opportunity to advance her own cause but chose not to do so. Bill's efforts did not directly hurt Susan but only helped himself. On the other hand, we might argue that Bill's actions violated the canons of justice because clearly defined data on which to base the decision were available; thus, Bill's calculated introduction of additional information into the decision was unjust.

This model has not been tested empirically. Indeed, its very nature may make it impossible to test. Further, as the preceding demonstrates, giving an unequivocal yes or no answer to the questions, even under the simplest circumstances, often is difficult. Thus, the model serves as a general framework for understanding the ethical implications of various courses of action managers might take.

How, then, should managers approach the phenomenon of political behavior? Trying to eliminate political behavior will seldom, if ever, work. In fact, such action may well increase political behavior because of the uncertainty and ambiguity it creates. At the other extreme, universal and freewheeling use of political behavior probably will lead to conflict, feuds, and turmoil.[20] In most cases, a position somewhere in between is best: the manager does not attempt to eliminate political activity, recognizing its inevitability, and may try to use it effectively, perhaps following the ethical model just described. At the same time, the manager can take certain steps to minimize the potential dysfunctional consequences of abusive political behavior.

Managing Political Behavior

Managing organizational politics is no easy task. Because of the very nature of political behavior, it is tricky to approach rationally and systematically. Success will require a basic understanding of three factors: the reasons for political behavior,

20. Pfeffer, *Power in Organizations.*

Effective management of political behavior requires an understanding of the reasons it occurs, common political behavior techniques, and strategies for limiting its effects.

common techniques for using political behavior, and strategies for limiting the effects of political behavior.

Reasons for Political Behavior Political behavior occurs in organizations for five basic reasons: ambiguous goals, scarce resources, technology and environment, nonprogrammed decisions, and organizational change (see Figure 13.4).[21]

Most organizational goals are inherently ambiguous. Organizations frequently espouse goals such as "increasing our presence in certain new markets" or "increasing our market share." The ambiguity of such goals provides an opportunity for political behavior because people can view a wide range of behaviors as potential contributors to goal accomplishment. In reality, of course, many of these behaviors may actually be designed for the personal gain of the individuals involved. For example, a top manager might argue that the corporation should pursue its goal of entry into a new market by buying out another firm instead of forming a new division. The manager appears to have the good of the corporation in mind. But what if he owns some of the target firm's stock and stands to make money on a merger or acquisition?

Whenever resources are scarce, some people will not get everything they think they deserve or need. Thus, they are likely to engage in political behavior as a means for inflating their share of resources. In this way, a manager seeking a larger budget might present accurate but misleading or incomplete statistics to inflate the perceived importance of her department. Because no organization has unlimited resources, incentives for this kind of political behavior are always present.

Technology and environment may influence the overall design of the organization and its activities. The influence stems from the uncertainties associated with nonroutine technologies and dynamic, complex environments. These uncertainties favor the use of political behavior because in a dynamic and complex environ-

FIGURE 13.4

Reasons for, Techniques of, and Possible Consequences of Political Behavior

Reasons	Political Behavior	Possible Results
Ambiguous Goals	Controlling Information	Personal Gain Disguised as
Scarce Resources	Controlling Lines of	Pursuit of Goals
Technology and Environment	Communication	Pursuit of Maximum Share
Nonprogrammed Decisions	Using Outside Experts	of Resources
Organizational Change	Controlling the Agenda	Personal Gains via Uncertainty
	Game Playing	Parochial Decision Making
	Image Building	Pursuit of Political Ends
	Building Coalitions	During Reorganization
	Controlling Decision	
	Parameters	

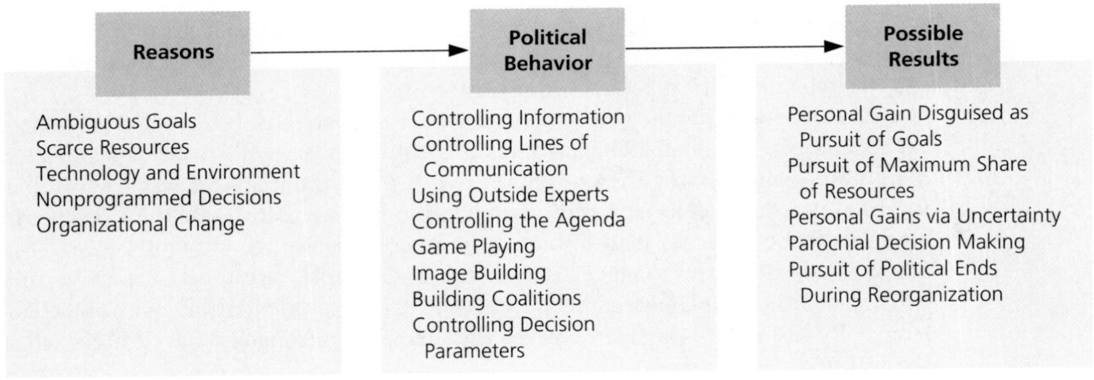

21. Robert H. Miles, *Macro Organizational Behavior* (Glenview, Ill.: Scott, Foresman, 1980). See also Carrie R. Leana, "Power Relinquishment versus Power Sharing: Theoretical Clarification and Empirical Comparison of Delegation and Participation," *Journal of Applied Psychology*, Vol. 72, 1987, pp. 228–233.

ment, it is imperative that an organization respond to change. An organization's response generally involves a wide range of activities, from purposeful activities to uncertainty to a purely political response. In the last case, a manager might use an environmental shift as an argument for restructuring his or her department to increase his or her own power base.

Political behavior is also likely to arise whenever many nonprogrammed decisions need to be made. Nonprogrammed-decision situations involve ambiguous circumstances that allow ample opportunity for political maneuvering. The two faculty members competing for one tenured position is an example. The nature of the decision allowed political behavior, and in fact, from Bill's point of view, the nonprogrammed decision demanded political action.

As we discuss in Chapter 18, changes in organizations occur regularly and can take many forms. Each such change introduces some uncertainty and ambiguity into the organizational system, at least until it has been completely institutionalized. This period usually affords much opportunity for political activity. For instance, a manager worried about the consequences of a reorganization may resort to politics to protect the scope of his or her authority.

The Techniques of Political Behavior   Several techniques are used in practicing political behavior. Unfortunately, because these techniques have not been systematically studied, our understanding of them is based primarily on informal observation and inference.[22] To further complicate this problem, the participants themselves may not even be aware that they are using particular techniques. Figure 13.4 summarizes the most frequently used techniques.[23]

One technique of political behavior is to control as much information as possible. The more critical the information and the fewer the people who have access to it, the larger the power base and influence of those who do. For example, a top manager has a report compiled as a basis for future strategic plans. Rather than distributing the complete report to peers and subordinates, he shares only parts of it with those few managers who must have the information. Because no one but the manager has the complete picture, he has power and is engaging in politics to control decisions and activities according to his own ends.

Similarly, some people create or exploit situations to control lines of communication, particularly access to others in the organization. Secretaries frequently control access to their bosses. A secretary may put visitors in contact with the boss, send them away, delay the contact by ensuring that phone calls are not returned promptly, and so forth. People who control information often find that they can use this type of political behavior quite effectively.

Using outside experts, such as consultants or advisers, can be an effective political technique. The manager who hires a consultant may select one whose views match her own. Because the consultant realizes that the manager was responsible for his selection, he feels a certain obligation to her. Although the consultant attempts to be objective and unbiased, he unconsciously recommends courses of action favored by the manager. Given the consultant's presumed expertise and neutrality, others in the organization accept his recommendations without challenge. By using an outside expert, the manager ultimately has gotten what she wants.

22. Pfeffer, *Power in Organizations*; Mintzberg, *Power in and around Organizations*.
23. The techniques in Figure 13.4 are based on Pfeffer, *Power in Organizations*; Mintzberg, *Power in and around Organizations*, and Galbraith, *The Anatomy of Power*.

Controlling the agenda is another common political technique. Suppose that a manager wants to prevent a committee's approval of a certain proposal. The manager first tries to keep the decision off the agenda entirely, claiming that it is not yet ready for consideration (or attempts to have it placed last on the agenda). As other issues are decided, he sides with the same set of managers on each decision, building up a certain expectation that they are a team. When the controversial item comes up, he is able to defeat it through a combination of everyone's fatigue and wish to get the meeting over with and the support of his carefully cultivated allies. This technique, then, involves group polarization. A less sophisticated tactic is to prolong discussion of prior agenda items so that the group never reaches the controversial one. Or the manager may raise so many technicalities and new questions about the proposal that the committee decides to table it. In any of these cases, the manager will have used political behavior for his or her own ends.

Game playing is a complex technique that may take many forms. When playing games, managers simply work within the rules of the organization to increase the probability that their preferred outcomes will come about. Suppose that a manager is in a position to cast the deciding vote on an upcoming issue. She does not want to alienate either side by voting on it. One game she might play is to arrange to be called out of town on a crucial business trip when the vote is to take place. Assuming no one questions the need for the trip, she will successfully maintain her position of neutrality and avoid angering either of the opposing camps.[24] Another game involves using any of the techniques of political behavior in a purely manipulative or deceitful way. For example, a manager who will soon be making recommendations about promotions tells each subordinate, in "strictest confidence," that he or she is a leading candidate and needs only to increase his or her performance to have the inside track. Here the manager is using his control over information to play games with his subordinates.

The technique of building coalitions has as its general goal convincing others that everyone should work together to get certain things accomplished. A manager who believes that she does not control enough votes to pass an upcoming agenda item may visit with other managers before the meeting to urge them to side with her. If her preferences are in the best interests of the organization, this may be a laudable strategy for her to follow. But if she herself is the principal beneficiary, the technique is not desirable from the organization's perspective.

At its extreme, coalition building, which is frequently used in political bodies, may take the form of blatant reciprocity. In return for Roberta Kline's vote on an issue that concerns him, José Montemayor agrees to vote for a measure that does not affect his group at all but is crucial to Kline's group. Depending on the circumstances, this practice may benefit or hurt the organization as a whole.

The technique of controlling decision parameters can be used only in certain situations and requires much subtlety. Instead of trying to control the actual decision, the manager backs up one step and tries to control the criteria and tests on which the decision is based. This allows the manager to take a less active role in the actual decision but still achieve his or her preferred outcome. For example, suppose that a district manager wants a proposed new factory to be constructed on a site in his region. If he tries to influence the decision directly, his arguments will be seen as biased and self-serving. Instead, he may take a very active role in defining the criteria on which the decision will be based, such as target population, access to rail transportation, tax rates, and distance from other facilities. If he is a

24. Michael Macoby, *The Gamesman* (New York: Simon & Schuster, 1976).

skillful negotiator, he may be able to influence the decision parameters such that his desired location subsequently appears to be the ideal site as determined by the criteria he has helped shape. Hence, he gets just what he wants without playing a prominent role in the actual decision.

Limiting the Effects of Political Behavior   Although it is virtually impossible to eliminate political activity in organizations, managers can limit its dysfunctional consequences. The techniques for checking political activity target the reasons it occurs in the first place as well as the specific techniques that people use for political gain.

Opening communication is one very effective technique for constraining the impact of political behavior. For instance, open communication can make the basis for allocating scarce resources known to everyone. This knowledge, in turn, will tend to reduce the propensity to engage in political behavior to acquire those resources because people already know how decisions will be made. Open communication also limits the ability of any single person to control information or lines of communication.

A related technique is to take steps to reduce uncertainty. Several of the reasons for political behavior—ambiguous goals, nonroutine technology and an unstable environment, and organizational change—as well as most of the political techniques themselves are associated with high levels of uncertainty. Political behavior can be limited if the manager can reduce uncertainty. Consider an organization about to transfer a major division from Florida to Michigan. Many people will resist the idea of moving north and may resort to political behavior to forestall the possibility of their own transfer. If the manager in charge of the move announces who will stay and who will go at the same time that news of the change spreads throughout the company, however, political behavior related to the move may be curtailed.

The adage "forewarned is forearmed" sums up the final technique for controlling political activity: simply being aware of the causes and techniques of political behavior can help a manager check its effects. Suppose that a manager anticipates that several impending organizational changes will increase the level of political activity. As a result of this awareness, the manager quickly infers that a particular subordinate is lobbying for the use of a certain consultant only because the subordinate thinks the consultant's recommendations will be in line with his own. Attempts to control the agenda, engage in game playing, build a certain image, and control decision parameters often are transparent to the knowledgeable observer. Recognizing such behaviors for what they are, an astute manager may be able to take appropriate steps to limit their impact.

Impression Management in Organizations

Impression management is a direct and intentional effort by someone to enhance his or her own image in the eyes of others.

Impression management is a subtle form of political behavior that deserves special mention. **Impression management** is a direct and intentional effort by someone to enhance his or her image in the eyes of others.[25] People engage in impression management for a variety of reasons. For one thing, they may do so to further

25. See William L. Gardner, "Lessons in Organizational Dramaturgy: The Art of Impression Management," *Organizational Dynamics*, Summer 1992, pp. 51–63; Elizabeth Wold Morrison and Robert J. Bies, "Impression Management in the Feedback-Seeking Process: A Literature Review and Research Agenda," *Academy of Management Review*, July 1991, pp. 522–541.

their own career. By making themselves look good, they think that they are more likely to receive rewards, to be given attractive job assignments, and to receive promotions. They may also engage in impression management to boost their own self-esteem. When people have a solid image in an organization, others make them aware of it through compliments, respect, and so forth. Still another reason people use impression management is in an effort to acquire more power and hence more control.

People attempt to manage how others perceive them through a variety of mechanisms. Appearance is one of the first things people think of. Thus, a person motivated by impression management will pay close attention to choice of attire, selection of language, and the use of manners and body posture. People interested in impression management are also likely to jockey to be associated only with successful projects. By being assigned to high-profile projects led by highly successful managers, a person can begin to link his or her own name with such projects in the minds of others.

Sometimes people too strongly motivated by impression management become obsessed by it and may resort to dishonest or unethical tactics (or both). For example, some people have been known to take credit for others' work in an effort to make themselves look better. Recall from our opening incident that this charge has been levied at Christopher Steffen. People have also been known to exaggerate or even falsify their personal accomplishments in an effort to build an enhanced image.[26]

Leadership Substitutes

An implicit assumption made by each leadership and influence perspective described thus far is that the leader and the follower can be differentiated. That is, one person is trying to influence or control another. Recently, though, experts have recognized that in some cases leadership may not be necessary. This perspective is called the leadership substitutes approach.

The Nature of Leadership Substitutes

Leadership substitutes are individual, task, and organizational characteristics that tend to outweigh the leader's ability to affect subordinates' satisfaction and performance.

Leadership substitutes are individual, task, and organizational characteristics that tend to outweigh the leader's ability to affect subordinates' satisfaction and performance.[27] In other words, if certain factors are present, the employee will perform his or her job capably without the direction of the leader. In contrast to traditional theories, which assume that hierarchical leadership is always important, the premise of the leadership substitutes perspective is that leader behaviors are irrelevant in many situations.

26. Ibid.
27. See Steven Kerr and John M. Jermier, "Substitutes for Leadership: Their Meaning and Measurement," *Organizational Behavior and Human Performance*, Vol. 22, 1978, pp. 375–403. See also Charles C. Manz and Henry P. Sims, Jr., "Leading Workers to Lead Themselves: The External Leadership of Self-Managing Work Teams," *Administrative Science Quarterly*, March 1987, pp. 106–128.

These stove-manufacturers are part of a largely self-managing workgroup. In an example of superleadership, their leader has turned power over to the group itself, allowing it to function independently, with only occasional guidance from the leader, who now serves only as a facilitator.

Workplace Substitutes

Individual characteristics that may neutralize leader behaviors are ability, experience, training, knowledge, need for independence, professional orientation, and indifference toward organizational rewards. For example, an employee who has the skills and abilities to perform her job and a high need for independence may not need—and may even resent—a leader who provides direction and structure.

A task characterized by routineness, a high degree of structure, frequent feedback, and intrinsic satisfaction may also render leader behavior irrelevant. Thus, if the task provides the subordinate with an adequate level of intrinsic satisfaction, she or he may not need support from a leader.

Characteristics of the organization that may substitute for leadership include explicit plans and goals, rules and procedures, cohesive work groups, a rigid reward structure, and physical distance between supervisor and subordinate. For example, if job goals are explicit and there are many rules and procedures for task performance, a leader providing directions may not be necessary. Preliminary research has provided support for the concept of leadership substitutes, but additional research is needed to identify other potential substitutes and their impact on leadership effectiveness.[28]

Superleadership

Superleadership occurs when a leader gradually and purposefully turns over power, responsibility, and control to a self-managing work group.

A relative newcomer to the literature on leadership substitutes is the notion of superleadership. **Superleadership** occurs when a leader gradually turns over power, responsibility, and control to a self-managing work group. As we discussed more fully in Chapter 11, firms like Clorox and Johnson Wax are making ever

28. Jon P. Howell, David E. Bowen, Peter W. Dorfman, Steven Kerr, and Philip Podsakoff, "Substitutes for Leadership: Effective Alternatives to Ineffective Leadership," *Organizational Dynamics*, Summer 1990, pp. 20–38.

greater use of worker teams that function without a formal manager.[29] A big challenge faced by these firms is what to do with the existing group leader. Although some managers will not be effectively able to handle this change and will leave, superleaders are able to alter their own personal style and become more of a coach or facilitator, rather than a supervisor.[30]

Summary of Key Points

- Influence can be defined as the ability to affect the perceptions, attitudes, or behaviors of others. Influence is a cornerstone of leadership. Whereas the basic leadership models discussed in Chapter 12 acknowledge influence, they do not directly include it as part of the leadership process.
- In recent years, new leadership approaches have attempted to more directly incorporate influence. Transformational leadership, one such approach, is the set of abilities that allow a leader to recognize the need for change, to create a vision to guide that change, and to execute the change effectively. Another influence-based approach to leadership is charismatic leadership. Charisma, the basis of this approach, is a form of interpersonal attraction that inspires support and acceptance.
- Power is the potential ability of a person or group to exercise control over another person or group. The five bases of power are legitimate power (granted by virtue of one's position in the organization), reward power (control of rewards valued by others), coercive power (the ability to punish or harm), expert power (control over information that is valuable to the organization), and referent power (power through personal identification). Position power is tied to a position regardless of the individual who holds it, and personal power is power that resides in a person regardless of position. Attempts to use power can result in commitment, compliance, or resistance.
- Organizational politics are activities people perform to acquire, enhance, and use power and other resources to obtain their preferred outcomes in a situation where uncertainty or disagreement exists. Research indicates that most managers do not advocate political behavior but acknowledge it as a necessity of organizational life. Political behavior is also closely related to ethical behavior. Because managers cannot eliminate political activity in the organization, they must learn to cope with it. Understanding how to manage political behavior requires understanding the reasons for political behavior, the techniques of political behavior, and strategies for limiting its effects.
- Another important form of influence in organizations is impression management. Impression management is a direct and intentional effort by someone to enhance her or his image in the eyes of others. People engage in impression management for a variety of reasons and adopt a variety of methods in an effort to influence how others see them.
- Leadership substitutes are individual, task, and organizational characteristics that tend to outweigh the leader's ability to affect subordinates' satisfaction and

29. Brian Dumaine, "The New Non-Managers," *Fortune*, February 22, 1993, pp. 80–84.
30. Manz and Sims, "Leading Workers to Lead Themselves." See also Dean W. Tjosvold and Mary M. Tjosvold, *Leading the Team Organization* (New York: Lexington Books, 1991).

performance. Superleadership, a special type of leadership substitute, occurs when a leader gradually and purposefully turns over power, responsibility, and control to a self-managing work group.

Discussion Questions

1. Can a person be a leader without influence? Does having influence automatically make someone a leader?
2. Do all organizations need transformational leaders? Do all organizations need transactional leaders? Why are some leaders able to play both roles, while others are able to perform only one role?
3. Who are some of the more charismatic leaders today?
4. What might happen if two people, each with significant and equal power, attempt to influence each other?
5. Cite examples in a professor-student relationship to illustrate each of the five bases of organizational power.
6. Is there a logical sequence for the use of power bases that a manager might follow? That is, should the use of legitimate power usually precede the use of reward power, or vice versa?
7. Cite examples in which you have been committed, compliant, and resistant as a result of efforts to influence you. Think of times when your attempts to influence others led to commitment, compliance, and resistance.
8. Do you agree or disagree with the assertion that political behavior is inevitable in organizational settings?
9. Given its general association with governmental bodies, why do you think the term *politics* has also come to be associated with behavior in organizations as described in the chapter?
10. Recall examples of how you have either used or observed others using the techniques of political behavior identified in the chapter. What other techniques can you suggest?
11. Have you ever engaged in impression management? Some people might think that, as long as it doesn't get out of hand, impression management is fine, while others may think it is misleading and is always inappropriate. What do you think?

EXPERIENTIAL EXERCISE

Purpose   This exercise will help you appreciate some of the ambiguities involved in assessing the ethics of political activity and impression management in organizations.

Format   First, you will create scenarios that you think represent different ethical perspectives on impression management. Then your classmates will assess your interpretations and you will evaluate theirs.

Procedure   Your instructor will divide the class into an even number of small groups of three to four. Using the model of ethical political behavior presented in Figure 13.3, write three short scenarios that represent different ethical perspectives to your group. Each scenario should have some connection to impression management. For example, one scenario might describe a person applying for a new position, whereas another could focus on people competing for a promotion. (You might reread the hypothetical case of the two professors up for a tenure vote on pages 126–127 to get an idea of how to approach these scenarios.) Write one scenario that follows only the "yes" branches in the model, one that follows only "no" branches, and one that follows different combinations of "yes" and "no" branches.

Number your scenarios randomly from 1 to 3. Do not write down anything that might indicate which branches are to be followed. On a separate page, write a brief description of the rationale for the path your group thinks each scenario most logically follows.

Next, exchange scenarios with another group. Evaluate each of its scenarios, and determine the most logical path through the model. Then exchange "answer sheets" and compare your interpretation of each scenario with that of the other group.

The two pairs of groups will then meet to discuss their results. Discussion should center on reasons for any disagreement between the two groups.

Follow-up Questions

1. How realistic was this exercise? What did you learn from it?
2. Could you assess real-life situations relating to the ethics of political activity using the same approach?

C A S E 1 3 . 1	**Getting Warnaco on Track**

Warnaco is an unusual firm in a number of different respects. For one, it is growing rapidly in an industry beset by cutbacks and decline. For another, most of the products it makes are sold under the names of others businesses. And for yet another, Warnaco is the only Fortune 500 industrial company with a female CEO.

Warnaco makes apparel, primarily intimate apparel and menswear. Most of it is sold under such brand names as Fruit of the Loom, Warner's, Olga, Christian Dior, Hathaway, Chaps by Ralph Lauren, and Puritan. In addition, however, Warnaco supplies large quantities of the private label lingerie sold by Victoria's Secret.

In 1986, Warnaco's management team decided to take the firm private in a leveraged buyout. Enter Linda Wachner. Wachner had enjoyed a rapid rise through the ranks of retailing, working for such firms as Federated Department Stores, Foley's, and R. H. Macy. But she desperately wanted to run her own company. After an unsuccessful effort to buy Max Factor, she heard about Warnaco's plans and decided to make her own bid for the firm.

Backed by a Los Angeles investor and Drexel Burnham Lambert, Wachner and her team bought Warnaco for $550 million. From her first day on the job as CEO, she knew that the firm needed to be changed in big ways. At the time Warnaco consisted of fifteen businesses. Each was struggling and needed a major overhaul. Given the need to generate cash and service the debt incurred during the buyout, Wachner knew that she could not take the time necessary to deal with the problems in all fifteen businesses.

Thus, her first order of business was to sell off several of the divisions that needed the most attention but still had some market appeal. These included

---

White Stag and Geoffrey Beene sportswear and Pringle of Scotland sweaters. The remaining businesses were combined into two divisions, intimate apparel and menswear.

Wachner then turned her attention to improving the effectiveness and productivity of each of these divisions. Wachner is highly concerned with detail, is aggressive and forceful, demands tight controls, and insists that things be done quickly. For example, she requires each of her top executives to carry a spiral notebook at all times labeled "do it now." Whenever she instructs one of them to get something done, he or she is supposed to write it down and then go and do it.

She also checks cash reports on a daily basis. If actual receipts do not total projected receipts, she is on the telephone immediately trying to find out why. Not surprisingly, some executives have resisted Wachner's driven, control-oriented approach to managing the firm. For example, one manager brought in from Calvin Klein to run Warnaco's Christian Dior business left after only eight months, citing difficulties in getting along with Wachner.

Still, few people can argue with her results. From 1986 to 1991, she cut the firm's debt by 40 percent, increased cash flow from $50 million to $92 million, and took the firm public again. Warnaco's stock price jumped 75 percent in less than a year, and the firm continues to be among the healthiest in the industry.

But she also is not sitting on her laurels. In 1990, for example, she sold Warnaco's activewear division, which includes Speedo bathing suits, to a private group of investors, of which she is a member. When this new firm, Authentic Fitness, goes public, Wachner stands to make a small fortune.

Case Questions

1. What examples of influence-based leadership can you identify in this case?
2. Have power and political behavior played a role at Warnaco? Speculate as to how these forces may have affected the firm.
3. Do you think men and women use different leadership styles? Why or why not?
4. Is there a question of ethics in Wachner's selling a division to herself?

SOURCES: Susan Caminiti, "America's Most Successful Businesswoman," *Fortune*, June 15, 1992, pp. 102–108; "Leaders of Corporate Change," *Fortune*, December 14, 1992, pp. 104–114; and "Avon Sales Test to Pitch Customers Warnaco Apparel," *Wall Street Journal*, May 14, 1993, p. B1.

| CASE 13.2 | **The Struggle for Power at Ramsey Electronics** |

A vice president's position is about to open up at Ramsey Electronics, maker of components for audio and visual equipment and computers. Whoever fills the position will be one of the four most powerful people in the company and may one day become its chief executive officer. So the whole company has been watching the political skirmishes among the three leading candidates: Arnie Sander, Laura Prove, and Billy Evans.

Arnie Sander, currently head of the research and development division, worked his way up through the engineering ranks. Of the three candidates, he alone has a Ph.D. (in electrical engineering from MIT), and he is the acknowledged genius behind the company's most innovative products. One of the current vice presidents—Harley Learner, himself an engineer—has been pushing hard for Sander's promotion.

Laura Prove spent five years on the road, earning a reputation as an outstanding salesperson of Ramsey's products before coming to company headquarters and working her way up through the sales division. She knows only enough about what she calls the "guts" of Ramsey's electronic parts to get by, but she is very good at selling them and at motivating the people who work for her. Frank Barnwood, another current vice president, has been filling the chief executive officer's ear with Prove's praises.

Of the three candidates, Billy Evans is the youngest and has the least experience at Ramsey. Like the chief, he has an M.B.A. from Harvard Business School and a very sharp mind for finances. The chief has credited him with turning the company's financial situation around, although others in the company believe that Sander's products or Prove's selling ability really deserves the credit. Evans has no particular champion among Ramsey's top executives, but he is the only other handball player the chief has located in the company, and the two play every Tuesday and Thursday after work. Learner and Barnwood have noticed that the company's financial decisions often get made during the cooling-off period following a handball game.

In the month preceding the chief's decision, the two vice presidents have been busy. Learner, head of a national engineering association, worked to have Sander win an achievement award from the association, and two weeks before the naming of the new vice president, he threw the most lavish banquet in the company's history to announce the award. When introducing Sander, Learner made a long, impassioned speech detailing Sander's accomplishments and heralding him as "the future of Ramsey Electronics."

Frank Barnwood has moved more slowly and subtly. The chief had asked Barnwood years before to keep him updated on "all these gripes by women and minorities and such," and Barnwood did so by giving the chief articles of particular interest. Recently he gave the chief one from a psychology magazine about the cloning effect—the tendency of powerful executives to choose successors who are most like themselves. He also passed on to the chief a *Fortune* article arguing that many U.S. corporations are floundering because they are being run by financial people rather than by people who really know the company's business. He also flooded bulletin boards and the chief's desk with news clippings about the value of having women and minorities at the top levels of a company.

Billy Evans has seemed indifferent to the promotion. He spends his days on the phone and in front of the computer screen, reporting to the chief every other week on the company's latest financial successes—and never missing a handball game.

Case Questions

1. Whom do you think the chief will pick as the new vice president? Why?
2. Who do you think should get the job? Why?
3. What role might impression management play?

Interpersonal Communication

OBJECTIVES

After studying this chapter, you should be able to:

Define communication and discuss its purposes
in organizations.

Summarize the basic methods of communication.

Describe the basic communication process.

Describe small-group and organizational
communication networks.

Discuss the impact of computerized information processing
and telecommunications on organizations.

Identify and discuss several barriers to communication in
organizations and how they can be overcome.

UNUM Corporation is a relatively small company with headquarters in Portland, Maine. Its primary business is underwriting of life, health, and accident insurance. Its 5,760 employees are spread around more than 100 offices in the United States and England. With employees spread over such great distances, it was quite difficult for employees to communicate and get the information needed to make timely decisions. UNUM addressed its communication problems in two ways. First UNUM connected all employees—including chief executive officer Jim Orr— to an on-line electronic mail (e-mail) system. Employees on both continents are encouraged to use e-mail to communicate with every other employee at any level as needed and to make suggestions for improvement. Suggestions received through the e-mail system have resulted in notable improvements in every aspect of the business. Orr is now exploring the use of televideo conferencing to further enhance communication across long distances.

Second, UNUM initiated week-long training programs that focus on communication for middle and lower-level managers. CEO Orr attends at least one day of each program to emphasize top management's commitment to better communication. At UNUM, employees are trained in all aspects of communication—from personal to electronic—and the importance of communication is reinforced with management commitment and action.[1]

Many companies have adopted e-mail systems in an effort to increase communication among departments, offices, and individuals, which has raised the level of performance throughout.

■ ■ ■ ■ The use of electronic mail is only one way that new technology is affecting interpersonal communication. Regardless of new technology, however, the basics of interpersonal communication remain important. In this chapter, we focus on the important processes of interpersonal communication and information processing. Communication is important for all phases of organizational behavior, but it is especially crucial in decision making, performance appraisal, and motivation and in ensuring that the organization functions effectively. First, we discuss the purpose and importance of communication in organizations. We describe the methods of organizational communication and examine the basic communication process. Next, we explore the development of communication networks in organizations. Then we examine the potential effects of computerized information processing and telecommunications, and finally, we discuss several common problems of organizational communication and methods for managing communication.

1. Faye Rice, "Champions of Communication," *Fortune*, June 3, 1991, pp. 111–120; and *Annual Report of UNUM Corporation*, 1992.

The Purpose of Communication in Organizations

Communication is the process by which two or more parties exchange information and share meaning.

Communication is the process by which two or more parties exchange information and share meaning.[2] Communication has been studied from many perspectives. In this section, we present the purposes of dynamic communication in organizations.

Communication among individuals and groups is vital in all organizations. Three purposes of organizational communication are shown in Figure 14.1. The primary purpose is to achieve coordinated action.[3] Just as the human nervous system responds to stimuli and coordinates responses by sending messages to the various parts of the body, communication coordinates the actions of the parts of an organization. Without communication, an organization would be merely a collection of individual workers attending to separate tasks. Organizational action would lack coordination and be oriented toward individual rather than organizational goals.

A second purpose of communication is information sharing. The most important information relates to organizational goals, which provide members with a sense of purpose and direction. Another information-sharing function of communication is the giving of specific task directions to individuals. Whereas information on organizational goals gives employees a sense of how their activities fit into the overall picture, task communication tells them what their job duties are and what they are not. Employees must also receive information on the results of their efforts, as in performance appraisals. Communication is essential to the decision-making process as well, as we discuss in Chapter 10. Information, and thus information sharing, is needed to define problems, generate and evaluate alternatives, implement decisions, and control and evaluate results.

Finally, communication expresses feelings and emotions. Organizational communication is far from a collection of facts and figures. People in organizations, like people anywhere else, often need to communicate emotions such as happiness, anger, displeasure, confidence, and fear.

2. Charles A. O'Reilly III and Louis R. Pondy, "Organizational Communication," in Steven Kerr (Ed.), *Organizational Behavior* (Columbus, Ohio: Grid, 1979), p. 121.
3. Otis W. Baskin and Craig E. Aronoff, *Interpersonal Communication in Organizations* (Santa Monica, Calif.: Goodyear, 1980), p. 2.

FIGURE 14.1

Three Purposes of Organizational Communication

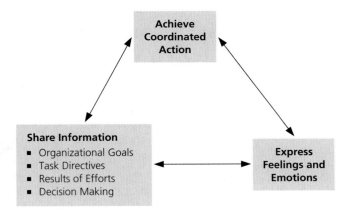

Methods of Communication

The three primary methods of communicating in organizations are written, oral, and nonverbal. Often the methods are combined. Considerations that affect the choice of method include the audience (whether it is physically present), the nature of the message (its urgency or secrecy), and the costs of transmission. Figure 14.2 shows various forms each method can take.

Written Communication

Typically organizations produce a great deal of written communication of many kinds. A letter is a formal means of communicating with an individual, generally someone outside the organization. Probably the most common form of written communication in organizations is the office memorandum, or memo. Memos usually are addressed to a person or group inside the organization.[4] They tend to address a single topic and are more impersonal (as they often are destined for more than one person) but less formal than letters.

Other common forms of written communication include reports, manuals, and forms. Reports generally summarize the progress or results of a project and often

4. William J. Seiler, E. Scott Baudhuin, and L. David Shuelke, *Communication in Business and Professional Organizations* (Reading, Mass.: Addison-Wesley, 1982).

FIGURE 14.2

Methods of Communication in Organizations

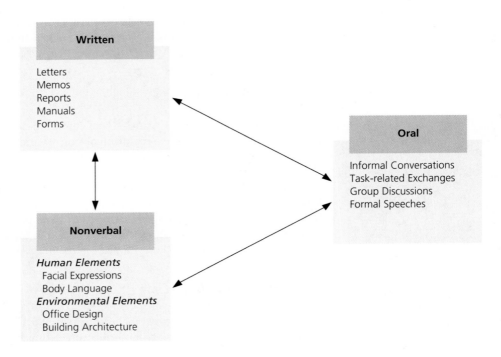

Although new methods of interpersonal communication continue to appear, oral communication continues to be the most common, and effective, method of organizational communication. The recipient of an oral message has the speaker's variations in tone, pitch, speed, and volume to aid them in understanding the true import of the message.

provide information to be used in decision making. Manuals have various functions in organizations. Instruction manuals tell employees how to operate machines, policy and procedures manuals inform them of organizational rules, and operations manuals describe how to perform tasks and respond to work-related problems. Forms are standardized documents on which to report information. As such, they represent attempts to make communication more efficient and information more accessible. A performance appraisal form is an example.

Oral Communication

The most prevalent form of organizational communication is oral. Oral communication takes place everywhere—in informal conversations, in the process of doing work, in meetings of groups and task forces, and in formal speeches and presentations. This form of communication is particularly powerful because it includes not only speakers' words but also their changes in tone, pitch, speed, and volume. As listeners, people use all of these cues to understand oral messages. Moreover, receivers interpret oral messages in the context of previous communications and, perhaps, the reactions of other receivers. Quite often top management of the organization sets the tone for oral communication throughout the organization.

Nonverbal Communication

Most forms of communication usually are associated with some form of nonverbal communication.

Most forms of communication, including written and oral, usually are associated with some form of nonverbal communication. Nonverbal communication includes all the elements associated with human communication that are not expressed orally or in writing. Sometimes it conveys more meaning than words. Human elements include facial expressions and physical movements, both conscious and unconscious. Facial expressions have been categorized as (1) interest-excitement, (2) enjoyment-joy, (3) surprise-startle, (4) distress-anguish, (5) fear-terror, (6) shame-humiliation, (7) contempt-disgust, and (8) anger-rage.[5] The eyes are the most expressive component of the face.

Physical movements and "body language" are also highly expressive human elements. Body language includes both actual movement and body positions during communication. The handshake is a common form of body language. Other examples include eye contact, which expresses a willingness to communicate; sitting on the edge of a chair, which may indicate nervousness or anxiety; and sitting back with arms folded, which may mean an unwillingness to continue the discussion.

Environmental elements such as buildings, office space, and furniture can also convey messages. A spacious office, expensive draperies, plush carpeting, and elegant furniture can combine to remind employees or visitors that they are in the office of the president and chief executive officer of the firm. In contrast, the small metal desk in the middle of the shop floor accurately communicates the organizational rank of a first-line supervisor. Thus, office arrangements convey status, power, and prestige and create an atmosphere for doing business. The physical setting can also be instrumental in the development of communication networks because a centrally located person can more easily control the flow of task-related information.[6]

The Communication Process

Communication is a social process in which information is exchanged or a common understanding is established between two or more parties. The process is social because it involves two or more persons. It is a two-way process and takes place over time rather than instantaneously. The communication process illustrated in Figure 14.3 is a loop between the source and the receiver.[7] Note the importance of the feedback portion of the loop; on receiving the message, the receiver responds with a message to the source to verify the communication. Each element of the basic communication process is important. If one part is faulty, the message may not be communicated as it was intended.

Source

The **source** is the individual, group, or organization interested in communicating something to another party.

The **source** is the individual, group, or organization interested in communicating something to another party. In group or organizational communication, an individual may send the message on behalf of the organization. The source is responsible for preparing the message, encoding it, and entering it into the transmission medium. In

5. Silvan S. Tompkins and Robert McCarter, "What and Where Are the Primary Affects? Some Evidence for a Theory," *Perceptual and Motor Skills*, February 1964, pp. 119–158.
6. Robert T. Keller and Winfred E. Holland, "Communicators and Innovators in Research and Development Organizations," *Academy of Management Journal*, December 1983, pp. 742–749.
7. See Everett M. Rogers and Rekha Agarwala-Rogers, *Communication in Organizations* (New York: Free Press, 1976), for a brief review of the background and development of the source-message-channel-receiver model of communication.

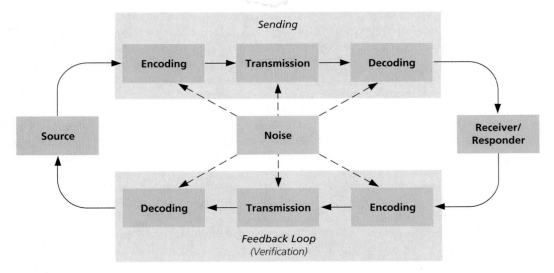

FIGURE 14.3

The Communication Process

some situations, the receiver chooses the source of information,[8] as when a decision maker seeks information from trusted and knowledgeable individuals.

Encoding

Encoding is the process by which the message is translated from an idea or thought into transmittable symbols.

Encoding is the process by which the message is translated from an idea or thought into symbols that can be transmitted. The symbols may be words, numbers, pictures, sounds, or physical gestures and movements. The source must encode the message in symbols that the receiver can decode properly; that is, the source and the receiver must attach the same meaning to the symbols. When we use the symbols of a common language, we assume that those symbols have the same meaning to everyone who uses them. Yet the inherent ambiguity of symbol systems can lead to decoding errors. In verbal communication, for example, some words have different meanings for different people. The meaning of words used by the sender may differ depending on the nonverbal cues, such as facial expression, that the sender transmits along with them.

Transmission

Transmission is the process through which the symbols that represent the message are sent to the receiver.

Transmission is the process through which the symbols that carry the message are sent to the receiver. The **medium** is the channel or path of transmission. The medium for face-to-face conversation is sound waves. The same conversation conducted over the telephone involves not only sound waves but electrical impulses and the line that connects the two phones. Communications media can range from

8. Charles A. O'Reilly III, "Variations in Decision Makers' Use of Information Sources: The Impact of Quality and Accessibility of Information," *Academy of Management Journal*, December 1982, pp. 756–771.

The **medium** is the channel or path through which the message is transmitted.

an interpersonal medium, such as talking or touching, to a mass medium, such as a newspaper, magazine, or television broadcast. Different media have different capacities for carrying information. For example, a face-to-face conversation generally has more carrying capacity than a letter because it allows the transmission of more than just words.[9] In addition, the medium can help determine the effect the message has on the receiver. Calling a prospective client on the telephone to make a business proposal is more personal than sending a letter and is likely to elicit a different response. A manager must choose the medium that is most likely to correspond to the type of message that needs to be sent and understood.[10]

Decoding

Decoding is the process by which the receiver of the message interprets the message's meaning.

Decoding is the process by which the receiver of the message interprets its meaning. The receiver uses knowledge and experience to interpret the symbols of the message and, in some situations, may consult an authority such as a dictionary or a code book. The meaning the receiver attaches to the symbols may be the same as or different from the meaning intended by the source. If the meanings differ, of course, communication breaks down and a misunderstanding is likely to occur.

Receiver/Responder

The **receiver** is the individual, group, or organization that perceives the encoded symbols and may or may not decode them and try to understand the intended message.

The **receiver** of the message may be an individual, a group, an organization, or an individual acting as the representative of a group. Until decoding, the source has been active and the receiver passive. The receiver, however, decides whether to decode the message, to make an effort to understand it, and to respond. Moreover, the intended receiver may not get the message at all, whereas an unintended receiver may, depending on the medium and symbols used by the source and the attention level of potential receivers.

The important skill necessary for proper reception of the message is good listening. The receiver may not concentrate on the sender, the message, or the medium, and the message may be lost. Listening is an active process that requires as much concentration and effort on the part of the receiver as sending the message does by the sender. *Developing Management Skills* gives you an opportunity to assess your personal listening skills.

The expression of emotions by the sender and receiver enters into the communication process in several places. First, the emotions may be part of the message, entering into the encoding process. Second, as the message is decoded, the receiver may let his or her emotions perceive a message different than what the sender intended. Third, emotion-filled feedback from the intended receiver can cause the sender to modify her or his subsequent message.[11]

9. See Richard L. Daft and Robert H. Lengel, "Information Richness: A New Approach to Managerial Behavior and Organization Design," in Barry M. Staw and L. L. Cummings (Eds.), *Research in Organizational Behavior*, Vol. 6 (Greenwich, Conn.: JAI Press, 1984), pp. 191-233, for further discussion of media and information richness.
10. See Janet Fulk and Brian Boyd, "Emerging Theories of Communication in Organizations," *Journal of Management*, 1991, pp. 407–446, for a good review of the research on choice of medium for message transmission.
11. Anat Rafaeli and Robert I. Sutton, "The Expression of Emotion in Organizational Life," in Larry L. Cummings and Barry M. Staw (Eds.), *Research in Organizational Behavior*, Vol. 11 (Greenwich, Conn.: JAI Press, 1989), pp. 1–42.

DEVELOPING MANAGEMENT SKILLS

Diagnosing Your Listening Skills

Introduction   Good listening skills are essential for effective communication and are often overlooked when communication is analyzed. This self-assessment questionnaire examines your ability to listen effectively.

Instructions   Go through the following statements, checking "yes" or "no" in the space next to each one. Mark each question as truthfully as you can in light of your behavior in the last few meetings or gatherings that you attended.

Yes   No

_____ _____ 1. I frequently attempt to listen to several conversations at the same time.

_____ _____ 2. I like people to give me only the facts and then let me make my own interpretation.

_____ _____ 3. I sometimes pretend to pay attention to people.

_____ _____ 4. I consider myself a good judge of nonverbal communications.

_____ _____ 5. I usually know what another person is going to say before he or she says it.

_____ _____ 6. I usually end conversations that don't interest me by diverting my attention from the speaker.

_____ _____ 7. I frequently nod, frown, or in some other way let the speaker know how I feel about what he or she is saying.

Yes   No

_____ _____ 8. I usually respond immediately when someone has finished talking.

_____ _____ 9. I evaluate what is being said while it is being said.

_____ _____ 10. I usually formulate a response while the other person is still talking.

_____ _____ 11. The speaker's "delivery" style frequently keeps me from listening to content.

_____ _____ 12. I usually ask people to clarify what they have said rather than guess at the meaning.

_____ _____ 13. I make a concerted effort to understand other people's point of view.

_____ _____ 14. I frequently hear what I expect to hear rather than what is said.

_____ _____ 15. Most people feel that I have understood their point of view when we disagree.

Feedback

Feedback is the process by which the receiver returns a message to that sender that indicates receipt of the message.

The receiver's response to the message constitutes the feedback loop of the communication process. **Feedback** verifies the message by telling the source whether the message has been received and understood. The feedback may be as simple as a phone call from the prospective client expressing interest in the business proposal or as complex as a written brief on a complicated point of law sent from an attorney to a judge.

Noise

Noise is any disturbance in the communication process that interferes with or distorts communication.

Channel noise is a disturbance in communication that is due primarily to the medium.

Noise is any disturbance in the communication process that interferes with or distorts communication. Noise can be introduced at virtually any point in the communication process. The principal type, called **channel noise,** is associated with the medium.[12] Radio static and television "ghosts" are examples of channel noise. When noise interferes with the encoding and decoding processes, poor encoding and decoding can result. Emotions that interfere with an intended communication may also be considered a type of noise.

Communication Networks

Communication links individuals and groups in a social system. Initially, task-related communication links develop in an organization so that employees can get the information they need to do their jobs and coordinate their work with that of others in the system. Over a long period, these communication relationships become a sophisticated social system composed of both small-group communication networks and a larger organizational network. These networks serve to structure both the flow and the content of communication and to support the organizational structure.[13] The pattern and content of communication also support the culture, beliefs, and value systems that enable the organization to operate.

Small-Group Networks

To examine interpersonal communication in a small group, we can observe the patterns that emerge as the work of the group proceeds and information flows

12. See Jerry C. Wofford, Edwin A. Gerloff, and Robert C. Cummins, *Organizational Communication* (New York: McGraw-Hill, 1977), for a discussion of channel noise.
13. See Daniel Katz and Robert L. Kahn, *The Social Psychology of Organizations*, 2nd ed. (New York: Wiley, 1978), for more about the role of organizational communication networks.

from some people in the group to others.[14] Four such patterns are shown in Figure 14.4. The lines identify the communication links most frequently used in the groups.

In a **wheel network**, information flows between the person at the end of each spoke and the person in the middle.

The **wheel network** describes a pattern in which information flows between the person at the end of each spoke and the person in the middle. Those on the ends of the spokes do not directly communicate with each other. The wheel network is a feature of the typical work group, in which the primary communication occurs between the members and the group manager. In the **chain network,** each member communicates with the person above and below, except for the individuals on each end, who communicate with only one person. The chain network is typical of communication in a vertical hierarchy, in which most communication travels up and down the chain of command. Each person in the **circle network** communicates with the people on both sides but not with anyone else. The circle pattern often is found in task forces and committees. Finally, all the members of an **all-channel network** communicate with all the other members. The all-channel

In a **chain network**, each member communicates with the person above and below, but not with the individuals on each end.

In a **circle network**, each member communicates with the people on both sides but with no one else.

14. For good discussions of small-group communication networks and research on this subject, see Wofford, Gerloff, and Cummins, *Organizational Communication*, and Marvin E. Shaw, *Group Dynamics: The Psychology of Small Group Behavior*, 3rd ed. (New York: McGraw-Hill, 1981), pp. 150–161.

FIGURE 14.4

Small-Group Communication Networks

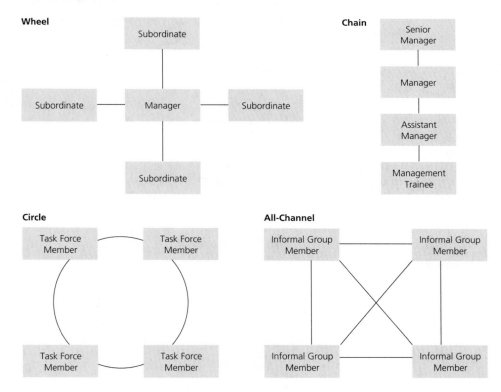

In an **all-channel network**, all members communicate with all other members.

Communication networks form spontaneously and naturally as the interactions among workers continue over time.

network often is found in informal groups that have no formal structure, leader, or task to accomplish.

When there is a lot of communication or when communication must travel a great distance, the chance is greater that the communication will be distorted by noise.[15] Improvements in electronic communication technology, such as computerized mail systems, are reducing this effect. A relatively central position provides an opportunity for the person to communicate with all of the other members. Thus, a member in a relatively central position can control the information flow and may become a leader of the group. This leadership position is separate and distinct from the formal group structure, although a central person in a group may also emerge as a formal group leader over a long period. This has been called emergent leadership.

Communication networks form spontaneously and naturally as the interactions among workers continue. They are rarely permanent because they change as the tasks, interactions, and memberships change. The patterns and characteristics of small-group communication networks are determined by the factors summarized in Table 14.1. The task is crucial in determining the pattern of the network. If the group's primary task is decision making, an all-channel network may develop to provide the information needed to evaluate all possible alternatives. If, however, the group's task mainly involves the sequential execution of individual tasks, a chain or wheel network will likely develop because communication among members may not be important to the completion of the tasks.

The environment (the type of room in which the group works or meets, the seating arrangement, the placement of chairs and tables, the geographical dispersion, and other aspects of the group's setting) can affect the frequency and types of interactions among members. For example, if most members work on the same floor of an office building, the members who work three floors down may be considered outsiders and develop weaker communication ties to the group. They may even form a separate communication network.

Personal characteristics also influence the development of the communication network. These include technical expertise, openness, speaking ability, and the degree to which members are acquainted with one another. For example, in a

15. Peter R. Monge, Jane A. Edwards, and Kenneth K. Kirste, "Determinants of Communication Network Involvement: Connectedness and Integration," *Group and Organization Studies*, March 1983, pp. 83–112.

TABLE 14.1

Factors Influencing the Development of Small-Group Networks

Factor	Example
Task	Decision making Sequential production
Environment	Type of room, placement of chairs and tables, dispersion of members
Personal Characteristics	Expertise, openness, speaking ability, degree of familiarity among group members
Group Performance Factors	Composition, size, norms, cohesiveness

group concerned mainly with highly technical problems, the person with the most expertise may dominate the communication flow during a meeting.

The group performance factors that influence the communication network include composition, size, norms, and cohesiveness. Group norms in one organization may encourage open communication across different levels and functional units, whereas the norms in another organization may discourage such lateral and diagonal communication. These performance factors are discussed in Chapter 11.

Because the outcome of the group's efforts depends on the coordinated action of its members, the communication network strongly influences group effectiveness. Thus, to develop effective working relationships in the organization, managers need to make a special effort to manage the flow of information and the development of communication networks. Managers can, for example, arrange offices and work spaces to foster communication among certain employees. Managers may also attempt to involve members who typically contribute little during discussions by asking them direct questions such as "What do you think, Tom?" or "Maria, please tell us how this problem is handled in your district." Methods such as the nominal group technique, discussed in Chapter 11, can also encourage participation.

One other factor that is becoming increasingly important in the development of communication networks is the advent of electronic groups, fostered by electronic distribution lists for computer network systems.[16] Known as "electronic group mail," this form of communication results in a network of people (or computers) who may have little or no face-to-face communication but still may be considered a group communication network.

Organizational Communication Networks

An organization chart shows reporting relationships from the line worker up to the chief executive officer of the firm. Although the lines of an organization chart may represent channels of communication through which information flows, communication may also follow paths that cross traditional reporting lines. Information moves not only from the top down—from the chief executive officer to group members—but upward from group members to the CEO.[17] In fact, a good flow of information to the CEO is an important determinant of an organization's success.[18]

A free flow of information to the CEO or president of the organization is essential to the organization's success.

Several companies have realized that improved internal communication was essential to their continuing success. General Motors was known for its extremely formal, top-down communication system. In the mid-1980s, however, the formality of its system came under fire from many sources: labor leaders, employees, managers, and even Ross Perot, who became a major shareholder in GM after he sold his company, Electronic Data Systems, to GM in 1984 for $250 million.[19] GM's response was to embark on a massive communication improvement program that included sending employees to public-speaking workshops, improving the more than 350 publications it sends out, providing videotapes of management

16. Tom Finholt and Lee S. Sproull, "Electronic Groups at Work," *Organization Science*, Vol. 1, pp. 41–64.
17. Michael J. Glauser, "Upward Information Flow in Organizations: Review and Conceptual Analysis," *Human Relations*, August 1984, pp. 613–644.
18. Irving S. Shapiro, "Managerial Communication: The View from the Inside," *California Management Review*, Fall 1984, pp. 157–172.
19. "GM Boots Perot," *Newsweek*, December 15, 1986, pp. 56–62.

meetings to employees, and using satellite links between headquarters and field operations to establish two-way conversations around the world.[20]

Downward communication generally provides directions, whereas upward communication provides feedback to top management. Communication that flows horizontally or crosses traditional reporting lines usually is related to task performance. It often travels faster than vertical communication because it need not follow organizational protocols and procedures.

Organizational communication networks may diverge from reporting relationships as employees seek better information with which to do their jobs. Employees often find that the easiest way to get their jobs done or to obtain necessary information is to go directly to employees in other departments rather than communicate through the formal channels shown on the organization chart. Figure 14.5 shows a simple organization chart and the organization's real communication network. The communication network links the individuals who most frequently communicate with one another; the firm's CEO, for example, communicates most often with employee 5. (This does not mean that individuals not linked in the communication network never communicate but only that they communicate relatively infrequently.) Perhaps the CEO and the employee interact often through.

20. Bruce H. Goodsite, "General Motors Attacks Its Frozen Middle," *IABC Communication World*, October 1987, pp. 20–23.

FIGURE 14.5

Comparison of an Organization Chart and the Organization's Communication Network

Organization Chart

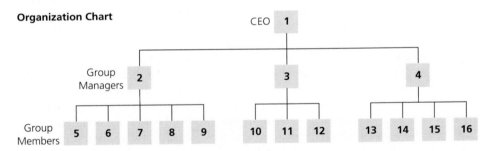

Communication Network of Most Frequent Communications for the Same Organization

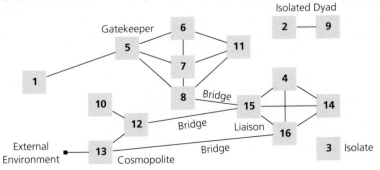

other means, such as church, outside organizations, or sporting events. Such inter-actions may lead to close friendships that carry over into business relationships. The figure also shows that the group managers do not have important roles in the communication network, contrary to common-sense expectations.

The roles that people play in organizational communication networks can be analyzed in terms of their contribution to the functioning of the network.[21] The most important roles are labeled in the bottom portion of Figure 14.5. A gatekeeper (employee 5) has a strategic position in the network that allows him or her to control information moving in either direction through a channel. A liaison (employee 15) serves as a bridge between groups, tying groups together and facilitating the communication flow needed to integrate group activities. Employee 13 performs the interesting function of cosmopolite; he or she links the organization to the external environment by, for instance, attending conventions and trade shows, keeping up with outside technological innovations, and having more frequent contact with sources outside the organization. This person may also be an opinion leader in the group. Finally, the isolate (employee 3) and the isolated dyad (employees 2 and 9) tend to work alone and to interact and communicate little with others.

Each of these roles and functions plays an important part in the overall functioning of the communication network and in the organization as a whole. Understanding these roles can help both managers and group members facilitate communication. For instance, the manager who wants to be sure that the CEO receives certain information is well advised to go through the gatekeeper. If the employee who has the technical knowledge necessary for a particular project is an isolate, the manager can take special steps to integrate the employee into the communication network for the duration of the project.

Recent research has indicated some possible negative impacts of communication networks. Employee turnover has been shown to occur in clusters related to employee communication networks.[22] That is, employees who communicate regularly in a network may share feelings about the organization and thus influence one another's intentions to stay or quit. Communication networks therefore may have both positive and negative consequences.

As we discuss in Chapters 15 and 16, a primary function of organization structure is to coordinate the activities of many people doing specialized tasks. Communication networks in organizations provide this much-needed integration.[23] In fact, in some ways communication patterns influence the way an organization is structured.[24] Some companies are finding that the need for better communication forces them to create smaller divisions. The fewer managerial levels and improved team spirit of these divisions tend to enhance communication flows.[25]

Another company that found it necessary to improve its communication is Tandem Computers. Tandem, known for its open communication and Friday afternoon parties at which its founder and president, Jimmy Treybig, gave motivational speeches to rally employees around company goals, was extremely successful. Communication was casual and friendly, but information flow usually was top

21. See R. Wayne Pace, *Organizational Communication: Foundations for Human Resource Development* (Englewood Cliffs, N.J.: Prentice-Hall, 1983), for further discussion of the development of communication networks.
22. David Krackhardt and Lyman W. Porter, "The Snowball Effect: Turnover Embedded in Communication Networks," *Journal of Applied Psychology*, February 1986, pp. 50–55.
23. Monge, Edwards and Kirste, "Determinants of Communication Network Involvement."
24. Karl E. Weick and Larry D. Browning, "Argument and Narration in Organizational Communication," *Journal of Management*, Summer 1986, pp. 243–259.
25. "Small Is Beautiful Now in Manufacturing," *Business Week*, October 22, 1984, pp. 152–156.

Most offices today have integrated computer systems: many workers send interdepartmental information through an office network, while others rely on their computers even for international communication. Computer systems often speed up office communication, transmitting relevant information to everyone who needs it instantaneously.

down. When revenues began to fall, Treybig found that he needed to have regular business meetings with managers and department heads to get more job- and task-related information flowing from the bottom up. After some tough decisions were made during regular staff meetings, the company got back on track.[26]

Electronic Information Processing and Telecommunications

Changes in the workplace are occurring at an astonishing rate. Many innovations are based on new technologies—computerized information-processing systems, new types of telecommunication systems, and combinations of these. Managers now send and receive memos and other types of communications on their computer terminals. In addition, a whole new industry is developing in the long-distance transmission of data between computers.

The "office of the future" is here. Most offices now have a facsimile (fax) machine, a copier, and personal computers often linked into a single integrated system with access to numerous databases and electronic mail systems. The electronic office links managers, clerical employees, professional workers, and sales personnel in a communication network that uses a combination of computerized data storage, retrieval, and transmission systems.

In fact, the computer-integrated organization is becoming commonplace. Ingersoll Milling Machine Co. of Rockford, Illinois, boasts a totally computer-integrated operation in which all major functions—sales, marketing, finance, distribution, and manufacturing—exchange operating information quickly and continuously via computers. For example, product designers can send specifications directly to machines on the factory floor, and accounting personnel receive on-line information about sales, purchases, and prices instantaneously. The computer system parallels and greatly speeds up the entire process.[27]

26. Brian O'Reilly, "How Jimmy Treybig Turned Tough," *Fortune*, May 25, 1987, pp. 102–104.
27. Jeremy Main, "Computers of the World, Unite!" *Fortune*, September 24, 1990, pp. 115–122.

Another system is the totally computerized human resource information system (HRIS) used by the Rorer Group, the world's twenty-sixth largest manufacturer of pharmaceuticals.[28] This system manages information on all of the company's 8,000 employees, including name, position, education, employment history, and pay. Through a network of personal computers, every properly authorized office in the company can gain access to the information on the system. That means HRIS data are available any time they are needed—not only to computer experts who know the system but to authorized managers throughout the company. Such systems make information available to aid decision making on a daily basis.

Computers are facilitating the increase in telecommuting across the United States and reducing the number of trips to the office to get work done. International Business Machines (IBM) provided many of its employees with think pads and notebook computers and told them to not come to the office but to use the computers to do the work out in the field and send it in electronically.[29] Other companies, such as Motorola and AT&T, have encouraged telecommuting by employees. Employees report increased productivity, less fatigue caused by commuting, reduced commuting expenses, and increased personal freedom. In addition, air pollution and overcrowding may be reduced. Some employees have reported, however, that they have missed the social interaction of the office. Some managers have expressed concerns about the quantity and quality of the work telecommuting employees do when away from the office.

New information-processing and transmission technologies have created new media, symbols, message transmission methods, and networks for organizational communication.

The effects of automated office systems on the communication system and the management of the organization are only now being studied. Research conducted among office workers using a new electronic office system indicated that attitudes toward the system generally were favorable. The users reported improvements in "communications, information access, preparation of written material, and worker collaboration."[30] On the other hand, reduction of face-to-face meetings may depersonalize the office. Some individuals are also concerned that companies are installing electronic systems with little consideration of the social structures of the office.[31] As departments adopt computerized information systems, activities of work groups throughout the organization are likely to become more interdependent, which may alter power relationships among the groups.[32] Most employees quickly learn the system of power, politics, authority, and responsibility in the office. A radical change in work and personal relationships caused by new office technology may disrupt normal ways of accomplishing tasks, thereby reducing productivity. Other potential problems include information overload, loss of records in a "paperless" office, and the dehumanizing effects of electronic equipment. In effect, new information processing and transmission technologies mean new media, symbols, message transmission methods, and networks for organizational communication.

28. Tony Pompili, "Rapid Expansion Smoothed with LAN Personnel System," *PC Week*, August 25, 1987, pp. C1, C9.
29. Kym France, "Computer Commuting Benefits Companies," *Arizona Republic*, August 16, 1993, pp. E1, E4.
30. Don Tapscott, "Investigating the Electronic Office," *Datamation*, March 1982, pp. 130–138.
31. Mary Gruhn, "Trends and Analysis in Word Processing," *Office Administration and Automation*, November 1983, pp. 100–101; and Julie A. Lacity, "The Wait Is Over," *Business Credit*, January 1991, pp. 8–10.
32. Starr R. Hiltz, "User Satisfaction with Computer-Mediated Communication Systems," *Management Science*, June 1990, pp. 739–764; and Carol S. Saunders, "Management Information Systems, Communications, and Department Power: An Integrative Model," *Academy of Management Review*, July 1981, pp. 431–442.

Managing Communication

As simple as the process of communication may seem, messages are not always understood. The degree of correspondence between the message intended by the source and the message understood by the receiver is called **communication fidelity.**[33] Fidelity can be diminished anywhere in the communication process, from source to feedback. Moreover, organizations may have characteristics that impede the flow of information. Table 14.2 summarizes the most common types of breakdowns and barriers in organizational communication.

Communication fidelity is the degree of correspondence between the message intended by the source and the message understood by the receiver.

Improving the Communication Process

Understanding potential problems is essential to improving organizational communication. Using the basic communication process, we can identify several ways to overcome typical problems.

Source   The source may intentionally withhold or filter information on the assumption that the receiver does not need it to understand the communication. Withholding information, however, may render the message meaningless or cause an erroneous interpretation. For example, during a performance appraisal interview a manager may not tell the employee all of the sources of information used to make the evaluation, thinking that the employee does not need to know. If the employee knew, however, he or she might be able to explain certain behaviors or otherwise alter the manager's perspective of the evaluation and thereby improve

33. Pace, *Organizational Communication*.

TABLE 14.2

Communications Problems in Organizations

Root of the Problem	Type of Problem
Source	Filtering
Encoding and Decoding	Lack of common experience Semantics; jargon Medium problems
Receiver	Selective attention Value judgments Lack of source credibility Overload
Feedback	Omission
Organizational Factors	Noise Status differences Time pressures Overload Communication structure

its accuracy. Selective filtering may cause a breakdown in communication that cannot be repaired, even with good follow-up communication.[34]

To avoid filtering, the communicator needs to understand why it occurs. Filtering can result from lack of understanding of the receiver's position, the sender's need to protect his or her own power by limiting the receiver's access to information, or doubts about what the receiver might do with the information. The sender's primary concern, however, should be the message. In essence, the sender must determine exactly what message she or he wants the receiver to understand, send the receiver enough information to understand the message but not enough to create an overload, and trust the receiver to use the information properly.

Encoding and Decoding   Encoding and decoding problems occur as the message is translated into or from the symbols used in transmission. Such problems can relate to the meaning of the symbols or to the transmission itself. As Table 14.2 shows, encoding and decoding problems include lack of common experience between source and receiver, problems related to semantics and the use of jargon, and difficulties with the medium.

Clearly, the source and the receiver must share a common experience with the symbols that express the message if they are to encode and decode them in exactly the same way. People who speak different languages or come from different cultural backgrounds may experience problems in this category. But even people who speak the same language can misunderstand each other.

Semantics is the study of language forms, and semantic problems occur when people attribute different meanings to the same words or language forms. For example, when discussing a problem employee, the division head may tell her assistant, "We need to get rid of this problem." Although the division head may have meant that the employee should be scheduled for more training or transferred to another division, the assistant may interpret the statement differently and fire the problem employee.

The specialized or technical language of a trade, field, profession, or social group is called *jargon*. Jargon may be a hybrid of standard language and the specialized language of a group. The use of jargon makes communication within a close group of colleagues more efficient and meaningful, but outside the group it has the opposite effect. Sometimes a source who is comfortable with jargon uses it unknowingly to communicate with receivers who do not understand it, thus causing a communication breakdown. In other cases, the source may use jargon intentionally to obscure meaning or to show outsiders that he or she belongs to the group that uses the language.

The use of jargon is acceptable if the receiver is familiar with it. Otherwise, it should be avoided. Repeating a message that contains jargon in clearer terms should help the receiver understand the message. In general, the source and the receiver should clarify the set of symbols to be used before they communicate. Also, the receiver can ask questions frequently and, if necessary, ask the source to repeat all or part of the message.

The source must send the message through a medium appropriate to the message itself and to the intended receiver. For example, a commercial run on an AM radio station will not have its intended effect if the people in the desired market segment listen only to FM stations.

34. Losana E. Boyd, "Why 'Talking It Out' Almost Never Works Out," *Nations's Business*, November 1984, pp. 53–54.

Communication problems
that originate in the receiver
include problems with selective attention, value judgments, source credibility,
and overload.

Receiver Several communication problems originate in the receiver, including problems with selective attention, value judgments, source credibility, and overload. Selective attention exists when the receiver attends to only selected parts of a message—a frequent occurrence with oral communication. For example, in a college class some students may hear only part of the professor's lecture as their minds wander to other topics. To focus receivers' attention on the message, senders often engage in attention-getting behaviors such as varying the volume, repeating the message, and offering rewards.

Value judgments involve the degree to which a message reinforces or challenges the receiver's basic personal beliefs. If a message reinforces the receiver's beliefs, he or she may pay close attention and believe it completely, without examination. On the other hand, if the message challenges those beliefs, the receiver may entirely discount it. Thus, if a firm's sales manager had predicted that the demand for new baby care products will increase substantially over the next two years, he may ignore reports that the birth rate is declining.

The receiver may also judge the credibility of the source of the message. If the source is perceived to be an expert in the field, the listener may pay close attention to the message and believe it. Conversely, if the receiver has little respect for the source, she or he may disregard the message. The receiver considers both the message and the source in making value judgments and determining credibility. An expert in nuclear physics may be viewed as a credible source in building a nuclear power plant and yet be disregarded, perhaps rightly, on evaluating the birth rate. This is one reason that a trial lawyer asks an expert witness about his or her education and experience at the beginning of testimony: to establish credibility.

A receiver experiencing communication overload is receiving more information than she or he can process. In organizations, this can happen very easily: a receiver can be bombarded with computer-generated reports and messages from superiors, peers, and sources outside the organization. Unable to take in all the messages, decode them, understand them, and act on them, the receiver may use selective attention and value judgments to focus on the messages that seem most important. Although this type of selective attention is necessary for survival in an information-glutted environment, it may mean that vital information is lost or overlooked.

Verification is the feedback
portion of communication in
which the receiver sends a
message to the source indicating receipt of the message
and the degree to which
he or she understood
the message.

Feedback The purpose of feedback is **verification,** in which the receiver sends a message to the source indicating receipt of the message and the degree to which it was understood. The lack of feedback can cause at least two problems. First, the source may need to send another message that depends on the response to the first; if no feedback is received, the source may not send the second message or may be forced to send the original message again. Second, the receiver may act on the unverified message; if the message was misunderstood, the resulting act may be inappropriate.

Because feedback is so important, the source must actively seek it and the receiver must supply it. Often it is appropriate for the receiver to repeat the original message as an introduction to the response, although the medium or symbols used may be different. Nonverbal cues can provide instantaneous feedback. These include body language and facial expressions, such as anger and disbelief.[35]

35. Robert A. Snyder and James H. Morris, "Organizational Communication and Performance," *Journal of Applied Psychology*, August 1984, pp. 461–465.

The source needs to be concerned with the message, the symbols, the medium, and the feedback from the receiver. Of course, the receiver is concerned with these things too, but from a different point of view. In general the receiver needs to be source oriented just as the source needs to be receiver oriented. Table 14.3 gives specific suggestions for improving the communication process.

Improving Organizational Factors in Communication

Organizational factors that can create communication breakdowns or barriers include noise, status differences, time pressures, and overload. As previously stated, disturbances anywhere in the organization can distort or interrupt meaningful communication. Thus, the noise created by a rumored takeover can disrupt the orderly flow of task-related information. Status differences between source and receiver can cause some of the communication problems just discussed. For example, a firm's chief executive officer may pay little attention to communications from employees far lower on the organization chart, and employees may pay little attention to communications from the CEO. Both are instances of selective attention prompted by the organization's status system.

Time pressures and communication overload are also detrimental to communication. When the receiver is not allowed enough time to understand incoming messages, or when there are too many messages, he or she may misunderstand or ignore some of them.

TABLE 14.3

Improving the Communication Process

Focus	Source		Receiver	
	Question	Corrective Action	Question	Corrective Action
Message	What idea or thought are you trying to get across?	Give more information. Give less information. Give entire message.	What idea or thought does the sender want you to understand?	Listen carefully to the entire message, not just to part of it.
Symbols	Does the receiver use the same symbols, words, jargon?	Say it another way. Employ repetition. Use receiver's language or jargon. Before sending, clarify symbols to be used.	What symbols are being used—for example, foreign language, technical jargon?	Clarify symbols before communication begins. Ask questions. Ask sender to repeat message.
Medium	Is this a channel that the receiver monitors regularly? Sometimes? Never?	Use multiple media. Change medium. Increase volume (loudness).	What medium or media is the sender using?	Monitor several media.
Feedback	What is the receiver's reaction to your message?	Pay attention to the feedback, especially nonverbal cues. Ask questions.	Did you correctly interpret the message?	Repeat message.

Effective organizational communication provides the right information to the right person at the right time and in the right form. Figure 14.6 summarizes how this goal can be achieved.

Reduce Noise   Noise is a primary barrier to effective organizational communication. A common form of noise is the rumor grapevine, an informal system of communication that coexists with the formal system.[36] The grapevine usually transmits information faster than official channels do. Because the accuracy of this information often is quite low, however, the grapevine can distort organizational communication. Management can reduce the effects of the distortion by using the grapevine as an additional channel for the dissemination of information and by constantly monitoring it for accuracy.

Foster Informal Communication   Thomas J. Peters and Robert H. Waterman have described communication in well-run companies as "a vast network of informal, open communications."[37] Informal communication fosters mutual trust, which minimizes the effects of status differences. Open communication can also contribute to better understanding between diverse groups in the organization. *Diversity in the Workplace* describes how Monsanto is using better communications to improve diversity management within the company. Open communication also allows information to be communicated when needed rather than when the formal information system allows it to emerge. Peters and Waterman further describe communication in effective companies as chaotic and intense, supported by the reward structure and the physical arrangement of the facilities. This means that the performance appraisal and reward system, offices, meeting rooms, and work areas are designed to encourage frequent, unscheduled, and unstructured communication throughout the organization.

Develop a Balanced Information System   Many large organizations have developed elaborate formal information systems. In many organizations, however, the systems have created problems rather than solved them. Often they produce more information than managers and decision makers can comprehend and use in their jobs. They also often use only formal communication channels and ignore various informal lines of communication. Furthermore, the systems frequently provide whatever information the computer is set up to provide—information that may not apply to the most pressing problem at hand. The result of all these drawbacks is a loss of communication effectiveness.

36. Keith Davis and John W. Newstrom, *Human Behavior at Work: Organizational Behavior*, 7th ed. (New York: McGraw-Hill, 1985), pp. 314–323.
37. Thomas J. Peters and Robert H. Waterman, Jr., *In Search of Excellence: Lessons from America's Best-Run Companies* (New York: Harper & Row, 1982), p. 121.

FIGURE 14.6

Improving Organizational Communication

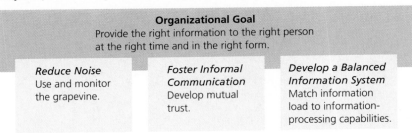

Organizational Goal
Provide the right information to the right person at the right time and in the right form.

Reduce Noise
Use and monitor the grapevine.

Foster Informal Communication
Develop mutual trust.

Develop a Balanced Information System
Match information load to information-processing capabilities.

Monsanto's Diversity Mission

Monsanto Company is a big firm on a big mission. The company, with 1991 revenues of $8.86 billion, is the third-largest U.S. chemical company; its diverse products include sweeteners (NutraSweet) and herbicides (Roundup). Its products can be segmented into chemicals, pharmaceuticals, agricultural, NutraSweet, Fisher Controls, and Biotechnology Research and Development. Although the entire company is involved in doing a better job of managing diversity, improving communication, and creating competitive advantage in every market it serves, two divisions are taking major steps to establish, recognize, and reward new management behaviors. Both programs focus on communication.

Monsanto Agricultural Group started a fifteen-member team, Eliminating Subtle Discrimination (ESD), in 1989, comprising volunteer women, minorities, and white men. This team and thirteen others discovered that discrimination was often so subtle that it was hard to define and describe. They soon found that all differences, including race, gender, ethnicity, speech patterns, culture, dress, and age, could create biases that affect working relationships. As the group's focus changed to finding ways to capitalize on the differences that were inherent in the heterogenous workforce, the name of the group soon changed to Valuing Diversity. The primary goal of the group was to increase consciousness and awareness through sensitivity training for all employees. Rather than create a single course for people who generally claim that they do not need such training, they introduced awareness and communication skills training into more than thirty existing training programs, such as supervisory training and team-building courses.

The Process for Diversity Management (PDM) program at the Chemical Group of Monsanto also focused on increasing awareness and establishing better working relationships within its increasingly diverse workforce. Exit interviews indicated that poorer retention rates of workers not associated with the dominant mainstream were due to poor relationships with supervisors who were in the mainstream. With the help of a consultant, join-up pairs of a boss and an employee were created. For example, pairs included one black and one white or one male and one female. Many different dimensions of diversity were included: age, race, ethnicity, gender, disability, and sexual preference. With the assistance of previously trained consulting pairs of employees, the join-up pairs met for two hours to discuss relationships, work expectations, and job relationships. More than 1,000 join-up pairs have been created, and new ones are created for every new boss-employee relationship. Written evaluations indicate that discussions covered issues that would never have taken place otherwise. The program has helped create a new way of managing people through breaking down the barriers and creating a great place to work, which is necessary to accomplishing business objectives.

SOURCES: "Trading Places at Monsanto," *Training and Development Journal*, April 1993, pp. 45–49; Shari Caudron, "Monsanto Responds to Diversity," *Personnel Journal*, November 1990, pp. 72–78; and Gary Hoover, Alta Campbell, and Patrick J. Spain, *Hoover's Handbook of American Business 1993* (Austin, Tex.: The Reference Press), 1992, p. 410.

Organizations need to balance information load and information-processing capabilities.

New information-processing and transmission technologies have created new media, symbols, message transmission methods, and networks for organizational communication.

Organizations need to balance information load and information-processing capabilities.[38] In other words, they must take care not to generate more information than people can handle. Producing sophisticated statistical reports that managers have no time to read is useless. Furthermore, the new technologies that are making more information available to managers and decision makers must be unified to produce usable information.[39] Information production, storage, and processing capabilities must be compatible with one another and, equally important, with the needs of the organization.

Some companies—for example, General Electric, McDonnell Douglas, Anheuser-Busch, and McDonald's—have formalized an upward communication system that uses a corporate "ombudsman."[40] This position usually is held by a highly placed executive who is available outside the formal chain of command to hear employees' complaints. The system provides an opportunity for disgruntled employees to complain without fear of losing their jobs and may help some companies achieve a balanced communication system.

Summary of Key Points

- Communication is involved in all activities of the organization and is the process by which two or more parties exchange information and share meaning. The purposes of communication in organizations are to achieve coordinated action, share information, and to express feelings and emotions.
- People in organizations communicate through written, oral, and nonverbal means. Written communication includes letters, memos, reports, manuals, and forms. Oral communication is the type most commonly used. Personal elements, such as facial expressions and body language, and environmental elements, such as office design, are forms of nonverbal communication.
- Communication among individuals, groups, or organizations is a process in which a source sends a message and a receiver responds. The source encodes a message into symbols and transmits it through a medium to the receiver, who decodes the symbols. The receiver then responds with feedback, which is an attempt to verify the meaning of the original message. Noise—anything that distorts or interrupts communication—may interfere in virtually any stage of the process.
- Communication networks are systems of information exchange within organizations. Patterns of communication emerge as information flows from person to person in a group. Typical small-group communication networks include the wheel, chain, circle, and all-channel networks.
- The organizational communication network, which describes the real communication links in an organization, usually differs from the arrangement on an organization chart. Roles people play in organizational communication networks include the gatekeeper, liaison, cosmopolite, and isolate.

38. Charles A. O'Reilly, "Individual and Information Overload in Organizations: Is More Necessarily Better?" *Academy of Management Journal*, December 1980, pp. 684–696.
39. James L. McKenney and F. Warren McFarlan, "The Information Archipelago—Maps and Bridges," *Harvard Business Review*, September–October 1982, pp. 109–119.
40. Michael Brody, "Listen to Your Whistleblower," *Fortune*, November 24, 1986, pp. 77–78.

- The fully integrated communication-information office system—the electronic office—links personnel in a communication network through a combination of computers and electronic transmission systems. The effects of such systems have not yet been fully realized.
- Managing communication in organizations involves understanding the numerous problems that can interfere with effective communication. Problems relate to the communication process itself and to organizational factors such as status differences.

Discussion Questions

1. How is communication in organizations an individual process as well as an organizational process?
2. Discuss the three primary purposes of organizational communication.
3. Describe a situation in which you tried to carry on a conversation when no one was listening. Were any messages sent during the "conversation"?
4. The typical college classroom provides an example of attempts at communication: the professor tries to communicate the subject to the students. Describe classroom communication in terms of the basic communication process described in the chapter.
5. Does the class in which you are using this book have a communication network (other than professor-to-student)? If so, identify any specific roles that people play in the network. If not, why has no network developed? What would be the benefits of having a communication network in this class?
6. Why might educators typically focus most communication training on the written and oral methods and pay little attention to the nonverbal methods? Do you think that more training emphasis should be placed on nonverbal communication? Why or why not?
7. Is the typical classroom form of transferring information from professor to student an effective form of communication? Where does it break down? What are the communication problems in the college classroom?
8. Whose responsibility is it to solve classroom communication problems: the students', the professor's, or the administration's?
9. Have you ever worked in an organization in which communication was a problem? If so, what were some causes of the problem?
10. What methods were used, or should have been used, to improve communication in the situation you described in question 9?
11. Would the use of advanced computer information processing or telecommunications have helped solve the communications problem you described in question 9?
12. What types of communication problems will new telecommunications methods most likely be able to solve? Why?

Purpose   This exercise demonstrates the importance of feedback in oral communication.

Format   You will be an observer or play the role of either a manager or an assistant manager trying to tell a coworker the location at which a package of important materials is to be picked up. The observer's role is to make sure that the other two participants follow the rules and to observe and record any interesting occurrences.

Procedure   The instructor will divide the class into groups of three. (Any extra members can be roving observers.) The three persons in each group will take the roles of manager, assistant manager, and observer. In the second trial, the manager and the assistant manager will switch roles.

Trial 1:   The manager and the assistant manager should turn their backs to each other so that neither can see the other. Here is the situation: the manager is in a city that he or she is not familiar with but that the assistant manager knows quite well. The manager needs to find the office of a supplier to pick up drawings of a critical component of the company's main product. The supplier will be closing for the day in a few minutes; the drawings must be picked up before closing time. The manager has called the assistant manager to get directions to the office. The connection is faulty, however; the manager can hear the assistant manager but the assistant manager can hear only enough to know the manager is on the line. The manager has redialed once, but there was no improvement in the connection. Now there is no time to lose. The manager has decided to get the directions from the assistant without asking questions.

Just before the exercise begins, the instructor will give the assistant manager a detailed map of the city that shows the locations of the supplier's office and the manager. The map will include a number of turns, stops, stoplights, intersections, and shopping centers between these locations. The assistant manager can study it for no longer than a minute or two. When the instructor gives the direction to start, the assistant manager, using the map, describes to the manager how to get from his or her present location to the supplier's office. As the assistant manager gives the directions, the manager draws the map on a piece of paper.

The observer makes sure that the manager asks no questions and records the beginning and ending times as well as the way in which the assistant manager tries to communicate particularly difficult points (including points about which the manager obviously wants to ask questions) and any other noteworthy occurrences.

After all pairs have finished, each observer "grades" the quality of the manager's map by comparing it with the original and counting the number of obvious mistakes. The instructor will ask a few managers who believe that they have drawn good maps to tell the rest of the class how to get to the supplier's office.

Trial 2:   In trial 2, the manager and the assistant manager switch roles, and a second map is passed out to the new assistant managers. The situation is the same as in the first trial, except that the telephones are working properly and the manager can ask questions of the assistant manager. The observer's role is the same as in trial 1—record the beginning and ending times, the methods of communication, and any other noteworthy occurrences.

After all pairs have finished, the observers grade the maps, just as in the first trial. The instructor will then select a few managers to tell the rest of the class how to get to the supplier's office. The subsequent class discussion should center on the experiences of the class members and the follow-up questions.

Follow-up Questions

1. Which trial resulted in more accurate maps? Why?
2. Which trial took longer? Why?
3. How did you feel when a question needed to be asked but it could not be asked in trial 1? Was your confidence in the final result different in the two trials?

CASE 14.1	**Mattel Executives Communicate in Unusual Ways**

Las Vegas-style singing and dancing by the CEO and two other executives singing "There's no business like toy business" as they announce earnings to employees is not the most common way to communicate with employees. Mattel's John Amerman did it, and then announced that all 1,100 headquarters employees would receive a bonus of two weeks' pay from the senior management bonus pool. This followed his rap-singing act of the previous year. In 1987 when Amerman became CEO of Mattel, he announced that there would be "fresh air" in the company and making toys would be fun. In addition, he started talking with employees while eating lunch in the cafeteria, walking around the plant, and holding regular meetings. Probably the most important difference was that he showed that he was available and listened to what employees had to say.

When Amerman took over, Mattel was losing money fast ($113 million in 1987) and had several big losers in new-toy ventures. The turn-around has been dramatic; 1991 earnings were more than $118 million on sales of $1.62 billion. The communication openness with employees had clearly been a major reason. The open communication convinced employees that management and labor were working toward the same objective. Suggestions by employees on plant closings and departments to be shut down were followed by management.

The difference has been dramatic. Barbie has been the base from which Mattel has been able to survive amid its losses in other toys. The Barbie line sales were around $485 million in 1988 and have increased to almost $1 billion in 1992. The company is continuing to grow by expanding its international sales in every product line and adding the production and marketing rights to toys based on Disney characters. A new communication challenge came when Mattel bought Fisher-Price for $1.1 billion in 1993. With its headquarters in California and Fisher-Price headquarters in New York, seeing how the new communication works long distance will be interesting.

Case Questions

1. What is wrong, or right, with the ways that Amerman chooses to communicate?
2. What do you expect to be the major communication problems for Mattel as the merger with Fisher-Price becomes final?
3. What communication methods and techniques would you use to enhance communication when the merger is completed?

SOURCES: "Mattel/Fisher-Price Merger Creates Toy Giant, Hasbro Rival," *Discount Store News*, September 6, 1993, p. 4; Faye Rice, "Champions of Communication," *Fortune*, June 3, 1991, pp. 111–120; "Five Magic Words: 'Give Me a Bigger Challenge,'" *Fortune*, September 21, 1992, p. 56; "The Man Who Mends Toy Companies," *Business Week*, September 13, 1993, p. 62; and Gary Hoover, Alta Campbell, and Patrick J. Spain, *Hoover's Handbook of American Business 1993* (Austin, Tex.: The Reference Press, 1992), p. 384.

Mindy Martin was no longer speaking to her co-worker, Al Sharp. She had been wary of him since her first day at Alton Products; he had always seemed distant and aloof. She thought at first that he resented her M.B.A. degree, her fast rise in the company, or her sense of purpose and ambition. But she was determined to get along with everyone in the office, so she had taken him out to lunch, praised his work whenever she could, and even kept track of his son's Little League feats.

But all that ended with the appointment of the new Midwest marketing director. Martin had her sights on the job and thought her chances were good. She was competing with three other managers on her level. Sharp was not in the running because he did not have a graduate degree, but his voice was thought to carry a lot of weight with the top brass. Martin had less seniority than any of her competitors, but her division had become the leader in the company, and upper management had praised her lavishly. She believed that with a good recommendation from Sharp, she would get the job.

But Walt Murdoch received the promotion and moved to Topeka. Martin was devastated. That she did not get the promotion was bad enough, but she could not stand that Murdoch had been chosen. She and Al Sharp had taken to calling Murdoch "Mr. Intolerable" because neither of them could stand his pompous arrogance. She felt that his being chosen was an insult to her; it made her rethink her entire career. When the grapevine confirmed her suspicion that Al Sharp had strongly influenced the decision, she determined to reduce her interaction with Sharp to a bare minimum.

Relations in the office were very chilly for almost a month. Sharp soon gave up trying to get back in Martin's favor, and they began communicating only in short, unsigned memos. Finally, William Attridge, their immediate boss, could tolerate the hostility no longer and called the two in for a meeting. "We're going to sit here until you two become friends again," he said, "or at least until I find out what's bugging you."

Martin resisted for a few minutes, denying that anything had changed in their relationship, but when she saw that Attridge was serious, she finally said, "Al seems more interested in dealing with Walter Murdoch." Sharp's jaw dropped; he sputtered but could not say anything. Attridge came to the rescue.

"Walter's been safely kicked upstairs, thanks in part to Al, and neither of you will have to deal with him in the future. But if you're upset about that promotion, you should know that Al had nothing but praise for you and kept pointing out how this division would suffer if we buried you in Topeka. With your bonuses, you're still making as much as Murdoch. If your work here continues to be outstanding, you'll be headed for a much better place than Topeka."

Embarrassed, Martin looked up at Sharp, who shrugged and said, "You want to go get some coffee?"

Over coffee, Martin told Sharp what she had been thinking for the past month and apologized for treating him unfairly. Sharp explained that what she saw as aloofness was actually respect and something akin to fear: he viewed her as brilliant and efficient. Consequently he was very cautious, trying not to offend her.

The next day, the office was almost back to normal. But Martin and Sharp established a new ritual: they took a coffee break together every day at ten. Soon their teasing and friendly competition loosened up everyone with whom they worked.

Case Questions

1. What might have happened had William Attridge not intervened?
2. Are the sources of the misunderstanding between Martin and Sharp common or unusual?

CHAPTER 15

Dimensions of Organization Structure

OUTLINE

[handwritten notes: "hasn't been explained to us yet they don't been functionalized by function"]

[handwritten: "Purchasing / etc..."]

OBJECTIVES

After studying this chapter, you should be able to:

Define organization structure and discuss its purpose.

Describe structural configuration and summarize its four basic dimensions.

Discuss two structural policies that affect operations.

Explain the dual concepts of authority and responsibility.

Describe the classic views of organization structure.

[handwritten: "Division"]

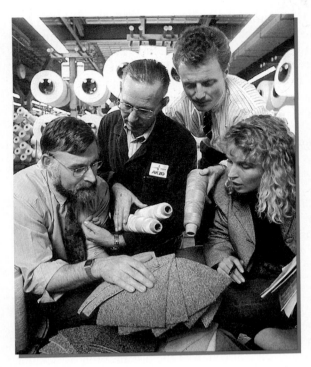

Allied-Signal Incorporated, a multi-business conglomerate, has recently been reorganized. Instead of a traditional departmental system, Allied-Signal employees are assigned to particular products and processes. Here, two workers inspect carpet samples at Azko, a European company in which Allied-Signal has acquired a majority interest.

The Signal Company started in the oil and gas business in 1922 and merged with Garrett Corporation, the aircraft engine and equipment giant, in 1964. Allied Chemical & Dye Corporation, founded in 1920, moved into the oil and gas business with the purchase of Union Texas Natural Gas in 1962, into the aerospace business through the purchase of the Bendix Corporation in 1983, into electronics with Eltra and Bunker Ramo, and into health and scientific products with Fisher Scientific. Finally, in 1985 the two companies merged to become Allied-Signal Incorporated, putting together Signal's Garrett division and Allied's Bendix division to make aerospace Allied-Signal's largest business sector. It had a typical conglomerate structure with the different businesses run somewhat independently, each with the typical functional organization structure. More change is coming, however, at Allied-Signal.

In response to changes in information technology (the speed with which information is manipulated, stored, retrieved, and disseminated) and the need for increases in productivity, quality, service delivery, and job satisfaction, Allied-Signal is moving toward what they think will be the way most organizations will be organized in the twenty-first century. Rather than have departments with the basic business functions of marketing, accounting, human resources, engineering and others, Allied-Signal plans to organize around processes. Its chief executive officer, Lawrence A. Bossidy, predicts that there will be an organizational revolution. He expects that organizations will organize around the materials and product flows rather than the traditional functions. The lack of departments in the new organization means that Allied-Signal will have no department of engineering, accounting, purchasing, or marketing. All employees have already gone through the company's training program on total quality management, which Bossidy expects will aid in changing employee attitudes and work behaviors.

Most companies have several basic processes: for example, new product development, flow of materials, and order-delivery billing cycle. At Allied-Signal, specialists will be assigned to one of the basic processes and make their functional contributions to that process. A marketing specialist may be involved in new product-development, from concept to design to actual manufacturing. A specialist in finance will be involved in each process as needed. These specialists will be available to contribute their expertise to each process. Engineers will know each other and be able to share information with each other but will not necessarily work with each other every day. Although the new structure may be somewhat confusing at first, Allied-Signal expects the benefits to be worth it.[1]

Organizations such as Allied-Signal do not make major structural changes arbitrarily; rather, they must have some compelling reason. Allied-Signal was already known as the industry leader in aerospace and automotive prod-

1. "The Search for the Organization of Tomorrow," *Fortune,* May 18, 1992, pp. 92–98; Thomas A. Stewart, "Allied Signal's Turnaround Blitz," *Fortune,* November 30, 1992, pp. 72–77; and Gary Hoover, Alta Campbell, and Patrick J. Spain, *Hoover's Handbook of American Business 1993* (Austin, Tex.: The Reference Press, 1992), p. 99.

ucts, electronics, and health and scientific products, but its managers believed that reorganizing would help focus the company's efforts to serve customers better. In this chapter, we explore how the structure of an organization can be a major factor in how successfully the organization achieves its goals. We begin with an overview of organizations and organization structure that defines each and puts organization structure in the context of organizational goals and strategy. Second, we discuss the two major perspectives of organizing, the structural configuration view and the operational view. Then, we discuss the often confusing concepts of responsibility and authority and present an alternative view of authority. Finally, we show several of the classic views of how organizations should be structured.

The Nature of Organization Structure

In Parts 1 through 4 we discussed major elements of the individual and the factors that tie the individual and the organization together. In a given organization, these factors must fit together within a common framework: the organization's structure.

Organization Defined

An **organization** is a group of people working together to attain common goals.

An **organization** is a group of people working together to achieve common goals.[2] Top management determines the direction of the organization by defining its purpose, establishing the goals to meet that purpose, and formulating strategies to achieve the goals.[3]

The definition of purpose is the organization's reason to exist; in effect, it answers the question, "What business are we in?" The establishment of goals converts the defined purpose into specific, measurable performance targets. **Organizational goals** are objectives that management seeks to achieve in pursuing the purpose of the firm. Goals motivate people to work together. Although each individual's goals are important to the organization, the organization's overall goals are the most important. Goals keep the organization on track by focusing the attention and actions of the members. They also provide the organization with a forward-looking orientation. They do not address past success or failure; rather, they force members to think about and plan for the future. Finally, strategies are specific action plans that enable the organization to achieve its goals and thus its purpose. They involve the development of an organization structure and the processes to do the organization's work.

Organizational goals are objectives that management seeks to achieve in pursuing the firm's purpose.

Organizational goals keep the organization on track by focusing the attention and actions of its members.

Organization Structure

Organization structure is a system of task, reporting, and authority relationships within which the organization does its work.

Organization structure is a system of task, reporting, and authority relationships within which the work of the organization is done. Thus, structure defines the form and function of the organization's activities. Structure also defines how the parts of an organization fit together, as in an organization chart.

2. See Richard Daft, *Organization Theory and Design*, 2nd ed. (St. Paul, Minn.: West, 1986), p. 9, for further discussion of the definition of organization.
3. John R. Montanari, Cyril P. Morgan, and Jeffrey S. Bracker, *Strategic Management* (Hinsdale, Ill.: Dryden Press, 1990), pp. 1–2.

The purpose of organization structure is to order and coordinate the actions of employees to achieve organizational goals. The premise of organized effort is that people can accomplish more by working together than they can separately. If the potential gains of collective effort are to be realized, however, the work must be coordinated. Suppose that the thousands of employees at Ford Motor Co. worked without any kind of structure. Each person might try to build a car that he or she thought would sell. No two automobiles would be alike, and each would take months or years to build. The costs of making the cars would be so high that no one would be able to afford them. To produce automobiles that are both competitive in the marketplace and profitable for the company, Ford must have a structure in which its employees and managers work together in a coordinated manner.

The task of coordinating the activities of thousands of workers to produce cars that are not only drivable but guaranteed for 60,000 miles may seem monumental. Yet whether for mass producing cars or making soap, the requirements of organization structure are similar. First, the structure must identify the tasks or processes that must be performed for the organization to reach its goals. This is often called *division of labor*. Even small organizations (those with fewer than one hundred employees) use division of labor.[4] Second, the structure must combine and coordinate the divided tasks to achieve a desired level of output. The more interdependent the divided tasks, the more coordination is required.[5] Every organization structure addresses these two fundamental requirements.[6] The various ways that they do so are what make one organization structure different from another.

Organization structure can be analyzed in three ways. First, we can examine its configuration, or its size and shape as depicted on an organization chart. Second, we can analyze its operational aspects or characteristics, such as separation of specialized tasks, rules and procedures, and decision making. Finally, we can examine responsibility and authority within the organization. In this chapter, we look at organization structure from all three points of view.

Structural Configuration

An **organization chart** is a diagram showing all people, positions, reporting relationships, and lines of formal communication in the organization.

The structure of an organization is most often described in terms of its organization chart. A complete **organization chart** shows all people, positions, reporting relationships, and lines of formal communication in the organization. (As we discuss in Chapter 14, however, communication is not limited to these formal channels.) Large organizations may need several charts to show all positions. For example, one chart may show top management, including the board of directors, the chief executive officer, the president, all vice presidents, and important headquarter staff units. Subsequent charts may show the structure of each department and staff unit. Figure 15.1 shows two organization charts for a large firm; the upper portion of the figure shows top management and the lower portion shows the manufacturing department. Notice that the structure of the different manufacturing groups is given in separate charts.

4. A. Bryman, A. D. Beardsworth, E. T. Keil, and J. Ford, "Organizational Size and Specialization," *Organization Studies*, September 1983, pp. 271–278.
5. Joseph L. C. Cheng, "Interdependence and Coordination in Organizations: A Role System Analysis," *Academy of Management Journal*, March 1983, pp. 156–162.
6. See Henry Mintzberg, *The Structuring of Organizations* (Englewood Cliffs, N.J.: Prentice-Hall, 1979), for further discussion of the basic elements of structure.

FIGURE 15.1

Examples of Organization Charts

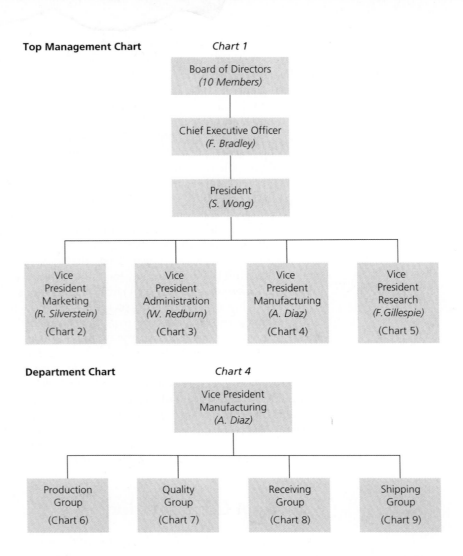

Top Management Chart — *Chart 1*

Board of Directors
(10 Members)

Chief Executive Officer
(F. Bradley)

President
(S. Wong)

Vice President Marketing
(R. Silverstein)
(Chart 2)

Vice President Administration
(W. Redburn)
(Chart 3)

Vice President Manufacturing
(A. Diaz)
(Chart 4)

Vice President Research
(F. Gillespie)
(Chart 5)

Department Chart — *Chart 4*

Vice President Manufacturing
(A. Diaz)

Production Group
(Chart 6)

Quality Group
(Chart 7)

Receiving Group
(Chart 8)

Shipping Group
(Chart 9)

An organization chart depicts reporting relationships and work group memberships and shows how positions and small work groups are combined into departments, which together make up the **configuration,** or shape, of the organization. The configuration of organizations can be analyzed in terms of how the two basic requirements of structure—division of labor and coordination of the divided tasks—are fulfilled.

Configuration is the shape of the organization, made up of division of labor and the means of coordinating the divided tasks.

Division of Labor

Division of labor is the extent to which the organization's work is divided into different jobs to be done by different people.

Division of labor is the extent to which the organization's work is separated into different jobs to be done by different people. Division of labor is one of the seven primary characteristics of structuring described by Max Weber,[7] but the concept

7. Max Weber, *The Theory of Social and Economic Organization*, trans. A. M. Henderson and Talcott Parsons (New York: Free Press, 1947).

can be traced back to the eighteenth-century economist Adam Smith. As we noted in Chapter 1, Smith used a study of pin making to promote the idea of dividing production work to increase productivity.[8] Division of labor continued to increase in popularity as large organizations became more prevalent in a manufacturing society. This has continued, and most research indicates that large organizations usually have more division of labor than small ones.[9]

Division of labor has also been found to have both advantages and disadvantages (see Table 15.1). Modern managers and organization theorists are still struggling with the primary disadvantage: division of labor often results in repetitive, boring jobs that undercut worker satisfaction, involvement, and commitment.[10] In addition, extreme division of labor may be incompatible with new, integrated computerized manufacturing technologies that require teams of highly skilled workers.[11]

Division of labor, however, need not result in boredom. Visualized in terms of a small organization such as a basketball team, it can be quite dynamic. A basketball team consists of five players, each of whom plays a different role on the team. In professional basketball the five positions typically are center, power forward, small forward, shooting guard, and point guard. The tasks of the players in each position are quite different, resulting in players of different sizes and skills being on the floor at any one time. The teams that won championships, such as the Los Angeles Lakers and the Chicago Bulls, used division of labor by having players specialize in specified tasks and do them impeccably. Similarly, organizations must have specialists who are highly trained and know their specific jobs very well.

Coordinating the Divided Tasks

Three basic mechanisms are used to help coordinate the divided tasks: departmentalization, span of control, and administrative hierarchy. These mechanisms focus on grouping tasks in some meaningful manner, creating work groups of manageable size, and establishing a system of reporting relationships among supervisors and managers.

8. Adam Smith, *An Inquiry into the Nature and Causes of the Wealth of Nations* (London: Dent, 1910).
9. Nancy M. Carter and Thomas L. Keon, "The Rise and Fall of the Division of Labour, the Past 25 Years," *Organization Studies*, 1986, pp. 54–57.
10. Glenn R. Carroll, "The Specialist Strategy," *California Management Review*, Spring 1984, pp. 126–137.
11. "Management Discovers the Human Side of Automation," *Business Week*, September 29, 1986, pp. 70–75.

TABLE 15.1

Advantages and Disadvantages of Division of Labor

Advantages	Disadvantages
Efficient use of labor	Routine, repetitive jobs
Reduced training costs	Reduced job satisfaction
Increased standardization and uniformity of output	Decreased worker involvement and commitment
Increased expertise from repetition of tasks	Increased worker alienation
	Possible incompatibility with computerized manufacturing technologies

Basketball teams use the organizational principle of the division of labor as a means to success. Each player on the floor at a given time has an assigned position and task, for which he has been specifically trained. Here, forward Scottie Pippin of the Chicago Bulls tries to evade guard A.C. Green of the Los Angeles Lakers.

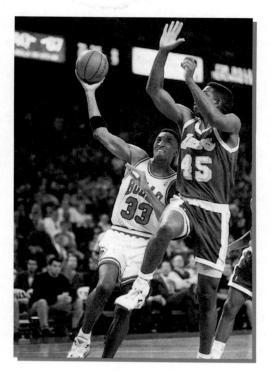

Departmentalization is the manner in which divided tasks are combined and allocated to work groups.

Divided tasks can be combined into departments by function, process, product or service, customer, and geography.

Departmentalization **Departmentalization** describes the manner in which divided tasks are combined and allocated to work groups. It is a consequence of the division of labor. Because employees engaged in specialized activities can lose sight of overall organizational goals, their work must be coordinated to ensure that it contributes to the welfare of the organization.

Tasks can be grouped, or departmentalized, in many possible ways. The five most often used methods are by business function, by process, by product or service, by customer, and by geography. The first two, function and process, derive from the internal operations of the organization; the others are based on external factors. Most organizations tend to use a combination of methods, and departmentalization often changes as organizations evolve.[12]

Departmentalization by business function is based on the traditional business functions such as marketing, manufacturing, and human resource administration (see Figure 15.2). In this configuration employees most frequently associate with those engaged in the same function, which helps in communication and cooperation. In a functional group, employees who do similar work can learn from one another by sharing ideas about opportunities and problems they encounter on the job. Unfortunately, the functional grouping lacks an automatic mechanism for coordinating the flow of work through the organization.[13] In other words, employees in a functional structure tend to associate little with those in other parts of the organization. The result can be a narrowness of focus that limits the coordination of work among functional groups, as when the engineering department fails to provide marketing with product information because it is too busy testing materials to think about sales.

12. See Robert H. Miles, *Macro Organizational Behavior* (Santa Monica, Calif.: Goodyear, 1980), pp. 28–34, for a discussion of departmentalization schemes.
13. Mintzberg, *The Structuring of Organizations*, p. 125.

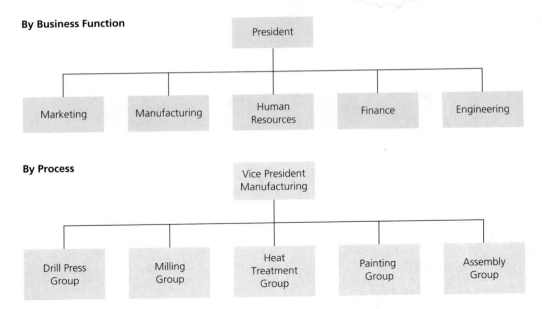

By Business Function

President

Marketing | Manufacturing | Human Resources | Finance | Engineering

By Process

Vice President Manufacturing

Drill Press Group | Milling Group | Heat Treatment Group | Painting Group | Assembly Group

FIGURE 15.2

Departmentalization by Business Function and by Process

Departmentalization by process is similar to functional departmentalization except that the focus is more on specific jobs grouped according to the activity. Thus, as Figure 15.2 illustrates, the firm's manufacturing jobs are divided into well-defined manufacturing processes: drilling, milling, heat treating, painting, and assembly. Hospitals often use process departmentalization, grouping professional employees such as therapists according to the types of treatment they provide.

Process groupings encourage specialization and expertise among employees, who tend to concentrate on a single operation and share information with departmental colleagues. A process orientation may develop into an internal career path and managerial hierarchy within the department. As in functional grouping, however, narrowness of focus can be a problem in process departmentalization. Employees in a process group may become so absorbed in the requirements and execution of their operations that they disregard broader considerations such as overall product flow.[14]

Departmentalization by product or service occurs when employees who work on a particular product or service are members of the same department regardless of their business function or the process in which they are engaged. This configuration is shown in Figure 15.3. In the late-1980s IBM reorganized its operations into five autonomous business units: personal computers, medium-size office systems, mainframes, communications equipment, and components.[15] Although this reorganization worked for a while, the company took quite a downturn in the early 1990s.

Colgate-Palmolive changed its organization structure by eliminating the typical functional divisions, such as basic research, processing, and packaging. Instead,

14. Miles, *Macro Organizational Behavior*, pp. 122–133.
15. "Big Blue Wants to Loosen Its Collar," *Fortune*, February 29, 1988, p. 8.

FIGURE 15.3

Departmentalization by Product

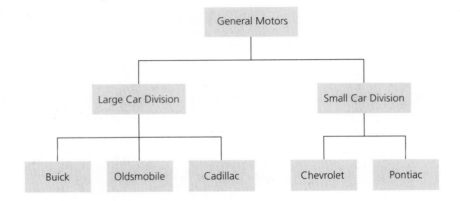

employees were organized into teams based on products such as pet food, household products, and oral hygiene products. Since the reorganization, new-product development has increased significantly and cost savings are estimated to be about $40 million.[16]

Departmentalization according to product or service obviously enhances interaction and communication among employees who produce the same product or provide the same service. Such a grouping may reduce product- or service-related coordination problems. In this type of configuration, there may be less process specialization but more specialization in the peculiarities of the specific product or service. IBM expected that the new alignment would allow all employees, from designers to manufacturing workers to marketing experts, to become specialists in a particular product line. The disadvantage is that employees may become so interested in their particular product or service that they miss technological improvements or innovations developed in other departments. Honda Motor Co. chose a product departmentalization strategy when it introduced the Acura.[17] Honda, however, later changed its structure, as discussed in the *Global Perspective*.

Departmentalization by customer often is referred to as *departmentalization by market*. Many lending institutions in Texas, for example, have separate departments for retail, commercial, agriculture, and petroleum loans, as shown in Figure 15.4. When important groups of customers differ substantially from one another, organizing along customer lines may represent the most effective way to provide the best product or service possible. This is why hospital nurses often are grouped by the type of illness they handle; the various maladies demand different treatment and specialized knowledge.[18]

With customer departmentalization, there usually is less process specialization because employees must remain flexible to do whatever is necessary to enhance the relationship with customers. This configuration offers the best coordination of the work flow to the customer; however, it may isolate employees from others in their special areas of expertise. For example, if each of a company's three metallurgical specialists is assigned to a different market-based group, these individuals are unlikely to have many opportunities to discuss the latest technological advances in metallurgy.

16. Ronald Henkoff, "Cost Cutting: How to Do It Right," *Fortune*, April 9, 1990, pp. 40–50;
17. "The Selling of Acura—a Honda That's Not a Honda," *Business Week*, March 17, 1986, p. 93.
18. Peggy Leatt and Rodney Schneck, "Criteria for Grouping Nursing Subunits in Hospitals," *Academy of Management Review*, March 1984, pp. 150–165.

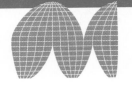

Does Honda Have Too Little Structure?

Honda of America Manufacturing (HAM) has always run one of the leanest car companies in the United States. In fact, it has prided itself on that fact. The supervision of its plant in Ohio has always been based on participation of all employees, the team concept, and everyone as a decision maker with authority and responsibility. Before 1993, Honda's cars, mostly made in the United States, were sold almost as fast as dealers could get them into the showroom. There was little need for an elaborate support staff to assist dealers in marketing, promotion, sales, and service. In 1993, however, sales took a sharp nosedive, and Honda dropped to number six in unit sales during the first half of the year. Intense competition has been part of the problem. Toyota's Lexus and Nissan's Infiniti have set very high standards in sales and service and cut Honda's Acura's sales by 17 percent. Adding to the problem was a potential scandal that alleged that dealers were accepting payoffs from Honda. Denials from the executives notwithstanding, the image of the company was damaged. Its lean structure may have contributed to the problem.

The result has been a restructuring of the company by redeploying almost 2,000 employees into new training programs and new positions. The company is trying to change the old way of thinking and make employees more flexible and responsive to customer needs. As Toyota and Nissan beat them to the showroom floors with new models of minivans, luxury cars, and utility vehicles, Honda had to do something to increase its response time. The new training is expected to increase the company's flexibility and adaptability in the coming market upswing.

SOURCES: Alison Rogers, "GM vs. Honda: A Morality Tale," *Fortune*, February 8, 1993, pp. 11–12; "The Dangers of Running Too Lean," *Fortune*, June 14, 1993, pp. 114–116; Roger Schreffler, "A Decade of Progress," *Automotive Industries*, November 1992, pp. 46-48; and Brian S. Moskal, "Supervision (or Lack of It)," *Industry Week*, December 3, 1990, pp. 54–57.

Departmentalization by geography means that groups are organized according to a region of the country or world. Sales or marketing groups often are arranged by geographic region. As Figure 15.4 illustrates, the marketing effort of a large, multinational corporation can be divided according to major geographical divisions. Using a geographically based configuration may result in major cost savings and better market coverage. On the other hand, it may isolate work groups from activities in the organization's home office or in the technological community because the focus of the work group is solely on the affairs within the region. This may foster loyalty to the work group that exceeds commitment to the larger organization. In addition, work-related communication and coordination among groups may be somewhat inefficient.

Many large organizations use a mixed departmentalization scheme. Such organizations may have separate operating divisions based on products, but within each division departments may be based on business function, process, customers, or geographic region (see Figure 15.5). Which methods work best depends on the organization's activities, communication needs, and coordination requirements. Another type of mixed structure often occurs in joint ventures, which are becoming increasingly popular. For example, Caterpillar, a long-time industry leader in heavy earth-moving equipment, faced major competition from the Japanese company Komatsu. In response, Caterpillar contracted with Daewoo Corporation of

FIGURE 15.4

Departmentalization by Customer and by Geographic Region

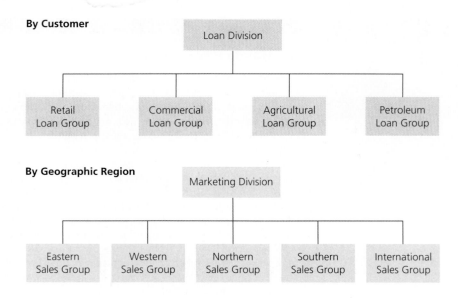

By Customer

Loan Division

Retail Loan Group · Commercial Loan Group · Agricultural Loan Group · Petroleum Loan Group

By Geographic Region

Marketing Division

Eastern Sales Group · Western Sales Group · Northern Sales Group · Southern Sales Group · International Sales Group

South Korea to make some of its trucks. Then it formed a joint venture, Shin Caterpillar-Mitsubishi, to make excavators. The new venture drew on Mitsubishi's expertise in designing and manufacturing quality excavators and on Caterpillar's unrivaled dealer network and manufacturing capacity.[19]

The **span of control** is the number of people who report to a manager.

Span of Control Another dimension of organizational configuration, **span of control,** is the number of people reporting to a manager; thus, it defines the size of the organization's work groups. Span of control is also referred to as *span of management.* A manager who has a small span of control can maintain close control over workers and stay in contact with daily operations. If the span of control is large, close control is not possible. Figure 15.6 shows examples of small and large spans of control. Supervisors in the upper portion of the figure have a span of control of sixteen, whereas in the lower portion their span of control is eight.

Experts have offered a number of formulas and rules for determining the optimal span of control in an organization,[20] but research on the topic has not conclusively identified a foolproof method.[21] Henry Mintzberg concluded that the optimal unit size depends on the coordination requirements within the unit, including factors such as the degree of job specialization in the unit, the similarity of the tasks in the unit, the type of information available or needed by unit members, differences in the members' need for autonomy, and the extent to which members need direct access to the supervisor.[22] Because results so far are inconclusive, research on span of control continues.[23]

19. Tsukasa Furukawa, "Global Construction Machinery Battle Looms," *Metalworking News,* July 27, 1987, p. 5, 31; "A Weakened Komatsu Tries to Come Back Swinging," *Business Week,* February 22, 1988, p. 48.
20. Lyndall F. Urwick, "The Manager's Span of Control," *Harvard Business Review,* May-June 1956, pp. 39–47.
21. Dan R. Dalton, William D. Tudor, Michael J. Spendolini, Gordon J. Fielding, and Lyman W. Porter, "Organization Structure and Performance: A Critical Review," *Academy of Management Review,* January 1980, pp. 49–64.
22. Mintzberg, *The Structuring of Organizations,* pp. 133–147.
23. See David Van Fleet, "Span of Management Research and Issues," *Academy of Management Journal,* September 1983, pp. 546-552, for an example of research on span of control.

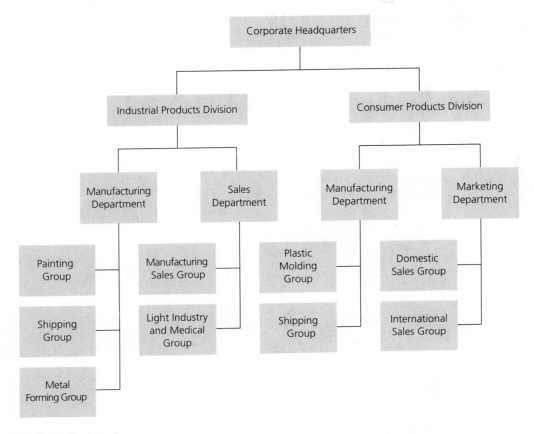

FIGURE 15.5
Mixed Departmentalization

The **administrative hierarchy** is a system of reporting relationships in the organization from the lowest to the highest managerial levels.

Administrative Hierarchy   The **administrative hierarchy** is a system of reporting relationships in the organization, from the first level up through the president or CEO. It results from the need for supervisors and managers to coordinate the activities of employees. The size of the administrative hierarchy is inversely related to the span of control: in organizations with a small span of control, there are many managers in the hierarchy; organizations with a large span of control have a smaller administrative hierarchy.

Using Figure 15.6 again, we can examine the effects of small and large spans of control on the number of hierarchical levels. The smaller span of control for the supervisors in the lower portion of the figure requires that there be four supervisors rather than two. Correspondingly, another management layer is needed to keep the department head's span of control at two. Thus, the span of control is small, the workers are under tight supervision, and there are more administrative levels. In the upper portion of the figure, production workers are not closely supervised, and there are fewer administrative levels. As a measure of the number of management personnel, or administrators, in the organization, the administrative hierarchy sometimes is called the administrative component, administrative intensity, or administrative ratio.

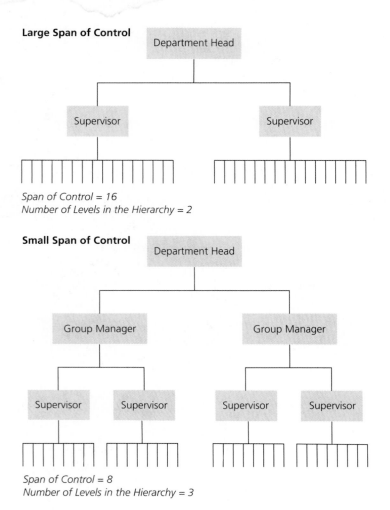

FIGURE 15.6

Span of Control and Levels in the Administrative Hierarchy

Large Span of Control

Department Head

Supervisor   Supervisor

Span of Control = 16
Number of Levels in the Hierarchy = 2

Small Span of Control

Department Head

Group Manager   Group Manager

Supervisor   Supervisor   Supervisor   Supervisor

Span of Control = 8
Number of Levels in the Hierarchy = 3

The size of the administrative hierarchy also relates to the overall size of the organization. As an organization's size increases, so do its complexity and the requirements for coordination, necessitating proportionately more people to manage the business. This conclusion, however, defines the administrative component as including all of the administrative hierarchy—that is, all of the support staff groups such as personnel, financial services, and legal staff. Defined in this way, the administrative component in a large company may seem huge when compared to the number of production workers. On the other hand, research that separates the support staff and clerical functions from the management hierarchy has found that the ratio of managers to total employees actually decreases with increases in the organization's size. Still other, more recent research has shown that the size of the administrative hierarchy and the overall size of the organization are not related in a straightforward manner, especially during periods of growth and decline.[24]

24. John R. Montanari and Philip J. Adelman, "The Administrative Component of Organizations and the Rachet Effect: A Critique of Cross-Sectional Studies," *Journal of Management Studies*, March 1987, pp. 113–123.

The popular movement of downsizing has been partially a reaction to the complexity of increasing organizational size. Much of the literature on organizational downsizing has proposed that downsizing results in lower overhead costs, less bureaucracy, faster decision making, smoother communications, and increases in productivity.[25] This expectation is due to the effort to reduce the administrative hierarchy by cutting layers of middle managers from the middle of the hierarchy. Unfortunately, many downsizing efforts have resulted in poorer communication, reduced productivity, and lower employee morale because the downsizing is done indiscriminately, without regard for the jobs that people actually do, the coordination needs of the organization, and the additional training that may be necessary for the survivors.[26]

Structure and Operations

Some important aspects of organization structure do not appear on the organization chart and thus are quite different from the configurational aspects discussed in the previous section. In this section, we examine the structural policies that affect operations and prescribe or restrict how employees behave in their organizational activities.[27] The two primary aspects of these policies are centralization of decision making and formalization of rules and procedures.

Centralization

Centralization is a structural policy wherein decision-making authority is concentrated at the top of the organizational hierarchy. In contrast, **decentralization** means that decisions are made at many different levels in the hierarchy.

The first structural policy that affects operations is **centralization,** wherein decision-making authority is concentrated at the top of the organizational hierarchy. This structural aspect is in contrast to **decentralization**, in which decisions are made throughout the hierarchy.[28] Increasingly, centralization is being discussed in terms of participation in decision making.[29] In decentralized organizations, lower-level employees participate in making decisions. The changes that Jack Smith made in 1993 at General Motors were intended to decentralize decision making throughout the company. Smith dismantled the old divisional structure and created a single unit called North American Operations and abolished a tangle of management committees that slowed down decision making. Managers are now encouraged to make decisions on new designs and pricing that used to take weeks to circulate through the committee structure on their way to the top.[30]

Decision making in organizations is more complex than indicated by the simple centralized/decentralized classification. In Chapter 10, we discuss organizational decision making in depth. One of the major distinctions we made there was that

25. D. A. Heenan, "The Downside of Downsizing," *The Journal of Business Strategy*, November–December 1989, pp. 18–23.
26. Wayne F. Cascio, "Downsizing: What Do We Know? What Have We Learned?" *Academy of Management Executive*, February 1993, pp. 95–104.
27. Dalton, Tudor, Spendolini, Fielding, and Porter, "Organization Structure and Performance."
28. See John Child, *Organization: A Guide to Problems and Practice*, 2nd ed. (New York: Harper & Row, 1984), pp. 145-153, for a detailed discussion of centralization.
29. Richard H. Hall, *Organization: Structure and Process*, 3rd ed. (Englewood Cliffs, N.J.: Prentice-Hall, 1982), pp. 87–96.
30. "Can Jack Smith Fix GM?" *Business Week*, November 1, 1993, pp. 126–131.

General Motors recently decentralized its organization structure, enabling employees throughout the hierarchy of the company to participate in decision making. At all administrative levels, employees are now more involved in the design, manufacturing, and marketing of GM's automotive products.

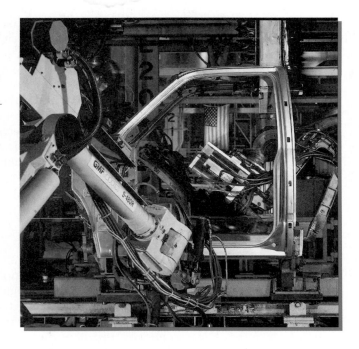

some decisions are relatively routine and require only the application of a decision rule. These decisions are programmed decisions, whereas those that are not routine are nonprogrammed. The decision rules for programmed decisions are formalized for the organization. This difference between programmed and nonprogrammed decisions tends to cloud the distinction between centralization and decentralization. For even if decision making is decentralized, the decisions themselves may be programmed and tightly circumscribed.

If employees participate little in decision making, the organization structure is centralized, regardless of the nature of the decisions being made. At the other extreme, if individuals or groups participate extensively in making nonprogrammed decisions, the structure can be described as truly decentralized. If individuals or groups participate extensively in making mainly programmed decisions, the structure is said to be formalized decentralization. Formalized decentralization is a common way to provide decision-making involvement for employees at many different levels in the organization while maintaining control and predictability.

Participative management has been described as a total management system in which people are involved in the daily decision making and management of the organization. As part of an organization's culture, it can contribute meaningfully to the long-run success of the organization.[31] It has been described as effective and, in fact, morally necessary in organizations. Thus, for many people, participation in decision making has become more than a simple aspect of organization structure. Caution is required, however, because if middle managers are to make effective decisions, as participative management requires, they must have sufficient information.[32]

31. Daniel R. Denison, "Bringing Corporate Culture to the Bottom Line," *Organizational Dynamics*, Autumn 1984, pp. 4–22.
32. Leonard W. Johnson and Alan L. Frohman, "Identifying and Closing the Gap in the Middle of Organizations," *Academy of Management Executive*, May 1989, pp. 107–114.

Formalization

Formalization is the degree to which rules and procedures shape the jobs and activities of employees.

Formalization is the degree to which rules and procedures shape employees' jobs and activities. The purpose of formalization is to predict and control how employees behave on the job.[33] Rules and procedures can be both explicit and implicit. Explicit rules are set down in job descriptions, policy and procedures manuals, or office memos. (One large company continually issues directives attempting to limit employee activities, and workers refer to them as "Gestapo" memos because of their prescriptive tone.) Implicit rules may develop as employees become accustomed to doing things a certain way over a period of time.[34] Though unwritten, these established ways of getting things done become standard operating procedures (SOPs) with the same effect on employee behavior as written rules.

We can assess formalization in organizations by looking at the proportion of jobs that are governed by rules and procedures and the extent to which those rules permit variation. More formalized organizations have a higher proportion of rule-bound jobs and less tolerance for rule violations.[35] Increasing formalization may affect the design of jobs throughout the organization,[36] as well as employee motivation,[37] and work group interactions.[38] The specific effects of formalization on employees are still unclear, however.[39]

Organizations tend to add more rules and procedures as the need for control of operations increases. For example, Lotus Development Corp. instituted more rules and procedures, especially in the areas of hiring and personnel, to gain control of its operations in the face of rapid growth.[40] Some organizations have become so formalized that they have rules for how to make new rules! One large state university created such rules in the form of a three-page document entitled "Procedures for Rule Adoption" that was added to the four-inch-thick *Policy and Procedures Manual*. The new procedure first defines terms such as *University, Board,* and *rule* and lists ten exceptions that describe when this procedure on rule adoptions does not apply. It then presents a nine-step process for adopting a new rule within the university.

Other organizations are trying to become less formalized by reducing the number of rules and procedures employees must follow. In this way, Chevron recently cut the number of its rules and procedures from more than four hundred to eighteen. Highly detailed procedures for hiring were eliminated in favor of letting managers make hiring decisions based on common sense.[41]

33. Mintzberg, *The Structuring of Organizations*, pp. 83-84.
34. Arthur P. Brief and H. Kirk Downey, "Cognitive and Organizational Structures: A Conceptual Analysis of Implicit Organizing Theories," *Human Relations*, December 1983, pp. 1065–1090.
35. Jerald Hage, "An Axiomatic Theory of Organizations," *Administrative Science Quarterly*, December 1965, pp. 289–320.
36. Gregory Moorhead, "Organizational Analysis: An Integration of the Macro and Micro Approaches," *Journal of Management Studies*, April 1981, pp. 191–218.
37. J. Daniel Sherman and Howard L. Smith, "The Influence of Organizational Structure on Intrinsic versus Extrinsic Motivation," *Academy of Management Journal*, December 1984, pp. 877–885.
38. John A. Pearce II and Fred R. David, "A Social Network Approach to Organizational Design-Performance," *Academy of Management Review*, July 1983, pp. 436–444.
39. Eileen Fairhurst, "Organizational Rules and the Accomplishment of Nursing Work on Geriatric Wards," *Journal of Management Studies*, July 1983, pp. 315–332.
40. "Coming of Age at Lotus: Software's Child Prodigy Grows Up," *Business Week*, February 25, 1985, pp. 100–101.
41. "Chevron Corp. Has Big Challenge Coping with Worker Cutbacks," *Wall Street Journal*, November 4, 1986, pp. 1, 25.

A relatively new approach to organizational formalization attempts to describe how, when, and why good managers should bend or break a rule.[42] Although rules exist in some form in almost every organization, how strictly they are enforced may vary notably from one organization to another and even within a single organization. Some managers argue that "a rule is a rule" and all rules must be enforced to control employee behaviors and prevent chaos in the organization. Other managers act as if "all rules are made to be broken" and see rules as stumbling blocks to effective action. Neither point of view is better for the organization; rather, a balanced attitude is recommended. The test of a good manager in a formalized organization may be how well he or she uses appropriate judgment in making exceptions to rules.

A balanced approach to making exceptions to rules should do two things. First, it should recognize that individuals are unique and that the organization can benefit from making exceptions that capitalize on exceptional capabilities. For example, an engineering design department with a rule mandating equal access to tools and equipment acquires a limited amount of specialized equipment, such as personal computers. The department manager decides to make an exception to the equal-access rule by assigning the computers to designers the manager believes will use them most and with the best results instead of making them available for use by all. Second, a balanced approach should recognize the commonalities among employees. Managers should make exceptions to rules only when individuals truly and meaningfully differ rather than base exceptions on features such as race, gender, appearance, or social factors.

Responsibility and Authority

Responsibility and authority are related to both configurational and operational aspects of organization structure. For example, the organization chart shows who reports to whom at all levels in the organization. From the operational perspective, the degree of centralization defines the locus of decision-making authority in the organization. Often there is some confusion about what responsibility and authority really mean for managers, however, and how the two terms relate to each other.

Responsibility

Responsibility is an obligation to do something with the expectation that some act or output will result.

Responsibility is an obligation to do something with the expectation that some act or output will result. For example, a manager may expect an employee to write and present a proposal for a new program by a certain date; thus, the employee is "responsible" for preparing the proposal.

Responsibility ultimately derives from the ownership of the organization. The owners hire or appoint a group, often a board of directors, to be responsible for managing the organization, making the decisions, and reaching the goals set by the owners. A downward chain of responsibility is then established. The board

42. Neil F. Brady, "Rules for Making Exceptions to Rules," *Academy of Management Review*, July 1987, pp. 436–444.

hires a president to be responsible for running the organization. The president hires more people and holds them responsible for accomplishing designated tasks that enable the president to produce the results expected by the board and the owners. The chain extends throughout the organization because each manager has an obligation to fulfill: to appropriately employ organizational resources (people, money, and equipment) to meet the owners' expectations. Although managers seemingly pass responsibility on to others to achieve results, each manager is still held responsible for the outputs of those to whom he or she delegates tasks.

A manager responsible for a work group assigns tasks to members of the group. Each group member is then responsible for doing his or her task. Yet the manager remains responsible for each task and for the work of the group as a whole. This means that managers can take on the responsibility of others but cannot shed their own onto those below them in the hierarchy.

Authority

Authority is power that has been legitimized within a particular social context.

Authority is power that has been legitimized within a specific social context.[43] (Power is discussed in Chapter 13.) Only when power is part of an official organizational role does it become authority. Authority includes the legitimate right to use resources to accomplish expected outcomes. As we discussed in the previous section, the authority to make decisions may be restricted to the top levels of the organization or dispersed throughout the organization.

Like responsibility, authority originates in the ownership of the organization. The owners establish a group of directors who are responsible for managing the organization's affairs. The directors, in turn, authorize people in the organization to make decisions and to use organizational resources. Thus, they delegate authority, or power in a social context, to others.

Authority is linked to responsibility because a manager responsible for accomplishing certain results must have the authority to use resources to achieve those results.[44] The relationship between responsibility and authority must be one of parity; that is, the authority over resources must be sufficient to enable the manager to meet the output expectations of others.

But authority and responsibility differ in important ways. Responsibility cannot be delegated down to others, but authority can. One complaint often heard from employees is that they have too much responsibility but not enough authority to get the job done. This indicates a lack of parity between responsibility and authority. Managers usually are quite willing to hold individuals responsible for specific tasks but are reluctant to delegate sufficient authority to do the job. In effect, managers try to rid themselves of responsibility for results (which they cannot do), yet they rarely like to give away their cherished authority over resources.

The delegation of authority to make decisions to lower-level managers is common in organizations today, but giving lower-level managers authority to carry out the decisions they make is essential. Managers typically have difficulty in delegating successfully. *Developing Management Skills* gives twelve suggestions that should help you develop your delegating skills.

43. See Jeffrey Pfeffer, *Power in Organizations* (Boston: Pittman, 1981), pp. 4–6, for a discussion of the relationship between power and authority.
44. John B. Miner, *Theories of Organizational Structure and Process* (Hinsdale, Ill.: Dryden Press, 1982), p. 360.

The Iran/Contra affair of 1987 and 1988 is a good example of the difference between authority and responsibility. Some believe that the Reagan administration confused delegation of authority with abdication of responsibility.[45] President Reagan delegated a great deal of authority to subordinates but did not require that they keep him informed. The subordinates thus made no effort to keep the president informed of their activities. Hence, delegation of authority by the administration was appropriate and necessary, but failing to require progress reports to keep informed and in control of operations resulted in the administration's trying to avoid responsibility. Although the president did hold his subordinates responsible for their actions, he ultimately—and rightfully—retained full responsibility.

An Alternative View of Authority

Authority and responsibility are closely related in that managers must have the authority to carry out their responsibilities. The **acceptance theory of authority** is the perspective that the authority of a manager depends on the subordinate's acceptance of the manager's right to give and expect compliance with the directive.

So far we have described authority as a "top-down" function in organizations; that is, authority originates at the top and is delegated downward as the managers at the top consider appropriate. In Chester Barnard's alternative perspective, authority is seen as originating in the individual who can choose whether to follow a directive from above.[46] The choice of whether to comply with a directive is based on the degree to which the individual understands it, feels able to carry it out, and believes it to be in the best interests of the organization and consistent with personal values. This perspective has been called the **acceptance theory of authority** because it means that the manager's authority depends on the subordinate's acceptance of the manager's right to give the directive and expect compliance.

For example, suppose that you are a marketing analyst. Your company has a painting crew, but for some reason your manager has told you to repaint your own office over the weekend. You probably would question your manager's authority to make you do this work. In fact, you would likely refuse to do it. A similar request to work over the weekend to finish a report would more likely be accepted and carried out. Thus, workers can either accept or reject the directives of a supervisor and thus limit supervisory authority.[47] In most organizational situations, employees accept a manager's right to expect compliance on normal, reasonable directives because of the manager's legitimate position in the organizational hierarchy or in the social context of the organization. When they do not accept the manager's right, they may choose to disobey the directive and must accept the consequences.

Classic Views of Organization Structure

The earliest views of organization structure combined the elements of organization configuration and operation into recommendations on how organizations should be structured. These views have often been called **classical organization theory** and include the ideal bureaucracy of Max Weber, the classic organizing

---

45. "Management Lesson of Irangate," *Wall Street Journal*, March 24, 1987, p. 36.
46. Chester Barnard, *The Functions of the Executive* (Cambridge, Mass.: Harvard University Press, 1938), pp. 161–184.
47. Pfeffer, *Power in Organizations*, pp. 366–367.

Pointers on Making Delegation Work

With all of the downsizing that has occurred recently, managers who are left must do more with less time and fewer resources. In addition, the essence of total quality management is allowing others—teams and individuals—to make decisions about their work. On the other hand, many managers and supervisors complain that they do not know how to delegate effectively. Delegating tasks and decision making to others is essential if what remains of middle management is to survive. The following points should help you delegate more effectively.

1. Choose a specific task and time frame. Know exactly what task is to be delegated and by when.
2. Specify in writing exactly why you are delegating this task.
3. Put down in writing exactly what you expect to be done and how it will be measured.
4. Be sure that the person or team is competent to do the task, or at least knows how to find the competence if they do not have it initially.
5. Be certain that those who will have to do the tasks really want to take on more responsibility.
6. Know what the costs of making errors are and that they can be absorbed, just in case errors are made.
7. Measure or oversee the work without being conspicuous and bothersome to those doing the task.
8. Make sure that *your* boss knows that you are delegating this task and approves.
9. Be sure that you will be able to provide the appropriate rewards to the person or team who takes on this additional responsibility if they succeed.
10. Be ready with another task to delegate when the person or team is successful with this one.
11. Be sure to delegate both the responsibility for the task and the authority to utilize the appropriate resources to get the job done.

SOURCES: Janet Houser Carter, "Minimizing the Risks from Delegation," *Supervisory Management*, February 1993, pp. 1–2; John Lawrie, "Turning Around Attitudes About Delegation," *Supervisory Management*, December 1990, pp. 1–2; and Selwyn W. Becker, "TQM Does Work: Ten Reasons Why Misguided Attempts Fail," *Management Review*, May 1993, pp. 30–33.

principles of Henri Fayol, and the human organization of Rensis Likert. All three are universal approaches, and their concerns and structural prescriptions differ significantly.

Ideal Bureaucracy

Weber's **ideal bureaucracy** is characterized by a hierarchy of authority and a system of rules and procedures designed to create an optimally effective system for large organizations.

Weber's **ideal bureaucracy**, presented in Chapter 1, was an organizational system characterized by a hierarchy of authority and a system of rules and procedures that, if followed, would create a maximally effective system for large organizations. Weber claimed that the bureaucratic form of administration is superior to other forms of management with respect to stability, control, and predictability of outcomes.[48]

48. Weber, *The Theory of Social and Economic Organization.*

Weber's ideal bureaucracy had seven essential characteristics, including the division of labor, hierarchy of authority, and rules and procedures. Weber intended these characteristics to ensure order and predictability in relationships among people and jobs in the bureaucracy. But it is easy to see how these same features can lead to sluggishness, inefficiency, and red tape. If any of the characteristics are carried to an extreme or are violated, the administrative system can easily break down. For example, if never-ending rules and procedures bog down employees with finding the precise rule to follow every time they do something, responses to routine client or customer requests may slow to a crawl. Moreover, subsequent theorists have said that Weber's view of authority is too rigid and have suggested that the bureaucratic organization may impede creativity and innovation and result in a lack of compassion for the individual in the organization.[49] In other words, the impersonality that is supposed to foster objectivity in a bureaucracy may result in serious difficulties for both employees and the organization. However, some organizations retain some characteristics of a bureaucratic structure while remaining innovative and productive.

The Classic Principles of Organizing

A second classic view was presented at the turn of the century by Henri Fayol, a French engineer and chief executive officer of a mining company. Drawing on his experience as a manager, Fayol was the first to classify the essential elements of management—now usually called **management functions**—as planning, organizing, command, coordination, and control.[50] In addition, he presented fourteen principles of organizing that he considered an indispensable code for managers. These principles are shown in Table 15.2.

The **management functions** set forth by Henri Fayol include planning, organizing, command, coordination, and control.

Fayol's principles have proved extraordinarily influential; they have served as the basis for the development of generally accepted means of organizing. For example, Fayol's unity of command means that employees should receive directions from only one person, and unity of direction means that tasks with the same objective should have a common supervisor. Combining these two principles with division of labor and authority and responsibility results in a system of tasks and reporting and authority relationships that is the very essence of organizing. Fayol's principles thus provide the framework for the organization chart and the coordination of work.

The classic principles have been criticized on several counts. First, they ignore factors such as individual motivation, leadership, and informal groups—the human element in organizations. This line of criticism asserts that the classic principles result in a mechanical organization into which people must fit, regardless of their interests, abilities, or motivations. The principles also have been criticized for their lack of operational specificity in that Fayol described the principles as universal truths but did not specify the means of applying many of them. Finally, Fayol's classic principles have been discounted because they were not supported by scientific evidence; Fayol presented them as universal principles, backed by no evidence other than his experience.[51]

49. For more discussion of these alternative views, see Miner, *Theories of Organizational Structure and Process*.
50. This summary of the classic principles of organizing is based on Henri Fayol, *General and Industrial Management*, trans. Constance Storrs (London: Pittman, 1949); and the discussions in Arthur G. Bedeian, *Organizations: Theory and Analysis*, 2nd ed. (Hinsdale, Ill.; Dyrden Press, 1984), pp. 58–59, and Miner, *Theories of Organizational Structure and Process*, pp. 358–381.
51. Miner, *Theories of Organizational Structure and Process*, pp. 358–381.

TABLE 15.2

Fayol's Classic Principles
of Organizing

Principle	Fayol's Comments
1. Division of work	Individuals and managers work on the same part or task.
2. Authority and responsibility	Authority—right to give orders; power to exact obedience; goes with responsibility for reward and punishment.
3. Discipline	Obedience, application, energy, behavior Agreement between firm and individual.
4. Unity of command	Employee receives orders from one superior.
5. Unity of direction	One head and one plan for activities with the same objective.
6. Subordination of individual interest to general interest	Objectives of the organization come before objectives of the individual.
7. Remuneration of personnel	Pay should be fair to the organization and the individual; discussed various forms.
8. Centralization	Proportion of discretion held by the manager compared to that allowed to subordinates.
9. Scalar chain	Line of authority from lowest to top.
10. Order	A place for everyone and everyone in their place.
11. Equity	Combination of kindness and justice; equality of treatment.
12. Stability of tenure of personnel	Stability of managerial personnel; time to get used to work.
13. Initiative	Power of thinking out and executing a plan.
14. Esprit de corps	Harmony and union among personnel is strength.

SOURCE: From *General and Industrial Management* by Henri Fayol. Copyright © Lake Publishing 1984, Belmont, CA 94002. Used by permission.

The Human Organization

Rensis Likert's **human organization** approach is based on supportive relationships, participation, and overlapping work groups.

Rensis Likert called his approach to organization structure the **human organization**.[52] Because Likert and others had criticized Fayol's classic principles for overlooking human factors, not surprisingly his approach centered on the principles of supportive relationships, employee participation, and overlapping work groups.

The term **supportive relationships** suggests that in all organizational activities, individuals should be treated in such a way that they experience feelings of support, self-worth, and importance. Participation means that the work group needs

52. See Rensis Likert, *New Patterns of Management* (New York: McGraw-Hill, 1961), and Rensis Likert, *The Human Organization: Its Management and Value* (New York: McGraw-Hill, 1967), for a complete discussion of the human organization.

Supportive relationships occur when individuals are treated so that they experience feelings of self-worth, support, and importance.

Overlapping work groups are work groups that are connected to each other by a common manager, who serves as a linking pin.

to be involved in decisions that affect it, thereby enhancing the sense of supportiveness and self-worth. The principle of **overlapping work groups** means that work groups are linked with managers, who serve as linking pins between groups. Each manager (except the highest ranking) is a member of two groups: a work group that he or she supervises and a management group composed of the manager's peers and their supervisor. Coordination and communication grow stronger when the managers perform the linking function by sharing problems, decisions, and information both upward and downward in the groups to which they belong. The human organization concept rests on the assumption that people work best in highly cohesive groups oriented toward organizational goals. Management's function is to ensure that the work groups are linked for effective coordination and communication.

Likert described four systems of organizing, whose characteristics are summarized in Table 15.3. System 1 is called Exploitive Authoritative and can be characterized as the classic bureaucracy. System 4, the Participative Group, is the organization design Likert favored. System 2, the Benevolent Authoritative system, and System 3, the Consultative system, are less extreme than either System 1 or System 4.

Likert described all four systems in terms of eight organizational variables: leadership processes, motivational forces, communication processes, interaction-influence processes, decision-making processes, goal-setting processes, control processes, and performance goals and training. Likert believed that work groups should be able to overlap horizontally as well as vertically where necessary to accomplish tasks. This feature is directly contrary to the classic principle that advocates unity of command. In addition, Likert favored the linking-pin concept of overlapping work groups for making decisions and resolving conflicts over the hierarchical chain of command.

Research support for Likert's human organization emanates primarily from Likert and his associates' work at the Institute for Social Research at the University of Michigan. Although their research has upheld the basic propositions of the approach, it is not entirely convincing. One review of the evidence has suggested that although research has shown characteristics of System 4 to be associated with positive worker attitudes and, in some cases, increased productivity, it is not clear that the characteristics of the human organization "caused" the positive results.[53] Possibly, positive attitudes and high productivity allowed the organization structure to be participative and provided the atmosphere for the development of supportive relationships. Likert's design has also been criticized for focusing almost exclusively on individuals and groups and not dealing extensively with structural issues. Overall, the most compelling support for this approach has come from research that focused on the individual and work group levels. Support for System 4 as a universally applicable organizational system is not strong.

Thus, the major elements of organization structure were embodied in the classic views of organization. Each view, however, combined these important features in different ways and with other management elements. These three classic views are typical of how the early writers attempted to prescribe a universal approach to organization structure that would be best in all situations. In the next chapter we describe other views of organization structure that are effective depending on the organizational situation.

53. Miner, *Theories of Organizational Structure and Process*, pp. 17–53.

TABLE 15.3

Characteristics of Likert's Four Management Systems

Characteristic	System 1: Exploitive Authoritative	System 2: Benevolent Authoritative	System 3: Consultative	System 4: Participative Group
Leadership				
■ Trust in subordinates	None	None	Substantial	Complete
■ Subordinates' ideas	Seldom used	Sometimes used	Usually used	Always used
Motivational Forces				
■ Motives tapped	Security, status	Economic, ego	Substantial	Complete
■ Level of satisfaction	Overall dissatisfaction	Some moderate satisfaction	Moderate satisfaction	High satisfaction
Communication				
■ Amount	Very little	Little	Moderate	Much
■ Direction	Downward	Mostly downward	Down, up	Down, up, lateral
Interaction-Influence				
■ Amount	None	None	Substantial	Complete
■ Cooperative teamwork	None	Virtually none	Moderate	Substantial
Decision Making				
■ Locus	Top	Policy decided at top	Broad policy decided at top	All levels
■ Subordinates involved	Not at all	Sometimes consulted	Usually consulted	Fully involved
Goal Setting				
■ Manner	Orders	Orders with comments	Set after discussion	Group participation
■ Acceptance	Covertly resisted	Frequently resisted	Sometimes resisted	Fully accepted
Control Processes				
■ Level	Top	None	Some below top	All levels
■ Information	Incomplete, inaccurate	Often incomplete, inaccurate	Moderately complete, accurate	Complete, accurate
Performance	Mediocre	Fair to good	Good	Excellent

SOURCE: Adapted from Rensis Likert, *New Patterns of Management* (New York: McGraw-Hill, 1961), pp. 223–233, and Rensis Likert, *The Human Organization* (New York: McGraw-Hill, 1967) pp. 197, 198, 201, 203, 210, and 211. Reprinted by permission of McGraw-Hill, Inc.

Summary of Key Points

- Organization structure is a system of task, reporting, and authority relationships within which the work of the organization is done. The purpose of organization structure is to order and coordinate the actions of employees to achieve organizational goals. Every organization structure addresses two fundamental issues: the division of available labor according to the tasks to be performed and the combination and coordination of divided tasks to ensure task accomplishment.

- An organization chart shows people, positions, reporting relationships, work group memberships, departments, and formal lines of communication. In a broader sense, an organization chart shows the configuration, or shape, of the organization. Configuration can be analyzed in two ways: division of labor and coordination of tasks. Division of labor is the extent to which the work is separated into different jobs to be done by different people. Coordination of tasks involves departmentalization, span of control, and the administrative hierarchy. Departmentalization is the manner in which the divided tasks are combined and allocated to work groups for coordination. Tasks can be combined into departments on the basis of business function, process, product or service, customer, and geographic region. Span of control is the number of people reporting to a manager; it also defines the size of work groups and is inversely related to the number of hierarchical levels in the organization. The administrative hierarchy is the system of reporting relationships in the organization.

- Structural policies that affect operations prescribe how employees should behave in their organizational activities. Such policies include centralization of decision making and formalization of rules and procedures. Centralization concentrates decision-making authority at the top of the organizational hierarchy; in decentralized organizations, decisions are made throughout the hierarchy. Formalization is the degree to which rules and procedures shape employees' jobs and activities. Its purpose is to predict and control how employees behave on the job. Explicit rules are set down in job descriptions, policy and procedures manuals, and office memos. Implicit rules develop over time as employees become accustomed to doing things a certain way.

- A final aspect of organization structure is the dual concepts of authority and responsibility. Responsibility is an obligation to do something. Authority is power that has been legitimized within a specific social context and includes the legitimate right to use resources to accomplish expected outcomes. The relationship between responsibility and authority needs to be one of parity; that is, authority over resources must be adequate to enable the employee to meet the expectations of others.

- Weber's ideal bureaucracy, Fayol's classic principles of organizing, and Likert's human organization include many of the major features of organization structure. Weber's ideal bureaucracy is characterized by rules and procedures, division of labor, hierarchy of authority, technical competence, separation of ownership, rights and property differentiation, and documentation. Fayol's classic principles included departmentalization, unity of command, and unity of direction and became generally accepted means of organizing. Likert's human organization was based on the principles of supportive relationships, employee participation, and overlapping work groups.

Discussion Questions

1. Define organization structure and explain how it fits into the process of managing the organization.
2. What is the purpose of organization structure? What would an organization be like without a structure?
3. In what ways are aspects of the organization structure similar to the structural parts of the human body?
4. How is labor divided in your college or university? In what other ways could your college or university be departmentalized?
5. What types of organizations could benefit from a small span of control? What types might benefit from a large span of control?
6. Discuss how increasing formalization might affect the role conflict and role ambiguity of employees. How might the impact of formalization differ for research scientists, machine operators, and bank tellers?
7. How might centralization or decentralization affect the job characteristics specified in job design?
8. When a group makes a decision, how is the responsibility for the decision apportioned among the members?
9. Why do employees typically want more authority and less responsibility?
10. Considering the job you now hold or one that you have held in the past, does your boss have the authority to direct your work? Why does he or she have this authority?
11. Describe at least four features of organization structure that were important parts of the classic views of organizing.

EXPERIENTIAL EXERCISE

Purpose   This exercise will help you understand the configurational and operational aspects of organization structure.

Format   You will interview employees of a small- to medium-size organization and analyze its structure. (Your instructor may coordinate this exercise with the exercise in Chapter 16.)

Procedure   Your first task is to find a local organization with fifty to five hundred employees. (It should not be part of your college or university.) The organization should have more than two hierarchical levels, but it should not be too complex to understand in a short period of study. You may want to check with your professor before contacting the company. Your initial contact should be with the highest-ranking manager that you can reach. Make sure that top management is aware of your project and gives its approval.

Using the material in this chapter, interview employees to obtain the following information on the structure of the organization:

1. The type of departmentalization (business function, process, product, customer, geographic region)
2. The typical span of control at each level in the organization
3. The number of levels in the hierarchy
4. The administrative ratio (number of managers to total employees and number of managers to production employees)
5. The degree of formalization (To what extent are rules and procedures written down in job descriptions, policy and procedures manuals, and memos?)
6. The degree of decentralization (To what extent are employees at all levels involved in making decisions?)

Interview at least three employees of the company at different levels and in different departments. One should hold a top-level position. Be sure to ask the questions in a way the employees will understand; they may not be familiar with the terminology used in this chapter.

The result of the exercise should be a report with a paragraph on each configurational and operational aspect of structure listed in this exercise, an organization chart of the company, a discussion of differences in responses from the employees you interviewed, and a discussion of any unusual structural features (for example, a situation in which employees report to more than one person or to no one). You may want to send a copy of your report to the cooperating company.

Follow-up Questions

1. Which aspects of structure were the hardest to obtain information about? Why?
2. If there were differences in the responses of the employees you interviewed, how do you account for them?
3. If you were president of the organization you analyzed, would you structure it in the same way? Why or why not? If not, how would you structure it differently?

CASE 15.1 Becton Dickinson Lets Tasks Form the Structure

Becton Dickinson and Company is the world's leading producer of single-use medical devices, selling to doctors, hospitals, laboratories, and medical schools. Products include syringes and needles, gloves, blood collection equipment, operating room products, surgical blades, thermometers, and diagnostic equipment. Price competition from internationally based firms, especially the Japanese, threatens its market share. Major changes worldwide as well as continued new product development are needed to keep the company on its growth track.

As other companies rush to reorganize, Becton Dickinson has kept its traditional functional departments. The work does not always get done through those departmental arrangements, however. For the past several years, Becton Dickinson has encouraged employees to form cross-functional teams to do things in new, different, and better ways. Management continually develops and presents to employees a broad vision for the future of each division and then lets each division develop the strategies and plans to accomplish the vision.

The consumer products division, for example, reorganized itself and created cross-functional teams that included suppliers, vendors, and personnel from other divisions. When a new instrument was developed in 1990, the company assigned a team leader who picked a team of engineers, marketers, manufacturing personnel, and suppliers to launch the product. The new product was launched 25 percent faster than the previous fastest launches in the company. The chief executive officer, Raymond Gilmartin, believed that it could have been done even faster. The problem, they discovered, was structural. During the planning phase, there was constant bickering between marketing and engineering. Marketing wanted an increased number of unique features to better satisfy customers. Engineering insisted that all of the unique features would make the product harder to design and produce and increase its cost. Division management found that the team leader, who was an engineer, continued to report to the head of engineering throughout the process and thus could not ever resolve the conflict between the groups. Since that situation, all team leaders have reported directly to the head of the division so they can make decisions for the division's best interests. In addition, when conflicts did result, the team leader could go to the "top" for division-wide authority. In other words, within each division, the structure now fits the tasks or projects that need to be done, rather than the other way around.

In other divisions, the heads of the cross-functional teams still maintained tight control on every decision.

Although everyone had been trained in how to avoid the bureaucracy, managers would not give it up. Finally, upper management kept moving decision making so far down throughout each division that middle managers had to give up some of their tasks and do the same. Finally, the teams were really involved in making decisions that affected their work.

Case Questions

1. What elements of structure were really changed by Becton Dickinson?
2. How is authority related to the configurational and operational aspects of structure at Becton Dickinson?
3. Was top management delegating authority or responsibility to middle managers? Why?

SOURCES: Brian Dumaine, "The Bureaucracy Busters," *Fortune*, June 17, 1991, pp. 36–50; Bernard C. Reimann, "Getting Value From Strategic Planning," *Planning Review*, March/April 1990, pp. 28–48; and Gary Hoover, Alta Campbell, and Patrick J. Spain, *Hoover's Handbook of American Business 1993* (Austin, Tex.: The Reference Press, 1992), p. 153.

| CASE 15.2 | **Changing the Rules at Cosmo Plastics** |

When Alice Thornton took over as chief executive officer at Cosmo Plastics, the company was in trouble. Cosmo had started out as an innovative company, known for creating a new product just as the popularity of one of the industry's old stand-bys was fading. In two decades, it had become an established maker of plastics for the toy industry. Cosmo had grown from a dozen employees to four hundred, and its rules had grown haphazardly with it. Thornton's predecessor, Willard P. Blatz, had found the company's procedures chaotic and had instituted a uniform set of rules for all employees. Since then, both research output and manufacturing productivity had steadily declined. When the company's board of directors hired Thornton, they emphasized the need to evaluate and revise the company's formal procedures in an attempt to reverse the trends.

First, Thornton studied the rules Blatz had implemented. She was impressed to find that the entire procedures manual was only twenty pages long. It began with the reasonable sentence: "All employees of Cosmo Plastics shall be governed by the following. . . ." Thornton had expected to find evidence that Blatz had been a tyrant who ran the company with an iron fist. But as she read through the manual, she found nothing to indicate this. In fact, some of the rules were rather flexible. Employees could punch in anytime between 8:00 and 10:00 A.M. and leave nine hours later, between 5:00 and 7:00 P.M. Managers were expected to keep monthly notes on the people working for them and make yearly recommendations to the human resources committee about raises, bonuses, promotions, and firings. Except for their one-hour lunch break, which they could take at any time, employees were expected to be in the building at all times.

Puzzled, Thornton went down to the lounge where the research and development people gathered. She was surprised to find a time clock on the wall. Curious, she fed a time card into it and was even more flabbergasted when the machine chattered noisily, then spit it out. Apparently R&D was none too pleased with the time clock and had found a way to rig it so it registered no time. When Thornton looked up in astonishment, only two of the twelve employees who had been in the room were still there. They said the others had gone back to work when they saw the boss coming.

Thornton asked the remaining pair to tell her what was wrong with company rules, and she got an earful. The researchers, mostly chemists and engineers with advanced graduate degrees, resented punching a time clock and having their work evaluated once a month, when they could not reasonably be expected to come up with something new and worth writing about more than twice a year. Before the implementation of the new rules, they often had gotten inspirations from going down to the local dime store and picking up $5 worth of cheap toys, but now they felt they could make such trips only on their own time. And when a researcher came up with an innovative idea, it often took months for the proposal to work its way up the company hierarchy to the attention of someone who could put it into production. In short, all these sharp minds felt shackled.

Concluding that maybe she had overlooked the rigidity of the rules, Thornton walked over to the manufacturing building to talk to the production supervisors. They responded to her questions with one word: anarchy. With employees drifting in between 8:00 and 10:00 and then starting to drift out again by 11:00 for lunch, the supervisors never knew if they had enough people to run a particular operation. Employee turnover was high, but not high enough in some cases; supervisors believed the rules prevented them from firing all but the most incompetent workers before the end of the yearly evaluation period. The rules were so "humane" that discipline was impossible to enforce.

By the time Alice Thornton got back to her office, she had a plan. The following week, she called in all the department managers and asked them to draft formal rules and procedures for their individual areas. She told them she did not intend to lose control of the company, but she wanted to see if they could improve productivity and morale by creating formal procedures for their individual departments.

Case Questions

1. Do you think Alice Thornton's proposal to decentralize the rules and procedures of Cosmo Plastics will work?
2. What risks will the company face if it establishes different procedures for different areas?

Organization Design

OUTLINE

OBJECTIVES

After studying this chapter, you should be able to:

Describe the basic premise of contingency approaches to organization design.

Discuss the three structural imperatives.

Describe the sociotechnical systems approach to organization design.

Summarize Mintzberg's classification of the five organizational forms.

Define matrix organization design and summarize its advantages and disadvantages.

Discuss contemporary approaches to organization design.

One of the greatest success stories in modern retailing has fallen on hard times and is restructuring in an effort to turn things around. The Limited, Inc., started in 1963 by Leslie Wexner with one store, grew to more than four thousand stores of Limited, Lerner, Express, Victoria's Secret, Lane Bryant, and other outlet chains. Throughout the growth stages in the decades of the 1970s and 1980s, each chain of stores had its own identity, marketing niche, and management. Victoria's Secret sold lingerie. The Limited focused on trendy fashions that were virtually "throw-away" clothes, which was quite appropriate for the times. Lerner concentrated on lower-cost clothes for the budget-conscious shopper.

Wexner, founder and chief executive officer, has admitted to a bit of neglect in the operation of The Limited and Lerner. Sales were down in both chains in 1991 and 1992. In 1993, Wexner, blaming major shifts in shopping patterns, announced major shake-ups in both. Both chains have new management and new strategies. The Limited stores had relied on "glitz and image" in trendy shopping malls and were not known for offering quality merchandise. Times have changed, however, and the twenty-year-old woman of the previous decade is now in her thirties and looking for quality, longer wear life, as well as fashion. The move in the 1990s is toward higher-quality cloth and manufacturing. Lerner, with its image of lower-cost clothes, has lost many customers to the discount stores. Its changes include higher quality, higher fashion, and higher cost, all at the same time. The changes were not so much structural changes as reorienting the activities of both chains toward the changing purchasing patterns of its customers. New managers now head both chains and there is a new customer focus throughout. These changes may result in head-to-head competition between the two chains.[1]

Leslie Wexner, who started the Limited in 1963, was responsible for the chain's timely transformation from purveyor of trendy "throw-away" clothes to well-made clothing better suited to today's wealthier, older market. Wexner has imposed a similar shift toward quality on his Lerner's stores, potentially causing competition between the two.

■ ■ ■ ■

T he Limited, Inc., had been so successful for so many years. Suddenly, the environment shifted and changes had to be made to respond and reposition the company for the different operating environment. Why is it that when products mature, the economy changes, or low-cost foreign competition enters the market, some companies die but other firms adjust and become stronger than ever? One major reason is the organization's design. Within the organization, design coordinates the efforts of the people, work groups, and departments. Designing a system of task, reporting, and authority relationships that leads to the efficient accomplishment of organizational goals is a challenge managers must be prepared to face. In Chapter 15, we discussed the tools with which managers design a system that enable the organization to be effective. In this chapter, we

1. "Did Leslie Wexner Take His Eye Off the Ball?" *Business Week*, May 24, 1993, pp. 104–108; "No Off-the-Rack Solutions Here," *Business Week*, May 25, 1992, pp. 116–118; Gary Hoover, Alta Campbell, and Patrick J. Spain, *Hoover's Handbook of American Business, 1993* (Austin: Tex.: The Reference Press, 1992), p. 366; and David Moin, "Limited Does Shuffle to Put Muscle in Stores," *WWD*, June 10, 1993, p. 2.

integrate these basic elements of structure, consider other factors such as the environment and technology, and present several perspectives on organization design. We begin this chapter by discussing organization designs based on the contingency approach. In this discussion we describe how the organization's size, environment, and technology combine with its strategy to determine various choices for organization design. Closely related is the sociotechnical systems approach which combines both the technical and human systems into organization design. Next, we examine the Mintzberg framework for classifying organization structures. We conclude with an examination of the matrix design and contemporary organization design.

Contingency Approaches to Organization Design

With the universal approach to organization design, prescriptions or propositions are designed to work in any circumstance.

Organization designs vary from rigid bureaucracies to flexible matrix systems. Most theories of organization design represent either a universal or a contingency approach. A universal approach is one whose prescriptions or propositions are designed to work in any situation. Thus, a universal design prescribes the "one best way" to structure the jobs, authority, and reporting relationships of the organization, regardless of factors such as the organization's external environment, the industry, and the type of work to be done.

With the contingency approach to organization design, the desired outcomes for the organization can be achieved in several ways.

A contingency approach, on the other hand, suggests that the desired outcome of organizational efficiency can be achieved in several ways. In a contingency design, specific conditions such as the environment, technology, and the organization's workforce determine the structure. Figure 16.1 shows the distinction between the universal and contingency approaches. This distinction is similar to that between universal and contingency approaches to motivation (Chapters 4, 5, and 6), job design (Chapter 7), and leadership (Chapters 12 and 13). Although no one particular form of organization is generally accepted, the contingency approach to organization design most closely represents current thinking.

Weber, Fayol, and Likert each proposed an organization design that is independent of the nature of the organization and its environment. Although each of these approaches contributed to an understanding of the organizing process and the practice of management, none has proved universally applicable. In this chapter we turn to several contingency designs that attempt to specify the conditions, or contingency factors, under which they are likely to be most effective. These contingency factors include such things as the technology, the environment, the organization's size, and the social system within which the organization operates. The contingency approach to organization structure has been criticized as being unrealistic in that managers are expected to observe a change in one of the contingency factors and to make a rational structural alteration. On the other hand, Donaldson has argued that it is reasonable to expect that organizations respond to lower organizational performance that may result from a lack of response to some important change in one or several contingency factors.[2]

2. Lex Donaldson, "Strategy and Structural Adjustment to Regain Fit and Performance: In Defense of Contingency Theory," *Journal of Management Studies*, January 1987, pp. 1–24.

FIGURE 16.1

Universal and
Contingency Approaches
to Organization Design

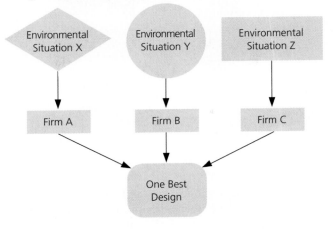

Universal Designs (Ideal Bureaucracy, Classic Principles
of Organizing, Human Organization)

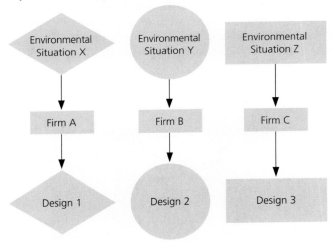

Contingency Designs (Sociotechnical Systems, Structural
Imperatives, Strategy and Strategic Choice)

Structural Imperatives and Strategy

The structural imperatives approach to organization design probably has been the most discussed and researched contingency approach of the last thirty years. The perspective was not formulated by a single theorist or researcher, and it has not evolved from a systematic and cohesive research effort; rather, it gradually emerged from a vast number of studies that sought to address the question, "What are the compelling factors that determine how the organization must be structured to be effective?" As Figure 16.2 shows, the three factors that have been identified as **structural imperatives** are size, technology, and environment.

Structural imperatives—size, technology, and environment—are the three primary determinants of organization structure.

FIGURE 16.2

**The Structural
Imperatives Approach**

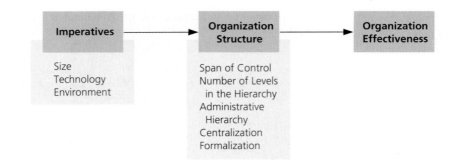

Imperatives	Organization Structure	Organization Effectiveness
Size Technology Environment	Span of Control Number of Levels in the Hierarchy Administrative Hierarchy Centralization Formalization	

Size

The size of an organization can be gauged in many ways. Usually it is measured in terms of total number of employees, value of the organization's assets, total sales in the previous year (or the number of clients served), or physical capacity. The method of measurement is a very important consideration, although the different measures usually are correlated.[3]

Larger organizations tend to have more complex organization structures than smaller organizations.

Research on the relationship between size and structure supports the view that larger organizations have a more complex structure than smaller ones. Peter Blau and his associates concluded that large size is associated with greater specialization of labor, a larger span of control, more hierarchical levels, and greater formaliza-

3. John R. Kimberly, "Organizational Size and the Structuralist Perspective: A Review, Critique, and Proposal," *Administrative Science Quarterly*, December 1976, pp. 571–597.

Pleasant Co., a small, high-end doll manufacturer, has managed to compete with the ubiquitous Barbie doll through ingenious marketing. The company sells the dolls, each of which represents a different period in American history, solely through a catalog which offers historically accurate doll-sized furniture and clothing, accompanying novels with a moral bent, and matching dresses for the dolls' owners.

tion.[4] These multiple effects are shown in Figure 16.3. Increasing size leads to more specialization of labor within a work unit, which increases the amount of differentiation among work units and the number of levels in the hierarchy and, consequently the need for more intergroup formalization. With greater specialization within the unit, there is less need for coordination among groups; thus, the span of control can be larger. Larger spans of control mean fewer first-line managers, but the need for more intergroup coordination may require more second- and third-line managers and staff personnel to coordinate them. Large organizations therefore may be more efficient because of their large spans of control and reduced administrative overhead; however, the greater differentiation among units makes the system more complex. Studies by researchers associated with the University of Aston in Birmingham, England, and others have shown similar results.[5]

Economies of scale are another advantage of large organizations. In a large operation, fixed costs—for example, plant and equipment—can be spread over more units of output, thereby reducing the cost per unit. In addition, some administrative activities, such as purchasing, clerical work, and marketing, can be accomplished for a large number of units at the same cost as for a small number. Their cost then can be spread over the larger number of units, again reducing unit cost.

Companies such as AT&T, General Electric's Aircraft Engine Products Group, and S. C. Johnson & Son, Inc., have gone against the conventional wisdom that larger is always better in manufacturing plants. They cite the smaller investment required for smaller plants, the reduced need to produce a variety of products, and the desire to decrease organizational complexity (that is, reduce the number of hierarchical levels and shorten lines of communication) as the main reasons. In a number of instances, the smaller-size plant has resulted in increased team spirit, improved productivity, and higher profits.[6] See the *Global Perspective* for more on how Hyundai is getting smaller to be more competitive.

4. Peter M. Blau and Richard A. Schoenherr, *The Structure of Organizations* (New York: Basic Books, 1971).
5. The results of these studies are thoroughly summarized in Richard H. Hall, *Organizations: Structure and Process*, 3rd ed. (Englewood Cliffs, N.J.: Prentice-Hall, 1982), pp. 89–94. For a recent study in this area, see John H. Cullen and Kenneth S. Anderson, "Blau's Theory of Structural Differentiation Revisited: A Theory of Structural Change or Scale?" *Academy of Management Journal*, June 1986, pp. 203–229.
6. "Small Is Beautiful Now in Manufacturing," *Business Week*, October 22, 1984, pp. 152–156.

FIGURE 16.3

Impact of Large Size on Organization Structure

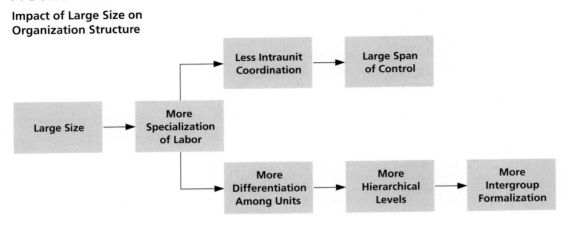

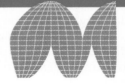
The Downsizing of Hyundai

Organizations around the world are downsizing, dismantling, and reorganizing. Even some of the most powerful, effectively managed organizations in the world are making major changes. One example is the Hyundai Corp., the largest conglomerate (*chaebol*) in South Korea, with estimated 1992 sales of $52 billion. Hyundai's empire includes automobiles, construction, heavy manufacturing, shipping, department stores, hotels, and insurance companies and accounts for approximately 10 percent of the country's gross national product. Hyundai is selling off the Hyundai Heavy Industries Co., Hyundai Merchant Marine Co., and its other interests in hotels, department stores, and insurance, and emphasizing its personal computer business by moving it to San Jose, California, to be closer to the U.S. market. The new company is expected to be smaller, leaner, and able to react more quickly to dynamic changes in the global marketplace for automobiles and construction.

The other major conglomerates in South Korea, including Samsung, Daewoo, and Lucky-Goldstar, are also reorganizing. Samsung is selling ten of its subsidiaries and focusing its efforts on improving quality and increasing its international operations. Pressured by changes in the nature of the workforce in South Korea and rapid changes in the environment, these companies are decentralizing decision making and turning over the top management roles to new, professional managers.

SOURCES: "Hyundai's Gutsy Gambit," *Business Week*, June 7, 1993; Sohn Jie-Ae, "Embracing Breathtaking Changes," *Business Korea*, August 1993, pp. 15–18; and H. Garrett DeYoung, "Hyundai's Gambit to Be a Big Player in PCs," *Electronic Business*, February 1993, pp. 61–64.

Organizational downsizing is a popular trend aimed at reducing the size of corporate staff and middle management to reduce costs.

Traditionally, as organizations have grown, several layers of advisory staff have been added to help coordinate the complexities inherent in any large organization. In contrast, a current trend is to cut staff throughout the organization. Known as **organizational downsizing**, this popular trend is aimed primarily at reducing the size of corporate staff and middle management to reduce costs. Companies such as Mobil, AT&T, and Burlington Northern Railroad Co. recently cut back headquarters and corporate staff significantly.[7] The results have been mixed, with some observers noting that indiscriminate across-the-board cuts may leave the organization weak in certain major areas. Positive results often include quicker decision making, however, because fewer layers of management must approve every decision. One review of research on organizational downsizing found both psychological and sociological results of downsizing.[8] This study suggested that the relationship between size in a downsizing environment affects organization design in very complex ways.

Other studies have found that the relationship between size and structural complexity is less clear than Blau's results indicated.[9] Instead, these studies suggest that size must be examined in relation to the technology of the organization.

7. Thomas Moore, "Goodbye, Corporate Staff," *Fortune*, December 21, 1987, pp. 65–76.
8. Robert I. Sutton and Thomas D'Anno, "Decreasing Organizational Size: Untangling the Effects of Money and People," *Academy of Management Review*, May 1989, pp. 194–212.
9. Richard H. Hall, J. Eugene Haas, and Norman Johnson, "Organizational Size, Complexity, and Formalization," *American Sociological Review*, December 1967, pp. 903–912.

Technology

In systems theory, **organizational technology** refers to the mechanical and intellectual processes that transform inputs into outputs. For example, the primary technology employed by Mobil transforms crude oil (input) into gasoline, motor oil, heating oil, and other petroleum-based products (outputs). Prudential Insurance Co. uses actuarial tables and information-processing technologies to produce its insurance services. Of course, most organizations use multiple technologies. Mobil uses research and information processing technologies in its laboratories where new petroleum products and processes are generated.

Although researchers generally agree with the systems view of technology, the means by which this technology has been evaluated and measured have varied widely. Five approaches to examining the technology of the organization are shown in Table 16.1. For convenience, we have classified these approaches according to the names of their proponents.

In an early study of the relationship between technology and organization structure, Joan Woodward categorized manufacturing technologies by their complexity: unit or small batch, large batch or mass production, and continuous processes.[10] Tom Burns and George Stalker proposed that the rate of change in the technology determines the best method of structuring the organization.[11] Charles

10. Joan Woodward, *Management and Technology: Problems of Progress in Industry*, No. 3 (London: Her Majesty's Stationery Office, 1958); and Joan Woodward, *Industrial Organizations: Theory and Practice* (London: Oxford University Press, 1965).
11. Tom Burns and George M. Stalker, *The Management of Innovation* (London: Tavistock, 1961).

TABLE 16.1

Summary of Approaches to Technology

Approach	Classification of Technology	Example
Woodward (1958 and 1965)	Unit or small-batch or in small batches	Customized parts made one at a time
	Large-batch or mass production	Automobile assembly line
	Continuous process	Chemical plant; petroleum refinery
Burns and Stalker (1961)	Rate of technological change	Slow: large manufacturing; rapid: computer industry
Perrow (1967)	Routine	Standardized products (Procter & Gamble, General Foods)
	Nonroutine	New technology products or processes (computers, telecommunications)
Thompson (1967)	Long-linked	Assembly line
	Mediating	Bank
	Intensive	General hospital
Aston studies: Hickson, Pugh, and Pheysey (1969)	Work flow integration; operations, materials, and knowledge technologies	Technology differs in various parts of the organization

Perrow developed a technological continuum, with routine technologies at one end and nonroutine technologies at the other, and claimed that all organizations could be classified on his routine-to-nonroutine continuum.[12] Thompson claimed that all organizations could be classified into one of three technological categories: long-linked, mediating, and intensive.[13] Finally, a group of English researchers at the University of Aston developed three categories of technology based on the type of work flow involved: operations, material, and knowledge.[14]

These perspectives on technology are somewhat similar in that all (except the Aston typology) reflect the adaptability of the technological system to change. Large-batch or mass production, routine, and long-linked technologies are not very adaptable to change. At the opposite end of the continuum, continuous-process, nonroutine, and intensive technologies are readily adaptable to change. For example, if the rate of change in technology is slow, the most effective design is bureaucratic or, to use Burns and Stalker's term, mechanistic. But if the technology is changing rapidly, the organization needs a structure that allows more flexibility and quicker decision making so that it can react quickly to change. This design is called organic. As summarized in Table 16.2, a **mechanistic structure** is primarily hierarchical, interactions and communications are mostly vertical, instructions come from the boss, knowledge is concentrated at the top, and continued membership requires loyalty and obedience. In contrast, the **organic structure** is structured like a network, interactions and communications are lateral and horizontal, work directions are in the form of information and advice, knowledge resides wherever it is most useful to the organization, and membership requires a commitment to the tasks of the organization.

One of the major contributions of the study of organizational technology is the revelation that organizations have more than one important "technology" that

A **mechanistic structure** is primarily hierarchical, interactions and communications typically are vertical, instructions come from the boss, knowledge is concentrated at the top, and loyalty and obedience are required to sustain membership.

An **organic structure** is set up like a network, interactions and communications are lateral and horizontal, knowledge resides wherever it is most useful to the organization, and membership requires a commitment to the organization's tasks.

12. Charles B. Perrow, "A Framework for the Comparative Analysis of Organizations," *American Sociological Review*, April 1967, pp. 194–208.
13. James D. Thompson, *Organizations in Action* (New York: McGraw-Hill, 1967).
14. David J. Hickson, Derek S. Pugh, and Diana C. Pheysey, "Operations Technology and Organization Structure: An Empirical Reappraisal," *Administrative Science Quarterly*, September 1969, pp. 378–397.

TABLE 16.2

Mechanistic and Organic Organization Designs

Characteristic	Mechanistic	Organic
Structure	Hierarchical	Network based on interests
Interactions, communication	Primarily vertical	Lateral throughout
Work directions, instructions	From supervisor	Through advice, information
Knowledge, information	Concentrated at top	Throughout
Membership, relationship with organization	Requires loyalty, obedience	Commitment to task, progress, expansion

Part 5   Organizational Processes and Characteristics

enables them to accomplish their tasks. Instead of examining technology in isolation, the Aston group also recognized that size and technology are related in determining organization structure.[15] They also found that in smaller organizations, technology had more direct effects on the structure. In large organizations, however, they found, like Blau, that structure depended less on the operations technology and more on size considerations such as the number of employees. In other words, in small organizations the structure depended primarily on the technology, whereas in large organizations the need to coordinate complicated activities was the most important factor. Thus, both organizational size and technology are important considerations in organization design.

> In small organizations the structure depends primarily on the technology, whereas in large organizations the need to coordinate complicated activities may be more important.

Environment

> The **organizational environment** includes all elements—people, other organizations, economic factors, objects, and events—that lie outside the boundaries of the organization.

The **organizational environment** includes all elements—people, other organizations, economic factors, objects, and events—that lie outside the boundaries of the organization. People in the organizational environment include customers, donors, regulators, inspectors, and shareholders. Among the other organizations are competitors, legislatures, and regulatory agencies. Economic factors include interest rates, the trade deficit, and the growth rate of the gross national product. Objects include things such as buildings, vehicles, and trees. Events that may affect organizations involve occurrences of weather, elections, or war.

The General Environment Determining the boundaries of the organization is necessary to understand where the environment begins. These boundaries may be somewhat elusive, or at least changeable, and thus difficult to define. But for the most part we can say that certain people, groups, or buildings are either in the organization or in the environment. For example, a college student shopping for a personal computer is part of the environment of Apple, Compaq, IBM, and other computer manufacturers. If the student works for one of these computer manufacturers, however, he or she is not part of that company's environment but is within the boundaries of the organization.

This definition emphasizes the expanse of the general environment within which the organization operates. Managers may indeed have the false impression that the environment is outside their control and interest. But because the environment completely encloses the organization, managers must be constantly concerned about it.

The manager, then, faces an enormous, only vaguely specified environment that somehow affects the organization. Managing the organization within such an environment may seem an overwhelming task. The alternatives for the manager are to (1) ignore the environment because of its complexity and focus on managing the internal operations of the company; (2) exert maximum energy in gathering information on every part of the environment and trying to react to every environmental factor; and (3) pay attention to specific aspects of the environment, responding only to those that most clearly affect the organization.

To ignore environmental factors entirely and focus on internal operations leaves the company in danger of missing major environmental shifts, such as changes in customer preferences, technological breakthroughs, and new regulations. To

15. Hickson, Pugh, and Pheysey, "Operations Technology and Organization Structure: An Empirical Reappraisal."

expend inordinate amounts of energy, time, and money exploring each and every facet of the environment may take more out of the organization than it returns.

The third alternative—to carefully analyze those segments of the environment that most affect the organization and to respond accordingly—represents the most prudent course of action. The issue, then, is to determine which parts of the environment are appropriate for the manager's attention. In the remainder of this section, we examine two perspectives on the organizational environment: the analysis of environmental components and environmental uncertainty.

Environmental Uncertainty   Not all forces in the general environment affect all organizations in the same way. Hospital Corporation of America, for example, is very much influenced by government regulations and medical and scientific developments. McDonald's, on the other hand, is affected by quite different environmental forces: consumer demand, disposable income, cost of meat and bread, and gasoline prices. Thus, the **task environment**—the specific set of environmental forces that affect the operations of an organization—varies among organizations.

The environmental characteristic that appears to have the most influence on the structure of the organization is uncertainty. **Environmental uncertainty** exists when managers have little information about environmental events and their effect on the organization.[16] Uncertainty has been described as resulting from complexity and dynamism in the environment. **Environmental complexity** is the number of environmental components that impinge on organizational decision making. **Environmental dynamism** is the degree to which these components change.[17] With these two dimensions, we can determine the degree of environmental uncertainty as illustrated in Figure 16.4.

In cell 1, a low-uncertainty environment, the few important components change infrequently. A company in the cardboard container industry might have a highly certain environment when demand is steady, manufacturing processes are stable, and government regulations have remained largely unchanged.

In cell 4, in contrast, many important components are involved in decision making, and they change often. Thus, cell 4 represents a high-uncertainty environment. The banking environment is now highly uncertain. With deregulation and the advent of interstate operations, banks today must compete with insurance companies, brokerage firms, real estate firms, and even department stores. The toy industry also has a highly uncertain environment. As they develop new toys, toy companies must stay in tune with movies, television shows, and cartoons as well as with public sentiment. Between 1983 and 1988, Saturday morning cartoons were little more than animated stories about children's toys. Recently, however, because of disappointing sales of many toys presented in cartoons designed to promote them, most toy companies have left the toy-based cartoon business.[18]

Environmental characteristics and uncertainty have been important factors in explaining organization structure, strategy, and performance. For example, the characteristics of the environment affect how managers perceive the environment, which in turn affects how they adapt the structure of the organization to meet

16. Richard L. Daft, *Organization Theory and Design*, 2nd ed. (St. Paul, Minn.: West, 1986), p. 55.
17. Robert B. Duncan, "Characteristics of Organizational Environments and Perceived Uncertainty," *Administrative Science Quarterly*, September 1972, pp. 313–327.
18. "Toy Makers Lose Interest in Tie-Ins with Cartoons," *Wall Street Journal*, April 28, 1988, p. 29.

	Cell 1: **Low Perceived Uncertainty** 1. Small number of factors and components in the environment 2. Factors and components are somewhat similar to one another 3. Factors and components remain basically the same *Example: Cardboard Container Industry*	**Cell 2:** **Moderately Low Perceived Uncertainty** 1. Large number of factors and components in the environment 2. Factors and components are not similar to one another 3. Factors and components remain basically the same *Example: State Universities*
	Cell 3: **Moderately High Perceived Uncertainty** 1. Small number of factors and components in the environment 2. Factors and components are somewhat similar to one another 3. Factors and components of the environment continually change *Example: Fashion Industry*	**Cell 4:** **High Perceived Uncertainty** 1. Large number of factors and components in the environment 2. Factors and components are not similar to one another 3. Factors and components of environment continually change *Example: Banking Industry*

Static / *Dynamic* — **Rate of Environmental Change**

Simple / *Complex* — **Environmental Complexity**

FIGURE 16.4

Classification of Environmental Uncertainty

environmental demands.[19] The environment has also been shown to affect the degree to which a firm's strategy enhances its performance.[20] That is, a certain strategy will enhance organizational performance to the extent that it is appropriate for the environment in which the organization operates. Finally, the environment is directly related to organizational performance.[21] The environment and the organization's response to it are crucial to success.

An organization attempts to continue as a viable entity in a dynamic environment. The environment completely encloses the organization, and managers must be constantly concerned about it. The organization as a whole, as well as departments and divisions within it, is created to address different challenges, problems, and uncertainties. James Thompson suggested that organizations design a structure

19. Masoud Yasai-Ardekani, "Structural Adaptations to Environments," *Academy of Management Review*, January 1986, pp. 9–21.

20. John E. Prescott, "Environments as Moderators of the Relationship between Strategy and Performance," *Academy of Management Journal*, June 1986, pp. 329–346.

21. Timothy M. Stearns, Alan N. Hoffman, and Jan B. Heide, "Performance of Commercial Television Stations as an Outcome of Interorganizational Linkages and Environmental Conditions," *Academy of Management Journal*, March 1987, pp. 71–90.

to protect the dominant technology of the organization, smooth out any problems, and keep down coordination costs.[22] Thus, organization structures are designed to coordinate relevant technologies and protect them from outside disturbances. Structural components such as inventory, warehousing, and shipping help buffer the technology used to transform inputs into outputs. For instance, demand for products usually is cyclical or seasonal and is subject to many disturbances, but the warehouse inventory helps the manufacturing system function as if the environment accepted output at a steady rate, maximizing technological efficiency and helping the organization respond to fluctuating demands of the market.

Strategy and Strategic Choice

Strategy is the plans and actions necessary to achieve organizational goals.

Another determinant of the design of the organization is the organization's strategy. **Strategy** is the plans and actions necessary to achieve organizational goals.[23] Kellogg, for example, has pursued a strategy that combines product differentiation and market segmentation in attempting to be the leader in the ready-to-eat cereal industry. Over the years Kellogg has successfully introduced new cereals from various grains in different shapes, sizes, colors, and flavors to provide any type of cereal the consumer might want.[24]

After studying the history of seventy companies, Alfred Chandler drew certain conclusions about the relationship between an organization's structure and its business strategy.[25] Chandler observed that a growth strategy to expand into a new product line usually is matched with some type of decentralization, a decentralized structure being necessary to cope with the problems of the new product line.

Chandler's "structure follows strategy" concept seems to appeal to common sense. Yet it is contradicted by the structural imperatives approach, which recommends that design decisions be based on size, technology, and environment, not on strategy. This apparent clash has been resolved by refining the strategy concept to include the role of the top management decision maker in determining the organization's structure.[26] In effect, this view inserts the manager–decision maker between the structural imperatives and the structural features of the organization. This distinction can be understood by comparing Figure 16.5 with Figure 16.2.

Strategy and the imperatives of size, technology, and environment combine to be primary determinants of organization design.

Figure 16.5 shows the structural imperatives as contextual factors within which the organization must operate and that affect the purposes and goals of the organization. The manager's choices for organization structure are affected by the organization's purposes and goals, the imperatives, and the manager's personality, value system, and experience.[27] Organizational effectiveness depends on the fit among the size, the technology, the environment, the strategies, and the struc-

---

22. Thompson, *Organizations in Action*, pp. 51–82.

23. John R. Montanari, Cyril P. Morgan, and Jeffrey Bracker, *Strategic Management* (Hinsdale, Ill.: Dryden Press, 1990), p. 114.

24. See Arthur A. Thompson, Jr., and A. J. Strickland III, *Strategic Management*, 3rd ed. (Plano, Tex.: Business Publications, 1984), pp. 19–27.

25. Alfred D. Chandler, *Strategy and Structure: Chapters in the History of the American Industrial Enterprise* (Cambridge, Mass.: MIT Press, 1962).

26. For more information on managerial choice, see John R. Montanari, "Managerial Discretion: An Expanded Model of Organizational Choice," *Academy of Management Review*, April 1978, pp. 231–241; and John Child, "Organizational Structure, Environment, and Performance: The Role of Strategic Choice," *Sociology*, Vol. 6, 1972, pp. 1–22.

27. H. Randolph Bobbitt and Jeffrey D. Ford, "Decision Maker Choice as a Determinant of Organizational Structure," *Academy of Management Review*, January 1980, pp. 13–23.

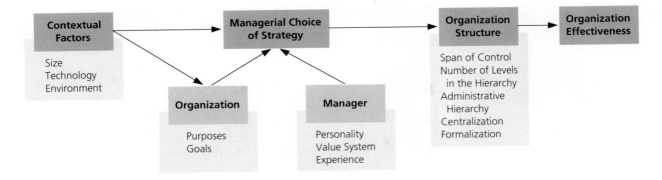

FIGURE 16.5

The Strategic Choice Approach to Organiza-tion Design

ture. *Developing Management Skills* illustrates how the Thermos company recognized environmental conditions, reinvented its traditional ways of doing things, and developed an innovative new product.

Another perspective on strategy-structure linkage is that the relationship may be reciprocal; that is, structure may be set up to implement the strategy, but it may also affect the strategic decision-making process via the centralization or decentralization of decision making and formalization of rules and procedures.[28] Thus, strategy determines structure, which in turn affects strategic decision making. A more complex view, however, suggested by Herman Boschken, is that strategy is a determinant of structure and long-term performance when the subunits doing the planning have distinctive competence in how to do planning.[29]

The role of strategic choice in determining organization structure actually goes a step beyond the view that structure follows strategy. However, it has received less research attention than have structural imperatives. And of course, some might simply view strategy as another imperative along with size, technology, and environment. Strategy does, though, seem to differ from the imperatives because it is a product of the analysis of the imperatives and an articulation of the organization's direction, purpose, and plans for the future.

Sociotechnical Systems Design

The foundation of the sociotechnical systems approach to organizing is systems theory, discussed in Chapter 1. There we defined a system as an interrelated set of elements that function as a whole. A system has numerous subsystems, each of which, like the overall system, includes inputs, transformation processes, outputs, and feedback. We also defined an **open system** as one that interacts with its environment. A complex system is made up of numerous subsystems in which the out-

28. James W. Fredrickson, "The Strategic Decision Process and Organization Structure," *Academy of Management Review*, April 1986, pp. 280–297.
29. Herman L. Boschken, "Strategy and Structure: Reconceiving the Relationship," *Journal of Management*, March 1990, pp. 135–150.

DEVELOPING MANAGEMENT SKILLS

Thermos Reinvents the Company

Barbecue grills have become all just alike, and everybody already has one. Therefore, Thermos Co., which makes gas and electric cookout grills in addition to its namesake Thermos bottles and lunch boxes, did not see much future for another outdoor grill. Chief executive officer Monte Peterson decided to reinvent the company's traditional way of doing things—its functional organization structure—to invent a totally new product. Although the product line for outdoor grills may be stagnant, the external environment has changed quite a bit. Thermos's experience can teach us a lot about the environment and organization structure.

The following five steps show how managers at Thermos reinvented their organization with positive results. Note that the analysis and changes moved from environmental analysis to organization structural change, to altering tasks, to altering the reward system, and to making the project personal to each individual involved.

The environment. The environment was changing fast. Customers can no longer be tricked by glitzy advertising. Women are grilling more. People are tired of the mess of traditional charcoal. Some cities are banning the use of gas in townhouses, apartments, and condominiums. Gas bottles can be dangerous, heavy, and often empty at the wrong time. Therefore, something new was needed.

The structure. Thermos eliminated its functional structure organized around marketing, manufacturing, and engineering, replacing it with multifunctional teams. The original team had ten persons from different functions, plus outsiders from design consulting firms and suppliers. There was no single team leader. The leadership and direction of the team rotated to whomever could direct the current task. Early in the process, marketing took the lead. Later, the design engineers were leading. Eventually, manufacturing took control. It is important to note that everyone was fully involved in the team throughout; only the leadership varied according to the task. Throughout the process, top management was solidly in support of the team.

The **sociotechnical systems approach** to organization design views the organization as an open system structured to integrate the technical and social subsystems into a single management system.

puts of some are the inputs to others. The **sociotechnical systems approach** views the organization as an open system structured to integrate the two important subsystems: the technical (task) subsystem and the social subsystem.

The **technical (task) subsystem** is the means by which inputs are transformed into outputs. The transformation processes may be the way steel is formed, cut, drilled, chemically treated, and painted or the ways information is processed in an insurance company or financial institution. Often major scientific and engineering expertise is applied to these transformation processes to get the highest productivity at the lowest cost. For example, Fireplace Manufacturers Inc. of Santa Ana, California, a manufacturer of prefabricated metal fireplaces, implemented new just-in-time (JIT) manufacturing and inventory systems to improve the productivity of its plant.[30] JIT is a system in which component parts arrive just in time to be used in the manufacturing process, thereby reducing the costs of storing them in a

---

30. "Small Manufacturers Shifting to 'Just-In-Time' Techniques," *Wall Street Journal*, December 21, 1987, p. 25.

Parallel tasks. While marketing was out getting in touch with consumers, engineering was working on new grilling technology, to get the flavor and look of gas and charcoal grilling with electricity. Manufacturing was also involved as designs were proposed by pointing out the difficulty or ease of manufacture of various designs.

The task is the reward. Thermos found that traditional monetary compensation was not as important to team members as being part of a team that was doing something innovative and meaningful. Everyone knew that the project was important to the company because top management supported it but did not meddle too closely, and plenty of time and money was available for research and product development.

Clear agendas. Top management made sure that this project was the primary responsibility of every team member, so that other things would not get in the way. Team members and other employees also got to home–field test the first one hundred manufactured. The results of this difficult testing were a few improvements that might not have been found until well after market introduction.

The results for the first year were quite good following its introduction in late 1992. It has won four design awards and may revolutionize the market for outdoor grills. More importantly, the redesigned company is expecting to create more new products that are equally successful in the near future.

These changes took place at five different levels of organizational analysis. Examine the different levels and write a list of other things at each level that Thermos also could have changed. For example, at the organizational level it could have initiated a matrix structure.

SOURCES: Brian Dumaine, "Payoff from the New Management," *Fortune*, December 13, 1993, pp. 103–110; "The Cleaner Patio Sizzler," *Business Week*, June 7, 1993, pp. 60–61; and "Thermos Fires Up Grill Lines," *The Weekly Home Furnishings Newspaper*, August 24, 1992, p. 54.

warehouse until they are needed. In effect, it redesigns the transformation process, from the introduction of raw materials to the shipping of the finished product. In three years, Fireplace Manufacturers' inventory costs dropped from $1.1 million to $750,000, and sales doubled over the same period. The transformation process usually is regarded as technologically and economically driven; that is, whatever process is most productive and costs the least generally is the most desirable.

The **social subsystem** includes the interpersonal relationships that develop among people in organizations. Employees learn one another's work habits, strengths, weaknesses, and preferences while developing a sense of mutual trust. The social relationships may be manifested in personal friendships and interest groups. Communication, about both work and employees' common interests, may be enhanced by friendship or hampered by antagonistic relationships. The Hawthorne studies (discussed in Chapter 1) were the first serious studies of the social subsystems in organizations.[31]

The sociotechnical systems approach was developed by members of the Tavistock Institute in England as an outgrowth of a study of coal mining. The study concerned new mining techniques that were introduced to increase productivity but

The **social subsystem** refers to the interpersonal relationships that develop among people in organizations.

31. Elton Mayo, *The Human Problems of an Industrial Civilization* (New York: Macmillan, 1933); and F. J. Roethlisberger and W. J. Dickson, *Management and the Worker* (Cambridge, Mass.: Harvard University Press, 1939).

failed because they entailed splitting up well-established work groups.[32] The Tavistock researchers concluded that the social subsystem had been sacrificed to the technical subsystem. Thus, improvements in the technical subsystem were not realized because of problems in the social subsystem. Recently, Lifeline Systems Inc., a manufacturer of electronic medical equipment that implemented JIT systems, recognized the potential problems of employee acceptance and emphasized the role of management in getting employees to go along with the changes.[33]

The Tavistock group proposed that an organization's technical and social subsystems could be integrated through autonomous work groups. **Autonomous work groups** are related to task design, particularly job enrichment, but also bring in concepts of group interaction, supervision, and other characteristics of organization design. The aim of autonomous work groups is to make technical and social subsystems work together for the benefit of the larger system. Accordingly, to structure the task, authority, and reporting relationships around work groups, organizations should delegate decisions regarding job assignments, training, inspection, rewards, and punishments to the work groups. Management has the responsibility of coordinating the groups according to the demands of the work and task environment.

Organizations in turbulent environments tend to rely less on hierarchy and more on the coordination of work among autonomous work groups. Sociotechnical systems theory asserts that the role of management is twofold: to monitor the environmental factors that impinge on the internal operations of the organization and to coordinate the social and technical subsystems. Although the sociotechnical systems approach has not been thoroughly tested, it has been tried with some success in the General Foods plant in Topeka, Kansas, the Saab-Scania project in Sweden, and the Volvo plant in Kalmar, Sweden (the last discussed in Chapter 7).[34] The development of the sociotechnical systems approach is meaningful in its departure from the universal approaches to organization design and in its emphasis on jointly harnessing the technical and human subsystems. The popular movements in management today include many of the principles of the sociotechnical systems design approach. The development of cross-functional teams for the development and design of new products and service are good examples.

Autonomous work groups are concerned with task design, but also include group interaction, supervision, and other aspects of organization design.

The Mintzberg Framework

In the remainder of this chapter, we describe two concrete organization designs and look at contemporary design issues. The universe of possible designs is large, but fortunately it is possible to identify a few basic forms that designs take.

Henry Mintzberg proposed a range of coordinating mechanisms that are found in operating organizations.[35] In his view, organization structure corresponds to the

32. Eric L. Trist and K. W. Bamforth, "Some Social and Psychological Consequences of the Longwall Method of Coal-Getting," *Human Relations*, February 1951, pp. 3–38.
33. "Small Manufacturers Shifting to 'Just-In-Time' Techniques."
34. Richard E. Walton, "How to Counter Alienation in the Plant," *Harvard Business Review*, November–December 1972, pp. 70–81; Richard E. Walton, "Work Innovations at Topeka: After Six Years," *Journal of Applied Behavioral Science*, July–August–September 1977, pp. 422–433; and Pehr G. Gyllenhammar, "How Volvo Adapts Work to People," *Harvard Business Review*, July–August 1977, pp. 102–113.
35. Henry Mintzberg, *The Structuring of Organizations: A Synthesis of the Research* (Englewood Cliffs, N.J.: Prentice-Hall, 1979).

Rather than focus on structural imperatives, people, or rules, Mintzberg's description of structure emphasizes the ways activities are coordinated.

way tasks are first divided and then coordinated. Mintzberg described five major ways in which tasks are coordinated: by mutual adjustment, by direct supervision, and by standardization of worker (or input) skills, work processes, or outputs (see Figure 16.6). These five methods can exist side by side within an organization.

Coordination by mutual adjustment simply means that workers use informal communication to coordinate with one another, whereas *coordination by direct supervision* means that a manager or supervisor coordinates the actions of workers. As noted, *standardization* may be used as a coordination mechanism in three different ways: we can standardize the *worker skills* that are inputs to the work process; the *processes* themselves (that is, the methods workers use to transform inputs into outputs); or the *outputs*, meaning the products or services or the performance levels expected of workers. Standardization usually is developed by staff analysts and enforced by management such that skills, processes, and output meet predetermined standards.

Mintzberg further suggested that the five coordinating mechanisms roughly correspond to stages of organizational development and complexity. In the very small organization, individuals working together communicate informally, achieving coordination by mutual adjustment. As more people join the organization, coordination needs become more complex, and direct supervision is added. For example, two or three persons working in a small fast-food business can coordinate the work simply by talking to each other about the incoming orders for hamburgers, fries, and drinks. In a large restaurant with complex cooking and warming equipment and several shifts of workers, however, direct supervision becomes necessary.

FIGURE 16.6

Mintzberg's Five Coordinating Mechanisms

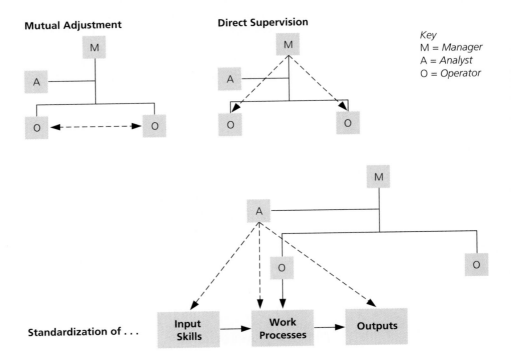

SOURCE: Henry Mintzberg, *The Structuring of Organizations: A Synthesis of the Research.* ©1979, p. 4. Reprinted by permission of Prentice-Hall, Inc., Englewood Cliffs, N.J.

In large organizations, standardization is added to mutual adjustment and direct supervision to coordinate the work. What type of standardization depends on the nature of the work situation—that is, the organization's technology and environment. When the organization's tasks are fairly routine, standardization of work processes may achieve the necessary coordination. Thus, the larger fast-food outlet may standardize the making of hamburger patties: the meat is weighed, put into a hamburger press, and compressed into a patty. McDonald's is well known for this type of standardized process.

In other complex situations, standardization of the output may allow employees to do the work in any appropriate manner as long as the output meets specifications. Thus, the cook may not care how the hamburger is pressed, only that the right amount of meat is used and the patty is the correct diameter and thickness. In other words, the worker may use any process as long as the output is a standard burger.

A third possibility, most often adopted in situations when processes and outputs are difficult to standardize, is to coordinate work by standardizing worker skills. In a hospital, for example, each patient must be treated as a special situation; the hospital process and output therefore cannot be standardized. Similar diagnostic and treatment procedures may be used with more than one patient, but management relies on the skills of the physicians and nurses, which are standardized through their professional training, to coordinate the work. In the most complex work situations, however, organizations may have to depend on workers' mutual adjustment to coordinate their own actions; here the salient elements of coordination are the workers' professional training and communication skills. In effect, mutual adjustment can be an appropriate coordinating mechanism in both the simplest and most complex situations.

Mintzberg pointed out that the five methods of coordination can be combined with the basic components of structure to develop five structural forms: the simple structure, the machine bureaucracy, the professional bureaucracy, the divisionalized form, and the adhocracy. Mintzberg called these structures *pure* or *ideal* types of designs.

Simple Structure

The **simple structure,** typical for relatively small or new organizations, has little specialization or formalization, and power and decision making are concentrated in the chief executive.

The **simple structure** characterizes relatively small, usually young organizations in a simple, dynamic environment. The organization has little specialization and formalization, and its overall structure is organic. Power and decision making are concentrated in the chief executive, often the owner-manager, and the flow of authority is from the top down. Direct supervision is the primary coordinating mechanism. Given its dynamic and often hostile environment, the organization must adapt quickly to survive. Most small businesses—a car dealership, a locally owned retail clothing store, or a candy manufacturer with only regional distribution—have a simple structure.

Machine Bureaucracy

The **machine bureaucracy** is typical of a large, well-established company in a simple and stable environment. Work is highly specialized and formalized, and deci-

In a machine bureaucracy, which typifies large, well-established organizations, work is highly specialized and formalized and decision making usually is concentrated at the top.

sion making usually is concentrated at the top. Standardization of work processes is the primary coordinating mechanism. Because the environment is both simple and stable, this highly bureaucratic structure does not have to adapt quickly to changes. Examples include large mass-production firms such as Container Corporation of America, some automobile companies, and providers of services to mass markets such as insurance companies.

Professional Bureaucracy

A professional bureaucracy is characterized by horizontal specialization by professional area of expertise, little formalization, and decentralized decision making.

Usually found in a complex and stable environment, the **professional bureaucracy** relies on standardization of skills as the primary means of coordination. There is much horizontal specialization by professional area of expertise but little formalization. Decision making is decentralized and takes place where the expertise is. The only means of coordination available to the organization is standardization of skills—the professionally trained employees. Although it lacks centralization, the professional bureaucracy stabilizes and controls its tasks with rules and procedures developed in the relevant profession. Hospitals, universities, and consulting firms are examples.

Divisionalized Form

The **divisionalized form,** typical of old, very large organizations, is divided according to the different markets served, has horizontal and vertical specialization between divisions and headquarters, divides decision making between headquarters and divisions, and standardizes outputs.

The **divisionalized form** characterizes old and very large firms operating in a relatively simple, stable environment with several diverse markets. It resembles the machine bureaucracy except that it is divided according to the various markets it serves. There is some horizontal and vertical specialization between the divisions (each defined by a market) and headquarters. Decision making is clearly split between headquarters and the divisions, and standardization of outputs is the primary means of coordination. The mechanism of control required by headquarters encourages the development of machine bureaucracies in the divisions.

The classic example of the divisionalized form is General Motors, which, in a reorganization in the 1920s, adopted a design that created divisions for each major car model.[36] Although the divisions have been reorganized and the cars changed several times, the concept of the divisionalized organization is still very evident at GM.[37] General Electric uses a two-tiered divisionalized structure, dividing its numerous businesses into strategic business units, which are further divided into sectors.[38]

Adhocracy

The **adhocracy** typically is found in young organizations engaged in highly technical fields with complex and dynamic environments. Decision making is spread throughout the organization, and power is in the hands of experts. There is horizontal and vertical specialization but little formalization, resulting in a very

36. See Harold C. Livesay, *American Made: Men Who Shaped the American Economy* (Boston: Little, Brown, 1979), pp. 215-239, for a discussion of Alfred Sloan and the development of the divisionalized structure at General Motors.
37. Anne B. Fisher, "GM Is Tougher Than You Think," *Fortune*, November 10, 1986, pp. 56–64.
38. Thompson and Strickland, *Strategic Management*, p. 212.

In an **adhocracy,** typically found in young organizations in highly technical fields, decision making is spread throughout the organization, power resides with the experts, horizontal and vertical specialization exist, and there is little formalization.

organic structure. Coordination is by mutual adjustment through frequent personal communication and liaison devices. Specialists are not grouped together in functional units but are deployed into specialized market-oriented project teams.

The typical adhocracy usually is established to foster innovation, something to which the other four types of structures are not particularly well suited. Numerous U.S. organizations—Johnson & Johnson, Procter & Gamble, Monsanto, and 3M, for example—are known for their innovation and constant stream of new products.[39] These organizations are either structured totally as an adhocracy or have large divisions set up as an adhocracy. Johnson & Johnson established a new-products division more than thirty years ago to encourage continued innovation, creativity, and risk taking. The division continues to succeed; more than two hundred new products have been introduced by Johnson & Johnson in the United States in the past several years.

Mintzberg believed that the most important consideration in designing an organization is the fit among parts. Not only must there be a fit among the structure, the structural imperatives (technology, size, and environment), and organizational strategy, the components of structure (rules and procedures, decision making, specialization) also must fit together and be appropriate for the situation. Mintzberg suggested that when these characteristics are not put together properly, an organization will not function effectively.[40]

Matrix Organization Design

One other organizational form deserves attention here: the matrix organization design. Matrix design is consistent with the contingency approach because it is useful only in certain situations. One of the earliest implementations of the matrix design was at TRW Systems Division in 1959.[41] Following TRW's lead, other firms in aerospace and high-technology fields created similar matrix structures.

The **matrix design** combines two different designs to gain the benefits of each; typically combined are a product or project departmentalization scheme and a functional structure.

The **matrix design** attempts to combine two different designs to gain the benefits of each. The most common matrix form superimposes product or project departmentalization on a functional structure (see Figure 16.7). Each department and project has a manager; each employee, however, is a member of both a functional department and a project team. The dual role means that the employee has two supervisors, the department manager and the project leader.

A matrix structure is appropriate when three conditions exist:

1. There is external pressure for a dual focus, meaning that factors in the environment require the organization to focus its efforts equally on responding to multiple external factors and emphasizing internal operations.
2. There are pressures for a high information-processing capacity.
3. There are pressures for shared resources.[42]

In the aerospace industry in the early 1960s, all these conditions were present. Private companies had a dual focus: their customers, primarily the federal government, and the complex engineering and technical fields in which they were

39. Kenneth Labich, "The Innovators," *Fortune*, June 6, 1988, pp. 51–64.
40. Henry Mintzberg, "Organization Design: Fashion or Fit," *Harvard Business Review*, January–February 1981, pp. 103–116.
41. Harvey F. Kolodny, "Managing in a Matrix," *Business Horizons*, March–April 1981, pp. 17–24.
42. Stanley M. Davis and Paul R. Lawrence, *Matrix* (Reading, Mass.: Addison-Wesley, 1977), pp. 11–36.

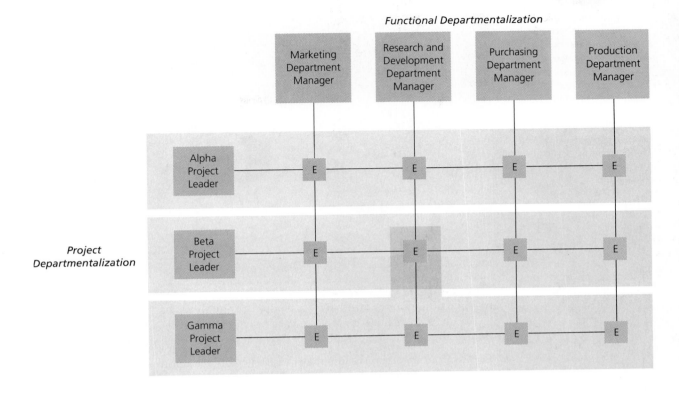

Functional Departmentalization

Marketing Department Manager | Research and Development Department Manager | Purchasing Department Manager | Production Department Manager

Project Departmentalization

Alpha Project Leader — E — E — E — E

Beta Project Leader — E — E — E — E

Gamma Project Leader — E — E — E — E

Key
E = Employee

FIGURE 16.7

A Matrix Design

engaged. Moreover, the environments of these companies were changing very rapidly. Technological sophistication and competition were increasing, resulting in growing environmental uncertainty and, consequently, an added need for information processing. The final condition stemmed from the pressure on the companies to excel in a very competitive environment despite limited resources. The companies concluded that it was inefficient to assign their highly professional—and highly compensated—scientific and engineering personnel to just one project at a time.

> The matrix structure attempts to build into the organization structure the ability to be flexible and provide coordinated responses to both internal and external pressures.

Built into the matrix structure is a flexible and coordinated response to internal and external pressures. Members can be reassigned from one project to another as demands for their skills change. They may work for a month on one project, be assigned to the functional home department for two weeks, and then be reassigned to another project for the next six months. The matrix form improves project coordination by assigning project responsibility to a single leader rather than dividing it among several functional department heads. Furthermore, communication is improved because employees can communicate about the project with the members of the project team as well as with members of the functional unit to which they belong. In this way, solutions to project problems may emerge from

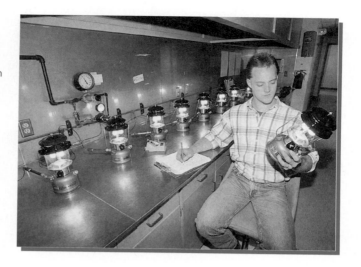

Re-engineering allows an organization to redesign itself around the most important processes it performs. Unnecessary steps can be eliminated, and routines made more efficient. At Coleman, where re-engineering has increased productivity by 35%, a worker inspects a lamp according to a newly streamlined procedure.

either group. Many different types of organizations have used the matrix form of organization, notably large-project manufacturing firms, banks, and hospitals.[43]

The matrix organizational form thus provides several benefits for the organization. It is not, however, trouble free. Typical problems include the following:

1. The dual reporting system may cause role conflict among employees.
2. Power struggles may occur over who has authority on which issues.
3. Matrix organization often is misinterpreted to mean that all decisions must be made by a group; as a result, group decision-making techniques may be used when they are not appropriate.
4. If the design involves several matrices, each laid on top of another, there may be no way to trace accountability and authority.[44]

Only under the three conditions listed earlier is the matrix design likely to work. In any case, it is a complex organizational system that must be carefully coordinated and managed to be effective.

Contemporary Organization Design Issues

The current proliferation of design theories and alternative forms of organization provide the practicing manager with a dizzying array of choices. The task of the practicing manager or organization designer is to examine the firm within its situation and to design a form of organization that meets its needs. A partial list of the contemporary alternatives include such things as downsizing, rightsizing, reengineering the organization, and the virtual organization. These approaches often include total quality management, employee empowerment, employee involvement and participation, reduction in force (RIF), process innovation, and networks of alliances. Practicing managers must learn new terminology, resist the

43. Lawton R. Burns, "Matrix Management in Hospitals: Testing Theories of Matrix Structure and Development," *Administrative Science Quarterly*, September 1989, pp. 355–358.
44. Ibid., pp. 129–154.

temptation to treat new approaches as fads, and examine their own organizational situation before making major organization design shifts. In this section we describe two currently popular approaches.

Reengineering the Organization

Reengineering is the radical redesign of organizational processes to achieve major gains in cost, time, and the provision of services. It forces the organization to start from scratch to redesign itself around its most important processes rather than take its current form and make incremental changes. If the company had no existing structure, departments, jobs, rules, or established ways of doing things, reengineering could design the organization as it should be for future success instead of what it has been. The process starts with discovering what the customers actually want from the organization and then developing a strategy to provide it. Once the strategy is in place, strong leadership from top management can create a core team of people to design an organizational system to achieve the strategy.[45] Reengineering is a process of redesigning the organization that does not necessarily result in a certain organizational form.

Reengineering is the radical redesign of organizational processes to achieve major gains in cost, time, and provision of services.

Rethinking the Organization

Another currently popular view of the organization is the concept of rethinking the organization. In addition to being a process of redesign, Robert Tomasko makes some suggestions for new organizational forms for the future.[46] Tomasko suggests that the traditional pyramid shape of organizations may be inappropriate for current business practices. He suggests that traditional structures have too many levels of management arranged in a hierarchy to be efficient and respond to dynamic changes in the environment. Rethinking organizations might include thinking of the organization structure as a dome rather than a pyramid. Top management needs to act as a dome, much like an umbrella that covers and protects those underneath but leaves them alone to do their work. Rather than have fixed internal units with walls like a pyramid, underneath a dome units would be flexible to interact with each other and with environmental forces. Companies such as Microsoft and Royal Dutch/Shell Group have some of the characteristics of this dome approach to organizational design.

Rethinking the organization means that managers need to look at the organization design in totally different ways, maybe even abandoning the classic view of organization as a pyramid.

Dominant Themes of Contemporary Design

The three dominant themes of current design strategies are the effects of technological and environmental change, the importance of people, and the necessity of staying in touch with the customer. Technology and the environment are changing so fast and in so many unpredictable ways that no organization structure will be appropriate for long. The changes just in electronic information processing, transmission, and retrieval are so vast that employee relationships, information distribution, and

There is no "one best way" to design an organization.

45. Thomas A. Stewart, "Reengineering: The Hot New Managing Tool," *Fortune*, August 23, 1993, pp. 41–48.
46. Robert Tomasko, *Rethinking the Corporation* (New York: AMA-COM, 1993).

task coordination need to be reviewed almost daily.[47] The emphasis on productivity through people that was energized by Thomas Peters and Robert Waterman, Jr., in the 1980s continues in almost every aspect of contemporary organization design.[48] In addition, Peters and Austin further emphasized the importance of staying in touch with customers as the initial stage in organization design.[49]

These two popular contemporary approaches (reengineering and rethinking the organization) and the three dominant factors argue for a contingency design perspective. Unfortunately, there is no "one best way." The designer must consider the impact of multiple factors—sociotechnical systems factors, the structural imperatives, strategy, changing information technology, people, and a concern for end users—on his or her particular organization.

Summary of Key Points

- Universal approaches to organization design attempt to specify a one best way to structure organizations for effectiveness. Contingency approaches, on the other hand, propose that the best way to design an organization structure depends on a variety of factors. Important contingency factors are technology, the environment, the organization's size, and the social system within which the organization operates.

- The structural imperatives are size, technology, and environment. In general, large organizations have more complex structures and usually more than one technology. The structure of small organizations, on the other hand, may be dominated by one core operating technology. The structure of the organization is also established to fit with the environmental demands and buffer the core operating technology from environmental changes and uncertainties.

- Initially, strategy was seen as the determinant of structure: the structure of the organization was designed to implement its purpose, goals, and strategies. The concept of managerial choice in determining organization structure represents a modification of this view. The manager designs the structure to accomplish organizational goals, guided by an analysis of the contextual factors, the strategies of the organization, and personal preferences.

- The sociotechnical systems approach viewed the organization as an open system structured to integrate two important subsystems: the technical (task) subsystem and the social subsystem. According to this approach, organizations should structure the task, authority, and reporting relationships around the work group by delegating to it decisions regarding job assignments, training, inspection, rewards, and punishments. Management's task is to monitor the environment and coordinate the structures, rules, and procedures.

- Mintzberg's ideal types of organization design were derived from a framework of coordinating mechanisms. The five types are simple structure, machine bureaucracy, professional bureaucracy, divisionalized form, and adhocracy. Most organizations have some characteristics of each type, but one is likely to

47. John Child, *Organizations: A Guide to Problems and Practice* (New York: Harper & Row, 1984), p. 246.
48. Thomas J. Peters and Robert H. Waterman, Jr., *In Search of Excellence: Lessons from America's Best-Run Companies* (New York: Harper & Row, 1982), pp. 235–278.
49. Thomas J. Peters and Nancy K. Austin, "A Passion for Excellence," *Fortune*, May 13, 1985, pp. 20–32.

predominate. Mintzberg believed that the most important consideration in designing an organization is the fit among parts of the organization.

- The matrix design combines two types of structure (usually functional and product or project departmentalization) to gain the benefits of each. It usually results in a multiple command and authority system. Benefits of matrix form are increased flexibility, cooperation, communication, and use of skilled personnel. Its problems typically are associated with the dual reporting system and the complex management system needed to coordinate work.
- Contemporary organization design is contingency oriented. Currently popular design approaches are reengineering the organization and rethinking the organization. Three dominant themes of current design strategies are the changing technological environment, concern for people as a valued resource, and the need to keep in touch with customers.

Discussion Questions

1. What is the difference between universal approaches and contingency approaches to organization design?
2. Define *organizational environment* and *organizational technology*. In what ways do these concepts overlap?
3. Identify and describe some of the environmental and technological factors that affect your college or university. Give specific examples of how they affect you as a student.
4. How does the organization design usually differ for large and small organizations?
5. What might be the advantages and disadvantages of structuring the faculty members at your college or university as an autonomous work group?
6. What do you think are the purpose, goals, and strategies of your college or university? How are they reflected in its structure?
7. Which of Mintzberg's pure forms is best illustrated by a major national political party (Democratic or Republican)? Religious organizations? A football team? The U.S. Olympic Committee?
8. In a matrix organization would you rather be a project leader, a functional department head, or a highly trained technical specialist? Why?
9. Discuss what you think the important design considerations will be for organization designers in the year 2000.
10. How would your college or university be different if you tried to rethink or reengineer the way that it is designed?

EXPERIENTIAL EXERCISE

Purpose This exercise will help you understand the factors that determine the design of organizations.

Format   You will interview employees of a small- to medium-size organization and analyze the reasons for its design. (Your instructor may coordinate this exercise with the one in Chapter 15.)

Procedure   Your first task is to find a local organization with between fifty and five hundred employees. (It should not be part of your college or university.) If you did the exercise for Chapter 15, you can use the same company for this exercise. The organization should have more than two hierarchical levels, but it should not be too complex to understand in a short period of study. You may want to check with your professor before contacting the company. Your initial contact should be with the highest-ranking manager that you can reach. Make sure that top management is aware of your project and gives its approval.

Using the material in this chapter, interview employees to obtain the following information on the design of the organization:

1. What is the organization in business to do? What are its goals and its strategies for achieving them?
2. How large is the company? What is the total number of employees? How many work full time? How many work part time?
3. What are the most important components of the organization's environment?
4. Is the number of important environmental components large or small?
5. How quickly or slowly do these components change?
6. Would you characterize the organization's environment as certain, uncertain, or somewhere in between? If in between, describe in detail approximately how certain or uncertain.
7. What is the organization's dominant technology, that is, how does it transform inputs into outputs?
8. How rigid is the company in its application of rules and procedures? Is it flexible enough to respond to environmental changes?
9. How involved are employees in the daily decision making related to their jobs?
10. What methods are used to ensure control over the actions of employees?

Interview at least three employees of the company at different levels and in different departments. One should hold a top-level position. Be sure to ask the questions in a way the employees will understand; they may not be familiar with some of the terminology used in this chapter.

The result of the exercise should be a report describing the technology, environment, and structure of the company. You should discuss the extent to which the structure is appropriate for the organization's strategy, size, technology, and environment. If it does not seem appropriate, you should explain the reasons. If you also used this company for the exercise in Chapter 15, you can comment further on the organization chart and its appropriateness for the company. You may want to send a copy of your report to the cooperating company.

Follow-up Questions

1. Which aspects of strategy, size, environment, and technology were the most difficult to obtain information about? Why?
2. If there were differences in the responses of the employees you interviewed, how do you account for them?

3. If you were the president of the organization you analyzed, would you design it in the same way? Why or why not? If not, how would you design it differently?
4. How did your answers to questions 2 and 3 differ from those in the exercise in Chapter 15?

| CASE 16.1 | **Virtual Organizations** |

Some companies do one or two things very well, but struggle with most others. For example, one company might very effectively sell to government clients, but have trouble manufacturing products with very tight precision. Another company might be great at close tolerance manufacturing, but ineffective at reaching out to certain types of clients. Wouldn't it be nice if those two organizations could get together to utilize each other's strengths but still retain their independence? Many companies are doing just that and calling it the *virtual organization*.

A virtual organization is a temporary alliance between two or more organizations that band together to accomplish a specific venture. Each partner contributes to the partnership what it does best. Usually, organizations form virtual organizations to take advantage of a situation that needs a quick response to maximize the market opportunity. A slow response will likely result in losses. Therefore, a virtual organization allows different organizations to bring their best capabilities together and not have to worry about learning how to do something that they have never done before. Thus, the reaction time is faster, mistakes are fewer, and profits are quicker. The sharing of information among partners is usually facilitated by electronic technology such as computers, faxes, and electronic mail systems, thereby avoiding the expenses of renting new office space for the venture or costly travel time between companies.

There is no limit on how large an organization or project needs to be to take advantage of this type of alliance. In fact, some very small organizations are working together quite well. In Phoenix, Arizona, a public relations firm, a graphic design firm, and an advertising firm are working together on projects that have multiple needs beyond the capabilities of any one firm. Rather than turn down the business or try to hire additional staff to do the extra work, the three firms work together to better serve client needs. The clients like the arrangement because they get high-quality work and do not have to shop around for someone to do little pieces of work. The networking companies feel that there is better creativity, more teamwork, more efficient use of resources, and better service for their clients.

Virtual organizations are more typically created by large companies. IBM, Apple, and a Japanese partnership are working on a multimedia software that will work on any machine. Corning Inc. is involved in nineteen partnerships on many different types of projects. Corning is pleased with most of its ventures and plans to do more. Intel worked with two Japanese organizations to manufacture the flash memory chips for computers. One of the Japanese companies was not able to complete its part of the project, leaving Intel with a major product delivery problem. Intel's chairman, Andrew Grove, was not too happy about that venture and may not participate in others.

The virtual organization may be just another management fad. On the other hand, it may be the wave of the future for organizations to capitalize on certain types of projects. Management scholars are mixed on the effectiveness of such arrangements. Although it may be an odd arrangement, its can offer considerable benefits.

Case Questions

1. How does the virtual organization differ from the traditional organization design?
2. Why would something like the virtual organization occur at this point in time?
3. In what type of situations do you think a virtual organization would work best?

SOURCES: "The Virtual Corporation," *Business Week*, February 8, 1993, pp. 98–102; and William H. Carlile, "Virtual Corporation a Real Deal," *The Arizona Republic*, August 2, 1993, pp. E1, E4.

Wild Wear, Inc., makes clothing, raingear, and sleeping bags for hikers and other outdoor enthusiasts. The company began when Myrtle Kelly began sewing pile jackets that her husband Ray sold on college campuses. It now employs almost five hundred persons organized into traditional divisions such as marketing, manufacturing, and research and development.

Recently it became apparent that although Wild Wear's balance sheet appeared healthy, the company was stagnant. Everyone seemed to work hard, and the company's products seldom flopped. Yet Wild Wear seemed to have developed a "me too" posture, bringing new products to market a season or a full year after competitors.

The Kellys, who still run the company, pored over performance appraisals looking for the weak points that might be holding the company back. But it seemed that the human resources department had been doing its work. R&D was coming up with a respectable number of new products, the manufacturing facility was modern and efficient, and the marketing tactics often won praise from customers.

Baffled, the Kellys called a meeting of middle-level managers, hoping that they could provide some answers they had missed. They were shocked when they noticed that the managers were introducing themselves as they came in and sat down. People who had been working in the same company for years had never even met! The meeting began with this observation, and for ninety minutes the Kellys sat back and listened to the problems their managers raised.

It became clear that in the attempt to grow from a family operation into a larger company, the Kellys had assumed the two needed to be very different. When they started out, the two of them handled all aspects of the business. Ray would hear from a customer that backpackers really needed a certain product, would pass the idea on to Myrtle and order the materials she needed, and within a few weeks would offer the product to the same—now delighted—customer. As the company grew, the Kellys began to worry about their lack of formal business training and hired professionals to run each division and set up appropriate rules and procedures.

What they had created, the middle managers informed them, was a number of very efficient, productive divisions that might as well have been separate companies. The R&D people might come up with a new breathable fabric for raingear only to find that production had just begun making a new rainwear line out of the old fabric and that marketing was turning all its attention to selling the big inventory of sleeping bags. Each division did the best it could with the information it had, but that information was very incomplete. Products progressed linearly from one division to the next, but it always seemed as though an idea that had been ahead of its time did not yield a product until the time had passed.

To remedy the problem, the Kellys decided to call in a management consultant to create more of a matrix structure for Wild Wear. While they were waiting for the consultant's solutions, they began holding weekly "Horizon" meetings. The group of middle managers would get together every Monday and discuss what they saw on their horizon. After less than a month of such meetings, the excitement generated promised better things for Wild Wear as the managers stretched to expand their own horizons and to help others bring their ideas to light.

Case Questions

1. What would be the ideal organizational design for a company like Wild Wear?
2. What does Wild Wear's experience say about the need for periodic corporate restructuring?

Organization Culture

OBJECTIVES

After studying this chapter, you should be able to:

Define *organization culture,* explain how it affects employee behavior, and understand its historical roots.

Describe two different approaches to culture in organizations.

Identify two emerging issues in organization culture.

Discuss the important elements of managing the organization culture.

Johnson & Johnson is the world's largest producer of health-care products with sales of more than $12 billion. Its many products include disposable contact lenses, surgical instruments, vitamins, birth control products, cancer treatments, and pain relievers, all of which are produced and distributed through 166 autonomous companies whose sales range from $100,000 to more than $1 billion each year. Each company has a president who reports to one of nineteen group heads, who then report to one of three sector heads, who then report to chief executive officer Ralph S. Larsen. As far back as 1932, when Robert W. Johnson, Jr., became chairman, the company has been known for its decentralized operations, letting the companies operate as independently as possible.

This independent style has become part of Johnson & Johnson's culture. The relatively small headquarters staff in New Brunswick, New Jersey, provides the capital, picks the people to run each company, and oversees the network of sectors, groups, and companies. The dominant culture is that the companies are expected to operate independently: each decides which products to produce and sell, whom to hire, how and how much to advertise, and to whom to sell. Everyone is expected—and pressured—to produce. Managers know that they are expected to take risks and run their own show, without interference or protection from corporate headquarters. Headquarters can provide financial support for investment in new technologies and products, but local management must make it work. The result is a freewheeling environment with entrepreneurial managers who are driven to be creative in research and innovative in marketing and sales, just as if they were running their own business. Promising new ideas may be assigned to an existing division with a separate management team to let it incubate and develop. When it is ready for the market, it may break out into an existing company or even a stand-alone company and set free. This type of independent culture is what many companies are striving to create. Johnson & Johnson already has it fine tuned and operating.[1]

As CEO of Johnson & Johnson, Ralph Larsen oversees a conglomerate of companies. Although Larsen and the others at the headquarters provide capital and make major decisions, each company must operate independently. This approach both fuels managerial creativity while providing enough structure to pressure the companies to produce.

Many organizations attribute their success to a strong and firmly entrenched culture. The culture at Johnson & Johnson is evidently one that has worked quite well for many years. Other companies may want to have a similar culture, or at least one that works as well, but creating this kind of successful culture for many 7organizations is not so easy.

We begin this chapter by exploring the nature and historical foundations of organization culture. Then we examine two basic approaches to defining the characteristics of organization culture. Next, we discuss two emerging issues in the area of organization culture. Finally, we show how organization culture can be managed to enhance the organization's effectiveness.

1. Brian Dumaine, "Is Big Still Good?" *Fortune*, April 20, 1992, pp. 50–60; "A Big Company That Works," *Business Week*, May 4, 1992, pp. 124–132; and Gary Hoover, Alta Campbell, and Patrick J. Spain, *Hoover's Handbook of American Business 1993* (Austin, Tex.: The Reference Press, 1992), p. 347.

The Nature of Organization Culture

In the early 1980s, organization culture became a central concern in the study of organizational behavior. Hundreds of researchers began to work in this area. Numerous books were published, important academic journals dedicated entire issues to the discussion of culture, and—almost overnight—organizational behavior textbooks that omitted culture as a topic of study became obsolete.

Interest in organization culture was not limited to academia. Businesses expressed an interest in culture that was far more intense than their concern with other aspects of organizational behavior. *Business Week*, *Fortune*, and other business periodicals published articles that claimed culture was essential to an organization's success and suggested that managers who could manage through their organization's culture almost certainly would rise to the top.[2]

Although the enthusiasm of the early 1980s has waned somewhat, the study of organization culture remains important. Many researchers have begun to weave the important aspects of organization culture into their research in the more traditional topics. Now there are relatively few headline stories in the popular business press about culture and culture management, but organization culture has become a common topic in the study of management. The enormous amount of research on culture completed in the early 1980s has fundamentally shifted the way both academics and managers look at organizations. Some of the concepts developed in the analysis of organization culture have become basic parts of the business vocabulary, and the analysis of organization culture is one of the most important specialties in the field of organizational behavior.

What Is Organization Culture?

A surprising aspect of the recent rise in interest in organization culture is that the concept, unlike virtually any other concept in the field of organizational behavior, has no single widely accepted definition. Indeed, it often appears that authors feel compelled to develop their own definitions, which range from very broad to highly specific. For example, Deal and Kennedy define a firm's culture as "the way we do things around here."[3] This very broad definition presumably could include the way a firm manufactures its products, pays its bills, treats its employees, and performs any other organizational operation. More specific definitions include those of Schein ("the pattern of basic assumptions that a given group has invented, discovered, or developed in learning to cope with its problems of external adaptation and internal integration"[4]) and Peters and Waterman ("a dominant and coherent set of shared values conveyed by such symbolic means as stories, myths, legends, slogans, anecdotes, and fairy tales"[5]). Table 17.1 lists these and other important definitions of organization culture.

2. See "Corporate Culture: The Hard to Change Values That Spell Success or Failure," *Business Week*, October 27, 1980, pp. 148–160; and Charles G. Burck, "Working Smarter," *Fortune*, June 15, 1981, pp. 68–73.
3. T. E. Deal and A. A. Kennedy, *Corporate Cultures: The Rites and Rituals of Corporate Life* (Reading, Mass.: Addison-Wesley, 1982), p. 4.
4. E. H. Schein, "The Role of the Founder in Creating Organizational Culture," *Organizational Dynamics*, Summer 1983, p. 14.
5. Thomas J. Peters and Robert H. Waterman, Jr., *In Search of Excellence: Lessons from America's Best-Run Companies* (New York: Harper & Row, 1982), p. 103.

TABLE 17.1

Definitions of
Organization Culture

Definition	Source
"A belief system shared by an organization's members"	J. C. Spender, "Myths, Recipes and Knowledge-Bases in Organizational Analysis" (Unpublished manuscript, Graduate School of Management, University of California at Los Angeles, 1983), p. 2.
"Strong, widely-shared core values"	C. O'Reilly, "Corporations, Cults, and Organizational Culture: Lessons from Silicon Valley Firms" (Paper presented at the Annual Meeting of the Academy of Management, Dallas, Texas, 1983), p.1.
"The way we do things around here"	T. E. Deal and A. A. Kennedy, *Corporate Cultures: The Rites and Rituals of Corporate Life* (Reading, Mass.: Addison-Wesley, 1982), p. 4.
"The collective programming of the mind"	G. Hofstede, *Culture's Consequences: International Differences in Work-related Values* (Beverly Hills, Calif.: Sage, 1980), p.25.
"Collective understandings"	J. Van Maanen and S. R. Barley, "Cultural Organization: Fragments of a Theory" (Paper presented at the Annual Meeting of the Academy of Management, Dallas, Texas, 1983), p. 7.
"A set of shared, enduring beliefs communicated through a variety of symbolic media, creating meaning in people's work lives"	J. M. Kouzes, D. F. Caldwell, and B. Z. Posner, "Organizational Culture: How It Is Created, Maintained, and Changed" (Presentation at OD Network National Conference, Los Angeles, October 9, 1983).
"A set of symbols, ceremonies, and myths that communicate the underlying values and beliefs of that organization to its employees"	W. G. Ouchi, *Theory Z: How American Business Can Meet the Japanese Challenge* (Reading, Mass.: Addison-Wesley, 1981), p. 41.
"A dominant and coherent set of shared values conveyed by such symbolic means as stories, myths, legends, slogans, anecdotes, and fairy tales"	T. J. Peters and R. H. Waterman, Jr., In *Search of Excellence: Lessons from America's Best-Run Companies* (New York: Harper & Row, 1982), p. 103.
"The pattern of basic assumptions that a given group has invented, discovered, or developed in learning to cope with its problems of external adaptation and internal integration"	E. H. Schein, "The Role of the Founder in Creating Organizational Culture," *Organizational Dynamics*, Summer 1985, p. 14.

Despite the apparent diversity of these definitions, a few common attributes emerge. First, all the definitions refer to some set of values held by individuals in a firm. These values define what is good or acceptable behavior and what is bad or unacceptable behavior. In some organizations, for example, blaming customers when problems arise is unacceptable. Here the value "the customer is always right" tells managers what actions are acceptable (not blaming the customer) and what actions are not acceptable (blaming the customer). In other organizations, the dominant values might support blaming customers for problems, penalizing employees who make mistakes, or treating employees as the firm's most valuable assets. In each case, values help members of an organization understand how they should act in that organization.

A second attribute common to many of the definitions in Table 17.1 is that the values that make up an organization's culture often are taken for granted; that is, rather than being written in a book or made explicit in a training program, there are basic assumptions made by the firm's employees. It may be as difficult for an organization to articulate these basic assumptions as it is for people to express their personal beliefs and values. Several authors have argued that organization culture is a powerful influence on individuals in firms precisely because it is not explicit but becomes an implicit part of employees' values and beliefs.[6]

Some organizations have been able to articulate the essential values in their cultures. Some have even written down these values and made them part of formal training procedures. For example, Lotus Development has written "Operating Principles" to guide interactions between employees (see Figure 17.1). At Hewlett-Packard a brief summary of "The HP Way" is given to all new employees. This pamphlet describes the basic values of the culture at Hewlett-Packard.[7] NCR recently began a national advertising campaign featuring its statement of organizational values.[8] Levi Strauss & Co. has embarked on an intense effort to communicate its values through the development of an "Aspirations Statement."[9]

Even when firms are able to articulate and describe the basic values that make up their cultures, however, the values most strongly affect actions when people in the organization take them for granted. An organization's culture is not likely to powerfully influence behavior when employees must constantly refer to a handbook to remember what the culture is. When the culture becomes part of them—when they can ignore what is written in the book because they already have embraced the values it describes—the culture can have an important impact on their actions.

Most definitions of organization culture include an emphasis on the values, symbols, and other factors that communicate the culture to employees.

The final attribute shared by many of the definitions in Table 17.1 is an emphasis on the symbolic means through which the values in an organization's culture are communicated. Although, as we noted, companies sometimes can directly describe these values, their meaning perhaps is best communicated to employees through the use of stories, examples, and even what some authors call "myths" or "fairy tales." Stories typically symbolize important implications of values in a firm's culture. Often they develop a life of their own. As they are told and retold,

6. See M. Polanyi, *Personal Knowledge* (Chicago: University of Chicago Press, 1958); E. Goffman, *The Presentation of Self in Every Day Life* (New York: Doubleday, 1959); and P. L. Berger and T. Luckman, *The Social Construction of Reality* (Garden City, N.Y.: Anchor, 1967).

7. W. G. Ouchi, *Theory Z: How American Business Can Meet the Japanese Challenge* (Reading, Mass.: Addison-Wesley, 1981).

8. See the NCR advertisement in *Fortune*, February 29, 1988, pp. 62–63.

9. Robert Howard, "Values Make the Company: An Interview with Robert Haas," *Harvard Business Review*, September–October 1990, pp. 133–144.

FIGURE 17.1

Statement of an Organization's Values

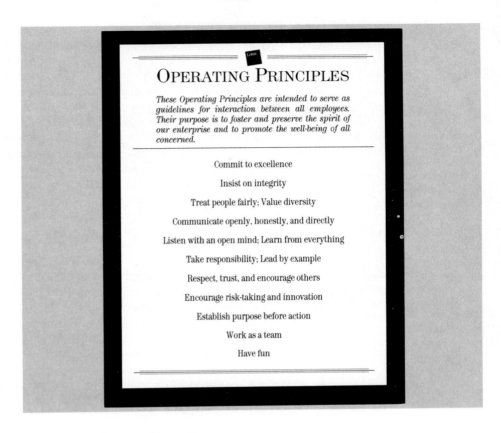

OPERATING PRINCIPLES

These Operating Principles are intended to serve as guidelines for interaction between all employees. Their purpose is to foster and preserve the spirit of our enterprise and to promote the well-being of all concerned.

Commit to excellence

Insist on integrity

Treat people fairly; Value diversity

Communicate openly, honestly, and directly

Listen with an open mind; Learn from everything

Take responsibility; Lead by example

Respect, trust, and encourage others

Encourage risk-taking and innovation

Establish purpose before action

Work as a team

Have fun

SOURCE: Courtesy of Lotus Development Corp.

shaped and reshaped, their relationship to what actually occurred becomes increasingly tenuous. Yet such stories communicate the meaning of organizational values much more powerfully than does a listing of values in a booklet.

Some organization stories have become famous. Two examples from Hewlett-Packard demonstrate how stories help communicate and reinforce important organizational values. One of the major values listed in "The HP Way" is that Hewlett-Packard avoids bank debt. A story is told of a senior manager in the finance area who was given free rein to develop a financing plan for a new investment. As she applied the best of finance theory, it became clear to her that part of the financial package should include bank debt. When her proposal reached Mr. Hewlett and Mr. Packard, however, it was rejected—not because the financial reasoning was unsound but because at Hewlett-Packard, "We avoid bank debt."[10] This story shows that avoiding bank debt is more than a slogan at Hewlett-Packard; it is a fact.

Another value at Hewlett-Packard is that "employees are our most important asset." A story that helps communicate the reality of this value tells what happened when the company was struggling through some difficult financial times. While virtually all other firms in the industry were laying people off, HP asked all its

10. A. Wilkins, "Organizational Stories as Symbols Which Control the Organization," in Louis R. Pondy, Peter J. Frost, Gareth Morgan, and Thomas C. Dandridge (Eds.), *Organizational Symbolism* (Greenwich, Conn.: JAI Press, 1983), pp. 81–82.

employees to take one day of unpaid vacation every two weeks. By working nine days and then taking one day off, the firm was able to avoid layoffs. All employees were hurt because all received a reduction in pay, but none had to bear the total cost of the firm's reduced performance.[11] The message communicated by this story is that Hewlett-Packard will go to great lengths to avoid layoffs to keep its employment team intact.

Organization culture is the set of values that helps the organization's employees understand which actions are considered acceptable and which are unacceptable.

We can use the three common attributes of definitions of culture just discussed to develop a definition with which most authors probably could agree: **organization culture** is the set of values, often taken for granted, that help people in an organization understand which actions are considered acceptable and which are considered unacceptable. Often these values are communicated through stories and other symbolic means.[12]

Historical Foundations

Our basic understanding of organization culture includes contributions from research in anthropology, sociology, social psychology, and economics.

Although research on organization culture exploded onto the scene in the early 1980s, the antecedents of this research can be traced to the origins of social science. Understanding the contributions of the social science disciplines is particularly important in the case of organization culture because many of the dilemmas and debates that continue in this area reflect differences in historical research traditions. Table 17.2 summarizes the disciplinary approaches.

Anthropologic Contributions   Of all the social science disciplines, anthropology is most closely related to the study of culture and cultural phenomena. Indeed,

11. Ibid.
12. This definition is very similar to the definition of culture proposed in M. R. Lewis, "Culture Yes, Organization No" (Paper presented at the Annual Meeting of the Academy of Management, Dallas, Texas, 1983).

TABLE 17.2

Social Science Contributions to Organization Culture Analysis

Contributor	Areas of Study	Methods of Study
Anthropology	■ Human cultures ■ Values and beliefs of society	■ Thick description ■ Interviews and observations
Sociology	■ Categorization of social system structures	■ Systematic interviews ■ Questionnaires ■ Statistics
Social Psychology	■ Creation and manipulation of symbols ■ Use of stories	■ Surveys ■ Observations ■ Statistics
Economics	■ Economic conditions of a company in a society	■ Statistics ■ Mathematical modeling

anthropology can be defined as the study of human cultures.[13] Anthropologists seek to understand how the values and beliefs that make up a society's culture affect the structure and functioning of that society. Many anthropologists believe that to understand the relationship between culture and society, it is necessary to look at a culture from the viewpoint of the people in a society—from the "native's point of view."[14] To reach this level of understanding, anthropologists immerse themselves in the values, symbols, and stories that people in a society use to bring order and meaning to their lives.

Whether the culture is that of a large, modern corporation or a primitive tribe in New Guinea or the Philippines, the questions asked are the same: how do people in this culture know what kinds of behavior are acceptable and what kinds are unacceptable? How is this knowledge understood? How is this knowledge communicated to new members?

Thick description research methods attempt to describe the totality of daily life through in-depth questioning and observation.

Practitioners of this anthropological approach usually use **thick description research methods**, which involve attempting to describe the totality of day-to-day life through in-depth questioning and observation.[15] Such methods are quite different from those used in other areas of organizational behavior research—experiments and questionnaire-based surveys, for example. Through this intense descriptive effort, the values and beliefs that underlie actions in an organization become clear. These values can be fully understood, however, only in the context of the organization in which they developed. In other words, a description of the values and beliefs of one organization is not transferable to other organizations.

Sociological Contributions

Sociologists also have had a long-term interest in studying the causes and consequences of culture. Many sociological methods and theories have found expression in the analysis of organization cultures.

In studying culture, sociologists most often have focused on informal social structure. Émile Durkheim, an important early sociologist, argued that the study of myth and ritual is an essential complement to the study of structure and rational behavior in societies.[16] By studying rituals, Durkheim argued, we can understand the most basic values and beliefs of a group of people. The same argument was developed by another sociologist, Max Weber, in his now famous description of the relationship between the Protestant ethic and the development of capitalism in Western Europe.[17] Weber argued that the religious values and beliefs of individuals in Western Europe supported the accumulation of material goods. The effort to accumulate material goods, in turn, was an important prerequisite for the development of capitalist economies.

This sociological approach to the study of culture perhaps is most evident in the methods used to study organization culture. Sociologists use systematic interviews, questionnaires, and other quantitative research methods rather than the thick description methods of anthropologists. Whereas anthropologists usually produce a book-length description of values, attitudes, and beliefs that underlie

---

13. A. L. Kroeber and C. Kluckhohn, "Culture: A Critical Review of Concepts and Definitions," in *Papers of the Peabody Museum of American Archaeology and Ethnology*, Vol. 47, No. 1 (Cambridge, Mass.: Harvard University Press, 1952).
14. C. Geertz, *The Interpretation of Cultures* (New York: Basic Books, 1973).
15. Ibid. pp. 5–6.
16. E. Durkheim, *The Elementary Forms of Religious Life*, trans. J. Swain (New York: Collier, 1961), p. 220.
17. H. H. Gerth and C. Wright Mills, *From Max Weber* (New York: Oxford University Press, 1976), pp. 267–362.

the behaviors of people in one or two organizations,[18] practitioners using the sociological approach generally produce a fairly simple typology of cultural attributes and then show how the cultures of a relatively large number of firms can be analyzed with this typology.[19]

Although both the anthropological and sociological approaches to studying organization culture are important, the recent emergence of organization culture as a major field of research primarily reflects work done in the sociological tradition. The major pieces of research on organization culture that later spawned widespread business interest—including Ouchi's *Theory Z*, Deal and Kennedy's *Corporate Cultures*, and Peters and Waterman's *In Search of Excellence*[20]—used sociological methods. Later in this chapter, we review some of this work in more detail.

Social Psychology Contributions Most research on organization culture has used anthropological or sociological methods and theories. Some research, however, has borrowed heavily from social psychology. Social psychological theory, with its emphasis on the creation and manipulation of symbols, provides a natural setting within which to analyze organization culture.

For example, research in social psychology suggests that people tend to use stories or information about a single event more than they use multiple observations to make judgments.[21] Thus, the fact that your neighbor had trouble with a certain brand of automobile means that you probably will conclude that the brand is bad even though the car company can generate reams of statistical data to prove your neighbor's car was a rarity.

The impact of stories on decision making suggests an important reason why organization culture has such a powerful influence on the people in an organization. Unlike other organizational phenomena, culture is best communicated through stories and examples, and these become the basis on which individuals in the organization make judgments. If a story says that blaming customers is a bad thing to do, then blaming customers *is* a bad thing to do. This value is communicated much more effectively through the cultural story than through some statistical analysis of customer satisfaction.[22]

Economics Contributions The influence of economics on the study of organization culture, although it has been less important than the influence of anthropology and sociology, is substantial enough to warrant attention. Economic analysis treats organization culture as one of a variety of tools that managers can use to give some economic advantage to the organization.

When sociological and anthropological research on culture moves beyond simply describing the cultures of companies, it usually focuses on linking the cultural attributes of firms with their performance. In *Theory Z*, for example, Ouchi does not just say that Type Z companies differ from other kinds of companies; rather,

18. See, for example, B. Clark, *The Distinctive College* (Chicago: Adline, 1970).
19. See Ouchi, *Theory Z*, and Peters and Waterman, *In Search of Excellence*.
20. See Ouchi, *Theory Z*, Deal and Kennedy, *Corporate Cultures*, and Peters and Waterman, *In Search of Excellence*.
21. E. Borgida and R. E. Nisbett, "The Differential Impact of Abstract vs. Concrete Information on Decisions," *Journal of Applied Social Psychology*, July–September 1977, pp. 258–271.
22. J. Martin and M. Power, "Truth or Corporate Propaganda: The Value of a Good War Story," in Louis R. Pondy, Peter J. Frost, Gareth Morgan, and Thomas C. Dandridge (Eds.), *Organizational Symbolism* (Greenwich, Conn.: JAI Press, 1983), pp. 93–108.

Within the Ouchi framework, U.S. Type Z firms, like Lotus, place a high value on keeping employees. Such firms fire workers only as a last resort and are attentive to the needs of their employees, even outside of the workplace. Here, the children of Lotus employees play at a corporate day care center.

he asserts that Type Z firms will outperform other firms.[23] When Peters and Waterman say they are in search of excellence, they define excellence, in part, as consistently high financial performance.[24] These authors are seeking cultural explanations of financial success.

Researchers disagree about the extent to which culture affects organization performance. The conditions under which organization culture is linked with superior financial performance have been investigated by several authors.[25] This research suggests that under some relatively narrow conditions, this culture-performance link may exist. But, simply because a firm has a culture does not mean that it will perform well. A variety of cultural traits can actually hurt performance.

Consider, for example, a firm whose culture includes values like "customers are too ignorant to be of much help," "employees cannot be trusted," "innovation is not important," and "quality is too expensive." This firm has a strong culture, but its financial success is far from assured. Clearly, the relationship between culture and performance depends, to some extent at least, on the content of the values that exist in the organization's culture.

Approaches to Describing Organization Culture

No single framework for describing the values in organization cultures has emerged; however, several frameworks have been suggested. Taken together, these models provide insights into the dimensions along which organization cultures vary.

23. A. Wilkins and W. G. Ouchi, "Efficient Cultures: Exploring the Relationship Between Culture and Organizational Performance," *Administrative Science Quarterly*, September 1983, pp. 468–481; and W. G. Ouchi, "Markets, Bureaucracies, and Clans," *Administrative Science Quarterly*, March 1980, pp. 129–141.
24. Peters and Waterman, *In Search of Excellence*.
25. J. B. Barney, "Organizational Culture: Can It Be a Source of Sustained Competitive Advantage?" *Academy of Management Review*, July 1986, pp. 656–665.

The Ouchi Framework

A number of authors have attempted to develop models for analyzing the cultural systems of specific groups of organizations. One of the first researchers to focus explicitly on analyzing the cultures of a limited group of firms was William G. Ouchi. Ouchi analyzed the organization cultures of three groups of firms, which he characterized as typical U.S. firms, typical Japanese firms, and U.S. **Type Z firms**.[26]

Through his analysis, Ouchi developed a list of seven points on which these three types of firms can be compared. Ouchi argued that the cultures of typical Japanese firms and U.S. Type Z firms are very different from those of typical U.S. firms and that these differences explain the success of many Japanese firms and U.S. Type Z firms at the expense of the latter. The seven points of comparison developed by Ouchi are presented in Table 17.3.

Commitment to Employees   According to Ouchi, typical Japanese and Type Z U.S. firms share the cultural value of trying to keep employees. Thus, both types of firms lay off employees only as a last resort. In Japan, the value of "keeping employees on" often takes the form of lifetime employment. A person who begins working at some Japanese firms has a virtual guarantee that she or he will never be fired. In U.S. Type Z companies, this cultural value is manifested in a commitment to what Ouchi called "long-term employment." Under Japanese lifetime employment, employees usually cannot be fired. Under U.S. long-term employment, workers and managers can be fired, but only if they are not performing acceptably.

Ouchi suggested that typical U.S. firms do not have the same cultural commitment to employees as do Japanese firms and U.S. Type Z firms. For this reason, typical U.S. firms have an expectation of short-term employment for their workers and managers. In reality, U.S. workers and managers spend their entire careers in a relatively small

The **Type Z firm** is committed to retaining employees; evaluates workers' performance based on both qualitative and quantitative information; emphasizes broad career paths; exercises control through informal, implicit mechanisms; requires that decision making occur in groups and be based on full information sharing and consensus; expects individuals to take responsibility for decisions; and emphasizes concern for people.

26. Ouchi, *Theory Z.*

TABLE 17.3

The Ouchi Framework

Cultural Value	Expression in Japanese Companies	Expression in Type Z U.S. Companies	Expression in Typical U.S. Companies
Commitment to Employees	Lifetime employment	Long-term employment	Short-term employment
Evaluation	Slow and qualitative	Slow and qualitative	Fast and quantitative
Careers	Very broad	Moderately broad	Narrow
Control	Implicit and informal	Implicit and informal	Explicit and formal
Decision Making	Group and consensus	Group and consensus	Individual
Responsibility	Group	Individual	Individual
Concern for People	Holistic	Holistic	Narrow

number of companies. Still, the cultural expectation exists that if there were a serious downturn in a firm's fortunes, workers and maybe even managers would be let go.[27]

Evaluation   Ouchi observed that in Japanese and U.S. Type Z companies, appropriate evaluation of workers and managers is thought to take a very long time—up to ten years—and requires the use of qualitative, as well as quantitative, information about performance. For this reason, promotion in these firms is relatively slow, and promotion decisions are made only after interviews with many people who have had contact with the person being evaluated.

In typical U.S. firms, on the other hand, the cultural value concerning evaluation suggests that evaluation can and should be done rapidly and should emphasize quantitative measures of performance. This value tends to encourage short-term thinking among workers and managers.

Careers   Ouchi next observed that the careers most valued in Japanese and Type Z U.S. firms span multiple functions. In Japan this value has led to very broad career paths, which may lead to experience in six or seven distinct business functions. The career paths in Type Z U.S. firms are somewhat narrower.

However, the career path valued in typical U.S. firms is considerably narrower. Ouchi's research indicated that most U.S. managers perform only one or two different business functions in their careers. This narrow career path reflects, according to Ouchi, the value of specialization that is part of so many U.S. firms.

Control   All organizations must exert some level of control. Without control, achieving coordinated action is impossible. Thus, not surprisingly, firms in the United States and Japan have developed cultural values related to organizational control and how to manage it.

Most Japanese and Type Z U.S. firms assume that control will be exercised through informal, implicit mechanisms. One of the most powerful of these mechanisms is the organization's culture. Managers expect to obtain guidance in what actions to take from the cultures of their firms. Stories, for example, communicate important information about what upper-level managers expect lower-level managers to do.

In contrast, typical U.S. firms expect that guidance will come not from informal and implicit cultural values but through explicit directions in the form of job descriptions, delineation of authority, and various rules and procedures. Stories about control may exist in these firms, but they typically communicate the message that to stay out of trouble it is best to follow explicit, written guidelines.

Decision Making   Japanese and Type Z U.S. firms hold the strong cultural expectation that decision making will occur in groups and be based on principles of full information sharing and consensus. In most typical U.S. firms, individual decision making is considered appropriate. Managers and workers given the responsibility of making decisions are not expected—and certainly not required—to obtain information or suggestions from others in the firm.

Responsibility   Closely linked with Ouchi's discussion of group versus individual decision making is his discussion of responsibility. Here, however, the parallels

27. "The Next Act at Chrysler," *Business Week*, November 3, 1986, pp. 66–69.

between Japanese firms and Type Z U.S. firms break down. Ouchi showed that in Japan, strong cultural norms support collective responsibility; that is, the group as a whole, rather than a single person, is held responsible for decisions made by the group. In both Type Z U.S. firms and typical U.S. firms, individuals expect to take responsibility for decisions.

Linking individual responsibility with individual decision making, as typical U.S. firms do, seems logically consistent. After all, if individuals are expected to make decisions, it makes sense that they should be held responsible for the decisions they make. Similarly, group decision making and group responsibility, the situation in Japanese firms, seem to go together. But how do Type Z U.S. firms combine the cultural values of group decision making and individual responsibility?

Ouchi suggested that the answer to this question depends on a cultural value we already discussed: slow and qualitative evaluation. The first time a manager uses a group to make a decision, it is not possible to tell whether the outcomes associated with that decision resulted from the manager's influence or the quality of the group. If a manager works with many groups over time, however, and if these groups consistently generate positive results for the organization, the manager is likely skilled at getting the most out of groups. This manager can be held responsible for the outcomes of group decision-making processes. Similarly, managers who consistently fail to work effectively with the groups assigned to them can be held responsible for the lack of results from the group decision-making process.

Ouchi suggested that the value of individual responsibility in U.S. Type Z firms reflects very strong cultural norms of individuality and individual responsibility in U.S. society as a whole. Organization cultures do not exist in isolation from broader cultural influences. Societal expectations and values can strongly influence the values in an organization's culture.

Concern for People   The last cultural value examined by Ouchi deals with a concern for people. Not surprisingly, in Japanese firms and Type Z firms, the cultural value that dominates is a holistic concern for workers and managers. Holistic concern extends beyond concern for a person simply as a worker or manager to concern with that person's home life, hobbies, personal beliefs, hopes, fears, and aspirations. In typical U.S. firms, the concern for people is narrow and focuses on the workplace. A culture that emphasizes a strong concern for people, rather than one that emphasizes a work/task orientation, can have a positive effect in terms of lower worker turnover.[28]

Theory Z and Performance   Ouchi argued that the cultures of Japanese and Type Z firms help them outperform typical U.S. firms. Toyota has imported the management style and culture that have succeeded in Japan into its manufacturing facilities in North America. The reasons for Toyota's success often have been attributed to the ability of Japanese and Type Z firms to systematically invest in their employees and in their operations over long periods of time and thus to obtain steady and marked improvements in long-term performance.

28. Lisa A. Mainiero, "Is Your Corporate Culture Costing You?" *Academy of Management Executive*, November 1993, pp. 84–85; and John E. Sheridan, "Organizational Culture and Employee Retention," *Academy of Management Journal*, 1992, pp. 1036–1056.

The Peters and Waterman Approach

Tom Peters and Robert Waterman, in their best seller *In Search of Excellence*, focused even more explicitly than Ouchi on the relationship between organization culture and performance. Peters and Waterman chose a sample of highly successful U.S. firms and sought to describe the management practices that led to their success.[29] Their analysis rapidly turned to the cultural values that led to successful management practices. These "excellent" values are listed in Table 17.4.

Bias for Action   According to Peters and Waterman, successful firms have a bias for action. Managers in these firms are expected to make decisions even if all the facts are not "in." Peters and Waterman argued that for many important decisions, all the facts will never "be in." Delaying decision making in these situations is the same as never making a decision. Meanwhile, other firms probably will have captured whatever business initiative existed. On average, according to Peters and Waterman, organizations with cultural values that include a bias for action outperform firms without such values.

Stay Close to the Customer   Peters and Waterman believe that firms whose organization cultures value customers over everything else will out-perform firms without this value. According to these authors, the customer provides a source of information about current products, a source of ideas about future products, the ultimate source of a firm's current financial performance, and the source of future performance. Focusing on the customer, meeting the customer's needs, and pampering the customer when necessary are all actions that lead to superior performance. After losing money for years, Scandinavian Airlines System focused its culture on customer service and finally started making money in 1989 when many other airlines were experiencing financial difficulties.[30]

Peters and Waterman also suggest that firms that adhere to keeping close to the customer do so not because the sales manager or the marketing handbook says it is a good idea. For true customer-satisfying companies, customer satisfaction lies at the core of the organization culture.

29. Peters and Waterman, *In Search of Excellence*.
30. Kenneth Labich, "An Airline That Soars on Service," *Fortune*, December 31, 1990, pp. 94–96.

TABLE 17.4

The Peters and Waterman Framework

Attributes of an Excellent Firm	
1. Bias for action	5. Hands-on management
2. Stay close to the customer	6. Stick to the knitting
3. Autonomy and entrepreneurship	7. Simple form, lean staff
4. Productivity through people	8. Simultaneously loosely and tightly organized

Autonomy and Entrepreneurship   Peters and Waterman maintain that successful firms fight the lack of innovation and the bureaucracy usually associated with large size. They do this by breaking the company into small, more manageable pieces and then encouraging independent, creative, even risk-taking activity within these smaller business segments. Stories often exist in these organizations about the junior engineer who, by taking a risk, is able to influence major product decisions or of the junior manager, dissatisfied with the slow pace of a product's development, who implements a new and highly successful marketing plan. These kinds of actions are not merely encouraged; they are the "stuff of organizational legends."

Productivity Through People   Like Ouchi, Peters and Waterman believe successful firms recognize that their most important assets are their people—both workers and managers—and that the organization's purpose is to let its people flourish. Again, this commitment to people is not simply written on plaques or announced in company magazines. Rather, it is a basic value of the organization culture—a belief that treating people with respect and dignity is not only appropriate but essential to success.

Hands-on Management   Peters and Waterman note the tendency in many large companies for senior managers to lose touch with the basic businesses they are in. For example, presidents of large electronics firms end up knowing less about electronics than they do about office politics, and presidents of large automobile companies inevitably learn less about cars than about finance.

   Peters and Waterman also note that to counter this tendency, the firms they studied insisted that their senior managers stay in touch with the firms' essential business. It is an expectation, reflecting a deeply embedded cultural norm, that managers should manage not from behind the closed doors of their offices but by "wandering around" the plant, the design facility, the research and development department, and so on.

"Stick to the knitting" is a popular management practice in which management chooses not to diversify into many unrelated businesses.

Stick to the Knitting   Another cultural value characteristic of excellent firms is their reluctance to engage in business outside their expertise. These firms reject the concept of diversification, the practice of buying and operating businesses in unrelated industries. If managers in such a company suggest that the firm begin operations in an unrelated business, the response to their efforts is not likely to be, "Where are the figures that justify this business move?" Rather, others in the firm are likely to simply shake their heads and say, "That's not the way we do business around here." This notion is also referred to as relying on the core competencies, or what the company does best.

Simple Form, Lean Staff   According to Peters and Waterman, successful firms tend to have few administrative layers and relatively small corporate staff groups. In many organizations, managers measure their status, prestige, and importance by the number of people who report to them. In excellently managed companies, however, importance is measured not by the number of people who report to a manager but by the manager's impact on the organization's performance. The cultural values in these firms tell managers that their staffs' performance rather than their size is important.

Simultaneously Loosely and Tightly Organized   The final attribute of organization culture identified by Peters and Waterman appears contradictory. How can a firm be simultaneously loosely organized and tightly organized? The resolution of this apparent paradox is found in the firms' values. The firms are tightly organized because all their members understand and believe in the firms' values. This common cultural bond makes a strong glue that holds the firms together. At the same time, however, the firms are loosely organized because they tend to have less administrative overhead, fewer staff members, and fewer rules and regulations. All this, Peters and Waterman believe, encourages innovation and risk taking.

This loose structure is possible only because of the common values held by people in the firm. When these people must make decisions, they can evaluate their options in terms of the organization's underlying values—whether the options are consistent with a bias for action, service to the customer, and so on. By referring to commonly held values, individuals often can make their own decisions about what actions to take. In this sense, the tight structure of common cultural values makes the loose structure of fewer administrative controls possible.

Emerging Issues in Organization Culture

As research into the importance of organization culture matures, it inevitably changes and develops new perspectives. Many new ideas about the environment in which employees become productive in organizations build on earlier views such as those of Ouchi, Peters and Waterman, Schein, and Deming. Typical of these approaches are total quality management, worker participation, and team-based management—all discussed in earlier chapters. We briefly discuss two other movements in this section: empowerment and procedural justice.

Empowerment

One of the most popular "buzz words" in management today is empowerment. Almost every new approach to quality, meeting the competition, enhancing employee performance and productivity, and corporate turnarounds includes employee empowerment. As we discuss in Chapter 5, **empowerment** is the process of enabling workers to set their own work goals, make decisions, and solve problems within their sphere of responsibility and authority. Like most fads and buzz words often dismissed as meaningless and without substance because of misuse and overuse, empowerment can be taken too lightly.

Empowerment is the process of enabling workers to set their own work goals, make decisions, and solve problems within their sphere of responsibility and authority.

Empowerment is both simple and complex at the same time. It is simple in that managers need to quit bossing people around and let them do their jobs. It is complex in that managers and employees typically are not trained to do that, and training may take meaningful amounts of time and practice. In Chapter 5, we discuss some techniques for utilizing empowerment and conditions in which empowerment can be effective in organizations.

Empowerment, however, can be much more than a motivational technique. In some organizations, it is the cornerstone of the organization culture. At Nissan, for example, middle-level managers and staff do not just participate in making some decisions, they are responsible for decisions. Plant managers have substantial control over budgets, personnel, and training, and cross-functional development

An Empowering Culture: What It Is and What It Is Not

What does it mean to empower people? Below is a brief definition, along with three behaviors that masquerade as empowerment, often with devastating results. See how well you can distinguish among them by choosing the one that best describes the supervisory behavior. Compare your answers to those at the end of the box. The quiz and answers were prepared by Donna Deeprose of Deeprose Consulting in New York.

Empower: to enable an employee to set work goals, make decisions, and solve problems.

Exploit: to take advantage of an employee to meet an unspoken goal of one's own.

Abandon: to delegate, but provide no support.

Delude: to give the appearance of empowering, but to withhold the freedom the employee needs to be successful.

1. A supervisor gives an employee authority to handle a project. When the employee complains about difficulties, the supervisor responds, "Don't worry, I'll handle it from now on."
   Behavior: _____

2. Same situation as (1), except that when the employee comes to the supervisor for help, the supervisor's response is, "This is your project. You take care of it."
   Behavior: _____

3. Same as (1) and (2), except that the supervisor discusses the problem with the employee and guides the employee into determining an appropriate next move.
   Behavior: _____

4. An employee has asked for additional responsibilities. The supervisor delegates to the employee total responsibility for a time-consuming report. The supervisor leaves at 5 P.M. each day while the employee works late to complete the report.
   Behavior: _____

5. A supervisor keeps up with the company's changing mission, objectives, and plans, and keeps employees informed of how all these changes impact the work unit.
   Behavior: _____

teams have complete responsibility for new cars and include people from design, manufacturing, and marketing.[31]

Another perspective that further broadens the concept of empowerment is to view it as liberating employees. In some uses empowerment is little more than delegating tasks to employees and then watching over them too closely. Employees may feel that this type of participation often has face value only and that they are not really making meaningful decisions. The concept of liberating employees

31. Matthew J. Kiernan, "The New Strategic Architecture: Learning to Compete in the Twenty-First Century," *Academy of Management Executive*, February 1993, pp. 7–21.

Answers

1. **Delude.** Whether the supervisor performed a misguided show of support, staged a Machiavellian act to maintain control, or fell prey to the employee's adroit manipulation of the situation, any display of empowerment here was a delusion. If you delegate responsibility and then retract it when the going gets rough, even for the most magnanimous of motives, you undermine the employee's development into a fully responsible worker and deprive the organization of that person's potential contribution.

2. **Abandon.** Here's a supervisor whose behavior was the exact opposite of that in the first situation. Yet this one, too, fails the empowerment test. The definition of empower began with the works "to enable . . . ," and turning your back on an employee's problems is not enabling. What this shows is that empowering employees doesn't necessarily mean less work for the boss, at least not at the outset. While it's not empowering to solve employee's problems for them, it is necessary to give them direction, provide necessary resources, and open the right doors to get them the help they need.

3. **Empower.** Finally, the supervisor got it right. Helping an employee who is having difficulties often means acting as a sounding board as the employee suggests his or her own solutions, offering suggestions as necessary, and supporting the employee as the person chooses a course of action and implements it.

4. **Exploit.** Delegating responsibility and authority for entire projects is one way to empower employees, but what's described in this situation isn't delegating, it's dumping. Dumping your own onerous work onto someone else is exploiting them. True, one person's poison may be someone else's fish; a task you don't want may be a developmental opportunity for someone else. But before you "empower" an employee to take over a task you want to be rid of, make sure the person understands what he or she is getting into. And provide assistance without hanging on to the reins.

5. **Empower.** Perhaps the first key to empowerment is information. With most organizations in a state of continuous change, employees all too often feel powerless because they don't know what's going on. In fact, supervisors very often feel the same way, so they sit back and wait for whatever happens to them. You can empower yourself and your employees if you relentlessly pursue knowledge about your organization's mission, goals and plans. Then you and your employees can have input into what your unit can do to contribute to carrying out those plans and fulfilling those goals.

suggests that employees should be free to do what they think is best without fear that the boss is standing by to veto or change the work done by the employee.[32] *Developing Management Skills* can help you differentiate between what is empowerment and what is not.

Procedural Justice

Another movement in management that may be viewed as a cultural issue is procedural justice. **Procedural justice** is the extent to which the dynamics of an organi-

---

32. Oren Harari, "Stop Empowering Your People," *Management Review*, November 1993, pp. 26–29.

Procedural justice is the extent to which the dynamics of an organization's decision-making processes are judged to be fair by those who are most affected by it.

zation's decision-making processes are judged to be fair by those who are most affected by it. Especially in the United States, employees are demanding more involvement with the employer in terms of work rules, health and safety on the job, and the provision of certain benefits for all employees. Furthermore, each generation of new employees may feel more entitled to certain things from the organization, especially in terms of being able to make decisions regarding their work. Employees who expect to have more input into decision making may or may not comply with decisions or directives from top management that they have little or no part in.

The lack of procedural justice may lead to less compliant attitudes on the part of lower-level managers. This has been shown to come into play in strategic decision making in multinational organizations. The exercise of procedural justice can be an effective way to engender compliance from subsidiary managers in large multinational companies.[33] The extent to which this movement continues may depend on the overall cultural shifts in society and the extent to which the employee empowerment becomes entrenched in organizations and management practice.

Managing Organization Culture

The work of Ouchi, Peters and Waterman, and many others demonstrates two important facts. First, organization cultures differ among firms; second, these different organization cultures can affect a firm's performance. Based on these observations, managers have become increasingly concerned about how to best manage the cultures of their organizations. There are three elements of managing organization culture—taking advantage of the existing culture, teaching organization culture, and changing organization culture.

Taking Advantage of the Existing Culture

It may be easier and faster to alter employee behaviors within the existing culture than it is to change the history, traditions, and values that already exist within the organization.

Most managers are not in a position to create an organization culture; rather, they work in an organization that already has cultural values. For these managers, the central issue in managing culture is how best to use the cultural system that already exists. Altering employee behaviors within the existing culture may be easier and faster than changing the history, traditions, and values that already exist within the organization.[34]

To take full advantage of an existing cultural system, managers must first be fully aware of what values the culture includes and what behaviors or actions those values support. Becoming fully aware of an organization's values usually is not easy, however. It involves more than reading a pamphlet about what the company believes in. It requires that managers develop a deep understanding of how organizational values operate in the firm—an understanding that usually comes only through experience.

33. W. Chan Kim and Renee A. Mauborgne, "Procedural Justice, Attitudes, and Subsidiary Top Management Compliance with Multinationals' Corporate Strategic Decisions," *Academy of Management Journal*, 1993, pp. 502–526.
34. See Warren Wilhelm, "Changing Corporate Culture—Or Corporate Behavior? How To Change Your Company," *Academy of Management Executive*, November 1992, pp. 72–77.

Hazel O'Leary, executive vice president of Northern States Power in Minneapolis, advises that "Without losing your personality, its important to be part of the prevailing corporate culture." Most successful managers work to understand the cultural values of their organization and to operate within the strictures of those values.

Understanding, once achieved, can be used to evaluate the performances of others in the firm. Articulating organizational values can be useful in managing others' behavior. For example, suppose that a subordinate in a firm with a strong cultural value of "sticking to its knitting" develops a business strategy that involves moving into a new industry. Rather than attempting to argue that this business strategy is economically flawed or conceptually weak, the manager who understands the corporate culture can point to this organizational value: "In this firm, we believe in sticking to our knitting."

Senior managers who understand their organization's culture can communicate that understanding to lower-level individuals. Over time, as these lower-level managers begin to understand and accept the firm's culture, they will require less direct supervision. Their understanding of corporate values will guide their decision making.

Teaching the Organization Culture: Socialization

Socialization is the process through which individuals become social beings.[35] As studied by psychologists, it is the process through which children learn to be adults in a society—the way they learn what is acceptable and polite behavior and what is not, the way they learn to communicate, the way they learn to interact with others, and so on. In complex societies, the socialization process may take many years.

Organizational socialization is the process through which employees learn about their firm's culture and pass their knowledge and understanding on to others. Just as people are socialized into societies, so are they socialized into organiza-

Organizational socialization is the process through which employees learn about the firm's culture and pass their knowledge and understanding on to others.

35. Socialization also has been defined as "the process by which culture is transmitted from one generation to the next." See J. W. M. Whiting, "Socialization: Anthropological Aspects," in D. Sils (Ed.), *International Encyclopedia of the Social Sciences*, Vol. 14 (New York: Free Press, 1968), p. 545.

tions; that is, they come to know over time what is acceptable in the organization and what is not, how to communicate their feelings, and how to interact with others. They learn through observation and through efforts by managers to communicate this information to them. Research into the process of socialization indicates that for many employees, socialization programs do not necessarily change their values but make them more aware of the differences between personal and organization values and help them develop ways to cope with the differences.[36]

A variety of organizational mechanisms have been shown to affect the socialization of workers in organizations.[37] Most important are the examples that people new to a firm see in the behavior of experienced people. Through example, new employees develop a repertoire of stories that they can use to guide their actions. When a decision needs to be made, new employees can ask, "What would my boss do in this situation?" This is not to suggest that formal training, corporate pamphlets, and corporate statements about organization culture are unimportant in the socialization process. These factors, however, tend to support the socialization process based on people closely observing the actions of others.

In some organizations, the culture written in pamphlets and presented in formal training sessions conflicts with the values of the organization as they are expressed in the actions of its people. For example, a firm may say that employees are its most important asset but may treat employees badly. In this setting, new employees quickly learn that the rhetoric of the pamphlets and formal training sessions has little to do with the reality of the organization culture. Employees who are socialized into this system usually come to accept the actual cultural values rather than those formally espoused.

Changing the Organization Culture

Much of our discussion to this point has assumed that an organization's culture enhances its performance. When this is the case, learning what an organization's cultural values are and using those values to help socialize new workers and managers is very important, for such actions help the organization succeed. As Ouchi's and Peters and Waterman's research indicates, however, not all firms have cultural values that are consistent with high performance. Ouchi found that Japanese firms and U.S. Type Z companies have performance-enhancing values, whereas typical U.S. firms have performance-reducing values. Peters and Waterman identified performance-enhancing values associated with successful companies. By implication, some firms not included in Peters and Waterman's study must have had performance-reducing values. What should a manager who works in a company with performance-reducing values do?

The answer to this question is, of course, that top managers in such firms should try to change their organizations' cultures. However, this is a difficult thing to do.[38] For all the reasons that culture is a powerful influence on behavior—the fact that it embodies the basic values in the firm, is often taken for granted, and typically is communicated most effectively through stories or other symbols—it resists

---

36. J. E. Hebden, "Adopting an Organization's Culture: The Socialization of Graduate Trainees," *Organizational Dynamics*, Summer 1986, pp. 54–72.
37. Barney, "Organizational Culture."
38. Ibid.

THE ETHICAL DILEMMA

Teledyne: A New Culture

Teledyne, Inc., is a conglomerate with businesses in many diverse fields, including consumer products such as Water Pik shower massage, and government and defense products such as electronic navigation systems, machine tools, and specialty metals. About one-third of the business is with the U.S. government. Total sales in 1988 were $4.5 billion but fell to about $3 billion in 1991. Its founder, Henry E. Singleton, effectively managed the more than 130 companies that made up Teledyne during its largest point in 1990.

Controls were very loose, but coordination of the diverse units was accomplished by Singleton's personal style. As revenues dropped, Teledyne was hit with a series of federal indictments alleging widespread cheating on government contracts, whistle-blower claims by employees in its defense businesses, and shareholder lawsuits. The allegations included inflated cost estimates on government contracts, problems with gear boxes for jet engines, faked missile relay systems test results, and illegal payments to an Egyptian Air Force general to secure lucrative contracts. Company officials have had little comments on the allegations. In late 1992, however, it has paid $19 million in fines and settled claims worth $10 million. In addition, three subsidiary presidents, three vice presidents, and nine managers have quit or been fired.

When Singleton retired, William P. Rutledge became chairman and CEO, and former Air Force secretary, Donald B. Rice, became second in command. Their task was to rebuild the company's credibility. Paying the fines and settling the claims has been the first step in that process. The company is stressing a new way of doing business at every level in the organization. The independent and loosely structured companies have been organized into a centralized structure with more controls in place. Fifty-six small companies have been reorganized into 12, with the total number of companies reduced from 130 to just 21. Although some downsizing and divestiture of certain divisions were accomplished, the goal for this decade is to increase sales to $5 billion by acquisitions and internal growth.

SOURCES: James R. Norman, "A New Teledyne," *Forbes*, September 27, 1993, pp. 44–45; Tim Deady, "Teledyne Will Overhaul Operations to Bring Company Out of Tailspin," *Los Angeles Business Journal*, September 2, 1991, p. 6; "At Teledyne, A Chorus of Whistle-Blowers," *Business Week*, December 14, 1992, p. 40; and Gary Hoover, Alta Campbell, and Patrick J. Spain, *Hoover's Handbook of American Business 1993* (Austin, Tex.: The Riverside Press, 1992), p. 529.

change. When managers attempt to change a culture, they are attempting to change people's basic assumptions about what is and what is not appropriate behavior in the organization. *The Ethical Dilemma* describes how Teledyne is trying to change its culture, which may have contributed to earlier ethical problems.

Despite these difficulties, some organizations have changed their cultures from performance-reducing to performance-enhancing.[39] This change process is described in more detail in Chapter 18. Here we briefly summarize several elements of the cultural change process.

Managing Symbols   Research suggests that organization culture is understood and communicated through the use of stories and other symbolic media. If this is

39. Main, "Westinghouse's Cultural Revolution," and "Corporate Culture: The Hard to Change Values That Spell Success or Failure," *Fortune*, June 15, 1981, p. 74.

correct, managers interested in changing cultures should attempt to substitute stories and myths that support new cultural values for those that support old ones. They can do so by creating situations that give rise to new stories.

Suppose that an organization traditionally has held the value that "employee opinions are not important." When management meets in this company, the ideas and opinions of lower-level people—when discussed at all—normally are rejected as foolish and irrelevant. The stories that support this cultural value tell about managers who tried to make a constructive point only to have that point lost in personal attacks from superiors.

An upper-level manager interested in creating a new story, which shows lower-level managers that their ideas are important and valuable, might ask a subordinate to prepare to lead a discussion in a meeting and follow through by asking the subordinate to take the lead when the topic arises. The subordinate's success in the meeting will become a new story, one that may displace some of the many stories suggesting that the opinions of lower-level managers do not matter.

The Difficulty of Change   Changing a firm's culture is a long and difficult process. A primary problem is that upper-level managers, no matter how dedicated they are to implementing some new cultural value, may sometimes inadvertently revert to old patterns of behavior. This happens, for example, when a manager dedicated to implementing the value that lower-level employees' ideas are important vehemently attacks a subordinate's ideas.

This mistake generates a story that supports old values and beliefs. After such an incident, lower-level managers believe that the boss may say she or he wants their input and ideas, but nothing could be further from the truth. No matter what the boss says or how consistent his or her behavior, some credibility has been lost, and cultural change has been made more difficult.

The Stability of Change   The process of changing a firm's culture starts with a need for change and moves through a transition period wherein efforts are made to adopt new values and beliefs. In the long run, a firm that successfully changes its culture will find that the new values and beliefs are just as stable and influential as the old ones. Value systems tend to be self-reinforcing. Once they are in place, changing them requires an enormous amount of effort.[40] Thus, if a firm can change its culture from performance-reducing to performance-enhancing, the new values will likely remain in place for a long time.

Summary of Key Points

- Organization culture has become one of the most discussed subjects in the field of organizational behavior. Interest has not been restricted to academics, however. Practicing managers also are interested in organization culture, especially as it relates to performance. There is relatively little agreement about how to define organization culture. We define organization culture as the set of values, often taken for granted, that help people in organizations understand which actions are considered acceptable and which are considered unacceptable.

40. Barney, "Organizational Culture."

Often these values are communicated through stories and other symbolic means. Research on organization culture burst on the scene in the 1980s with books by Ouchi, Peters and Waterman, and others. Current research on organization culture reflects various research traditions. The most important contributions have come from anthropology and sociology. Two other influences on current work in organization culture are social psychology, with its emphasis on the manipulation of symbols in organizations, and economics. The economics approach sees culture both as a tool used to manage and as a determinant of performance.

- Although no single framework for describing organization culture has emerged, several have been suggested. Most popular efforts in this area have been Ouchi's comparison of U.S. and Japanese firms and Peters and Waterman's description of successful firms in the United States. Ouchi and Peters and Waterman suggested several important dimensions along which organizational values vary, including treatment of employees, definitions of appropriate means for decision making, and assignment of responsibility for the results of decision making.

- Emerging issues in the area of organization culture include employee empowerment and procedural justice. In addition to being similar to employee participation as a technique of motivation, some now view empowerment as a type of organization culture. Empowerment is the process of enabling employees to make decisions, set their own work goals, and solve problems in their own area of responsibility. Procedural justice is the extent to which the dynamics of an organization's decision-making processes are judged to be fair by those who are most affected by it.

- Managing organization culture requires attention to three factors. First, managers can take advantage of cultural values that already exist and use their knowledge to help subordinates understand them. Second, employees need to be properly socialized, or trained, in the cultural values of the organization, either through formal training or by experiencing and observing actions of higher-level managers. Third, managers can change the culture of the organization through managing the symbols, dealing with the extreme difficulties of change, and relying on the permanence of the new organization culture once the change has been implemented.

Discussion Questions

1. A sociologist or anthropologist might suggest that the culture in U.S. firms simply reflects the dominant culture in the society as a whole. Therefore, to change the organization culture of a company, one must first deal with the inherent values and beliefs of the society. How would you respond to this claim?

2. Psychology has been defined as the study of individual behavior. More specifically, organizational psychology is the study of individual behavior in organizations. Many of the theories described in the early chapters of this book are based in organizational psychology. Why was this field not identified as a contributor to the study of organization culture along with anthropology, sociology, social psychology, and economics?

3. Describe the culture of an organization with which you are familiar. It might be one in which you currently work, one in which you have worked, or one in which a friend or family member works. What values, beliefs, stories, and symbols are meaningful to employees of the organization?

4. Discuss the similarities and differences between the organization culture approaches of Ouchi and Peters and Waterman.

5. Describe how symbols and stories are used in organizations to communicate values and beliefs. Give some examples of how symbols and stories have been used in organizations with which you are familiar.

6. What is the role of leadership (discussed in Chapters 12 and 13) in developing, maintaining, and changing organization culture?

7. Review the characteristics of organization structure described in earlier chapters, and compare them with the elements of culture described by Ouchi and Peters and Waterman. Describe the similarities and differences, and explain how some characteristics of one may be related to characteristics of the other.

8. Discuss the role of organization rewards in developing, maintaining, and changing the organization culture.

9. How are empowerment and procedural justice similar to each other? How are they different?

EXPERIENTIAL EXERCISE

Purpose This exercise will help you appreciate the fascination as well as the difficulty of examining culture in organizations.

Format The class will divide into groups of four to six. Each group will analyze the organization culture of a college class. Students in most classes that use this book will have taken many courses at the college they attend and therefore should have several classes in common.

Procedure The class is divided into groups of four to six on the basis of classes the students have had in common.

1. Each group should first decide which class it will analyze. Each person in the group must have attended the class.

2. Each group should list the cultural factors to be discussed. Items to be covered should include the following:
   a. Stories about the professor
   b. Stories about the exams
   c. Stories about the grading
   d. Stories about other students
   e. The use of symbols that indicate the values of the students
   f. The use of symbols that indicate the values of the instructor
   g. Other characteristics of the class as suggested by the frameworks of Ouchi and Peters and Waterman

3. Students should carefully analyze the stories and symbols to discover their underlying meanings. They should seek stories from other members of the group to ensure that all aspects of the class culture are covered. Students should take notes as these items are discussed.
4. After twenty to thirty minutes of work in groups, the instructor will reconvene the entire class and ask each group to share its analysis with the rest of the class.

Follow-up Questions

1. What was the most difficult part of this exercise? Did other groups experience the same difficulty?
2. How did your group overcome this difficulty? How did other groups overcome it?
3. Do you believe that your group's analysis accurately describes the culture of the class you selected? Could other students who analyzed the culture of the same class come up with a very different result? How could that happen?
4. If the instructor wanted to try to change the culture in the class you analyzed, what steps would you recommend that he or she take?

| CASE 17.1 | **UPS Turning Around from the Inside Out—Or the Outside In?** |

United Parcel Service, Inc. (UPS)—the world's largest package delivery service—was started in Seattle as America Messenger Company in 1907. From the tiny telephone message service, it has gone through several names and headquarters locations; it has added ground-based parcel delivery, next-day air delivery, and international service. Operating in relative obscurity until 1972, when the United States Postal Service announced that UPS was its prime competitor, the company has branched out to include worldwide and express delivery. Throughout its history, it has had a policy of employee ownership of stock. As a result, almost all of the company stock is owned by its employees and their families and heirs, which gives the employees the genuine feeling that what goes on at the company affects them directly.

UPS had always prided itself on its door-to-door delivery services, making its way through local neighborhoods in its easily recognizable brown delivery trucks and charging everyone the same price. As profits dropped and big companies turned to other shippers who offered more personal attention, prompt service, and volume discounts, however, UPS knew that something had to change. As strong as its culture has been, social and market changes are forcing UPS to adapt its culture in two ways.

UPS found that it had to reach out to get more in touch with its customers. The marketing department, which grew from 7 persons to 175, conducted face-to-face interviews with more than 25,000 customers to find out what they wanted in terms of package delivery. New services and pricing policies were developed in response. Three-day delivery service at a lower cost was fine for some people, whereas next-day air was important to others. Electronic tracking of packages begins with the driver who picks up the package and begins the tracking from a cellular phone in the truck. Corporate business is receiving more attention, sometimes at the expense of the neighborhood customer and the catalog sellers. To facilitate the shift in culture, thousands of employees have undergone extensive training in providing customer service. The trucks are still brown, but additional artwork now emphasizes the worldwide nature of the business.

Until recently little was known about the diversity training program that has been going on at UPS for twenty-five years. Approximately forty managers have participated in the company's Community Internship Program. This program removes the manager from normal duties and requires that the manager spend one month away from the company, working in a community service or agency. Typical assignments include serving meals to the homeless, cleaning drug paraphernalia out of the inner-city ghetto, helping migrant farm workers build temporary houses, and helping teachers manage a classroom of kids in a Head Start program. Managers finish the program with more than a diversity awareness education. They have a wealth of experiences that transfer back into their jobs for UPS. Some "graduates" have stayed close to the problems that they worked on during the program and continue to fight for the cause involved. These managers begin to see that the poor and disadvantaged are not as different as they first thought. On the other hand, however, they begin to appreciate the vast differences between what is important to a mother struggling to find clothes for her children to attend school and the importance of getting a package to Detroit by noon tomorrow. UPS figures that it costs approximately $10,000 per manager for the program, and about forty participate per year. At $400,000 per year for twenty-five years, UPS is making quite a contribution.

Case Questions

1. Describe the two different types of cultural programs at UPS.
2. The two programs are essentially unrelated. Describe how they may, in fact, be more related than it first appears.
3. How could the management of UPS make them work together?

SOURCES: "After a U-turn, UPS Really Delivers," *Business Week*, May 31, 1993, pp. 92–93; Bob Filipczak, "25 Years of Diversity at UPS," *Training*, August 1992, pp. 42–46; and Gary Hoover, Alta Campbell, and Patrick J. Spain, *Hoover's Handbook of American Business 1993* (Austin, Tex.: The Riverside Press, 1992) p. 553.

CASE 17.2   Surviving Plant World's Hard Times

In ten years, Plant World had grown from a one-person venture to the largest nursery and landscaping business in its area. Its founder, Myta Ong, combined a lifelong interest in plants with a botany degree to provide a unique customer service. Ong had managed the company's growth so that even with twenty full-time employees working in six to eight crews, the organization culture was still as open, friendly, and personal as it had been when her only "employees" were friends who volunteered to help her move a heavy tree.

To maintain that atmosphere, Ong increasingly involved herself with people and less with plants as the company grew. With hundreds of customers and scores of jobs at any one time, she could no longer say without hesitation whether she had a dozen arborvitae bushes in stock or when Mrs. Carnack's estate would need a new load of bark mulch. But she knew when Rose had been up all night with her baby, when Gary was likely to be late because he had driven to see his sick father over the weekend, and how to deal with Ellen when she was depressed because of her boyfriend's behavior. She kept track of the birthdays of every employee and even those of their children. She was up every morning by 5:30, arranging schedules so that John could get his son out of day care at 4:00 or Martina could be back in town for her afternoon equivalency classes.

All this attention to employees may have led Ong to make a single bad business decision that almost destroyed the company. She provided extensive landscaping to a new mall on credit and, when the mall never opened and its owners went bankrupt, Plant World found itself in deep trouble. The company had virtually no cash and had to pay off the bills for the mall plants, most of which were not even salvageable.

One Friday, Ong called a meeting with her employees and leveled with them: either they would not get paid for two weeks or Plant World would fold. The news hit the employees hard. Many counted on the

Friday paycheck to buy groceries for the week. The local unemployment rate was low, however, and they knew they could find other jobs.

But as they looked around, they wondered whether they could ever find this kind of job. Sure, the pay was not the greatest, but the tears in the eyes of some were not because of pay or personal hardship; they were for Ong, her dream, and her difficulties. They never thought of her as the boss or called her anything but "Myta." And leaving the group would not be just a matter of saying goodbye to fellow employees. If Bernice left, the company softball team would lose its best pitcher, and the Sunday game was the height of everyone's week. Where else would they find people who spent much of the weekend working on the best puns with which to assail one another on Monday morning? At how many offices would everyone show up twenty minutes before starting time just to catch up with friends on other crews? What other boss would really understand when you simply said,

"I don't have a doctor's appointment, I just need the afternoon off"?

Ong gave her employees the weekend to think over their decision: whether to take their pay and look for another job or to dig into their savings and go on working. Knowing it would be hard for them to quit, she told them they did not have to face her on Monday; if they did not show up, she would send them their checks. But when she arrived at 7:40 Monday morning, she found the entire group already there, ready to work even harder to pull the company through. They were even trying to top one another with puns about being "mall-contents."

Case Questions

1. How would you describe the organization culture at Plant World?
2. How large can such a company get before it needs to change its culture and structure?

Organization Change and Development

OBJECTIVES

After studying this chapter, you should be able to:

Summarize the dominant forces for change in organizations.

Describe the process of planned organization change.

Discuss several approaches to organization development.

Explain resistance to change.

Identify five keys to managing successful organization change and development.

It is the same old story. Someone with an idea of how to do something better starts a new company and blows away the competition for a few years. Then the things that contributed to its early success have to be changed for the company to stay in business. Dell Computer is no different. In 1984 Michael Dell started PC's Limited at age nineteen in his apartment at college. He figured that he could sell personal computers by telephone, assemble parts on demand, and ship cheaply directly to the consumer, thereby cutting out costs associated with dealers, inventory, manufacturing plants, traditional advertising, and a large sales staff. Everything was rented, based on reducing costs, and fast. He was right. In less than ten years sales in 1992 were more than $2 billion and on the way to $10 billion. He had gone up against the major manufacturers such as IBM and Compaq and won.

In late 1991, Michael Dell and others realized that major changes were needed if the company were to survive. The company was still profitable, but profit margins were down as the competition began to meet Dell's low-price strategy with new products at lower prices and with faster

Seven years ago, Michael Dell started Dell Computer out of his college apartment with the successful combination of low prices and speedy mail-order service. Since then, Dell has had to re-organize the company to accommodate what has grown into a $2 billion a year international business.

service. First, Dell has 5,650 employees, more than forty different models, and sells in ninety-five countries. To forge the dramatic growth plans, in 1993 Dell was hiring, although now only ten or fifteen employees a week, instead of the 1992 levels of more than sixty per week. Instead of selling only through telephone and mail order, Dell is trying to sell through dealers, which may be difficult because his primary winning strategy over the years has been to bypass the dealers. He is now building plants and moving assembly in-house rather than contracting it out to others. He is hiring a top management team of executives from other large companies to run design, finance, and manufacturing. Sophisticated systems and management controls are being developed and put in place like other large companies. The loose and fast ways of doing things were not adequate for running a $2 billion a year company, even in the computer business.[1]

Companies such as Dell Computer are constantly faced with pressures to make changes. Forecasts of changing economic conditions, consumer purchasing patterns, technological and scientific factors, and foreign competition force top management to evaluate their organization and consider major changes.

This chapter first presents a view of change in organizations by examining the forces for change and then discusses several approaches to planned organization change. Then we discuss organization development and the resistance to change that usually occurs. Finally, we present the management of organization change and development efforts in organizations.

1. "The Education of Michael Dell," *Business Week*, March 22, 1993, pp. 82–88; "Dell Computer Goes Into the Shop," *Business Week*, July 12, 1993, pp. 138–140; and "Compaq: Turning the Tables on Dell?" *Business Week*, March 22, 1993, p. 87.

Forces for Change

The complexity of events and the rapidity of change make it difficult to predict future sources of pressure for change.

An organization is subject to many pressures for change from a variety of sources—far too many to discuss here. Moreover, because the complexity of events and the rapidity of change are increasing, predicting what type of pressure for change will be most meaningful in the next decade is difficult. Discussing the broad categories of pressures that probably will have major effects on organizations is possible, however—and important. The four areas in which the pressures for change appear most powerful involve people, technology, information processing and communication, and competition. Table 18.1 gives examples of each of these categories.

People

Approximately 56 million people were born between 1945 and 1960. These baby boomers differ notably from previous generations with respect to education, expectations, and value systems.[2] As this group has aged, the median age of the U.S. population has gradually increased as it passed thirty-two for the first time.[3] The special characteristics of baby boomers show up in distinct purchasing patterns that affect product and service innovation, technological change, and marketing and promotional activities.[4] Employment practices, compensation systems, promotion and managerial succession systems, and the entire concept of human resource management are also affected.

Other population-related pressures for change involve the generations that sandwich the baby boomers: the increasing numbers of senior citizens and those born after 1960. The parents of the baby boomers are living longer, healthier lives

2. "Baby Boomers Push for Power," *Business Week*, July 2, 1984, pp. 52–56.
3. "Americans' Median Age Passes 32," *The Arizona Republic*, April 6, 1988, pp. A1, A5.
4. Geoffrey Colvin, "What the Baby Boomers Will Buy Next," *Fortune*, October 15, 1984, pp. 28–34.

TABLE 18.1

Pressures for Organization Change

Category	Examples
People	Baby boomers Senior citizens Coming generations Workforce diversity
Technology	Manufacturing in space Robotics Artificial intelligence
Information Processing and Communication	Computer, satellite communications Videoconferencing
Competition	Worldwide markets International trade agreements Emerging nations

than previous generations, and today they expect to live the "good life" that they missed when they were raising their children. The impact of the large number of senior citizens is already evident in part-time employment practices, in the marketing of everything from hamburgers to packaged tours of Asia, and in the service areas such as health care, recreation, and financial services. The post-1960 generation of workers entering the job market differ from the baby boomers in terms of their willingness to work overtime, to accept transfers that require moving to different cities or even countries, and to conform to corporate norms.

The increasing diversity of the workforce in the coming years will mean major changes for organizations. This increasing diversity is discussed in more detail in Chapter 20. In addition, employees will be faced with a different work environment in the next century. The most descriptive word for this new work environment is change. Employees must be prepared for constant change. Change is occurring in organizations' cultures, structures, work relationships, customer relationships, as well as the actual jobs that people do. People will have to be completely adaptable to new situations while maintaining productivity under the existing system.[5]

Technology

Not only is technology changing, the rate of technological change is itself increasing. In 1970, for example, all engineering students owned slide rules and used them in almost every class. By 1976, slide rules had given way to portable electronic calculators. In the mid-1980s, some universities began issuing microcomputers to entering students or assuming that students already owned them. In 1993, the Scholastic Assessment Test (SAT), which many college-bound students take to get into college, allowed students to use calculators during the test! And students cannot make it through the university without owning or at least having ready access to a personal computer.

Interestingly, change as it affects organizations is self-perpetuating. Advances in information technology mean that more information is generated within organizations and it circulates more quickly. Consequently, employees are able to respond more quickly to problems, which enables the organization to respond more quickly to demands from other organizations, customers, and competitors.[6] New technology will affect organizations in ways that we cannot yet predict. Artificial intelligence—computers and software programs that think and learn in much the same way as human beings do—already is assisting in geological exploration.[7] Several companies are developing systems to manufacture chemicals and exotic electronic components in space. Robotics was developing so rapidly in the 1980s, that annual U.S. sales of robots were expected to exceed $7 billion by 1990.[8] Robot sales in other countries, most notably Japan, were expected to increase even faster. Thus, as organizations respond more quickly to changes, change occurs more rapidly, which in turn necessitates more rapid response.

---

5. John Huey, "Managing in the Midst of Chaos," *Fortune*, April 5, 1993, pp. 38–48.
6. Peter Nulty, "How Personal Computers Change Managers' Lives," *Fortune*, September 3, 1984, pp. 38–48.
7. "Artificial Language Is Here," *Business Week*, July 9, 1984, pp. 54–62.
8. Robert U. Ayres and Steven M. Miller, *Robotics: Applications and Social Implications* (Cambridge, Mass.: Ballinger, 1983).

Many markets are now international. In light of this trend towards globalization, many companies find it useful to employ talented workers from the newly accessible international pool to handle their foreign markets. These Dubliners have been employed by a California software company to answer international sales questions.

Information Processing and Communication

Advances in information processing and communication have paralleled each other. A new generation of computers, which will mark another major increase in processing power, is being designed. Satellite systems for data transmission already are in use. Today people can carry telephones in their briefcases along with their portable computers and pocket-size televisions.

In the future, people may not need offices as they work with computers and communicate through new data transmission devices. Workstations, both inside and outside of offices, will be increasingly electronic instead of paper- and pencil-based. For years the capability existed to generate, manipulate, store, and transmit more data than managers could use, but the benefits were not fully realized. Now, managers can utilize all of that information-processing potential, and companies are making the most of it. Typically, companies received orders by mail in the 1970s, by 800 number in the 1980s, by facsimile machine in the late 1980s and early 1990s, and by electronic data exchange in the mid-1990s. From orders in a week to orders in an instant, companies must now be able to receive and respond to orders immediately, all because of changes in information processing and communication.[9]

Competition

Although competition is not a new force for change, competition today has a meaningful new twist: most markets are international because of decreasing transportation and communication costs and the increasing export orientation of business. The adoption of trade agreements such as the North American Free Trade Agreement (NAFTA) and the General Agreement on Trade and Tariffs (GATT) has changed the way businesses operate. In the future, competition from the industrialized countries such as Japan and Germany will take a back seat to compe-

9. Thomas A. Stewart, "Welcome to the Revolution," *Fortune*, December 13, 1993, pp. 66–80.

Mercedes-Benz Makes Major Changes

Mercedes-Benz is the world's oldest and certainly one of the most visible names in automobiles. Based in Germany, the Daimler-Benz organization, the company which makes Mercedes-Benz, sits atop the car world in prestige, quality, and engineering. As first Japanese manufacturers, and then U.S. manufacturers, made major changes in automotive production methods, Mercedes refused to change its old ways of doing things. After peaking in sales in 1991, sales of Mercedes have dropped in almost every market: down 23 percent in Europe and 8.8 percent in the United States. Other luxury car makers in Europe also experienced slumps, but at lower levels. In the United States, luxury cars such as Jaguar and BMW actually experienced increases. Mercedes finally got the message that maybe it was guilty of ignoring changes in both the market and manufacturing technology.

Mercedes has begun to respond to these pressures and is in the middle of massive changes internally as well as in the way the buying public views its cars. In the marketplace, it introduced a new C-class that has all of the luxury features and a sticker price of less than $30,000. It also unveiled plans to develop a supersmall city car for less than $20,000 by 1995. It seems firmly committed to being an exclusive, full-line manufacturer. Internally, it has eliminated two layers of management and 25,000 jobs, almost 4,000 of which came from headquarters. It is building a new plant in the United States with state-of-the-art manufacturing technology. Overall, the company is experiencing quite a revolution. All of the companies in the automobile business are affected by the same forces for change.

SOURCES: "Making Up for Lost Time," *Fortune,* October 18, 1993, pp. 78–80; "Downshift at Daimler: A Mercedes World Slump Rattles It to the Core," *BusinessWeek,* November 16, 1992, pp. 88–90; and Diana T. Kurylko, "Daimler: Earnings to Plummet in '93," *Automotive News,* April 12, 1993, p. 6.

tition from the booming industries of developing nations. Developing nations may soon offer different, newer, cheaper, or higher-quality products while enjoying the benefits of low labor costs, abundant supplies of raw materials, expertise in certain areas of production, and financial protection from their governments that may not be available in the older industrialized states. Daimler-Benz, the parent company of Mercedes-Benz, has painfully experienced competitive pressures which have necessitated the internal changes (see the *Global Perspective*). Organizations that are not ready for these new sources of competition in the next decade may not exist by the year 2000.

Processes for Planned Organization Change

External elements may force change on an organization. Ideally, however, the organization will not only respond to change but anticipate it, prepare for it through planning, and incorporate it in the organization strategy. Organization change can be viewed from a static point of view, such as that of Lewin, or from a dynamic perspective.

FIGURE 18.1

Lewin's Process of Organization Change

Lewin's Process Model

Lewin's three-stage model of planned organization change suggests that change is a systematic process of moving from one stage to another.

Unfreezing is the process by which people become aware of the need for change.

Refreezing is the process of making new behaviors relatively permanent and resistant to further change.

Planned organization change requires a systematic process of moving from one condition to another. Kurt Lewin suggested that efforts to bring about planned change in organizations should approach change as a multistage process.[10] His model of planned change is made up of three steps—unfreezing, change, and refreezing—as shown in Figure 18.1

Unfreezing is the process by which people become aware of the need for change. Satisfaction with current practices and procedures may result in little or no interest in making changes. The important factor in unfreezing is making employees knowledgeable about the importance of a change and how their jobs will be affected by it. The employees who will be most affected by the change must be made aware of the need for it, in effect making them dissatisfied enough with current operations to be motivated toward change.

Change is the movement from an old stage to a new one. Change may mean installing new equipment, restructuring the organization, or implementing a new performance appraisal system—anything that alters existing relationships or activities.

Refreezing makes new behaviors relatively permanent and resistant to further change. Examples of refreezing include repeating newly learned skills in a training session and role playing to teach how the new skill can be used in a real-life work situation. Refreezing is necessary because without it, the old ways of doing things might soon reassert themselves while the new ways were forgotten. For example, many employees who attend special training sessions apply themselves diligently and resolve to change things in their organizations. But when they return to the workplace, they find it easier to conform to the old ways than to make waves. There usually are few, if any, rewards for trying to change the organizational status quo. In fact, the personal sanctions against doing so may be difficult to tolerate. Learning theory and reinforcement theory (Chapter 6) can play important roles in the refreezing phase.

The Continuous Change Process Model

The continuous change process model utilizes the Lewin three-stage model of organization change and emphasizes that change is continuous in organizations.

Perhaps because Lewin's model is very simple and straightforward, virtually all models of organization change use his approach. The model, however, does not address several important issues. A more complex, and more helpful, approach is illustrated in Figure 18.2. This approach looks at planned change from the per-

10. Kurt Lewin, *Field Theory in Social Science* (New York: Harper & Row, 1951).

spective of top management and indicates that change is continuous. Although we discuss each step as if it were separate and distinct from others, it is important to note that as change becomes continuous in organizations these steps are most likely occurring simultaneously throughout the organization. The model incorporates Lewin's concept into the implementation phase.

In this approach, top management perceives that certain forces or trends call for change, and the issue is subjected to the organization's usual problem-solving and decision-making processes (see Chapter 10). Usually, top management defines its goals in terms of what the organization or certain processes or outputs will be like after the change. Alternatives for change are generated and evaluated, and an acceptable one is selected.

The **change agent** is the person responsible for managing the change effort.

Early in the process, the organization may seek the assistance of a **change agent**—a person who will be responsible for managing the change effort. The change agent may also help management recognize and define the problem or the need for the change and may be involved in generating and evaluating potential plans of action. The change agent may be a member of the organization or an outsider such as a consultant or even someone from headquarters whom employees view as an outsider. An internal change agent is likely to know the organization's people, tasks, and political situations, which may be helpful in interpreting data and understanding the system; an insider, however, may also be too close to the situation to view it objectively. (In addition, a regular employee has to be removed from his or her regular duties to concentrate on the transition.) An outsider, then, often is received better by all parties because of her or his assumed impartiality. Under the direction and management of the change agent, the organization implements the change through Lewin's unfreeze, change, and refreeze process.

In the final step, evaluation and control, the change agent and top management assess the degree to which the change is having the desired effect; that is, they

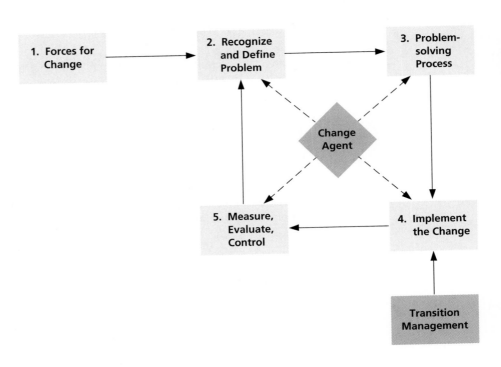

FIGURE 18.2

Continuous Change Process Model of Organization Change

1. Forces for Change

2. Recognize and Define Problem

3. Problem-solving Process

Change Agent

5. Measure, Evaluate, Control

4. Implement the Change

Transition Management

measure progress toward the goals of the change and make appropriate changes if necessary. The more closely the change agent is involved in the change process, the less distinct the steps become. As the change agent becomes immersed in defining and solving the problem with members of the organization, she or he becomes a "collaborator" or "helper" to the organization. When this happens, the change agent may be working with many individuals, groups, and departments within the organization on different phases of the change process. Because of the total involvement of the change agent in every phase of the project, it may not be readily observable when the change process is moving along from one stage to another. Throughout the process, however, the change agent brings in new ideas and viewpoints that help members look at old problems in new ways. Change often comes from the conflict that results when the change agent challenges the organization's assumptions and generally accepted patterns of operation.

Transition management is the process of systematically planning, organizing, and implementing change, from the disassembly of the current state to the realization of a fully functional future state within an organization.[11] Once change begins, the organization is in neither the old state nor the new state; yet business must continue. Transition management ensures that business continues during the change, and thus it must begin before the change occurs. The members of the regular management team must take on the role of transition managers and coordinate organizational activities with the change agent. An interim management structure or interim positions may be created to ensure continuity and control of the business during the transition. Communication of the changes to all involved, including employees, customers, and suppliers, play an important role in transition management.[12]

Transition management is the process of systematically planning, organizing, and implementing change.

Organization Development

On one level, organization development is simply the way organizations change and evolve. Organization change can involve personnel, technology, competition, and other areas. Employee learning and formal training, transfers, promotions, terminations, and retirements are all examples of personnel-related changes. Thus, in the broadest sense, organization development means organization change.[13] The term as used here, however, means something more specific. Over the past twenty years, organization development (OD) has emerged as a distinct field of study and practice. Researchers now substantially agree on what OD is in general, although arguments about details continue.[14] Our definition of organization development is an attempt to simply describe a very complex process. It is also an attempt to capture the best points of several definitions offered by writers in the field.

11. Linda S. Ackerman, "Transition Management: An In-Depth Look at Managing Complex Change," *Organizational Dynamics*, Summer 1982, pp. 46–66; and David A. Nadler, "Managing Transitions to Uncertain Future States," *Organizational Dynamics*, Summer 1982, pp. 37–45.
12. Noel M. Tichy and David O. Ulrich, "The Leadership Challenge—A Call for the Transformational Leader," *Sloan Management Review*, Fall 1984, pp. 59–68.
13. W. Warner Burke, *Organization Development: Principles and Practices* (Boston: Little, Brown, 1982).
14. See Burke, *Organization Development*; and Michael Beer, *Organization Change and Development* (Santa Monica, Calif.: Goodyear, 1980).

Organization development (OD) is the process of planned change and improvement of the organization through the application of knowledge of the behavioral sciences.

Organization development (**OD**) is the process of planned change and improvement of organizations through the application of knowledge of the behavioral sciences. Three points in this definition make it simple to remember and use. First, OD involves attempts to *plan* organization changes, thus excluding spontaneous, haphazard initiatives. Second, the specific intention of OD is to *improve* organizations. This point excludes changes that merely imitate those of another organization, are forced on the organization by external pressures, or are undertaken merely for the sake of changing. Third, the planned improvement must be based on *knowledge of the behavioral sciences*, such as psychology, sociology, cultural anthropology, and related fields of study, rather than on financial or technological considerations. Under our definition, the replacement of manual personnel records with a computerized system would not be considered organization development. Although such a change has behavioral effects, it is a technology-driven reform rather than a behavioral one. Likewise, alterations in record keeping necessary to support new government-mandated reporting requirements are not a part of organization development because the change is obligatory and the result of an external force. The three most basic types of techniques are systemwide, task-technological, and group and individual.

Systemwide Organization Development

Systemwide organization development can be a major restructuring of the organization or the implementation of programs such as quality of work life.

The most comprehensive type of organization change involves a major reorganization, usually referred to as a structural change—a systemwide rearrangement of task division and authority and reporting relationships. A structural change affects performance appraisal and rewards, decision making, and communication and information processing systems. As we discuss in Chapter 16, reengineering and rethinking the organizations are two contemporary approaches to systemwide structural change.

An organization may change the way it divides tasks into jobs, groups jobs into departments and divisions, and arranges authority and reporting relationships among positions. It may move from functional departmentalization to a system based, for example, on products or geography or from a conventional linear design to a matrix design. Other changes may include dividing large groups into smaller ones or merging small groups into larger ones. In addition, the degree to which rules and procedures are written down and enforced, as well as the locus of decision-making authority, may be altered. If the organization makes all these changes, it will have transformed both the configurational and operational aspects of its structure.

No systemwide structural change is simple.[15] A company president cannot just issue a memo notifying company personnel that on a certain date they will report to a different supervisor and be responsible for new tasks. Employees have months, years, and sometimes decades of experience in working with people and tasks in certain ways. When these patterns are disrupted, employees need time to learn the new tasks and to settle into the new relationships. Moreover, the change may be resisted for a number of reasons; we discuss resistance to change later in this chapter. Therefore, organizations must manage the change process.

15. Danny Miller and Peter H. Friesen, "Structural Change and Performance: Quantum versus Piecemeal-Incremental Approaches," *Academy of Management Journal*, December 1982, pp. 867–892.

Quality of work life is the degree to which workers are able to satisfy important personal needs through their experiences in the organization.

Another systemwide change is the introduction of quality-of-work-life (QWL) programs. J. Lloyd Suttle has defined **quality of work life** as the "degree to which members of a work organization are able to satisfy important personal needs through their experiences in the organization."[16] QWL programs focus strongly on providing a work environment conducive to the satisfaction of individual needs. The emphasis on improving life at work developed during the 1970s, a period of increasing inflation and deepening recession. The development was rather surprising because an expanding economy and substantially increased resources are the conditions that usually induce top management to begin people-oriented programs. Improving life at work was viewed by top management as a means of improving productivity.

Any movement with broad and ambiguous goals tends to spawn diverse programs, each claiming to be based on the movement's goals, and QWL is no exception. QWL programs differ substantially, although most espouse a goal of "humanizing the workplace." Richard Walton has divided QWL programs into the eight categories shown in Figure 18.3.[17] Obviously, many types of programs can be accommodated by the categories, from changing the pay system to establishing an employee bill of rights that guarantees workers the rights to privacy, free speech, due process, and fair and equitable treatment.

16. J. Lloyd Suttle, "Improving Life at Work—Problems and Prospects," in J. Richard Hackman and J. Lloyd Suttle (Eds.), *Improving Life at Work: Behavioral Science Approaches to Organizational Change* (Santa Monica, Calif.: Goodyear, 1977), p. 4.
17. Richard E. Walton, "Quality of Work Life: What Is It?" *Sloan Management Review*, Fall 1983, pp. 11–21.

FIGURE 18.3

Walton's Categorization of Quality-of-Work-Life (QWL) Programs

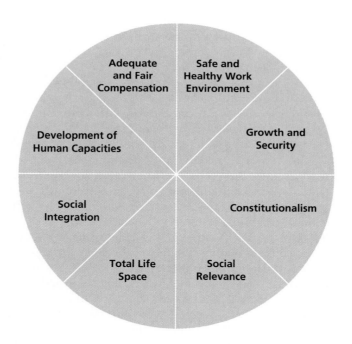

SOURCE: Reprinted (adapted) from Richard E. Walton, "Quality of Work Life: What Is It?" *Sloan Management Review*, Fall 1973, pp. 11-21, by permission of the publisher. Copyright © 1973 by the Sloan Management Review Association. All rights reserved.

Total quality management (TQM), which has been discussed in Chapter 8, can also be viewed as a systemwide OD program. In fact, some might consider TQM as a broad program that includes structural change as well as QWL. It differs from QWL in that TQM emphasizes satisfying customer needs by making quality-oriented changes rather than focusing on satisfying employee needs at work. Often, however, the two programs are very similar.

The benefits gained from QWL programs differ substantially, but generally they are of three types. A more positive attitude toward the work and the organization, or increased job satisfaction, perhaps is the most direct benefit.[18] Another is increased productivity, although it often is difficult to measure and separate the effects of the QWL program from the effects of other organizational factors. A third benefit is increased effectiveness of the organization as measured by its profitability, goal accomplishment, shareholder wealth, or resource exchange. The third gain follows directly from the first two: if employees have more positive attitudes about the organization and their productivity increases, everything else being equal, the organization should be more effective.

Task-Technological Change

Another way to bring about systemwide organization development is through changes in the task or technology (or both) involved in doing the work. The direct alteration of jobs usually is called *task redesign*. Changing the way inputs are transformed into outputs is called technological change and also usually results in task changes. Strictly, changing the technology typically is not part of organization development, whereas task redesign usually is.

The structural changes discussed in the preceding section are explicitly systemwide. Those we examine in this section are more narrowly focused and may not seem to have the same far-reaching consequences. It is important to remember, however, that their impact is felt throughout the organization. The discussion of task design in Chapter 7 focused on job definition and motivation and gave little attention to implementing changes in jobs. Here we discuss task redesign as a mode of organization change.

Several approaches to introducing job changes in organizations have been proposed. One approach is by a coauthor of this book, Ricky W. Griffin. Griffin's approach is an integrative framework of nine steps that reflect the complexities of the interfaces between individual jobs and the total organization.[19] The process, shown in Table 18.2, includes the steps usually associated with change, such as recognition of the need for a change, selection of the appropriate intervention, and evaluation of the change. But Griffin's approach inserts four additional steps into the standard sequence: diagnosis of the overall work system and context, including examination of the jobs, workforce, technology, organization design, leadership, and group dynamics; evaluation of the costs and benefits of the change; formulation of a redesign strategy; and implementation of supplemental changes.

Diagnosis includes analysis of the total work environment within which the jobs exist. When job changes are being considered, the organization structure must be

18. Daniel A. Ondrack and Martin G. Evans, "Job Enrichment and Job Satisfaction in Greenfield and Redesign QWL Sites," *Group and Organization Studies*, March 1987, pp. 5–22.
19. Ricky W. Griffin, *Task Design: An Integrative Framework* (Glenview, Ill.: Scott, Foresman, 1982).

Step 1: Recognition of a need for a change
Step 2: Selection of task redesign as a potential intervention
Step 3: Diagnosis of the work system and context
       a. Diagnosis of existing jobs
       b. Diagnosis of existing workforce
       c. Diagnosis of technology
       d. Diagnosis of organization design
       e. Diagnosis of leader behavior
       f. Diagnosis of group and social processes
Step 4: Cost/benefit of proposed changes
Step 5: Go/no-go decision
Step 6: Formulation of the strategy for redesign
Step 7: Implementation of the task changes
Step 8: Implementation of any supplemental changes
Step 9: Evaluation of the task redesign effort

SOURCE: Ricky W. Griffin, *Task Design: An Integrative Framework* (Glenview, Ill.: Scott, Foresman, 1982), p. 208. Used by permission.

evaluated, especially the work rules and decision-making authority within a department.[20] For example, if jobs are to be redesigned to give employees more freedom in choosing work methods or scheduling work activities, diagnosis of the present system must determine whether the rules will allow that to happen. Diagnosis must also include evaluation of the work group and intragroup dynamics (discussed in Chapter 11). Furthermore, it must determine whether workers have or can easily obtain the new skills to perform the redesigned task.

Recognizing the full range of potential costs and benefits associated with a job redesign effort is extremely important. Some are direct and quantifiable; others are indirect and not quantifiable. Redesign may involve unexpected costs or benefits; although these cannot be predicted with certainty, they can be weighed as possibilities. Factors such as short-term role ambiguity, role conflict, and role overload can be major stumbling blocks to a job redesign effort.

Implementing a redesign scheme takes careful planning, and developing a strategy for the intervention is the final planning step. Strategy formulation is a four-part process. First, the organization must decide who will design the changes. Depending on the circumstances, the planning team may consist of only upper-level management or may include line workers and supervisors. Next, the team undertakes the actual design of the changes based on job design theory and the needs, goals, and circumstances of the organization. Third, the team decides the timing of the implementation, which may require a formal transition period during which equipment is purchased and installed, job training takes place, new physical layouts are arranged, and the "bugs" in the new system are worked out. Fourth, strategy planners must consider whether the job changes require adjustments and supplemental changes in other organizational components, such as reporting relationships and the compensation system.

20. Gregory Moorhead, "Organizational Analysis: An Integration of the Macro and Micro Approaches," *Journal of Management Studies*, April 1981, pp. 191–218.

At Anderson Consulting, the world's leader in systems integration, a group of new employees learn computer languages. In their years at Anderson, they will spend an average of 135 hours a year in formal training. Employee training is one of the most important steps an organization can take in the direction of change and of increased employee effectiveness.

Group and Individual Change and Development

Groups and individuals can be involved in organization change in a vast number of ways. Retraining a single employee can be considered an organization change if the training affects the way the employee does her or his job. Familiarizing managers with the principles of Groupthink (Chapter 11) or the Vroom-Yetton-Jago decision tree (Chapter 12) are attempts at change. In the first case, the goal is to help managers and groups make better decisions; in the second, it is to increase the participation of rank-and-file employees in the organization's decision making. In this section, we present an overview of four popular types of people-oriented change techniques: training, management development programs, team building, and survey-feedback.

Training Training generally is designed to improve employees' job skills. Employees may be trained to run certain machines, taught new mathematical skills, or exposed to personal growth and development methods. Stress management programs are becoming popular for helping employees, particularly executives, understand organizational stress and develop ways to cope with it.[21] Training may also be used in conjunction with other, more comprehensive organization changes. For instance, if an organization is implementing an MBO program, training in establishing goals and reviewing goal-oriented performance likely is needed. One important type of training that is becoming increasingly common is training people to work in other countries. *Developing Management Skills* describes some of the issues that might be addressed when U.S. managers are trained to work with Japanese managers.

Among the many training methods, the most common are lecture, discussion, a lecture-discussion combination, experiential methods, case studies, and films or videotapes. Training can take place in a standard classroom, either on company property or in a hotel, at a resort, or at a conference center. On-the-job training

21. James C. Quick and Jonathan D. Quick, *Organizational Stress and Preventive Management* (New York: McGraw-Hill, 1984).

Getting Ready to Do Business with the Japanese

When you greet someone in Japan, instead of shaking hands and saying the name of the person you meet, bow deeply from the waist and present your business card with two hands. Accept the business card of your new acquaintance with two hands. To call the person by name, say the last name followed by "san," as in Moorhead-san. In addition, you will probably take off your shoes when you enter a traditional Japanese home, sit on the floor to eat, and offer a gift to your host, again with two hands while bowing. Be sure to offer the gift several times because it may be turned down more than once. If offered a gift, turn it down at least once before accepting. Never chew gum or yawn in public.

When doing business with the Japanese, several things are more important than just learning the language. Lisa Gianotti teaches courses in Scottsdale, Arizona, in beginning Japanese that go far beyond the language. She outlines five steps that are essential to doing business with the Japanese:

1. Always use the person's position and title, followed by the person's last name. Never address Japanese business people by their first names; doing so is considered rude.
2. Always exchange business cards when meeting Japanese people. It is a casual ritual similar to shaking hands in other cultures.
3. Volunteer and pitch in. The Japanese consider failure to volunteer a sign of disrespect.
4. Think collectively rather than individually as in Western cultures.
5. Always stay at work well after the normal quitting time. The Japanese assume that leaving work at the exact quitting time is a sign of losing interest in the job.

Whether negotiating a big business deal with Japanese companies or simply taking care of Japanese customers, Gianotti suggests that these five principles will make the process much smoother.

SOURCES: "Class Gives Broad Look at Japan," *The Arizona Republic*, March 6, 1991, p. 9; Robert E. Axtell (Ed.), *Do's and Taboos around the World* (New York: Wiley, 1990); and *Culturgram for the '90s* (Provo, Utah: Brigham Young University, David M. Kennedy Center for International Studies, 1990).

provides a different type of experience, in which the trainee learns from an experienced worker. Most training programs use a combination of methods determined by the topic, the trainees, the trainer, and the organization.

A major problem of training programs is transferring employee learning to the workplace. Often an employee learns a new skill or a manager learns a new management technique but, on returning to the normal work situation, finds it easier to go back to the old way of doing things. As we discuss earlier, the process of refreezing is a vital part of the change process, and some way must be found to make the accomplishments of the training program permanent.

Management development
programs attempt to develop
managers' skills, abilities,
and perspectives.

Management Development Programs   Management development programs, like employee training programs, attempt to foster certain skills, abilities, and perspectives. Often, when a highly qualified technical person is promoted to manager of a work group, he or she lacks training in how to manage or deal with people. In such cases, management development programs can be important to organizations, both for the new manager and for his or her subordinates.

Typically, management development programs use the lecture-discussion method to some extent but rely most heavily on participative methods, such as case studies and role playing. Participative and experiential methods allow the manager to experience the problems of being a manager as well as the feelings of frustration, doubt, and success that are part of the job. The subject matter of this type of training program is problematic, however, in that management skills, including communication, problem diagnosis, problem solving, and performance appraisal, are not as easy to identify or to transfer from a classroom to the workplace as the skills required to run a machine. In addition, rapid changes in the external environment can make certain managerial skills obsolete in a very short time. As a result, some companies are approaching the development of their management team as an ongoing, career-long process and are requiring their managers to attend refresher courses periodically.

One training approach involves managers in an intense exercise that simulates the daily operation of a real company. Such simulations emphasize problem-solving behavior rather than competitive tactics and usually involve extensive debriefing, in which a manager's style is openly discussed and criticized by trained observers as the first step to improvement. IBM and AT&T have commissioned experts who created simulations specifically for their managers. Although the cost of custom simulations is high, it is reportedly repaid in benefits from individual development.[22]

As U.S. businesses invest hundreds of millions of dollars in management development, certain guiding principles are evolving: (1) Management development is a multifaceted, complex, and long-term process for which there is no quick or simple solution; (2) organizations should pay close attention to the systematic identification of their unique developmental needs and evaluate their programs accordingly; (3) management development objectives must be compatible with organizational objectives; and (4) the utility and value of management development remains more an article of faith than a proven fact.[23]

Team Building   When interaction among group members is critical to group success and effectiveness, team development, or team building, may be useful. **Team building** emphasizes members' working together in a spirit of cooperation and generally has one or more of the following goals:

1. To set team goals, priorities, or both
2. To analyze or allocate the way work is performed
3. To examine the way a group is working—that is, to examine processes such as norms, decision making, and communications
4. To examine relationships among the people doing the work[24]

Total quality management (TQM) efforts usually utilize teams as the focal point of the quality effort. The principles of team building are essential to making TQM work. Participation is especially important in the data-gathering and evaluation phases of team development. In data gathering, the members share information on the functioning of the group. The opinions of the group thus form the founda-

---

22. Peter Petre, "Games That Teach You to Manage," *Fortune*, October 29, 1984, pp. 65–72.
23. Kenneth N. Wexley and Timothy T. Baldwin, "Management Development," *1986 Yearly Review of Management of the Journal of Management*, pp. 277–294.
24. Richard Beckhard, "Optimizing Team-Building Efforts," *Journal of Contemporary Business*, Summer 1972, pp. 23–27, 30–32.

tion of the development process. In the evaluation phase, the members are the source of information about the effectiveness of the development effort.[25]

Just like TQM and many other management techniques, team building should not be thought of as a one-time experience, perhaps something undertaken on a retreat from the workplace; rather, it is a continuing process. It may take weeks, months, or years for a group to pull together and function as a team. Team development can train the group to solve its own problems in the future. Research on the effectiveness of team building as an OD intervention tool thus far is mixed and inconclusive.

Survey-Feedback Survey-feedback techniques can form the basis for a change process in which data are gathered, analyzed, summarized, and returned to those who participated in its generation for identification, discussion, and solution of problems. A survey-feedback process often is set in motion by either the organization's top management or a consultant to management. By providing information about employees' beliefs and attitudes, a survey can help management diagnose and solve an organization's problems. A consultant or change agent usually coordinates the process and is responsible for data gathering, analysis, and summary.

The use of survey-feedback techniques in an organization development process differs from their use in traditional attitude surveys. In an organization development process, data are (1) returned to employee groups at all levels in the organization and (2) used as the basis for problem identification and solution by all employees working together in their normal work groups. In traditional attitude surveys, top management reviews the data and may or may not initiate a new program to solve problems the survey has identified.

The three-stage survey-feedback process is shown in Figure 18.4.[26] In the data-gathering stage, the change agent interviews selected personnel from appropriate levels to determine the major issues to be examined. From the interviews, a survey questionnaire is developed and distributed to a large sample of employees. The questionnaire may be a standardized instrument, an instrument developed specifically for the organization, or a combination of the two. The questionnaire data are analyzed and aggregated by group or department to ensure anonymity of individual respondents.[27] Then the change agent prepares a summary of the results for the group feedback sessions. From this point on, the consultant is involved in the process as a resource person and expert.

25. William M. Vicars and Darrel D. Hartke, "Evaluating OD Evaluations: A Status Report," *Group and Organization Studies*, June 1984, pp. 177-188; and Bernard M. Bass, "Issues Involved in Relations between Methodological Rigor and Reported Outcomes in Evaluations of Organizational Development," *Journal of Applied Psychology*, February 1983, pp. 197–201.
26. Beer, *Organization Change and Development*.
27. Jerome L. Franklin, "Improving the Effectiveness of Survey Feedback," *Personnel*, May–June 1978, pp. 11–17.

FIGURE 18.4

The Survey-Feedback Process

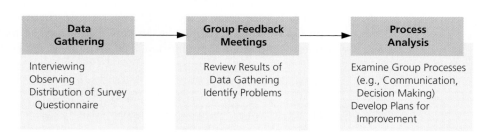

Part 5   Organizational Processes and Characteristics

The group feedback meetings generally involve only two or three levels of management, or family groups. Meetings usually are held serially, beginning with a meeting of the top management group, which is followed by meetings of employees throughout the organization. Sessions typically are led by the group manager rather than the change agent to transfer "ownership" of the data from the change agent to the work group. The feedback consists primarily of profiles of the groups' attitudes toward the organization, the work, the leadership, and other topics on the questionnaire. During the feedback sessions, participants discuss reasons for the scores and the problems that the data reveal.

In the process analysis stage, the group examines its process for making decisions, communicating, and accomplishing work, usually with the help of the consultant. Unfortunately, groups often overlook this stage as they become absorbed in the survey data and the problems revealed during the feedback sessions. Occasionally, group managers simply fail to hold feedback and process analysis sessions. Change agents should ensure that managers hold these sessions and that they are rewarded for doing so. The process analysis stage is important because its purpose is to develop action plans for making improvements. Several sessions may be required to discuss the process issues fully and settle on a strategy for improvements. Groups often find it useful to document the plans as they are discussed and to appoint a member to follow up on implementation. Generally, the follow-up concerns whether communication and communication processes have actually been improved. A follow-up survey can be administered several months to a year later to assess how much these processes have changed since they were first reported.

The survey-feedback method probably is one of the most widely used organization change and development interventions. If any of its stages are compromised or omitted, however, the technique becomes less useful. A primary responsibility of the consultant or change agent, then, is to ensure that the method is fully and faithfully carried through.

Resistance to Change

Resistance to change within the organization can come from sources that are either external or internal to the organization.

Just as change is inevitable, so is resistance to change. Paradoxically, organizations both promote and resist change. As an agent for change, the organization asks prospective customers or clients to change their current purchasing habits by switching to the company's product or service and asks current customers to change by increasing their purchases. At the same time, the organization resists change in that its structure and control systems protect the daily tasks of producing a product or service from uncertainties in the environment. Because an organization is constantly buffeted by the forces of change, it must have some elements of permanence to avoid mirroring the instability of the environment. Yet it also must react to external shifts with internal change to maintain currency and relevance in the marketplace.

Managing resistance to change means working with the sources of resistance rather than trying to overpower or overcome resistance.

A commonly held view is that all resistance to change needs to be overcome, but that is not always the case. Resistance to change need not be eliminated entirely but can be used and controlled for the benefit of the organization. By revealing a legitimate concern that a proposed change may not be good for the organization, or that there might be other alternatives, resistance may alert the organization to investigate and reexamine the change.[28] For example, an organization may be considering the acquisition of a company in a completely different industry. Resistance to such a proposal may cause the organization to examine the advantages and disadvantages of the move more carefully. Without resistance, the decision might be made before the pros and cons have been sufficiently explored.

Resistance may come from the organization, the individual, or both. Determining the ultimate source is often difficult, however, because organizations are composed of individuals. Table 18.3 summarizes various types of organizational and individual sources of resistance.

Organizational Sources of Resistance

Daniel Katz and Robert Kahn have identified six major organizational sources of resistance: overdetermination, narrow focus of change, group inertia, threatened expertise, threatened power, and changes in resource allocation.[29] Of course, not every organization or every change situation displays all six sources.

28. Paul R. Lawrence, "How to Deal with Resistance to Change," *Harvard Business Review*, May–June 1954, reprinted in Gene W. Dalton, Paul R. Lawrence, and Larry E. Greiner (Eds.), *Organizational Change and Development* (Homewood, Ill.: Irwin, 1970), pp. 181–197.
29. Daniel Katz and Robert L. Kahn, *The Social Psychology of Organizations*, 2nd ed. (New York: Wiley, 1978), pp. 36–68.

TABLE 18.3

Organizational and Individual Sources of Resistance

Organizational Sources	Examples
Overdetermination	Employment system, job descriptions, evaluation and reward system
Narrow Focus of Change	Structure changed with no concern given to other issues, e.g., jobs, people
Group Inertia	Group norms
Threatened Expertise	People move out of area of expertise
Threatened Power	Decentralized decision making
Resource Allocation	Increased use of part-time help

Individual Sources	Examples
Habit	Altered tasks
Security	Altered tasks or reporting relationships
Economic Factors	Changed pay and benefits
Fear of the Unknown	New job, new boss
Lack of Awareness	Isolated groups not heeding notices
Social Factors	Group norms

Overdetermination Organizations have several systems designed to maintain stability. For example, consider how organizations control employees' performance. To ensure that as employees they will do the job the organization desires, job candidates must meet specific requirements to be hired. As soon as a person is hired, he or she is given a job description, and the supervisor trains, coaches, and counsels the employee in job tasks. The new employee usually serves some type of probationary period that culminates in a performance review; thereafter, the employee's performance is regularly evaluated. Finally, rewards, punishment, and discipline are administered depending on the level of performance. Such a system is said to be characterized by **overdetermination, or structural inertia,**[30] in that the same effect on employee performance probably could be achieved with fewer procedures and safeguards. In other words, the structure of the organization provides resistance to change because it was designed to maintain stability.

Overdetermination occurs because numerous organizational systems are in place to ensure that behavior of employees and systems is as expected to maintain stability.

Narrow Focus of Change Many efforts to create change in organizations adopt too narrow a focus. Any effort to force change in the tasks of individuals or groups must take into account the interdependencies among organizational elements such as people, structure, tasks, and the information system. For example, some attempts at redesigning jobs are unsuccessful because the organization structure within which jobs must function is inappropriate for the redesigned jobs.[31]

Group Inertia When an employee attempts to change his or her work behavior, the group may resist by refusing to change other behaviors that are necessary complements to the individual's changed behavior. In other words, group norms may act as a brake on individual attempts at behavior change.

Threatened Expertise A change in the organization may threaten the specialized expertise that individuals and groups have developed over the years. A job redesign or a structural change may transfer the responsibility for a specialized task from the current expert to someone else, thus threatening the specialist's expertise and building his or her resistance to the change.

Threatened Power Any redistribution of decision-making authority may threaten an individual's power relationships with others. If an organization is decentralizing its decision making, managers who wielded their decision-making powers in return for special favors from others may resist the change because they do not want to lose their power base.

Resource Allocation Groups that are satisfied with current resource allocation methods may resist any change that they believe will threaten their future allocations. Resources in this context can mean anything from monetary rewards and equipment to additional seasonal help to more computer time.

These six sources explain most types of organization-based resistance to change. All except the second (narrow focus of change) are based on people and social relationships. Furthermore, many of these sources of resistance can be traced to groups or individuals afraid of losing something—resources, power, or comfort in a routine.

30. See Michael T. Hannah and John Freeman, "Structural Inertia and Organizational Change," *American Sociological Review*, April 1984, pp. 149–164, for an in-depth discussion of structural inertia.
31. Moorhead, "Organizational Analysis."

Individual Sources of Resistance

Individual sources of resistance to change are rooted in basic human characteristics such as needs and perceptions. Researchers have identified six reasons for individual resistance to change: habit, security, economic factors, fear of the unknown, lack of awareness, and social factors (see Table 18.3).[32]

Habit   Doing a job the same way every day is easy. If the steps in the job are repeated over and over, the job becomes increasingly easier. But learning an entirely new set of steps increases the job's difficulty. For the same amount of return (pay), most people prefer to do easy rather than hard work.

Security   Some employees like the comfort and security of doing things the same old way. They gain a feeling of constancy and safety in knowing that some things stay the same despite all the change going on around them. Thus, people who believe that their security is threatened by a change are likely to resist the change.

Economic Factors   Change may also threaten employees' steady paychecks. Workers may fear that change will make their jobs obsolete.

Fear of the Unknown   Some people fear anything unfamiliar. Changes in reporting relationships and job duties create anxiety for such employees. Employees become familiar with their boss, their job, and relationships with others within the organization, such as contact people for certain situations. These relationships and contacts help facilitate their work. Any disruption of familiar patterns may create fear because it can cause delays and the belief that nothing is getting accomplished.

Lack of Awareness   Because of perceptual limitations, such as lack of attention or selective attention, a person may not recognize a change in a rule or procedure and thus may not alter behavior. People may pay attention only to those things that support their point of view. As an example, employees in an isolated regional sales office may not notice—or may ignore—directives from headquarters regarding a change in reporting procedures for expense accounts. They therefore may continue the current practice as long as possible.

Social Factors   People may resist change for fear of what others will think. As we have mentioned before, the group can be a powerful motivator of behavior. Employees may believe that change will hurt their image, result in ostracism from the group, or simply make them "different." For example, an employee who agrees to conform to work rules established by management may be ridiculed by others who openly disobey the rules.

32. David A. Nadler, "Concepts for the Management of Organizational Change," in J. Richard Hackman, Edward E. Lawler III, and Lyman W. Porter (Eds.), *Perspectives on Behavior in Organizations*, 2nd ed. (New York: McGraw-Hill, 1983), pp. 551–561; and G. Zaltman and R. Duncan, *Strategies for Planned Change* (New York: Wiley, 1977).

Managing Successful Organization Change and Development

In conclusion, we offer five keys to managing change in organizations. They relate directly to the problems identified in this chapter and to our view of the organization as a social system. Each can influence the elements of the social system and may help the organization avoid some of the major problems in managing the change. Table 18.4 lists the points and their potential impacts.

Take a Holistic View

Managers must take a holistic view of the organization and the change project. Because the organization's subsystems are interdependent, a limited view can endanger the change effort. A holistic view encompasses the culture and dominant coalition as well as the people, tasks, structure, and information subsystems.

Secure Top Management Support

The support of top management is essential to the success of any change effort. As the organization's probable dominant coalition, it is a powerful element of the social system, and its support is necessary for addressing control and power problems. For example, a manager who plans a change in the way tasks are assigned and responsibility is delegated in his or her department must notify top management and gain its support. Complications may arise if disgruntled employees complain to high-level managers who have not been notified of the change or do not support it. The employees' complaints may jeopardize the manager's plan—and perhaps her or his job.

TABLE 18.4

Managing Successful Organization Change and Development

Key	Impact
Take a holistic view of the organization.	Anticipate effects on social system and culture.
Secure top management support.	Get dominant coalition on the side of change; safeguard structural change; head off problems of power and control.
Encourage participation by those affected by the change.	Minimize transition problem of control, resistance, and task redefinition.
Foster open communication.	Minimize transition problems of resistance and information and control systems.
Reward those who contribute to change.	Minimize transition problems of resistance and control systems.

Encourage Participation

Problems related to resistance, control, and power can be overcome by broad participation in planning the change. Giving people a voice in designing the change may give them a sense of power and control over their own destinies, which may help win their support during implementation.

Foster Open Communication

Open communication is an important factor in managing resistance to change and overcoming information and control problems during transition. Employees typically recognize the uncertainties and ambiguities that arise during a transition and seek information on the change and their place in the new system. In the absence of information, the gap may be filled with inappropriate or false information, which may endanger the change process. Rumors tend to spread through the grapevine faster than accurate information can be disseminated through official channels. A manager should always be sensitive to the effects of uncertainty on employees, especially in a period of change; any news, even bad news, seems better than no news.

Reward Contributors

This last point, although simple, can easily be neglected. Employees who contribute to the change in any way need to be rewarded. Too often the only people who are acknowledged after a change effort are those who tried to stop it. Those who quickly grasp new work assignments, work hard to cover what otherwise might not get done in the transition, or help others adjust to changes deserve special credit—perhaps a mention in a news release or the internal company newspaper, special consideration in performance appraisal, a merit raise, or a promotion. From a behavioral perspective, individuals need to benefit in some way if they are to willingly help change something that eliminates the old, comfortable way of doing the job.

In the current dynamic environment, managers must anticipate the need for change and satisfy it with more responsive and competitive organization systems. Because organizations must change or face elimination, these five keys to managing organization change may also serve as general guidelines for managing organizational behavior.

Summary of Key Points

■ Change may be forced on an organization, or an organization may change in response to the environment or an internal need. The forces for change influence organizations in many ways. Currently, the areas in which the pressures for change seem most powerful involve people, technology, information processing and communication, and competition.

- Planned organization change involves anticipating change and preparing for it. Lewin described organization change in terms of unfreezing, change, and refreezing. In the continuous change process model, top management recognizes forces that call for change, engages in a problem-solving process to design the change, and implements and evaluates the change.
- Organization development is the process of planned change and improvement of organizations through the application of knowledge of the behavioral sciences. OD uses a systematic change process and focuses on managing the culture of the organization. The most comprehensive change involves altering the structure of the organization through a systemwide reorganization of departments, reporting relationships, and authority systems. Quality-of-work-life programs focus on providing a work environment in which employees can satisfy individual needs. Task-technological changes alter the way the organization accomplishes its primary tasks. Task redesign includes, along with the steps usually associated with change, diagnosis, cost/benefit analysis, formulation of a redesign strategy, and implementation of supplemental changes. Frequently used group and individual approaches to organization change are training and management development programs, team building, and survey-feedback techniques.
- Resistance to change may arise from several individual and organizational sources. Resistance may indicate a legitimate concern that the change is not good for the organization and may warrant a reexamination of plans.
- The management of change in organizations requires a holistic view of the organization, top management support, participation by those most affected, open communication, and rewarding those who contribute to the change effort.

Discussion Questions

1. Is most organization change forced on the organization by external factors or created from within? Explain.
2. What broad category of pressures for organization change other than the five discussed in the chapter can you think of? Briefly describe it.
3. Which sources of resistance to change present the most problems for an internal change agent? For an external change agent?
4. Which stage of the Lewin model of change do you think is the most often overlooked? Why?
5. What are the advantages and disadvantages of having an internal change agent rather than an external change agent?
6. How does organization development differ from organization change?
7. How and why would OD differ if the elements of the social system were not interdependent?
8. Do quality-of-work-life programs rely more on individual or organizational aspects of organizational behavior? Why?
9. Describe how the job of your professor could be redesigned. Include a discussion of other subsystems that would need to be changed.
10. Which of the five suggestions for successfully managing an organizational change effort seem to be the most difficult to manage? Why?

Purpose This exercise will help you understand the complexities of change in organizations.

Format Your task is to plan the implementation of a major change in an organization.

Procedure **Part 1.** The class will divide into five groups of approximately equal size. Your instructor will assign each group one of the following changes:

1. A change from the semester system to the quarter system (or the opposite, depending on the school's current system)
2. A requirement that all work—homework, examinations, term papers, problem sets—be done on computer
3. A requirement that all students live on campus
4. A requirement that all students have reading, writing, and speaking fluency in at least three languages, including English and Japanese, to graduate
5. A requirement that all students room with someone in the same major

First, decide what individuals and groups must be involved in the change process. Then decide how the change will be implemented using Lewin's process of organization change (Figure 18.1) as a framework. Consider how to handle resistance to change, using Tables 18.3 and 18.4 as guides. Decide whether a change agent (internal or external) should be used. Develop a realistic timetable for full implementation of the change. Is transition management appropriate?

After all groups have developed plans, they will present them to the class.

Part 2. Using the same groups as in part 1, your next task is to describe the techniques that you would use to implement the change described in part 1. You may use structural changes, task-technology methods, group and individual programs, or any combination of these. You may need to go to the library to gather more information on some techniques.

You should also discuss how you will use the five keys to successful change management discussed at the end of the chapter.

Your instructor may make this exercise an in-class project, but it is also a good semester-ending project for groups to work on outside class. Either way, the exercise is most beneficial when the groups report their implementation programs to the entire class. Each group should report on which change techniques are to be used, why they were selected, how they will be implemented, and how problems will be avoided.

Follow-up Questions

Part 1
1. How similar were the implementation steps for each change?
2. Were the plans for managing resistance to change realistic?
3. Do you think that any of the changes could be successfully implemented at your school? Why or why not?

Part 2
1. Did various groups use the same technique in different ways or to accomplish different goals?

2. If you did outside research on OD techniques for your project, did you find any OD techniques that seemed more applicable than those in this chapter? If so, describe one of them.

| C A S E   1 8 . 1 | **Procter & Gamble Reengineers at Home and Abroad** |

The Procter & Gamble Co. (P&G) probably has more recognized names on the grocery store shelves in the United States than any other company. It currently has more than 160 household products including Head & Shoulders, Citrus Hill, Scope, Secret, Clearasil, Cover Girl, Tide, Mr. Clean, and Ivory soap, which it launched in 1879. Its products are number one in twenty-two of forty product categories in the United States. Its branding and marketing image has always focused on the premium brand image, with heavy advertising directly to the consumer.

In 1990 and 1991, however, P&G began to notice subtle shifts in the way that consumers shopped for household items. These shifts caused P&G's operating profits to drop significantly for those years. Customers seemed to be less brand loyal and more price sensitive. In its biggest business, disposable diapers, private-label brands increased their market share to 31 percent, mostly at the expense of Pampers and Luv, both P&G brands. For decades P&G relied on the assumption that customers would choose brand name products because they were assured of value, quality, and consistency. The timing finally may have run out on that assumption.

P&G is making wholesale changes in the way it does its business. First, it is studying its internal operations in an effort to reduce manufacturing overhead by $750 million. In some plants, the changeover from manufacturing one product to another has been reduced from two days to two hours. Second, it is cutting back on coupons and in-store promotions to provide lower daily prices rather than one-time promotions. The price of Folgers coffee was reduced by almost 15 percent from 1991 to 1993. Prices for Tide and Cheer were dropped by almost 10 percent. Third, in a major reversal of time-honored practice, it is consolidating some of its brand names. Its normal practice was to produce and market two or three (or more) brand names in a single product category to appeal to every consumer's different tastes and preferences. The different names, colors, and flavors were reduced by almost 25 percent by late 1993. White Cloud toilet paper joins the Charmin line as Charmin Ultra. Puritan cooking oil joins Crisco/Puritan.

With all of these changes going on in its U.S. operations, P&G is considering the same changes worldwide. Price pressures are occurring around the world, as brand loyalty means less. Prices of private-label products are able to undercut brand-name products by as much as 15 percent in some European countries. Off-brand buying is becoming more popular throughout Europe as retailing is modernized and the effects of the recession continue to be felt. P&G, Nestlé, Philip Morris, and Unilever are all beginning to feel the pinch. In addition to pricing, across Europe each country has its own local and national brands that have strong followings.

Case Questions

1. Identify as many forces for change that P&G is experiencing as you can.
2. How is P&G responding to the pressures for change described in the case?
3. Ask the manager of a local grocery store how the changes in P&G's marketing and promotions have affected the store, its pricing, local private label brands, and overall profitability.

SOURCES: "Procter & Gamble Hits Back," *Business Week*, July 19, 1993, pp. 20–22; Gary Hoover, Alta Campbell, and Patrick J. Spain, *Hoover's Handbook of American Business 1993* (Austin, Tex.: The Reference Press, 1992), p. 466; and "The Eurosion of Brand Loyalty," *Business Week*, July 19, 1993, p. 22.

The New England Arts Project had its headquarters above an Italian restaurant in Portsmouth, New Hampshire. The project had five full-time employees, and during busy times of the year, particularly the month before Christmas, it hired as many as six part-time workers to type, address envelopes, and send out mailings. Although each of the five full-timers had a title and a formal job description, an observer would have had trouble telling their positions apart. Suzanne Clammer, for instance, was the executive director—the head of the office—but she could be found typing or licking envelopes just as often as Martin Welk, who had been working for less than a year as office coordinator, the lowest position in the project's hierarchy.

Despite a constant sense of being a month behind, the office ran relatively smoothly. No outsider would have had a prayer of finding a mailing list or a budget in the office, but project employees knew where almost everything was, and after a quiet fall they did not mind having their small space packed with workers in November. But a number of the federal funding agencies on which the project relied began to grumble about the cost of the part-time workers, the amount of time the project spent on handling routine paperwork, and the chaotic condition of its financial records. The pressure to make a radical change was on. Finally Martin Welk said it: "Maybe we should get a computer."

To Welk, fresh out of college, where he had written his papers on a word processor, computers were just another tool to make a job easier. But his belief was not shared by the others in the office, the youngest of whom had fifteen years' more seniority than he. A computer would eat the project's mailing list, they said, destroying any chance of raising funds for the year. It would send the wrong things to the wrong people, insulting them and convincing them that the project had become another faceless organization that did not care. They swapped horror stories about computers that had charged them thousands of dollars for purchases they had never made or had assigned the same airplane seat to five people.

"We'll lose all control," Suzanne Clammer complained. She saw some kind of office automation as inevitable, yet she kept thinking she would probably quit before it came about. She liked hand-addressing mailings to arts patrons whom she had met, and she felt sure that the recipients contributed more because they recognized her neat blue printing. She remembered the agonies of typing class in high school and believed she was too old to take on something new and bound to be much more confusing. Two other employees, with whom she had worked for a decade, called her after work to ask if the prospect of a computer in the office meant they should be looking for other jobs. "I have enough trouble with English grammar," one of them wailed. "I'll never be able to learn Pascal or Lotus or whatever these new languages are."

One morning Clammer called Martin Welk into her office, shut the door, and asked him if he could recommend any computer consultants. She had read an article that explained how a company could waste thousands of dollars by adopting integrated office automation in the wrong way, and she figured the project would have to hire somebody for at least six months to get the new machines working and to teach the staff how to use them. Welk was pleased because Clammer evidently had accepted the idea of a computer in the office. But he also realized that as the resident authority on computers, he had a lot of work to do before they went shopping for machines.

Case Questions

1. Is organization development appropriate in this situation? Why or why not?
2. What kinds of resistance to change have the employees of the project displayed?
3. What can Martin Welk do to overcome the resistance?

CHAPTER 19

International Aspects of Organizations

OUTLINE

OBJECTIVES

After studying this chapter, you should be able to:

Describe the emergence of international management.

Discuss individual behavior in an international context.

Describe various means of enhancing performance in
international settings.

Discuss interpersonal processes in an international context.

Describe organization processes in an international context.

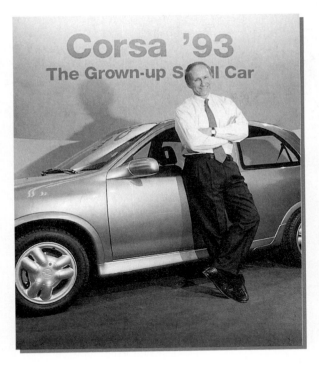

Corsa '93
The Grown-up Small Car

Louis Hughes, president of the European Operations division of General Motors, has capitalized on the combination of streamlined production, flexible teams of workers, and constant attention to efficiency. This approach has made GM's European cars, such as the new Opel, much more successful than their American counterparts. ▪ ▪ ▪ ▪

General Motors Corp. is not only the world's largest maker of automobiles, it is the world's largest company. In 1991 GM also had the largest losses ever reported by a U.S. company—almost $5 billion. On the other hand, GM's European operations— led by Jack Smith, who moved on to become chief executive officer of GM, and Louis Hughes, president of European operations— have been quite successful. Its primary line of cars, the Vauxhall in Great Britain and the Opel in the rest of Europe, increased sales every year from 1985 through 1992. In 1992 GM's market share in Europe was 12.6 percent, which put it in second place only to Volkswagen. General Motors Europe (GME) also added the new Opel Corsa line in 1993.

The new Corsa was built utilizing the best of all auto manufacturing technologies from around the world. Its engineering and design was put together in just thirty-six months. It has 30 percent fewer parts and costs 25 percent less to assemble than previous models. The primary plant is in Eisenach in former East Germany and utilizes low inventory, just-in-time parts delivery, flexible teams of workers, and continuous improvement. The plant is dedicated to the principles of lean manufacturing practices, major gains in quality every year, team-based manufacturing, and improvements in productivity of 7 to 8 percent every year. It has to put together parts and subassemblies from plants all over Europe.

The plan is to make GM operations worldwide as lean as the Eisenach plant, beginning with the rest of the European plants. The crisis is even worse in the United States. Jack Smith is expected to take the successes that he engineered in Europe to the company's worldwide operations as quickly as possible.[1]

The experience of General Motors represents something different than the expected: a U.S. company that is losing money at home and making money abroad. To save the company—and some thought that was impossible—the U.S. component of the company had to learn some hard lessons from its international divisions. Some lessons were technologically based, and others were based in management style and the management of groups and teams. The lesson for General Motors is that it truly is a world economy, and managers must learn to manage globally.

This chapter is about organizational behavior in an international context. First, we trace the emergence of international management. In subsequent discussions, we parallel the overall organization of the book by relating international issues to individual behavior, performance enhancement issues, interpersonal processes, and organizational processes and characteristics.

1. Alex Taylor III, "Why GM Leads the Pack in Europe," *Fortune*, May 17, 1993, pp. 83–87; "GM Europe Grows in Importance," *Automotive News*, November 9, 1992, p. 61; "GM's German Lessons," *Business Week*, December 20, 1993, pp. 67–68; and Gary Hoover, Alta Campbell, and Patrick J. Spain, *Hoover's Handbook of American Business 1993* (Austin, Tex.: The Reference Press, 1992), p. 293.

Many businesses, aided by vast improvements in communication and transportation, have moved into the international realm in an effort to cut costs. IBM, among others, has found well-trained workers and lower production costs in Mexico. Here, an employee tests computers at IBM's highly successful Mexican plant.

The Emergence of International Management

In many ways, international management is nothing new. Centuries ago, the Roman army was forced to develop a management system to deal with its widespread empire.[2] Likewise, the Olympic games, the Red Cross, and many similar organizations have international roots. From a business standpoint, however, international management is relatively new, at least to the United States.

The Growth of International Business

The rapid growth in international business makes an understanding of organizational behavior all the more important for contemporary managers.

In 1990, the volume of international trade in current dollars was almost thirty times greater than that amount in 1960, and the figures are projected to continue escalating during the remainder of this decade. What has led to this dramatic increase? As Figure 19.1 shows, four major factors account for much of the momentum.

2. M. J. Gent, "Theory X in Antiquity, or the Bureaucratization of the Roman Army," *Business Horizons*, January–February 1984, pp. 53–54.

FIGURE 19.1

Forces That Have Increased International Business

Domestic Business → *International Business*

Improved Communication and Transportation Facilities
Larger Potential Market
Lower Costs of Production and/or Distribution
Response to International Activity of Competitors

Worldwide Cigarette Advertising

Cigarette smoking in the United States has declined for eight straight years, probably because of increased awareness of the health dangers of cigarette smoking, strict limits on advertising tobacco by certain media, and increased public pressure against smoking in public places. Tobacco companies have been more and more creative through the outlets that are available and finding new ways to reach young people, nonsmokers, and existing smokers. The international market is something else, however. The major tobacco companies have turned to previously untapped markets around the world to take up the slack where U.S. sales have dropped.

Advertising is controlled in the European Community as it is in the United States. Still, young people are starting to smoke at increasing rates there. In less-developed countries with improving economies, increased media penetration, and increased general awareness of affluence, power, and status, smoking is also increasing—more than tripling in some places since 1985. In the Philippines, 22.7 percent of people younger than eighteen smoke. The teenage smoking rate is 50 percent in some Latin American cities.

Advertising is the way that tobacco companies are attracting new customers. In Europe, pressure to stop some advertising is increasing, but sponsorship of sports teams, participants, and events is quite common. In addition, major efforts to make people aware of the dangers of smoking are having some impact. In other countries the balance between the smoking and antismoking forces is not even close. Tobacco companies are advertising and sponsoring direct give-away programs to young people at rock music discos and sporting events, on clothing and in clothing stores, and in every place where affluence, power, and status can be marketed.

The results have been staggering. The advertising is not just appealing to the existing smoker as the U.S. tobacco companies contend. For example, Taiwanese high school student smoking has doubled to more than 30 percent since 1985. The numbers are similar or worse in most other countries. The companies claim that they should not be prohibited from selling their products and making a profit. The antismoking lobby claims that the companies are preying on an unsuspecting public.

SOURCES: "America's New Merchants of Death," *Readers' Digest*, April 1993, pp. 50–57; Karen Hoggan and John Warden, "Tobacco-Sports Link Under Fire," *Marketing*, February 21, 1991, pp. 2–3; and Dermont McKeone, "Smoking Out the PR Impact," *Marketing*, March 4, 1993, p. XII.

First, communication and transportation have advanced dramatically over the past few decades. Telephone service has improved, communication networks span the globe and can interact via satellite, and access to remote areas has been vastly facilitated. Facsimile machines allow managers to send documents around the world in seconds as opposed to days just a few years ago. In short, conducting international business is simply easier today.

Second, businesses have expanded internationally to increase their markets. Companies in smaller countries, such as Nestlé in Switzerland, recognized long ago that their domestic markets were too small to sustain much growth; they therefore moved into international activities. Many U.S. firms, on the other hand, had all the business they could handle until recently; hence, they are just beginning to consider international opportunities. Companies in the tobacco industry have significantly increased their global efforts and are currently embroiled in a global controversy, as discussed in *The Ethical Dilemma*.

Third, more and more firms are moving into the international realm to control costs, especially to reduce labor costs. The attempts to cut costs this way do not always work out as planned, but many firms are successfully using inexpensive labor in the Far East and Mexico.[3] In searching for lower labor costs, some companies have discovered well-trained workers and built more efficient plants that are closer to international markets.[4]

Finally, many organizations have become international in response to competition. If an organization starts gaining strength in international markets, its competitors often must follow suit to avoid falling too far behind in sales, profitability, and so forth. Mobil, Texaco, and Exxon realized that they had to increase their international market share to keep pace with foreign competitors such as British Petroleum and Royal Dutch/Shell Group.

Trends in International Business

The most striking trend in international business is obvious: growth. More and more businesses are entering the international marketplace, including many smaller firms. We read a great deal about the threat of foreign companies. For example, successful Japanese automobile firms like Toyota and Nissan produce higher-quality cars for lower prices than do U.S. firms. What we often overlook, however, is the success of U.S. firms abroad. Ford, for example, has long had a successful business in Europe and today employs less than half its total workforce on U.S. soil. And U.S. firms make dozens of products better than anyone else in the world.[5] General Motors Europe has had strong sales in Europe since 1985, rising to a 12.6 percent market share, the second best in Europe behind Volkswagen.[6]

Business transactions are also becoming increasingly blurred across national boundaries. Ford owns 25 percent of Mazda, General Motors and Toyota have a joint venture in California, Ford and Volkswagen have one in Argentina, and Honda and British Sterling have one worldwide. Indeed, some experts have predicted that some multinational firms will soon start to lose their national identity altogether and become truly global corporations.

International involvement has also increased across nonbusiness organizational forms. Universities offer study programs abroad, health care and research programs span national boundaries, international postal systems are working more closely together, and athletic programs are increasingly being transplanted to different cultures.

Recent events in other parts of the world also will have a major effect on business. The unification of Germany and the movement of the formerly communist-controlled countries in Central Europe toward a free-market economy will provide many new opportunities and challenges to business in the years to come.

3. Henry W. Lane and Joseph J. DiStefano, *International Management Behavior* (Ontario: Nelson, 1988).
4. Brian O'Reilly, "Your New Global Workforce," *Fortune*, December 14, 1992, pp. 58–66.
5. Christopher Knowlton, "What America Makes Best," *Fortune*, March 28, 1988, pp. 40–54.
6. Taylor, "Why GM Leads the Pack in Europe."

In many ways, then, we are becoming a truly global economy. No longer will a firm be able to insulate itself from foreign competitors or opportunities. Thus, it is imperative that every manager develop and maintain at least a rudimentary understanding of the dynamics of international management.[7]

Cross-cultural Differences and Similarities

Because the primary concern of this discussion is human behavior in organizational settings, we focus on differences and similarities in behavior across cultures. Unfortunately, research in this area is still relatively new. Thus, many of the research findings we can draw on are preliminary at best.

Although we can present a few ideas about differences and similarities at a general level, we must first note that cultures and national boundaries do not necessarily coincide. Some areas of Switzerland are very much like Italy, other parts like France, and still other parts like Germany. Similarly, within the United States there are profound cultural differences among southern California, Texas, and the East Coast.[8]

Given this basic assumption, one recent review of the literature on international management reached five basic conclusions.[9] First, behavior in organizational settings indeed varies across cultures. Thus, employees in companies based in Japan, the United States, and Germany are likely to have different attitudes and patterns of behavior. The behavior patterns are likely to be widespread and pervasive within an organization.

Second, culture itself is one major cause of this variation. Thus, while the behavioral differences just noted may be caused in part by different standards of living, different geographical conditions, and so forth, culture itself is a major factor apart from other considerations.

Third, although behavior within organizational settings (e.g., motivation and attitudes) remains quite diverse across cultures, organizations themselves (e.g., organization design and technology) appear to be increasingly similar. Hence, managerial practices at a general level may be very much alike, but the people who work within organizations still differ markedly.

Fourth, the same manager behaves differently in different cultural settings. A manager may adopt one set of behaviors when working in one culture but change those behaviors when moved to a different culture. For example, Japanese executives who come to work in the United States slowly begin to act more like U.S. managers and less like Japanese managers. This often is a source of concern for them when they are transferred back to Japan.[10]

Finally, cultural diversity can be an important source of synergy in enhancing organizational effectiveness. More and more organizations are coming to appreciate the virtues of cultural diversity, but they still know surprisingly little about how to manage it.[11] Organizations that adopt a multinational strategy can—with effort—become

Behavior in organizational settings varies across cultures.

Culture is a major cause of behavioral variation.

Behavior across cultures remains diverse, but organizations themselves are becoming more similar.

The same manager behaves differently in different cultures.

Cultural diversity can be an important ingredient in achieving synergy.

7. Richard M. Steers and Edwin L. Miller, "Management in the 1990s: The International Challenge," *Academy of Management Executive*, February 1988, pp. 21–22.

8. Simcha Ronen and Oded Shenkar, "Clustering Countries on Attitudinal Dimensions: A Review and Synthesis," *Academy of Management Review*, July 1985, pp. 435–454.

9. Nancy J. Adler, Robert Doktor, and Gordon Redding, "From the Atlantic to the Pacific Century," *Journal of Management*, Summer 1986, pp. 295–318.

10. Brian O'Reilly, "Japan's Uneasy U.S. Managers," *Fortune*, April 25, 1988, pp. 245–264.

11. "Learning to Accept Cultural Diversity," *Wall Street Journal*, September 12, 1990, pp. B1, B9.

more than a sum of their parts. Operations in each culture can benefit from operations in other cultures through an enhanced understanding of how the world works.[12] Chapter 20 discusses the issues involved in managing diversity in detail.

Individual Behavior in an International Context

The first two conclusions we just noted clearly suggest that individual behavior varies across cultures. These variations can be viewed in terms of individual differences, managerial behavior, and motivation.

Individual Differences across Cultures

Figure 19.2 highlights some of the more important dimensions along which behavior varies. These dimensions were identified in a large-scale study of 160,000 persons working in sixty countries.[13]

12. Tamotsu Yamaguchi, "The Challenge of Internationalization," *Academy of Management Executive*, February 1988, pp. 33–36.
13. See the work by Geert Hofstede including Geert Hofstede, "Cultural Constraints in Management Theories," *Academy of Management Executive*, February 1993, pp. 81–91; and Geert Hofstede, *Culture's Consequences: International Differences in Work Related Values* (Beverly Hills, Calif.: Sage, 1980).

FIGURE 19.2

Differences in Individual Behaviors among Cultures

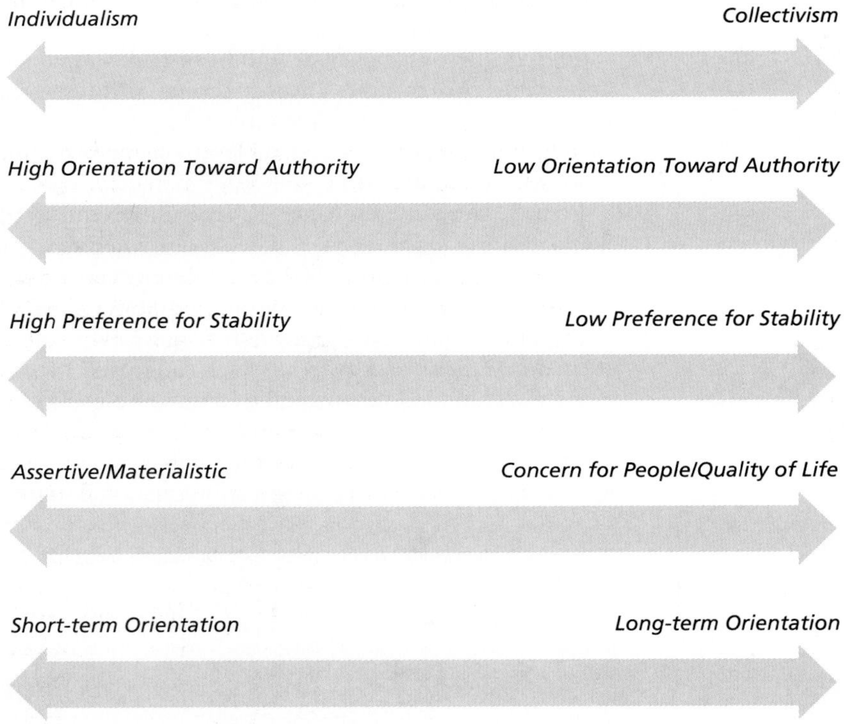

Individualism ⟷ Collectivism

High Orientation Toward Authority ⟷ Low Orientation Toward Authority

High Preference for Stability ⟷ Low Preference for Stability

Assertive/Materialistic ⟷ Concern for People/Quality of Life

Short-term Orientation ⟷ Long-term Orientation

Individualism and **collectivism** reflect whether individuals place primary value on themselves or on the good of the group or society.

Individualism/Collectivism

Individualism is a state of mind in which people view themselves first as individuals and believe that their own interests and values take priority. **Collectivism**, on the other hand, is a feeling that the good of the group or society should come first.

People in a culture characterized by individualism tend to put their careers before their organizations and usually assess situations in terms of how decisions and alternative courses of action will affect them personally. People in a culture dominated by collectivism, in contrast, often put the needs of the organization before their own needs and view decisions and alternatives in terms of their impact on the organization.

The United States, Australia, Great Britain, the Netherlands, Canada, and New Zealand are among the most individualistic cultures. Colombia, Pakistan, Taiwan, Peru, Singapore, Japan, Mexico, Greece, and Hong Kong are among the countries in which collectivism is stronger.

Orientation toward authority is the extent to which people accept the right of organizations to grant power.

Orientation to Authority

Orientation to authority reflects the extent to which employees accept the idea that people in an organization rightfully have different levels of power. In a high authority-oriented culture, for example, a boss makes decisions simply because he or she is the boss; others do not question those decisions but merely follow instructions. In a low authority-oriented culture, employees recognize few power differences and follow the boss's lead only when they believe that the boss is right or when they feel explicitly threatened.

The United States, Israel, Austria, Denmark, Ireland, Norway, Germany, and New Zealand are cultures with a low orientation toward authority. Spain, France, Japan, Singapore, Mexico, Brazil, and Indonesia are examples of cultures with a strong orientation toward authority.

Preference for stability reflects how much certainty or uncertainty people will accept.

Preference for Stability

Preference for stability is the extent to which people accept or avoid feelings of uncertainty. Some people, for example, thrive on the excitement and stimulation they experience from the prospect of new opportunities and challenges. Other people want predictable and certain futures.

Employees in Denmark, the United States, Canada, Norway, Singapore, Hong Kong, and Australia are among those who can tolerate uncertainty. Workers in Israel, Austria, Japan, Italy, Argentina, Peru, France, and Belgium are more highly motivated to avoid uncertainty in their work lives.

Assertiveness and **materialism** are indicators of a culture's values regarding being forceful and interested in acquisition of goods rather than being interested in people and quality of life.

Assertiveness/Materialism

The degree of **assertiveness** or **materialism** is seen as the extent to which cultures value qualities like forcefulness and achievement on the one hand and people and the quality of life on the other. Materialistic societies define male-female roles more rigidly than do less materialistic societies. Japan and Austria are highly materialistic; the United States is slightly assertive and materialistic; and Norway, Sweden, Denmark, and Finland are much less so.

Long-term versus **short-term orientation** reflects whether people focus on the future or the past or present.

Short-term versus Long-term Orientation

This dimension was developed on the basis of a study that followed the study that was the basis for the first four dimensions. Values with a **long-term orientation** focus on the future, projects that have a long payoff, persistence, and thrift. **Short-term orientation** values are more oriented toward the past and the present, such as respect for traditions and social obligations. Japan, Hong Kong, and China are highly long-term oriented. The Netherlands and Germany are moderately long-term oriented. The United States, Indonesia, West Africa, and Russia are more short-term oriented.

Managerial Behavior across Cultures

Individual differences across cultures obviously can shape managerial as well as employee behavior. Beyond those differences are others specific to managerial behavior.[14]

In general, these differences relate to managerial beliefs about the role of authority and power in the organization. For example, managers in Indonesia, Italy, and Japan tend to believe that the purpose of an organization structure is to let everyone know who his or her boss is. Managers in the United States, Germany, and Great Britain, in contrast, believe that the organization structure is intended to coordinate group behavior and effort. On another dimension, Italian and German managers believe that it is acceptable to bypass one's boss to get things done, whereas managers in Sweden and Great Britain hold the strongest prohibitions against bypassing one's superior.

Figure 19.3 illustrates findings on another interesting point. Managers in Japan strongly believe that a manager should be able to answer any question he or she is

14. André Laurent, "The Cultural Diversity of Western Conceptions of Management," *International Studies of Management and Organization*, Spring-Summer 1983, pp. 75–96.

SOURCE: Reprinted from International Studies of Management and Organization, Vol, XIII, No. 1–2, Spring–Summer 1983, by permission of M. E. Sharpe, Inc., Armonk, N. Y. 10504.

FIGURE 19.3

Differences across Cultures in Managers' Beliefs about Answering Questions from Subordinates

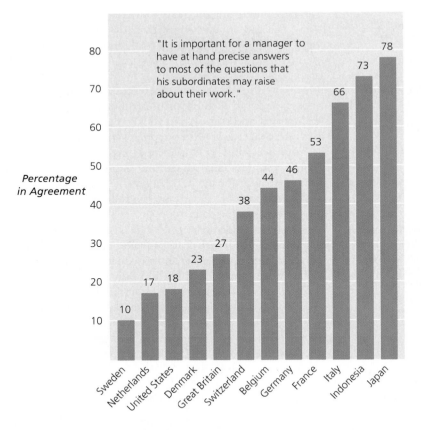

"It is important for a manager to have at hand precise answers to most of the questions that his subordinates may raise about their work."

Percentage in Agreement

Sweden 10, Netherlands 17, United States 18, Denmark 23, Great Britain 27, Switzerland 38, Belgium 44, Germany 46, France 53, Italy 66, Indonesia 73, Japan 78

asked. Thus, they place a premium on expertise and experience. In contrast, Swedish managers have the lowest concern for knowing all the answers. They view themselves as problem solvers and facilitators who make no claim to omnipotence.

Some recent evidence also suggests that managerial behavior is rapidly changing, at least among European managers. In general, these managers are becoming more career oriented, better educated, more willing to work cooperatively with labor, more willing to delegate, and more cosmopolitan.[15]

Motivation across Cultures

Some specific implications can also be drawn regarding motivation across cultures. Maslow's hierarchy of needs, for example, has been shown to vary across some cultures and remain stable across others. In some countries, such as Japan and Greece, security needs are most important, whereas social needs tend to dominate in Sweden and Norway.[16] On the other hand, the hierarchy seems to be fairly stable in Peru, India, Mexico, the Middle East, and parts of Canada.[17]

Research has also found that the need for achievement, Herzberg's dual structure theory, and the expectancy theory of motivation all vary across cultures. For example, many U.S. managers have a high expectancy that their hard work will lead to high performance. In contrast, Moslem managers believe their success is determined solely by God.[18]

Enhancing Performance in an International Context

Approaches to enhancing individual and interpersonal processes vary across cultures.

In Part 3, we describe several ways that organizations can enhance individual performance. In this section, we consider a few of the international extensions and implications that parallel those topics.

Job Design across Cultures

Job design clearly varies across cultures.[19] We noted many such differences in Chapter 7 and will summarize them here. Scandinavian companies, especially Volvo in Sweden, pioneered the use of work teams as a basis for job design. Workers in Germany, especially formerly West Germany, also have enjoyed innovative and progressive approaches to the design of their jobs. And in many ways, the participative management systems and quality circle programs so widespread in Japan represent aspects of job design. Beyond simple case analyses, however, job design has not been systematically studied across cultural boundaries.

15. See Brian O'Reilly, "Your New Global Workforce," *Fortune*, December 14, 1992, pp. 58–66; and Richard I. Kirkland, Jr., "Europe's New Managers," *Fortune*, September 29, 1986, pp. 56–60.
16. Adler, Doktor, and Redding, "From the Atlantic to the Pacific Century."
17. Nancy J. Adler, *International Dimensions of Organizational Behavior*, 2nd ed. (Boston: Kent, 1991).
18. Ibid.
19. Ricky W. Griffin, *Task Design* (Glenview, Ill.: Scott, Foresman, 1982).

Performance Measurement and Rewards across Cultures

Cross-cultural variation in performance evaluation includes two points of particular interest: what constitutes performance and how people respond to evaluation.

Measures of Performance   Unfortunately, little has been written about what constitutes performance in various cultures. Some insights, however, can be inferred from our earlier discussion of motivation in Chapters 4, 5, and 6. Some workers may view the number of hours they work as the measure of their performance, while others may view their personal effort as the proper measure. Still others might count their output as the measure of their performance. Workers in a highly group-focused culture such as Japan's might shy away from performance measures that assess the individual's contributions. Instead, they may see their performance in terms of what they contribute to the group.

Reactions to Evaluation   Similar differences characterize responses to actual evaluations of performance. People in some cultures accept critical evaluation, and negative feedback about performance may be appreciated and may result in improved performance. In other cultures, people take criticism much more seriously. Indeed, a recipient of criticism may be embarrassed enough to withdraw from the organization. The manager dealing with a new culture should develop a clear understanding of the role of performance feedback and its likely effects before undertaking any form of performance evaluation.

Rewards across Cultures   To date no one has systematically studied reward systems across cultures. Given that motivational processes vary across cultures, however, it follows that the rewards people want also vary. For example, job security clearly is more valued in some cultures than in others. Similarly, employees in some cultures, like the United States, put greater emphasis on individual rewards such as recognition, promotion, and merit salary increases. In other cultures, such as Japan, employees place a higher value on group rewards and recognition.

Whatever the situation, the manager must be prepared to thoroughly assess what employees want before presuming to know. Adler provides two examples in which U.S. managers overgeneralized from their own experiences and failed to anticipate problems. In one, salaries were increased for a group of Mexican workers. Unexpectedly, they started working fewer hours. Why? Because their higher salaries allowed them a better lifestyle, and they wanted to enjoy it. In the other case, a Japanese employee was promoted by a U.S. manager as a reward for high performance. This made him feel less a part of the group and led to a performance decline.[20]

Stress and Conflict across Cultures

In Chapter 9 we describe many of the individual and organizational consequences of excessive stress. Given the variations across cultures in the role of work in people's lives, their motivation, and other factors, we can logically conclude that both

20. Adler, *International Dimensions of Organizational Behavior*, pp. 132–133.

the causes and consequences of stress can vary across cultures. So too can individual coping levels, tolerance for stressors, and so forth. Different executives from various countries report very different levels of experienced stress. We still know little about stress among operating employees in other countries, but future research no doubt will yield some insights soon.

In the United States, conflict is a normal part of work life. When we see two people arguing, we think nothing of it. In general, we accept that these situations, as long as they do not become too dysfunctional, are just a part of doing business. In some other countries, however, conflict is even more pronounced. Great Britain, for example, is more prone to conflict in the workplace. This stems in part from the generally hostile nature of labor-management relations in that country. Bitter strikes make conflict commonplace.

Decision Making across Cultures

Chapter 10 describes the steps involved in making decisions. Nancy Adler recently explained how these steps, in a slightly modified form, can vary across cultures.[21] Table 19.1 shows the steps she identified and the range of variation.

First, managers in different cultures are likely to recognize problems and decision situations differently. Managers in the United States, for example, see problems as situations that require change. In contrast, managers in cultures like Indonesia and Thailand argue that one should accept the situation as it is instead of trying to change it.

Second, managers in some cultures see information as fact and make decisions accordingly. Others see information in terms of its possibilities and use it as a means of generating alternatives. For example, managers in some countries might see the citizens of an underdeveloped nation as being too poor to buy the products their companies make and therefore choose not to introduce the products there. Other managers might see the same reality but figure out how to lower the products' cost to make them more affordable.

Third, people in different cultures see different alternative solutions to problems. For example, managers in the United States tend to see future-oriented alternatives, whereas managers in Great Britain focus more on the past. Thus, U.S. managers may be more inclined to figure out a new technology for doing something, whereas the British may concentrate on modifying an existing technology to do the same thing.

Next, people's perceptions about making choices vary. The notion of orientation to authority we discussed earlier has clear implications as to who is expected to make the choices. Time urgency also varies. For example, U.S. managers make decisions very rapidly, whereas managers in some other cultures, as in the Middle East, are more deliberate and dislike having to make snap decisions.

Finally, cultures differ in how chosen alternatives are implemented. In the United States, managers tend to believe the implementation of decisions should be managed from the top and be the responsibility of one person. In contrast, Japanese managers believe participation is needed at all levels and responsibility should be shared.

21. Ibid.

TABLE 19.1

Cultural Variations
in Decision Making

Steps in Decision Making	Cultural Variations	
1. Problem Recognition	**Problem solving**	**Situation accepting**
	Situation should be changed	Some situations should be accepted, not changed
2. Information Search	**Gather "facts"**	**Gather ideas and possibilities**
3. Constructing Alternatives	**New, future-oriented alternatives**	**Focus includes past, present, and future alternatives**
	People can learn and change	Adults cannot change substantially
4. Choice	**Individuals make decisions**	**Groups make decisions**
	Decision-making responsibility delegated	Only senior management makes decisions
	Decisions made quickly	Decisions made slowly
	Decision rule: Is it true or false?	Decision rule: Is it good or bad?
5. Implementation	**Fast**	**Slow**
	Managed from the top	Involves the participation of all levels
	Responsibility of one person	Responsibility of the group

SOURCE: Nancy J. Adler, *International Dimensions of Organizational Behavior*, 2nd ed. (PWS-Kent Publishing Company, 1991), p. 163. Copyright © 1991 by South-Western College Publishing. All rights reserved.

Interpersonal Processes in an International Context

Interpersonal processes vary across cultures.

Just as individual behavior varies from culture to culture, so do interpersonal processes. The important areas of variation are group dynamics, leadership and influence, and communication.

Group Dynamics across Cultures

As we already noted, cultures differ in the importance they place on group membership. Writers have also focused attention on how to deal with groups made up of people from different cultures.[22]

22. Ibid.

In general, a manager in charge of a culturally diverse group can expect several things. First, the probability is high that distrust will exist among group members. Stereotyping also will present a problem. Finally, communication problems almost certainly will arise. Thus, the manager needs to recognize that such groups will seldom function smoothly, at least at first. Therefore, he or she may need to spend additional time helping the group through the rough spots as it matures and should allow a longer than normal time before expecting it to carry out its assigned task.

Leadership and Influence Processes across Cultures

We already noted variations in managerial behavior across cultures. Leadership is another important dimension. In many ways, the issue of leadership in an international context parallels our discussions of leadership as a situational process in Chapter 12. Specifically, cultural factors comprise another important set of situational elements that dictate appropriate leadership style.

One highly important situational factor we already discussed is orientation to authority. In a culture with a high orientation to authority, employees routinely expect the leader to make decisions, solve problems, and assign tasks. Thus, when a leader in such a culture tries to promote participation, his or her efforts will likely be rebuked. Under conditions of low orientation to authority, on the other hand, employees expect a greater say in how they do their jobs. Too much directive behavior and too few opportunities to participate may create problems.[23]

Finally, we should note the different roles leaders play in various cultures. Only recently have managers in Europe, for example, recognized that their jobs extend beyond the formal boundaries of managerial roles. In China, leaders are expected to remain formal and behave only within the clear confines of their legitimate power. In Japan, leaders serve more to facilitate group performance than as a control or supervisory mechanism.

In the United States, the use of power is considered a normal part of work life. When we see people striving to increase their power, we think nothing of it. These situations, within reason, are part of normal business.

Communication across Cultures

Communication is an aspect of interpersonal relations that obviously is affected by the international environment, partly because of language issues and partly because of coordination issues.

Language   Differences in languages are compounded because the same word can mean different things in different cultures. For example, Table 19.2 shows that Chevrolet's Nova did not fare well in Italy until managers there changed its name; in Italian, *no va* means "doesn't go." The table lists other interesting examples of communication foibles across cultures.

23. See James B. Shaw, "A Cognitive Categorization Model for the Study of Intercultural Management," *Academy of Management Review*, October 1990, pp. 626–645.

TABLE 19.2

Examples of
International
Communication
Problems

Source of Problem	Examples
Language	One firm, trying to find a name for a new soap powder, tested the chosen name in fifty languages. In English, it meant *dainty*. Translations into other languages meant *song* (Gaelic), *aloof* (Flemish), *horse* (African), *hazy* or *dimwitted* (Persian), and *crazy* (Korean). The name was obscene in several Slavic languages.
	The Chevy Nova was *no va* in Italian, which means "doesn't go."
	Coca-Cola in Chinese meant "Bite the head of a dead tadpole."
	Idioms cannot be translated literally: "to murder the King's English" becomes " to speak French like a Spanish cow" in French.
Nonverbal Signs	Shaking your head up and down in Greece means *no*, and swinging it from side to side means *yes*.
	In most European countries, it is considered impolite not to have both hands on the table.
	The American sign for *OK* is an obscenity in Spain.
Colors	Green: Popular in Moslem countries 　　　　Suggests disease in jungle-covered countries 　　　　Suggests cosmetics in France, Sweden, and the 　　　　　Netherlands
	Red: Blasphemous in African countries 　　　Stands for wealth and masculinity in Great Britain
Product	Campbell Soup Co. was unsuccessful in Britain until the firm added water to its condensed soup so the cans would be the same size as the cans of soup the British were used to purchasing.
	Long-life packaging, which is commonly used for milk in Europe, allows milk to be stored for months at room temperature if it is unopened. Americans are still wary of it.
	Coca-Cola had to alter the taste of its soft drink in China when the Chinese described it as "tasting like medicine."

SOURCE: Adapted from David A. Ricks, *Big Business Blunders*: *Mistakes in Multinational Marketing* (Homewood, Ill.: Dow Jones–Irwin, 1983); Nancy Bragganti and Elizabeth Devine, *The Traveler's Guide to European Customs and Manners* (St. Paul, Minn.: Meadowbrook Books, 1984); and several *Wall Street Journal* articles.

Note in the table that elements of nonverbal communication also vary across cultures. For example, colors and body language can convey quite a different message in one culture than in another. Thus, managers should be forewarned that they can take nothing for granted in dealing with people from another culture.

They must take the time necessary to become as fully acquainted as possible with the verbal and nonverbal languages of that culture.

Coordination   International communication is closely related to issues of coordination. For example, a U.S. manager who wants to talk with his or her counterpart in Hong Kong or Singapore must contend not only with differences in language but with a time difference of several hours. When the U.S. manager needs to talk on the telephone, the Hong Kong executive may be home asleep. Organizations are having to find increasingly innovative methods for coordinating their activities in scattered parts of the globe. Merrill Lynch, for example, has developed its own satellite-based telephone network to monitor and participate in the worldwide money and financial markets.[24]

Organizational Processes in an International Context

Organizational processes vary across cultures, particularly in terms of cultural influences on environment and technology, the ways that organizations are structured, and the importance of organization change.

> Organizational processes vary across cultures, particularly in terms of cultural influences on environment, and technology, organization structure and design, and the importance of organization change.

Organizational processes vary across cultures, particularly in terms of cultural influences on environment and technology, the ways that organizations are structured, and the importance of organization change. In Chapters 17 and 20 we discuss important issues related to organization culture and workforce diversity, respectively. A discussion of the combination of these two issues in the context of international issues is presented in *Diversity in the Workplace*. In this section, we examine cultural influences on environment, organization structure and design, and organization change.

Environment and Technology across Cultures

Variation in environment across cultures can be assessed at several levels. As we describe in Chapter 16, environments can be viewed in terms of their complexity and their dynamism. Organizations with international operations must contend with additional levels of complexity and dynamism, both within and across cultures.

Environmental Complexity and Dynamism   Many cultures have relatively stable environments. For example, the economies of Sweden, Japan, and the United States are fairly stable. Although competitive forces within them vary, they generally remain strong, free-market economies. In contrast, the environments of other countries are much more dynamic. For example, France's policies on socialism versus private enterprise tend to change dramatically with each election. At present, far-reaching changes in the economic and management philosophies of most Western European countries make their environments far more dynamic.

Environments also vary widely in terms of their complexity. The Japanese culture, which is fairly stable, is also quite complex. Japanese managers are subject to an array of cultural norms and values that are far more encompassing and resistant to change than those U.S. managers face. India too has an extremely complex environment, which remains influenced by its old caste system.

24. "How Merrill Lynch Moves Its Stock Deals All Around the World," *Wall Street Journal*, November 9, 1987, pp. 1, 8.

DIVERSITY IN THE WORKPLACE

International Workforce Diversity

In earlier chapters we stressed the importance of the organization culture, which we defined as the set of values that help people in an organization understand which actions are considered acceptable and which are considered unacceptable. The most important part of that definition is the values of the organization's employees. In other countries, the people's values may be quite different than the values of the people in a company's home country. Thus, the culture of an organization may clash with the culture of the host country for organizations that have operations in many different countries (cultures).

Clashes such as this are quite common. Compensation plans that require peers to evaluate each other with publicly known results are becoming common in the United States, but are totally unacceptable in Japan, where coworkers are highly respected and a worker cannot allow a coworker to lose face in front of others. Individually based performance and incentive plans are unacceptable in Scandinavian countries where teamwork and group productivity are most important.

Additional problems are created by the fact that the typical international workforce will be fully diverse and comprise people from many different cultures. This means that coworkers will likely have vastly different value systems and beliefs. With such a diverse workforce it will be more difficult to forge a cohesive set of values on which most employees can agree, believe, and be committed to. Companies in Europe have understood this for several years. Employees in Europe are quite mobile and comfortable moving from one country to another country to follow a particular job with a particular company. In such cases the company may try to develop a culture and set of values for its employees that transcends differences in beliefs that may occur between countries.

The globally diverse workforce will also be highly trained and willing to work. In the countries of Central Europe, such as Hungary, the former East Germany, and Slovenia, the engineers are highly trained, have worked apprenticeships, and are eager for full-time paying jobs with companies from the United States, Japan, and countries in Western Europe. The productivity payoffs for developing a globally and culturally diverse workforce will most certainly be positive if companies are willing to work hard to understand and work with the differences that will occur.

SOURCES: Cresencio Torres and Mary Bruxelles, "Capitalizing on Global Diversity," *HR Magazine*, December 1992, pp. 30–33; Barry Louis Rubin, "Europeans Value Diversity," *HR Magazine*, January 1991, pp. 38–78; and Brian O'Reilly, "Your New Global Workforce," *Fortune*, December 14, 1992, pp. 58–66.

Technology   Technological variations come in two forms: variations in available technology and variations in attitudes toward technology. Available technology affects how organizations can do business. Many underdeveloped countries, for example, lack electric power sources, telephones, and trucking equipment, not to mention computers and robots. A manager working in such a country must be prepared for many frustrations. A few years ago, some Brazilian officials convinced a U.S. company to build a high-tech plant in their country. Midway through construction, however, the government of Brazil decided it would not allow the company to import some accurate measuring instruments it needed to produce its products. The new plant was abandoned before it ever opened.[25]

25. Andrew Kupfer, "How to Be a Global Manager," *Fortune*, March 14, 1988, pp. 52–58.

Companies that have entered the international market must adapt their corporate structure to accommodate not only increased business, but also the demands of other cultures. A company such as Pepsi, shown here in Moscow, must have foreign market managers to handle the business it conducts all over the globe.

Attitudes toward technology also vary across cultures. Surprisingly, Japan has only recently begun to support basic research. For many years, the Japanese government encouraged its companies to take basic research findings discovered elsewhere (often in the United States) and figure out how to apply them to consumer products (applied research). In the mid-1980s, however, the government changed its stance and started to encourage basic research as well.[26] Most of the Western nations have a generally favorable attitude toward technology, whereas China and other Asian countries (with the exception of Japan) do not.

Organization Structure and Design across Cultures

Cross-cultural considerations related to organization structure and design include not only similarities and differences among firms in different cultures but structural features of multinational organizations.

Between-Culture Issues   "Between-culture issues" refers to comparisons of the organization structure and design of companies operating in different cultures. As might be expected, there are both differences and similarities. For example, one study compared the structures of fifty-five U.S. and fifty-one Japanese manufacturing plants. Results suggest that Japanese plants have less specialization, more "formal" centralization (but less "real" centralization), and taller hierarchies than their U.S. counterparts. The Japanese structures are also less affected by their technology than are the U.S. plants.[27]

Many cultures still take a traditional view of organization structure not unlike the approaches used in this country during the days of classical organization theory. For example, Tom Peters, a leading U.S. management consultant and coauthor of *In Search of Excellence*, recently spent some time lecturing to managers in

26. "Going Crazy in Japan—In a Break from Tradition, Tokyo Begins Funding a Program for Basic Research," *Wall Street Journal*, November 10, 1986, p. 20D.
27. James R. Lincoln, Mitsuyo Hanada, and Kerry McBride, "Organizational Structures in Japanese and U.S. Manufacturing," *Administrative Science Quarterly*, September 1986, pp. 338–364.

China. They were not interested in his ideas about decentralization and worker participation, however. Instead, the question most often asked involved how a manager determined the optimal span of control.[28]

In contrast, many European companies are increasingly patterning themselves after successful U.S. firms. This stems in part from corporate raiders in Europe emulating their U.S. counterparts and partly from a better educated managerial workforce. Taken together, these two forces have caused many European firms to become more decentralized and to adopt divisional structures by moving from functional to product departmentalization.[29]

Multinational Organization More and more firms have entered the international arena and have found it necessary to adapt their designs to better cope with different cultures.[30] For example, after a company has achieved a moderate level of international activity, it often establishes an international division, usually at the same organizational level as other major functional divisions. Levi Strauss uses this organization design. One division, Levi Strauss International, is responsible for the company's business activities in Europe, Canada, Latin America, and Asia.

For an organization that has become more deeply involved in its international activities, a logical form of organization design is the international matrix, illustrated in Figure 19.4. This type of matrix arrays product managers across the top. Project teams headed by foreign market managers cut across the product departments. A company with three basic product lines, for example, might establish

28. "The Inscrutable West," *Newsweek*, April 18, 1988, p. 52.
29. Kirkland, "Europe's New Managers"; Shawn Tully, "Europe's Takeover Kings," *Fortune*, July 20, 1987, pp. 95–98.
30. Lane and DiStefano, *International Management Behavior*.

FIGURE 19.4

An International Matrix

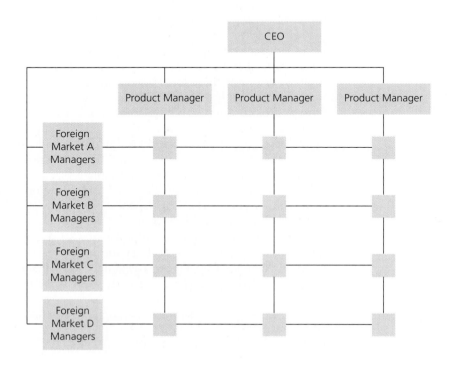

Part 6   Emerging Dimensions of Organizational Behavior

three product departments (of course, it contains domestic advertising, finance, and operations departments as well). Foreign market managers can be designated for, say, Canada, Japan, Europe, Latin America, and Australia. Each foreign market manager is then responsible for all three of the company's products in his or her market.[31]

Finally, at the most advanced level of multinational activity, a firm might become an international conglomerate. Nestlé and Unilever fit this typology. Each has an international headquarters (Nestlé in Vevey, Switzerland, and Unilever in Rotterdam, Netherlands) that coordinates the activities of businesses scattered around the globe. Nestlé has factories in fifty countries and markets its products in virtually every country in the world. More than 96 percent of its business is done outside of Switzerland, and only about 7,000 of its 160,000 employees reside in its home country.

Organization Change in an International Context

Managing organization change and development processes also vary significantly across cultures.

Organization change and development are the topics of Chapter 18, so our discussion at this point will be brief. One factor to consider is how international environments dictate organization change. As we already noted, the environment can be a major factor in bringing about organization change. Given the additional environmental complexities multinational organizations face, it follows that organization change may be even more critical to them than to purely domestic organizations.

A second point to remember is that acceptance of change varies widely around the globe. In some cultures, as we noted earlier, change is a normal and accepted part of organization life. In other cultures, change causes many problems. The manager should remember that techniques for managing change that have worked routinely back home may not work at all and may even trigger negative responses if used indiscriminately in other cultures.[32]

Careers across Cultures

An understanding of careers, which we discuss in Appendix 2 at the end of the book, is also becoming increasingly important for managers. It should come as no surprise that there are international implications to be drawn from career-related concerns. Some of these center on career paths in different cultures; others involve career concerns for managers in international businesses.

Cultural Variations in Careers Perhaps the most important career-related issue for the manager to understand is that different cultures have different norms and standards relevant to career paths. The U.S. culture, for example, generally supports people who are ambitious, want to succeed, and strive for advancement. In other cultures, personal ambition is less acceptable. The Japanese, for example, are expected to put organizational concerns and priorities above personal ones. Working to better one's own position in the organization is considered unseemly.

31. William H. Davison and Philippe Haspeslagh, "Shaping a Global Product Organization," *Harvard Business Review*, July–August 1982, pp. 125–132.

32. Alfred M. Jaeger, "Organization Development and National Culture: Where's the Fit?" *Academy of Management Review*, January 1986, pp. 178–190.

Widespread gender discrimination exists in many parts of the world. In Japan and Finland, women are quite restricted in their opportunities for advancement. Japanese women are expected to become wives and mothers. Even those who graduate from college usually take jobs as clerks and seldom move up the corporate ladder. This is beginning to change somewhat, although the changes are still indiscernible in most organizations.[33] In Finland, women have a strong heritage of working outside the home but still lag behind men in both income and opportunities for advancement.[34]

International Career Paths As businesses become increasingly international, they must devote more attention to how this change affects their managers' careers. For example, a manager who is transferred from New York to Dallas to Seattle obviously experiences a certain amount of trauma and stress. But this pales in comparison to what happens to the manager transferred from New York to Tokyo to Bangkok. Thus, the firm must carefully consider both the advantages and disadvantages of international assignments.[35]

Summary of Key Points

- International business has rapidly become an important part of almost every manager's life and is likely to become even more so in the future. Thus, managers need to recognize that both similarities and differences exist across cultures.
- One important concern is individual behavior. Managers must recognize that patterns of individual differences, managerial behavior, motivation, and rewards vary across cultures.
- Similarly, just as domestic managers work to enhance individual and interpersonal processes, the international manager confronts the same opportunities and challenges. Concerns regarding job design, performance measurement and rewards, stress, and decision making are as important in an international context as they are in a domestic one.
- Interpersonal processes also vary across cultures. Particularly important are concerns related to group dynamics, leadership and influence processes, and communication.
- International management involves an understanding of how organizational processes vary in an international context. Environment, technology, and organization structure and design are especially important characteristics to understand. Forces for and techniques of organization change also vary systematically across cultures. Career-related issues are another special consideration for managers receiving international assignments.

33. "Look Whose Sun Is Rising Now: Career Women," *Business Week*, August 25, 1986, p. 50.

34. Kaisa Kauppinen-Toropainen, Irja Kandolin, and Elina Haavio-Mannila, "Sex Segregation of Work in Finland and the Quality of Women's Work," *Journal of Organizational Behavior*, Vol. 9, 1988, pp. 15–27.

35. Mark Mendenhall and Gary Oddou, "The Dimensions of Expatriate Acculturation: A Review," *Academy of Management Review*, January 1985, pp. 39–47.

Discussion Questions

1. Identify ways in which international business affects businesses in your community.
2. All things considered, do you think people from diverse cultures are more alike or more different? Why?
3. What stereotypes exist about the motivational patterns of workers from other cultures?
4. What can U.S. managers learn about individual behavior from other cultures? What can managers in other cultures learn about individual behavior from U.S. managers?
5. Which dimension of the individual-organization interface is most likely to vary across cultures? Which is least likely to vary?
6. If you had just been appointed leader of a group of employees from another culture, what would you do first to be more effective?
7. At present, the United States limits the importation of many products into this country. Do you agree or disagree with this policy? Why?
8. If you were offered a temporary assignment abroad, would you be inclined to take it? Why or why not?
9. Suppose you work for a firm that recently transferred in a manager from another country. The transfer represents this manager's first international exposure. What might you do to help the manager adjust?
10. What are the advantages and disadvantages of transferring managers across a variety of locations scattered around the world?

EXPERIENTIAL EXERCISE

Purpose This exercise will help you develop a better understanding of the complexities involved in international management.

Format The instructor will divide the class into small groups of three to four. Assume that you are a task force for a medium-size manufacturing company. Top management has just decided to open a new facility overseas. Your instructor will specify the location for your group.

Procedure Your assignment is to learn as much about the culture of your location as possible and report back to top management about the advantages and disadvantages of the location. Try to identify three major advantages and three major concerns that need to be addressed. Report your findings to the class.

Follow-up Questions

1. In a situation like this, can you ever learn all you need to know about a different culture and how it will affect a business?
2. How easy or difficult is it to learn about other cultures?

Traditionally, companies chose to move manufacturing outside the United States because the labor costs were so much lower: they sometimes paid only a few dollars a day compared to fifteen to twenty dollars per hour in the United States. Although lower labor costs used to be a good enough reason, today there are many additional reasons for producing outside the United States. These reasons are some of the factors that have contributed to the truly global economy.

First, by having manufacturing and service operations in other countries, it is possible to be closer to markets that are rapidly developing and that will be a major part of corporate growth in the next few decades. Being closer to the new markets often results in lower transportation costs and lower import tariffs and duties. Locating manufacturing plants in developing economies also helps them grow faster and have large appetites for new products and services.

Another reason is that there is a worldwide surplus of labor that, combined with the increased mobility of the workforce and technology, comprises a workforce that will go where the jobs are. New factories are combining new technologies of manufacturing with a newly trained workforce that is not burdened with long-standing union work rules. The result is highly efficient production systems: the elimination of one million jobs in the United States may create only 100,000 jobs in other countries. Historically, U.S. companies have been almost totally vertically integrated from the manufacture of the smallest parts to the finished products, based on the assumption that the big company could make all the parts and sub-assemblies faster, cheaper, and better than could suppliers. In other countries, following the lead of the Japanese system, there are likely to be a whole host of suppliers of small parts and supplies that feed off of the manufacturing plant. Thus, the workforce is not solely dependent on the "mother" company and the economy is more likely to develop independently.

Many different types of processes are now being done around the world. For example, the simple process of entering data on keyboards can now be done in many places other than the United States for a fraction of the cost: fifty cents per 10,000 characters in the Philippines and twenty cents per 10,000 in China. Insurance claims can be processed in other countries such as Ireland. Airline reservations and ticket processing is done in Montego Bay and Kingston.

Training of engineers and high-tech workers is improving worldwide. The engineers of Central Europe, formerly Eastern Europe and communist controlled, are highly skilled and ready to work. Their formal university-based education is excellent, plus most have served several years of apprenticeships. Jobs are also available in the management ranks. The demands for managers who are globally experienced, who speak more than one language, and are willing to relocate are increasing rapidly. The abilities of local managers are increasing in all of the developing economies, so that expatriate managers are not always the dominant force anymore. However, the future will most likely bring a complete integration of managers from around the world to meet the challenges at any one location. Finally, strategic alliances between companies based in different countries will force an increased integration of managers. All of these factors are forcing managers of the future to rethink the previously held assumption about the workforce of the future.

Case Questions

1. Identify three factors in this case that illustrate individual behavior in an international context.
2. How are factors that affect individual and group performance in organizations illustrated in this case?
3. One of the most obvious impacts of internationalization on organizations is the need for managers to be multilingual. How many people in your class can speak more than one language? What can you do to make yourself more internationally aware?

SOURCES: E. B. Baatz, "Survey: Go Global!" *Electronic Business*, April 1993, pp. 38–44; Cecil G. Howard, "Profile of the 21st-Century Expatriate Manager," *HR Magazine*, June 1992, pp. 93–100; and Brian O'Reilly, "Your New Global Workforce," *Fortune*, December 14, 1992, pp. 58–62.

Warren Oats was a highly successful executive for American Auto Suppliers (AAS), a Chicago-based company that makes original equipment specialty parts for Ford, GM, and Chrysler. Rather than retreat before the onslaught of Japanese automakers, AAS decided to counterattack and use its reputation for quality and dependability to win over customers in Japan. Oats had started in the company as an engineer and worked his way up to become one of a handful of senior managers who had a shot at the next open vice presidential position. He knew he needed to distinguish himself somehow, so when he was given a chance to lead the AAS attack on the Japanese market, he jumped at it.

Oats knew he did not have time to learn Japanese, but he had heard that many Japanese executives speak English, and the company would hire a translator anyway. The toughest part about leaving the United States was persuading his wife, Carol, to take an eighteen-month leave from her career as an attorney with a prestigious Chicago law firm. Carol finally persuaded herself that she did not want to miss an opportunity to learn a new culture. So, armed with all the information they could gather about Japan from their local library, the Oats headed for Tokyo.

Known as an energetic, aggressive salesperson back home, Warren Oats wasted little time getting started. As soon as his office had a telephone—and well before all his files had arrived from the home office—Oats made an appointment to meet with executives of one of Japan's leading automakers. Oats reasoned that if he was going to overcome the famous Japanese resistance to foreign companies, he should get started as soon as possible.

Oats felt very uncomfortable at that first meeting. He got the feeling that the Japanese executives were waiting for something. It seemed that everyone but he was in slow motion. The Japanese did not speak English well and appeared grateful for the presence of the interpreter, but even the interpreter seemed to take her time in translating each phrase. Frustrated by this seeming lethargy and beginning to doubt the much-touted Japanese efficiency, Oats got right to the point. He made an oral presentation of his proposal, waiting patiently for the translation of each sentence.

Then he handed the leader of the Japanese delegation a packet containing the specifics of his proposal, got up, and left. The translator trailed behind him as if wanting to drag out the process even further.

By the end of their first week, both Oats and his wife were frustrated. Oats' office phone had not rung once, which did not make him optimistic about his meeting with another top company the following week. Carol could scarcely contain her irritation with what she had perceived to be the Japanese way of life. She had been sure that a well-respected U.S. lawyer would have little trouble securing a job with a Japanese multinational corporation, but the executives she had met with seemed insulted that she was asking them for a job. And the way they treated their secretaries! After only a week in Japan, both Carol and Warren Oats were ready to go home.

A month later, their perspective had changed radically, and both looked back on those first meetings with embarrassment. Within that month, they had learned a lot about the Japanese sense of protocol and attitudes toward women. Warren Oats believed he was beginning to get the knack of doing business with the Japanese in their manner: establishing a relationship slowly, almost ritualistically, waiting through a number of meetings before bringing up the real business at hand, and then doing so circumspectly. It was difficult for Oats to slow his pace, and it made him nervous to be so indirect, but he was beginning to see some value in the sometimes humbling learning process he was going through. Perhaps, he thought, he and Carol could become consultants for other executives who needed to learn the lessons he was beginning to understand.

Case Questions

1. What specific errors did Warren and Carol Oats make during their first week in Japan?
2. If you were talking to a non–U.S. businessperson making a first contact with a U.S. company, what advice would you give?

Managing Diversity in Organizations

OBJECTIVES

After studying this chapter you should be able to:

Define diversity and describe why diversity is important
in organizations.

Identify primary and secondary dimensions of diversity.

Describe several ways that diversity issues affect individual
behavior in organizations.

Discuss several ways that diversity issues affect interpersonal
processes in organizations.

Explain how organizational processes are affected
by diversity.

Describe how to create a multicultural organization.

Avon Products, Inc., may be more aware of the issues involved in workforce diversity than other companies: its salesforce and primary customers have been women since it began its door-to-door sales more than forty years ago and, currently, 73 percent of its managers are women. In the 1970s, Avon women formed groups—Concerned Women of Avon; these groups became the Women and Minorities Committee in the 1980s, and later the Minorities and Women Council. The Council has now branched out into several networks to address the needs of special groups. The most active networks are the Avon Asian Network, the Avon Hispanic Network, and the Black Professional Association (BPA). Although not formally established by management, these networks are supported by Avon top management and are very important to the company's multicultural movement. Avon's chairman of the board and chief executive officer, Jim Preston, was instrumental in supporting the networks in his earlier position as executive vice president and continues to support them today.

The networks contribute in many ways to the growth of individual members and to the organization. Networks

In the past twenty years, many ethnic groups have formed organizations within the workplace. These networks, with the support of top management, may hold educational workshops and seminars on the subject of workforce diversity, sponsor ethnicity-focused special events, or simply serve as support systems for their members.

hold seminars and workshops such as the BPA academy, which presents regular workshops on a variety of topics such as perspectives of black employees, managing personal growth, and managing upward mobility. Other networks hold open question-and-answer sessions with top management. Some special events are intended to familiarize all employees with various multicultural issues. For example, the Avon Asian Network sponsors Avon Asian Day each year to demonstrate traditional aspects of Asian culture such as flower arranging, ancient calligraphy, Indian spices and teas, and jewelry. Days such as these help employees who are not Asian to better understand the history and traditions of Asian cultures, which aids in breaking down cultural stereotypes, increases communication across all levels, improves understanding of different management styles, and has helped the career development of many Asians.[1]

■ ■ ■ ■ **D**iversity councils, workshops on managing diversity, and minority networks are now common in organizations. Rather than force diverse people to hide their differences to fit the corporate mold, minority councils and networks focus on diversity and aid in destroying biases and stereotypes that inhibit organizational productivity.

The growing diversity of the workforce will have a major impact on our work lives and is posing a growing managerial challenge. This chapter is about managing the differences among people in organizations. First, we examine the nature of the diverse workforce. Then we describe the dimensions and the complexities of

1. Charlene Marmer Solomon, "Networks Empower Employees," *Personnel Journal*, October 1991, pp. 51–54; "Past Tokenism," *Newsweek*, May 14, 1990, pp. 37–38; Charlene Marmer Solomon, "The Corporate Response to Work Force Diversity," *Personnel Journal*, August 1989, pp. 42–54; and Gary Hoover, Alta Campbell, and Patrick J. Spain (Eds.), *Hoover's Handbook of American Business 1993* (Austin, Tex.: The Reference Press, 1992), p. 138.

the diverse workforce. Next, we parallel the overall organization of the book by relating workforce diversity to individual behavior, to interpersonal processes, and to organizational processes. Finally, we discuss how to create a multicultural organization that utilizes the benefits of the diverse workforce.

The Nature of Diversity in Organizations

Diversity is all about being different! And we are all different in many ways. In the workplace this diversity may be called "cultural diversity," "workforce diversity," or "cultural variety" and is often referred to as "Workforce 2000," which was the title of a book that reported a 1987 study by the Hudson Institute of the nature of the future U.S. workforce.[2] This study found that the workforce of the year 2000 and beyond will be very different than the workforce that has characterized the United States in the recent past. The opportunities and problems inherent in managing a culturally diverse workforce will be the most challenging aspects of managing human resources in the next twenty years.

Definition of Diversity

Workforce diversity is the differences, such as in age, gender, ethnic heritage, physical ability/disability, race, and sexual orientation, that make up the employees of organizations. To manage diversity in organizations, we must first recognize that differences exist among the people in the organization.

These differences are reflected in how people conceive of work, what rewards they expect from the organization, and how they relate to others.[3] Managers of diverse work groups need to know about people, to understand how their social conditioning affects their beliefs about work, and to have the communication skills to develop confidence and self-esteem among diverse work groups. Many managers tend to stereotype people in organizations.

As we discuss in Chapter 3, a *stereotype* is a generalization about a person or a group of persons based on certain characteristics or traits. Unfortunately, most managers initially think that workers are like themselves in their orientation toward work, rewards, and relationships to coworkers. Coworkers who differ in race, age, gender, and other ways, however, may not share those same beliefs, and thus may be treated as "different." In this situation managers may tend to stereotype different workers according to their particular characteristics. Stereotypes tend to ignore individual differences and become rigid judgments about others that do not take into account the specific person and the current situation.[4]

Stereotypes can lead to the even more dangerous process of prejudice. **Prejudices** are judgments made about others that reinforce a superiority/inferior-

> **Workforce diversity** is the differences, such as in age, gender, ethnic heritage, physical ability/disability, race, and sexual orientation, that make up the employees of organizations.
>
> We must recognize that diversity exists in organizations before we can begin to manage this diversity.

2. William B. Johnston and Arnold H. Packer, *Workforce 2000: Work and Workers for the 21st Century* (Indianapolis: Hudson Institute, 1987).
3. Elaine Carter, Elaine Kepner, Malcolm Shaw, and William Brooks Woodson, "The Effective Management of Diversity," *S.A.M. Advanced Management Journal*, Autumn 1982, pp. 49–53.
4. Marilyn Loden and Judy B. Rosener, *Workforce America! Managing Employee Diversity as a Vital Resource* (Homewood, Ill.: Business One Irwin, 1991), pp. 58–62.

Prejudices are judgments made about others that reinforce a superiority/inferiority belief system and can lead to exaggerating the worth of one group while diminishing the worth of others.

ity belief system and can lead to exaggerating the worth of one group while diminishing the worth of others.[5] For example, some people may assume that all people from Asia are superior in mathematics. A manager might therefore assign the team member from Asia to the mathematical part of the assignment based on that stereotype. When we prejudge others we use the categories that we have put people in and then build job descriptions, reward systems, performance appraisal systems, and management systems and policies that fit our stereotypes. In other words, we assume things about the nature of the workers that may or may not be true, and then we manage accordingly.

Management systems built on stereotypes and prejudices can then be inappropriate for a diverse workforce. Examples include compensation systems that do not foster higher performance, job descriptions that do not fit the jobs and the people who do them, and performance appraisal systems that measure the wrong things, such as similarity to the boss or fitting in with the dominant group. In addition, stereotypes and prejudices tend to reduce the individuality of people who have been stereotyped. Their distinctiveness and individual talents are minimized, resulting in a loss of self-esteem, which can lead to lower levels of satisfaction and performance. Stereotypes can also become self-fulfilling prophesies.[6] If we assume people are incompetent and treat them accordingly, then over time they may begin to believe themselves to be incompetent. This can lead to reduced productivity, lower creativity, and lower morale.

Thus, the first step is to recognize that diversity exists in organizations so that we can begin to manage this diversity accordingly. The danger of not recognizing this diversity is a workforce that may have problems working cooperatively and is unhappy, disillusioned, and underutilized.

Workforce Demographics

Employment statistics provide one perspective for understanding the radically different workforce of the future. Figure 20.1 shows the workforce composition of 1985 compared to projections for 2000. All segments of the workforce will increase as a percentage of the total workforce *except* the white male segment, which declines from 47 percent to 41 percent. Although this decline may not seem dramatic, it follows decades in which the white male segment has been the dominant segment of the workforce, making up well over 50 percent of the workforce. This expected 6 percent drop is an important decline, considering that the total U.S. workforce is expected to be more than 140 million in 2000.

Another way to view these changes is to examine the nature of the growth in the workforce during the fifteen-year period from 1985 to 2000. Figure 20.2 shows the percentage of the growth attributable to each segment. White men are expected to account for only 15 percent of the growth. In other words, 85 percent of the growth in the workforce by 2000 is expected to be in the nonwhite-male segments. White women are expected to make up 42 percent of the expected growth, resulting in the expectation that more than 61 percent of women in the United States will be working in 2000.

5. Loden and Rosener, *Workforce America!* p. 60.
6. Ibid., pp. 68–70.

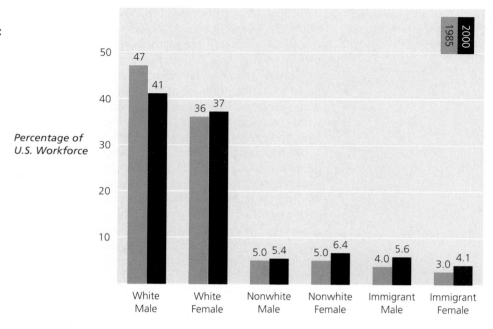

FIGURE 20.1

Workforce Composition: 1985 and 2000

Percentage of U.S. Workforce

	White Male	White Female	Nonwhite Male	Nonwhite Female	Immigrant Male	Immigrant Female
1985	47	36	5.0	5.0	4.0	3.0
2000	41	37	5.4	6.4	5.6	4.1

SOURCE: William B. Johnston and Arnold H. Packer, *Workforce 2000* (Indianapolis: Hudson Institute, 1987).

Another view of the changes is to examine the age ranges of the workforce. In the last few decades, the workforce was dominated by young workers, but these young workers are growing older. In fact, workers aged 16 to 24 will decline by almost 2 million, or about 8 percent, by 2000. The number of workers between 35 and 54 years of age is expected to increase from 38 percent to 51 percent (from 1985 to 2000), or by more than 25 million.[7]

This situation is not unique to the United States. The numbers for Canada are much the same. Minorities are the fastest-growing segment of the population and the workforce in Canada. In addition, women make up two-thirds of the growth in the workforce, increasing their percentage from 35 percent in the 1970s to 45 percent in 1991.[8]

Increasing diversity in the workplace is even more dramatic in Europe. Employees have been crossing borders for many years, and this phenomenon simply increased markedly when borders were opened in 1992. It was expected that opening borders for the twelve European Community members primarily meant relaxing trade restrictions so goods and services could move among the member countries. In addition, however, workers were also free to move and have taken advantage of the opportunity. Currently, it is estimated that more than two million Europeans are working in countries they were not born in.

Companies throughout Europe are learning to adjust to the changing workforce. Amadeus Global Travel Distribution serves the travel industry primarily in Europe, but its staff of 650 comprises individuals from thirty-two different countries. Amadeus developed a series of workshops to teach upper management how to lead multicultural teams and how to interact better with peers, subordinates, and superiors from a variety of countries.[9] Other companies experiencing much the same and

Opening borders for the twelve European Community members meant relaxing trade restrictions so that workers, goods, and services could move among the member countries. More than two million Europeans work in European countries they were not born in.

7. Johnston and Packer, *Workforce 2000*, p. 7.
8. Michael Crawford, "The New Office Etiquette," *Canadian Business*, May 1993, pp. 22–31.
9. Barry Louis Rubin, "Europeans Value Diversity," *HR Magazine*, January 1991, pp. 38–41, 78.

FIGURE 20.2

Percentage of Growth in Workforce: 1985–2000*

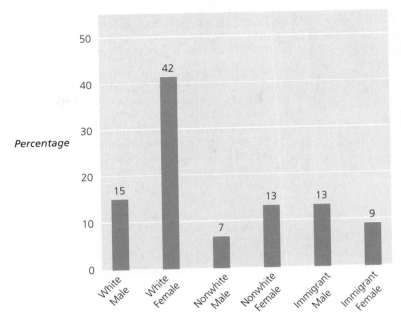

Percentage

*Due to rounding, percentages do not add up to 100%.
SOURCE: William B. Johnston and Arnold H. Packer, *Workforce 2000* (Indianapolis: Hudson Institute, 1987).

doing something about it include Mars Incorporated, Digital Equipment Corp., Hewlett-Packard Spain, Fujitsu Ltd. in Spain, and British Petroleum. For more on diversity internationally, see the *Global Perspective*. These changes have initiated a workforce revolution in offices and factories. Managers must learn to adapt to changing demographics. Employees also will need to be tolerant of the differences among their coworkers and be more flexible to work rule changes.

From Assimilation to Valuing Diversity

The issue of workforce diversity is receiving increased attention in the last few years because employees, managers, consultants, and the government are finally realizing that the composition of the workforce is very important to organizational productivity. They are also realizing that managing a diverse workforce is not as simple as it was once thought to be. Although the impact of equal employment opportunity and accompanying affirmative action legislation has been great, initial attempts focused on bringing people from culturally different groups into the workplace and fully assimilating them into the existing organization. The United States has often been referred to as a melting pot of people from many different countries, cultures, and backgrounds. For centuries, these differences have been covered up as people who were different tried to integrate into the existing culture.

In organizations, however, integration proved to be difficult as people were slow to change, usually resistant to change, and opportunities for true career advancement rarely materialized for those who were different. So, rather than a melting pot, the workplace now resembles a tossed salad of different flavors, colors, and textures. Rather than assimilate those who are different into a single organizational culture, the current view is that organizations need to celebrate the differences and use the variety of talents, perspectives, and backgrounds of all employees.

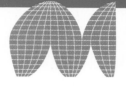

Global Workforce Diversity Is a Worldwide Issue

Managing workforce diversity is truly international in scope. In the United States, diversity at work formerly referred to having more women and minorities in the organization. Later management recognized that diversity had many other dimensions including age, disabilities, ethnicity, and sexual orientation. Now the issues of managing a diverse workforce are being felt all over the world.

In Europe, organizations commonly have workers who come from many different countries. At Mars the finance manager is French, the personnel director is Swiss, and the general manager is English; executive movement between countries is considered a normal transfer, not an "international" transfer. The experience of Mars is that the international mobility is primarily with professional, white-collar workers because of the company's desire to move the people with specialized expertise to where there is a problem to solve, regardless of nationality.

Some problems are international in scope. Japanese companies doing business in the United States have often run into trouble with U.S. laws regarding equal employment rights. For example, Sumitomo Corp. was sued for discriminating against non-Japanese employees in filling management positions. It settled by agreeing to raise the base salaries of some non-Japanese employees, integrate more U.S. workers into senior management, provide back pay to some U.S. employees, and implement a career development program. Honda of America Manufacturing Inc. was sued (and eventually settled for $6 million) for racial and sexual bias at its Ohio plant.

One of the biggest problems for companies that move people internationally is the mix of company culture with country culture. The question of how much to force the company culture or adapt the country culture is faced by every multinational. Companies have found that the notion of a single company culture into which employees from all countries must fit may not be the best. Often the company learns that their company culture must be adapted to fit the host country. Mars, for example, has learned some things from the southern Europeans about creativity and human relations that has forced it to adapt its tough English management style to fit the host country. Fujitsu Ltd.'s operation in Spain had to adapt its Japanese operating style to the culture of Spain and realized that to develop a truly international culture, it must have a core culture flexible enough to work in countries all over the world. Digital Equipment of Canada requires all employees to go through its two-day "Valuing Diversity" program and its training on improper workplace behavior, such as sexual harassment.

SOURCES: Martin F. Payson and Philip B. Rosen, "Playing by Fair Rules," *HR Magazine*, April 1991, pp. 42–43; Michael Crawford, "The New Office Etiquette," *Canadian Business*, May 1993, pp. 22–31; and Barry Louis Rubin, "Europeans Value Diversity," *HR Magazine*, January 1991, pp. 38–41, 78.

Assimilation is the process in which a minority group learns the ways of the dominant group. In organizations this is the attempt to mold people who are different to fit the existing organization culture.

Assimilation   **Assimilation** is the process in which a minority group learns and adopts the ways of the dominant group. In organizations this is the attempt to mold people who are different to fit the existing organization culture. Most organizations develop systems, such as performance standards and compensation systems, to reflect and reinforce the values of the dominant group. Under the assumptions of assimilation, the values of the dominant group are universally applied throughout the organization, which tends to perpetuate any falsely held stereotypes and prejudices. Workers who are different are expected to meet the standards for dominant group members.

Assimilation has several consequences for people not included in the dominant group. For example, communication channels and decision making remain closed to anyone not in the dominant group. Because members of the dominant group often tend to avoid people who are different simply because they do not understand them, informal discussions over coffee, lunch, and after-hours socializing tend to be limited to people in the dominant group. The result is that those not in the dominant group miss out on the informal communication opportunities at which office politics, company policy, and other issues may be discussed in great detail. Subsequently, they often do not understand more formal communication and may not be included in necessary action taken in response.

Similarly, decisions are made by the dominant group based on their values and beliefs because those who are different are not in the dominant group. Thus, the non-dominant group's views and perspectives are not included in decisions regarding compensation, facility location, benefit plans, performance standards, and other work issues that pertain directly to all workers. Workers who are different from the dominant group very quickly learn that to succeed in such a system, one must be like the dominant group in terms of values and beliefs, dress, and most other ways. Therefore, assimilation is required to succeed, and the differences are hidden even more.

In most organizations the dominant group is fairly predictable. Table 20.1 shows the results of interviews with members of several organizations who were asked to list the attributes that were reinforced by the organization's cultures. For the most part, these are characteristics of white men, traditionally the dominant group in U.S. organizations. Typically, white men in organizations see themselves as quite diverse. On the other hand, others in the organizations view white men as homogeneous, similar to those attributes listed. And also typically, working in such a homogeneous dominant group tends to decrease its members' awareness of the problems that can be caused by such a homogeneous dominant group. Usually only those not in the dominant group are most affected by it.

Ignoring cultural diversity, or assimilation, can be very costly to the organization. In addition to blocking the involvement in communication and decision making, ignoring diversity can also cause tensions among workers; lower productivity;

TABLE 20.1

Attributes Reinforced by the Culture in Typical Organizations

- Rational, linear thinker
- Impersonal management style
- Married with children
- Quantitative
- Adversarial
- Careerist
- Individualistic
- Experience in competitive team sports
- In control
- Military veteran
- Age 35–49
- Competitive
- Protestant or Jewish
- College graduate
- Tall
- Heterosexual
- Predictable
- Excellent physical condition
- Willing to relocate

SOURCE: Marilyn Loden and Judy B. Rosener, *Workforce America! Managing Employee Diversity as a Vital Resource* (Homewood, Ill.: Business One Irwin, 1991), p. 43. Copyright © 1991 by Business One Irwin. Used with permission.

increase costs because of absenteeism, turnover, and EEO and harassment suits; and lower morale among workers.[10]

Benefits of Valuing Diversity   Valuing diversity means ending the assumption that assimilation is required for all nondominant group members. It is not easily accomplished in most organizations. Ending assimilation is not just an ideal, a necessary evil, developing a level of tolerance for those who are different, or the latest fad. It is an opportunity to develop and use all of the human resources available to the organization for the benefit of the workers as well as the organization.

Valuing diversity is not just the right thing to do for workers, it is the right thing to do for the organization, financially and economically. One of the most important benefits is the richness of the ideas and perspectives available within the organization. When diversity is valued, rather than relying on the homogeneous dominant group for new ideas and alternative solutions to increasingly complex problems, more perspectives on the problem are available and more issues are considered. Entirely new solutions can result that may develop a new product, open new markets, or improve service to existing customers.

A worker who is valued by the organization will be more creative, more productive, and more committed to accomplishing the goals of the organization. In addition to personal commitment and morale, there is usually less interpersonal conflict among employees because employees understand each other. When employees of different cultural groups, backgrounds, and values understand each other better, there is a greater sense of teamwork, identification with the team and the organization, and commitment to the organization. Overall, the organization wins when diversity is valued within the organization.

Dimensions of Diversity

Race and gender were considered the primary dimensions of diversity during the past two decades. The earliest civil rights laws were aimed at correcting racial segregation. Other laws have dealt with discrimination on the basis of gender, age, and disability. Diversity, however, includes more than just these dimensions. In the largest sense, workforce diversity refers to all of the ways that employees differ. The focus of the valuing diversity movement is on utilizing all of the differences among workers for the benefit of the workers and the organization. To organize our discussion, however, we have divided the many different dimensions of diversity into primary and secondary dimensions.

Primary Dimensions of Diversity

The primary dimensions of diversity include those factors that either are inborn or exert extraordinary influence on early socialization. These include age, ethnicity, gender, physical abilities, race, and sexual orientation.[11] These are factors that make up the essence of who we are as human beings. They define us to others and, because of how

---

10. Lennie Copeland, "Making the Most of Cultural Differences at the Workplace," *Personnel*, June 1988, pp. 52–60.
11. Loden and Rosener, *Workforce America!* p. 19.

Valuing diversity means ending the assumption that assimilation is required for all nondominant group members.

The primary dimensions of diversity include those factors that either are inborn or exert extraordinary influence on early socialization: age, ethnicity, gender, physical abilities, race, and sexual orientation.

The workplace of the future will have to be flexible enough to accommodate an increasingly diverse work-force. As people of different ages and physical abilities, as well as those of different genders, ethnicities, and sexual preferences, work together, changes in equipment and in training methods that better accommodate diversity will be necessary.

others react to these factors about us, these factors define us to ourselves. These are considered enduring characteristics of our human personality, are not easily changed, and, thus, present extremely complex problems to managers. In this section, we highlight a few of the issues surrounding some of these primary dimensions.

Age The issue of the age of workers is multifaceted and very personal. As the United States' and the world's economy and labor productivity resume expected growth rates, the demand for labor is expected to grow at 2 percent annually. At the same time, the number of new entrants into the workforce is decreasing, and the overall age of the workforce is growing older as the "baby boomers" reach age 45. Thus, experienced workers older than age 50 will be at a premium, and the labor force participation rate for workers older than age 65 is expected to increase from 16 to 20 percent.[12] To add more complexity, more of the increase in older workers will be women, as the participation rate of women older than age 50 is increasing faster than that of men older than age 50.

These data indicate several areas that will require managerial attention. First, benefit packages may need to be changed to appeal to older workers. For example, with no children at home, family benefit packages may not be as attractive. Second, as the population ages, more people are living well into their 80s! A man who reaches age 65 is expected to live fourteen more years. A woman who reaches age 65 is expected to live another eighteen and a half years. Persons older than age 85 comprise the fastest-growing segment of the population.[13] Therefore, their children, who may be older than age 50 and still active in the workforce, may need to become primary caregivers for their elderly parents. Primary caregivers for the elderly present problems of increased stress, more unscheduled days off, more late arrivals and early departures, above-average use of telephones, and more absenteeism.

The older workers may need additional and different training in new technologies and equipment that will accommodate their special needs. As an example, consider

Changing workforce demographics means changing benefit packages, compensation systems, training programs, equipment, physical facilities, and other organizational processes.

12. Sar A. Levitan, "Older Workers in Today's Economy," presentation at the Textbook Authors Conference, Washington, D.C., October 21, 1992.
13. Beverly Hynes-Grace, "To Thrive, Not Merely Survive," presentation at the Textbook Authors Conference, Washington D.C., October 21, 1992.

the functioning of the eye. As people get older the amount of light that reaches the retina of the eye is reduced by about 50 percent because of the gradual yellowing of the lens. This also makes slight differences of shading of the colors of blue, green, and gray. The average 60-year-old needs two and a half times as much light to read comfortably as does the average 20-year-old.[14] Differences also exist in manual dexterity, auditory function, perception, cognition, strength, and agility. Managers will need to adjust physical facilities, equipment, and training methods to obtain maximum productivity from all of the workforce. In the past, little allowance was made for a worker who could not conform to the standard equipment and expectations of the workplace. In the future, the workplace will need to adjust to the diverse worker.

Race and Ethnicity   Racial and ethnic cultural differences may be more important than most managers initially realize. One way that these differences may be organized is to use the categories that were described in Chapter 19: individualism/collectivism, orientation toward authority, preference for stability, and assertiveness/materialism.[15] Table 20.2 summarizes these differences for ten different countries. Because of different countries' or cultures' values and beliefs, employees may be stereotyped on the basis of their race or ethnic heritage.

Gender   Much of the expected growth of the workforce—64 percent, according to Figure 20.2—by the year 2000 is expected to come primarily from women. This category was one of the first to be emphasized in the early attempts at equal

14. Ibid.
15. Geert Hofstede, *Culture's Consequences: International Differences in Work-Related Values* (Beverly Hills: Sage Publications, 1980); and Nancy J. Adler, *International Dimensions of Organizational Behavior*, 2nd ed. (Boston: PWS-Kent, 1991), pp. 46–47.

TABLE 20.2

Work-related Differences in Ten Countries

Country	Individualism/ Collectivism	Orientation to Authority	Preference for Stability	Assertiveness/ Materialism
Canada	H	M	M	M
Germany	M	M	M	M
Italy	H	M	M	H
Israel	M	L	M	M
Japan	M	M	H	H
Mexico	H	H	H	M
Pakistan	L	M	M	M
Sweden	H	M	L	L
United States	H	M	M	M
Venezuela	L	H	M	H

Note: H=high; M=moderate; L=low. These are only ten of the more than sixty countries that Hofstede and others have studied. Titles of the categories have been adapted from Hofstede's original titles to make them more easily understood.

SOURCE: Adapted from Geert Hofstede, "Motivation, Leadership, and Organization: Do American Theories Apply Abroad?" *Organizational Dynamics*, Summer 1980, pp. 42–63.

employment opportunity and affirmative action. Most organizations have always had at least some female employees. The issue now is that women currently hold more and different positions than secretary, nurse, teacher, and receptionist. Many companies discovered that women were in many other types of jobs and moving into more all the time. Apple Computer found in 1987 that more than 40 percent of its salesforce were women who were generating more than $1.5 billion in sales.[16] Managing this diverse salesforce was clearly important to the company. Xerox noted that its workforce changed significantly from 1978 to 1988. For example, women had increased from only 29 to 32 percent of the workforce, but the number of female managers had doubled from 10 to 20 percent, the number of female professionals had increased from 18 to 29 percent, and the number of women in the salesforce had almost doubled from 22 to 41 percent.[17] After these revelations, Xerox increased its efforts to move more women into sales, professional, and managerial jobs and developed programs to help all employees work together in the new diversity of its workforce.

Until recently, most managers assumed that women should be treated the same as men and that their reactions to issues were no different. Following a sales meeting, for example, men often go to the hotel bar for relaxation and the inevitable continuation of discussions. Women, however, often do not feel comfortable having social drinks with the men in the bar and, therefore, are often excluded from the continued discussions. Similar feelings arise when men leave a meeting to go to a golf club, many of which are off-limits to women. Situations such as these may keep women from valuable socialization processes necessary for groups to coordinate activities and accomplish goals and may be an unintended but systematic method of excluding women from top management positions. Companies have found simple solutions to some of these situations by having sales meetings in conference centers and bringing refreshments into the meeting rooms after the meetings so all can participate in the follow-up sessions. Hosting dinners in the conference center can also assist in keeping everyone involved after the formal meeting. Increasing numbers of women in the workforce means that there are different employees with different attitudes, backgrounds, and capabilities that need to be utilized, possibly in different ways than has been the norm in many organizations.

Physical Abilities   An often misunderstood group that is more diverse than any other includes those people who have abilities that are in some way limited when compared to those of the general population. These limitations include amputated or nonfunctioning limbs, limited or no eyesight or hearing, mental limitations of various kinds, and diseases such as multiple sclerosis.

The rights of these people are protected under the Americans with Disabilities Act and the Rehabilitation Act. First, employers cannot discriminate in any way regarding the employment of persons with disabilities, and furthermore, employers must make reasonable accommodations in the workplace to assist employees on the job. These workers are best referred to as "physically challenged" to indicate respect for the abilities that they have that make them unique and able to make valuable contributions to the organizations.[18]

16. Lennie Copeland, "Making the Most of Cultural Differences at the Workplace," *Personnel*, June 1988, pp. 52–60.
17. Charlene Marmer Solomon, "The Corporate Response to Work Force Diversity," *Personnel Journal*, August 1989, pp. 42–54.
18. Loden and Rosener, *Workforce America!* pp. 85–86.

People with disabilities are, for the most part, just like everyone else. They have to live, eat, sleep, and support themselves by working and—like everyone else—are often found to be excellent employees in jobs appropriate for their skill types and levels. Reasonable accommodations to allow people to work include equipment purchase or modification, job restructuring or reassignment, increasing the accessibility of facilities, and modifying work schedules and examination and training materials.[19] There is usually no one guaranteed way to make these accommodations. Each situation must be studied to determine the appropriate accommodations. One accommodation that is often important is the reaction of coworkers to the hiring of someone who has a disability. It may take some training and personal accommodation for the other members of the group to adjust.

Many companies have made major efforts to make the appropriate accommodations for differently abled workers. Lotus Development Corp. has a hiring program that works in conjunction with Greater Boston Rehabilitation Services to hire workers with disabilities in assembly, packing, and shipping departments. Lotus provides a shuttle bus to the plant from the local train station and provides job coaches, special equipment, and new training programs to ensure the success of each worker. In addition, other Lotus employees participate in awareness programs to ease the entry of the new workers into the company. Eastman Kodak's warehouse in Oak Brook, Illinois, includes five employees who are both deaf and mute. The order-filling accuracy of these employees—more than 99 percent—exceeds that of other employees. Special accommodations were made by placing them in an area that had no forklifts or other heavy equipment and by adding special telephones that use a keyboard and screen for communication.[20]

Sexual Orientation   Another dimension that may make some people uncomfortable but is receiving increasing attention in organizations is sexual orientation. It is estimated that 10 percent of the workforce is homosexual, and homosexuals are working in all types of industries, including finance, insurance, science, engineering, and computers.[21] Although some homosexuals are no longer trying to hide their sexual preference, many still feel that they must continue to keep it a secret. A California judge recently ordered a Shell Oil subsidiary to pay $5.3 million in damages to a worker who was fired because of his homosexuality.[22] On the other hand, some companies such as Levi Strauss, Apple Computer, Digital Equipment Corp., Boeing, Du Pont, and Xerox have lesbian and gay groups that openly hold meetings, orientation sessions, and special gay pride weeks. As open as some companies have become, however, many people still complain that a glass ceiling exists for managers ready to advance to executive positions. Regardless of a company's comfort level, tolerance, and openness, managers of the future will have workers who may have different sexual orientation than themselves.

19. Richard L. Drach, "Making Reasonable Accommodations under the ADA," *Employment Relations Today*, Summer 1992, pp. 167–175.
20. Toby B. Gooley, "Ready, Willing, and Able!" *Traffic Management*, October 1993, pp. 63–67.
21. Thomas A. Stewart, "Gay in Corporate America," *Fortune*, December 16, 1991, pp. 42–56.
22. Ibid., p. 45.

Secondary Dimensions of Diversity

Secondary dimensions of diversity include factors that are important to us as individuals and to some extent define us to others but are less permanent and can be adapted or changed. These include educational background, geographic location, income, marital status, military experience, parental status, religious beliefs, and work experience.

These factors may exert just as much impact on our lives as the primary dimensions. Many veterans of the Vietnam war, for example, were profoundly affected by their experiences serving in that devastating war. The impact of these secondary dimensions may differ at various times in our lives, also. For example, moving to another part of the country or world may be a traumatic experience that requires notable adjustment, followed by several years of outstanding work performance. The ages and stages of childhood growth and development may affect some employees more than others. For example, a manager who has not raised children may not understand the sudden increase in telephone calls, tardiness, or absenteeism caused by a major illness of an employee's child.

Employees enter the workforce with unique experiences and backgrounds that affect their perspective of work rules, expectations of work, and personal concerns, as discussed in more detail in Chapter 3. Although employees may have essentially the same work hours, job description, tenure with the company, and compensation, their reactions to the work situation may differ notably because of the primary and secondary dimensions of diversity

Individual Behavior and Diversity

Diversity in the workforce will have many effects on employees and managers. Many of these effects are on the individual aspects of organizational behavior, which we discuss in Part 2.

Diversity and the Foundations of Individual Behavior

As we discuss earlier and in Chapter 3, the process of stereotyping is a major problem in dealing with diversity. If managers stereotype older workers as unable to work or untrainable, then hiring and training programs may overlook a valuable segment of the workforce. Motor skills, especially speed, begin to decline between the ages of 27 and 30 but can continue at acceptable work levels well into a worker's 60s.[23] Machines, which can be run by workers of any age, now do much of the heavy lifting in many companies. Older workers may also be able to pace their work better by working smarter rather than manually lifting everything in short bursts of speed. In either case, stereotyping the older worker as unsuitable in the machine shop may markedly reduce the pool of available workers and rob many workers of the opportunity to work.

23. Robert J. Paul and James B. Townsend, "Managing the Older Worker—Don't Just Rinse Away the Gray," *Academy of Management Executive*, August 1993, pp. 67–74.

Secondary dimensions of diversity include factors that are important to us as individuals and to some extent define us to others but are less permanent and can be adapted or changed: educational background, geographic location, income, marital status, military experience, parental status, religious beliefs, and work experience.

Stereotyping older workers as not motivated and unwilling to learn is likewise inaccurate. Training programs for workers of all ages were first established by the Manpower Development and Training Act of 1962. Since that time studies have shown that older workers have a higher completion rate than younger workers and consistently have jobs within one year of completion.[24]

The development of prejudices against those who are different or prejudices in favor of those who are similar also can become major stumbling blocks for managers. Objective performance appraisals, promotion systems, and compensation systems may be threatened when managers are biased against workers from a particular ethnic, age, or gender group. In the selection of new employees, a manager who may not understand the values and beliefs of a whole class of potential workers who happen to be different could result in eliminating an entire group of potentially good workers. In interpersonal relations between coworkers the dimensions of diversity may prevent the building of lasting relationships. In effect, the primary and secondary dimensions of diversity can serve as roadblocks to mutual understanding, trust, and effective communication.

Diversity and Motivation

If the manager of a diverse workforce assumes that workers have similar needs and designs a reward system accordingly, workers may not respond in the way that the manager expects.

Many theories of motivation that were developed in a unique culture may not be universally applicable. The need theories of motivation, for example, discussed in Chapter 4, assume that workers are motivated to satisfy certain needs. If the manager of a diverse workforce assumes that workers have similar needs and designs a reward system accordingly, some of the workers may not respond in the way that the manager expects. For example, workers in highly collectivist cultures such as Pakistan's tend to emphasize social needs over the more individualistic ego and personal goal accomplishment needs.[25] Other approaches to motivation, discussed in Chapters 5 and 6, suggest that behavior is initiated and reinforced in certain ways. However, people with different beliefs and values, experience, education, or physical abilities may value different outcomes and have different beliefs regarding effort, performance, rewards, and equity in the workplace. Thus, consideration for the diversity of the workforce is important to understanding many aspects of organizational behavior.

Interpersonal Processes and Diversity

Interpersonal processes that are notably affected by diversity issues include group dynamics, leadership, and communication.

Interpersonal processes in organizations include group dynamics, leadership, and communication and are markedly affected by diversity issues. Diverse groups function differently than others. Leaders must take into account the makeup of the group in determining leadership practices. And the exchange of meaning is more difficult when sender and receiver have different backgrounds. In this section all of these three areas are discussed in terms of the impact of diversity in the workforce.

24. Ibid., p. 70.
25. Adler, *International Dimensions of Organizational Behavior*, p. 153.

Diverse Work Groups

As we discuss in Chapter 11, groups that differ notably on major characteristics are called heterogeneous. Therefore, a culturally mixed work group will have the characteristics and performance tendencies of heterogeneous groups. If, however, a group has only one member who is markedly different from the other members (i.e., only one woman), the group might be called a **token group**. The tendency of token groups is to expect the token member to conform to the behaviors and attitudes of the dominant group. Many organizations are currently attempting to focus more attention on the contributions of token members.[26]

Groups in which the membership is approximately equally divided between two groups are called **bicultural groups**. Bicultural groups must recognize and integrate the perspectives of both sets of members. A **multicultural group** is fully heterogeneous and has membership that represents more than two diverse segments.

The effects of diversity on group processes depend on two factors: the type of tasks that the group must perform and the early socialization processes that serve to integrate the diverse members and contribute to cohesiveness within the group. Homogeneous groups easily become cohesive. On tasks that require physical performance and cooperation among group members, the early socialization is very important to the eventual performance of the group. In addition, because performance often depends on the most effective allocation of tasks to member skills, diversity may affect member perception of skills and their proper matching with tasks to be performed. On intellectual, or cognitively based, tasks that require cooperative problem solving, a heterogeneous and culturally diverse group may perform quite well. On idea-generation and decision-making tasks, a culturally diverse group may be able to add significantly more perspectives and thus help the group generate more ideas. This may depend on the quality of the early socialization process, which can help a diverse group recognize their differences and be more tolerant of the different perspectives.

In general, more cohesive groups tend to outperform less cohesive groups. At the same time, heterogeneous groups tend to be less cohesive than homogeneous groups. Early socialization processes that involve more interactions over time can be notably helpful in establishing the cohesiveness necessary for a diverse group to reach its performance potential.[27]

*A **token group** has only one member different from the dominant group and usually expects the token member to conform to behaviors and attitudes of the dominant group. A **bicultural group's** membership is approximately equally divided between two groups. A **multicultural group** is fully heterogeneous and has membership that represents more than two diverse segments.*

Leadership and Diversity

As we discuss in Chapters 12 and 13, leadership is the process of social influence. The diversity of the work group has major impact on how the leader exerts influence on followers. The theories of leadership discussed in earlier chapters note how leaders often adapt their behaviors to the situation and the particular needs of the group. The diversity of the group is one important aspect of the group and the situation.

One way in which diversity is important is in the expectations that employees have of the leader. Employees from cultures that have a high orientation to

The diversity of the group is one important aspect of the group and the situation that a leader must consider when making leadership decisions.

---

26. Ibid., p. 127.
27. Warren E. Watson, Kamalesh Kumar, and Larry K. Michaelsen, "Cultural Diversity's Impact on Interaction Process and Performance: Comparing Homogeneous and Diverse Task Groups," *Academy of Management Journal*, June 1993, pp. 590–602.

The early socialization processes that serve to integrate diverse members of a group are vital to the group's ultimate performance. Although homogeneous groups tend to cohere more quickly, heterogeneous groups, such as this one at New York's law firm of Shearman and Sterling, have a great ability to generate ideas and add new perspectives to decision-making processes.

authority such as Mexico and Venezuela may expect the leader to make all the decisions and tell the followers what to do. On the other hand, other employees may expect the leader to share decision making. Thus, in a multicultural work team, the leader may have difficulty in satisfying both sets of expectations. Older workers may also have a different set of expectations of the leader than do younger workers, thus creating a difficult situation for the leader.

Interpersonal Communication and Diversity

Interpersonal communication within a diverse workforce can be extremely difficult because even when the native language is the same, employees from different cultures may often assign different meanings to the same word.

Interpersonal communication within a diverse workforce can be extremely difficult. Even when the native language is the same (i.e., English in the United States compared to English in Great Britain), employees from different cultures may often assign different meanings to the same word. Symbols of respect differ from generation to generation. To the older worker, "Yes, sir" and "No, sir" convey respect, and "Yeah" and "Nah" indicate a lack of respect. The younger worker may not see the difference in the two styles of speaking. Communication difficulties may also arise when employees speak a different language than their supervisor, as described in *The Ethical Dilemma*.

The purpose of communication is to convey a meaning or an idea to another person by encoding the message into symbols, sending the symbols through a medium, and decoding the symbols into a message by the receiver in the presence of noise and interference. Clearly, diversity can create problems at many places in this process. When employees with diverse backgrounds encode and decode differently, the intended message may not be understood. As we caution in Chapter 14, overcoming communication problems requires that both sender and receiver pay close attention to each other, the symbols, the medium, and the possible noise and interference.

To Tagalog or Not at Pomona Valley Hospital

Immigrants will make up 22 percent of the growth in the labor force in the United States through the year 2000. Along with their cultures, values, and beliefs they bring their native languages, most of which are not English. A growing issue is the extent to which a language other than English can be spoken at work.

Filipinos are the largest ethnic Asian group in the United States, many of whom live in California. Some have been in the United States for many years, as has Adelaida Dimaranan, an assistant head nurse at Pomona Valley Hospital Medical Center. Dimaranan and her fellow Filipino nurses often spoke their native language, Tagalog, while on break, on personal time, on the phone with family, and occasionally and unintentionally on the job. After Dimaranan had worked at the hospital for ten years, a new supervisor ruled that she could no longer speak Tagalog at work.

Dimaranan and her Filipino coworkers claimed that they were more comfortable speaking Tagalog among themselves, and sometimes Tagalog just came out. The supervisor objected to her violation of the rule and demoted her and transferred her to another department. Dimaranan felt humiliated and that she could no longer feel like a Filipino and sued the hospital. When mediation failed, the American Civil Liberties Union and the Asian Pacific American Legal Center filed suit for her, alleging a violation of Title VII of the Civil Rights Act of 1964, based on discrimination on the basis of race or national origin.

The issue is more than a legal one, however. Should employers require that employees speak English? If so, when and under what circumstances? When employees gather and speak their native language among themselves, possibly highly animated with laughter, does the supervisor think the laughter is at her or his expense? Should this be allowed? Or should only job-related speech be regulated? To what extent are the employees' identity and character stripped away by not allowing them to speak their native language?

In the legal case, a U.S. district judge ruled that the hospital's rule was not discriminatory but was an effort to improve patient care. In addition, the hospital was ordered to reinstate Dimaranan to a comparable position, give her back pay, and remove any negative evaluations from her personnel file. Both sides decided to appeal. How would you rule, as the judge and as hospital management?

SOURCES: Norman Sklarewitz, "American Firms Lash Out at Foreign Tongues," *Business and Society Review*, Fall 1992, pp. 24–28; "Appeals of Discrimination Ruling Expected," *Modern Healthcare*, November 18, 1991, p. 26; Julie Solomon, "Firms Grapple with Language," *Wall Street Journal*, November 7, 1989, pp. b1, b10; and Joe Schwartz, "Who's Ahead: Population Growth of Asian Ethnic Groups in the U.S.," *American Demographics*, April 1988, pp. 16–17.

Organizational Processes and Diversity

The organizational processes of organization structure and design, organization culture, and organization change and development are also affected by the diversity of the workforce. The ways that organizations set up systems to coordinate the work of employees must depend on the nature of the people who do the work. And naturally the culture of the organization is related to the culture of the country in which it operates. In addition, different cultures may prefer different types of change processes. In this section each of these areas is discussed in terms of the impact of diversity on the workforce.

Organization Structure and Diversity

As we discuss in Chapter 15, organization structure is the system of task, reporting, and authority relationships within which the work of the organization gets done and includes the hierarchy of authority, chain of command, rules and procedures, and decision making within the organization. All of these characteristics are affected by the diversity of the workforce.

Employees from countries that have a high orientation to authority may be most comfortable in a mechanistic organization structure with strict rules and procedures. Other employees may prefer a loose organization structure in which decision making is decentralized, few rules and procedures exist, and activities are diverse and unpredictable. This is more than just a preference: employees who expect the organization to dictate work rules and exercise major authority over the work of employees may be extremely uncomfortable and unable to perform their jobs in an organic structure with few rules and procedures and decentralized decision making. An employee from Sweden, where organizations are decentralized and more loosely organized, who goes to work in a country such as Italy, where companies are highly centralized and have more work rules, might have trouble understanding the system and might violate the rules when she or he makes a decision without asking for higher-level approval.

Organization Culture and Diversity

Organization culture, discussed in Chapter 17, plays an important role in how workforce diversity is managed. Because organization culture is essentially the way that things are done in an organization, it reflects some of the major aspects of the country of which it is a part. Although there are some differences among organizations within a country, just as there are differences among people within a country, a company tends to reflect the values and beliefs of the country in which it does its dominant work or in which it was founded. Orientation to authority, time, uncertainty, and collective action are typically shared within a culture. Therefore, organization culture tends to vary similarly.

Some organization cultures are closed to new and different ideas as well as employees. This type of culture may tend to assimilate diverse employees into the existing culture and get them to become like the dominant group. On the other hand, some cultures are more open to differences among employees and may even seek to establish an open organization culture. Employees who are different from the dominant group might be encouraged to seek out companies that value diversity in the workforce. Considering the statistics discussed earlier in this chapter, all organizations will have an increasingly diverse workforce in the future and should begin to develop an organization culture that values diversity.

Organization Change and Diversity

Making major changes in the organization—whether it be in the reward systems, the leadership, the organization structure, or the organization culture—requires major attention to the change process. This involves making employees aware of the need to change the organization or its culture, overcoming the resistance to change that will inevitably occur, and rewarding those who contribute to making the change. Employees who have a high preference for stability, such as those from Mexico or Japan, may resist the change. To properly address this type of resistance, managers must be able to evaluate the various sources of resistance to change. When top management knows that the preference for stability differs for a certain segment of the workforce, it might be able to develop a specific communication program to address the difficulties created by the differences in cultural factors. As in all major organization changes, managers need to pay close attention to the differences in the workforce and the reasons for those differences in planning change.

Managing the Multicultural Organization

In a **multicultural organization**, employees of mixed backgrounds, experiences, and cultures can contribute and achieve their fullest potential for the benefit of themselves and the organization.

Taking advantage of diversity in the various parts of the organizational system is a difficult challenge full of opportunities. It is more than just announcing that the organization values diversity. It requires that management develop a **multicultural organization** in which employees of mixed backgrounds, experiences, and cultures can contribute and can achieve their fullest potential for the benefit of themselves and the organization. Management must plan for managing diversity throughout the organization and work hard to implement the plan. Developing a program for managing diversity is the subject of the last section of this chapter.

The Multicultural Organization as Competitive Advantage

A company begins to better manage its diverse workforce usually for one (or more) of three reasons. First, some companies are forced into developing ways to better manage their increasingly diverse workforce because of affirmative action. That is, companies such as Xerox realize that their employees are increasingly different, mostly because of affirmative action efforts. Second, other companies, such as Digital Equipment and Hewlett-Packard, develop a sense of urgency to respond to various constituencies after they grow very quickly to remain competitive. A third group of companies such as Avon Products need to have a diverse workforce to match the diversity in the marketplace. So, for all three reasons, companies have a diverse workforce and are developing ways to manage it.[28] They feel the need to better manage the workforce by developing a multicultural organization to obtain or maintain competitive advantage in the marketplace.

Diversity is to be highly valued and effectively managed not only because it is the socially responsible thing to do. Business leaders, consultants, and academic scholars contend that the multicultural organization also can create competitive

28. Bill Leonard, "Ways to Make Diversity Programs Work," *HR Magazine*, April 1991, pp. 37–39, 98.

A multicultural organization can be one important factor in the development of competitive advantage for the company for six reasons: cost, resource acquisition, marketing, creativity, problem solving, and organizational flexibility.

advantage.[29] Competitive advantage can be created in the six ways shown in Table 20.3: cost, resource acquisition, marketing, creativity, problem solving, and organizational flexibility.

Because the workforce is becoming more diverse, the companies that value and integrate diverse employees the fastest and the best will be able to realize their contributions the most. Decreased personnel costs and the improvement of the quality of personnel are two obvious benefits for the company. In addition, the benefits of the inclusion of diverse perspectives in problem solving, decision making, creativity, and product development and marketing activities are essential to creating competitive advantage in the increasingly dynamic global marketplace.

Creating the Multicultural Organization

Creating the multicultural organization utilizes extensive training programs in diversity awareness, language and cultures, conflict management, and bias reduction.

The multicultural organization has six characteristics: pluralism, full structural integration, full integration of informal networks, an absence of prejudice and discrimination, equal identification with organizational goals for majority and minority groups, and low levels of intergroup conflict.[30] Developing the multicultural organization requires a commitment on the part of top management and a clear vision of the benefits of the multicultural organization for the future of the organization. For a multicultural organization to achieve each of these positive characteristics, specific activities are required, as shown in Table 20.4.

29. Taylor H. Cox and Stacy Blake, "Managing Cultural Diversity: Implications for Organizational Competitiveness," *Academy of Management Executive*, August 1991, pp. 45–56.
30. Taylor H. Cox, "The Multicultural Organization," *Academy of Management Executive*, May 1991, pp. 34–47.

TABLE 20.3

Six Ways That Managing Diversity Can Create Competitive Advantage

Advantage	Contribution
Cost	Trim the costs of integrating diverse workers.
Resource Acquisition	Companies that have the best reputation for managing diverse employees will have the best chance of hiring the best available diverse personnel.
Marketing	Increased insight and cultural sensitivity will improve the development and marketing of products and services for diverse segments of the population.
Creativity	Diversity of perspectives will improve levels of creativity throughout the organization.
Problem Solving	Problem solving and decision making will improve through groups with more diverse perspectives.
System Flexibility	Tolerance and valuing of diverse perspectives throughout the organization will make the organization more fluid, more flexible, and more responsive to environmental changes.

SOURCE: Adapted from Taylor H. Cox and Stacy Blake, "Managing Cultural Diversity: Implications for Organizational Competitiveness," *Academy of Management Executive*, August 1991, p. 47.

TABLE 20.4

Creating the Multicultural Organization: Above All—Top Management Support Throughout!!

Characteristic	Tools
Pluralism	Training and orientation programs, ensuring minority group input, putting diversity into mission statements
Full Structural Integration	Education, training, affirmative action, performance appraisal and reward systems, benefits, work schedules
Integration of Formal Networks	Mentoring, social events, support groups
Absence of Prejudice	EEO seminars, focus groups, bias-reduction training programs, task forces
Equal Identification with Goals	Input of minority group into mission, goals, and strategies
Minimal Intergroup Conflict	Survey feedback, conflict reduction training

SOURCE: Adapted from Taylor Cox, Jr., "The Multicultural Organization," *Academy of Management Executive*, May 1991, p. 41.

A **pluralistic organization** has heterogeneous membership and takes steps to achieve the full participation and integration of people who are different from the organization's dominant group.

Using focus groups, networks, minority groups, and mentoring; involving minority groups in mission, goal, and strategy sessions; creating mixed-culture social events; and changing reward systems, benefits, and work schedules can also assist in the development of a multicultural organization.

A **pluralistic organization** has heterogeneous membership and takes steps to achieve the full participation and integration of people who are different from the organization's dominant group. Creating pluralism requires training and orientation programs that increase awareness of cultural differences and build skills for working together. Programs that describe how people of various ages and genders are both different and similar can be included in new employee orientation programs and in programs for existing employees. Language and culture training can help employees in the dominant group better understand people from different cultures. Companies such as Motorola and Pace Foods offer language training on company time and at company expense.

Minority group input into the organization can be accomplished in several ways. First, minority representation should be included in regular meetings at all levels. For example, members of racial, ethnic, education, and geographic groups are represented at *USA Today*'s daily news meetings.[31] Second, the organization must foster the development of minority advisory groups that meet regularly to discuss organizational issues and are consulted by top management on important issues. Organizations can also foster pluralism throughout the organization by explicitly stating that pluralism is an integral part of the organization in its mission statements and strategic policies.

Creating full structural integration requires that minority group members are represented at all levels, functions, and work groups. This requires that education and skills be equally distributed throughout all levels, functions, and work groups. Therefore, organizations will need to be active in supporting and developing educational programs and skill building at all levels. Organizations must also be active in hiring and in promoting minority group members into positions at all levels and functions.

31. Ibid., p. 42.

Performance measurement and reward systems, discussed in Chapter 8, must also be changed to promote full structural integration. This requires measuring the extent to which managers incorporate multiculturalism into their work groups and hire and promote in a multicultural manner. In addition, these behaviors will need to be rewarded through the formal organizational reward system. Benefit plans and work schedules will also need to be altered to accommodate differences in employee family situations, needs, and values.

Creating integration in informal networks requires establishing mentoring programs, creating special social events, and developing support groups for minority groups. Such special groups and events might be viewed as creating more differences, but in practice they have had the opposite effect. They provide outlets for minority groups to express their cultural identity and share part of themselves with dominant groups. Dominant group members then are better able to understand the cultural heritage and traditions of minority members.

Creating a bias-free organization can be accomplished by several means. Equal opportunity seminars have been used to increase awareness among employees for quite a while. In addition, organizations are using in-house focus groups to examine attitudes and beliefs about cultural differences and organizational practices. Bias-reduction training programs are one- or two-day workshops designed to help employees identify and begin to modify negative attitudes toward people who are different. These programs usually include exercises and role plays that expose stereotypes about minority group members and help build the skills to eliminate biased views. Another way to move toward a bias-free organization is to create task forces that monitor organizational policies and practices for evidence of unfairness. Such task forces must be composed of members from all levels, functions, and minority groups to ensure a balanced view and the commitment of top management.

Ensuring that all groups develop a sense of identity with the organization's mission, goals, and strategies comes about as a result of all of the tools and techniques already discussed. When members of different groups participate fully in developing the organization's direction and how it intends to get there (that is, its mission, goals, and strategies), there is more understanding of the organization and their places in it. Through training programs, mentoring programs, support groups, social events, and bias-free organization practices, employees who are different from the dominant group can become an integral part of the organization.

Minimizing intergroup conflict can be accomplished in several ways. As we discuss in Chapter 9, a form of conflict can be considered healthy if it stimulates creativity in problem solving and decision making. However, conflict that is based on cultural differences and divides employees along cultural lines is unhealthy and detrimental to the multicultural organization. Survey feedback processes can be used to expose beliefs and attitudes toward others and to measure the success of the multicultural effort. The feedback to all relevant groups is important to ensure openness throughout the organization. Special training in conflict resolution has also been shown to be effective in helping managers learn the skills of mediation and listening that are so important to managing conflict.

Taken together as an integrated program, these activities can help management create a truly multicultural organization. The transition to a multicultural organization is neither easy nor quick. However, its benefits can help the organization achieve the competitive advantage necessary for success.

Summary of Key Points

- Workforce diversity is the differences in people, such as in age, gender, ethnic heritage, physical ability/disability, race, and sexual orientation, that make up the employees of organizations. Managers of diverse work groups need to know about people, to understand how their social conditioning affects their beliefs about work, and to have the communication skills to develop confidence and self-esteem among diverse work groups. Stereotypes, which are judgments made about others that reinforce a superiority/inferiority belief system and can lead to exaggerating the worth of one group while diminishing the worth of others, can lead to the dangerous process of prejudice. Management systems built on stereotypes and prejudices can then be inappropriate for a diverse workforce. Employment statistics provide one perspective for understanding the radically different workforce of the future.

- The focus of the valuing diversity movement is on utilizing all of the differences among workers for the benefit of the workers and the organization. The many different dimensions of diversity can be categorized into primary and secondary dimensions of diversity. The primary dimensions of diversity are those factors that either are inborn or exert extraordinary influence on early socialization and include age, ethnicity, gender, physical abilities, race, and sexual orientation. Secondary dimensions of diversity include factors that are important to us as individuals and to some extent define us to others but are less permanent and can be adapted or changed: educational background, geographic location, income, marital status, military experience, parental status, religious beliefs, and work experience.

- Diversity in the workforce will have many effects on the individual aspects of organizational behavior. The processes of stereotyping can lead to prejudging those who are different from the dominant group, and these processes become a major problem in dealing with others. Many theories of motivation were developed in a unique culture and may not be universally applicable, especially the need theories of motivation.

- Interpersonal processes in organizations include group dynamics, leadership, and communication and are markedly affected by diversity issues. Diverse groups function differently than others. Leaders must take into account the makeup of the group in determining leadership practices. And the exchange of meaning is more difficult when sender and receiver have different backgrounds.

- The diversity of the workforce may also affect the processes and characteristics of the organization. Employees who have a high orientation to authority may be most comfortable in a mechanistic organization structure with strict rules and procedures. Other employees may prefer a loose organization structure in which decision making is decentralized, few rules and procedures exist, and activities are diverse and unpredictable.

- A multicultural organization is one in which employees of mixed backgrounds, experiences, and cultures can contribute and can achieve their fullest potential for the benefit of themselves and the organization. Developing a multicultural organization can be an important step in managing a diverse workforce and may be crucial to obtaining and maintaining competitive advantage in the marketplace. A multicultural organization has six characteristics: pluralism, full structural integration, full integration of informal networks, an absence of prejudice and discrimination, equal identification with organizational goals for majority and minority groups, and low levels of intergroup conflict.

Discussion Questions

1. Why does an organization need to be interested in managing diversity? Is it a legal obligation, a moral obligation, or something else?
2. Summarize in your own words what the statistics tell us about the workforce of the future.
3. What is the difference between assimilating minority groups and valuing diversity in organizations?
4. What are the two major differences in the primary and secondary dimensions of diversity? Which particular dimension seems to you to be the most difficult to deal with in organizations?
5. Discuss three ways that managing individual behavior in organizations is affected by diversity issues.
6. Describe the token group, the bicultural group, and the multicultural group, and describe the different ways that productivity may be affected for each. How does early socialization affect the productivity of the different types of groups?
7. How is interpersonal communication affected by cultural diversity? Describe an example.
8. Why might employees from different countries or cultural backgrounds prefer different organizational structures? Give two examples that illustrate these preferences.
9. Why does the multicultural organization contribute to competitive advantage for the organization?
10. What are the characteristics of a multicultural organization?
11. Discuss three techniques that can contribute to the development of a multicultural organization.

EXPERIENTIAL EXERCISE

Purpose   This exercise will help you better understand your own stereotypes and attitudes toward others.

Format   You will be asked to evaluate a situation and the assumptions you make in doing so. Then you will compare your results with those of the rest of the class.

1. Read the situation to yourself, and decide who it is that is standing at your door and why you believe it to be that person. Make some notes as to your rationale for eliminating the other possibilities and selecting the one that you did. Answer the Follow-up Questions.
2. Working in small groups or with the class as a whole, discuss who might be standing at your door and why you believe it to be that person. Using the grid at the end of this exercise, record the responses of class members.
3. In class discussion, consider the stereotypes used to reach a decision, and consider the following:
    a. How hard was it to let go of your original decision once you had made it?
    b. What implications do first impressions of people have about how you treat them, the expectations you have of them, and whether the acquaintance is likely to go beyond the initial stage?
    c. What implications do your responses to these questions have about how you, as a manager, might treat a new employee? What will the impact be on that employee?
    d. What are the implications for yourself in terms of job hunting and so forth?

Situation You have just checked into a hospital room for some minor surgery the next day. When you get to your room, you are told that the following people will be coming to speak with you within the next several hours:

1. The surgeon who will do the operation
2. A nurse
3. The secretary for the department of surgery
4. A representative of the company that supplies televisions to the hospital rooms
5. A technician who does laboratory tests
6. A hospital business manager
7. The dietician

You have never met any of these people before and don't know what to expect.

About half an hour after your arrival, a woman who seems to be of Asian ancestry appears at your door dressed in a straight red wool skirt, a pink-and-white-striped polyester blouse with a bow at the neck, and red medium-high-heeled shoes that match the skirt. She is wearing gold earrings, a gold chain necklace, a gold wedding band, and a white hospital laboratory coat. She is carrying a clipboard.

Follow-up Questions

1. Of the seven people listed, which of them is standing at your door? How did you reach this conclusion?
2. If the woman had not been wearing a white hospital laboratory coat, how might your perceptions of her have differed? Why?
3. If you find out that she is the surgeon who will be operating on you in the morning, and you thought initially that she was someone different, how confident do you now feel in her ability as a surgeon? Why?

SOURCE: Adapted from *OB in Action: Cases and Exercises* by Janet W. Wohlberg and Scott Weighart (Boston: Houghton Mifflin, ©1992), pp. 31–33.

	Reasons	Number who make this selection
Surgeon		
Nurse		
Secretary		
Television Representative		
Laboratory Technician		
Business Manager		
Dietician		

Valuing Diversity at Digital Equipment Corp.

Digital Equipment Corp. is recognized as one of the leaders in the field of managing diversity. Its program began in the 1970s as a combination of its Equal Employment Opportunity and Affirmative Action programs and its corporate values. For years, in an effort to be fair and treat everyone the same, managers did not discuss the issues of race and gender at work. Women and minorities were treated the same as the white men, the dominant group throughout most of the company. An employee attitude survey regarding management practices showed that women and minorities were very uncomfortable about how they were treated.

Once employees began to talk to each other about their differences, people throughout the company realized that there were important differences among employee groups that needed to be discussed. In the early 1980s, the director of EEO and Affirmative Action established core groups of senior and district managers to openly discuss what the differences were and what the value of diversity might be at Digital. The resulting "Valuing Differences" program was initially aimed at the differences between women and minorities and the dominant group. Discussions slowly evolved to the point that participants realized that everyone is different in some way. Gradually, people of both genders and all races and ethnicities were included in the discussion groups. People of all types began to feel less alienated and more involved in the company.

In 1985, Digital institutionalized the core groups in the "Valuing Differences" program, and they meet at least four hours each month. It established the Affirmative Action University to teach employees

how to become leaders in the area of valuing differences. In addition, more than 4,000 persons annually complete the "Understanding the Dynamics of Difference" program to help employees understand the behavioral and business implications of a diverse workforce.

These programs include the following features: stripping away stereotypes, learning to listen for differences, building relationships, enhancing personal empowerment, and exploring group differences. The company is now developing ways to measure the contribution of the valuing diversity programs to the bottom line of the company. Employees know that it has made a lot of difference, especially in making Digital a more comfortable place to work.

Case Questions

1. Compare the features of Digital's programs to the characteristics of a multicultural organization.
2. How have the programs evolved over the past two decades?
3. What do you think will be the next phase of its valuing diversity programs?

SOURCES: Barbara Mandell and Susan Kohler-Gray, "Management Development That Values Diversity," *Personnel*, March 1990, pp. 41–47; Stephenie Overman, "Managing the Diverse Work Force," *HR Magazine*, April 1991, pp. 32–36; Charlene Marmer Solomon, "The Corporate Response to Work Force Diversity," *Personnel Journal*, August 1989, pp. 42–54; Lennie Copeland, "Making the Most of Cultural Differences at the Workplace," *Personnel*, June 1988, pp. 53–60; and Kimberly Blanton, "Utilizing Human Resources at DEC," *Boston Globe*, Special Section: Working Together: Exploring Diversity in the Workplace, March 7, 1994, pp. 12, 14.

Diversity on the Search Committee

Joe Don Barker had been assigned the task of putting together a search committee for the new head of the county's Library and Media Systems Department. He knew that selecting the new head of the department would be especially important because the recent bond issue provided the money for new buildings and media

systems throughout the county, and the head would be responsible for spending the bond money wisely. The citizens and taxpayers of the county would be watchdogs every step of the way and over each penny. Department employees would also keep a close eye on the process because their jobs were at stake.

He knew that he needed a committee that could work well together under the pressures of media attention, taxpayer scrutiny, and employee self-interests. He thought that the committee needed to have members with diverse backgrounds and represent the many constituency and special interest groups within the department. Media services had only recently been added to the library department, on the advice of a consultant who convinced someone in county government that library and media services belonged together. He knew that the media services added new technology and skill requirements that the current department did not have.

Here is how he broke down the requirements for the committee: one African American, one Hispanic American, one Asian American, one woman, at least one-fourth of the committee from internal library staff, at least one-fourth from the general citizenship of the county, at least one-fourth from other related departments in the county government, at least one person with some type of physical disability, at least one student high school level or younger, at least one person 55 years of age or older, at least one administrator from approximately the same level in the hierarchy that the new head would be, at least one specialist in the new field of library and media systems, and one person specially trained in affirmative action laws to ensure compliance with legalities. His boss had instructed him to keep the total membership to ten persons or fewer. He had no idea what he was going to do. The way he counted, with all of the requirements, the committee could have as many as fourteen members if he were not careful.

He feared that members of minority groups were being overworked by being the token representative on every committee. He worried that such a diverse group would get sidetracked too easily by special interests. He was also concerned that he could not find anyone for the committee who knows the area of media systems.

Case Questions

1. Do you think Joe Don's worries have merit? Which one will cause the most problems for the committee? Why?
2. Describe the tradeoffs between having an extremely diverse committee and having a committee that is very homogeneous.

Research Methods in Organizational Behavior

T hroughout this book, we referred to theories and research findings as a basis for our discussion. In this appendix, we further examine how theories and research findings are developed. First, we highlight the role of theory and research. Then we identify the purposes of research and describe the steps in the research process, types of research designs, and methods of gathering data. We conclude with a brief discussion of some related issues.

The Role of Theory and Research

Some managers—and many students—fail to see the need for research. They seem confused by what appears to be an endless litany of theories and by sets of contradictory research findings. They often ask, "Why bother?"

Indeed, few absolute truths have emerged from studies of organizational behavior. Management in general and organizational behavior in particular, however, are in many ways fields of study still in their infancy. Thus, it stands to reason that researchers in these fields have few theories that always work. In addition, their research cannot always be generalized to settings other than those in which it was originally conducted.

Still, theory and research play valuable roles.[1] Theories help investigators organize what they do know. They provide a framework that managers can use to diagnose problems and implement changes. They also serve as road signs that help managers solve many problems involving people. Research too plays an important role. Each study conducted and published adds a little more to the storehouse of knowledge available to practicing managers. Questions are posed and answers developed. Over time, researchers can become increasingly confident in findings as they are applied across different settings.[2]

Purposes of Research

Scientific research is the systematic investigation of hypothesized propositions about the relationships among natural phenomena.

Basic research involves discovering new knowledge rather than solving specific problems.

As much as possible, researchers try to approach problems and questions of organizational behavior scientifically. **Scientific research** is the systematic investigation of hypothesized propositions about the relationships among natural phenomena. The aims of science are to describe, explain, and predict phenomena.[3] Research can be classified as basic or applied. **Basic research** is concerned with discovering new knowledge rather than solving particular problems. The knowledge made available through basic research may not have much direct application to organizations, at least when it is first discovered.[4] Research scientists and university professors are the people who most often conduct basic research in organizational behavior.

1. Jeffrey Pfeffer, "The Theory-Practice Gap: Myth or Reality?" *Academy of Management Executive*, February 1987, pp. 31–33.
2. Eugene Stone, *Research Methods in Organizational Behavior* (Santa Monica, Calif.: Goodyear, 1978).
3. Fred N. Kerlinger, *Foundations of Behavioral Research*, 3rd ed. (New York: Holt, Rinehart & Winston, 1987).
4. Richard L. Daft, Ricky W. Griffin, and Valerie Yates, "Retrospective Accounts of Research Factors Associated with Significant and Not-So-Significant Research Outcomes," *Academy of Management Journal*, December 1987, pp. 763–785.

Applied research is conducted to solve particular problems or answer specific questions.

Applied research, on the other hand, is conducted to solve particular problems or answer specific questions. The findings of applied research are, by definition, immediately applicable to managers. Consultants, university professors, and managers themselves conduct much of the applied research performed in organizations.

The Research Process

To result in valid findings, research should be conducted according to the scientific process shown in Figure A1.1. The starting point is a question or problem.[5] For example, a manager wants to design a new reward system to enhance employee motivation but is unsure about what types of rewards to offer or how to tie them to performance. This manager's questions therefore are "What kinds of rewards will motivate my employees?" and "How should those rewards be tied to performance?"

The next step is to review the literature to determine what is already known about the phenomenon. Something has quite likely been written about most problems or questions today's managers face. Thus, the goal of the literature review is to avoid "reinventing the wheel" by finding out what others have already learned. Basic research generally is available in journals such as the *Academy of Management Journal, Academy of Management Review, Administrative Science Quarterly, Journal of Applied Psychology, Organizational Behavior and Human Decision Processes, Journal of Management*, and *Organization Science*. Applied research findings are more likely to be found in sources such as the *Harvard Business Review, Academy of Management Executive, Organizational Dynamics, HR Magazine*, and *Personnel Psychology*.

5. Richard L. Daft, "Learning the Craft of Organizational Research," *Academy of Management Review*, October 1983, pp. 539–546.

FIGURE A1.1
The Research Process

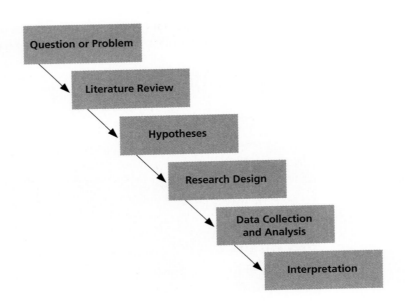

Based on the original question and the review of the literature, researchers formulate hypotheses—statements of what they expect to find. The hypothesis is an important guide for the researcher's design of the study because it provides a very clear and precise statement of what the researcher wants to test. That means that study can be specifically designed to test the hypothesis.

The research design is the plan for doing the research. (We discuss the more common research designs later.) As part of the research design, the researcher must determine how variables will be measured. Thus, if satisfaction is one factor being considered, the researcher must decide how to measure it.

After data have been collected, they must be analyzed. (We also discuss common methods for gathering data later.) Depending on the study design and hypotheses, data analysis may be relatively simple and straightforward or require elaborate statistical procedures. Methods for analyzing data are beyond the scope of this discussion.

Finally, the results of the study are interpreted; that is, the researcher figures out what they mean. They may provide support for the hypothesis, fail to support the hypothesis, or suggest a relationship other than that proposed in the hypothesis. An important part of the interpretation process is recognizing the limitations imposed on the findings by weaknesses in the research design.

Some researchers go a step further and try to publish their findings. Several potential sources for publication are the journals mentioned in the discussion of literature review. Publication is important because it helps educate other researchers and managers and also provides additional information for future literature reviews.[6]

Types of Research Designs

A **research design** is the set of procedures used to test the predicted relationships among natural phenomena.

A **research design** is the set of procedures used to test the predicted relationships among natural phenomena. The design addresses issues such as how the relevant variables are to be defined, measured, and related to one another. Managers and researchers can draw on a variety of research designs, each with its own strengths and weaknesses. Four general types of research designs often are used in the study of organizational behavior (see Table A1.1); each type has several variations.[7]

6. Larry L. Cummings and Peter Frost, *Publishing in Organizational Sciences* (Homewood, Ill.: Irwin, 1985).
7. D. T. Campbell and J. C. Stanley, *Experimental and Quasi-Experimental Designs for Research* (Chicago: Rand McNally, 1963).

TABLE A1.1

Types of Research Designs

Type	Dominant Characteristic
Case Study	Useful for thorough exploration of unknown phenomena
Field Survey	Provides easily quantifiable data
Laboratory Experiment	Allows researcher high control of variables
Field Experiment	Takes place in realistic setting

Case Study

A **case study** in an in-depth analysis of one setting.

A **case study** is an in-depth analysis of a single setting. This design frequently is used when little is known about the phenomena being studied and the researcher wants to look at relevant concepts intensively and thoroughly. A variety of methods are used to gather information, including interviews, questionnaires, and personal observation.[8]

The case study research design offers several advantages. First, it allows the researcher to probe one situation in detail, yielding a wealth of descriptive and explanatory information. The case study also facilitates the discovery of unexpected relationships. Because the researcher observes virtually everything that happens in a given situation, she or he may learn about issues beyond those originally chosen for study.

The case study design also has several disadvantages. The data it provides cannot be readily generalized to other situations because the information is so closely tied to the situation studied. In addition, case study information may be biased by the researcher's closeness to the situation. Case study research also tends to be very time consuming.

Nevertheless, the case study can be an effective and useful research design as long as the researcher understands its limitations and takes them into account when formulating conclusions.

Field Survey

A **field survey** typically relies on a questionnaire distributed to a sample of people selected from a larger population.

A **field survey** usually relies on a questionnaire distributed to a sample of people chosen from a larger population. If a manager is conducting the study, the sample often is drawn from a group or department within her or his organization. If a researcher is conducting the study, the sample typically is negotiated with a host organization interested in the questions being addressed. The questionnaire generally is mailed or delivered by hand to participants at home or at work and may be returned by mail or picked up by the researcher. The respondents answer the questions and return the questionnaire as directed. The researcher analyzes the responses and tries to make inferences about the larger population from the representative sample.[9]

Field surveys can focus on a variety of topics relevant to organizational behavior, including employees' attitudes toward other people (such as leaders and coworkers), attitudes toward their jobs (such as satisfaction with the job and commitment to the organization), and perceptions of organizational characteristics (such as the challenge inherent in the job and the degree of decentralization in the organization).[10]

Field surveys provide information about a much larger segment of the population than do case studies. They also provide an abundance of data in easily quantifiable form, which facilitates statistical analysis and the compilation of normative data for comparative purposes.

8. R. Yin and K. Heald, "Using the Case Study Method to Analyze Policy Studies," *Administrative Science Quarterly*, June 1975, pp. 371–381.
9. Kerlinger, *Foundations of Behavioral Research*.
10. Ramon J. Aldag and Timothy M. Stearns, "Issues in Research Methodology," *Journal of Management*, June 1988, pp. 253–276.

Field surveys also have several disadvantages. First, survey information may reveal only superficial feelings and reactions to situations rather than deeply held feelings, attitudes, or emotions. Second, the design and development of field surveys require a great deal of expertise and can be very time consuming. Further-more, relationships among variables tend to be accentuated in responses to questionnaires because of what is called *common method variance*. This means that people tend to answer all the questions in the same way, creating a misleading impression. Finally—and very important—field surveys give the researcher little or no control. The researcher may lack control over who completes the questionnaire, when it is filled out, the mental or physical state of the respondent, and many other important conditions. Thus, the typical field survey has many inherent sources of potential error.[11]

Nonetheless, surveys can be a very useful means of gathering large quantities of data and assessing general patterns of relationships among variables.

Laboratory Experiment

A **laboratory experiment** involves creating an artificial setting similar to a real work situation to allow control over almost every possible factor in that setting.

The **laboratory experiment** gives the researcher the most control. By creating an artificial setting similar to a real work situation, the researcher can control almost every possible factor in that setting. He or she can manipulate the variables in the study and examine their effects on other variables.[12]

As an example of how laboratory experiments work, consider the relationship between how goals are developed for subordinates and the subordinates' subsequent level of satisfaction. To explore this relationship, the researcher structures a situation in which some subjects (usually students but occasionally people hired or recruited from the community) are assigned goals while others determine their own goals. Both groups then work on a hypothetical task relevant to the goals, and afterward all subjects fill out a questionnaire designed to measure satisfaction. Differences in satisfaction between the two groups could be attributed to the method used for goal setting.

Laboratory experiments prevent some of the problems of other types of research. Advantages include a high degree of control over variables and precise measurement of variables. A major disadvantage is the lack of realism; rarely does the laboratory setting exactly duplicate the real-life situation. A related problem is the difficulty in generalizing the findings to organizational settings. Finally, some organizational situations, such as plant closings or employee firings, cannot be simulated in a laboratory.

Field Experiment

A **field experiment** is similar to a laboratory experiment but is conducted in a real organization.

A **field experiment** is similar to a laboratory experiment except that it is conducted in a real organization. In a field experiment, the researcher attempts to control certain variables and manipulate others to assess the effects of the manipulated variables on outcome variables. For example, a manager interested in the

---

11. See C. A. Schriesheim et al., "Improving Construct Measurement in Management," *Journal of Management*, Summer 1993, pp. 385–418.
12. Cynthia D. Fisher, "Laboratory Experiments," in Thomas S. Bateman and Gerald R. Ferris (Eds.), *Method and Analysis in Organizational Research* (Reston, Va.: Reston, 1984); and Edwin Locke (Ed.), *Generalizing from Laboratory to Field Settings* (Lexington, Mass.: Lexington Books, 1986).

effects of flexible working hours on absenteeism and turnover might design a field experiment in which one plant adopts a flexible work schedule program and another plant, as similar as possible to the first, serves as a control site. Attendance and turnover are monitored at both plants. If attendance increases and turnover decreases in the experimental plant and there are no changes at the control site, the manager probably will conclude that the flexible work schedule program was successful.

The field experiment has certain advantages over the laboratory experiment. The organizational setting provides greater realism, making generalization to other organizational situations more valid. Disadvantages include the lack of control over other events that might occur in the organizational setting (such as additional changes the firm introduces), contamination of the results if the various groups discover their respective roles in the experiment and behave differently because of that knowledge, greater expense, and the risk that the experimental manipulations will contribute to problems within the company.

Methods of Gathering Data

Data-gathering methods may be grouped into four categories: questionnaires, interviews, observation, and nonreactive measures.

The method of gathering data is a critical concern of the research design. Data-gathering methods may be grouped into four categories: questionnaires, interviews, observation, and nonreactive measures.[13]

Questionnaires

A *questionnaire* is a collection of written questions about the respondents' attitudes, opinions, perceptions, and/or demographic characteristics. Usually the respondent fills out the questionnaire and returns it to the researcher. To facilitate scoring, the researcher typically uses multiple-choice questions. Some questionnaires have a few open-ended questions that allow respondents to elaborate on their answers. Designing a questionnaire that will provide the information the researcher desires is a very complex task and one that has received considerable attention.

Interviews

An *interview* resembles a questionnaire, but the questions are presented to the respondent orally by an interviewer. The respondent usually is allowed to answer questions spontaneously rather than asked to choose among alternatives defined by the researcher. Interviews generally take much more time to administer than questionnaires, and they are more difficult to score. The benefit of interviews is the opportunity for the respondent to speak at length on a topic, thereby providing a richness and depth of information not normally yielded by questionnaires.

13. Stone, *Research Methods in Organizational Behavior.*

Observation

Observation, in its simplest form, is watching events and recording what is observed. Researchers use several types of observation. In structured observation, the observer is trained to look for and record certain activities or types of events. In participant observation, the trained observer actually participates in the organizational events as a member of the work team and records impressions and observations in a diary or daily log. In hidden observation, the trained observer is not visible to the subjects. A hidden camera or a specially designed observation room may be used.

Nonreactive Measures

When a situation is changed because of data gathering, we say the activity has caused a reaction in the situation. *Nonreactive*, or unobtrusive, *measures* have been developed for gathering data without disturbing the situation being studied. When questionnaires, interviews, and obtrusive observations may cause problems in the research situation, the use of nonreactive measures may be an appropriate substitute. Nonreactive measures include examination of physical traces, use of archives, and simple observation. At some universities, for example, sidewalks are not laid down around a new building until it has been in use for some time. Rather than ask students and faculty about their traffic patterns or try to anticipate them, the designers observe the building in use, see where the grass is most heavily worn, and put sidewalks there.

Related Issues in Research

Three other issues important to research are causality, reliability and validity, and ethical concerns.

Three other issues are of particular interest to researchers: causality, reliability and validity, and ethical concerns.[14]

Causality

Scientific research attempts to describe, explain, and predict phenomena. In many cases, the purpose of the research is to reveal causality; that is, researchers attempt to describe, explain, and predict the cause of a certain event. In everyday life, people commonly observe a series of events and infer causality about the relationship among them. For example, you might observe that a good friend is skipping one of her classes regularly. You also know that she is failing that class. You might infer that she is failing the class because of her poor attendance. But the causal relationship may be just the reverse: your friend may have had a good attendance record until her poor performance on the first test destroyed her motivation and led her to stop attending class. Given the complexities associated with human behavior in organizational settings, the issues of causality, causal inference, and causal relations are of considerable interest to managers and researchers alike.

14. Philip M. Podsakoff and Dan R. Dalton, "Research Methodology in Organizational Studies," *Journal of Management*, Summer 1987, pp. 419–441.

In the behavioral sciences, causality is difficult to determine because of the interrelationships among variables in a social system. Causality cannot always be empirically proven, but it may be possible to infer causality in certain circumstances. In general, two conditions must be met for causality to be attributed to an observed relationship among variables. The first is temporal order: if x causes y, then x must occur before y. Many studies, especially field surveys, describe the degree of association among variables with highly sophisticated mathematical techniques, but inferring a causal relationship is difficult because the variables are measured at the same point in time. On the basis of such evidence, we cannot say whether one variable or event caused the other, whether they were both caused by another variable, or whether they are totally independent of each other.

The second condition is the elimination of spuriousness. If we want to infer that x caused y, we must eliminate all other possible causes of y. Often a seemingly causal relationship between two variables may be due to their joint association with a third variable, z. To be able to say the relationship between x and y is causal, we must rule out z as a possible cause of y. In the behavioral sciences, so many variables may influence one another that tracing causal relationships is like walking in an endless maze. Yet despite the difficulties of the task, we must continue trying to describe, explain, and predict social phenomena in organizational settings if we are to advance our understanding of organizational behavior.[15]

Reliability and Validity

The **reliability** of a measure is the extent to which it is
consistent over time.

The **reliability** of a measure is the extent to which it is consistent over time. Suppose that a researcher measures a group's job satisfaction today with a questionnaire and then measures the same thing in two months. Assuming nothing has changed, individual responses should be very similar. If they are, the measure can be assessed as having a high level of reliability. Likewise, if question 2 and question 10 ask about the same thing, responses to these questions should be consistent. If measures lack reliability, little confidence can be placed in the results they provide.

Validity is the extent to
which a measure actually
reflects what it was intended
to measure.

Validity describes the extent to which research measures what it was intended to measure. Suppose that a researcher is interested in employees' satisfaction with their jobs. To determine this, he asks them a series of questions about their pay, supervisors, and working conditions. He then averages their answers and uses the average to represent job satisfaction. We might argue that this is not a valid measure. Pay, supervision, and working conditions, for example, may be unrelated to the job itself. Thus, the researcher has obtained data that do not mean what he thinks they mean—they are not valid. The researcher, then, must use measures that are valid as well as reliable.[16]

Ethical Concerns

Last, but certainly not least, the researcher must contend with ethical concerns. Two concerns are particularly important.[17] First, the researcher must provide ade-

15. Stone, *Research Methods in Organizational Behavior*.
16. Kerlinger, *Foundations of Behavioral Research*.
17. Mary Ann Von Glinow, "Ethical Issues in Organizational Behavior," *Academy of Management Newsletter*, March 1985, pp. 1–3.

quate protection for participants in the study and not violate their privacy without their permission. For example, suppose that a researcher is studying the behavior of a group of operating employees. A good way to increase people's willingness to participate is to promise that their identities will not be revealed. Having made such a guarantee, the researcher is obligated to keep it.

Likewise, participation should be voluntary. All prospective subjects should have the right to not participate or to withdraw their participation after the study has begun. The researchers should explain all procedures in advance to participants and should not subject them to any experimental conditions that could harm them either physically or psychologically. Many government agencies, universities, and professional associations have developed guidelines for researchers to use to guarantee protection of human subjects.

The other issue involves how the researcher reports the results. In particular, it is important that research procedures and methods be reported faithfully and candidly. This enables readers to assess for themselves the validity of the results reported. It also allows others to do a better job of replicating (repeating) the study, perhaps with a different sample, to learn more about how its findings generalize.

Career
Dynamics

Baby boomers are finally moving up the corporate ladder, having now moved into middle management. The problem is that the people of the following generation, often called the busters, do not like working for the boomers. In fact, the busters are leaving the corporate world for small businesses, often starting their own.[1] Career paths are not what they used to be. As every company downsizes, reengineers, and rethinks the corporation, there are fewer jobs in the middle and at the top, so fewer opportunities to climb the ladder. Many of the boomers have also become disillusioned with their middle-level management position and resigned. Many managers have quit their jobs for a variety of personal and professional reasons. Some finally discover that they are in the wrong occupation. After a long career in corporate finance with numerous companies, Douglas Flaherty admitted that if he had it all to do over again, he would have gone to medical school.[2] In a recent study initiated by Robert Half International, vice presidents and human resources directors from one hundred of the nation's top one thousand corporations estimated that 24.3 percent of employees (that is, almost one of four workers) are unhappy or unsuccessful (or both) because they are in the wrong occupation or profession.[3] This means that nearly 30 million people are unhappy in their jobs. The impact on organizational productivity is immense. Clearly, if this problem is to be solved, both individuals and organizations need to know more about careers, career choices, and career management.

Almost one-fourth of U.S. workers are dissatisfied with their occupations.

Why are so many people dissatisfied with their jobs and careers? How can organizations help employees pursue the careers that offer the greatest benefit to both employees and the organization? Why do many people change not only their jobs but the type of work they do several times during their work lives? How can organizations ensure that when employees leave the company, by either quitting or retiring, they will be quickly and efficiently replaced by highly qualified people? The issues reflected in these questions have led organizations to invest large amounts of money, time, and effort in developing career management programs. In addition, researchers have begun to systematically study careers.

In this appendix, we examine individual and organizational perspectives on careers. We describe several aspects of career choices. Then we explore the career stages and conclude by discussing organizational career planning.

Individual and Organizational Perspectives on Careers

People often use the word "career" to refer to professional occupations of others and not to their own work or job. Indeed, many people do not even expect to have careers, they expect to have jobs.[4] A **career** is a "perceived sequence of atti-

---

1. Suneel Ratan, "Generational Tension in the Office: Why Busters Hate the Boomers," *Fortune,* October 4, 1993, pp. 56–70.
2. "Stars of 1962: How the Top Students at Harvard Business School Fare 20 Years Later," *Wall Street Journal,* December 20, 1982, pp. 1, 12.
3. *Banker's Digest,* June 22, 1987, p. 8.
4. M. W. McCall and E. E. Lawler III, "High School Students' Perceptions of Work," *Academy of Management Journal,* March 1976, pp. 17–24.

tudes and behaviors associated with work-related experiences and activities over
the span of the person's life."[5] Whereas a job is what a person does at work to
bring home a paycheck, a career means being engaged in a satisfying and productive activity.[6] Thus, a career involves a long-term view of a series of jobs and
work experiences.

Individuals may have personal interests in careers, specifically their own. As people evaluate job opportunities, those with a career perspective usually are concerned with factors such as those listed in Table A2.1. Note how these concerns
have a long-term perspective: concerns for the future of technological change,
economic conditions, and personal advancement. Many individuals see opportunities for advancement slowing as more people enter popular career fields. They see
the rate of technical obsolescence accelerating with the advent of new and better
computers and automated manufacturing processes. Individuals trying to establish
their careers may have serious concerns when the rate of economic growth is
declining. Individuals also perceive that new entrants are treated better than people already in the labor market—getting higher starting salaries, better opportunities, and the like. Furthermore, companies are reorganizing and downsizing,
which is increasing uncertainty and decreasing opportunities for advancement.
Finally, aging is a concern; as people get older, their career options frequently narrow and their opportunities shrink.[7]

Organizations have a different perspective on careers.[8] They want to ensure that
managerial succession is orderly and efficient so that when managers need to be
replaced because of promotion, retirement, accident or illness, termination, or resignation, they can be replaced quickly and easily by highly qualified people.

5. D. T. Hall, *Careers in Organizations* (Santa Monica, Calif.: Goodyear, 1976), p. 4.
6. M. Breidenbach, *Career Development: Taking Charge of Your Career* (Englewood Cliffs, N.J.: Prentice-Hall,
1988).
7. "Stable Cycles of Executive Careers Shattered by Upheaval in Business," *Wall Street Journal*, May 26, 1987, p. 31.
8. D. B. Miller, *Careers '79* (Saratoga, Calif.: Vitality Associates, 1979).

TABLE A2.1

**Individual Career
Issues**

Career Issues	Examples
Opportunity for advancement slowing	More people entering popular careers
Technical obsolescence accelerating	Rapidly changing automation, computerization
Rate of economic growth declining	Economy not expanding, fewer jobs created
New entrants into the labor market receiving more favorable treatment	Higher starting salaries and prerequisites for new hires
Companies reorganizing	Downsizing, reducing layers of middle management
Aging	Career options narrow, fewer opportunities

SOURCE: Adapted from C. Hymowitz, "Stable Cycles of Executive Careers Shattered by Upheaval in
Business," *Wall Street Journal*, May 26, 1987, p. 31. Reprinted by permission of *The Wall Street Journal*,
©1987 Dow Jones & Company, Inc. All rights Reserved Worldwide.

Organizations also want their employees to pursue careers in which they are interested and for which they have been properly trained. If individuals are unhappy with their career choices and opportunities, they may not perform well or may choose to leave the organization. Thus, organizations have an investment in ensuring that people-career matches will achieve high levels of performance and lower levels of turnover.

Clearly, although their perspectives are not identical, individual employees and organizations can benefit from working together to improve career management. Career choices, however, remain in the hands of individuals.

Career Choices

Career choices arise more than once during a lifetime because both people and career opportunities change. People need not be "locked in" to a particular career choice. Knowing that a change can be made should help individuals avoid becoming poor performers in their jobs as a result of career frustration.

Career choices are not something to take lightly, however; they are important in their own right and form the basis for future career decisions. As Figure A2.1 indicates, making a career choice involves six steps. First, an individual must become aware that a career choice is needed. This awareness may come about in a variety of ways. A recent high-school graduate may recognize the need to make a choice after being urged to find a job or declare a college major. A person already pursuing a career may consider choosing a new one after receiving a negative performance evaluation, being turned down for a big promotion, or being fired or laid off.

Second, the individual must obtain information about himself or herself and about available career options. Personal interests, skills, abilities, and desires can be identified by self-reflection as well as by formal and informal consultation with others. In addition, information about the demands and rewards of various careers is available from numerous sources, including career counselors, placement officers, friends, and family.

Career advisors and counselors can help people find and analyze career information, but the ultimate career decision must be made by the individual.

The third step in the career choice process involves evaluating the information and looking for matches between the wants and needs of the individual and the characteristics of potential careers. This can be a frustrating and confusing time as the person finds there are advantages as well as disadvantages to every career. Although the help of a competent adviser or counselor is valuable, the next step—the career decision—rests with the individual. In the fourth step, the individual must make a commitment to a career or a set of highly similar careers. Commitment means making the decision and initiating the next step implementation.

Implementing the decision involves actively pursuing the career; preparing through training, education, or internships; obtaining a position; and, finally, working. After a time, the individual must assess the choice. As long as the result of the assessment is satisfactory, the individual continues to pursue the career. If the conclusion is not satisfactory, the individual becomes aware of the need for another career choice, and the process begins again.

In making career decisions, people are subjected to a number of pressures. As indicated in Figure A2.2, these pressures may be personal, work-related, or social. An individual's personality and goals may be better suited to certain careers than

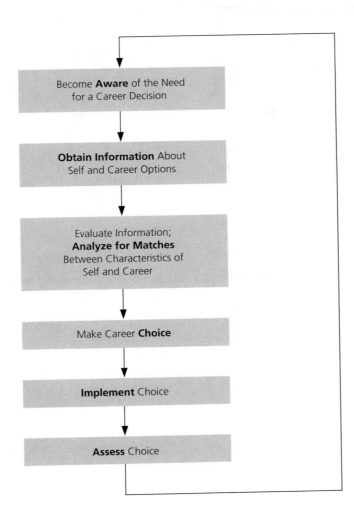

to others, and a lack of agreement between the types of careers that suit the person's personality and those appropriate to his or her personal goals can create internal conflicts.

Work-related factors can also create career-related pressures. A person's current position in an organization may open certain career options; other options may simply be unavailable to one in that position. This is true of some state government jobs; if one wants to run for political office, one must resign any other government job first. In addition to formal requirements, informal expectations are associated with most positions in organizations. Certain job and career-related behaviors may be expected from a person in a particular position, which usually will put pressure on the job holder to do the things expected. For example, coworkers may expect a colleague to seek managerial jobs to advance in the organization, whereas the person may enjoy her or his current position and not wish to move into management.

Social factors that create career pressure include urging from family or friends to quit a job or to take one job rather than another. Religious dictates can impose powerful career-related pressures on some individuals.

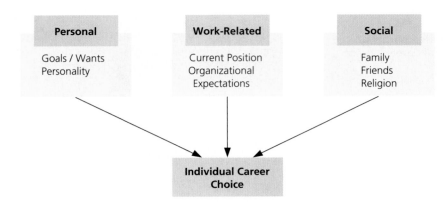

Choice of Occupation

An **occupation** is a group of jobs that are similar with respect to the type of tasks and training involved.

One major career choice confronting individuals is the choice of occupation. An **occupation**, or **occupational field**, is a group of jobs that are similar in terms of the type of tasks and training involved. Occupations usually are found in many different organizations, whereas jobs are organization specific. The United States Bureau of the Census identifies hundreds of occupations, including such diverse ones as accountant, auctioneer, baker, carpenter, cashier, dancer, embalmer, farmer, furrier, huckster, loom fixer, railroad conductor, receptionist, stock handler, waiter, weaver, and weigher.[9] Of course, these occupations are not equally appealing to people. Rankings of the desirability of occupations have shown a general stability. For instance, professions dominate the upper end of such evaluations. Physicians are nearly always among the occupations with the highest prestige, as are college and university professors, judges, and lawyers. The lowest-prestige occupations are more mixed. Bellhops, bootblacks, cleaners and janitorial workers, teamsters, and ushers are among those consistently low in prestige.

Theories that explain how people choose among the many occupations available to them emphasize either content or process.[10] Content theories deal with factors—prestige, pay, and working conditions, for example—that influence career decisions. Process theories, on the other hand, deal with how people make these decisions.

Content theories focus on six major factors that influence the occupations people choose:

1. Values and attitudes of the individual's family, especially parents[11]
2. Interests and needs[12]
3. Skills and abilities[13]
4. Education
5. General economic conditions
6. Political and social conditions

9. U.S. Bureau of the Census, *1980 Census of the Population: Alphabetical Index of Industries and Occupations* (Washington, D.C.: U.S. Government Printing Office, 1981).

10. D. C. Feldman, *Managing Careers in Organizations*, (Glenview, Ill.: Scott, Foresman, 1988), pp. 189–192.

11. P. M. Blau, J. W. Gustad, R. Jesson, H. S. Parnes, and R. C. Wilcox, "Occupational Choices: A Conceptual Framework," *Industrial and Labor Relations Review*, July 1956, pp. 531–543.

12. Hall, *Careers in Organizations;* and J. L. Holland, *Making Vocational Choices* (Englewood Cliffs, N.J.: Prentice-Hall, 1973).

13. D. C. Feldman and H. J. Arnold, "Personality Types and Career Patterns: Some Empirical Evidence on Holland's Model," *Canadian Journal of Administrative Science*, June 1985, pp. 192–210.

Process theories suggest that people make occupational choices in stages over time, seeking a match between their needs and their occupational demands. According to this approach, although people begin considering occupations when they are very young, their thinking evolves and becomes more specific over time.[14]

One process model of occupational choice has been proposed by J. L. Holland. According to Holland, there are six basic personality types—realistic, investigative, artistic, social, enterprising, and conventional—each of which is characterized by a set of preferences, interests, and values. Occupations can also be grouped: working with things, working with observations and data, working with people, working in very ordered ways, exercising power, and using self-expression.[15] As people evaluate occupations over time, they attempt to match their occupational activities to their personality types. Table A2.2 shows Holland's proposed matching between personality types and various occupational activities.

Another process model is similar to the expectancy model of motivation introduced in Chapter 5. This framework assumes that people base their occupational choices on their probability of success.[16] Thus, in an expectancy approach, a person uses information on the anticipated outcomes of being employed in a given occupation and the probability of obtaining those outcomes to try to assess the attractiveness of the occupation.

This process may be used in comparing two occupations. For example, some people face a new occupational choice after several years in their chosen field. From an expectation point of view, the person may attempt to compare the costs and benefits of remaining in his or her current field against the advantages and disadvantages of a new occupation. The costs may be the loss of things such as seniority, pension benefits, and earning power if extensive retraining is involved. Benefits may include higher long-term earnings, different lifestyles, and daily activities that seem inherently more enjoyable.

Choice of Organization

People must choose not only an occupation but an organization in which to pursue that occupation. This is an important choice because, for example, being an engineer for a municipal government may be far different from being an engineer for a private aerospace corporation. Indeed, some organizational differences—profit versus not-for-profit, large versus small, private versus governmental, and military versus nonmilitary, for instance—may be very important for the individual's ability to reach his or her goals and have a satisfying career.

Research suggests that in choosing an organization, individuals generally seek companies that can provide some minimally acceptable level of economic return—a sort of "base pay." Beyond that, the most frequently sought-after features of an organization involve the opportunity it offers the individual to engage in interest-

14. E. Ginzberg, S. W. Ginzberg, W. Axelrod, and J. L. Herna, *Occupational Choice: An Approach to a General Theory* (New York: Columbia University, 1951); and Hall, *Careers in Organizations.*
15. J. L. Holland, *Making Vocational Choices: A Theory of Careers* (Englewood Cliffs, N.J.: Prentice-Hall, 1973).
16. T. R. Mitchell and B. W. Knudsen, "Instrumentality Theory Predictions of Students' Attitudes toward Business and Their Choice of Business as an Occupation," *Academy of Management Journal*, March 1973, pp. 41–52; and S. L. Rynes and J. Lawler, "A Policy-Capturing Investigation of the Role of Expectancies in Decisions to Pursue Job Alternatives," *Journal of Applied Psychology*, November 1983, pp. 620–631.

Appendix 2   Career Dynamics

Realistic		
Personal characteristics		Shy, genuine, materialistic, persistent, stable
Sample occupations		Mechanical engineer, drill press operator, aircraft mechanic, dry cleaner, waitress
Investigative		
Personal characteristics		Analytical, cautious, curious, independent, introverted
Sample occupations		Economist, physicist, actuary, surgeon, electrical engineer
Artistic		
Personal characteristics		Disorderly, emotional, idealistic, imaginative, impulsive
Sample occupations		Journalist, drama teacher, advertising manager, interior decorator, architect
Social		
Personal characteristics		Cooperative, generous, helpful, sociable, understanding
Sample occupations		Interviewer, history teacher, counselor, social worker, clergy
Enterprising		
Personal characteristics		Adventurous, ambitious, energetic, domineering, self-confident
Sample occupations		Purchasing agent, real estate salesperson, market analyst, attorney, personnel manager
Conventional		
Personal characteristics		Efficient, obedient, practical, calm conscientious
Sample occupations		File clerk, CPA, typist, keypunch operator, teller

SOURCE: Table from *Career Management* by Jeffrey H. Greenhaus, copyright ©1987 by The Dryclen Press, reprinted by permission of the publisher. Adapted from J. L. Holland, *Making Vocational Choices: A Theory of Careers.* Englewood Cliffs, N.J.: Prentice Hall, 1973. Used with permission of the author.

ing, challenging, or novel activities.[17] The type and size of the organization, its reputation, and its geographic location do not seem as important to people making career choices as the level of economic return and the nature of the activities in which they can expect to engage.[18]

Changing Careers

As people change, grow older, and mature, they may need to reevaluate their careers and make new choices. Someone who dropped out of school early in life, for example, may decide the career options that resulted from that choice are no longer acceptable and may return to school to open up new career opportunities.

17. P. A. Renwick, E. E. Lawler III, and staff, "What You Really Want From Your Job," *Psychology Today*, May 1978, pp. 53–65.
18. D. C. Feldman and H. J. Arnold, "Position Choice: Comparing the Importance of Job and Organizational Factors," *Journal of Applied Psychology*, December 1978, pp. 706–710.

Life experiences may broaden a person's skills so that new career options become available. One increasingly popular career change option is to take one or more part-time jobs. Some research suggests that the part-time option may benefit the employee as well as the organization.[19]

Sometimes people find that as they have changed, their careers have changed. Although these people may not need to move from one occupation to another, some adaptation may be in order. Career adaptation may involve retraining to perform better on the job or to move to another job within the same career field. Adaptation may also mean changing organizations while pursuing the same career.

Career Stages

Career stages are the periods in which the person's work life is characterized by specific needs, concerns, tasks, and activities.

The gradual changes that occur over time in careers are called **career stages**, which are periods in which the individual's work life is characterized by distinctive needs, concerns, tasks, and activities. Career stages are closely associated with but not identical to the adult life stages identified by Erikson: adolescence, young adulthood, adulthood, and senescence.[20] As shown in Figure A2.3, there are five general career stages: entry, socialization, advancement, maintenance, and withdrawal.

Entry

The **entry stage (exploration stage)** is characterized by self-examination, role tryouts, and occupational exploration.

The **entry stage** is also known as the **exploration stage**. **Exploration** may be the more accurate label for the early part of the stage, in which self-examination, role

19. Ellen F. Jackofsky and Lawrence H. Peters, "Part-Time Versus Full-Time Employment Status Differences: A Replication and Extension," *Journal of Occupational Behaviour*, 8, 1987, 1–9.
20. E. H. Erikson, *Childhood and Society* (New York: Norton, 1963).

FIGURE A2.3
A Model of Career Stages

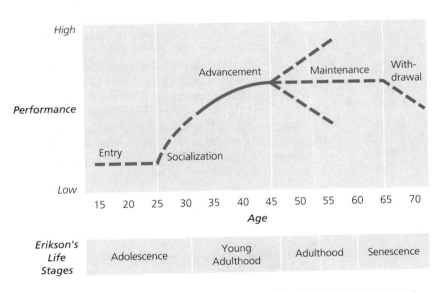

SOURCE: From *Careers in Organizations* by Douglas T. Hall. Copyright ©1976 by Scott, Foresman and Company. Reprinted by permission.

tryouts, and occupational exploration occur. Individuals in this stage are usually, but not necessarily, young. This is the stage during which education and training are most commonly pursued. During the latter part of the stage, the individual enters a career, albeit tentatively, by trying out jobs associated with the career. This trial period may involve many different jobs as the individual explores a variety of organizations, occupations, and careers. Performance during this stage is represented in Figure A2.3 as a dashed line to indicate unpredictability.[21]

Socialization

During the **socialization stage (establishment stage)**, individuals more specifically explore jobs, and performance begins to improve.

The **socialization stage** has also been called the **establishment stage**. It usually begins with a trial period (shown in the figure by a dashed line) during which the individual continues to explore jobs, but much more narrowly than before. Then, as the individual becomes focused on a specific job, performance begins to improve. The individual is becoming established in the career. The sequence of getting established has been found to consist of three phases: "getting in" (entry), "breaking in" (trial period), and "settling in" (establishment).[22]

During the socialization stage, people begin to form attachments and make commitments, both to others (new friends and coworkers) and to their employing organizations. Employees begin to learn the organization's goals, norms, values, and preferred ways of doing things; in other words, they learn the culture of the organization (see Chapter 17). In particular, they learn an appropriate set of role behaviors and develop work skills and abilities particular to their jobs and organizations. They begin to demonstrate that, at least to some degree, they are learning to accept the values and norms of the organization.[23]

During the socialization stage, individuals must make many adjustments. They must learn to accept that the organization and its people may be quite different from what they had anticipated. When they learn, for example, that other people do not appreciate their ideas, they must learn to handle such resistances to change. Employees must also be prepared to face dilemmas that involve making on-the-job decisions. Dilemmas may pit loyalties to the job, to good performance, to the boss, and to the organization against one another. Career dilemmas may also involve ethical considerations.[24]

An organization can take actions to ensure that the socialization stage is successful.[25] It can provide a relaxed orientation program for new personnel. It can see to it that the first job is challenging and that relevant training is provided. It can ensure that timely and reliable feedback is provided to people in this early stage of their careers. Finally, it can place new personnel in groups with high standards to encourage modeling of acceptable norms.

21. Hall, *Careers in Organizations.*
22. D. C. Feldman, "A Socialization Process That Helps New Recruits Succeed," *Personnel*, March–April 1980, pp. 11–23.
23. D. C. Feldman, "The Multiple Socialization of Organization Members," *Academy of Management Review*, April 1981, pp. 309–318.
24. E. Schein, *Career Dynamics: Matching Individual and Organizational Needs* (Reading, Mass.: Addison-Wesley, 1978); and R. A. Webber, "Career Problems of Young Managers," *California Management Review*, Summer 1976, pp. 19–33.
25. D. C. Feldman, "A Practical Program for Employee Socialization," *Organizational Dynamics*, Autumn 1976, pp. 64–80.

Advancement

In the **advancement stage (settling-down stage)**, the individual gets more recognition for improved performance.

The **advancement stage**, also known as the **settling-down stage**, evolves as the individual is recognized for the improved performance that comes with development and growth. The individual is learning his or her career and performing well in it. Soon he or she becomes less dependent on others.

As in the socialization stage, adjustments often are necessary within the advancement stage. Some individuals, of course, are less likely to make adjustments and learn than others. Those who are unsuccessful may change careers or adapt in another way—by job hopping. **Job hopping** occurs when individuals make fewer adjustments within organizations and instead move to different organizations to advance their careers. This practice is becoming more characteristic of the advancement stage. It has gained acceptance and increased in recent years as more organizations have used outsiders to replace important managers to improve organization performance.[26]

Job hopping occurs when an individual makes fewer adjustments within the organization and moves to different organizations to advance his or her career.

Vertical and horizontal, or lateral, movement also occurs frequently in the advancement stage. Vertical movement involves promotions, whereas lateral movement involves transfers. These kinds of movements teach people about various jobs in the organization, a broadening experience that can benefit both the individuals and the organization. Organizations meet their staffing needs through such movement, and individuals satisfy their needs for achievement and recognition.

Job moves, whether to a new organization or within the same organization, can cause problems, however. Invariably, higher-level jobs bring increased demands for performance, and frequently there is less preparation for managers moving into these jobs. They usually are expected to step right into top executive positions and perform well, with little time for socialization into a new system. Furthermore, moves often necessitate relocation to other parts of the country, placing stress on not only the job holder but also his or her family.

Organizations can take steps to manage promotions and transfers to reduce problems. Longer-term, careful career planning may reduce the need to relocate because much of the broadening may be accomplished at one location. The timing and spacing of moves can be coordinated with, or at least adjusted to, the individual's family situation. More important, better training can be provided to enable the individual to make the move more readily and with substantially less stress.

Maintenance

As people move into the **maintenance** and **withdrawal stages** of their careers, there are still many contributions they can make to the organization.

In the **maintenance stage**, individuals develop a stronger attachment to their organizations and, hence, lose some career flexibility. Performance varies considerably in this stage. It may continue to grow, level off, or decline. If performance continues to grow, this stage progresses as a direct extension of the advancement stage. If performance levels or drops, career changes may result.

If leveling off occurs, the individual is said to have reached a "plateau" in her or his career. Responses to plateauing can be effective or ineffective for the individual and the organization. Those who respond effectively to plateaus have been termed "solid citizens"; they have little chance for further advancement but continue to make valuable contributions to the organization. Those whose responses are inef-

---

26. "Should Companies Groom New Leaders or Buy Them?" *Business Week*, September 22, 1986, pp. 94–96.

fective are referred to as "deadwood"; they too have little chance for promotion, but they also contribute little to the organization.[27]

Solid citizens become interested in establishing and guiding the next generation of organization members. As a result, they frequently begin to act as mentors for younger people in the organization (we discuss mentoring later). As mentors, they show younger members the "ins and outs" of organization politics and help them learn the values and norms of the organization. These individuals also begin to reexamine their goals in life and rethink their long-term career plans. In some cases, this leads to new values (or the reemergence of older ones) that cause the individuals to quit their jobs or pass up chances for promotions.[28] In other cases, individuals achieve new insights and begin to move upward again; such individuals are known as "late bloomers."[29]

Individuals who have become deadwood are more difficult to deal with. Their knowledge, loyalty, and understanding of plateauing, however, represent value to the organization and could make them salvageable. Perhaps rewards other than advancement would keep these persons productive. Their jobs may be redesigned (see Chapters 7 and 18) to facilitate performance, or they may be reassigned within the organization. And, of course, career counseling programs (discussed later in this chapter) could help them reach a better understanding of their situations and opportunities.[30]

If performance declines, the individual may be experiencing some type of midlife crisis, which is associated with effects such as awareness of physical aging and the nearness of death, a reduction in career performance, the recognition that life goals may not be met, and changes in family and work relationships. Individuals handle midlife crises differently. Some develop new patterns for coping with the pressures of careers. They may change careers or modify the way that they are handling their current careers. Others have a more difficult time and may need professional assistance.

Changing jobs has become fairly common during the maintenance stage. Many such moves have proven highly beneficial to the person. Several "executive dropouts," for example, have become successful entrepreneurs, such as James L. Patterson, who left IBM to cofound Quantum Corp.[31] Of course, not all job changes at this stage lead to success. Some job changers find, much to their dismay, that the grass is not greener in the new job, and they experience just as much frustration and disappointment as they did in the old job.[32]

Withdrawal

The final stage—the **withdrawal**, or **decline**, stage—frequently involves the end of full-time employment as the individual faces retirement and other end-of-career options. Some individuals begin new careers at this stage and others level off, but the general pattern is one of decreasing performance. Again, individual adaptation

27. T. P. Ference, J. A. F. Stoner, and E. K. Warren, "Managing the Career Plateau," *Academy of Management Review*, October 1977, pp. 602–612.
28. D. LaBier, "Madness Stalks the Ladder Climbers," *Fortune*, September 1, 1986, pp. 79–84.
29. F. Rice, "Lessons from Late Bloomers," *Fortune*, August 31, 1987, pp. 87–91.
30. R. C. Payne, "Mid-Career Block," *Personnel Journal*, April 1984, pp. 38–48.
31. J. Main, "Breaking Out of the Company," *Fortune*, May 25, 1987, pp. 81–88.
32. "Crushed Hopes: When a New Job Proves to Be Something Different," *Wall Street Journal*, June 10, 1987, p. 27.

may be positive—beginning a new career, helping others, or learning to accept retirement—or negative—becoming indifferent, giving up, or developing abnormally high dependence on family and friends. Although legislation may restrict an organization's power to force retirement at age sixty-five, many individuals nevertheless quit full-time employment at about that age, and a number of organizations encourage even earlier retirement for many of their members. Problems may arise for people who are not prepared for the changes retirement brings. An individual who is not ready to retire or feels forced to do so may have an especially difficult time adapting to those changes. To help employees adjust, many organizations are initiating preretirement programs that include information on health, housing, financial planning, legal issues, time management, and social programs for maintaining involvement in the community.

Hall and Hall have argued that the use of the career growth cycle can help organizations manage careers, especially at this crucial stage.[33] The career growth cycle suggests that the organization should provide employees with challenging job goals, support, feedback, and proper counseling to foster career growth for employees. Initially, the organization ensures that jobs offer challenging goals and supports employees' efforts to achieve those goals. If feedback is positive, the employees experience psychological success, which enhances their self-esteem and leads to greater involvement. Less positive feedback, however—which people often receive in the withdrawal stage—has the opposite effect. In this instance, the organization provides counseling to help the individual adapt to the changing circumstances.

Mentoring

Mentoring occurs when an older, more experienced person helps a younger employee grow and advance by providing advice, support, and encouragement.

Mentoring programs can be an excellent way for an organization to help manage the career stages of its employees. **Mentoring** occurs when an older, more experienced person helps a younger individual grow and advance by providing advice, support, and encouragement. Despite some criticisms of formal mentoring programs, many organizations recently have implemented formal mentoring programs, and many others rely on more traditional informal networks. These companies believe that creating a bond between a senior and a junior employee helps both individuals and benefits the company as well. The mentor often gets in touch with the feelings and attitudes of a younger generation and can learn about new research and techniques from the protégé. The younger colleague can pick up practical skills from the mentor and also gain insights into the organization culture and philosophy that otherwise might take years to discover. A strong, secure bond between the two can lead one or both to do more innovative, important work than they might do on their own.[34]

For the company, this kind of bond can pay off in a number of ways. As the baby-boom generation ages, businesses have to try harder to find and keep good employees. An employee who feels secure in the company because of a good mentoring relationship is less likely to think about looking for another job. Mentors can be especially important for employees who might have trouble fitting into the

33. D. T. Hall and F. S. Hall, "What's New in Career Management," *Organizational Dynamics*, Summer 1976, pp. 17–33.
34. Dan Hurley, "The Mentor Mystique," *Psychology Today*, May 1988, pp. 39–43.

organization. To move up in a company dominated by an "old-boy" network, for instance, women and minority employees often need contacts of their own in the company's higher ranks. Similarly, multinational corporations may find mentors useful in helping managers from other countries fit into the culture of the corporation. Mentors can also help executives of merged companies adjust to the philosophies and expectations of their new employers.[35]

To get the most out of mentoring programs, experts say, companies must do more than just put two people together and hope for the best.[36] They need to determine the goals of the program: to teach specific skills, help new people get along with other employees, or introduce employees to corporate philosophies. Clarifying these goals should help the organization decide who will make the best mentors. Middle managers may be best at helping new people develop specific skills, whereas senior managers may be more effective at passing on the company's vision. In any case, an important element in any mentoring program is matching the two individuals, for the protégé needs to believe that he or she is gaining a friend rather than another boss.

Research into the career stages of people in organizations continues. A recent phenomenon among managers is the occurrence of gaps in career development. These may occur because of changing lifestyles, taking time off for childbearing and child rearing, and for a variety of other reasons. A recent study, however, showed that such career gaps seem to have more negative effects on the careers of men than on those of women.[37]

Organizational Career Planning

In **career planning**, individuals evaluate their abilities and interests, consider alternative career opportunities, establish career goals, and plan practical development activities.

Career planning is the process of planning one's life work and involves evaluating abilities and interests, considering alternative career opportunities, establishing career goals, and planning practical development activities.[38] Organizations have a vested interest in the careers of their members, and career planning and development programs help them enhance employees' job performance and thus the overall effectiveness of the organization.

Purposes of Career Planning

Organizational career planning programs can help companies identify qualified personnel and future managers, improve job satisfaction and other attitudes, increase involvement of important employees, and improve the vital match between individual and organizational wants and needs.[39] The purposes of career planning, then, involve ensuring that such enhanced individual and organizational performance occurs.

35. Michael G. Zey, "A Mentor for All Reasons," *Personnel Journal*, January 1988, pp. 47–51.
36. "Guidelines for Successful Mentoring," *Training*, December 1984, p. 125.
37. Joy A. Schneer and Frieda Reitman, "Effects of Employment Gaps on the Careers of M.B.A.'s: More Damaging for Men Than for Women," *Academy of Management Journal*, June 1990, pp. 391–406.
38. J. Walker, "Does Career Planning Rock the Boat?" *Human Resource Management*, Spring 1978, pp. 2–7.
39. C. S. Granrose and J. D. Portwood, "Matching Individual Career Plans and Organizational Career Management," *Academy of Management Journal*, December 1987, pp. 699–720.

Organizational career planning is a complex process involving many conflicting concerns that involve employees, the organization, and social issues.

Organizational career planning is a complex process involving many conflicting concerns, some of which are listed in Figure A2.4. Reliable and valid personnel decision techniques must be used in organizations to ensure that career planning achieves its purposes. Careers should provide a breadth of experience for organizational members to foster skill development. The organization must act to ensure that women and minorities are hired, especially in managerial positions, and that these individuals are compensated fairly. These concerns also include issues such as nepotism, dual careers, age discrimination, and international opportunities. Career planning may also involve establishing a functional stress management program (see Chapter 9).

Types of Career Programs

Research suggests that organizational career planning programs fit into seven general categories: career pathing, career counseling, human resource planning, career information systems, management development, training, and special programs.[40]

Career pathing is the identification of a certain sequence of jobs in a career that represent a progression through the organization.

Career Pathing   **Career pathing** is the identification of career tracks, or sequences of jobs, that represent a coherent progression vertically and laterally through the organization. Figure A2.5 illustrates two such paths for college graduates, one for an engineering/technical career and one for a sales/marketing career. Paths like these may be clearly specified in some organizations, whereas

40. M. A. Morgan, D. T. Hall, and A. Martier, "Career Development Strategies in Industry—Where Are We and Where Should We Be?" *Personnel*, March–April 1979, pp. 13–30.

FIGURE A2.4

Organizational Career Planning Concerns

Path 1: Engineering / Technical Career

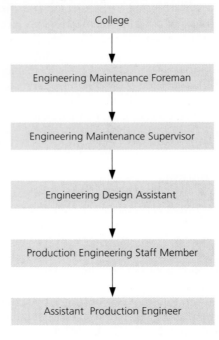

College

↓

Engineering Maintenance Foreman

↓

Engineering Maintenance Supervisor

↓

Engineering Design Assistant

↓

Production Engineering Staff Member

↓

Assistant Production Engineer

Path 2: Sales / Marketing Career

College

↓

Salesperson

↓

Sales Supervisor

↓

Marketing Research Staff Assistant

↓

Marketing Research Project Group Leader

↓

Product Planning Team Member

↓

New Product Development Staff

↓

New Product Development Team Leader

other organizations may allow far more flexibility. Most organizations do not adhere too strictly to specific career paths because doing so might limit the full utilization of individual potential, and there are always many exceptions to specified paths.[41] Such organizations provide opportunities for both horizontal and vertical movement to enable individuals to develop their skills and breadth of experience. Some career paths include assignments overseas to help prospective top managers gain an understanding of the organization's international operations. Career paths usually have a time frame (frequently five to ten years), may be updated periodically, and may be developed to ensure that the work experiences are relevant to a particular target (that is, higher-level) position in the organization.

Career Counseling Organizations use both informal and formal approaches to career counseling.[42] Counseling occurs informally as part of the day-to-day

41. T. A. DiPrete, "Horizontal and Vertical Mobility in Organizations," *Administrative Science Quarterly*, December 1987, pp. 422–444.
42. N. C. Hill, "Career Counseling: What Employees Should Do—and Expect," *Personnel*, August 1985, pp. 41–46.

supervisor-subordinate relationship and often during employment interviews and performance evaluation sessions as well (see Chapter 8). More formally, career counseling often is provided by the human resources department and is available to all personnel, especially those who are being moved up, down, or out of the organization.[43]

Human Resource Planning   Human resource planning involves forecasting the organization's human resource needs, developing replacement charts (charts showing planned succession of personnel) for all levels of the organization, and preparing inventories of the skills and abilities individuals need to move within the organization. Human resource planning and development systems can be quite complex and involve both individual and organizational activities. Basically, however, such systems involve developing plans, matching organizations and individuals, assessing needs, and implementing the plans. It is the specific applications that lead to the complexity of the system.

Career Information Systems   When internal job markets are combined with formal career counseling to establish a career information center for organization members, the result is a career information system. Internal job markets exist when job openings within the organization are announced first to organization members. News about openings may appear on bulletin boards, in newsletters, and in memoranda. A career information center keeps up-to-date information about such openings, as well as information about employees who are seeking other jobs or careers within the organization. Career information systems, then, can serve not only to develop the organization's resources but to provide information that may increase the motivation of organization members to perform.

Management Development   Management development programs vary considerably. They may consist simply of policies that hold managers directly responsible for the development of their successors, or they may set out elaborate formal educational programs. Management development is receiving increasing attention in all types of organizations. On average, managers are participating in between twenty and forty hours per year of education and development activities[44] dealing with topics such as time management, problem solving and decision making, strategic planning, and leadership. Developmental programs in smaller organizations (those with fewer than one thousand employees) tend to focus on management and supervisory skills, communication, and behavioral skills. In larger organizations, development activities typically concentrate on executive development, new management techniques, and computer literacy.[45] Management development is discussed in detail in Chapter 18.

Training   More specialized efforts to improve skills usually are termed "Training." These activities include on-the-job training, formalized job rotation programs, in-house training sessions for the development of specific technical job skills, programs on legal and political changes that affect specific jobs, tuition reimbursement pro-

---

43. W. Kiechel III, "Passed Over," *Fortune*, October 13, 1986, pp. 189–191; and J. C. Latack and J. B. Dozier, "After the Ax Falls: Job Loss as a Career Transition," *Academy of Management Review*, April 1986, pp. 375–392.
44. E. H. Burack, *Creative Human Resource Planning and Applications: A Strategic Approach* (Englewood Cliffs, N.J.: Prentice-Hall, 1988).
45. Ibid.

grams, and student intern programs. The emphasis usually is on specific job skills, with immediate performance being of greater concern than long-term career development. Of course, continued improvement in job performance carries implications for evolving career opportunities.

Special Programs   Training and development programs may be designed for and offered to special groups within the organization. Preretirement programs offer one example, as do programs designed to help organization members cope with midlife career crises. Many organizations now offer outplacement counseling—programs designed to help employees who are leaving the organization, either voluntarily or involuntarily.[46] Outplacement programs help people preserve their dignity and self-worth when they are fired and can reduce negative feelings toward the organization. Other special programs have been developed for women, minorities, and handicapped personnel to help them solve their special career problems.[47] Some organizations also have special programs to assist personnel in the career move from technical to managerial positions. Still other organizations have begun programs to deal with smokers because it has become clear that they pose health risks not only to themselves but to others.[48]

Career Management

Career management
is the process of implementing organizational career planning.

Career management is the process by which organizational career planning is implemented. As Table A2.3 shows, top management support is needed to establish a climate that fosters career development. All human resource activities within the organization must be coordinated, and human resource managers from various areas should be involved at least as consultants. The career planning programs must be open to all members of the organization and thus must be flexible to accommodate the variety of individual differences that will be encountered. Realistic feedback should be provided to participants with the focus on psychological success rather than simply advancement. Implementation of new programs should begin with small pilot programs that emphasize periodic assessment of employee skills and experiences of the program itself.[49]

Each supervisor and manager in the organization plays a key role in making the organization's career planning program work to the benefit of the organization and its employees.

It is extremely important that supervisors be involved and that they are trained carefully lest they neglect or mishandle their role and negate the positive effects of career planning programs. The role of supervisors includes communicating information about careers; counseling to help subordinates identify their skills and to understand their options; evaluating subordinates' performance, strengths, and weaknesses; coaching or teaching skills and behaviors to those who need support;

46. T. M. Camden, "Using Outplacement as a Career Development Tool," *Personnel Administrator*, January 1982, pp. 35–44.
47. See, for example, D. D. Bowen and R. D. Hisrich, "The Female Entrepreneur: A Career Development Perspective," *Academy of Management Review*, April 1986, pp. 393–407; "Male vs. Female: What a Difference It Makes in Business Careers," *Wall Street Journal*, December 9, 1986, p. 1; "In Dad's Footsteps: More Women Find a Niche in the Family Business," *Wall Street Journal*, May 28, 1987, p. 29; D. D. Van Fleet and J. Saurage, "Recent Research on Women in Leadership and Management," *Akron Business and Economic Review*, Summer 1984, pp. 15–24; and E. M. Van Fleet and D. D. Van Fleet, "Entrepreneurship and Black Capitalism," *American Journal of Small Business*, Fall 1985, pp. 31–40.
48. "Cigarette Smoking Is Growing Hazardous to Careers in Business," *Wall Street Journal*, April 23, 1987, pp. 1, 19.
49. Adapted from Feldman, *Managing Careers in Organizations*, pp. 189–192. See also K. B. McRae, "Career-Management Planning: A Boon to Managers and Employees," *Personnel*, May 1985, pp. 56–61.

TABLE A2.3

Key Ingredients for Career Management

- Top management support
- Coordination with other human resource activities
- Involvement of supervisors
- Use of human resource managers as consultants
- Periodic skill assessment
- Realistic feedback about career progress

- Equal access and open enrollment
- Focus on psychological success rather than advancement
- Flexibility for individual needs
- Climate setting for career development
- Small pilot programs
- Periodic program assessment

SOURCE: From *Managing Careers in Organizations* by Daniel C. Feldman. Copyright © by Scott, Foresman and Company. Reprinted by permission of HarperCollins Publishers.

advising about the realities of the organization; serving as a mentor or role model for subordinates; brokering, or bringing together subordinates and those who might have positions better suited to them; and informing subordinates about opportunities.[50]

Results of Career Planning

Organizational career planning has many important results.[51] Employees develop more realistic expectations of what is expected of them on the job and what their future with the organization will entail. Supervisory roles in career counseling are clarified, personal career planning ability is increased through knowledge and education, and human resource systems within the organization are more effectively utilized. All of these effects serve to strengthen career commitment as individuals develop plans to take charge of their careers. Ultimately, then, the organization is able to better use the talent of its members, turnover is reduced, and individual and corporate performance is increased.

These benefits are not, however, guaranteed. If the existence of an organizational career planning program raises individuals' expectations unrealistically, dysfunctional consequences may result. Anxiety may increase, supervisors may spend too much time counseling their subordinates, and human resource systems may become overloaded. These effects lead to frustration, disappointment, and reduced commitment. In the end, talent is inadequately used, turnover increases, and individual and organizational performances suffer. The key to keeping employee expectations realistic is for all supervisors and managers to be trained to provide only factual information about jobs and the true prospects for an employee. Clearly, organizations must use career planning programs carefully to ensure positive results.

50. Z. B. Leibowitz and N. K. Schlossberg, "Training Managers for Their Role in a Career Development System," *Training and Development Journal*, July 1981, pp. 72–79.
51. Walker, "Does Career Planning Rock the Boat?"

Glossary

abilities   The capacities an individual has to perform well in one or more areas of activity, such as physical, mental, or interpersonal work. (3)

absenteeism   Failure to report to work. (2, 3)

acceptance theory of authority   Suggests that the authority of the manager depends on the subordinate's acceptance of the manager's right to give the directive and expect compliance. (15)

accommodation   A type of intergroup interaction that occurs when the goals are compatible but not considered to be very important to goal attainment. (9)

adhocracy   A form of organization design that has horizontal and vertical specialization but little formalization, resulting in a very organic structure. Decision making is spread throughout the organization. It is one of Mintzberg's structural forms and is typically found in young organizations engaged in highly technical fields where the environment is complex and dynamic. (16)

administrative hierarchy   A system of reporting relationships in the organization, from the first level up through the president or CEO. (15)

advancement stage   Career stage in which the individual is recognized for the improved performance that comes with development and growth (App. 2)

affect   The individual's feelings toward something. (3)

all-channel network   A small-group network in which all members communicate with all other members. (14)

applied research   Research conducted to solve particular problems or answer specific questions. (App. 1)

assertiveness   An indicator of a culture's values regarding being forceful rather than being interested in people and quality of life. (19)

assimilation   The process in which a minority group learns the ways of the dominant group. In organizations this is the attempt to mold people who are different to fit the existing organization culture. (20)

attitudes   Complexes of beliefs and feelings that people have about specific ideas, situations, or other people. (3)

attribution theory   Suggests that we observe the behavior of others and then attribute causes to it. The theory is associated with Heider and Kelley. (3, 5)

authoritarianism   The extent to which a person believes that there should be power and status differences within a social system such as an organization. The stronger the belief, the more the individual is said to be authoritarian. (3)

authority   Power that has been legitimized within a specific social context. (15)

autonomous work groups   An innovation in task design whereby jobs are structured for groups rather than for individuals. The group itself is given considerable discretion in scheduling, individual work assignments, and other matters that have traditionally be management prerogatives. (7,16)

avoidance (negative reinforcement)   A concept of reinforcement theory that occurs when the individual is engaging in desired behavior in order to avoid an unpleasant, or aversive, consequence. The effect of avoidance is to increase the frequency of a desired behavior. (6)

avoidance   A type of intergroup interaction that occurs when the interaction is not considered to be important to any group's goal attainment and the goals are considered to be incompatible. (9)

Basic research   Research concerned with discovering new knowledge rather than solving particular problems. (App. 1)

behavioral approach (to decision making)   A decision-making model characterized by the use of procedures and rules of thumb, suboptimizing, and satisficing. (10).

behavioral approach (to leadership)   Approach designed to determine the behaviors associated with effective leadership. These approaches to the study of leadership began in the late 1940s. (12)

belongingness needs   Primarily social in nature, including, for example, the need for love and affection and the need to be accepted by peers. (4)

benefits   A major component of the employee compensation plan beyond wages. (8)

Note: The number in parentheses after each entry refers to the chapter in which the term was discussed.

bicultural group Membership is approximately divided equally between two groups. (20)

bounded rationality A decision-making process whereby the decision maker limits the inputs to the decision-making process and makes decisions based on judgment and personal biases as well as logic. (10)

brainstorming A technique for stimulating imaginative and novel ideas. Participants in brainstorming are encouraged to suggest as many innovative and extreme ideas as possible as solutions to the identified problem. Participants are forbidden to discourage the ideas of others and are encouraged to build on the ideas of others. (11)

bureaucracy A type of organizational structure proposed by Max Weber. The ideal bureaucracy is characterized by Weber as having a hierarchy of authority, a system of rules and procedures, and division of labor. (1,19)

burnout The overall feeling of exhaustion a person feels when simultaneously experiencing too much pressure and too few sources of satisfaction. (9)

Business strategy An outline of how a business intends to compete with other firms in the same industry. (2)

Career A perceived sequence of attitudes and behaviors associated with work-related experiences and activities over the span of the person's life. (App. 2)

career management The process by which organizational career planning is implemented. (App. 2)

career pathing The identification of career tracks, or sequences of jobs, that represent a coherent progression vertically and laterally through the organization. (App. 2)

career planning The process of planning one's life work; involves evaluating abilities and interests, considering alternative career opportunities, establishing career goals, and planning practical development. (App. 2)

career stages The gradual changes that occur over time in careers. (App. 2)

case study An in-depth analysis of one setting. This design is frequently used when little is known about the phenomena in question and the researcher wants to look at relevant concepts intensively and thoroughly. (App. 1)

causality The attempt by researchers to describe, explain, and predict the cause of a certain event. The purpose of scientific research is to reveal causality. (App. 1)

centralization Decision-making authority is concentrated at the top of the organizational hierarchy. (15)

certainty A condition where the outcome of each alternative is known. (10)

chain network A small group network in which each member communicates with the person above and below, except the individuals on each end, who communicate with only one person. (14)

change agent A person who is responsible for managing the change effort in the organization. The change agent may be a member of the organization or an outsider. (18)

channel noise The principal type of noise in the communication process. (14)

charisma A form of interpersonal attraction that inspires support and acceptance from others. (13)

charismatic leadership An approach to leadership that assumes charisma is an individual characteristic of the leader. It is presumed that a supervisor who is very charismatic may be more successful in influencing subordinate behavior than one lacking charisma. (13)

circle network A small group network in which each person communicates with the people on both sides but no one else. (14)

classic principles of organizing Fourteen principles that provide the framework for the organization chart and the coordination of work. These principles were identified by Fayol and have been criticized for ignoring the human element in organizations. (15)

classical conditioning An approach to learning stating that if a conditioned stimulus is repeatedly paired with an unconditioned stimulus, the conditioned stimulus will eventually become associated in the mind of the learner with the same response that is elicited by the unconditioned stimulus. The approach is associated with Pavlov and his experiments with dogs. (6)

classical organization theory A branch of management that was concerned with structuring organizations effectively. (1,15)

coercive power A base of power identified by French and Raven that exists when someone has the ability to punish or to inflict physical or psychological harm on someone else. (13)

cognition The knowledge a person presumes to have about something.

cognitive abilities An individual's power to think intelligently and to effectively analyze situations and data. (10)

cognitive dissonance The anxiety a person experiences when two sets of knowledge or perceptions are contradictory or incongruent. It also occurs when a person behaves in a way inconsistent with her or his attitudes.

cognitive process A process that assumes people are conscious, active participants in how they learn. People draw on their experiences and use past learning as a basis for present behavior. People make choices about their behavior and then recognize the consequences of their choices. Finally, people evaluate those consequences and add them to prior learning, affecting future choices. (6)

cohesiveness   See **group cohesiveness**.

collaboration   A type of intergroup interaction that occurs when the interaction is important to goal attainment and the groups' goals are compatible. (9)

collectivism   A feeling that the good of the group or society should come first. (19)

command group   A type of formal group that is relatively permanent. A command group is also referred to as a functional group. (11)

commitment   See **organizational commitment**.

communication   A process in which information is exchanged or a common understanding established between two or more parties. (14)

communication and decision-making stage of group development   When members discuss their feelings more openly and agree on group goals and individual roles of the group. (11)

communication fidelity   The degree of correspondence between the message intended by the source and the message understood by the receiver. (14)

communication network   Links that develop so that employees can obtain the necessary information to do their jobs and coordinate their work with others in the system. It serves to structure both the flow and the content of communication and support the organization structure. (14)

competencies   Refined skills that are honed by practice and experience and that enable the individual to develop a specialty. (3)

competition   A type of intergroup interaction that occurs when the goals of the groups are incompatible and interactions are important to goal attainment of each group. (9)

compressed workweek   A work schedule in which an employee works a full forty-hour week in less than the traditional five days. Typically, a employee may work ten hours a day for four days, with an extra day off. (7)

compromise   A type of intergroup interaction that occurs when the interactions are of moderate importance to goal attainment and goals are neither completely compatible nor incompatible. (9)

conceptual skills   The manager's ability to think about the abstract. (2)

configuration   The size and shape of an organization as depicted on an organization chart. (15)

conflict   A form of group interaction that occurs whenever one group perceives that its attempts to accomplish its goals have been frustrated by another group. (9)

conflict model   The Janis-Mann process of decision making based on research in social psychology and individual decision processes. The model makes five assumptions. (10)

conflict resolution   Conflict-handling strategies a manager needs to engage in when a potentially harmful conflict arises. (9)

conflict stimulation   The creation and constructive use of conflict by a manager. (9)

contingency approach to organization design   The structure determined by specific conditions such as the environment, technology, and the organization's work force. (16)

contingency perspective   A theory that suggests that in most organizations situations and outcomes are contingent on, or influenced by, other variables. (1)

contingency plans   Alternative actions that can be taken if the primary course of action is unexpectedly disrupted or rendered inappropriate. (10)

contingency theory of leadership   See **LDC theory of leadership**.

continuous reinforcement   The rewarding of behavior every time it occurs. (6)

contributions   An individual's input into the organization, such as effort, skills, ability, time and loyalty. (3)

control and organization stage of group development   When mature group members work together and are more flexible, adaptive, and self-correcting. (11)

controlling   The process of monitoring and correcting the actions of the organization and people and activities within it so as to keep them headed toward their goal. (2)

convergent validity   In performance appraisal, the extent to which different measures agree in the evaluations of the same performance. (14)

creativity   The process of developing original and imaginative perspectives on situations. (10)

cross-functional work teams   Comprised of representatives from different functional areas or the organization and work together on various projects and activities. (7)

Decentralization   A structural aspect in which decisions are made throughout the hierarchy. (15)

decision making   The process of choosing one alternative from several alternatives. (10)

decision rule   A statement that tells the decision maker which alternative to choose once she or he has information about the decision situation. (10)

decision-making roles   One of Mintzberg's three general categories of managerial roles including the entrepreneur, the disturbance handler, the resource allocator, and the negotiator roles. These roles closely relate to decision making (2)

decoding   The process by which the receiver of the message interprets its meaning. (14)

defensive avoidance   In the conflict model of decision making, making no changes in present activities and avoiding any further contact with issues affecting the activities because there seems to be no hope of finding a better solution. (10)

deficiency needs   The three sets (physiological, security, belongingness) of needs at the bottom of the hierarchy which must be satisfied for the individual to be fundamentally comfortable. (4)

Delphi technique   A method of improving group decision making that involves systematically gathering the judgments of experts and developing forecasts. When using the Delphi technique, groups do not meet face to face. (11)

demographic differences   Those differences associated with physical or biographical characteristics. (3)

departmentalization   The manner in which divided tasks are combined into work groups for coordination. The most common methods are by business function, process, product or service, customer, and geography. (15)

diagnostic skills   The manager's ability to understand cause-and-effect relationships and to recognize the optimal solutions to problems. (2)

discipline   An attempt to punish that is structured, official, and organizationally sanctioned. (6)

dispositional view of attitudes   A view that suggests that people respond in predictable ways depending on their affect, cognitions, and intentions. (3)

disseminator role   The manager who transmits the information gathered by the monitor to others. (2)

dissonance reduction   An attempt by an individual to reduce the tension and discomfort that attitudes and behaviors not consistent with each other cause. Generally, the person tries to change the attitude, change the behavior, or perceptually distort the circumstances. (3)

distress   A negative form of stress that can lead to dangerous side effects. (9)

disturbance handler role   The manager who helps settle disputes between various parties, such as other managers and their subordinates. (2)

division of labor   The extent to which the work of the organization is separated into different jobs to be done by different people. (15)

divisionalized form   An organization design that resembles the machine bureaucracy except that it is divided according to the different markets it serves. Standardization of outputs is the primary means of coordination. It is one of Mintzberg's structural forms that characterizes old, very large firms operating in a relatively simple, stable environment with several diverse markets. (16)

Dogmatism   Reflects the rigidity of a person's beliefs and his or her openness to other viewpoints. (13)

Downsizing   The process of purposely becoming smaller by reducing the size of the workforce or shedding divisions or businesses. (2)

dual-structure theory   Herzberg's theory which identifies motivation factors, which affect satisfaction, and hygiene factors, which determine dissatisfaction. (4)

Effort-to-performance expectancy   The perceived probability that effort will lead to performance. The probability may range between 0 and 1.0. It is a major concept of the expectancy theory. (5)

empowerment   The process of enabling workers to set their own work goals, make decisions, and solve problems within their sphere of responsibility and authority. (5,17)

encoding   The process by which the message is translated from an idea or thought into symbols that can be transmitted. (14)

entrepreneur role   The manager who voluntarily initiates change, such as innovations or new strategies. (2)

entry stage (exploration stage)   The first career stage in which self-examination, role tryouts, and occupational exploration occur. (App. 2)

environmental complexity   The number of environmental components that affect organizational decision making. (16)

environmental dynamism   The degree to which environmental components change. (16)

environmental uncertainty   A condition that exists when managers have little information about environmental events and their impact on the organization. It results from environmental complexity and environmental dynamism. (16)

equity theory   A theory based on the premise that people want to be treated fairly and that they compare their own input-to-outcome ratio in the organization to the ratio of a comparison-other. If they feel that, in a relative sense, they are being treated inequitably, they take steps to reduce the inequity. The theory was articulated by Adams. (5)

ERG theory　A theory that suggests that people may be motivated by more than one kind of need at the same time. The theory also includes a frustration-regression component and a satisfaction-progression component. Associated with Alderfer, this theory is an extension and refinement of Maslow's needs hierarchy. It identifies three basic need categories: existence, relatedness, and growth. (4)

escalation of commitment　The tendency to persist in an ineffective course of action when evidence indicates the project is doomed to failure. (10)

establishment stage　See **socialization stage**.

esteem needs　Encompasses two slightly different kinds of needs: the need for a positive self-image and self-respect and the need to be respected by others. (4)

ethics　Personal beliefs about what is right and wrong or good and bad. (2)

eustress　A positive form of stress that can motivate, stimulate, and, often, reward a person. (9)

existence needs　Needs perceived as necessary for basic human existence in the ERG theory of motivation as developed by Clayton Alderfer. (4)

expectencies　The probabilities linking effort and performance and performance and rewards in the expectancy model. (5)

expectancy theory　Assumes that motivation depends on how much we want something and how likely we think we are to get it. (5)

expert power　A base of power identified by French and Raven that relates to control over expertise or, more precisely, over information. (3)

exploration stage　See **entry stage**.

extinction　A concept of reinforcement theory that decreases the frequency of undesired behavior, especially behavior that was previously rewarded. Extinction occurs when rewards are removed from behaviors that were previously reinforced. (6)

feedback　Verification of a message sent from the receiver to the source. (14)

field experiment　A type of research design similar to a laboratory experiment, but it is conducted in a real organization. The researcher is able to control certain variables and manipulate others in order to assess the effects of the manipulated variables on outcome variables. (App. 1)

field survey　A type of research design that usually relies on a questionnaire distributed to a sample of people chosen from a larger population. The researcher analyzes the responses to the questionnaire and tries to make inferences about the larger population the sample was chosen to represent. (App. 1)

figurehead role　An interpersonal role sometimes taken by the manager wherein he or she serves as a symbol of the organization. (2)

fixed-interval reinforcement　Reinforcement provided on a predetermined, constant schedule. (6)

fixed-ratio reinforcement　Reinforcement where the number of behaviors needed to obtain reinforcement is constant. (6)

flexible reward system　A compensation system that lets employees choose the combination of benefits that best suits their needs. (8)

flexible work schedules (flextime)　A work schedule in which the work day is broken down into two categories: flexible time and core time. All employees must be at their work stations during core time, but they can choose their own schedules during flexible time. Flexible time enables employees to have some control over their working hours. (7)

flextime (flexible work schedules)　See **flexible work schedules**.

formal groups　Groups established by the organization to do its work and usually identifiable on an organization chart. Include the command (functional) group, which is relatively permanent, and task (special projects) group, which is relatively temporary. (11)

formalization　The degree to which the jobs and activities of employees are codified by rules and procedures. (15)

friendship group　A type of informal group that is relatively permanent. The association among the members is due to friendly relationships and the pleasure that comes from being together. (11)

functional group　See **command group**.

functional job analysis technique　Identifies the specific tasks that make up a job and examines how much each task involves data, people, and things. Each task's complexity in each respect is rated from 1 to 10. (8)

General adaptation syndrome (GAS)　Begins when a person first encounters a stressor. The basic threshold at which stress starts to affect individuals. The three stages of response to stress are alarm, resistance, and exhaustion. (9)

goal　A desirable objective individuals or organizations want to achieve. (5)

goal acceptance   The extent to which an individual accepts a goal as his or her own. (5)

goal commitment   The extent to which an individual is personally interested in reaching a goal. (5)

goal compatibility   The extent to which the goals of more than one group can be achieved at the same time. (9)

goal difficulty   The extent to which a goal is challenging and demands effort. (5)

goal setting theory of motivation   This theory, developed by Locke, assumes that behavior is the result of conscious goals and intentions. Goal difficulty and goal specificity shape performance. (5)

goal specificity   Setting a goal in quantitative terms. It is consistently related to performance. (5)

group   Two or more persons interacting with one another in such a manner that each person influences and is influenced by each other person. (11)

group cohesiveness   How strongly members of a group feel about remaining in the group. Attraction to the group, resistance to leaving the group, and motivation to remain a member of the group are forces that create cohesiveness. Group cohesiveness may be increased by competition or the presence of an external threat. (11)

group composition   The makeup of a group. It is often described in terms of the homogeneity of heterogeneity of the members. (11)

group development   The stages and activities groups progress through in order to become mature, effective groups. The four general stages are: mutual acceptance, communication and decision making, motivation and productivity, and control and organization. (11)

group performance factors   Factors that influence the formation and development of the group. They describe the way group members do their jobs and relate to each other. Primary factors are composition, size, norms, and cohesiveness. (11)

group polarization   The shift of member attitudes and opinions to a more extreme position following group discussion. It arises due to the expression of shared attitudes in the discussion, persuasive arguments by supporters of the extreme position, and the feeling that responsibility is diffused by the group process. (11)

group size   The number of members of a group. The size of a group can vary from two members to as many members as can interact and influence each other. (11)

groupthink   A mode of thinking that people engage in when they are deeply involved in a cohesive ingroup, when the members' strivings for unanimity override their motivation to realistically appraise alternative courses of action. (11)

growth needs   The top two sets of needs (esteem and self-actualization), focusing on personal growth and development. Also part of needs described in Alderfer's ERG theory. (4)

Hawthorne studies   A series of experiments that played a major role in developing the foundations of the field of organizational behavior. The studies were conducted at the Hawthorne Plant of Western Electric near Chicago between 1927 and 1932. The overall conclusion of the studies was that individual and social processes are too important to ignore. (1)

hedonism   A concept that dominated the earliest views on human motivation. Hedonism argues that people seek pleasure and comfort and try to avoid pain and discomfort. (4)

hierarchy of needs   Maslow theory that assumes human needs are arranged in a hierarchy of importance. (4)

human organization   A system that centers on the principles of supportive relationships, employee participation, and overlapping work groups. The human organization is an approach to organization design presented by Likert. (15)

human relations movement   A movement that played a major role in developing the foundations of the field of organizational behavior. The basic premise of the movement was that people respond primarily to their social environment. McGregor's Theory X and Theory Y and Maslow's hierarchy of needs were predominant theories of this period. (1, 4)

hygiene factors   Extrinsic to the work itself, including factors such as pay and job security. (4)

hypervigilance   In the conflict model of decision making, frantic and superficial pursuit of some satisficing strategy. (10)

Ideal bureaucracy   An organizational system characterized by a hierarchy of authority and a system of rules and procedures designed to create an optimally effective system for large organizations. (15)

impression management   A direct and intentional effort by someone to enhance his or her own image in the eyes of others. (13)

individual characteristics   One of five basic categories of organizational behavior concepts. Among such characteristics are learning, perception, attitudes, personalities, employee motivation, goal setting, rewards, and stress. (1)

individual differences   A set of factors that includes the ways we think, the ways we interpret our environment, and the ways we respond to that environment that vary from person to person. (3)

individualism   A state in which people view themselves first as individuals and believe their own interest and values take priority. (19)

individual-organization interface   One of the five basic categories of organizational behavior concepts. It includes job design, role dynamics, group and intergroup dynamics, leadership, power, politics, and conflict. (1)

inducements   What the organization provides the individual in the form of tangible and intangible rewards. (3)

influence   The ability to affect the perceptions, attitudes, or behaviors of others. (13)

informal groups   Groups formed by members of an organization. They include the relatively permanent friendship group and the interest group, which may be less long-lived. (11)

informational roles   One of Mintzberg's three general categories of managerial roles including the monitor, the disseminator, and the spokesperson roles. These roles involve some aspect of information processing. (2)

innovation   The process of creating and doing new things that are introduced into the marketplace as new products, processes, or services. (10)

inputs   An individual's contribution to the organization, such as experience, effort, and loyalty. (5)

intangible compensation   Rewards whose value is not easily defined or measured. (8)

Intention   Guides a person's behavior as a component of attitude. (3)

interactionalism   A perspective that attempts to explain how people select, interpret, and change various situations. The individual and the situation are presumed to interact continuously; this interaction determines the individual's behavior. (1)

interest group   A type of informal group that is relatively temporary. An interest group is organized around a common interest of the members. (11)

intergroup behavior   The ways groups interact with each other. (11)

interpersonal demands   The demands from other people or groups confronting those in organizational settings, such as group pressures, leadership style, and personalities and behavior. (9)

interpersonal roles   One of Mintzberg's three general categories of managerial roles including figurehead, leader, and liaison roles. These roles are primarily social in nature. (2)

Interpersonal skills   Comprise the manager's ability to communicate with, understand, and motivate individuals and groups. (2)

Interrole conflict   Occurs when a person experiences conflict among two or more roles. (9)

interview   A method of gathering data whereby questions are presented to the respondent by an interviewer. The respondent is usually allowed to answer questions spontaneously rather than asked to choose among alternatives defined by the researcher. (App. 1)

intrapreneurship   Entrepreneurial activity within the organization. (10)

intrarole conflict   Arises when a person gets contradictory messages from different people in the same role. (9)

intrasender conflict   When the same person sends contradictory messages to the recipient. (9)

involvement   See **job involvement**.

job analysis   The process of systematically gathering information about specific jobs for use in developing a performance appraisal system and in writing job descriptions. (8)

job characteristics approach   Began with the work of Turner and Lawrence, who believed that workers would prefer complex, challenging tasks to monotonous, boring ones, and who predicted that job complexity would be associated with employee satisfaction and attendance. (7)

Job Characteristics Theory   A model of job enrichment that defines job enrichment as increasing the amounts of certain core dimensions—skill variety, task identity, task significance, autonomy, and feedback. The core dimensions lead to three psychological states that result in positive personal and work-related outcomes. (7)

job design   The specification of an employee's task-related activities, including both structural and interpersonal aspects of the job, as determined by both the organization's and the individual's needs and requirements. (7)

Job Diagnostic Survey   A questionnaire that measures employee perceptions of job characteristics, the various psychological states, personal and work outcomes, and strength of growth needs. (7)

job enlargement   Expansion of a worker's job to include tasks previously performed by other workers. Also called horizontal job loading, it is one alternative to job specialization. (7)

job enrichment   A technique based on Herzberg's two-factor theory of motivation. Employees could be motivated by positive job-related experiences through job loading (giving employees more control over those tasks added by horizontal loading). (7)

job hopping   Moving to different organizations rather than making adjustments within the present organization. (App. 2)

job involvement   Results in an individual's tendency to exceed the normal expectations associated with his or her job. (3)

job rotation   Systematically shifting workers from one job to another, with the goal of sustaining worker motivation and interest. It is one alternative to job specialization. (7)

job satisfaction or dissatisfaction   An individual's attitude toward his or her job. It is one of the most widely studied variables in the entire field of organizational behavior. (3)

job sharing   An approach to work schedules whereby two part-time employees share one full-time job. For example, one person may perform the job from 8:00 A.M. until noon, and the other from 1:00 P.M. until 5:00 P.M. (7)

job specialization   An historical approach to the design of jobs whereby jobs are scientifically studied, broken down into their smallest component parts, and then standardized across all workers doing those jobs. It is a rational, seemingly efficient way to organize jobs, but it can also cause problems due to the monotony of highly specialized, standardized tasks. (7)

Laboratory experiment   A type of research design whereby the researcher creates an artificial setting similar to a real work situation. The experimenter has a great deal of control and can manipulate the variables in the study and examine their effects on the other variables in the experiment. (App. 1)

leader-member exchange (LMX) model   A model of leadership which stresses that leaders develop unique working relationships with each of their subordinates. (12)

leader role   A role sometimes served by the manager during which he or she works to hire, train, and motivate employees. (2)

leadership   Both a process and a property. As a process, leadership is the use of noncoercive influence to direct and coordinate the activities of group members toward goal accomplishment. As a property, leadership is the set of characteristics attributed to those who are perceived to employ such influence successfully. (12)

leadership grid   A framework for examining types of supervision developed by Blake and Mouton. Two dimensions are identified: concern for production and concern for

people. It is suggested that a manager who has a high concern for people and production will be very effective. (12)

leadership substitutes   Individual, task, and organizational characteristics that tend to negate the leader's ability to affect subordinate satisfaction and performance. (13)

leadership traits   Unique set of qualities or traits that early research leaders thought distinguished leaders from their peers. The traits were presumed to be relatively stable and enduring. (12)

leading   The process of getting members of the organization to work together in a fashion consistent with the goals of the organization. (2)

learning   A relatively permanent change in behavior or potential behavior that results from direct or indirect experience. (6)

legitimate power   A base of power identified by French and Raven that is granted by virtue of one's position in the organization.

liaison role   A role sometimes played by the manager that consists of relating to others outside the group or organization. (2)

life change   Any meaningful change in a person's personal or work situation. (9)

life cycle theory   According to this theory, appropriate leader behavior depends on the maturity of the leader's followers. The maturity is how motivated, competent, experienced, and interested in accepting responsibility the subordinates are. (12)

life stressors   Events taking place outside the organization that cause stress in organizational settings, generally categorized in terms of life change and life trauma. (9)

life trauma   Any single upheaval in an individual's life that disrupts his or her attitudes, emotions, or behaviors. (9)

locus of control   The extent to which a person believes that his or her behavior has a direct impact on the consequences of that behavior. Individuals with an internal locus of control believe that if they work hard, they will be successful. People who have an external locus of control tend to think that what happens to them is a function of fate or luck. (3)

long-term orientation   Focus on the future, projects that have a long payoff, persistence and thrift. (19)

LPC theory of leadership   A concept developed by Fred Fiedler which suggests that a leader's effectiveness depends on the situation. LPC stands for "least preferred coworker." (12)

Machiavellianism   A person's motivation to gain power and control the behavior of others. (3)

machine bureaucracy   An organization design in which work is highly specialized and formalized, and decision making is usually concentrated at the top. It is one of Mintzberg's structural forms and is typical of a large, well-established company in a simple and stable environment. (16)

maintenance stage   Individuals develop a stronger attachment to their organizations and, hence, lose some career flexibility. (App. 2)

management by objectives (MBO)   A process in which managers and employees collaborate to set verifiable employee goals. Progress is periodically reviewed, and at the end of the process, employee performance is evaluated. (5)

management functions   Elements of management set forth by Henri Fayol, including planning, organizing, command, coordination, and control. (15)

manifest needs theory   An abstract theory presented by Murray in 1938 and translated into a more concrete, operational framework by Atkinson. The theory assumes that people have a set of multiple needs that motivates behavior simultaneously rather than in a preset order. Each need has two components: direction and intensity. (4)

Maslow's hierarchy of needs   According to Maslow's theory, human needs are arranged in a five-tiered hierarchy of importance, from physiological needs at the bottom, to security needs, belongingness needs, esteem needs, and, at the top, self-actualization needs. (4)

materialism   An indicator of a culture's values regarding being forceful rather than being interested in people and quality of life. (19)

matrix design   An attempt to combine two different designs to gain the benefits of each. In the most common form, product or project departmentalization is superimposed on a functional structure. (16)

mechanistic structure   A type of organization design that is primarily hierarchical in nature, interactions and communications are primarily vertical, instructions come from the boss, knowledge is concentrated at the top, and continued membership requires loyalty and obedience. Burns and Stalker state that this type of structure is appropriate if the rate of change in technology is slow. (16)

medium   The channel or path by which the encoded message travels from the source to the receiver. (14)

mentoring   Occurs when an older, more experienced person helps a younger employee grow and advance by providing advice, support, and encouragement. (App. 2)

Michigan leadership studies   A program of research on leadership behavior conducted at the University of Michigan. Two basic forms of leader behavior were identified: job-centered and employee-centered leader behaviors. These styles are presumed to be at opposite ends of a single dimension. (12)

monitor role   An informational role that consists of actively seeking information that might be of value to the organization in general or to specific managers. (2)

motivating potential score (MPS)   A measurement included in the *Job Diagnostic Survey* that provides a summary index of a job's overall potential for motivating employees. (7)

motivation   The set of factors that cause people to behave in certain ways. (4)

motivation and productivity stage of group development   When members cooperate, help each other, and work toward task accomplishment. (11)

motivation factors   Intrinsic to the work itself and including factors such as achievement and recognition. (4)

motive   The individual's reason for choosing one certain behavior from among several choices. (4)

multicultural group   A fully heterogeneous group that has membership that represents more than two diverse segments. (20)

multicultural organization   Contains employees of mixed backgrounds, experiences, and cultures can contribute and achieve their fullest potential for the benefit of themselves and the organization. (20)

mutual acceptance stage of group development   Characterized by members sharing information about themselves and getting to know each other. (11)

Need for achievement   Reflects an individual's desire to accomplish a goal or task more effectively than in the past. High need achievers tend to set moderately difficult goals, assume personal responsibility for getting things done, want immediate feedback, and are preoccupied with the task. It is associated with the work of McClelland. (4)

need for affiliation   The need for human companionship. People with a high need for affiliation tend to want reassurance and approval from others, have a genuine concern for the feelings of others, and are likely to conform to the wishes of others, especially those with whom they strongly identify. (4)

need for power   The desire to control one's environment, including financial resources, material resources, information, and other people. (4)

need   A deficiency experienced by an individual. (4)

need theories of motivation   Assume that need deficiencies cause behavior. (4)

negative reinforcement (avoidance)   A concept of reinforcement theory that occurs when the individual is engaging in desired behavior in order to avoid an unpleasant, or aversive, consequence. The effect of negative reinforcement is to increase the frequency of a desired behavior. (3)

negotiator role   The manager who represents the organization in reaching agreements with other organizations, such as contracts between management and labor unions. (2)

noise   Any disturbance in the communication process that interferes with or distorts the intended communication. (14)

nominal group technique (NGT)   A method of improving group decision making whereby group members follow a generate-discussion-vote cycle until they reach an appropriate decision. (11)

nonprogrammed decision   A problem or decision situation that has not been encountered before such that the decision maker cannot rely on a previously established decision rule. A nonprogrammed decision is poorly structured because goals are vague, information is ambiguous, and there is no clear procedure for making the decision. (10)

norm   The expected behavior or behavioral pattern in a certain situation. A norm is usually associated with a group and is established during the group development process.

Objective judgment quotient (OJQ) method   A multiple-rater comparative system of evaluating employee performance differences. (14)

observation   A method of gathering data that may include observing and recording events, structured observations, participant observation, and hidden observation. (App. 1)

occupation   A group of jobs similar as to the type of tasks and training involved. (App. 2)

Ohio State leadership studies   A series of studies conducted by researchers at Ohio State University designed to assess subordinates' perceptions of their leaders' actual behavior. The studies identified two dimensions of leadership behavior: consideration and initiating structure. The two dimensions were presumed to be independent. (12)

oral communication   A form of communication in organizations whereby the message is encoded into audible sounds. It is the most prevalent form of organizational communication. (14)

organic structure   A type of organization design that is structured like a network, interactions are more lateral and horizontal, knowledge resides wherever it is most useful to the organization, and membership requires a commitment to the tasks of the organization. Burns and Stalker state that this type of structure is appropriate if the rate of change in technology is high. (16)

organization   A group of people working together to attain common goals. (15)

organization chart   Shows all people, positions, reporting relationships, and lines of formal communication in the organization. (15)

organization culture   That set of values that help people in an organization understand which actions are considered acceptable and which are considered unacceptable. (17)

organization development   The process of planned change and improvement of organizations through the application of knowledge of the behavioral sciences, such as psychology, sociology, cultural anthropology, and other related fields of study. (18)

organizational behavior (OB)   The study of human behavior in organizational settings, the interface between human behavior and the organizational context, and the organization itself. (1)

organizational behavior modification (OB Mod.)   The application of reinforcement principles and concepts to people in organizational settings to achieve motivational improvements. (6)

organizational characteristics   One of the five basic categories of organizational behavior concepts. Among such characteristics are organization structure, environment, technology, organization design, and organizational culture. (1)

organizational citizenship   The behavior of individuals who make a positive overall contribution to the organization. (3)

organizational commitment   An attitude that reflects an individual's identification with and attachment to the organization. (3)

organizational downsizing   A popular trend aimed at reducing the size of corporate staff and middle management to reduce costs (see **downsizing**). (16)

organizational environment   The people, other organizations, economic factors, and objects that are outside the boundaries of the organization. (16)

organizational goals   Objectives management seeks to achieve in pursuing the firm's purpose. (15)

organizational politics   Activities carried out by people to acquire, enhance, and use power and other resources to obtain their preferred outcomes in a situation where there is uncertainty or disagreement. (13)

organizational processes   One of the five basic categories of organizational behavior concepts. Includes decision making, creativity, communication, information processing, performance appraisal, careers, and international aspects of organizational behavior. (1)

organizational socialization   The process through which employees learn about a firm's culture and pass their knowledge and understanding on to others. (17)

organizational stressors   Factors in the workplace that can cause stress: task demands, physical demands, role demands, and interpersonal demands. (9)

organizational structure   A system of task, reporting, and authority relationships within which the organization does its work. (15)

organizational technology   The mechanical and intellectual processes that transform inputs and outputs. (16)

organizing   The process of designing jobs, grouping jobs into manageable units, and establishing patterns of authority among jobs and groups of jobs. (2)

orientation toward authority   The extent to which people accept the right of organizations to grant power. (19)

outcomes   Anything an individual receives from the organization as a result of performance such as pay, recognition, and intrinsic rewards, or anything that might possibly result from performance. (5)

overdetermination   Also called structural inertia: The structure of the organization provides resistance to change because it was designed to maintain stability. (18)

overlapping work groups   Situation where managers serve as linking pins between groups. (15)

overload   More information than the receiver can process. (14)

participation   The process of giving employees a voice in making decisions about their own work. (5)

participative management   A way of thinking about the human resources of an organization. Employees are viewed as valued human resources capable of making substantive and valuable contributions to organizational effectiveness. Employees are allowed the opportunity to participate in decisions. (15)

participative pay system   The participation of employees in either the design of the compensation system or the administration of it, or both. (8)

path-goal theory of leadership   A theory that focuses on appropriate leader behavior for various situations. The path-goal theory suggests that directive, supportive, participative, or achievement-oriented leader behavior may be appropriate, depending on the characteristics of the person and the environment. It was developed in the 1970s by Evans and House and is based on the expectancy theory of motivation. (12)

perception   The set of processes by which the individual receives and interprets information about the environment. (3)

Performance behaviors   The total set of work-related behaviors that the organization expects the individual to display. (3)

performance management system (PMS)   The organizational processes and activities involved in performance appraisals. It includes organizational policies, procedures, and resources that support the performance appraisal activity. (8)

performance measurement (performance appraisal)   The process of evaluating work behaviors by measurement and comparison to previously established standards, recording the results, and communicating them back to the employee. It is an activity between a manager and an employee. (8)

Performance plan   An understanding between an employee and manager of what and how a job is to be done so that both parties know what is expected and how success is defined and measured. (8)

performance-to-outcome expectancy   A person's perception of the probability that performance will lead to certain outcomes. The probability may range between 0 and 1.0. It is a major concept of expectency theory. (5)

perquisites   Means of compensation in the form of special privileges associated with employees of relatively high rank in the organization. (8)

Person-job fit   The extent to which the contributions made by the individual match the inducements offered by the organization. (3)

Person-role conflict   When there is some basic incongruence between the person and his or her job. (9)

personal power   Power that resides in the person, regardless of his or her position in the organization. (13)

personality   The set of distinctive traits and characteristics that can be used to compare and contrast individuals. (3)

physical demands   Demands relating to the setting of the job, such as temperature, office design, and poor lighting. (9)

physiological needs   The most basic needs in the hierarchy, including food, sex, and air. (4)

planning   The process of determining the organization's desired future position and the best means to get there. (2)

pluralistic organization   Has heterogeneous membership and takes steps to achieve the full participation and integration of people who are different from the organization's dominant group. (20)

Porter-Lawler extension   This model suggests that performance may lead to various intrinsic and extrinsic rewards. When an individual perceives the rewards as equitable, the rewards lead to satisfaction. (5)

position power   Power that resides in the position, regardless of the person involved. (13)

positive reinforcement   A concept of reinforcement theory in which positive reinforcement is a reward that follows desirable behavior. Its effect is to maintain or increase the frequency of a desired behavior. (6)

power   The potential ability of a person or group to influence another person or group. (13)

practical approach to decision making   Combines the steps of the rational approach with the conditions of the behavioral approach to create a more realistic process for making decisions in organizations. (10)

preference for stability   Reflection of how much certainty or uncertainty people will accept. (19)

prejudices   Judgements made about others that reinforce a superiority/inferiority belief system that can lead to exaggerating the worth of one group while diminishing the worth of others. (20)

primary needs   Things people require to sustain themselves. (4)

problem solving   A special kind of decision making in which the issue is unique. It requires development and evaluation of alternatives without the aid of a programmed decision rule. (10)

procedural justice   The extent to which the dynamics of an organization's decision-making processes are judged to be fair by those who are most affected by it. (17)

productivity   How many goods and services an organization creates relative to its inputs. (2)

professional bureaucracy   An organization design in which standardization of skills is the primary means of coordination. Specialization is horizontal, and decision making is decentralized. It is one of Mintzberg's structural forms and is usually found in a complex, stable environment. It is a special type of bureaucracy. (16)

programmed decision   A decision that recurs often enough for decision rules to be developed. A decision rule is a statement that tells the decision maker which alternative

to choose once she or he has information about the decision situation, such as outcomes, action-outcome probabilities, and values of outcomes. (10)

psychological contract   The overall set of expectations held by an individual with respect to what he or she will contribute to the organization and what the organization, in return, will provide to the individual. (3)

punishment   The presentation of unpleasant, or aversive, consequences as a result of undesirable behaviors. It is a concept of reinforcement theory that decreases the frequency of undesired behaviors. (6)

Quality   The total set of features and characteristics of a product or service that determines its ability to satisfy stated or implied needs. (2)

quality circles (QCs)   Small groups of volunteers who meet regularly to identify, analyze, and solve quality and related problems that pertain to their work. (5)

quality of work life   The degree to which members of a work organization are able to satisfy important personal needs through their experiences in the organization. (18)

questionnaire   A collection of written questions about the respondents' attitudes, opinions, perceptions, and/or demographic characteristics. (App. 1)

Rational decision-making approach   A systematic, step-by-step process that assumes objectivity and complete information. The steps are: statement of goal, identification of the problem, determination of decision type, generation of alternatives, evaluation and choice of alternatives, implementation, and control. (10)

receiver   An individual, or group, or an individual acting as the representative of a group that is the receiver of the message. (14)

reengineering   The radical redesign of organizational processes to achieve major gains in cost, time, and provision of services. (16)

referent power   A base of power identified by French and Raven that is basically power through identification. It usually manifests itself through emulation and imitation. (13)

refreezing   The process of making new behaviors relatively permanent and resistant to further change. It is the third step of Lewin's model of planned change. (18)

reinforcement   The consequences of behavior. The four basic kinds of reinforcement are positive, negative (avoidance), extinction, and punishment. (6)

---

reinforcement theory (operant conditioning) A theory that suggests that behavior is a function of its consequences. It is generally associated with the work of Skinner. (6)

relatedness needs Those involving the need to relate to others in the ERG theory as developed by Clayton Alderfer. (4)

reliability The extent to which a measurement system's results are consistent. (App. 1)

research design The set of procedures used to test the predicted relationships among natural phenomena. (App. 1)

resource allocator role The manager who decides how resources in the organization will be distributed among various individuals and groups. (2)

responsibility The obligation to do something under the expectation that some act will be done or certain outputs achieved. (15)

reward power A base of power identified by French and Raven that is the extent to which one person controls rewards that are valued by another. (13)

reward system All parts of the organization that are involved in the allocation of compensation and benefits to employees in exchange for their contributions to the organization. (8)

risk A condition where the decision maker does not know with certainty what the outcome of a given action will be, but has enough information to estimate the probabilities of occurrence of various outcomes. (10)

Risk propensity The degree to which an individual is willing to take chances and make risky decisions. (3)

role The part an individual plays in the work group. (9)

role ambiguity A situation that occurs when it is unclear or uncertain what behavior is expected of a role occupant. (9)

role conflict A situation that arises when demands of or messages about roles are essentially clear but also contradict each other somewhat. The four types of role conflict are interrole, intrarole, intrasender, and person-role. (9)

role demands The demands of the expected set of behaviors (role) associated with a particular position in a group or organization. (9)

Satisficing A situation that occurs in decision making when the decision maker examines alternatives only until a solution that meets minimal requirements is found and then ceases to look for a better one. (10)

schedules of reinforcement The various ways in which a manager may attempt to reinforce desired or undesired behavior. The five types of schedules include continuous reinforcement, fixed interval, variable interval, fixed ratio, and variable ratio. (6)

scientific management An approach to designing jobs emphasizing efficiency. It served as the foundation for job specialization and mass production. Employees performed a small part of a complete task and were paid on a piece-rate system. Primarily associated with the work of Taylor, it was one of the first approaches to the study of management. (1,4)

scientific research The systematic investigation of hypothesized propositions about the relationships among natural phenomena. (App. 1)

secondary needs Needs learned from the environment and culture in which the individual lives. (4)

security needs Things that offer safety and security, such as adequate housing and clothing and freedom from worry and anxiety. (4)

selection attention The receiver attends to only selected parts of the message. (14)

selective perception The process by which we pay attention to objects we are comfortable with and filter out those that cause us discomfort. (3)

self-actualization needs Needs that involve the realization of our full potential and becoming all that we can be. (4)

self-efficacy An individual's belief that she or he can still accomplish goals, even if that person has failed in the past. (3, 5)

self-esteem The extent to which a person believes that she or he is a worthwhile and deserving individual. (3)

self-reactions In the conflict model of decision making, comparisons of alternatives with internalized moral standards. (10)

settling down stage See **advancement stage**.

short-term orientation Values which focus on the past and present. (19)

simple structure An organization design that has little specialization and formalization, and its overall structure is organic. It is one of Mintzberg's structural forms and characterizes a relatively small, usually young organization in a simple, dynamic environment. (16)

situational view of attitudes A view that argues that attitudes evolve from socially constructed realities. (3)

skills More task specific than are abilities; reflected when applying abilities to a specialized area. (3)

social information processing model   A perspective presented by Salancik and Pfeffer. The model suggests that through various processes, commitment, rationalization, and information saliency are defined. These attributional and enactment processes then combine with social reality construction processes to influence perceptions, attitudes, and behaviors. (7)

social learning   A specific type of vicarious learning. It is assumed that people learn behaviors and attitudes partly in response to what others expect of them. (6)

social responsibility   The organization's obligation to protect and/or contribute to the social environment in which it functions. (2)

socialization stage   Second career stage in which an individual becomes more focused on a specific job and performance begins to improve. (App. 2)

social subsystem   Includes the interpersonal relationships that develop among people in organizations. (16)

sociotechnical systems approach   An approach that views the organization as an open system structured to integrate the two important subsystems: the technical (task) subsystem and the social subsystem. The approach is based on systems theory. (16)

source   The individual, group, or organization interested in communicating something to another party. (14)

span of control   The number of people reporting to a manager. It defines the size of the organization's work groups. (15)

specialization   The number of distinct occupational titles or activities accomplished within the organization. (15)

spokesperson role   The manager who speaks for the organization to outsiders. (2)

stereotyping   The process of categorizing people into groups on the basis of certain characteristics or traits. (3)

stimulus discrimination   The ability of the individual to recognize differences between stimuli. (6)

stimulus generalization   The process by which people recognize the same or similar stimuli in different settings. (6)

strategic choice   An approach to organization design whereby the manager is viewed as the decision maker. The manager's choices of how to structure the organization are affected by the purposes and goals, the imperatives, and her or his personality, value system, and experience. (16)

strategy   The plans and actions necessary to achieve organizational goals. (16)

stress   A person's adaptive response to a stimulus that places excessive psychological or physical demands on that person. (2,9)

structural change   A type of organizational change that consists of a system-wide rearrangement of task division and authority and reporting relationships. (18)

structural imperatives   Factors that determine how the organization must be structured in order to be effective. The three factors that have been identified as structural imperatives are size, technology, and environment. (16)

suboptimizing   Occurs in decision making when decision makers trade off the gains of some outcomes to avoid the potential negative aspects of those outcomes. Occurs when the less than best possible outcome is accepted. (10)

superleadership   When a leader gradually and purposefully turns over power, responsibility, and control to a self-managing workgroup. (13)

superordinate goal   A solution to goal displacement, it is usually a goal of the overall organization and is more important than the more specific goals of interacting groups. (9)

supportive relationships   Relationships where people are treated in a manner that fosters feelings of support, self-worth, and importance. (15)

surface value   Meaning that a reward has to the employee at an objective level. (8)

survey-feedback   A process of gathering, analyzing, and summarizing data and returning it to employees and groups for discussion, and identification and solution of problems. (18)

symbolic value   Messages below the surface of rewards which convey to the employee how much he or she is valued by the organization as well as his or her importance relative to others. (8)

system   An interrelated set of elements functioning as a whole. (1)

systems perspective   A theory popularized in the physical sciences and extended to the area of management. An organizational system receives various inputs from its environment, transforms these inputs into products or services, and creates various outputs of the system. The system receives feedback from the environment regarding those outputs. (1)

Tangible compensation   Rewards that have a definite value. (8)

task demands   Stressors associated with the specific job a person is performing, such as the job surgeons and coaches, for example, face. (9)

task environment   The particular environmental forces that affect an organization's operations. (16)

task group   A type of formal group that is relatively temporary. (11)

Glossary

task interdependence   The degree to which the activities of separate groups force them to depend on each other, thereby requiring more coordination to realize organizational goals. The three types of task interdependence are pooled, sequential, and reciprocal. (11)

task uncertainty   A situation that arises whenever employees or work groups lack information about what course of action to take or about future events that may affect them, the task, or the organization. (11)

team building   Programs designed to assist a work team (group) in developing into a mature, well-functioning team by helping it define its goals or priorities, analyze its tasks and the way they are performed, and examine relationships among people doing the work (18).

Technical skills   Those abilities necessary to accomplish specific tasks within the organization. (2)

technology   The mechanical and intellectual processes that transform inputs into outputs. (2, 16)

Theory X   A pessimistic view of managerial thinking consistent with the tenets of scientific management. (1)

Theory Y   An optimistic view of management representative of the human relations perspective. (1)

thick description methods   Attempts to describe the totality of day-to-day life through in-depth questioning and observation. (17)

token group   Has only one member different from the dominant group and usually expects that member to conform to the behaviors of the dominant group. (20)

Total Quality Management (TQM)   A fundamental change in an organization's culture that involves a focus on the customer, an environment of trust and openness, the formation of work teams, breaking down of internal organizational barriers, team leadership coaching, shared powers, and continuous improvement. (8)

training   Specialized efforts to improve specific employee job skills. Such activities include on-the-job training, formalized job rotation programs, and student intern programs. (21)

trait approaches   Attempts to identify stable and enduring traits that differentiate effective leaders from non-leaders. (12)

transformational leadership   The process of leading for change rather than for stability. (13)

transition management   The process of systematically planning, organizing, and implementing change, from the disassembly of the current state to the realization of a fully functional future state within an organization. (18)

transmission   The process through which the symbols that carry the message are sent to the receiver. (14)

turnover   The permanent cessation of working for the organization. (2, 3)

Type A person   A person who is extremely competitive, highly committed to work, has a strong sense of time urgency, is aggressive, impatient, and very work oriented, has much drive, and wants to accomplish as much as possible as quickly as possible. (9)

Type B person   A person who, in comparison with the Type A person, is less competitive, is less committed to work, has a weaker sense of time urgency, feels less conflict with people or time, has a more balanced and relaxed approach to life, has more confidence, and is able to work at a constant pace. (9)

Type Z (American firms)   One of the three types of firms analyzed by Ouchi. As compared to typical American and Japanese firms, Type Z American firms have a wholistic concern for workers and managers. The firms have a long-term employment commitment, evaluate employees slowly through both qualitative and quantitative information about performance, emphasize somewhat broad career paths, exercise control through informal, implicit mechanisms, have a strong cultural expectation that decision making will occur in groups and will be based on full information sharing and consensus, and expect individuals to take responsibility for decisions. (17)

Uncertainty   When a decision maker takes enough information to estimate the probability of outcomes. (10)

unconflicted adherence   In the conflict model of decision making, continuing with activities if doing so does not entail serious risks. (10)

unconflicted change   In the conflict model of decision making, making changes in present activities if doing so entails no serious risks. (10)

unfreezing   The process by which people become aware of the need for change. It is the first step of Lewin's model of planned change. (18)

universal approach   An approach whose prescriptions or propositions are designed to work in any situation or circumstance. This is the "one best way" to structure the jobs, authority, and reporting relationships of any organization's external environment, the industry, and the type of work to be done. (16)

Valences   The attractiveness or unattractiveness of any given outcome to any given person. It is a concept of expectancy theory. (5)

validity   The extent to which research measures what it is intended to measure. (App. 1)

value judgments   The degree to which a message reinforces or challenges the receiver's basic personal beliefs. (11)

variable-interval reinforcement   Using time as the basis for applying reinforcement, but varying the interval between reinforcements. (6)

variable-ratio reinforcement   Reinforcement where the number of behaviors between reinforcement varies. (6)

verification   The receiver indicates to the source that the receiver received the message and the degree to which it was understood. (14)

vertical-dyad linkage model   See **leader-member exchange model (LMX)**.

vigilant information processing   In the conflict model of decision making, thoroughly investigating all possible alternatives, weighing their costs and benefits before making a decision, and developing contingency plans. (10)

Vroom-Yetton-Jago model   First developed by Vroom and Yetton in 1973 and recently expanded by Vroom and Jago. Prescribes a leadership style appropriate to a given situation and presumes that one leader may display various leadership styles. The model is concerned with only one aspect of leader behavior: subordinate participation in decision making. The goals of the model are to protect the quality of the decision and ensure decision acceptance by subordinates. (12)

Wheel network   A small group network pattern in which information flows between the person at the end of each spoke and the person in the middle. (14)

withdrawal stage   Involves the end of full time employment as the individual faces retirement and other end-of-career options.

workforce diversity   The differences, such as age, gender, ethnic heritage, physical ability/disability, race, and sexual orientation that make up the employees of an organization. (20)

workplace behavior   A pattern of action by the members of an organization that directly or indirectly influences organizational effectiveness. (3)

written communication   A form of communication in organizations. Common forms of written communication include letters, memos, reports, manuals, and forms. (14)

Photo Credits

(continued from page ii)

Chapter 3:

p. 51, Alex Stewart, The Image Bank, p. 55, Spencer Grant III, Stock, Boston, p. 59, Phillip Wallick, The Stock Market;

Chapter 4:

p. 77, Alan MacWeeney, p. 84, Bob Daemmrich, Stock, Boston, p. 85, Spencer Grant, Stock, Boston;

Chapter 5:

p. 103, Michael Abramson, p. 113, John Madere, Fortune Magazine, p. 119, Karen Kasmauski, Matrix;

Chapter 6:

p. 129, Steve Winter, Black Star, p. 133, Brownie Harris, Courtesy General Electric, p. 137, N. R. Rowan, Stock, Boston;

Chapter 7:

p. 155, Tom Tracy, The Stock Market, p. 163, John Abbott, p. 171, Spencer Grant, Stock, Boston;

Chapter 8:

p. 181, National Institute of Standards and Technology, Office of Quality Programs, Gaitersburg, Maryland, p. 182, Spencer Grant, Stock, Boston, p. 192, Dennis MacDonald, Photo Edit;

Chapter 9:

p. 205, Bill Gentile, p. 221, Louie Psihoyos, Matrix, p. 226, Bob Daemmrich, Sygma;

Chapter 10:

p. 235, Ted Hardin, p. 244, Jeff Smith, p. 252, Joseph Schuyler, Stock, Boston;

Chapter 11:

p. 263, John Abbott, p. 277, Alan MacWeeney, Alcoa Technical Center, p. 282, James Schnepf;

Chapter 12:

p. 285, Joseph Nettis, Photo Researchers, p. 302, Peter Sibbald, Sygma, p. 308, Dana Fineman, Sygma;

Chapter 13:

p. 323, Bob Daemmrich, p. 329, John Abbott, p. 344, Jeff Smith;

Chapter 14:

p. 351, Forest McMullin, Black Star, p. 354, Richard Pasley, Stock, Boston, p. 365, Blair Seitz;

Chapter 15:

p. 379, Ted Horowitz, Courtesy Allied Signal Inc., p. 384, Jonathan Kirn, Gamma Liaison, p. 392, James Schnepf;

Chapter 16:

p. 409, John Abbott, p. 412, John Abbott, p. 430, Paul Chesley, Photographers Aspen;

Chapter 17:

p. 439, Louis Psihoyos, Matrix, p. 447, Seth Resnick, Stock, Boston, p. 457, Dana Fineman, Sygma;

Chapter 18:

p. 467, Bob Daemmrich, p. 470, Ted Rice, p. 479, John Abbott;

Chapter 19:

p. 495, Raphael Gaillarde, Gamma Liaison, p. 496, Peter Menzel, Stock, Boston, p. 511, Nikolai Ignatiev, Matrix;

Chapter 20:

p. 519, Joseph Nettis, Photo Researchers, p. 527, Blair Seitz, Photo Researchers, p. 534, Jeff Smith.

Name Index

Boyd, Brian, 357n
Boyd, Losana E., 368n
Bracker, Jeffrey S., 380n, 420n
Brady, Neil F., 394n
Braggantl, Nancy, 508n
Branan, Paul, 205
Brantner, Thomas M., 147n
Brehm, Jack W., 78n
Bridwell, Lawrence G., 85n
Brief, Arthur P., 393n
British Airways, 171
British Leyland, 7
British Petroleum, 498, 523
British Sterling, 498
Brockner, Joel, 251n
Brody, Michael, 373n
Brody, Pauline N., 186n
Bromet, Evelyn J., 215n
Browning, Larry D., 364n
Bruning, Nealia S., 214n
Bryman, A., 381n
Bryson, Vaughn, 295, 296
Buckley, M. Ronald, 186n
Bunker Ramo, 379
Burack, E.H., 574n
Burck, Charles G., 440n
Bureau of Labor Statistics, 193
Burke, W. Warner, 474n
Burlington Northern Railroad Company,
    414
Burnham, David H., 94n
Burns, James McGregor, 325n
Burns, Lawton R., 430n
Burns, Tom, 415
Burtt, H.E., 301n, 303n
Busse, Thomas V., 254n

Cable News Network (CNN), 77
Cage, Jack H., 312n
Calder, Bobby J., 62n
Caldwell, David F., 53n, 170n, 272n,
    441
California Public Employees Retirement
    System, 291
Calvin Klein, 348
Camden, T.M., 575n
Caminiti, Susan, 348n
Campbell, Alta, 151n, 202n, 326n,
    372n, 376n, 379n, 405n, 409n, 439n,
    459n, 464n, 491n, 495n, 519n
Campbell, Donald J., 168n, 170n
Campbell, D.T., 551n
Campbell, John P., 91n, 92n, 104n,
    111n
Campion, Michael A., 163n
Carey, Alex, 10n
Carlile, William H., 435n
Carlson, Chester, 256
Carnation, 39
Carroll, Glenn R., 383n

Carroll, John S., 132n
Carroll, Stephen J., 6n, 115n
Carsrud, Alan L., 93n
Carter, Elaine, 520n
Carter, Janet Houser, 397n
Carter, Nancy M., 383n
Cartwright, Darwin, 330n
Cartwright, Dorwin, 278n
Cascio, Wayne F., 391n
Case, Thomas, 324n
Casey, William, 275, 276
Cashman, J.F., 313n
Cass, E.L., 163n
Caterpillar Inc., 205, 387–388
Caudron, Shari, 273n, 372n
Cavanaugh, Gerald F., 337n
Cellar, Douglas F., 132n
Chai, Alan, 326n
Chandler, Alfred D., 420, 420n
Chaparral Steel, 172
Chatman, Jennifer A., 53n
Chaucer, 6
Chemers, Martin M., 307n
Cheng, Joseph L.C., 381n
Chicago Bulls, 383, 384
Child, John, 391n, 420n, 432n
Christie, R., 59n
Chrysler Corporation, 40, 196,
    253–254, 323
Citera, Maryalice, 94n
Citicorp, 32, 318–319, 323
Clark, Alfred W., 266n
Clark, B., 446n
Clorox, 344–345
CNN (Cable News Network), 77
Coca-Cola, 33, 39, 259–260
Coch, Lester, 283n
Cohen, A.R., 173n
Cohen, Ben, 38
Coleman, 430
Colgate-Palmolive, 187, 385–386
Colonial Life Insurance Company, 159
Colvin, Geoffrey, 194n, 468n
Compaq, 417, 467
Conant, H., 159n
Conger, Jay A., 297n, 327n
Conner, Mark, 55n
Container Corporation of America, 427
Continental Airlines, 333
Control Data Corporation, 174, 219
Cooper, Cary, 142n, 207
Copeland, Lennie, 526n, 529n, 545n
Cordery, John L., 168n
Corning Inc., 134, 283, 435
Cosier, Richard A., 107n
Costner, Kevin, 255
Cotton, John L., 284n
Cox, Taylor H., Jr., 538n, 539n
Crawford, Michael, 523n
Cropanzano, Russell, 94n

Cullen, John H., 413n
Cummings, Larry L., 4n, 12n, 20n, 52n,
    55n, 59n, 62n, 78n, 94n, 167n, 184n,
    357n, 551n
Cummings, L.L., 132n
Cummins, Robert C., 359n, 360n
Curie, Irene, 253
Curie, Marie, 253
Curie, Pierre, 253
Cyert, Richard M., 245n

Daewoo Corporation, 387, 414
Daft, Richard L., 357n, 380n, 418n,
    550n
Daimler-Benz, 471
Dalton, Dan R., 107n, 388n, 391n,
    555n
Dalton, Don, 56
Dalton, Gene W., 484n
Dandridge, Thomas C., 443n, 444n,
    446n
D'Anno, Thomas, 414n
Dansereau, Fred, Jr., 274n, 313
Datsun, 7
Datta, Deepak, K., 237n
David, Fred R., 393n
Davids, Keith, 175n
Davis, James H., 271n, 274n, 276n
Davis, Keith, 371n
Davis, Stanley M., 428n
Davis-Blake, Alison, 190n
Davison, William H., 513n
Day, D. David, 107n
Deady, Tim, 459n
Deal, T.E., 440, 441
Dean, John, 281
De Brabander, Bert, 57n
Deci, E.L., 121
Deeprose, Donna, 454
Deere, 205
Deese, J., 130n, 132n
Dehecq, Jean-Francois, 326
Deitcher, Janet, 251n
Dell, Michael, 467
Dell Computer, 467
DeLorean, John, 328
Deming, W. Edwards, 187, 453
Denison, Daniel R., 392n
Deutschman, Alan, 77n
Devine, Elizabeth, 508n
DeVos, Richard, 98
Dew, Mary A., 215n
DeYoung, H. Garrett, 414n
Dickson, William J., 10, 423n
Digital Equipment Corporation, 211,
    523, 530, 537, 545
Dimaranan, Adelaida, 535
DiPrete, T.A., 573n
DiStefano, Joseph J., 498n, 512n
Doktor, Robert, 499n, 503n

Dolphin, 192
Donaldson, Lex, 410
Dorfman, Peter W., 344n
Douglass, Frederick, 253
Downey, H. Kirk, 393n
Dozler, I.B., 574n
Drach, Richard L., 530n
Drexel Burnham Lambert, 347
Dreyfuss, Joel, 40n
Dubinsky, Alan J., 266n
Duchon, Dennis, 314n
Dumaine, Brian, 28n, 38n, 172n, 263n, 268n, 325n, 345n, 405n, 423n, 439n
Duncan, R., 486n
Duncan, Robert B., 418n, 419n
Dunegan, Kenneth J., 314n
Dunnette, Marvin D., 91n, 92n, 104n, 111n, 223n, 275n, 297n
Du Pont, 117, 150–151, 283, 530
Durkheim, Émile, 445

Earley, P. Christopher, 171n, 273n
Eastman Kodak, 20, 39, 120, 263, 291–292, 323, 326, 530
Edwards, Jane A., 361n, 364n
Edwards, Ward, 55n
Egeth, H., 130n, 132n
Ehrlich, Sanford B., 296n
Ehrlichman, John, 281
Eisen, Jerry, 189n, 199n
Eisenhardt, Kathleen M., 247n
Electrolux, 67
Electromation Inc., 283
Electronic Data Systems, 362
Elf Sanofi, 326
Eli Lilly and Company, 295
Eltra, 379
Emerson, Harrington, 6
Erickson, Rebecca J., 61n
Erikson, E.H., 566
ESPN, 23
Evans, Aaron, 77
Evans, Martin G., 307n, 477n
EXPO '86, 250
Express, 409
Exxon, 214, 259, 498
Eyres, Patricia S., 188n

Fairhurst, Eileen, 393n
Fayol, Henri, 8, 397, 398–399, 410
Federal Express Corporation, 73, 172
Federated Department Stores, 347
Fedor, Donald B., 186n
Feldman, Daniel C., 275n
Feldman, D.C., 563n, 565n, 567n, 575n
Ference, Richard, 280n, 281n
Ference, T.P., 569n
Ferris, G., 221n
Ferris, Gerald R., 265n, 553n
Festinger, Leon, 62n, 243n, 276n

Fiedler, Fred E., 298, 304, 305, 306, 307
Field, R.H. George, 312n
Fielding, Gordon J., 388n, 391n
Fierman, Jaclyn, 73n
Fiesta Mart, 37
Filipczak, Bob, 464n
Fine, Marlene G., 300n
Finholt, Tom, 362n
Fireplace Manufacturers Inc., 422, 423
First Boston, 8
Fischman, Joshua, 209n
Fisher, Anne B., 231n, 427n
Fisher, Cynthia D., 553n
Fisher-Price, 376
Fisher Scientific, 379
Flaherty, Douglas, 559
Fleishman, E.A., 54n
Fleishman, Edwin A., 301n, 302n, 303n
Foley's, 347
Folkins, C., 219n
Follett, Mary Parker, 9
Fombrun, Charles J., 183n
Food Lion Inc., 213
Forbes, 6
Ford, J., 381n
Ford, Jeffrey D., 68n, 420n
Ford, R.N., 161n
Ford Motor Company, 7, 39, 40, 41, 130, 158, 245, 381, 498
Forrer, Stephen, 129n
France, Kym, 366n
Franklin, Jerome L., 482n
Franklin Mint, 27
Fredrickson, James W., 421n
Freedman, David H., 29n
Freedman, Sara M., 181n, 185n
Freeman, John, 485n
French, John R.P., Jr., 283n, 330, 333n, 334n
Frenkel-Brunswick, E., 58n
Frew, David R., 214n
Friedman, Meyer, 208
Friedman-Jacobs Company, 198
Friesen, Peter H., 475n
Frigidaire, 103
Froggatt, Mark L., 284n
Frohman, Alan L., 392n
Frost, Peter J., 443n, 444n, 446n, 551n
Fujitsu Ltd., 523
Fulk, Janet, 357n
Furukawa, Tsukasa, 388n
Fusilier, Marcelline R., 220n

Gadon, H., 173n
Galbraith, John Kenneth, 329n
Galton, F., 253n
Gandz, Jeffrey, 336n
Ganster, Daniel C., 220n
Gantt, Henry, 6

Gardner, Donald G., 59n, 168n
Gardner, John W., 297n
Gardner, William L., 68n, 342n, 343
Garrett, Thomas M., 37n
Garrett Corporation, 379
Gault, Stanley, 32–33, 325–326
Gavaza, Charity, 85
Gavaza, Kristin, 85
Geertz, C., 445n
Gehrman, Douglas B., 191n
Geis, F. L., 59n
General Electric Company, 27, 133, 198, 202, 373, 413, 427
General Foods, 117, 161, 172, 424
General Mills, 172, 283
General Motors Corporation, 36, 177–178, 226, 245, 267, 362, 391, 392, 427, 495, 498
Gent, M.J., 496n
Gerloff, Edwin A., 359n, 360n
Gersick, Connie J.G., 271n
Gerstein, Marc S., 263n
Gerth, H.H., 445n
Gifford, Dale, 197n
Gilberg, Kenneth R., 184n
Gilbreth, Frank, 6
Gilbreth, Lillian, 6
Gillen, Dennis A., 6n
Gilmartin, Raymond, 405
Ginsberg, Ari, 243n
Ginzberg, E., 564n
Ginzberg, S.W., 564n
Gioia, Dennis A., 147n, 182n
Gist, Marilyn E., 57n
Glass, David, 32
Glauser, Michael J., 362n
Glenn, Ethel C., 359n
Glick, William, 167n, 168n
GME (General Motors Europe), 495, 498
Gobdel, Bruce C., 314n
Goffman, E., 442n
Goizueta, Robert, 33
Goodman, Paul S., 104n
Goodsite, Bruce H., 363n
Goodyear, 32
Gooley, Toby B., 530n
Graeff, Claude L., 315n
Graen, George, 307n, 313
Graf, Steffi, 147
Granrose, C.S., 571n
Graphic Controls Corporation, 198
Greater Boston Rehabilitation Services, 530
Green, Stephen G., 314n
Greenberg, Jerald, 107n, 155n, 185n
Greenfield, Jerry, 38
Greenpeace, 214
Greiner, Larry E., 484n
Griffin, Ricky W., 62n, 91n, 116, 120n,

Kast, Fremont, 17n, 19n
Katz, Daniel, 212n, 359n, 484
Katz, Robert L., 32n
Katzell, Raymond A., 9n
Kaufman, Gary M., 214n
Kauppinen-Toropainen, Kaisa, 514n
Keil, E.T., 381n
Keller, Robert T., 277n, 355n
Kelley, H.H., 68, 121n
Kellogg, 39, 420
Kemery, Edward R., 214n
Kendall, L.M., 64n
Kennedy, A.A., 440, 441, 446
Keon, Thomas L., 20n, 383n
Kepner, Elaine, 520n
Kerlinger, Fred N., 549n, 552n, 557n
Kerr, Jeffrey, 191n
Kerr, Steven, 343n, 344n
Kessler, David, 259, 260
Keys, Bernard, 324n
Kidwell, Roland E., Jr., 78n
Kiechel, W., 574n
Kiechel, Walter, III, 27n, 56, 155n, 181n, 299n
Kiernan, Matthew J., 454n
Kilbridge, M., 159n
Kim, W. Chan, 456n
Kimberly, John R., 412n
Kimble, Charles E., 60n
King, Martin Luther, 328
King, Nathan, 92n
King, Wesley C., Jr., 107n
Kirkland, Richard I., Jr., 503n, 512n
Kirkpatrick, Shelly A., 299n
Kirste, Kenneth K., 361n, 364n
Kitano, Mikio, 118
Kleiman, Carol, 208n
Klein, Howard J., 121n
Klonoski, Richard J., 37n
Kluckhohn, C., 445n
Knight, Patrick A., 60n
Knowlton, Christopher, 498n
Knudsen, B.W., 564n
Kobasa, Susan C., 215n
Kodak, 20, 39, 120, 263, 291–292, 323, 326, 530
Kofman, Fred, 130n
Kogan, N., 278n
Kohler-Gray, Susan, 545n
Kohn, Alfie, 225n
Kolodny, Harvey F., 428n
Komatsu, 387
Konovsky, Mary, 70n
Koresh, David, 328
Kouzes, J.M., 441
Krackhardt, David, 364n
Kreitner, Robert, 134n, 143n, 145n
Kroeber, A.L., 445n
Kubiak, Malgorzata, 59n
Kuhnert, Karl W., 325n

Kumar, Kamalesh, 533n
Kupfer, Andrew, 24n, 510n

Labich, Kenneth, 428n, 451n
LaBier, D., 569n
Labkh, Kenneth, 143n
Lacity, Julie A., 366n
Lacroix, Renee, 276n
Lambert, Drexel Burnham, 37
Landy, Frank J., 9n, 78n
Lane, Henry W., 498n, 512n
Lane Bryant, 409
Larack, J.C., 574n
Larsen, Ralph S., 439
Larson, L.L., 303n, 313n, 327n
Latham, Gary P., 114, 142n
Laud, Robert L., 183n
Laurent, André, 502n
Lawler, Edward E., III, 104n, 110, 112n, 164, 165n, 166, 190n, 193n, 198n, 199n, 486n, 559n, 564n, 565n
Lawrence, Paul R., 428n, 484n
Lawrence, P.R., 163, 164
Lawrie, John, 397n
Leana, Carrie R., 284n, 339n
Leatt, Peggy, 386n
Lechmere, 175
Lei, David, 243n
Leibowitz, Zandy, 129n
Leibowitz, Z.B., 576n
Lengel, Robert H., 357n
Lengnick-Hall, Mark L., 284n
Lenway, Stefanie Ann, 337n
Leonard, Bill, 537n
Lerner, 409
Levinson, D.J., 58n
Levi Strauss & Company, 39, 273, 442, 512, 530
Levitan, Sar A., 527n
Lewin, Kurt, 108, 472
Lewis, Laurie K., 256n
Lewis, M.R., 444n
Lewis, Philip, 325n
Lieber, Jill, 266n, 271n
Lifeline Systems, Inc., 424
Likert, Rensis, 283n, 300n, 301, 397, 399–401, 410
The Limited, Inc., 409
Lincoln, James F., 191n
Lincoln, James R., 64n, 65n, 511n
Lincoln Electric Company, 191
Litton Industries, 312
Livesay, Harold C., 427n
Lloyd, Kathy, 251n
Locke, Edwin A., 7n, 113, 114, 121n, 146n, 284n, 299n, 553n
Loden, Marilyn, 520n, 521n, 525n, 526n, 529n
Long, Susan, 270n
Longenecker, Clinton O., 182n

Loomis, Carol J., 292n, 319, 323n
Lorenzo, Frank, 64, 333
Lorsch, Jay W., 11n, 12n, 190n
Los Alamos National Laboratory, 185
Los Angeles Lakers, 383, 384
Lotus Development Corporation, 393, 442, 530
Lounsbury, John W., 219n
Luckman, T., 442n
Lucky-Goldstar, 414
Luthans, Fred, 134n, 143n, 145n
Lynch, Merrill, 509

Mabe, P.A., 185n
McBride, Kerry, 511n
McCall, M.W., 559n
McCanse, Anne Adams, 303n
McCarter, Robert, 355n
McCaw, 24
McClelland, David, 92, 93, 94n
McConnell, John, 125
McDonald's, 34, 39, 418, 426
McDonnell Douglas, 373
McFarlan, F. Warren, 373n
McFarlane, Robert, 275, 276
McGregor, Douglas, 11
McGuire, Joseph W., 15n
Machiavelli, Niccolo, 6, 59
McKeene, Dermont, 497n
McKenney, James L., 373n
McMahan, Gary C., 155n, 162n
McMahon, J. Timothy, 307n
Macoby, Michael, 341n
McRae, K.B., 575n
Maddi, S.R., 56n
Mael, Fred, 264n, 286n
Magnet, Myron, 47n, 77n
Mahar, Linda, 307n
Maher, J.R., 162n
Main, J., 569n
Main, Jeremy, 365n, 459n
Mainiero, Lisa A., 450n
Malik, S.D., 269n, 270n
Malone, John, 23–24
Mandell, Barbara, 545n
Mann, Leon, 247, 248n, 250
Manning, Michael R., 210n
Manpower, Inc., 174
Mansfield, Richard S., 254n
Manz, Charles C., 343n, 345n
March, James G., 244n, 245n
Markham, Steven E., 274n
Marrache, Myriam, 276n
Marriott Corporation, 235
Marriott International, 235
Mars Incorporated, 39, 523
Martella, J.A., 307n
Martier, A., 572n
Martin, J., 446n
Martinko, Mark J., 68n

Name Index

Shearman and Sterling, 534
Sheelen, Don, 67
Shell Oil Company, 18, 39, 530
Shenkar, Oded, 499n
Shepard, Herbert A., 224n
Sherman, J. Daniel, 393n
Sherman, Stratford P., 327n
Shimizu Corporation, 254
Shin-Caterpillar-Mitsubishi, 388
Shiseido, 254
Shuelke, L. David, 353n
Signal Company, 379
Sils, D., 457n
Simon, Herbert A., 237n, 244n, 245n
Simonds Rolling Machine Company, 7
Simonton, D.K., 253n
Sims, Henry P., Jr., 147n, 343n, 345n
Singh, B., 253n
Singleton, Henry E., 459
Skinner, B.F., 134
Sklarewitz, Norman, 535n
Skowcroft, Brent, 275n, 276n
Slocum, John W., Jr., 191n
Slutsker, Gary, 205n
Smith, Adam, 156, 159, 383
Smith, Bob, 283n
Smith, Howard L., 393n
Smith, Jack, 391, 495
Smith, Patricia, 91n
Smith, Patricia C., 64n
Snyder, Robert A., 369n
Snyderman, Barbara, 89n
Societe Nationale Elf Aquitaine, 326
Solomon, Charlene Marmer, 519n, 529n, 545n
Solomon, Julie, 535n
Sorrels, J. Paul, 265n
Southern California Edison, 300
Spain, Patrick J., 151n, 202n, 326n, 372n, 376n, 379n, 405n, 409n, 439n, 459n, 464n, 491n, 495n, 519n
Spender, J.C., 441
Spendolini, Michael J., 388n, 391n
Sproull, Lee S., 362n
Stahl, Michael J., 93n
Stalker, George, 415
Standard Oil of Ohio, 146
Stanley, J.C., 551n
Staw, Barry M., 12n, 20n, 52n, 55n, 62n, 63, 78n, 94n, 104n, 132n, 167n, 168n, 250, 251n, 357n
Stearns, Timothy M., 419n, 553n
Steel, Robert P., 70n
Steers, Richard M., 65, 78n, 83n, 104n, 193n, 499n
Steffen, Christopher J., 323, 324, 343n
Sterling Winthrop Drugs, 326
Stevenson, Howard H., 67n
Stewart, Thomas A., 155n, 213n, 263n, 292n, 332n, 379n, 431n, 470n, 530n

Stogdill, Ralph M., 296n
Stoka, Ann Marie, 7n
Stone, Eugene, 549n, 554n, 556n
Stoner, J.A.F., 569n
Stoner, James A.F., 278n
Storrs, Constance, 398n
Straw, Barry, 4n
Strickland, A.J., III, 191n, 420n, 427n
Sumitomo Corporation, 524
Suttle, J. Lloyd, 476
Suttle, J.L. 167n
Sutton, Robert I., 212n, 357n, 414n

Tabar, Thomas D., 314n
Tandem Computers, 19
Tane, Lance D., 197n
Tapscott, Don, 366n
Tavistock Institute, 423–424
Taylor, Alex, III, 495n, 498n
Taylor, Frederick W., 6–7, 82, 157, 282n
Tele-Communications, Inc. (TCI), 23–24
Teledyne, Inc., 459
Tenneco, 117
Terborg, James, 20n
Texaco, 498
Texas Instruments, 120, 161, 162, 167
Thayer, Paul W., 163n
Thermos Company, 422–423
Thomas, Joe, 169n
Thomas, Kenneth, 15n, 223n
Thompson, Arthur A., Jr., 191n, 420n
Thompson, James D., 416n, 419–420, 427n
Thornton, Emily, 254n
3M, 167, 172, 428
Tichy, Noel M., 474n
Tjosvold, Dean W., 345n
Tjosvold, Mary M., 345n
Tolman, Edward, 108
Tomasko, Robert, 431n
Tompkins, Silvan S., 355n
Tosi, Henry L., 115n
Touliatos, John, 214n
Tower, John, 275n, 276n
Townsend, James B., 531n, 532n
Toyota, 40, 89, 118, 119, 178, 243, 387, 450, 498
Toyota-General Motors, 173
Tracey, J. Bruce, 325n
Treacy, Michael E., 197n
Treybig, Jim, 19
Trist, Eric L., 424n
Trump, Donald, 20, 327
TRW, 428
Tubbs, Mark E., 115n
Tudor, William D., 388n, 391n
Tully, Shawn, 27n, 268n
Turban, Daniel B., 20n
Turner, A.N., 163, 164

Turner, Ted, 24
Tushman, Michael L., 327n
Tustin, 55
Tymon, Walter G., 15n

UAW (United Auto Workers), 205
Uhl-Bien, Mary, 314n
Ulrich, David O., 221n, 474n
Unilever, 491, 513
Union Carbide, 244
Union Texas Natural Gas, 379
United Auto Workers (UAW), 205
United Parcel Service, Inc. (UPS), 73, 463–464
U.S. Bank, 230–231
U.S. Civil Service, 159
U.S. Postal Service, 73, 463
UNUM Corporation, 351
UPS (United Parcel Service, Inc.), 73, 463–464
Urwick, Lyndall F., 8, 388n
USA Today, 77, 539
U S West, 273

Van Dyne, Linn, 171n
Van Fleet, David D., 297n, 299n, 388n
Van Fleet, D.D., 575n
Van Fleet, E.M., 575n
Van Maanen, J., 441
Van Velzen, Dawn, 218n
Vecchio, Robert P., 314n
Velasquez, Manuel, 337n
Ventrakaman, N., 243n
Vicars, William M., 482n
Victoria's Secret, 347, 409
Volkswagen, 498
Vollrath, David A., 284n
Volvo, 167, 172, 424
Von Glinow, Mary Ann, 557n
Vroom, Victor H., 78n, 108, 284n, 310, 311n, 312

Wachner, Linda, 329, 347
Wahba, Mahmond A., 85n
Walker, C.R., 157, 158
Walker, J., 571n, 576n
Wall, Toby D., 175n
Wallace Company, 181, 182, 185, 187
Wallach, M.A., 278n
Wal-Mart Discount City, 3
Wal-Mart Stores, Inc., 3, 32, 333
Walsh, Bill, 271
Walton, Richard, 476
Walton, Richard E., 424n
Walton, Sam, 3, 20, 332–333
Wanous, John P., 269n, 270n
Warden, John, 497n
Warnaco, 329, 347–348
Warr, Peter, 55n
Warren, E.K., 569n

Waterman, R.H., Jr., 441, 446, 447, 458
Waterman, Robert, 451–453
Waterman, Robert H., Jr., 371, 432, 440
Watkins, David W., 185n
Watson, Warren E., 533n
Weatherup, Craig, 259–260
Weber, Max, 8, 9, 382n, 396, 397, 410, 445
Weed, E.D., 162n
Weick, Karl E., 104n, 364n
Weinberger, Caspar W., 275
Weiss, H.M., 147n
Welch, John F., 202
Wells, Ronald G., 188n
Welsh, M. Ann, 167n
West, S.G., 185n
Western Electric, 10
Westinghouse, 120, 172
Westt, Inc., 27
Wexley, Kenneth N., 481n
Wexner, Leslie, 409
Weyerhaeuser, 114, 146, 307
Wharton, Amy S., 61n

Whirlpool, 103
Whisler, Timothy R., 7n
Whistler Corporation, 40
Whiting, J.W.M., 457n
Whitmire, Marshall, 188n
Whitmore, Kay, 291
Whitsett, David A., 10n
Wigdor, L., 92n, 162n
Wilcox, R.C., 563n
Wilhelm, Warren, 456n
Wilkins, A., 443n, 444n, 447n
Winchell, William O., 40n
Wofford, Jerry C., 359n, 360n
Wolfe, Richard A., 221n
Wood, Richard, 295, 296
Wood, Robert, 132n, 147n
Woodman, Richard W., 253n
Woodson, William Brooks, 520n
Woodward, Joan, 415n
Worthington Industries, 125
Wozniak, Steve, 33
Wrege, Charles D., 7n, 82n
Wren, D.A., 299n

Wren, Daniel, 82n
Wren, Daniel A., 6n
Wriston, Walter, 318

Xerox Corporation, 167, 256, 263, 529, 530, 537

Yamaguchi, Tamotsu, 500n
Yammarino, Francis, J., 266n
Yasai-Ardekani, Masoud, 419n
Yetton, Philip H., 310, 312
Yin, R., 552n
Yukl, Gary A., 114n, 297n, 298n, 299n, 303n, 310n, 325n, 329n, 332, 333n
Yves Saint Laurent, 326

Zaleznik, Abraham, 296n
Zaltman, G., 486n
Zavalloni, M., 278n
Zeleny, Milan, 242n
Zey, Michael G., 571n
Zimmer, F.G., 163n
Zimmerman, Paul, 276n

Subject Index

Charismatic leadership, 326–327
Choice
  of careers. *See* Career choice
  in social information processing model, 169
Circle network, 360
Classical conditioning, 131–132
Classical organization theory, 8, 396–400
  classification of management functions and, 398
  ideal bureaucracy and, 397–398
Close-mindedness, 59
Coalition building, political, 341
Coercive power, 330
Cognitive dissonance, 62–63
  in rational decision-making approach, 243
Cognitive processes. *See also* Information processing
  attitudes and, 61
  cognitive abilities and creativity and, 253
  learning as, 132–133
Cohesiveness of group, performance and, 276–278
Collaboration, conflict in organizations and, 225
Collateral stress programs, 221–222
Collectivism, 501
Command groups, 267
Commission programs, 194
Commitment
  to employees, in Type Z firms, 448–449
  escalation of, decision making and, 250–251
  to goals, 115
  to objectives, total quality management and, 188
  organizational, 64–65
  power and, 332–333
Communication, 350–374
  across cultures, 507–509
  defined, 352
  diversity and, 534, 535
  electronic information processing and telecommunications and, 365–366
  as force for organization change, 470
  improving organizational factors in, 370–373
  informal, fostering, 371
  nonverbal, 354–355
  oral, 354
  organization change and, 488
  purpose of, 352
  written, 353–354
Communication and decision-making stage of group development, 270
Communication fidelity, 367

Communication networks, 359–365
  all-channel, 360
  chain, 360
  circle, 360
  organizational, 362–365
  small-group, 359–362
  wheel, 360
Communication process, 355–359
  decoding and, 357, 368
  encoding and, 356, 368
  feedback and, 358, 369–370
  improving, 367–370
  noise and, 359, 371
  receiver/responder and, 357, 369
  source and, 355–356
  transmission and, 356–357
Compensation. *See also* Reward systems
  of executives, 194
  indirect, benefits as, 195–196
  long-term, 194
  tangible and intangible, 190
Competencies, 55
Competition, 39–41
  conflict in organizations and, 224–225
  as force for organization change, 470–471
  global, 39–40
  quality and productivity and, 40–41
  technology and, 41
Competitive advantage, diversity as, 537–538
Complexity, environmental, 418
Composition of group, performance and, 271–273
Compressed workweek, 173
Compromise, conflict in organizations and, 225–226
Computers, communication using, 365–366
Conceptual skills of managers, 33
Concern for people
  Leadership Grid and, 303
  Theory Z and, 450
Concern for production, Leadership Grid and, 303
Conditioning, classical. *See* Classical conditioning
Configuration, 382
Conflict
  across cultures, 504–505
  defined, 222
  interrole, 212
  intrarole, 213
  intrasender, 214
  minimizing, in pluralistic organizations, 540
  in organizations. *See* Organizational conflict
  person-role, 214
  role, 212

Conflict model of decision making, 247–250
Conflict resolution, 226
Conflict stimulation, 227–228
Consensus, 68
Consideration behavior, leadership and, 302
Consistency, 68
Contingency approaches to organization design, 410
Contingency perspective, 18–19
Contingency plans in rational decision-making approach, 242–243
Continuous change process model of organization change, 472–474
Continuous reinforcement, 136–137
Contracts, psychological, 52–53
Contributions, 52
Control
  of information, politics and, 340
  job enrichment and, 160
  as managerial function, 30
  in rational decision-making approach, 243
  span of, 388
  in Type Z firms, 449
Control and organization stage of group development, 270–271
Convergent thinking, 253
Coordination
  across cultures, 509
  by direct supervision, 425
  of divided tasks, 383–391
  by mutual adjustment, 425
Core job dimensions, in Job Characteristics Theory, 165–166
Corporate research, 257
Creativity, 252–255
  creative individuals and, 253–254
  creative process and, 254–255
  defined, 252
  in Japan, 254
Critical psychological states, in Job Characteristics Theory, 165
Cross-cultural differences and similarities, 499–500. *See also* Global perspective; Workforce diversity
Cross-functional work teams, 171
Culture. *See* Global perspective; Organization culture; Workforce diversity
Customer
  departmentalization by, 386
  in Peters and Waterman approach to organization culture, 451

Data collection in research, 554–555
Decentralization, 391–392

Subject Index

scientific management approach to, 82
Motivation and productivity stage of group development, 270
Motivation factors in dual-structure theory, 91
Motives, 80
MPS. *See* Motivating potential score (MPS)
Multicultural groups, 533
Multicultural organizations, 537–540. *See also* Workforce diversity
  as competitive advantage, 537–538
  creation of, 538–540
Multinational organization, 512–513
Mutual acceptance stage of group development, 269–270
Mutual adjustment, coordination by, 425

Need(s), 83–88, 92–96
  for achievement, 92–94
  for affiliation, 94
  belongingness, 84–85
  esteem, 84, 85
  existence, 86
  growth, 86
  integrating perspectives on, 94–96
  international, changing, 89
  physiological, 84
  for power, 94
  primary, 79
  relatedness, 86
  secondary, 79–80
  security, 84
  self-actualization, 84, 85
  workplace diversity and, 81
Need-based perspectives on motivation, 76–96. *See also* Need(s)
  dual-structure theory, 88–92
  ERG theory, 86–88
  hierarchy of needs and, 83–85
  historical perspectives on motivation and, 80–83
  integration of, 94–96
  manifest needs theory, 86
  nature of motivation and, 78–79
  need for achievement and, 92–94
  need for affiliation and, 94
  need for power and, 94
  needs and motives in organizations and, 79–80
Negative reinforcement, 136
Negotiator role of managers, 32
Networks, communication. *See* Communication networks
New ventures, 256
Noise in communication process, 359, 371
Nominal group technique (NGT), 285
Nonprogrammed decisions, 237

Nonreactive measures, 555
Nonverbal communication, 354–355
  process of. *See* Communication process
Norms
  of group, performance and, 274–275
  social, in social information processing model, 169

OB. *See* Organizational behavior (OB)
Objectives, commitment to, total quality management and, 188
OB Mod. *See* Organizational behavior modification (OB Mod.)
Observation, 555
Occupation, choice of, 563–564
Occupational field, 563–564
OD. *See* Organization development (OD)
Ohio State leadership studies, 301–303
Open-mindedness, 59
Open system, 421–422
Operations, organization structure and, 391–394
Oral communication, 354
Organic structure, 416
Organization (process)
  group development and, 270–271
  as managerial function, 29
Organization(s)
  choice of, 564–565
  consequences of stress for, 217–218
  coping strategies of, 220–222
  defined, 380
  human, 399–400
  learning in, 133
  multicultural. *See* Multicultural organizations; Workforce diversity
  multinational, 512–513
  pluralistic, 539–540
  reengineering, 431
  rethinking, 431
  sources of resistance to change in, 484–485
Organizational behavior (OB)
  basic concepts of, 15–16
  characteristics of field, 12–15
  classical organization theory and, 8, 9
  contemporary field of, 12–17
  contingency perspective on, 18–19
  defined, 4–5
  emergence as field of study, 9–12
  Hawthorne studies and, 10
  historical background of, 5–8
  human relations movement and, 11
  importance of, 17
  interactional view of, 20
  managerial perspectives on, 28–29
  popular-press perspectives on, 20–21
  precursors of, 9
  scientific management and, 6–7
  systems perspective on, 17–18

Organizational behavior modification (OB Mod.), 142–147
  effectiveness of, 146
  ethics of, 146–147
Organizational citizenship, 70
Organizational commitment, 64–65
Organizational communication networks, 362–365
Organizational conflict, 222–228
  managing, 226–228
  nature of, 223
  reactions to, 223–226
Organizational environment, 417–420
  across cultures, 509–511
  general, 417–418
  organization design and, 417–420, 431
  task, 418
  uncertainty in, 418–420
Organizational factors in communication, improving, 370–373
Organizational goals, 380
Organizational socialization, 457–458
Organizational stressors, 210
Organizational technology, 415–417. *See also* Technology
Organization change, 466–489. *See also* Organization development (OD)
  communication as force for, 470
  competition as force for, 470–471
  continuous change process model of, 472–474
  diversity and, 537
  information processing as force for, 470
  in international context, 513
  Lewin's process model of, 472
  management of, 487–488
  people as force for, 468–469
  resistance to, 483–486
  technology as force for, 469
Organization chart, 381–382
Organization culture, 438–461
  anthropologic contributions to, 444–445
  changing, 458–460
  defined, 440–444
  diversity and, 536
  economics contributions to, 446–447
  empowerment and, 453–455
  ethics and, 459
  existing, taking advantage of, 456–457
  Peters and Waterman approach to, 451–453
  procedural justice and, 455–456
  socialization and, 457–458
  social psychology contributions to, 446
  sociological contributions to, 445–446

expert, 330–331
legitimate, 330
nature of, 328–329
need for, 94
personal, 331–332
position, 306, 331–332
referent, 331
reward, 330
threat to, resistance to change and, 485
uses of, 332–336
Practical decision-making approach, 245–247, 249
Preference for stability across cultures, 501
Prejudices, 521
Primary needs, 79
Priming, external, in social information processing model, 169
Privacy of employees, 35
Problem identification in rational decision-making approach, 240
Problem solving, 237
in groups, 284–286
Procedural justice, 455–456
Process(es)
departmentalization by, 385
standardization of, 425
Process-based perspectives on motivation, 102–123
attribution theory, 121
empowerment and, 120–121
equity theory, 104–108
expectancy theory, 108–112
goal setting theory, 112–117
integration of, 121–122
participation and, 117–119
Product, departmentalization by, 385–386
Production, concern for, Leadership Grid and, 303
Productivity, 42–43
competition and, 40–41
group development and, 270
in Peters and Waterman approach to organization culture, 452
Professional bureaucracy, 427
Profit-sharing plans, 194
Programmed decisions, 237
Psychological consequences of stress, 217
Psychological contracts, 52–53
Psychology, relation to field of organizational behavior, 13
Publicness in social information processing model, 169
Punishment, 136
in organizations, 141–142

Quality. *See also* Total quality management (TQM)

competition and, 40
Quality circles (QCs), 120
Quality of work life (QWL), 476–477
Questionnaires, 554

Race of workers, 528. *See also* Workforce diversity
Radical innovation, 256
Rational decision-making approach, 240–244, 249
Receiver of communication, 357, 369
Reengineering, 431
Referent power, 331
Refreezing, organization change and, 472
Reinforcement
continuous, 136–137
defined, 134
fixed-interval, 137–138
fixed-ratio, 138
in Japan, 139
negative, 136
positive, 134–135
variable-interval, 138
variable-ratio, 138
Reinforcement theory, 134–138
schedules of reinforcement and, 136–138
types of reinforcement and, 134–136
Relatedness needs, 86
Relationship motivation in LPC theory of leadership, 304–305
Relaxation, stress management and, 219–220
Reliability in research, 556
Research, 548–557
causality and, 556
corporate, 257
data collection methods for, 554–555
ethical concerns in, 557
process for, 550–551
purposes of, 549–550
reliability and validity and, 556–557
research designs and, 551–554
theory and, 549
Research designs, 551–554
case study, 552
field experiment, 554
field survey, 552–553
laboratory experiment, 553–554
Research methods, thick description, 446
Resistance, power and, 333
Resistance to change, 483–486
individual sources of, 486
organizational sources of, 484–485
Resource allocation
resistance to change and, 485
as role of managers, 32

Responder in communication process, 357
Responsibility, 394–395
social, 37
in Type Z firms, 449–450
Rethinking, 431
Revocability in social information processing model, 169
Reward(s)
of contributors to organization change, 488
intrinsic and extrinsic, in expectancy theory of motivation, 110
learning and, 142
Reward power, 330
Reward systems, 190–199
across cultures, 504
defined, 190
encouraging diversity and, 187
flexible, 197–198
managing, 196–197
participative pay systems, 198
pay secrecy and, 198–199
in pluralistic organizations, 540
roles, purposes, and meanings of rewards and, 191–193
types of rewards and, 193–196
Rights of employees, 35
Risk, decision making under conditions of, 238–239
Risk propensity, 60
Robotics, job design and, 175
Role(s)
defined, 212
managerial, 30–32
Role ambiguity, 212
Role conflict, 212
Role demands, stress caused by, 212–214
Role management, stress management and, 220
Rotation of jobs, 158
Rules, 393–394

Satisfaction-progression component in ERG theory, 87
Satisficing, 245
Schedules
of reinforcement, 136–138
work, 173–175
Scientific management, 6–7
motivation and, 82
Scientific research, 549
Secondary needs, 79–80
Security
resistance to change and, 486
stress caused by, 211
Security needs, 84
Selective perception, 66
Self-actualization needs, 84, 85
Self-efficacy, 57–58, 112

Turnover, 69–70
Types A and B personality profiles, stress and, 208–210
Type Z firms, 448. *See also* Theory Z

Uncertainty
  decision making under conditions of, 239
  in organizational environment, 418–420
Unconflicted adherence, 249
Unconflicted change, 249
Unemployment compensation, 195
Unfreezing, organization change and, 472
Unionization, 36
Universal approach, 8
Unobtrusive measures, 555

Vacation time, 195
Valences in expectancy theory of motivation, 109–110
Validity in research, 557
Values, surface and symbolic, of rewards, 193–194
Variable-interval reinforcement, 138
Variable-ratio reinforcement, 138
Verification
  in communication process, 369
  in creative process, 255
Vertical dyad in leader-member exchange model of leadership, 313
Vigilant information processing, 250

Vroom-Yetton-Jago model of leadership, 310–312
  application of, 313
  evaluation and implications of, 312

Wheel network, 360
Withdrawal
  stress and, 217–218
  in workplace, 69–70
Withdrawal stage of careers, 569–570
Women in work force, 34, 521, 528–529. *See also* Workforce diversity
Workers. *See* Employee(s); Individual(s); Individual behavior; People; Workforce; Workforce diversity
Workers' compensation benefits, 195
Workforce. *See* Employee(s); Individual(s); Individual behavior; People
Workforce diversity, 33–34, 372, 518–541. *See also* Multicultural organizations
  across cultures, 510
  capitalizing on, 56
  communication and, 534, 535
  defined, 520–521
  demographics and, 521–523
  diversity groups and, 273
  ethics and, 535
  global perspective on, 524
  individual behavior and, 531–532
  interpersonal processes and, 532–534

leadership and, 300, 533–534
motivation and, 532
needs and, 81
organization change and, 537
organization culture and, 536
organization structure and, 536
performance evaluations and rewards to encourage, 187
primary dimensions of, 526–530
secondary dimensions of, 531
valuing, 523–526
work groups and, 533
Work groups, 171–173
  autonomous, 171, 424
  cross-functional, 171
  diverse, 533
  ethics of, 283
  job design for, 171–172
  overlapping, 400
Work life, quality of, 476–477
Work pace, job enrichment and, 160
Workplace
  issues and challenges in, 35–36
  leadership substitutes in, 344
  stress management in, 218–222
Workplace behavior, 68–70
  organizational citizenship, 70
  performance behaviors, 69
  withdrawal behaviors, 69–70
Work schedules, 173–175
Workweek, compressed, 173
Written communication, 353–354